Transactions of the Royal Historical Society

SIXTH SERIES

IX

CAMBRIDGE
UNIVERSITY PRESS

Published by the Press Syndicate of the University of Cambridge
The Edinburgh Building, Cambridge CB2 2RU, United Kingdom
40 West 20th Street, New York, NY 10011–4211, USA
10 Stamford Road, Oakleigh, Melbourne 3166, Australia

First published 1999

A catalogue record for the book is available from the British Library

ISBN 0 521 77286 9 hardback

SUBSCRIPTIONS. The serial publications of the Royal Historical Society, *Royal Historical Society Transactions* (ISSN 0080–4401), Camden Fifth Series (ISSN 0960–1163) volumes and volumes of the Guides and Handbooks (ISSN 0080–4398) may be purchased together on annual subscription. The 1999 subscription price (which includes postage but not VAT) is £60 (US$99 in the USA, Canada and Mexico) and includes Camden Fifth Series, volumes 13 and 14 (published in July and December) and Transactions Sixth Series, volume 9 (published in December). Japanese prices are available from Kinokuniya Company Ltd, P.O. Box 55, Chitose, Tokyo 156, Japan. EU subscribers (outside the UK) who are not registered for VAT should add VAT at their country's rate. VAT registered subscribers should provide their VAT registration number.

Subscription orders, which must be accompanied by payment, may be sent to a bookseller, subscription agent or direct to the publisher: Cambridge University Press. The Edinburgh Building, Shaftesbury Road, Cambridge CB2 2RU, UK; or in the USA, Canada and Mexico: Cambridge University Press 40 West 20th Street, New York, NY 10011–4211, USA. Prices include delivery by air.

SINGLE VOLUMES AND BACK VOLUMES. A list of Royal Historical Society volumes available from Cambridge University Press may be obtained from the Humanities Marketing Department at the address above.

Printed and bound in the United Kingdom by Butler & Tanner Ltd, Frome and London

CONTENTS

MEDIEVAL COMMUNITIES

TRANSACTIONS OF THE

ROYAL HISTORICAL SOCIETY

PRESIDENTIAL ADDRESS

By P.J. Marshall

BRITAIN AND THE WORLD IN THE EIGHTEENTH CENTURY: II, BRITONS AND AMERICANS

READ 20 NOVEMBER 1998

IN my address last year I tried to offer some explanations for the great change of direction in Britain's territorial empire in the second half of the eighteenth century: the failure of empire over much of North America coinciding with the beginnings of great acquisitions in India.[1] I would like now to look more closely at the American débâcle. In trying to account for it, I stressed the yawning gap between British ambitions as they developed from mid-century and any capacity to realise them in the colonies, where, in the absence of a strong imperial presence or adequate machinery to enforce metropolitan wishes, the effective working of the empire depended on the willingness of local populations to co-operate. In the 1760s the majority of the colonial elites refused to co-operate with what they regarded as new departures from the long-established constitutional conventions of the empire. British attempts to resolve the ensuing crisis by armed coercion were to be frustrated in seven years of unsuccessful war.

Underlying British policies, I suggested, was a sense of national danger from the supposed ambitions of France. These ambitions had been checked by the Seven Years War, but revenge for that check seemed inevitable. Both the British Isles and the colonies were at risk and they must act together. There seemed to be clear evidence that at

[1] P.J. Marshall, 'Britain and the World in the Eighteenth Century: I, Reshaping the World', *Transactions of the Royal Historical Society*, 6th ser., 8 (1998), 1–18.

least some colonies had pursued and were still pursuing narrow self-centred ends which were weakening the empire and might even fragment it. This would deprive Britain of the resources drawn from colonial trade that had been of crucial importance in enabling her to prevail against her enemies in the Seven Years War, and would leave the disunited colonies vulnerable to any renewed assault. Victory had given the empire an opportunity to regroup and by proper regulations to guarantee its strength and prosperity for the foreseeable future. Only the British parliament had the breadth of vision to lay down such regulations that would ensure that all parts of the empire would benefit. Resistance to the authority of parliament could not be countenanced.

The determination of successive British governments to try to exert an effective imperial authority over the American colonies, while paying scant regard to the practical means by which such authority might actually be enforced is, I hope, a sufficient explanation of Britain's role in precipitating the great crisis that was ultimately to lead to the reconfiguration of the British empire. It is not, however, a complete one. Other sections of British society apart from the political elite were involved in empire in America, and other issues were at stake apart from the questions of national wealth and power and the constitutional arrangements appropriate for the empire which so dominated parliamentary debates and contemporary pamphlets and which continue to dominate the historiography of the British side of the Revolution.

The ties of empire seem to have been growing stronger in the years immediately before the Revolution. These ties were diverse and affected wide sections of the British population. John M. Murrin has argued that 'economic, social and intellectual trends' were tying Britain and America ever closer to one another and were causing, in his suggestive phrase, a crisis of 'imperial *integration*' rather than preparing the ground for disintegration.[2] This suggests that disengagement from the thirteen colonies after a fruitless war would involve rather more than the fears for the loss of Britain's standing in the world which were to be quickly assuaged as the British elite began to recognise that the economic benefits of America could be harvested more effectively without the travails of trying to rule it. The loss of America would be the vivisection of a living empire in which many people were deeply committed for many different reasons.

---

[2] 'The Great Inversion, or Court versus Country: A Comparison of the Revolution Settlements in England (1688–1721) and America (1776–1816)', *Three British Revolutions: 1641, 1688, 1776*, ed. J. G. A. Pocock (Princeton, 1980), 387.

I

There seems to be one notable exception to a pattern of closer imperial integration on the eve of the Revolution. Politically, Britain and the colonies seem to have been drifting apart. The British politicians who were increasingly preoccupied with America as a vital source of wealth and as a critical constitutional problem had few direct contacts with the colonies.[3] Governors or colonial politicians appear to have been more removed from the British political world than had been the case under Walpole or the Pelhams.[4] The work of Alison Olson has described the withering of the contacts long maintained by a wide variety of colonial interest groups with the London bureaucracy. In the past these contacts had given the colonies 'an informal but effective voice in the making of English decisions', but she describes how the increasing dominance of parliament over colonial policy from mid-century reduced the effectiveness of colonial lobbying.[5] The limited nature of the representation of the mainland colonies in the House of Commons was notorious at the time. The self-confidence of British ministers in their own judgement as to where the interest of the whole empire lay in any case made them less responsive to any lobbying. The colonial agents were increasingly disregarded after they had been actively patronised by the Rockingham administration for the repeal of the Stamp Act.[6]

If the empire was drifting apart politically, it was being tied closer together in many other ways. Integration was greatly facilitated by the 'shrinking' of the Atlantic, brought about not by spectacular changes in maritime technology but by greatly increased numbers of ships being operated more effectively and more cheaply. The volume of people, goods, news and information crossing the ocean was growing year by year.[7] Between the Seven Years War and the outbreak of the Revolutionary War the Atlantic economy experienced spectacular growth, if

---

[3] Edmund Burke's *Speech on Conciliation with America* of 1775 is a pre-eminent exception to the failure of nearly all British politicians to envisage colonial America in concrete terms as a distinct society rather than as an abstract problem of governance and economic regulation.

[4] This is the theme of the later chapters of Alison Gilbert Olson, *Anglo-American Politics 1660–1775: The Relationship between Parties in England and Colonial America* (Oxford, 1973). See also Stanley Nader Katz, *Newcastle's New York: Anglo-American Politics 1732–53* (Cambridge, Mass., 1968), 242–4.

[5] *Making the Empire Work: London and American Interest Groups 1690–1790* (Cambridge, Mass., 1992).

[6] Jack M. Sosin, *Agents and Merchants: British Colonial Policy and the Origins of the American Revolution* (Lincoln, Neb., 1965); Michael G. Kammen, *A Rope of Sand: The Colonial Agents, British Politics and the American Revolution* (Ithaca, NY, 1968).

[7] Ian K. Steele, *The English Atlantic, 1675–1740: An Exploration of Communications and Community* (New York, 1986).

punctuated by sharp recessions. In the years from 1770 to 1774 American exports to Britain were worth more than twice as much as they had been in the years before the Seven Years War, while North America now took about a quarter of all British exports.[8] To sustain these trades the colonies drew heavily on British credit, which was being made available on an ever-larger scale. The expanding Atlantic commercial world brought more and more British and American people into personal contact with one another. Scottish and English factors were taking up residence for long periods in America, especially around the Chesapeake. American merchants were coming to Britain in increasing numbers and forming the kind of connections with their British correspondents that made the great British merchant Richard Oswald 'the most intimate and respected friend' of his former client in South Carolina, Henry Laurens, who was to sit on the other side of the table from him at the peace negotiations in 1782.[9] Anglo-American marriages often reinforced commercial ties.

The spurt of emigration to the colonies on the eve of the Revolution has been fully documented. Over 100,000 British emigrants are estimated to have gone to North America between 1760 and 1775.[10] These included a good many people of some substance and ambition, going to better themselves as factors and agents, merchants in their own right or in professions, as well as indentured servants and convicts. The military garrison kept permanently in America after 1763 became in some degree Americanised, as colonials sought commissions and British officers married in America and bought land there.[11] The scale of the emigration from Scotland and northern Ireland in particular aroused much concern. It was conventionally assumed that the loss of such people weakened Britain.[12] In the Revolutionary War, however, recent immigrants, especially Highland Scots, were to be greatly valued as a source of strength to the empire. The first three provincial loyalist regiments embodied to fight with the British army were predominantly recruited from migrants from the Highlands.[13] Such people often chose to stay in the empire after the loss of the thirteen colonies, becoming

[8] Table 4.6, Jacob M. Price, 'The Imperial Economy 1700–1776', *The Oxford History of the British Empire*, vol. II, *The Eighteenth Century*, ed. P. J. Marshall (Oxford, 1998), 103.

[9] David Hancock, *Citizens of the World: London Merchants and the Integration of the British Atlantic Community 1735–1785* (Cambridge, 1995), 391.

[10] James Horn, 'The British Diaspora: Emigration from Britain 1660–1815', *Oxford History of British Empire*, II, 32.

[11] John Shy, *Toward Lexington: The Role of the British Army in the Coming of the American Revolution* (Princeton, 1965), 354–7.

[12] Bernard Bailyn, *Voyagers to the West: Emigration from Britain to America on the Eve of the Revolution* (1987), 53–4.

[13] Paul H. Smith, *Loyalists and Redcoats: A Study in British Revolutionary Policy* (Chapel Hill, 1964), 67–8.

a major element among the loyalists who settled in Canada.[14]

Movements of people from the colonies to Britain were on a much smaller scale than transatlantic British emigration and most Americans who crossed the ocean probably returned home. People of substance, if they did not have cause to come on business, made trips of pleasure as tourists and sent their children to complete their education, especially to learn the law at the Inns of Court or to obtain medical qualifications at Scottish universities. Dr Julie Flavell's forthcoming study suggests that affluent colonial families, whatever their allegiance was to be during the Revolution, seem to have remained convinced of the value of exposing their offspring to the polished world of London and that young Americans, even if they were given to lamenting the corruption and vice that were, they thought, rampant in the metropolis, still readily accepted British values.[15]

Emulation of things British remained the norm among colonial elites. Increasing imports from Britain spread British consumer tastes very widely. English houses were the models for affluent colonial town houses and for rural mansions which were furnished in the English manner. Accounts of British upper-class mores appropriate for those who lived in such houses were widely disseminated through the 'courtesy books' that enjoyed a vogue in aspiring colonial families.[16] English rhetoric and belles-lettres were taught in American colleges on the Scottish model to instil proper standards of taste, writing and speech.[17]

The loyalist George Chalmers recalled that after the Seven Years War 'Every man, who had credit with the ministers at home, or influence over the governors in the colonies, ran for the prize of American territory. And many land-owners in Great Britain, of no small importance, neglected the possessions of their fathers, for a portion of wilderness beyond the Atlantic.'[18] This is only a slightly exaggerated account of a great scramble in Britain for land in North America between 1763 and 1775, both in some of the existing colonies and in new ones taken from the French or the Spanish. Claimants

---

[14] J. M. Bumsted, 'The Cultural Landscape of Early Canada', *Strangers within the Realm: Cultural Margins of the First British Empire*, ed. Bernard Bailyn and Philip D. Morgan (Chapel Hill, 1991), 384.

[15] I am grateful to Dr Flavell for letting me consult sections of her forthcoming work.

[16] Richard L. Bushman, *The Refinement of America: Persons, Houses, Cities* (New York, 1992), chap. ii.

[17] Robert Crawford, *Devolving English Literature* (Oxford, 1992), 39; William Smith, 'An Account of the College and Academy of Philadelphia', *Discourses on Several Public Occasions During the War in America* (1759), 218–21.

[18] *An Estimate of the Comparative Strengths of Great Britain during the Present and Four Preceding Reigns*, new edn (1794), 141. British interest in land, resources and profitable offices in North America is analysed in my 'Empire and Opportunity in Britain, 1763–1775', *Transactions of the Royal Historical Society*, 6th ser., 5 (1995), 111–28.

operated on their own, in partnerships and in great combines seeking grants for huge areas. People resident in the colonies and in Britain tended to join together in the more grandiose schemes, British people contributing their political influence, Americans their local knowledge. On the British side, interest was usually confined to illusory hopes of quick profits with the minimum outlay, but men of capital and commercial experience also bought land in the hopes of improving the resources of the empire as well as of making profits for themselves.[19] Similarly, although Americans complained that British manufacturing interests sought to impose restrictions wherever they saw competition, some in Britain took a wider imperial view, such as those members of the Society of Arts who offered premiums for colonial inventions regardless of 'unreasonable Jealousies'.[20] Americans were welcomed as corresponding members of the Society as they were to the Royal Society, which elected seven residents of North America to the fellowship after 1763.[21]

By the middle of the eighteenth century, some religious denominations, such as Congregationalists, Baptists or Presbyterians, had become 'Americanized', that is, unlike the Anglicans or the Quakers, they no longer owed allegiance to parent churches in Britain.[22] But whether Americanised or not, right up to the Revolution religious denominations still maintained close links with like-minded Christians across the Atlantic. Through these links they sought to enlist imperial authority to protect their interests or to gain new privileges, as for instance, in the conflicts over the project for a colonial bishop or over the rights of dissenters in Virginia. Religious denominations were also heavily engaged in the expansion of education in America, especially in trying to cope with the needs of the greatly increased populations in the middle colonies. Numerous British teachers and much British money crossed the Atlantic. Money was sent to set up schools for the Pennsylvania Germans. Presbyterians from Ulster and Scotland opened schools in the backcountry. Scottish Presidents and Scottish curricula had a formative influence on new colleges, notably in New Jersey and Philadelphia.[23] In all, American colleges are estimated to have collected

[19] Hancock, *Citizens of the World*, 170–1.

[20] W. Shipley to Franklin, 1 Sept. 1756, cited in D. G. C. Allen, ' "The Present Unhappy Disputes": The Society and the Loss of the American Colonies, 1774–83', *The Virtuoso Tribe of Arts and Sciences: Studies in the Eighteenth-century Work and Membership of the London Society of Arts*, ed. D. G. C. Allen and John L. Abbot (Athens, Ga., 1992), 216.

[21] R. P. Stearns, 'Colonial Fellows of the Royal Society of London, 1661–1788', *William and Mary Quarterly*, 3rd ser., 3 (1946), 246–65.

[22] Boyd Stanley Schlenther, 'Religious Faith and Commercial Empire', *Oxford History of the British Empire*, II, 135.

[23] Douglas Sloan, *The Scottish Enlightenment and the American College Ideal* (New York, 1971).

some £24,000 in Britain between 1749 and 1775,[24] money mostly being subscribed through denominational connections. The Anglican church in America received large subventions from Britain raised by the Society for the Propagation of the Gospel to support the seventy-seven missionary clergy in post on the eve of the Revolution. To sustain its work in America the Society was spending some £5,000 a year. Through many channels a flow of charitable donations from Britain was going to the colonies on a scale comparable to the sums being raised for major domestic appeals.

Evangelically minded people in England, Scotland and the colonies felt themselves to be united by a common experience of the Holy Spirit working through religious revivals that transcended denominational and geographical boundaries. Following Whitefield's missionary journeys in the 1740s, ministers in Boston, Edinburgh, Glasgow and London exchanged news among themselves about the progress of the awakening in different parts of the British world.[25] A 'concert of prayer' linked America and Scotland.

After the Seven Years War, missions to Native Americans became a special object of evangelical expectations and religious charity on both sides of the Atlantic. Missions to Indians were regarded as an inescapable obligation in return for the divine favour shown to Britain and British America in granting victories over the French anti-Christ in the late war. The conversion of the Indians seemed to be the next stage in the divine plan. America was said by the Massachusetts agent in 1759 to lie 'near the heart of the children of God in England', who were 'particularly importunate for the spread and success of the Gospel among the natives that the Heathen may hear and know the joyful sound, and your western end of the earth, become the willing subjects of the Divine Emanuel, who is promised the ends of the earth for his possession.'[26] Such millennial expectations were shared by some Anglicans. William Smith, Provost of the Philadelphia College, told the Archbishop of Canterbury that 'God has pre determined some future period in the Gospel for the final conversion of the Heathens inhabiting these parts and that the time of this Conversion seems to be near at hand.'[27] The Society for the Propagation of the Gospel was seeking support in 1771 for 'an extensive plan' for 'additional Settlements of

[24] Beverly McAnear, 'The Raising of Funds by the Colonial Colleges', *Mississippi Valley Historical Review*, 38 (1952), 606.
[25] Michael J. Crawford, *Seasons of Grace: Colonial New England's Revival Tradition in its British Context* (New York, 1991).
[26] D. de Berdt to E. Wheelock, 24 March 1759, 'Letters of Dennys de Berdt 1757–70', *Publications of the Colonial History Society of Massachusetts*, 13 (1910–11), 413.
[27] Letter of 26 Aug. 1760, Lambeth Palace Library, MS 1123, no. 196.

Missions and Schools' beyond the work it was already undertaking.[28] The Society in Scotland for Propagating Christian Knowledge had collected money to support the work of the famous missionary David Brainerd and was still very active in the North American missionary field. The sum of £12,000 was collected throughout England and Scotland in 1765–6 for Eleazor Wheelock's Indian school at Lebanon, Connecticut.[29]

II

On the eve of the Revolution the ties that bound the American colonies to the British Isles were very diverse indeed. The valuable material which Professor Jacob Price assembled in answer to his question, 'Who cared about the Colonies?' can be considerably amplified.[30] Many British people seem to have cared in ways that went beyond his careful quantification.

The multiplicity of ties suggests the growing vitality of empire up to the point of disruption, but it was a vitality marked by tensions as well as by many common interests. The gains of an expansive commerce seemed ambiguous to some. Old securities appeared to dissolve as more and more people were drawn into market transactions, arousing anxieties about the spread of luxury and a growing dependence on foreign goods. For all the opportunities created by an expanding British market and access to British credit, Americans became vulnerable to the importunities of their creditors and to economic disruptions across the Atlantic, such as that of 1772 caused by the failure of Scottish banks. As Jonathan Clark's *Language of Liberty* has stressed, competition between religious denominations was sharp and often bitter. A more assertive Anglicanism on both sides of the Atlantic was being matched by a militant heterodoxy of some sections of dissent.[31] The money expended by the new British garrison helped the colonies to balance their payments with Britain, but there was also anxiety about the presence of a standing army on American soil. In allocating American land the

---

[28] [Robert Lowth], *A Sermon Preached before the Incorporated Society for the Propagation of the Gospel at their Anniversary Meeting...* (1771), 24.

[29] William Kellaway, *The New England Company 1649–1776: Missionary Society to the American Indians* (1961), 191.

[30] 'Who Cared about the Colonies? The Impact of the Thirteen Colonies on British Society and Politics, circa 1714–1775', in *Strangers within the Realm*, 395–436.

[31] *The Language of Liberty: 1660–1832: Political Discourse and Social Dynamics in the Anglo-American World* (Cambridge, 1994).

crown was sometimes accused of favouring 'British gentlemen' rather than deserving colonials.[32]

Into these already turbulent waters British governments threw their sticks of dynamite, the Stamp Act, the Townshend Duties, the Coercive Acts and the eventual deployment of troops. The result was to create even greater turbulence in which a clear pattern is not always easy to see. Long-standing conflicts of debtor and creditor, Anglican and dissenter, tidewater and backcountry, western settler and native American, were exacerbated. Much of the fighting in America that spilled out beyond the operations of the continental army and the regular royal troops seems to have been about winning local supremacy or paying off old scores. Contention within English boroughs and counties as to whether to pledge loyalty to the king against his rebellious colonies or to beg him to call off the military repression of America could be an outlet for ideological divisions that went far beyond the specific question of America. To refer to petitioners for conciliation as 'pro-American', as is usually done, can be misleading; colonial grievances were generally seen in terms of a perceived threat by Lord North's government to the constitution and to religious liberty at home.[33]

Such a confused pattern of conflicts on both sides of the Atlantic suggests that the war that broke out in 1775 can perhaps best be interpreted as a civil war, or more accurately as a series of civil wars on both sides of the Atlantic. So in a real sense it was. Yet a single divide eventually superimposed itself on other antagonisms and rivalries: that was the divide between Britons and Americans. By measures which, until the clumsy attempts to isolate Massachusetts in 1774, were aimed at all the colonies, British governments did much to consolidate them into a united opposition, while by invoking the authority of parliament for these measures they created a situation in which it would be increasingly difficult for British opinion to condone this opposition.

This growing divide can be traced through linguistic usage. Colonial usage in the mid-eighteenth century varied considerably, but in general expressions of loyalty seem to have embraced two entities. There was talk of 'country' (*patria* by classical analogy), which usually meant the colony in which one lived, and there was talk of 'nation', which invariably meant 'Britain' or 'England', a term usually signifying much more than a geographical England, but extended to include values and rights associated with an ideal England. These two loyalties were in no way incompatible. The colonial American elites' view of their place in

[32] Paragraphs inserted by Franklin in the British press in 1767, *The Papers of Benjamin Franklin*, ed. L. W. Labaree *et al.*, 33 vols to date (New Haven, 1959–), XIV, 113, 131.

[33] For published collections of petitions, see *American Archives*, ed. Peter Force, 9 vols (Washington, 1837–53), 4th ser., III, and James E. Bradley, *Popular Politics and the American Revolution in England: Petitions, the Crown and Public Opinion* (Macon, Ga., 1986), 218–33.

the world, as recent scholarship has suggested, was not essentially different from that of the post-Union Scots or of Protestant Irish 'patriots'. Pride in one's homeland, be it South Carolina, Massachusetts, Jamaica, Lowland Scotland or Ireland, was not a kind of nationalism challenging what were taken to be the universal values of Englishness.[34] These values were proudly asserted and 'the rights of Englishmen' were endlessly cited as the inalienable rights of people in the colonies or in Ireland against anything that seemed to be discrimination against them by crown or parliament. A sense of 'America' that served either as an extended *patria* or as an alternative 'nation' seems not to have been well developed until the 1770s, when 'America', 'Americans' or Jefferson's term 'British Americans' became the standard usage, especially in controversy with Britain. When Americans finally renounced their loyalty to Britain, they often implied that they had been forced to do so because Britain had rejected them and betrayed its own English ideals.[35]

Until the 1770s, people in Britain were probably more given to generalising about Americans and to endowing them with common qualities than were people in the colonies. The Seven Years War encouraged such generalisations. Although British regular regiments recruited in America, the British and the 'American' soldier (from whatever colony he might come) were assumed to be different species. As a British officer put it, 'the native Americans are naturally an unmanageable and ungovernable people, utterly unacquainted with the nature of subordination in general' and therefore needing to be taught an entirely different pattern of drill.[36] The fighting qualities of 'Americans' or the contribution that 'America' as a whole appeared to be making to the war in terms of men, money and support for the British armies were frequently discussed in public debate, rarely to the advantage of America. A stereotype of a rich America, relying on Britain to defend it and making no adequate recompense for that defence, while even indulging in profitable trade with the enemy on the side, seems to have gained ground. Franklin took it upon himself in 1759 to correct items in the press that tended 'to render the colonies

---

[34] S. J. Connolly, 'Varieties of Britishness: Ireland, Scotland and Wales in the Hanoverian State', *Uniting the Kingdom? The Making of British History*, ed. Alexander Grant and Keith J. Stringer (London, 1995), 193–207; Jacqueline Hill, *From Patriots to Unionists: Dublin Civic Politics and Irish Patriotism, 1660–1840* (Oxford, 1997); Colin Kidd, 'North Britishness and the Nature of Eighteenth-century British Patriotisms', *Historical Journal*, 39 (1996), 361–82. For a warning against seeing the Revolution in nationalist terms, see Clark, *Language of Liberty*, 19–20, 50–7.

[35] See T. H. Breen, 'Ideology and Nationalism on the Eve of the American Revolution: Revisions *Once More* in need of Revising', *Journal of American History*, 34 (1997), 13–39.

[36] A. Johnson to Lord Loudoun, 20 Dec. 1756, Huntington Library MSS, LO. 2371.

despicable, and even odious to the mother country'.[37] William Smith, on a mission to raise funds for the college at Philadelphia, found such prejudices still alive after the war. He reported from Liverpool in 1763 that it was believed that Americans 'had got all the advantages of the war, had born little of the burden, and were impudent beggars that would do nothing for ourselves'.[38]

The war made British people increasingly aware of a generic category of 'Americans'. How they understood the connection between themselves and these Americans is not very clear. Imperial idealists, such as Thomas Whately, William Knox or Arthur Young, insisted that the people of the colonies and of the British Isles were 'the same people' and constituted 'one nation' in Whately's and Young's words.[39] On the other hand, Lord Halifax, another imperial enthusiast, thought it realistic to suppose that 'the people of England' considered the inhabitants of the colonies as 'foreigners'.[40] Use of that term can certainly be found, as when an exasperated MP complained in 1766 of concessions being made 'to please these foreigners'.[41] The legal and official view was that Americans were British subjects, that is fellow subjects of the crown, and as such that they should be permitted to enjoy as wide a share of the rights of British subjects in the British Isles as was appropriate for them. The extent of their rights was not, however, for them to determine. It became increasingly the complaint of Americans in Britain that British opinion in general accepted that Americans were British subjects, but interpreted this to mean, not that they shared in a common inheritance of rights but that they were subjects of the British people as well as of the British crown. As Franklin famously put it, 'Every Man in England seems to consider himself as a Piece of a Sovereign over America; seems to jostle himself into the Throne with the King, and talks of OUR *Subjects in the Colonies*.'[42]

The great controversy between imperial authority and colonial rights that began in 1765 gave British opinion a sharper sense of a collective American identity and of American difference. Reports of riots through-

---

[37] Letter to *London Chronicle*, 9 May 1759, *Franklin Papers*, VIII, 340–56.

[38] Letter to T. Penn, 23 July 1763, Pennsylvania Historical Society, Smith MSS, reel XR 439.1.

[39] Whately, *The Regulations lately made concerning the Colonies and the Taxes imposed upon them, Considered* (1765), 39; Young, *Political Essays Concerning the Present State of the British Empire* (London, 1772), 1. For Knox the peoples of the colonies were 'members of the British community or state', *The Controversy between Great Britain and her Colonies Reviewed* (1769), 18.

[40] Letter to Archbishop of Canterbury, 6–7 May 1763, *Calendar of Home Office Papers of the Reign of George III, 1760–5* (1873), 279.

[41] Diary of James Harris, 14 April 1766, *Proceedings and Debates of the British Parliament Respecting North America 1754–1783*, ed. R. C. Simmons and P. D. G. Thomas, 6 vols to date Milwood, NY, 1982–) II, 368–9.

[42] Letter to Lord Kames, 25 Feb. 1767, *Franklin Papers*, XIV, 67.

out the colonies, of a Stamp Act Congress claiming to speak for all 'the British colonies on this continent' and of co-ordinated non-importation agreements all implied an 'America' in opposition, according to one's point of view, to the policies of a specific British government or to the authority of Britain as a whole. This opposition seemed to adopt a uniformly radical tone with its stress on the natural right of the individual to consent to acts of government, above all to taxation. Allegations, which had been made during the Seven Years War, that Americans were infected with 'levelling' and old 'Oliverian' principles, seemed to be abundantly confirmed. The South Carolina Committee of Correspondence might complain in December 1765 that although the epithet 'republican' was being maliciously applied to the colonies, 'No people in the world can be more averse to republicanism than the British Americans',[43] but that was a lost cause and South Carolina did nothing to save it by voting a grant of £1,500 to Wilkes in 1769. As Americans appeared to identify their cause with the cause of English radicalism, what were taken to be American principles were increasingly seen as a challenge to properly constituted authority.

The Rockingham administration of 1765–6 was able to portray American recalcitrance as directed against specific policies and not against British authority in general. In so doing they were responding to, and in some degree stimulating, a considerable body of opinion outside parliament in petitions from ports and manufacturing areas for repeal of the Stamp Act. Thereafter the argument that American resistance was solely aimed at malign ministers and their tyrannical policies became increasingly difficult to sustain. From 1767 Americans in London noted with dismay the hardening of opinion, both among politicians and, as far as they could gauge it, out of doors, against Americans in general. 'America has few friends', William Johnson of Connecticut wrote on 9 June 1767. Though British opinion wished 'to keep all the colonies disunited, yet they seem too ready to impute to *all* the transgressions of any one of them, and consider them as all alike disaffected to this country and seeking an entire independency upon all Parliamentary restraint and authority...'.[44]

Governments after 1767 did not make policy for America in a vacuum. Even had they been inclined to do so, overtly renouncing parliamentary sovereignty or condoning some particularly flagrant piece of American defiance would have aroused strong opposition in parliament and outside it. Resorting to armed coercion in America in 1775 was another matter. That split the politicians, although not to an

[43] Letter to C. Garth, 16 Dec. 1765, Library of Congress, Force Transcripts, 7E.
[44] Letter to W. Pitkin, 9 June 1767, 'Trumbal Papers', *Massachusetts History Society Collections*, 5th ser., 9 (1885), 237.

extent that endangered the government, and, as James E. Bradley's meticulous research has clearly revealed,[45] it split opinion. Both members of the parliamentary opposition and some of those who signed petitions in such large numbers made efforts to reclaim Americans for the nation as an argument against war. Edmund Burke continued to refer to Americans as members of a single 'English' or, more rarely, 'British' 'race' or 'nation' until the later stages of the war.[46] Those who petitioned the king for conciliation referred to Americans not only as their 'fellow subjects', but often as their 'brethren'.[47]

For those who addressed the king with professions of loyalty, Americans were 'unnatural' rebels. Much was made of American ingratitude. They had been nurtured by Britain and saved in the last war by the expenditure of British blood and treasure.[48] Addresses from weaving towns in Wiltshire complained that Americans owed their 'Protection and Prosperity' to the exertions of their 'poorer Fellow Subjects' and would contribute nothing in return.[49] When the king's speech on 26 October 1775 invoked the high 'Spirit of the *British* Nation', Americans were most certainly not included.[50] The Prohibitory Act with its provisions that American ships and trade were 'the Ships and Effects of open Enemies' put the colonies out of the nation beyond any conceivable doubt.[51] Congress confirmed this by its declaration of independence and by seeking the alliance of the Bourbon powers.

III

At the end of the war Lord Shelburne and his colleagues in the peace-making process had aspirations for a continuing union of peoples, but once peace had been made and Britain had been able to dictate the terms of the post-war commercial relationship, her new political leadership seems to have taken as little interest in developments in the United States as their predecessors in the 1760s had done in developments in the thirteen colonies. It was therefore largely left to merchants, religious communities, promoters of emigration and indi-

[45] *Popular Politics and the American Revolution* and *Religion, Revolution and English Radicalism: Non-Conformity in Eighteenth-Century Politics and Society* (Cambridge, 1990).

[46] *The Speeches and Writings of Edmund Burke*, 7 vols to date (Oxford, 1980–), III, ed. Warren M. Elofson and John A. Woods, 248, 251, 303, 328, 350, 354.

[47] See, for instance, the protest of the Freeholders of Middlesex, 26 Sept. 1775, against sending 'armed legions of Englishmen thence to cut the throats of Englishmen' (*American Archives*, 4th ser., III, 786).

[48] For example, Dundee petition, *London Gazette*, 4–7 Nov. 1775.

[49] Ibid., 17–21 Oct. 1775.

[50] *Journals of the House of Commons*, XXXV, 398.

[51] 16 Geo. III, c. 5.

viduals of all sorts to try to knit together the arteries slashed through by war and separation.

Some things were restored relatively easily. British–American trade revived quickly, although there were casualties among the old British firms.[52] British emigration across the Atlantic also revived. Irish people began to return to the new republic almost at once in even larger numbers than before 1775; Scots at first tended to head further north to what was still British territory.[53] There was a forced emigration of loyalists to Britain. They continued to use the concepts of the 'country' from which they were exiled and the 'nation' to which they now looked for justice.[54] They rarely seem to have felt themselves at home when they crossed the Atlantic; 'Ironically the loyalists only realized how American they were after they had abandoned America.'[55] British opinion seems to have been in no doubt that they were his majesty's loyal American subjects, not part of the British nation, and the great bulk of them settled not in Britain but in surviving British colonies.

The Revolution produced a vigorous republican critique of imported tastes in favour of home-grown American simplicity, but, as Richard Bushman puts it, 'The multifaceted criticism of gentility did not impede in the slightest the pursuit of refinement.'[56] Refinement was still deemed to come from Europe, above all from England, and American visitors continued to come to Britain to improve themselves and their offspring.

The war weakened transatlantic religious networks. All American religious denominations asserted their independence from churches in Britain. A powerful sense of a unique American providential destiny replaced pre-revolutionary ideals of a single elect nation on both sides of the Atlantic. British–American projects for the redemption of the Indians foundered, although the enemies of slavery and the slave trade on both sides of the ocean increasingly made common cause after 1783.[57] The Society for the Propagation of the Gospel abandoned its mission to the old thirteen colonies, leaving the seriously damaged American Anglican church to fend for itself. British dissenters no longer acted as the patrons of their colonial brethren who were now nominally at least emancipated from religious establishments and any sort of

[52] Olson, *Making the Empire Work*, 182–3.

[53] T.C. Smout, N.C. Landsman and T.M. Devine, 'Scottish Emigration in the Seventeenth and Eighteenth Centuries', L.M. Cullen, 'The Irish Diaspora of the Seventeenth and Eighteenth Centuries', *Europeans on the Move: Studies on European Migration, 1500–1800*, ed. Nicholas Canny (Oxford, 1994), 97–8, 148.

[54] *The Case and Claim of the American Loyalists Impartially Stated and Considered* [1783], 2.

[55] Mary Beth Norton, *The British–Americans: The Loyalist Exiles in England 1774–89* (1974), 41.

[56] *The Refinement of America*, 195.

[57] Betty Fladeland, *Men and Brothers: Anglo-American Anti-Slavery Co-operation* (Urbana, 1972).

discrimination. The flow of charitable donations from Britain dried up.[58] Scots professors were still being imported, but a new basis for a national and republican education was being sought. When the Royal Society asked Arthur Lee for arrears in his subscription, he replied that 'since the establishment of American independence he had considered himself as no longer a fellow of the Royal Society'. In 1788 the Society duly elected the president of the American Academy of Arts and Sciences, but from the list of 'foreign candidates'.[59]

Although there were strong continuities with the pre-revolutionary past, much could not be restored. Links for which the empire had provided the framework weakened or snapped when that empire foundered. The proposition that British ministers, motivated by a high-minded sense of national necessity but abysmally ignorant of American realities, had driven the empire onto the rocks seems irrefutable. Yet responsibility for the wreck of empire by no means rests exclusively with ministers. Far from entreating the ship's officers to change course, a large contingent of the British passengers and crew, especially those who enjoyed the more comfortable berths, had cheered them on.

Ministerial policies had forced the peoples of the empire in the last resort to choose between a British or an American allegiance. British people might esteem individual Americans and value empire, but for most of them it must be an empire in proper subordination to Britain, which was the focus for their loyalty. Only during the campaign against the Stamp Act, a campaign which had the support of the then administration, is there evidence of significant dissent in parliament or outside it for the policies that had asserted parliamentary supremacy over the colonies. As the great petitioning movement of 1775 demonstrated, many British people who accepted the subordinate status of the colonies within the British empire did not wish to fight a war to enforce that subordination. Yet Bradley, who has done so much to reveal the strength of dissent against the war, shows that people of power and influence in society tended strongly to the government side in England in 1775: Anglican clergy, the law, office-holders, members of corporations, 'a large complement of gentlemen, baronets and esquires and at least half the merchants in any given setting'.[60] In Scotland the preponderance among such people would have been even greater. British army officers accepted the duty of suppressing rebellion with relatively little dissent.[61] Americans liked to believe that those with a practical interest in the empire would in general support conciliation.

[58] Olson, *Making the Empire Work*, 186.
[59] Stearns, 'Colonial Fellows', 251–2, 267–8.
[60] *Religion, Revolution and English Radicalism*, 394.
[61] Stephen Conway, 'British Army Officers and the American War for Independence', *William and Mary Quarterly*, 3rd ser., 41 (1984), 265–76.

This was not necessarily so. To care about the colonies did not always entail sharing colonial points of view. Merchants with colonial connections in London, Bristol and Lancashire seem to have been split over the war,[62] while Glasgow's delay, unlike other Scottish burghs, in formally pledging its loyalty seems to have been a tactical response to the vulnerability of the tobacco trade.[63]

In what they rejected in 'Americans', people of substance in British society defined their own beliefs. The American and the Irish doctrine of a series of autonomous *patriae*, enjoying the full rights of Englishmen, united by allegiance to the crown and at the best by the recognition of an ill-defined superiority owed to the Westminster parliament, was unacceptable. In the first place, the interpretation of the rights of Englishmen with its emphasis on individual consent was thought to be out of date. British people now enjoyed a freedom that depended on accepting the authority of the legislature and obeying the due processes of law. Secondly, autonomous *patriae* were incompatible with the needs of national survival in an age of fierce international rivalry. The British empire was based on freedom, but this must be tempered by obedience to central authority on vital issues. Those, like the Scots, who were willing to accept a full parliamentary union could be incorporated into the British nation. That solution was, however, impractical for trans-oceanic colonies and in any case the Americans by their reluctance to co-operate for the common good and later by their flagrant defiance of the British legislature had ruled themselves out of any such privilege. All that could be done was to attempt by persuasion and ultimately by force to bring them back to their obedience as subjects of crown and parliament. Those who dissented from the war against the colonies could later reassert their Britishness in the war against the traditional Bourbon enemies of Britain.

The American crisis brought out starkly the limitations on evolving British concepts of nationhood. It could not be exported beyond the British Isles. Nevertheless, a territorially limited doctrine of nationhood was by no means incompatible with grandiose imperial ambitions. Common subjecthood was not a status that need be confined to people of British origins. While British Americans were rejecting it, it was being extended to French people in America and events were taking place in India which would mean its eventual extension to millions of people in Asia.

---

[62] Bradley, *Popular Politics and the American Revolution*, 81–2, 190; John Sainsbury, *Disaffected Patriots: London Supporters of Revolutionary America 1769–1782* (Kingston, 1987), 117; Kathleen Wilson, *The Sense of the People: Politics, Culture and Imperialism in England, 1715–1785* (Cambridge, 1995), 270.

[63] T. M. Devine, *The Tobacco Lords: A Study of the Tobacco Merchants of Glasgow and their Trading Activities, c. 1740–90* (Edinburgh, 1975), 124.

THATCHERISM: AN HISTORICAL PERSPECTIVE*

READ BY E. H. H. GREEN, 23 JANUARY 1998

MARGARET THATCHER resigned as Prime Minister and leader of the Conservative party in November 1990, but both she and the political ideology to which her name has been appended[1] continue to fascinate pundits and scholars. Indeed, since Thatcher's resignation in November 1990, curiosity about her political legacy has, if anything, increased, fuelled in part by the memoirs produced by the ex-premier herself and a large number of her one-time Cabinet colleagues. Since the early 1980s the bulk of work that has appeared on Thatcherism has been dominated either by what one might describe as the 'higher journalism' or by political science scholarship,[2] both of which have been most exercised by the questions of what Thatcherism was and where it took British politics and society. In this essay I want to look at Thatcherism from an historical perspective and thus ask a different question, namely where did Thatcherism, and in particular the political economy of Thatcherism, come from?

Given that Margaret Thatcher became leader of the Conservative party in 1975 this might seem a logical starting-point from which to track Thatcherism's origins. Some have argued, however, that Thatcher's election in itself was of little importance, in that the Conservative party's leadership contest in 1975 was a competition not to be Edward Heath, and that Thatcher won because she was more obviously not Edward Heath than anyone else.[3] This emphasis on the *personal* aspects of the leadership issue necessarily plays down any ideological significance

---

*I am grateful to the Minda de Gunzberg Center for European Studies, Harvard University, which provided me with the opportunity to write and 'test' the ideas of this essay. I am also grateful to the Modern British History Seminar, Princeton University, the Politics and History Seminar, Duke University, and the Modern History Seminar, Georgia Institute of Technology.

[1] Robert Skidelsky, amongst others, has rightly pointed out that 'Mrs Thatcher is the only Prime Minister whose name has given rise to an "ism" ', 'Introduction' to *idem* (ed.), *Thatcherism* (London, 1988), p. 2.

[2] In the former category, see in particular, P. Jenkins, *Mrs Thatcher's Revolution* (London, 1985), P. Riddell, *The Thatcher Government* (London, 1989), H. Young, *One of Us* (London, 1990). For the latter see, for example, A. Gamble, *The Free Economy and the Strong State* (London, 1994, 2nd edn), K. Minogue and M. Biddiss (eds), *Thatcherism: Personality and Politics* (London, 1987), R. Skidelsky (ed.), *Thatcherism*, K. Hoover and R. Plant, *Conservative Capitalism in Britain and America* (London, 1989), T. Hames and A. Adonis (eds), *A Conservative Revolution* (Manchester, 1994).

[3] See Riddell, *Thatcher Government*, p. 21.

of Thatcher's victory, a point often reinforced by reference to the fact that key elements of the policy agenda that came to be associated with Thatcherism, notably privatisation, were by no means clearly articulated in the late 1970s and did not appear in the Conservative Election Manifesto of 1979.[4] On this basis Thatcherism had its ideological origins post 1975 and arguably post 1979 – it was simply what Thatcher's party did after it came to government.

But there are problems with the notion that the events of 1975 were ideologically innocent. Margaret Thatcher was the candidate of the Conservative Right in 1975. She stood only after the Right's main standard-bearer, Sir Keith Joseph, had ruled himself out with a clumsy, eugenics-sounding speech at Birmingham in the autumn of 1974. But, since the summer of 1974, Thatcher had developed a close relationship with Joseph, and their alliance was well established by the time of the leadership contest. Moreover, between 1975 and 1979 both Thatcher and Joseph outlined in keynote speeches many of the broad policy objectives of what came to be known as Thatcherism, and in the same period the think tank that Joseph established in 1974, the Centre for Policy Studies, produced a series of policy papers that foreshadowed the legislative developments of the Thatcher administrations.[5] There *was* more than contingency to Thatcher's gaining the Conservative leadership in 1975, and from 1975 to 1979 this became quite evident.[6]

Even if one admits an underlying ideological element to Thatcher's success in 1975 it could still be the case that it was a product of the 1970s. Thatcher's election could be viewed as a reaction to the failures of the Heath government of 1970–4. Arguably, this created within the party a desire for a change of approach as well as a change of leader, and this Thatcher, well tutored by Joseph and his acolytes at the CPS, seemed to offer. On a more general level the ending of the post-war boom in the early 1970s triggered a combination of economic difficulties which it had been assumed impossible to combine – in particular rising unemployment and rapid inflation. This posed problems for the supposedly dominant Keynesian paradigm of economic policy-making, in so far as (after Phillips) unemployment and inflation were supposed to enjoy an inverse relationship. This led to a questioning at various levels of the adequacy of Keynesianism, and especially to a renaissance of liberal-market and monetarist economics – ideas supposedly discarded in the boom years of the 1950s and 1960s. The political economy

---

[4] See, for example, Michael Biddiss' remark that in 1975 'Thatcher*ism* ... was ... still only quite imperfectly formed', 'Thatcherism: Concept and Interpretations', in Minogue and Biddiss (eds), *Thatcherism*, p. 6.

[5] See R. Cockett, *Thinking the Unthinkable* (London, 1993), pp. 254–74.

[6] See M. Wickham-Jones, 'Right Turn: A Revisionist Account of the 1975 Conservative Party Leadership Election', *TCBH*, viii, 1997.

of Thatcherism could thus be viewed as a product of the economic context of the 1970s, and part of a larger, international re-birth of interest in liberal-market and monetarist economics.[7] Undoubtedly, such an analysis of Conservative party politics in the early 1970s, and the changing climate of both economic performance and debate, carries some explanatory weight. But this essay would suggest that one needs to go back a lot further than the 1970s to establish the pedigree of Thatcherite political economy.

A definition of terms is perhaps appropriate at this juncture – what do I mean when I speak of Thatcherite political economy? I will define it in terms of the self-professed intentions of Margaret Thatcher and her administrations. They saw their main aim as being to 'roll back the frontiers of the State'. This was to be achieved by replacing the mixed economy with a private-sector dominated market economy. This in turn was to be complemented by a reform and reduction of the welfare state, by a lowering of direct personal taxation and the encouragement of wider property-ownership. Institutions which hampered the operation of the market, in particular trade unions, were to have their powers and legal privileges curbed. Finally, low inflation rather than full employment was to be the central goal of economic policy. In short, Thatcherism saw its task as being to challenge and ultimately to dismantle the institutions, practices and assumptions which underpinned what had come to be known by the mid-1970s as 'the post-war consensus', or what Thatcher herself referred to (without meaning to be complimentary) as 'the progressive consensus'.[8]

In terms of understanding Thatcherism *historically* the explicit assault on the 'post-war consensus' is important. To begin with it stemmed from Thatcherism's own historical interpretation of what had gone wrong with the British economy. Thatcherite interest in and use of history is best known in the context of eulogies about 'Victorian values',[9] but there is strong evidence to support the view that 'the values she [Thatcher] admired were the values of the inter-war years'.[10] Certainly the 1930s and the immediate post-war period played as important a role as the Victorian era in Thatcherism's construction of the past. Speaking to the CPS in January 1975, Keith Joseph argued that Britain

[7] For a summary of this argument, see Skidelsky, 'Introduction', pp. 10–13, and note Kenneth Minogue's remark that 'The real context of Thatcherism is to be found in the troubles ... in the 1970s', Minogue and Biddiss (eds), *Thatcherism*, xii.

[8] M. Thatcher in New York, 15 Sept. 1975, reprinted in *idem*, *The Revival of Britain* (London, 1989), p. 3.

[9] For a discussion of 'Victorian values' against this backdrop, see T. C. Smout (ed.), *Victorian Values* (London, 1992).

[10] J. Gould and D. Anderson, 'Thatcherism and British Society', in Minogue and Biddiss (eds), *Thatcherism*, pp. 42–3.

needed to embrace *embourgeoisement* 'which went so far in Victorian times *and even in the much-maligned "thirties"*'.[11] The importance of the 1930s to the Thatcherite schema was underscored by Thatcher herself in her second volume of memoirs. Commenting on 1930s life in her father's grocery in Grantham, she noted that that the experience gave her

> A sympathetic insight into what I would later come to think of as 'capitalism' or the 'free enterprise system'. Whereas for my ... political contemporaries it was the *alleged* failure of that system in the Great Depression that convinced them that something better had to be found, for me the reality of business in our shop and the bustling centre of Grantham demonstrated the opposite ... what I learned in Grantham ensured that abstract criticisms I would hear of capitalism came up against the reality of my own experience: I was thus inoculated against the conventional economic wisdom of post-war Britain.[12]

For Thatcher, like Joseph, the 1930s was a period to be praised, not condemned, and post-war acceptance of a 'pessimistic', Keynesian analysis of the period was seen to have informed a mistaken rejection of the liberal-market orthodoxies of the inter-war years and, therefore, an equally erroneous adoption of Statist, Keynesian forms of economic management after 1945. On this basis the reforms of the 1945–51 Attlee government, and more particularly the Conservative party's adaptation to them, had been a mistake based on a misinterpretation of the inter-war period and of the 1945 general election as a verdict on the 1930s. Sir Keith Joseph's speeches of 1974–5 were very precise in seeing the 'the past *thirty* years' as one long error of judgement.[13] Likewise, one of Thatcher's closest colleagues, Nicholas Ridley, noted that he had entered politics to reverse the Attlee government's reforms,[14] whilst Thatcher's favourite party chairman argued that 'the failure of the Conservative governments of 1951–64 to reverse the Attlee experiment was deplorable'.[15] More formal Thatcherite history was equally clear on this point, with Andrew Roberts noting that

> Instead of treating it as the freak result it was, an entire generation of Tory politicians was emasculated by the 1945 election result,

---

[11] Sir Keith Joseph, London, 1 Jan. 1975, reprinted in *idem, Reversing the Trend* (London, 1975), p. 57 (my emphasis).
[12] M. Thatcher, *The Path to Power* (London, 1994), p. 566, my emphasis.
[13] See, for example, Sir Keith Joseph at Upminster, 22 June 1974, in *idem, Reversing*, p. 7 (my emphasis).
[14] N. Ridley, *My Style of Government: the Thatcher Years* (London, 1991), p. 2.
[15] C. Parkinson, *Right at the Centre* (London, 1991), p. 191.

especially over the issues of nationalization, the growth of the State and trade union reform.[16]

Thatcherite history saw both the country and the Conservative party as having taken a wrong turning in and after 1945 as a consequence of misreading the 1930s.

To rely upon memoirs and assessments from the 1970s and 1990s to demonstrate a point could be regarded as a dangerous valorisation of post-hoc judgements. But whether Thatcherite memoirs and commentaries are 'accurate' is not the real issue here. The fact that they all construct the past in similar fashion underscores the *political* essence of their historical judgement. More important still is the fact that Thatcherite 'history' represented the culmination of a long-standing Conservative critique, extant since at least 1945, of developments in national and Conservative party economic policy. In this respect this essay will seek to establish that the first step in understanding the vehemence of Thatcherism's assault on the 'post-war settlement' is to grasp that the Conservative party never fully accepted that anything had been settled.

At present the history of post-war Conservative politics suggests that although the Conservatives were slow to appreciate the significance of the *Beveridge Report*'s proposals and the 1944 White Paper on Full Employment, they rapidly made up ground after 1945. The shock of the general election defeat, it has been argued, demonstrated the popularity of Labour's commitment to reform and thereby strengthened the hand of 'progressive' opinion in the Conservative ranks. As a consequence of the related pressures on the one hand of electoral necessity and on the other of internal reformers, the Conservative party, it has been suggested, shifted its position on issues of economic and social State intervention. The growing authority of 'progressive' figures such as R. A. Butler, Lord Hailsham and Harold Macmillan have been seen as evidence of the Conservatives' determination to discard their hard-faced inter-war image.[17] Likewise, Conservative deeds seemed to speak as loudly as the words of their 'progressives'. Apart from returning the steel and road-haulage industries to private ownership, successive Conservative administrations after 1951 made no great attempt to roll back the Attlee government's reforms. Indeed, in 1958 the Conservative premier, Harold Macmillan, proved willing to accept the resignation of his entire Treasury team in order, it seems, to defend and publicly demonstrate his government's commitment to full employment. The

[16] A. Roberts, *Eminent Churchillians* (London, 1994), p. 253.
[17] For this interpretation, see K. O. Morgan, *The People's Peace* (Oxford, 1991), pp. 31–2. For a different analysis, see H. Jones, 'The Conservative Party and the Welfare State, 1942–55', unpublished London University PhD thesis, 1992.

actions of Conservative governments in the 1950s appear to confirm a process which saw the party accommodate itself to the mixed economy and the welfare state.

As far as it goes this story of Conservative accommodation to the Attlee government's reforms is accurate, in so far as as the Conservative *leadership* after 1945 assumed that it would be impolitic to launch an assault on either the welfare state, full employment or the mixed economy. But to see Conservative politics in the 1950s in terms of a triumph of 'progressive' Conservatism is to tell, at best, only part of the story. From the publication of the *Beveridge Report* in 1942, through the post-war Labour reform legislation and on into the 1950s and 1960s, there is evidence of deep-seated Conservative hostility, especially in the middle and lower ranks of the party, to the development and impact of State intervention in the economic and social spheres. Moreover, the intensity of this hostility, which was firmly grounded in a liberal-market critique of Labour's post-war reforms, increased rather than decreased as time went by.

When the *Beveridge Report* appeared in 1942 the Conservative response was at best lukewarm.[18] Popular interest in and approval of the *Report* forced the Conservatives to take it seriously and a committee, chaired by Ralph Assheton, was set up to examine its proposals. Although there were aspects of Beveridge which this committee accepted, it made two fundamental criticisms. The first was voiced by Assheton personally when he told R. A. Butler in December 1942 that

> one of the chief troubles about the *Beveridge Report* is that whereas his diagnosis relates to Want, his proposals are very largely devoted to giving money to people who are not in want.[19]

In effect this was a critique of 'universality', a principle at the heart of Beveridge's proposals and which represented his attempt to remove Poor Law stigmatisation from the post-war welfare structure. The second criticism was the level of taxation that would be required for Beveridge's scheme. Here Assheton's committee reported that if the economy was to flourish after the war this would require 'a substantial reduction of taxation, especially in the rate of income tax'.[20] The argument was clear and (to a 1990s audience) familiar: a successful economy requires incentives, and a welfare system based on universality

---

[18] See K. Jeffreys, 'British Politics and Social Policy During the Second World War', *Historical Journal*, xxx, 1987, and Jones, 'Conservative Party', *passim*.

[19] R. Assheton to R. A. Butler, 21 Dec. 1942, Butler paper, Trinity College Library, Cambridge, MS RAB, H77, fol. 70.

[20] Report on the Beveridge Proposals, 19 Jan. 1943, Conservative Party Archive [hereafter CPA], Bodleian Library, Oxford, Conservative Research Department [hereafter CRD] 2/28/6.

hampers incentives, first by offering 'a sofa rather than a springboard' of benefits and, second, by requiring a level of taxation that reduced the rewards of productive enterprise.

In 1945 this liberal-market opposition to plans for extensive social reform set the tone for the Conservative election campaign. The previous year had seen the publication of F. A. Hayek's *The Road to Serfdom*, with its warnings about the loss of liberty, choice and efficiency that interventionist economies entailed. Mention of Hayek here is important: not simply because his *œuvre*, and *The Road to Serfdom* in particular, became essential referents for Thatcherism, but because *The Road to Serfdom* played a major role in the Conservatives' 1945 campaign. Ralph Assheton, by then party chairman, read Hayek's work soon after it was published, and was so impressed by it that he immediately advised Conservative election agents and candidates to read it, and wanted 12,000 copies of an abridged version to be distributed as campaign literature, which entailed promising the publishers one and a half tons of the party's paper ration for the election. Moreover, it was Assheton who wrote the outline notes for Churchill's 'Gestapo' speech of the 1945 campaign. This speech, which claimed that Labour's proposed reforms would have to be enforced by State police, expressed, albeit crudely, basic Hayekian themes.[21]

The Conservative defeat in 1945 weakened the liberal-market position within the party: that Assheton was replaced as party chairman by the emollient figure of Lord Woolton in 1946, and that R. A. Butler took over the Conservative Research Department (CRD) marked the increased strength of the 'progressive' Conservative cause. But two points need to made here about Conservative politics and the Conservative electoral revival from 1945 to 1951. First, although the liberal-market position was weakened it did not disappear, and such views played a major role in the Conservatives' ongoing criticisms of the Attlee government's reforms, particularly in the realms of the creation of the National Health Service (NHS), nationalisation and housing.[22] Second, the Conservatives' effort to revive their electoral fortunes saw them target middle-class floating voters, especially in the South and South-East of England, by presenting themselves as the party that would reduce government expenditure and taxation, remove controls, especially building controls, and rationing, and thereby free the private sector to provide for expanded consumer demand and aspirant home-

---

[21] For this information I am indebted to Jones, 'Conservative Party', pp. 107–8.

[22] For the Conservative critique of Labour's health policy, see in particular, C. Webster, 'Conflict and Consensus: Explaining the British Health Service', *TCBH*, I, 1990. On housing, see Jones, 'Conservative Party', pp. 127–46. *Parliamentary Debates* remain the best source for the conflicts over nationalisation.

owners.[23] Thus, although the liberal-market tone of the 1945 had been quietened by 1951, it is essential to remember that the Conservative leitmotif in 1950–1 was 'Set the People Free', not 'the welfare estate and the mixed economy are safe in our hands'.

It is worth dwelling briefly on the Conservative electoral revival of the late 1940s and early 1950s, and in particular on the Conservatives' underlying strategy, for this in itself brings home the importance Conservatives attached to opposing the Labour government's position. The basic Conservative aim was to target floating voters, particularly those antagonised by the rationing, austerity and government controls associated with Labour's period in office.[24] According to internal party research the profile and outlook of these floating voters was very similar to that of Liberal supporters,[25] and the Conservatives thus made every effort to attract Liberal voters. This included constructing an official pact with the National Liberal grouping, and equally important seeking to appeal to Liberal supporters 'where no [Liberal] organisation exists' – a large number of local Conservative associations even went so far as to rename themselves 'Conservative and Liberal'.[26] The *raison d'être* of this strategy was to construct an 'anti-Socialist' bloc such as Baldwin had built in the inter-war years. In this context it is significant that the supposedly 'progressive' Industrial Charter was welcomed by at least one local Conservative association on the grounds that there was 'nothing in it with which a Liberal would disagree'.[27] In 1951 this strategy paid dividends when the Conservatives gathered in the lion's share of the collapsing Liberal vote – not on the grounds of endorsing the Attlee govermnent's reforms but on the basis that they would at least ensure that there were no further extensions of State intervention.

The Conservative electoral revival by no means put an end to liberal-market activism. In 1950 Richard Law, the overlooked son of the unknown Prime Minister, published *Return from Utopia*, a sustained critique of Labour's post-war reforms from a liberal-market perspective.

[23] I. Zweiniger-Bargielowska, 'Rationing, Austerity and the Conservative Party Recovery After 1945', *Historical Journal*, xxxvi, 1993.

[24] See ibid., and also *idem*, 'Consensus and Consumption: Rationing, Austerity and Controls after the War', in H. Jones and M. Kandiah (eds), *The Myth of Consensus* (Basingstoke, 1996), pp. 78–96.

[25] 'The Floating Vote', 6 Dec. 1949, CRD 2/21/1, in M. Kandiah, 'Conservative Leaders' Strategy – and Consensus, 1945–64', in *The Myth of Consensus*, p. 63.

[26] Lord Woolton to Conservative Constituency Agents, 8 May 1947, Woolton papers, Bodleian Library, Oxford, MS WLTN, fols 66–7. For the Conservatives' view of the Liberals as subaltern anti-Socialists, see E. H. H. Green, 'The Conservative Party, the State and the Electorate, 1945–64', in M. Taylor and J. Lawrence (eds), *Party, State and Society in Modern Britain* (Aldershot, 1996).

[27] Sheffield Conservative Party Agent, quoted in J. Ramsden, *The Age of Churchill and Eden* (London, 1996), p. 150.

In particular Law attacked the high levels of taxation required to fund the welfare state, and argued that inflation was bound to exact a serious toll in an economy committed to full employment.[28] Law did not confine his criticism to publications. At the Conservative party conference in 1952 he was one of the principal speakers to a motion that 'public expenditure has increased, is increasing and ought to be diminished'[29] – a motion that was carried by an overwhelming majority. In 1952 most Conservative demands for 'economy' were directed at a 'bloated' Civil Service. However, by the 1955 party conference speakers were arguing that the welfare state was 'admirable, *so long as you can afford it*' and that full employment was only being sustained by the profligate spending of government departments and nationalised industries.[30] Given the stringent administrative processes designed to filter out hostile comment at conference, the fact that such criticisms were being voiced was indicative of significant rank-and-file displeasure. Furthermore, the language of these criticisms was informed by clear liberal-market imperatives.

Nor was it only the rank and file who expressed disquiet. As early as 1950 the backbench 1922 Committee was of the view that 'no more money can be spent on the welfare state, and they were keen to establish a Conservative approach to social policy that was not 'me-tooing Socialist solutions'. It was against this backdrop that the 'One Nation' group of Conservative MPs began to produce a series of publications which sought to define a distinctive Conservative approach to the economy and social policy. An interesting example of their thinking was provided by two young MPs, Iain Macleod and Enoch Powell, in a 1952 publication *The Social Services: Needs Not Means*, which asserted that 'the question ... which poses itself is not "should a means test be applied to a social service?" but "why should any social service be provided without a real test of need?" '.[31] Once again the universality of the Beveridge system was being challenged. The One Nation group, in the pamphlet *Change is Our Ally* (written by Enoch Powell and Angus Maude), also attacked Statist incursions into economic management. In spite of their Disraelian moniker, the One Nation group sought to bring liberal-market thinking to the centre of Conservative debate on social and economic policy.

The 1951 Conservative government did not embrace any significant liberal-market proposals.[32] The steel industry was denationalised, ration-

---

[28] R. Law, *Return from Utopia* (London, 1950).

[29] National Union, Conference Report, 1952, CPA, Microfilm Cards 8–9.

[30] Ibid.

[31] I. Macleod and E. Powell, *The Social Services: Needs Not Means* (London, 1952).

[32] Although the fact that the 'Robot' scheme to float the pound was so heavily canvassed, it is a significant indication that 'Keynesian' thinking was by no means

ing and controls were removed, and Butler at the Exchequer was able to reduce personal taxation. Systematic means tests for benefits were resisted, however, and there was no major attempt to reduce the scale of the public sector or to reform the welfare state. That the government was able to adopt this approach and still gain an increased majority in 1955 seemed to indicate that they were able to ignore liberal-market opinion in the party. But after 1955 there were signs that the Conservatives could not ignore these voices with impunity.

Significant problems began to emerge for the Conservatives in and after 1956. Although they sustained only one loss before 1958 the Conservative government experienced greatly reduced majorities in a number of by-elections. At the same time two protest organisations emerged, the Middle Class Alliance (MCA) and the People's League for the Defence of Freedom (PLDF), both of which were highly critical of post-war economic and social reform. I have dealt at length with these organisations elsewhere and I will not discuss their activities and the Conservative response to them in detail here.[33] Suffice it to say that the MCA had a shopping-list of liberal-market demands, whilst the PLDF campaigned on the single issue of trade-union reform, and that both groups were considered to have a membership made up of people who would normally have been considered 'natural' Conservative voters. What made these organisations particularly worrying for the Conservative leadership was that they were seen as symptomatic of a wave of dissatisfaction with Conservative policy among, in particular, members of the British middle class – the social group regarded as the core Conservative constituency. The MCA and PLDF were seen as an extreme, institutional manifestation of grievances voiced by the party rank and file at the disagreeable party conferences of 1955–8 and of the 'middle-class revolt' which brought about the drop in the Conservative vote in Tunbridge Wells in 1956, at Torquay, Edinburgh and Ipswich and the lost seat of Lewisham North in 1957, and the loss of Torrington in 1958. Harold Macmillan, as usual, sought to conceal any anxiety behind an appearance of *sang froid*, telling the party's chief research officer, 'I am always hearing about the middle classes. What is it they really want? Can you put it on a sheet of notepaper, and then I will see if I can give it to them.'[34] But the fact that he and others in the party hierarchy *were* always hearing about the middle classes was the point. From mid-1956 on Butler was constantly being warned that the 'oppressed middle classes' would cause the party problems. In early

---

entrenched in the party. See N. Rollings, 'Poor Mr. Butskell: A Short Life Wracked by Schizophrenia', *TCBH*, v, 1994.

[33] See Green, 'Conservative party', in Taylor and Lawrence (eds), *Party, State and Society*.

[34] Macmillan to M. Fraser, 17 Feb. 1957, Public Record Office, PREM 11/1816.

1957 some constituency parties were reporting difficulties of recruitment and subscription renewal, and in the autumn of 1957 both Oliver Poole and Lord Hailsham, the Conservative chairman and vice-chairman, referred to 'Poujadist' tendencies amongst the party's middle-class voters and rank and file.[35]

From the protests of the MCA and PLDF, and from party conference debates and constituency reports, it is possible to distil four main interrelated grievances behind the 'middle-class revolt'. First, inflation; second, the growing power and abuses of trade unions in general, and in particular their ability under full-employment conditions to achieve inflationary wage settlements. Third, the level of taxation required to fund an 'over-generous' welfare state and inefficient nationalised industries. Fourth, and perhaps most important, the apparent inability or unwillingness of the Conservative party to adopt 'real' Conservative policies to combat these problems and, as a corollary, the apparent tendency of successive Conservative governments to 'hang on to Socialist policies and legislation that should have been swept away long ago'.[36]

It was this pressure from the party rank and file and disaffected voters that explains Harold Macmillan's comments about the centrality of stable prices which he added as a rider to his 'never had it so good speech' at Bedford in 1957. It was also this pressure that provided the context for Peter Thorneycroft's attempt to prioritise the fight against inflation later in that year, which was to culminate in his and his Treasury team's resignation in January 1958.[37] Less publicly dramatic, but equally important, the Conservative hierarchy's establishment of a Policy Studies Group (PSG) in the summer of 1957, to examine possible changes of policy direction, the deliberations of the Party Commitee on the Nationalized Industries (PCNI) and the setting up of the Policy Committee on the Future Funding of the Social Services (PCFFSS) in 1959, were informed by a desire to find a means of quelling the concerns of the party's core constituents and its rank and file.[38]

None of the above-mentioned party committees produced proposals for sweeping changes of the kind advocated by the party rank and file, but their deliberations are indicative of an important debate on the merits of post-war economic and social policy that was taking place in

---

[35] See J. Ramsden, *Winds of Change: the Age of Macmillan and Heath* (London, 1996), pp. 19, 29.

[36] T. Constantine to O. Poole, 10 June 1956, CPA, CCO 120/3/4.

[37] See Green, 'Conservative party', and *idem*, 'The Treasury Resignations of 1958 Reconsidered' (forthcoming).

[38] For a discussion of the PSG's work, see Green, 'Conservative party', and for the PCFFSS, see R. Lowe, 'The Failure to Reform the Welfare State', in I. Zweiniger-Bargielowska and M. Francis (eds), *The Conservatives and British Society in the 20th Century* (Cardiff, 1997). For the deliberations of the PCNI, see CRD 2/6/2,3 in the CPA.

the party in the late 1950s and early 1960s. The PSG's sessions saw much deliberation of inflation, with Macmillan acknowledging at its ninth meeting that 'on the domestic front the reconciliation of full employment with a stable cost of living was the key problem', and he was prompted to ask 'could either aim be said to be electorally more important?'[39] The Prime Minister's response to his Treasury team's resignation seemed to indicate that, in the short term at any rate, he saw full employment as more significant,[40] but the PSG's discussions indicated that there was significant and growing pressure for a prioritisation of inflation.

With regard to the nationalised industries both the PCNI and the PSG saw much critical comment of the performance of public corporations. It is worth noting that the PCNI's initial remit was

> to examine and make recommendations regarding the position of the nationalized industries' ... with particular reference to the possibility of introducing any element of competitive enterprise[41]

and that its chairman felt that one purpose its deliberations served was 'to bridge the gulf that existed on the subject between the Ministers and the Backbench'.[42] The very acknowledgement of such a gulf is in itself interesting, as is the fact that when the party's Advisory Committee on Policy (ACP) discussed nationalised concerns the idea of a half-way house between public and private ownership, referred to as 'the BP model',[43] was floated. Equally interesting, the chairman of the 1922 Committee greeted this suggestion with approval, and added that such a 'hiving off' would receive support from the party as the first step to later more ambitious proposals'.[44] The PCNI, PSG and ACP were loath (partly for fear of treading on particular Ministers' toes) to endorse ideas of denationalisation, but their discussions revealed an awareness of a body of opinion in the party that favoured such a radical move.

On trade unions, Macmillan's Minister of Labour, Iain Macleod, constantly stressed at PSG meetings that the legal and political problems involved in legislating on strike action, picketing and the closed shop were too great to warrant action. Macleod was probably tired of having

---

[39] PSG, Minutes of the 4th Meeting, 15 July 1957, CPA, CRD 2/53/28.

[40] Through much of 1957 Macmillan offered a great deal of support to Thorneycroft and his team, which in part explains the legacy of bitterness which his 'back-pedalling' in the winter of 1957–8 engendered. See Green, 'Treasury Resignations'.

[41] PCNI, Terms of Reference, CRD 2/6/2, CPA.

[42] PCNI, Chairman's notes at the 17th Meeting, record by J. Douglas, CRD, 16 Dec. 1957, CPA, CRD 2/6/3.

[43] Minutes of the ACP, 25 Jan. 1957, CPA, ACP 2/1.

[44] J. G. Morrison, ibid.

to make this point, given that he, like his predecessor Walter Monckton,[45] had been repeatedly forced to make it to hostile party audiences after taking on his office.[46] But other members of the PSG were supporters of legal curbs on trade unions.[47] In April 1957 Reginald Maudling and John Simon 'reported strong feeling in the party against Trade Unions',[48] and in autumn that year James Douglas of CRD noted that 'since the 1955 election ... there seems to have been a slight move to the right on trade unions issues, nothing so definite as a People's League attitude, but the political centre of gravity ... seeems to have shifted appreciably'.[49] In 1958 the Conservative barristers' organisation, the Inns of Court Society, published *A Giant's Strength*, which advocated the removal of many of the legal immunities given to trade- union activities under the 1906 Trades Disputes Act.[50] In 1959 even Macleod felt that the pressure to do something had reached such a level that he included a promise to introduce legal reforms in the first draft of the Conservative election manifesto, only to have Macmillan intervene personally to remove it.[51] Conservative opinion on the trade-union question was clearly hardening.

On the question of public expenditure on the welfare state the PSG's discussions also saw strong sentiments in favour of reform. Enoch Powell argued that 'the whole machinery of social security has to be overhauled', that 'Lloyd George, Chamberlain and Beveridge have had their day', and that 'their theories and their system ... was simply the delayed reaction to Victorian poverty'.[52] Powell had two major criticisms to make. First, and here he restated earlier objections, he attacked the principle of universality – that the welfare structure was not needs-driven. Second, he pointed to the practical problem of finance, arguing that, for example, the National Insurance scheme was only solvent because of constant post-war inflation and that, with the population ageing and other demands increasing, targets and priorities had to be established. The PSG concurred with the idea of 'switching the emphasis of state expenditure away from services which, in a fully employed community, people ought to be able to provide at least in part for

[45] For rank-and-file criticisms of Conservative trade union policy in the early 1950s, see Roberts, *Eminent Churchillians*, pp. 259–71.

[46] For a particularly uncomfortable conference for Macleod on this issue, see the debate at the party conference at Llandudno in 1956.

[47] The most powerful advocates were the MP John Simon and Peter Goldman from the party's Research Department.

[48] PSG, Minutes of the 4th Meeting, 12 Apr. 1957, CPA, CRD 2/53/28.

[49] J. Douglas to J. Rodgers, 8 Aug. 1957, CPA, CRD 2/9/38.

[50] It is perhaps worth noting that one of the members of the Society who took part in the discussions leading to the publication of this document was Geoffrey Howe.

[51] See R. Shepherd, *Iain Macleod* (London, 1994), p. 149.

[52] E. Powell to J. Pain, n.d., Mar. 1957, CPA, CRD 2/53/26.

themselves',[53] but, in spite of this sympathy for Powell's views, the government produced no major action in 1957–8. However, even after the Conservatives' handsome success at the 1959 election, the party's Advisory Committee on Policy established that a key long-term issue was 'the future financing of the social services as a whole and to what extent we should break away ... from the principle of universality',[54] and it was precisely this issue that the PCFFSS was set up to examine, with a remit that echoed the concerns Powell had expressed at the PSG.

As the 1950s drew to a close the liberal-market critics of the supposed post-war settlement were on the march. The PSGs attempt in 1957–8 to frame the basis of what was referred to as 'the opportunity state' – an obvious attempt at differentiating Conservative thinking from the welfare state – laid emphasis on 'the opportunity to make money and get on' through a regime that would facilitate spending opportunities, encourage wider property- and share-ownership and lower personal taxation.[55] Such a regime, Lord Home argued, would serve to quell 'the restlessness amongst the middle class voters who fear that the standards which they have so painfully gained by work and thrift are going to be lost',[56] and also allow the party to identify itself more broadly with social mobility and aspirational consumerdom. Important question marks were being placed against the political and electoral viability of sustaining a system of social and economic policy that in the eyes of many in the party reflected 'Socialist' rather than Conservative values.

II

In September 1961 Harold Macmillan, after a Cabinet meeting about the economic situation, noted in his diary that there was a division of opinion between those who favoured 'old Whig, liberal, laissez faire traditions' and those who were 'not afraid of a little *dirigisme*'.[57] Not surprisingly, the author of *The Middle Way* sided with the *dirigistes*, and from 1961 to 1963 Macmillan sought to establish the institutional structure of a 'developmental state' through the creation of the National Economic Development Council (NEDC), a National Incomes Commission (NIC) and related actions such as the application to join the

[53] PSG, 13th Meeting, 24 Feb. 1958, CPA, CRD 2/53/28.
[54] Chairman's notes of the Meeting of the ACP, 9 Dec. 1959, CPA, ACP 1/10.
[55] P. Goldman, at PSG 2nd Meeting, 15 Mar. 1957, CPA, CRD 2/53/28.
[56] Home to R. A. Butler, 4 Mar. 1958, CPA, CRD 2/53/29.
[57] H. Macmillan, diary entry, 21 Sept. 1961, in *idem, At the End of the Day* (London, 1973), p. 37.

EEC and the abolition of Resale Price Maintenance.[58] But this served neither to quieten discontent in the lower echelons of the party nor to cement the Conservatives' electoral position, with the twin developments of a Liberal revival and adverse by-election reversals, most notably at Orpington in 1962, signalling a recurrence of the problems that had troubled the Conservatives in the mid- to late 1950s.

After Macmillan's resignation and the Conservative defeat at the 1964 general election calls for a change in policy direction gathered pace, and the election of Edward Heath as leader in 1965 seemed to many in the party to presage such a change. Heath inherited a party whose backbenches and grassroots were very restive.[59] At this juncture one senior Conservative politician, Enoch Powell, emerged as the most articulate spokesman of this unease and an eloquent critic of post-war economic policy. Although he was to be dismissed from the Shadow Cabinet in 1968 after his Birmingham speech on immigration, Powell's main contributions to Conservative intra-party debate from 1964 to 1970 were focused on the economy. Powell's basic message, condensed in his 1965 collection of speeches *A Nation Not Afraid*, was that the Conservative party had to stop apologising for being a 'capitalist' party and embrace true, that is liberal, market, capitalist policies. The grievances expressed by the party rank and file in the 1950s – inflation, high levels of public expenditure and high taxation – were all highlighted by Powell as the incubi of the post-war economy.[60] After the Conservatives' 1966 general election defeat Powell intensified his assault on post-war economic management, with a further series of speeches in the autumn of that year criticising State intervention and calling for a return to a liberal-market approach.[61] One novelty of Powell's critique, and one that was to become central to liberal-market thought in the 1970s, was an emphasis on government monetary policy as the chief cause of inflation. At the time, however, it was the general tenor of his economic liberalism rather than specifics that attracted attention.

Given that Powell had stood for the party leadership in 1965, and gained only 15 votes, his ideas could easily be dismissed as the public musings of a maverick. But it would be wrong to measure his significance in these formal, 'high political' terms. Powell's poor showing in the leadership election owed more to his lack of interest in the politics of the Commons' tea room than to indifference to his ideas. His old One Nation colleague, Iain Macleod, noted in a review of *A Nation Not Afraid*

[58] For the most detailed description of these initiatives, see K. Middlemass, *Power Competition and the State* (3 vols, 1986–91), ii, pp. 28–58.

[59] See Ramsden, *Winds of Change*, pp. 245–53.

[60] J. E. Powell, *A Nation Not Afraid* (London, 1965).

[61] See J. E. Powell, *Freedom and Reality* (London, 1969), where extracts from these speeches are collected.

in *The Spectator* that 'Powellism is gaining converts every day' and that 'much of our programme when the general election comes will be based on ideas in this book'.[62] To see the Conservatives in 1966 as espousing 'Powellite' economics would overstate the case, but the party's 1965 document, *Putting Britain Right Ahead*, had seen a shift to a more liberal-market agenda as the Conservatives sought to put, to use a 1990s expression, 'clear blue water' between Conservative and Labour approaches to economic management.[63] Moreover, Powell was not, as some of his biographers suggest, a lone voice crying in the wilderness. Through the 1960s a complex, often overlapping, set of liberal-market groups and intellectuals were establishing an influential voice in Conservative politics.[64] At an individual level people like Keith Joseph were identified as increasingly close to Powell, but the purchase of liberal-market ideas was also reflected in the policy groups Edward Heath established as part of his 'government in exile' strategy. For example, Frederick Corfield, a member of the Industrial Policy committee, told Edward Boyle in December 1967 that there was

> a somewhat bigger split in our ranks than we had anticipated between those who would give top priority to region, and those who would give the priority to ensuring that there are no obstacles to growth in the 'natural growth areas'.[65]

This would have come as no surprise to Boyle, who had warned the Shadow Cabinet in the summer about a group within the party trying to build an 'anti-planning orthodoxy'.[66] Nor would it have shocked Arthur Seldon of the Institute for Economic Affairs, who argued in the *Swinton Journal* in 1968 that

> the outsider has some difficulty in reconciling the views of Reginald Maudling, John Boyd-Carpenter and Edward Boyle ... with those of Powell, Joseph ... Thatcher, Maude, Maurice Macmillan, Home, Biffen, Bernard Braine, Patrick Jenkin and others.

Seldon concluded that on economic policy, 'Conservatives speak with two voices',[67] with one of those voices being decidedly liberal market in its accent. The *Sunday Times* comment of June 1965 that Powell had

[62] I. Macleod in *The Spectator*, quoted in D. E. Schoen, *Powell and the Powellites* (London, 1977), p. 15.

[63] For example, *Putting Britain Right Ahead* called for tax reductions, stimulation of competition, trade union reform and selectivity in the social services.

[64] See R. Cockett, *Thinking the Unthinkable* (London, 1994), pp. 159–99.

[65] F. Corfield to E. Boyle, 7 Dec. 1967, quoted in Ramsden, *Winds of Change*, p. 230.

[66] Boyle, Memorandum to Shadow Cabinet, 25 July 1967, ibid.

[67] A. Seldon, *Swinton Journal*, quoted in *Winds of Change*, p. 280.

'driven the true concept of market forces back into Tory thinking'[68] seemed, by 1967–8, no longer hyperbolic. But Powell was articulating, rather than leading, an important body of Conservative opinion.

That liberal-market views were moving towards a more prominent position in the Conservative party during the 1960s is confirmed by the outlook of the rank and file, by party policy deliberations and the reaction to the Selsdon Park conference of early 1970. With regard to grass-roots opinion John Ramsden's study of the 1960s' party has shown that local party opinion was insistent on establishing a distinctive Conservative approach to the economy. Hence the London Area conference of 1965 insisted on 'an assurance that the next Conservative Government will govern by true Conservative principles, not seeking electoral popularity by the adoption of quasi-Socialist measures', whilst the North Cornwall Conservatives demanded in February 1966 that there should be 'a return to Conservative principles with a greater emphasis on individual freedom and less control from government'.[69] The language and underlying message of these statements is strikingly similar to the arguments of the 1950s, namely that 'real' Conservatism meant a rejection of Statist economic and social policy and a return to liberal-market governance. What made the 1960s different, however, was that the party hierarchy was more responsive to grass-roots opinion.

In this last context, party policy with regard to trade unions was particularly significant. In the 1960s grass-roots pressure on this issue continued unabated. In 1963 Edward Martell, whose PLDF had caused the Conservative leadership some anxiety in the 1950s, reappeared as chairman of the Hastings Conservative association, and his journal the *New Daily*, still campaigning for trade-union reform, gained a circulation of 100,000.[70] Likewise, in November 1963, 279 constituency associations supported a Monday Club proposal for making trade unions liable for losses incurred by employers during strikes, and a large majority of local Conservative discussion groups were pressing for compulsory ballots before strikes.[71] After 1964 such arguments went from being local party pipe-dreams to central party policy, and Edward Martell could have been forgiven for thinking that his PLDF campaign had finally borne fruit. After 1964, and especially with the publication of the party's *Fair Deal At Work* in 1968, legal reform of trade-union law became a central feature of Conservative policy, and provided a basis for the Heath government's industrial relations initiatives of the early 1970s.

[68] *Sunday Times*, 25 June 1965, quoted in Schoen, *Powell*, p. 15.
[69] Ramsden, *Winds of Change*, pp. 219, 255.
[70] Ibid., pp. 146–8.
[71] Ibid., p. 218.

Nor was the trade-union question the only one which saw movement. With regard to the nationalised industries a Policy Group on the Nationalized Industries (PGNI), chaired by Nicholas Ridley, produced some ambitious statements. The PGNI's final report argued that 'the public sector is a millstone round our necks', that 'we have a built-in system of misallocation of capital in our economy', and that there was 'a very strong case for embarking on a course of gradually dismantling the public sector'.[72] The benefits of this course of action were to be increased efficiency, lower government costs and wider share-ownership.[73] Candidate industries for denationalisation were steel, BEA, BOAC, BAA and Thomas Cook, and it was suggested that, at some stage, other sectors could be put on a sound financial basis and then sold off, notably coal, buses, electricity, gas, telephones and Cable and Wireless.[74] As an interim measure the 'BP model', as floated in the late 1950s, was put forward as a first step. Edward Heath was unenthusiastic about this Report, and even Keith Joseph baulked at its radicalism.[75] The 1970 Conservative Manifesto was to reflect their caution rather than the PGNI's ambition, but, as the chief of CRD noted, the wording of the Manifesto's industrial section was sufficiently broad to give a mandate for as much of the Ridley–Eden policy as a Conservative government might wish to implement'.[76] Moreover, if one leaves aside the issue of direct policy influence, and compares the PGNI position to that of the 1957 PCNI, it is very apparent that liberal-market thinking on the question of nationalisation had become both more advanced and enjoyed greater latitude.

But it was the Selsdon Park conference of late January and early February 1970 that fully convinced liberal-market Conservatives that their time had come. This meeting of the Shadow Cabinet was convened by Heath as a 'brainstorming' weekend of discussion to focus attention on the policy ideas that would form the basis of the Conservatives' next election campaign. As such it was not very different from other so-called 'Chequers weekends' that Heath was wont to organise from time to time, but its impact was far greater than either Heath or his shadow team could have anticipated. The meeting enjoyed widespread publicity, partly because of the Labour goverrunent's response to the Conservatives' deliberations. Harold Wilson's reference to the

[72] Report of the PGNI, CRD 3/17/12, CPA.

[73] Ibid.

[74] Ibid.

[75] For Heath's attitude, see Ramsden, *Winds of Change*, p. 283; for Joseph's, see R. Taylor, 'The Heath Government, Industrial Policy and the "New Capitalism"', in A. Seldon and S. Ball (eds), *The Heath Government, 1970–74: A Reappraisal* (London, 1996), p. 145.

[76] M. Fraser to J. Douglas, 18 May 1970, quoted in *The Heath Government*, p. 146.

emergence of 'Selsdon Man' ensured that the conference took on almost instant mythopœic status: the notion of 'Selsdon Man' being that the Conservatives had revealed themselves to be advocates of stone-age economics, and were bent on clubbing the economy with laissez-faire, market economics and dragging Britain back to a Conservative cave.

The prevailing historiographical orthodoxy on Selsdon Park suggests the conference by no means represented an explicit Conservative endorsement of liberal-market ideas, and that 'Selsdon Man', like Piltdown Man, was a fraud.[77] Certainly those seeking evidence for such a development in Conservative thinking can find very little succour in the minutes of the conference discussions. There was minimal debate on the principles of economic policy, and there were few statements that could be regarded as unequivocally 'market' orientated.[78] There was talk, for example, of restoring a 'competitive framework' for the steel industry,[79] but it was also argued that the idea of denationalisation was 'of no great interest to the general public'.[80] On the question of combating inflation through incomes policy, an area where the Conservatives had been very critical of Labour, the conference's briefing documents simply advised avoiding the use of the phrase,[81] and Reginald Maudling conceded that there was a gap in Conservative policy on this issue that could not easily be filled.[82] There was general agreement that inflation and the level of direct personal taxation had the most direct electoral relevance, but as to methods of addressing these questions the conference was at best ambivalent. It is true that even the vague liberal-market sentiments that were expressed were treated with respect, but then so were most arguments. There was no clear, underlying philosophy in the discussions that would enable an historian to say that Selsdon Park saw a 'proto-Thatcherite' agenda in the making.

So why did the Selsdon conference gain the reputation it achieved within the party? The answer lies with the context of its reception. After 1964, and especially after 1966, the Conservative rank and file had been hoping for a Conservative move against the 'post-war settlement'. The Conservative Opposition's statements on trade unions, its denunciations of the Labour government's economic management,

[77] J. Campbell, *Edward Heath* (London, 1993), pp. 265–7.
[78] The only exception was the discussion of trade unions. See Shadow Cabinet Conference, Selsdon Park, 7th Session, 1 Feb. 1970, CRD 3/9/93, CPA.
[79] CRD document, 'Other Issues Requiring Policy Decisions', n.d., Jan. 1970, CRD 3/9/92, CPA.
[80] CRD document, 'Publication of Policy During 1070, n.d., Jan. 1070, CRD 3/9/92, CPA.
[81] CRD document, 'Controlling Prices', 21 Jan. 1970, CRD 3/9/92, CPA.
[82] Selsdon Park Shadow Cabinet Conference, 7th Session, 1 Feb. 1970, CRD 3/9/93, CPA.

particularly in the realms of inflation and prices and incomes policy, and its stress on the need for greater freedom for enterprise and personal incentives had all served to create a climate of expectation. The response of the press and, paradoxically, of the Labour leadership to Selsdon Park only served to heighten this expectation. As Ramsden has suggested, this response gave the Conservative position in 1970 a free-market coherence that went beyond the intentions of Edward Heath and many of his Shadow Cabinet.[83] But the party leadership's response to their own publicity also played a part here. It may well be that the depiction of Selsdon Park at the time gave the Conservatives an unsought-for identity as a liberal-market party, but it was an identity the leadership did not seek to repudiate. Indeed, their behaviour and statements during the 1970 election campaign and after the Conservative victory further heightened the sense that there had been a pronounced, liberal-market shift in Conservative thinking.[84] Edward Heath's speech to the Conservative conference in October 1970, which stood as both a victory celebration and statement of intent, declared that the government's aim was 'to change the course of history of this nation', which modest task was to be achieved by policies designed to

> reorganize the function of government, to leave more to individual or corporate effort, to make savings in government expenditure, to provide room for greater incentives for men and women and to firms and businesses ... to encourage them more and more to take their own decisions, to stand firm on their own feet, to accept responsibility for themselves and their families.

Furthermore, the government's actions in its first year of office appeared to confirm a bold start to this new approach. That Heath chose John Davies, the former Director-General of the CBI, to run the new Department of Trade and Industry, and appointed as his deputies Nicholas Ridley, John Eden and Frederick Corfield, all known liberal-market enthusiasts, could not but be seen as a statement about the direction of industrial policy. In 1970–1 this team lived up to its reputation. The Industrial Reorganization Corporation was abolished, the Industrial Expansion Act was repealed, seven of the regional Economic Development Councils ('little Neddies') were scrapped, the Mersey Docks and Harbour Board was allowed to go into liquidation, the Land Commission was abolished and the Prices and Incomes Board was wound up. All of these were regarded as key elements of 'Socialist'

---

[83] See Ramsden, *Winds of Change*, pp. 302–3.

[84] That the IEA, always quick to be critical of the Conservatives, greeted Heath's election with optimism is significant here. See Cockett, *Thinking*, p. 200, for the IEA's reaction.

economic management, and their removal was greeted with enthusiasm by the Conservative press and the party rank and file. With regard to prices and taxation the government was also making all the right noises and gestures. Heath's promise to cut prices 'at a stroke' was to prove a dangerous hostage to fortune, but a rhetorically tough stance on prices was precisely what the party faithful had been looking for. On taxation too the government's first budget saw a 6d (2.5p) cut in the basic rate of income tax, a 25 per cent reduction in corporation tax, and the phasing out of the Regional Employment Premium and Selective Employment Tax. The promise of new trade-union legislation was also rapidly fulfilled, with the publication in December 1970 of the Industrial Relations Bill. On all fronts the government seemed to be marching in its first year to the beat of a liberal-market drum.

However, by 1972–3 the government was engaged in what famously became known as an economic 'U-turn'. The notion that there was any such dramatic reversal of policy has been played down in some studies of the Heath government.[85] There is a logic to this argument if one accepts that 'Selsdon Man' was a myth and that the government did not have a coherent liberal-market strategy to start with. If that was the case then, of course, there could be no 'U-turn', and the argument that there was a change of direction becomes another piece of 'mythology' particularly attractive to Thatcherites. But this, once again, is to miss the point about historical myth. Without exception Thatcherite memoirs highlight the experience of 1970–4 as formative. For example, Lord Young comments that

> when Ted Heath paraded Selsdon Man I perked up. Here at long last was the realization that the wealth of a nation has to be created by its citizens and not by its government . . .

and that 'the 1970 election seemed to bring a ray of hope to us all'.[86] Likewise, Norman Tebbit notes that the 'Selsdon declaration . . . marked the Tory party's first repudiation of the post-war Butskellite consensus' and that 'the 1970 manifesto . . . was music to the ears of radical Conservatives like myself'.[87] It could be that Young, Tebbitt and others like them were just 'deceived' by the 'myth' of Selsdon, but two points are salient here. The first is that in terms of understanding Thatcherism it is important that this period, like the 1930s and the immediate post-war era, is singled out by Thatcherite protagonists. In terms of how Thatcherites understood (understand) each other a shared sense of the

---

[85] See Seldon and Ball, introduction to *idem* (eds), *The Heath Government*, and Campbell, *Heath*, pp. 451–6, 468–83.

[86] Lord Young, *The Enterprise Years* (London, 1991), p. 16.

[87] N. Tebbitt, *Upwardly Mobile* (London, 1988), p. 94.

'betrayal' of Selsdon and the promise of 1970 is a crucial point of contact. The second is that whilst 'Selsdon Man' and the liberal-market manifesto of 1970 may both have been 'myths' they became, because of the contemporary response to them, some of those 'myths we live by' – just as 'real' as any ' objective' assessment of the events of 1970. Why else should those Conservative MPs who dissented from the Government's policies in 1973 have formed themselves into the 'Selsdon Group' if the name in itself did not conjure up a particular political message? Why also should Edward Heath have been so keen to tell the party conference in 1973 that the promises of Selsdon Park had been fulfilled, unless he too understood its resonance?

For those in the party, in both the upper and lower echelons, who had had their hopes and expectations raised in 1970 the disappointment of 1972–4 was all too palpable. Without acknowledging this sense of 'betrayal' one cannot fully understand why Sir Keith Joseph should have felt able to say that 'It was only in April 1974 that I was converted to Conservatism', meaning that he had finally understood that the liberal-market approach was Conservatism. But equally one cannot understand the depth of the sense of betrayal unless one acknowledges that 1970 was itself seen by a powerful body of Conservative opinion as the climax of a twenty-five-year battle against not only the Labour party's Socialism, but the 'quasi-Socialism' represented by their party's failure to dismantle the 'post-war settlement'. Small wonder that in 1975 the party equipped itself with a leader who would commit herself to this battle with more vigour and 'conviction'. Nigel Lawson has commented that whereas 'Harold Macmillan had a contempt for the party, Alec Home tolerated it, [and] Ted Heath loathed it. Margaret genuinely liked it. She felt a communion with it.'[88] Harold Macmillan, albeit from a different perspective, expressed a similar view. After seeing Thatcher at a party conference he remarked on the contrast to his own period as leader, noting that

> we [his cabinet] used to sit there listening to these extraordinary speeches urging us to birch or hang them all or other such strange things. We used to sit quietly nodding our heads and when we came to make our speeches we did not refer to what had been said at all ... But watching her ... I think she agrees with them.[89]

It is difficult fully to grasp Thatcher's special hold over the party rank and file unless one appreciates that from 1975 to 1990 (and beyond) the Conservatives' middle and lower ranks felt they had a leader who shared their preferences and prejudices.

---

[88] N. Lawson, *The View from No. 11* (London, 1994), p. 14.
[89] Macmillan's comments are recorded in P. Walker, *Staying Power* (London, 1991), p. 138.

III

The Irish revolutionary James Connolly once remarked that any event, no matter how seemingly improbable, could be made by historians to appear to have been inevitable. This essay is content merely to argue that the triumph of Thatcherite political economy in the late 1970s and 1980s was unsurprising. From the very outset Conservative voices had been raised against the 'post-war settlement' and through the 1950s and 1960s elements of the Conservative party leadership, a substantial section of the backbenches and probably a majority of the middle and lower ranks of the party were predisposed to accept a liberal-market diagnosis of and prescription for their own and the nation's economic troubles. That the Churchill, Eden and Macmillan governments chose not to respond positively to liberal-market opinion is explicable for two reasons. The first is that the generation of Conservative leaders that was dominant into the 1960s was heavily influenced by the trauma of the 1945 defeat and accepted the view that it was a 'delayed punishment' for the 'hungry thirties'. As a consequence they were reluctant to take risks, particularly in the realm of unemployment. Equally important, the post-war boom that began in 1952 meant that for the most part Conservative governments were able to square the circle of high public expenditure and full employment with occasional tax cuts and relatively stable prices. Indeed, in the context of the 1950s, when inflation was reasonably low (albeit historically high), the economy was growing and living standards rising, the remarkable thing is the amount of discontent there was in the Conservative ranks. In this sense there was an indication in the disgruntled voices of the 1950s of how powerful the reaction might be if the post-war boom came to an end, inflation became more pressing, and the dilemma of the power of organised labour in a full employment economy was more graphically exposed. In short there was almost a ready-made Conservative audience for the Thatcherite agenda.

This may seem to lead back to the argument that it was the economic troubles of the 1970s that were crucial to Thatcherism's success. To a degree the 1970s *were* important, but whilst the immediate circumstances of that decade can help to explain the emergence of greater political space for Thatcherite political economy, they cannot explain why Thatcherism was chosen as opposed to any other potential strategy. History is perhaps a factor here, in so far as in the 'crisis' of the early 1960s the Conservative leadership had opted for Macmillan's *dirigiste* approach and Statist strategies had thereby become discredited. But there were other, broader, factors at work.

Staying with the Conservatives themselves, changes were taking place in the Parliamentary party in and after the 1960s that had important

implications for the party's outlook. After the 1966 election only 60 per
cent of Conservative MPs had sat continuously since 1959, and only 11
MPs had been in Parliament before 1945. This generational change
understandably continued, and by February 1974 only 50 per cent of
MPs had been in Parliament before 1964, and the bulk of them were
of the 1959 vintage. For historians of Conservative politics in the 1950s
and early 1960s the 'class of 1950' has had particular significance in
terms of its contribution to Cabinet personnel and the influence it
exercised. Arguably the 'class of 1959' should have equal importance
for scholars of Thatcherism. The 'class of 1950' had come into politics
with the memory of the 1945 defeat still strong and with the 'myth' of
the 'hungry thirties' seen as the explanation. The 'class of 1959' came
into politics in a climate dominated by the questions of 'slow growth',
the grumblings of grass-roots discontent, and a querying of the social
and economic achievements of the 'post-war settlement'. At the same
time the social and geographical base of the 'class of 1959' was markedly
different from that of their predecessors. The presence of the 'knights
of the shires', military and other public servants declined, and they
were replaced by representatives of the salaried, professional middle
classes. In short the new generation of Conservative MPs were closer
socially to the kind of people who had expressed discontent with the
'post-war settlement' – 'Orpington Man' (or woman for that matter)
had arrived in the Conservative ranks in strength by the mid-1960s.

Furthermore, the new generation of MPs were increasingly returned
from constituencies South of Birmingham. The changing, and narrowing, base of the Conservative Parliamentary party thus reflected
general economic and demographic shifts in the country, as employment
and population trends followed the decline of Britain's old industrial
heartlands. From 1951 to the 1970s, and accelerating through the 1980s,
demographic and economic change saw the population and, through
redistribution, the representation of the South and South-East of Britain
growing inexorably. This growth was fuelled, in particular, by a massive
surge in service-sector activity or what would once have been termed
white-collar and black-coated employment. Many of these occupations
were non-unionised. and, even if they were, employees showed a greater
degree of 'economic instrumentalism' in their voting allegiance than
workers in the older industrial communities.[90] The possibility that a
Conservative, liberal-market appeal could be made to this social and
regional constituency had been mooted in the late 1950s when the idea
of the 'opportunity state' had been in vogue. Although this concept
had been designed to meet the needs of the self-professed 'beleaguered
middle class' it was also seen as appealing to the aspirational lower-

---

[90] A. Heath *et al.*, *Understanding Political Change* (Oxford, 1991), pp. 102–19, 136–55.

middle and working-class voter on the basis that, as one Conservative minister put it, 'potentially the foreman class is ours'.[91] Likewise, the Conservative Lord Chancellor of the late 1950s hinted at a potential regional appeal of the 'opportunity state', noting that tax cuts, wider property-ownership and lower inflation were 'an acute political problem from the standpoint of Conservative workers South of the Trent, in the north they are much more concerned with their council houses, factories, schools and hospitals'. In the 1980s this constituency was to be labelled 'Essex Man', and was seen, rightly, as an electoral vanguard of Thatcherism.

Thatcherism did not emerge simply from a 'battle of ideas' within the Conservative party. Nor was it a product of 'high political' manœuvre in the leadership contest of 1975. Thatcher*ism* existed long before Margaret Thatcher became leader of the Conservative party, and 1975 was as much the occasion as the cause of the 'Thatcherite Revolution'. In the mid-1970s the Conservative party, at both the Parliamentary and grass-roots level, was looking for and found a leader in tune with their long-held aspirations, and one who was fortunate enough to reap the benefit of social and economic change that gave 'Thatcherite' political economy an opportunity to flourish. This is not to present a reductionist argument that simply collapses Thatcherite political economy into the liberal-market ideas of the 1950s and 1960s. In the 1970s and 1980s monetarism was a new, and powerful, ingredient that had been largely (although not wholly) absent in earlier decades. But important though monetarist theory was to Thatcherite political economy, it is crucial to realise that it was *one* ingredient. The title of Sir Keith Joseph's 1976 Stockton lecture was after all 'Monetarism is Not Enough', and he made it plain that reducing the size of the State, reducing public expenditure, curbing inflation, and providing tax incentives for individuals and businesses, were essential in their own right.[92] In this respect monetarism may have given a new theoretical cutting edge to liberal-market ideas, but the broader aims and desires of 1970s liberal economics were remarkably similar to earlier Conservative protests against the 'post-war settlement'.

The prefiguring of Thatcherite political economy in long-standing debates within the Conservative party has significance not only in the history of Conservatism. It also has relevance in terms of the notion of a 'post-war consensus'. In recent years a number of historians have questioned the historical veracity and helpfulness of the idea of 'consensus', and one of the implications of this essay is that they have been right to do so. One writer has recently argued that 'there was a certain amount of agreement at the elite level of British politics, but the extent

---

[91] C. Hill to R. A. Butler, 11 Feb. 1958, CPA, CRD 2/53/29.
[92] K. Joseph, *Monetarism is Not Enough* (London, 1976), pp. 17–19.

and depth of this agreement is by no means clear'.[93] In terms of the issue of depth, this essay would conclude that the Conservative party's reaction to the *Beveridge Report*, the tenor of its election campaign in 1945, and the attitude of the party's rank and file through the 1950s and 1960s, indicates a very shallow level of 'commitment' to a 'consensual' framework, and that the party's attitude generally indicates, with some individual exceptions, a 'pragmatic' or 'instrumental' acquiesence rather than a 'normative agreement' with the policy framework associated with the 'post-war settlement'.[94] But although one can seriously question the 'reality' of consensus, that does not mean the notion is robbed of historical importance. *The Myth of Consensus*, to use the title of a recent publication,[95] has been as politically and historically significant as the 'myth' of Selsdon Man. The idea of consensus, as constructed by Thatcherism, was crucial to the whole Thatcherite project. Likewise, Thatcherism's opponents, whether Labour left or Social Democratic, deployed the idea as, respectively, either a justification for a radical Socialist departure from the policies of post-war Labour governments, or for a return to a similar set of goals. Hence Tony Benn argued in 1981 that the SDP was not a new political force, because Britain had been governed by a centre party since 1945, and in 1982 a leading intellectual in the SDP, tongue firmly in cheek, informed this author that 'We want the policies that failed before.'[96] Perhaps the historical politics of the idea of consensus have as much, if not more, importance to historians than the actual existence of such a shared approach.

---

[93] J. D. Marlow, *Questioning the Post-War Consensus Thesis* (Aldershot, 1996), p. 13.
[94] The terminology deployed here is that of Marlow, ibid., pp. 24–5.
[95] Jones and Kandiah (eds), *Myth*.
[96] Professor Peter Clarke, personal remark to the author, c. May 1992.

GENERAL DE GAULLE AND HIS ENEMIES: ANTI-GAULLISM IN FRANCE SINCE 1940

By Julian Jackson

READ 6 MARCH 1998

ON the centenary of General de Gaulle's birth in November 1990, hundreds of historians, politicians and statesmen gathered in Paris to discuss his life. Their deliberations were published in seven volumes running to several thousand pages. The participants included former opponents who now declared themselves 'posthumous Gaullists' or 'remorseful' ones.[1] The whole occasion seemed to fulfil André Malraux's prediction: 'Everyone is, has been or will become Gaullist.' Of those who were not, never had been, or would never become Gaullist, little was said.

One purpose of this essay is to provide a corrective to the centenary consensus and remind us that de Gaulle was one of the most reviled figures of French history. In the twentieth century, the only rivals for this position have all been on the left (and two of them Jewish to boot): Jean Jaurès, Léon Blum, and Pierre Mendès France. But the intensity of hatred displayed towards de Gaulle was of a different order. There were people who defined their politics through anti-Gaullism. In some cases the hatred verges on pathology: André Figueras's immense output of anti-Gaullism includes books like *De Gaulle Will Die, The Gaullists in Hell, De Gaulle the Impotent.*[2] Some anti-Gaullists even worried if the intensity of their sentiments had distorted their perceptions. Talking to Salazar in 1962 Jacques Isorni, Marshal Pétain's defence counsel in 1945, wondered: 'Am I unjust towards de Gaulle by nature and by virtue of memories? Perhaps'.[3] De Gaulle was the last battleground of the *guerres franco-françaises* in which, for more than two hundred years, the French have fought over the legacy of the Revolution.

Why study anti-Gaullism? Partly to set a record straight. In the 1990 conference, anti-Gaullism was almost airbrushed out of the picture,

---

[1] Institut Charles de Gaulle, *De Gaulle en son siècle*, 7 vols (Paris, 1991–2). For the posthumous Gaullists, see vol. I, *De la mémoire des hommes et des peuples*, 525–31.

[2] A. Figueras, *De Gaulle l'Impuissant* (Paris, 1970).

[3] J. Isorni, *Jusqu'au bout de notre peine* (Paris, 1963), 130. Also Maurice Bardèche in Pol Vandromme, *La Droite buissonière* (Paris, 1960), 63.

and almost nothing has been published on it.[4] Yet anti-Gaullism is part of the history of France: a *contre-mémoire* standing relation to the grand narrative of Gaullism as the Vendée stands to the Revolution. It is a 'vision of the vanquished' which deserves to be rescued from the vast condescension of Gaullist historiography. Anti-Gaullism perhaps also provides insights into de Gaulle which do not come from his generally left-wing and favourable biographers. What gives right-wing anti-Gaullism its visceral, but also poignant, quality was the fact that its spokesmen recognised their adversary as one of their own: two visions of nationalism were in conflict. Reviewing de Gaulle's *War Memoirs*, one hostile commentator, Pierre Andreu, noted: 'we Maurrassians will recognise family memories'.[5] There was sense of a brother who had gone astray, a fellow-believer who had lapsed: 'How could de Gaulle, pupil of the Jesuits, protégé of the liberal Paul Reynaud' have done all this.[6] This made some right-wing anti-Gaullists sensitive to aspects of de Gaulle which his admirers did not wish to see.

I

So far I have only mentioned right-wing anti-Gaullists, but was there not also a rich tradition of anti-Gaullism on the left, especially in the Communist Party? I do not intend to discuss Communist perceptions of de Gaulle in any detail, partly because they have already been studied,[7] and partly because it is not quite accurate to talk of 'anti-Gaullism' in this context. Certainly the Communists were frequently – usually – opposed to de Gaulle. From June 1940 to June 1941 they depicted him as a warmonger and agent of British Imperialism. Even when he became an ally, after the German invasion of the Soviet Union, they remained wary. When he founded the RPF in 1947, overnight they started to portray him as a fascist.[8] Even when de Gaulle disappeared from the scene after 1953, the Communists remained in competition with him as custodians of the memory of the Resistance: for de Gaulle the founding act of the Resistance was his speech of 18 June 1940; for the Communists it was their 'Appeal' of 10 July 1940.

[4] The exceptions are the unpublished thesis by P. Foro 'L'Anti-Gaullisme. Réalités et représentations (1940–1953)', Doctorate, University of Toulouse II, 1997; and 'Les Anti-Gaullistes', in *De Gaulle en son siècle*, vol. VII, 357–80. I would also like to thank Richard Vinen for showing me his unpublished paper on right-wing anti-Gaullism.

[5] *La Nation française*, 4 November 1959.

[6] *Documents nationaux*, June 1946.

[7] S. Courtois and M. Lazar, *Cinquante ans d'une passion française: de Gaulle et les Communistes* (Paris, 1991).

[8] Foro, 'L'Anti-Gaullisme', 258.

This symbolic battle became all the more important after 1958 when de Gaulle returned to power as a result of the Algerian crisis. The Communists opposed his return, depicting him variously as Napoleon I, Napoleon III, Salazar, Hitler, Pétain.[9] In the 1960s, the Communists interpreted Gaullism as the instrument of State monopoly capitalism.[10] On de Gaulle's death, *L'Humanité* treated him briskly, emphasising his class origins, saying nothing about 18 June and minimising his Resistance record. A re-evaluation occurred after the election of Giscard d'Estaing in 1973. Since Giscard had 'betrayed' de Gaulle in 1969, the Communists offered themselves as an alternative for Gaullists who had 'grave problems of conscience' in voting for Giscard. Gradually the appreciation of de Gaulle shifted: Giscard, whose family had Vichy links, was portrayed as the incarnation of those financial interests which, as *L'Humanité* remarked in July 1974, 'General de Gaulle said he had not seen in London'; by the end of 1974, de Gaulle had become the 'unifier of the resistance'.[11]

In short, the Communists' attitude towards de Gaulle was instrumental, dictated unsentimentally by the contingencies of their political line. It lacks the quality of implacable hatred found on the right. Communist polemic against de Gaulle contains none of the bitterness of their attacks on Blum.[12] In some matters – hostility to America, national independence – there was even a certain complicity between the Communists and de Gaulle. Their relationship displayed the mutual respect and fascination of two rivals in the quest to incarnate French identity. Pierre Nora in his *Lieux de mémoire* rightly treats them, in a single chapter, as *frères ennemis*, complementary, even necessary, to each other.[13]

This does not mean that anti-Gaullism was exclusively confined to the right. There are two strands which can be identified with the left: one with the non-Communist Resistance and the other with the 'Republican' tradition.

Resistance leaders who met de Gaulle during the war found it a chastening experience and their relationship with him was very fraught. They resented de Gaulle's presumption that resistance had started with

---

[9] M. Mouillaud, *La Mystification* (Paris, 1958); *De Gaulle: ce qu'il est, ce qu'il veut* (Paris, 1958).

[10] H. Claude, *Gaullisme et Grand Capital* (Paris, 1960); J. Duclos, *Gaullisme, technocratie, corporatisme* (Paris, 1963).

[11] M. Lazar, 'De Gaulle et les Communistes: confrontation de deux légitimités', in *De Gaulle en son siècle*, vol. II, 328–39, and S. Courtois, 'Le PCF et le Gaullisme: 1958–1969', 340–56.

[12] A. Kriegel, 'Un Phénomène de haine fratricide: Léon Blum vu par les Communistes' in A. Kriegel, *et les roses* (Paris, 1968).

[13] P. Nora, 'Gaullistes et Communistes', in P. Nora (ed.), *Les Lieux de mémoire III. Les France. 1. Conflits et partages* (Paris, 1992), 347–93.

his speech of 18 June 1940. Most resisters had started by acting quite independently of de Gaulle – if indeed they had heard his speech at all. Some of them felt that the 'emigrés' of London did not share their dangers.[14] Rank-and-file resisters were unaware of these conflicts during the war, but their meeting with de Gaulle in 1944 was often a moment of terrible disillusion. De Gaulle behaved with studied coldness to the Resistance to signify that its role was now over and the State was to be restored. One resister commented on de Gaulle's visit to Toulouse in September 1944: 'I was stunned. Our meeting lasted an hour. He asked me no question. I discovered the existence of an immense abyss between this man who had lived all the war out of France and domestic Resistance which was the vehicle of an entirely different experience.'[15]

This disillusion was carried on into the post-war period. The Resistance had believed the Liberation would effect a regeneration of French politics. When this did not occur, some blamed de Gaulle. Claude Bourdet of the Combat movement described the Liberation as a Restoration.[16] He later wrote: 'De Gaulle was the principal adversary of the Resistance ... he could not bear the existence of a force which competed with his preeminence ... For de Gaulle, the Resistance was him ... this attitude did the veterans of the Resistance a lot of harm after the war.'[17] Of the three claimants to the inheritance of the Resistance, it was hardest for the non-Communist Resistance to find a satisfactory interpretation of the past between the two monoliths of Communist and Gaullist memory. The Gaullist and Communist mythology was that Vichy had not represented the 'real' France and the mass of the French people had, passively or actively, supported the Resistance. But many resented this down-playing of their role as an elite in a society that was initially indifferent, even hostile, to them. As one wrote in 1955: 'It is time to un-mask a pious myth which has not really deceived anyone. The great majority of the people of this country played only a small and fleeting part in the events. Their activity was passive, except at the last moments. In these circumstances how can one require them to keep a faithful memory?'[18] De Gaulle was no less aware that the Resistance had been a minority, but was ready to overlook this truth in the interests of restoring political unity and

[14] C. Pineau in O. Wieviorka, *Nous entrerons dans la carrière. De la Résistance à l'exercice du pouvoir* (Paris, 1994), 260.

[15] S. Ravanel, *Esprit de la Résistance* (Paris, 1995), 203.

[16] Bourdet, *L'Aventure incertaine: de la Résistance à la Restauration* (Paris, 1975), 202, 412, 418; also H. Frenay, *La Nuit finira* (Paris, 1973), 561–2.

[17] Wieviorka, *Nous entrerons*, 364.

[18] A. Vistel, *L'Héritage spirituel de la Résistance* (Lyon, 1955), 58. See also P. Viannay [Indomitus], *Nous sommes des rebelles* (Paris, 1945); Pineau in O. Wieviorka, *Nous entrerons*, 27; O. Wieviorka, 'Du Bon usage du passé. Résistance, politique, mémoire', *Mots*, 32 (1992), 67–79.

national self-respect. For the Resistance, whose objectives were as much moral as political, French renewal could not be built on a lie: an ethical vision of the Resistance competed with Gaullist *realpolitik*.

The other left-wing tradition of anti-Gaullism was represented among the French community in wartime London in two publications: the review *La France Libre* run by André Labarthe and the daily paper *France* run by the Socialist journalist Charles Gombault. Both doubted the genuineness of de Gaulle's commitment to democracy. The left traditionally distrusted generals in politics: Gombault remarked after his first meeting with de Gaulle that he had never expected to meet General Boulanger in person.[19] The most intellectually distinguished contributor to *La France Libre* was the philosopher Raymond Aron. Although based in London, he managed the feat of avoiding any mention of de Gaulle. In his article of August 1943, entitled 'the Shadow of Bonaparte', it was only too clear whom he had in mind.[20]

Labarthe took up the case of Admiral Muselier who had broken with de Gaulle in 1942. Constant criticism of de Gaulle's political ambitions was also expressed by the Jean Jaurès group which included many French Socialists present in London. In July 1942 the group voted that 'de Gaulle must remain a military leader ... if he becomes a head of government he would govern in too authoritarian a manner, with a dubious entourage'.[21] The 'entourage' was a reference to André Dewavrin, alias Colonel Passy, head of de Gaulle's intelligence service, the BCRA. Lurid rumours circulated to the effect that Passy was a former right-wing extremist – a 'Cagoulard' – who ran BCRA like a French Gestapo. This was one theme of Muselier's post-war anti-Gaullist tirade, *De Gaulle contre le Gaullisme*.[22]

Criticism of de Gaulle's allegedly lukewarm Republicanism was also strong in the French exile community in the United States which included many former Third Republic politicians. Among these was the talented polemical journalist Henri de Kérillis, the only conservative *député* to have voted against Munich. Initially a supporter of de Gaulle, de Kérillis turned against him in 1943, claiming he had become obsessed with the quest for personal power. The book he wrote attacking de Gaulle in 1945 was called *De Gaulle the Dictator*, and it contained criticism of de Gaulle's 'evil genius' Passy, the 'all powerful head of the Gaullist Gestapo' with its torture chambers in Duke Street.[23] But by the time de Kérillis's anti-Gaullist polemic appeared, this aspect of it was

[19] A. Gillois, *Histoire sécrète des Français à Londres* (Paris, 1972), 52.
[20] R. Aron, *Chroniques de guerre: la France libre 1940–1945* (Paris, 1990).
[21] Foro, 'L'Anti-Gaullisme' 165–6.
[22] Muselier, *De Gaulle contre le gaullisme* (Paris, 1948).
[23] H. de Kérillis, *De Gaulle dictateur* (Montreal, 1945). See also J.-Y. Boulic and A. Lavaure, *Henri de Kérillis. L'Absolu patriote* (Rennes, 1997).

somewhat out of date, since de Gaulle had adopted an explicitly Republican position. Anti-Gaullism was left open for the right.

II

For Vichy, de Gaulle was always 'ex-General de Gaulle'. Having deprived de Gaulle of his rank, condemned him to death for desertion (2 August 1940) and stripped him of French nationality (8 December 1940), Vichy was not sure how to react next. Mentioning de Gaulle directly gave him publicity; ignoring him allowed his broadcasts to go unanswered. Vichy propaganda tried to tread a middle way. De Gaulle's followers in France were described as 'dissidents', but no speech of Pétain's referred to him by name.

No such restraint was shown by the Paris collaborationist press which denounced the alleged predominance of Jews in de Gaulle's entourage – he was a 'marionette in the hands of the Judeo-British plutocrats' – and his reliance on the British. He was often portrayed in cartoons as a dim-looking aristocrat wearing a monocle, or even as what was taken to be the appearance of a fashionable Englishman.[24] Despite his eminently caricaturable features, few people knew what he looked like.

After the Gaullist attack on French Syria it became difficult for Vichy to ignore de Gaulle, and Vichyite and collaborationist rhetoric converged, although the latter remained more strident. De Gaulle was assimilated into a long tradition of extreme-right polemic: the fascist Robert Brasillach described Gambetta as a 'Jewish Gaullist before his time'.[25] The basic themes of wartime anti-Gaullism were now fixed: de Gaulle the deserter; de Gaulle the warmonger; de Gaulle the creature of the British, the Jews and the Freemasons.[26]

The line of Vichy's defenders after the war was that the Armistice had spared France from total occupation. If this position was arguable up to November 1942, after the American invasion of North Africa and subsequent German occupation of the Free Zone, it was no longer sustainable. Some former Pétainists now fell back on the figure of General Giraud, the conservative general whom the Americans installed in North Africa. Giraud had impeccably anti-German credentials as well as being ultra-conservative. He provided a bridge for Pétainists who wished to detach themselves from Vichy without needing to renounce their political

---

[24] Foro, 'L'Anti-Gaullisme', 105–6, 119–20; J. P. and M. Cointet, *La France à Londres 1940–1943* (Brussels, 1990) 110–11; P. Allard, *Ici-Londres* (Paris, 1942).

[25] Foro, 'L'Anti-Gaullisme', 108.

[26] Special issue of the collaborationist *Notre combat pour la Nouvelle France socialiste*, November 1942, devoted to Gaullism.

convictions: Giraud was a continuation of Pétainism by other means. De Gaulle, however, refused agreement with Giraud except on his own terms: commitment to Republican values and a clear break with Vichy policies.

The emergence of Giraudism as a middle way between Pétain and de Gaulle was a fundamental moment in the history of anti-Gaullism. It focused the image of de Gaulle as the general turned politician, refusing to embrace Giraud in the name of national unity. Giraud became the point of convergence between former Pétainists turned resisters and many London left-wing anti-Gaullists: Labarthe and Muselier went to join him in North Africa. There was a certain incongruity in this alliance between an anti-Republican general and those who opposed de Gaulle because he was insufficiently Republican. The circle was squared by arguing that Giraud was simply a military man without political ambitions who wanted to get back into the war: a conservative general with no interest in politics was preferable to a political one even if he claimed to be a Republican.

For former Pétainists, de Gaulle's rejection of Giraud was proof of his adventurism, partisanship and sectarianism. Everything that happened subsequently confirmed their image of de Gaulle as someone ready to sacrifice reconciliation with his former adversaries to his own pursuit of power. In eliminating Giraud, de Gaulle was supported by the Communist Party, and he took two Communists into his provisional government. The depiction of de Gaulle as the ally of Communism became a major theme of conservative anti-Gaullist polemic, especially after the execution of the ex-Vichy minister Pucheu who had come to North Africa. Since Pucheu was execrated by the Communists, his execution was seen as the price of Communist support for de Gaulle. The pact with the Communists was sealed in blood, and Pucheu was the first in a long line of martyrs which right-wing anti-Gaullists would accumulate over the next forty years. The Liberation – the purges, the imprisonment of Pétain, the execution of Robert Brasillach – confirmed this image of de Gaulle as sanguinary and vengeful.

At the Liberation, it was impossible for Pétainist apologetics to appear, except in the form of semi-clandestine roneo'd sheets reminiscent of the first Resistance tracts. Their authors gloried in the sense of participating in a new Resistance to a new tyranny.[27] But with the disintegration of post-Liberation unity and the development of Cold War anti-Communism, Vichy apologists emerged into the light of day. The clandestine sheets gave way to newspapers – *Ecrits de Paris* from 1947, *Rivarol* from 1951 – which endlessly recalled the horrors of the Liberation, and de Gaulle's part in them. A key text in the crystallisation

---

[27] The Resistance publishing house had been called Editions de Minuit; the anti-Gaullist Alfred Fabre-Luce published his writings under the imprint Editions de Midi.

of anti-Gaullist ideology was the *Lettre à François Mauriac* (1947) by Maurice Bardèche, brother-in-law of Brasillach. Bardèche became one of the most articulate exponents of fascism in France as well as a pioneer of Holocaust negationism. Another indefatigable anti-Gaullist polemicist was Professor Louis Rougier who had in 1940 briefly acted as semi-official emissary between Pétain and Churchill. He claimed on the strength of this that Vichy had been playing an anti-German double game.[28] Most of what was written in the early 1940s would be endlessly recycled over the next forty years, comprising the obligatory battle-kit of all right-wing anti-Gaullists. The palette of anti-Gaullism was enriched by subsequent testimonies about de Gaulle's perfidy, but little new was added to the argument.

From this emerged a reading of history which could be summarised in seven points:

(1) The armistice had shielded the French people from the worst effects of the war, but because de Gaulle had only an abstract vision of France, he was unable to grasp the importance of this. Pétainists loved France in a different way: 'they love the towns of their country, its harvests'.[29] Unlike de Gaulle, 'mad with pride', Pétain acted like an honest peasant, accepting the 'humble task of looking after the house and the fields'.[30] As Bardèche wrote: 'the nationalism ... which accepts risking the total destruction of the nation through anti-Communism or anti-nazism is a romantic deviation of nationalism ... de Gaulle incarnates the exact opposite of what is noble and fecund in nationalism ... ready to transform the country into a desert so that finally it conforms to the image of the Promised Land'.[31] De Gaulle was a cold and inhuman figure incapable of 'ordinary life' which is composed of 'work well done, love and friendship, contemplation, aesthetic enjoyment'. Instead he lived only for great catastrophes and 'the dreadful carnage of war', allowing him to live out 'dreams of grandeur'.[32]

(2) Vichy had in its own way resisted the Germans. 'Gaullism started as a dissidence which broke French unity with no other profit than to add an open resistance to the clandestine resistance of Vichy.' Vichy's 'apolitical resistance' had occurred 'under cover of collaboration in accord with the Anglo-Saxon powers like Prussia after Jena'.[33] One

[28] L. Rougier, *Le Bilan du Gaullisme* (n.p., 1946); *La France jacobine* (Brussels/Paris, 1947); *La Défaite des vainqueurs* (Paris/Brussels, 1947); *De Gaulle contre de Gaulle* (Paris, 1948).
[29] M. Bardèche, *Lettre à François Mauriac* (Paris, 1947), 173.
[30] *Rivarol*, 8 February 1951.
[31] Bardèche, *Lettre*, 183.
[32] A. Fabre-Luce, *Le Plus illustre des Français* (Paris, 1960), 22.
[33] *Documents nationaux*, April 1946.

Vichy apologist published a book favourably comparing Pétain's meeting with Hitler at Montoire to Verdun.[34]

(3) The armistice benefited the allies. Even if de Gaulle had correctly prophesied that Britain would not be defeated, this made it all the more necessary to keep North Africa free for an allied landing: 'General de Gaulle rightly predicted the future – British resistance – but it was Weygand who, without realising it, drew from this prediction the correct conclusion.'[35] The North African army which was France's main contribution to Allied victory, was the army which the Armistice had allowed France to preserve; it was infinitely more important to the war than the Resistance. Instead of viewing Vichy as the only government of the West which 'accepted the yoke of the conqueror', it should be seen as the government which retained a large Empire ready to re-enter the war.[36] The turning-point of the war was not Stalingrad but the invasion of North Africa.[37] Much was made of Churchill's alleged remark to General Georges in 1944 that the Armistice had helped the Allies.[38]

(4) De Gaulle in no way changed the history of France: 'Without de Gaulle France would have been liberated in 1944 by the English and Americans: neither earlier nor later nor with any greater difficulty nor at a higher price.'[39] Everything de Gaulle obtained from the allies after the war would have been secured by any French government. Indeed, had France not alienated America, she would probably have gained more.[40]

(5) De Gaulle was less interested in fighting the Germans than the French, more interested in politics than war. 'De Gaulle did not make war against the Germans for the Liberation of France, but against Vichy, and Giraud, for the conquest of power.'[41] Then in 1944 de Gaulle missed the chance for national reconciliation: 'How different would France's position be today if de Gaulle had grasped the hand offered by the Marshal.'[42] De Gaulle squandered his chance to be Henri IV.[43] The Liberation had become a bloodbath, a 'veritable St. Bartholomew of the French elite', in which more than 100,000 people had been executed (the real figure was closer to 10,000). Describing the horrors of the Liberation became an industry. A distinction was invented

[34] L.-D. Girard, *Montoire. Verdun diplomatique* (Paris, 1948).
[35] A. Fabre-Luce, *Au Nom des silencieux* (Paris, 1945), 118.
[36] Fabre-Luce, *Le Plus illustre*, 60.
[37] *Défense de l'Occident*, January 1953.
[38] M. Weygand, *Recalled to Service* (1952), 220.
[39] *Documents nationaux*, April 1946.
[40] Rougier, *Le Bilan*, 16.
[41] Rougier, *De Gaulle*, 93.
[42] *Documents nationaux*, April 1946.
[43] *Rivarol*, 26 April 1951.

between true resistance and 'resistentialisme', the exploitation of the resistance by fanatics and criminals motivated by personal hatred, revenge and profit.[44]

(6) De Gaulle had signed an infernal pact with Communism: he was the Kerensky to Thorez's Lenin. This was shown by his amnesty of the Communist leader Maurice Thorez; his visit to Stalin in December 1944; and his proto-Communist policy of socialisation of the economy.[45]

(7) De Gaulle was driven by an absurdly unrealistic view of France's role in the world. This theme was a particular favourite of one of the most talented anti-Gaullist writers, Alfred Fabre-Luce. The rich son of a banker, Fabre-Luce devoted his life to journalism and writing on public affairs. He wrote four books on de Gaulle whom, from the lofty heights of a marriage to the Princess de Faucigny-Lucinge, he sometimes affected to call 'Gaulle'.[46] Fabre-Luce's first book in 1924, *La Victoire*, had argued that Germany was not exclusively responsible for the outbreak of the First World War. This was a standard theme of the internationalist left in the 1920s. Its target was Poincaré, President of France in 1914 and the Premier who occupied the Ruhr in 1923. Fabre-Luce underlined the theme in 1933 in his favourable study of Poincaré's rival Joseph Caillaux, the symbol of Franco-German reconciliation since 1911. In the 1930s Fabre-Luce edited the left-of-centre review *Europe nouvelle* which was dedicated to the Briandist ideals of international co-operation. In the same spirit he supported Munich and after 1940 became an articulate exponent of collaboration. Fabre-Luce spent the rest of his long career justifying his wrong choice in 1940. Despite the special pleading, there was a coherence to the argument which places it in a foreign policy tradition running from Caillaux and Briand, through Laval, to Robert Schumann in the 1950s, and opposed to the tradition running from Clemenceau through Poincaré to de Gaulle.

That second tradition was, of course, also shared by the Maurrassian right which hated Germany as much as it revered the memory of Pétain. But Fabre-Luce's cosmopolitan pro-Germanism could converge with nationalist Maurrasianism around the proposition that de Gaulle harboured an over-elevated idea of France's role in the world. The Maurrassian *Documents nationaux* argued that while Pétain's government

[44] J.-M. Desgranges, *Les Crimes masqués du 'Résistentialisme'* (Paris, 1948).

[45] Recent versions of this line are H.-C. Giraud, *De Gaulle et les Communistes*, 2 vols (Paris, 1988–9), and H. Ronzyé, *Gaullisme ou gaulchévisme* (Paris, 1995).

[46] A. Fabre-Luce, *Gaulle deux* (Paris, 1958); *Le Plus illustre des Français* (Paris, 1960); *Haut cour* (Paris, 0000); *Le Général en Sorbonne* (Paris, 1960). See also *Vingt-cinq ans de liberté III. La Récompense 1946–61* (Paris, 1964); *Au Nom des silencieux* (Paris, 1944); *Double prison* (Paris, 1945).

had 'safeguarded our basic patrimony by an effective policy, but one without éclat', de Gaulle had 'opted for a romantic choice ... indulging in sensationalist demonstrations which did not correspond to our real state of weakness'. It was a lie to let the French believe that they had the means to pursue a policy of grandeur.[47] This Maurrassianism was pessimistic and inward-looking – 'la France seule' as Maurras said during the war – while Fabre-Luce was optimistic about France's prospects if she adopted an internationalist posture. This was the difference between Vichy and Paris, Pétainism and collaborationism, united only in contrasting their 'realism' with de Gaulle's futile romanticism.

III

The politics of anti-Gaullism were complicated after 1947 when de Gaulle, who had resigned in the previous year, founded the RPF whose anti-Communism, pro-Atlanticism and anti-parliamentarianism struck a chord with the nostalgic Pétainists while alienating the left with whom de Gaulle had been allied since the Liberation. The Socialists and the centre-left resuscitated the Republican critique of Gaullism in a more alarmist form: de Gaulle had become a Boulangist adventurer who threatened democracy.[48] The ex-Vichyite right found it harder to respond. Some were ready to accept the new-style de Gaulle. Even the implacable Maurras wrote from jail: 'so much the better for France if some rapid service ... can be obtained from this mind without understanding and this heart without warmth'.[49] But most others would not offer forgiveness without repentance, and this de Gaulle would not provide. The anti-Gaullist review *Réalisme* said that 'to the extent that de Gaulle recognises his past errors he will find us at his side', but each issue contained a litany of the horrors de Gaulle had inflicted on the nation.[50] It constantly reminded its few readers that 1944 had been worse than the Jacquerie, St Bartholemew's Day, the Terror or the Commune.[51] *Rivarol* shared de Gaulle's anti-Communism but reminded its readers of the past: 'If tomorrow a brainless electorate elected to the head of the State this soldier who has never won a battle and whose main glory was to pass the major part of the First War in a German prison with Marshal Tukachevsky ... they will celebrate in Moscow.'[52]

[47] *Documents nationaux*, November 1945.
[48] Foro, 'L'Anti-Gaullisme', 231–76.
[49] C. Bigegaray and P. Isoart, *Les Droites et le Général de Gaulle* (Paris, 1991), 26.
[50] *Réalisme*, 11 December 1948.
[51] For example, *Réalisme*, 15 February 1948.
[52] *Rivarol*, 8 February 1951.

The first steps towards European unity further complicated the politics of anti-Gaullism. Between 1950 and 1954, the European Defence Community was one of the most passionately debated issues in post-war French politics. De Gaulle, like the Communists, was opposed to the project. This allowed some of the anti-Gaullist right to reassert its pro-European credentials, but traditionalist Pétainists like Weygand found themselves on the same side as de Gaulle. A slightly different tune was played by Bardèche, the fascist, whose paper Défense de l'Occident was pro-European but preferred 'a voluntary association of European nations in a classic form' to any kind of supranationalism. He was also anti-American, believing that France should choose between a continental and an Atlantic destiny. As he realised, this was eminently 'Gaullist': 'that changes nothing in our point of view about the *impossibility* in the accession of de Gaulle to power ... the person of de Gaulle remains an obstacle for us as for millions of Frenchmen and millions of Germans'.[53]

Following a period of detachment from politics, de Gaulle returned to power after the Algerian revolt of May 1958. Most of the left and centre reluctantly accepted him as the man to save democracy from the army; for the anti-Gaullist right the dilemma was whether to overcome their historic opposition in the hope that de Gaulle would preserve French Algeria. The eerie and ironic echoes of 1940 – an ageing hero emerging from retirement and requesting full powers to reform the constitution – were only too evident. Jean-Louis Tixier-Vignancourt, who had held a junior post at Vichy, was resigned to having de Gaulle as premier, but refused to vote him full powers. He recalled that granting such powers to Pétain in 1940 was why parliamentarians had been punished in 1944. *Rivarol*, while not disguising its 'revulsion' towards de Gaulle and delighting in the irony that he was now seeking support from 'those whom with supreme incompetence – not to say lack of heart – he rejected from the national community when a mere gesture would have sufficed to associate them in the work of national reconstruction', felt it was necessary to gamble that 'for the first time the legendary intransigence of the General will benefit the country'.[54] One right-winger who did not vote for de Gaulle was Jacques Isomi, high priest of the cult of Pétain's memory. But his ostensible reason for opposing de Gaulle in 1958 was that de Gaulle was not truly committed to *Algérie française*.[55]

Over the next months conservatives began to see that Isomi had

---

[53] *Défense de l'Occident*, No. 1, December 1952.
[54] *Rivarol*, 11 May, 29 May 1958. A similar line was taken by M. Dacier in *Ecrits de Paris*, June 1958.
[55] J. Isorni, *Ainsi passent les républiques* (Paris, 1959).

been right.[56] Some were quicker to realise this than others – by October 1958 *Rivarol* was calling de Gaulle 'the prince of dissimulation'[57] – but by the end of 1961 everyone was clear: 'Nothing that will follow de Gaulle could be worse than what he is.'[58] The agony which de Gaulle's Algerian policy inflicted on the right is well illustrated by the case of *La Nation française*. Founded in 1955 by Pierre Boutang, an admirer of Maurras, out of dissatisfaction with the sterile politics of the official *Action française* paper, still living on the memories of the war, *La Nation française*, while theoretically monarchist and inspired by Maurras, wanted to look forward and update Maurrasianism. It was nationalist, opposed to democracy in general and to the Fourth Republic in particular, but culturally open-minded.[59] Its contributors, who included the historian Philippe Ariès, comprised both former Pétainists and former resisters. Among the latter was the historian Raoul Girardet whose review of de Gaulle's *War Memoirs* defined the editorial line: 'To bring together men who wish to remain faithful to the memory of the old Marshal whom they served, and others who fought in the ranks of the Resistance and in the uniform of the Free French ... All are rid of their dreary rancour and their acrid resentments which the sludge of the war and occupation still carries with it.'[60] This group supported de Gaulle's return to power without the reticence shown in other quarters: he was seen as the man who would both save Algeria and restore the authority of the State, providing the kind of authority which Maurras had believed only the monarchy could offer.[61]

By October 1959, however, *La Nation française* realised it might be necessary to choose between de Gaulle and Algeria.[62] As the choice loomed, the contributors split between those, like Boutang, who reluctantly chose de Gaulle, and those, like Girardet, who chose Algeria. They seceded and founded a new paper, *L'Esprit publique*, at the end of 1960. For Girardet, Boutang, by sacrificing Algeria to de Gaulle, had repeated the error of Maurras in 1940 when he sacrificed his anti-German patriotism to his belief in Pétain.[63] Ariès argued that the conflict was a turning-point in the history of the French right. In de Gaulle, the nationalist right had achieved many of the principles for which it had fought since before the First World War: 'a personal,

---

[56] *Rivarol*, 14 August 1958, 11 September 1958.

[57] *Rivarol*, 16 October 1958.

[58] *Ecrits de Paris*, December 1961.

[59] R. Girardet, 'L'Héritage de l'Action Française', *Revue française de science politique*, vii, 4 (1957), 765–92.

[60] *La Nation française*, 18 July 1956.

[61] Louis Salleron, a former supporter of the Vichy, wrote that he supported de Gaulle for the same reasons he had supported Pétain: *La Nation française*, 28 January 1959.

[62] *La Nation française*, 7 October 1959.

[63] R. Girardet, *Singulièrement libre* (Paris, 1990), 135.

anti-democratic and anti-parliamentary regime, inspired by quasi-monarchical principles of legitimacy'. But because of the 'central and obsessional place' which Algeria had assumed, it had lost interest in the question of institutions.[64]

Algeria was not merely a replay of the battle-lines of 1940–4 with the former Pétainists on one side, and former resisters on the other. Certainly few former collaborators or Pétainists were for withdrawal – Fabre-Luce was one – but many former resisters supported *Algérie française*. This created curious inversions of themes. De Gaulle, previously accused of being an unrealistic romantic, was now portrayed as a cynical realist. Former resisters, like Jacques Soustelle and Georges Bidault, claimed de Gaulle was betraying the spirit of Resistance and opposed him in the name of true Gaullism. Georges Bidault, chairman in 1944 of the National Council of the Resistance, now set up, in 1962, a new Council of the Resistance – this time to protect Algeria.[65] In this upside-down world, the terrorism of the OAS was assimilated to that of the Resistance, since the Gaullists were collaborating with the enemy – the FLN – as Vichy was accused of having done with the Germans.[66]

Former Pétainists easily fitted de Gaulle's Algerian policy into the logic of his career since 1940. Ever since the Anglo-Gaullist attack on Syria in 1941, it had been a theme of the Pétainists that de Gaulle's dissidence was a threat to the future of the Empire.[67] Bardèche noted in 1947 that de Gaulle had lit a fuse whose consequences would first be seen in Indo-China and then Algeria. In the long term de Gaulle's career was an enterprise of Imperial demolition with Algeria as the last stage.[68] As for his heartlessness towards the *pieds noirs*, this fitted into his abstract patriotism: for de Gaulle, France was not a 'terre, nor a people, but an idea.'[69]

The Empire had been central to the world view of Vichy: it had been the regime's main asset until 1942. After the war, the obsession with Empire was the corollary of the anti-Gaullist right's fundamental pessimism about French power. As a diminished nation, France had to cling on to the main source of influence left to her. Thus the defenders of *Algérie française* linked their defence of the Empire to ever-more violent attacks on what they saw as the excessive ambitions of Gaullist foreign policy: de Gaulle's anti-Americanism and anti-Europeanism risked the total isolation of France in a sterile neutralism. The atomic bomb was

---

[64] *La Nation française*, 7 December 1960.
[65] J. Soustelle, *L'Espérance trahie 1958–1961 (Paris, 1962)*.
[66] *Défense de l'Occident*, February 1962.
[67] Rougier, *De Gaulle*, 16, 20, 82; *Bilan du Gaullisme*, 28.
[68] *Rivarol*, 13 April 1961.
[69] Pleyber, *Esprit publique*, March 1961.

an absurdity which would make France a laughing-stock unless it were linked to a European defence policy.[70] There was a continuity from the *Munichois* advocates of a fall-back on the Empire in 1938 through Vichy to *Algérie française* in 1958.

L'Esprit publique had a slightly different angle. It fully embraced the romantic nationalism of de Gaulle, and turned it against him. Algeria could have been 'the great French adventure of the second half of the twentieth century', that 'collective dream' of which de Gaulle so often talked. Instead of rising to this challenge, de Gaulle had succumbed to the 'worst traditions of the petty bourgeois and Malthusian nineteenth century ... condemning us to live in a narrow Switzerland, a mediocre Sweden, deprived even of the alibi of prosperity'. Instead of being a new Carnot or a Clemenceau, de Gaulle was a cut-price Talleyrand.[71]

Algeria, then, was the second great moment in the history of anti-Gaullism – confirming traditional anti-Gaullists in their worst suppositions and adding new cohorts to the cause. The loss of Algeria was lived with an intensity no less great than the events of the war. Again there was a sense of having been duped in the name of the shared values. *Rivarol* commented that at least Mendès-France did not sing the *Marseillaise* for 'every piece of flesh torn off the body of the fatherland'.[72] The saintly cult of the victims of Gaullism in 1944–5 – Pétain and Brasillach – was enriched by new names: Salan, one of the putschist generals, and Bastien-Thiry, who was executed in 1963 for having tried to assassinate de Gaulle. In these cases, Isorni's 1945 role of defence counsel was now played by Tixier-Vignancourt.

IV

The cult of martyrs was all that was available to those who had – once again – lost. Algeria was independent: was there a future for anti-Gaullism? In theory anti-Gaullism after 1962 had the potential to become a broader movement than ever before because the left and centre had also turned against de Gaulle again. Until the Algerian question was solved, the Socialist and centrist politicians who brought de Gaulle back were reluctant to oppose him, although they were increasingly unhappy about his authoritarian style of government and his foreign policy: nuclear independence, anti-Americanism and anti-Europeanism.[73] The centrist Christian Democrats (MRP) broke

---

[70] *Rivarol*, 30 October 1958, 2 July 1960, 25 July 1960.
[71] *Esprit publique*, 23 December 1960. Also Mery [Girardet] in *La Nation française*, 18 March 1960.
[72] *Rivarol*, 6 October 1960.
[73] The government survived a censure motion on nuclear policy in October 1960.

with de Gaulle in April 1962, and when de Gaulle announced in August that he was proposing a reform of the constitution to allow the President to be elected by universal suffrage, he alienated almost the entire political class which saw this as a break with the traditions of parliamentary republicanism. One of the leaders of this opposition was the veteran liberal conservative Paul Reynaud, who had supported de Gaulle's return to power in 1958. As Reynaud put it in the debate on constitutional reform: 'Our admiration for his past remains intact, but this Assembly is not yet so degraded as to renounce the Republic.'[74] Reynaud later published an attack on de Gaulle's foreign policy which summarised most of the objections of the liberal right.[75]

In theory, this opened the way to all sorts of political re-alignments since the pro-*Algérie française* right was no less hostile to de Gaulle's foreign policy and was just as happy to play up the theme of authoritarianism. Girardet wrote: 'in the fullest sense of the term the Gaullist regime is a tyranny'.[76] Those who voted against de Gaulle in the referendum on constitutional reform ranged from fascists, ex-Pétainists, pro-*Algérie française* ex-Gaullists, pro-European Catholic centrists, liberal conservatives, Socialists and Communists. But this heterogeneity caused the weakness of anti-Gaullism, and thus jeopardised its future.

Just within the small world of *L'Esprit Publique* there was uncertainty about the future course of anti-Gaullism once Algeria was lost. There were those who wished to combat de Gaulle in the name of Europe and those for whom his crime was to have betrayed traditional French patriotism. The division was a continuation of that between Vichy and Paris, Pétainism and fascism. One contributor pointed out that Bastien Thiry had died for France not Europe;[77] not all the others agreed. In 1963 a split finally occurred, and the 'traditionalists', who included Girardet, left the paper.

Such divisions demonstrated the problem of defining a convincing vision of French nationalism in the shadow of de Gaulle. For one writer in *Ecrits de Paris* de Gaulle was the last Maurrassian, clutching desperately onto this 'outmoded national individualism' of 'La France seule'; for another writer, in the same number of the same journal, he was a Jacobin nationalist who did not understand the simple love of the country – 'love of the land of France, of her church bells, her tombs,

---

[74] The debate was held on 4 October 1962.

[75] P. Reynaud, *La Politique étrangère du gaullisme* (Paris, 1964).

[76] *Esprit Public*, November 1962. Boutang criticised de Gaulle's 'machine of police dictatorship' and his move to totalitarian dictatorship of one party: *La Nation française*, 17 October 1962, 14 November 1962. Bardèche, however, criticised him for consolidating democracy: he was a replay of Doumergue or Macmahon: *Défense de l'Occident*, May 1958, January 1959.

[77] Perret, *L'Esprit Publique*, June 1963.

her homes' – and was bent on the pursuit of futile glory, regardless of the sacrifices of lives and money.[78] On the other hand, the fascists of *Défense de l'Occident* could not deny that de Gaulle's anti-Americanism represented 'the policy we have been calling for for ten years' but this did not remove their historic objections to him, and the memory of the Liberation remained alive in the paper.[79]

Achieving coherence out of such factionalism was difficult, but in October 1963 the former *Algérie française* activist, Jean-Marie Le Pen, set up a committee to organise a single anti-Gaullist candidate of the right for the forthcoming presidential elections. The brief was clear: 'It is not a question of electing a specifically defined person ... we want to beat de Gaulle. The political past, height, hair or skin colour, age or profession of the man we will support matters little. What counts are his chances of beating de Gaulle.'[80] In the end the choice fell on Tixier-Vignancourt. Tixier's campaign received the support of most of the extreme right, but as the election approached, he also tried appealing to centrists alienated by de Gaulle's anti-Europeanism: he put flowers on the tomb of the Marshal as well as making favourable references to the Resistance hero Jean Moulin. This strategy was sabotaged by the late entry of a centrist candidate, Jean Lecanuet. As a result, at the first ballot Tixier received only 5 per cent of the vote, and even some on the extreme right, like Isorni and Pierre Poujade, preferred a 'useful' vote for Lecanuet than a wasted one for Tixier. In the second round Tixier advised voting for the leftist candidate Mitterrand.[81] But this *politique du pire* was not supported by everyone on the right, including Le Pen, and it led to the break up of the Tixier coalition.[82]

For anti-Gaullists the mid-1960s was a desperate period, although it witnessed the publication of some classic anti-Gaullist polemics, including two books by the right-wing novelist Jacques Laurent, who found himself facing prosecution for insulting the Head of State.[83] Soustelle, in exile for his involvement in the OAS plots to assassinate de Gaulle, wrote a book about the need to detach Gaullism from de Gaulle: he described the Fifth Republic as the triumph of neo-Gaullism which

---

[78] See, respectively, the articles of G. Aimel and J. Pleyber, *Ecrits de Paris*, March 1961.

[79] *Défense de l'Occident*, March 1964.

[80] Right-wing leader cited in Vinen's unpublished paper, 15.

[81] *Rivarol*, 16 December 1965, reminded its readers (incorrectly) that however distasteful Mitterrand might be, he did at least have a Cagoulard past.

[82] On the choices of the extreme right groups in the first round, see *Europe Action* supplement of December 1965. *Esprit publique* supported the centrist turn which led to another split and the departure of the more right-wing elements. The paper folded in February 1966. In general, see F. Duprat, *Les Mouvements d'extrême droite en France depuis 1944* (Paris, 1972); F. Bergeron and P. Vilgier, *De le Pen à le Pen* (Paris, 1985).

[83] J. Laurent, *Mauriac sous de Gaulle* (Paris, 1964); and *Année 40. Londres, de Gaulle, Vichy* (Paris, 1965). See also *Histoire égoïste* (Paris, 1976).

bore no relation to the genuine Gaullism of the war. But there seemed no hope until the events of 1968. The virulence of these attacks was in inverse proportion to any real chance of bringing de Gaulle down – until the sudden eruption of 1968.

The students of 1968 fitted none of the traditions of anti-Gaullism, and one of the most striking aspects of May is how little interest they showed in the person of de Gaulle: to them he was a museum-piece. They did not even bother to demonstrate outside the Elysée Palace to de Gaulle's perplexity. Some conservative anti-Gaullists, like Tixier, found the anarchy of 1968 even more alarming than their old adversary de Gaulle, and they joined the massive pro-de Gaulle demonstration of 30 May which brought 1968 to an end. This disgusted the less fainted-hearted anti-Gaullists. One of them wrote: 'How many nationalists – the eternal dupes of politics – were there in the columns which marched on 30 May? How many nostalgic for Marshal Pétain, how many partisans of *Algérie française*, victims of the 1944 purges, admirers of Bastien-Thiry, among the human masses who saved de Gaulle under the flags with the cross of Lorraine?'[84] Uncompromising anti-Gaullists for whom it was inconceivable to support de Gaulle in any cir-cumstances – even against leftist students – justified their position in various ways. *Rivarol* argued that de Gaulle was in fact the objective ally of the gauchiste students as he had always been of the Communists: the students wanted to destroy bourgeois society and it was because they understood the 'inestimable services' that de Gaulle had made to this cause since 1944 that they did not attack the Elysée.[85] From this perspective, politics resumed its reassuring grooves once the Com-munists came to de Gaulle's aid and restored him to his role as 'auxiliary number one of Communist imperialism'.[86]

There were, however, some on the anti-Gaullist right who welcomed 1968 not only because it represented a discomfiture for de Gaulle, but because it resonated with themes familiar to them. The language of the anti-Gaullist fascists was eerily similar to that of the gauchiste students. In the mid-1960s, the fascist review *Europe Action* had analysed the Fifth Republic as the incarnation of a 'technocratic vision of the world ... the transformation of men into machines to produce and consume'.[87] Thus Bardèche recognised that some of the fascist right 'were not far from feeling fraternally united to those who accuse this society of money and consumption'.[88] Ariès, who had written in *Esprit publique* in 1961, 'we do not repudiate fridges, cars or holidays, but we

[84] Duprat, *Les Mouvements*, 162.
[85] *Rivarol*, 16 May 1968.
[86] *Rivarol*, 6 June 1968.
[87] *Europe action*, January 1963, March 1963.
[88] *Défense de l'Occident*, June/August 1968.

refuse a regime which offers the fervour of the young French only fridges and cars',[89] found the anti-materialism and the anti-Jacobinism of the students recalled the aspirations of his own *Action française* youth: 'What a surprise for us! Under the deluge of speeches and graffiti we rediscovered the familiar theme of our reactionary youth, a distrust of the centralising state, an attachment to real liberties and small inter-mediary communities, to the region and to its language.'[90]

In this context, it is interesting that one of the most prescient anticipations of 1968 came from Ariès's friend Girardet in a 1963 article on 'Gaullist tyranny':

> The spirit of petit-bourgeois conservatism is tending gradually to spread throughout society … The new forms of collective life are organised around a narrow turning in on the self, around the organisation of holidays, the purchase of cars and refrigerators, the escape into the dreams of the official Television which have replaced the desire to participate in the great adventures of collective life … [But] inexorably the consequences of the demographic renewal will penetrate the interior of the Malthusian structures inherited from the last century. These numerous younger generations … [will not] be so easily contented with the satisfactions of their elders. .. We are in the great winter freeze. But under the apparently immobile surface of the land slow and mysterious germinations are taking place.[91]

That this prophecy was written by a conservative ex-Maurrassian deeply hostile to de Gaulle was a sign perhaps of the curious cross-currents of anti-Gaullism. For Girardet the Fifth Republic represented the total separation of politics and ethics. If this was so, it also made de Gaulle the supreme exemplar of the Maurrassian adage: *politique, d'abord.*

V

This essay has identified four traditions of anti-Gaullism. First, there is that of the Resistance generation. Secondly, there is a 'Republican' critique which runs from critics like Labarthe in wartime London, through the accusations of Boulangism in the late 1940s to defenders of the parliamentary Republic 1962. Thirdly, there is the 'realist'

[89] *L'Esprit publique*, July/August 1961.

[90] P. Ariès, *Historien de Dimanche* (Paris, 1980), 184. See also Bernard Fay in *Ecrits de Paris*, August 1968.

[91] *L'Esprit publique*, January 1963.

tradition which argues that de Gaulle was an outmoded nationalist, his anti-Americanism and anti-Europeanism dangerously isolating France and overestimating how much she counted in the contemporary world. Fourthly, there is the extreme-right tradition which remembers de Gaulle's rebellion against Pétain in 1940, his alleged sectarianism in 1944 and his betrayal of *Algérie française*.

These traditions vary in intensity. Resistance anti-Gaullism has none of the visceral hatred displayed on the right: it is a different telling of a shared history. Perhaps the description anti-Gaullist is inappropriate, but one should not underestimate depth of feeling. As the novelist Marguerite Duras, writing from within that tradition, put it in her memoir *La Douleur*: 'We shall never forgive.'[92]

The different anti-Gaullist traditions are not distinct. They weave in and out of each other, creating curious alliances of opposites: the pro-Europeanism of the Catholic centre and the Socialists is shared by the former collaborationist right; the moral language of the Resistance echoes the rhetoric of some of the defenders of *Algérie française*; resisters proud of their role as a tiny elite agreed with defenders of Vichy that in 1940 France had been almost unanimously Pétainist.

Anti-Gaullism has its generational strata. There are the implacable lifelong anti-Gaullists keeping the flame alive in the darkest days, and even beyond the grave. In the centenary year of 1990 *Ecrits de Paris* was at last able to triumph: 'He who cheated with life was not able to cheat with death which struck him down on the anniversary of 18 Brumaire turning him into a back to front Napoleon since his career had started on the anniversary of Waterloo with a lie, the lie of 18 June.'[93] There were repentant former Gaullists ready, when they joined the anti-Gaullist faith, to perform the necessary initiation rights even at the cost of repudiating their earlier convictions: Bidault, the former resister, was ready to lend his voice to the campaign for the transfer of Pétain's remains to Douaumont, the resting place of First War soldiers. There were others, like Soustelle, who claimed that it was de Gaulle himself who had betrayed a Gaullism to which they remained faithful. There were intermittent anti-Gaullists like Paul Reynaud.

In general these strands were too disparate to hold anti-Gaullism together. The differences were never overcome between Pétainists and fascists; resisters and Pétainists; Europeans and nationalists; Republicans and Maurrassians. But there is one man in whom the four strands intertwined with remarkable success providing a thread to guide us through what would otherwise be an incomprehensively sinuous tra-

[92] M. Duras, *La Douleur* (Paris, 1986), 32–3.
[93] *Ecrits de Paris*, June 1990.

jectory: François Mitterrand. If there is any consistency in the career of Mitterrand besides the pursuit of power, the key lies surely in anti-Gaullism: he represents the most perfect synthesis of all four traditions of anti-Gaullism I have tried to identify.

Mitterrand's Europeanism needs no emphasis from his presence at the Hague meeting on Europe in 1948 to his pursuit of European integration in the 1980s. This policy was the antithesis of everything in which de Gaulle believed, and represents the aspect of contemporary French policy most at variance with de Gaulle's vision of the world. Secondly, Mitterrand was one of the very few members of the left who refused to vote for de Gaulle's return to power in 1958 – because it had occurred under the threat of a military coup – and subsequently he wrote one of the classic statements of the Republican anti-Gaullist theme in his 1964 book denouncing the Fifth Republic as a 'permanent coup d'état'.[94] Thirdly, Mitterrand was one of those resisters who retained a strong animus against de Gaulle. In 1969, he wrote:

> the head of the Free French confiscated the Resistance's capital of sacrifice, suffering and dignity amassed by the obscure soldiers of the night. The Gaullist dictionary, like the Stalinist dictionary, scratched out the pages which recounted the true story of the struggle against the enemy and identified the services rendered to General de Gaulle as services rendered to France while services rendered to France without having contributed to the glory of General de Gaulle are considered negligible, even suspect.[95]

These attitudes can be found in the writings of many resisters, but in Mitterrand's case there is a special twist: he was a former Pétainist who had originally looked to Giraud as providing a possible third way between de Gaulle and Vichy. This takes us to the fourth aspect of Mitterrand's anti-Gaullism: his unhappiness with the Gaullist inter-pretation of Vichy. Mitterrand had been taken prisoner in 1940 and returned to France after escaping at the end of 1941. He then worked for a Vichyist organisation devoted to the reinsertion of Prisoners of War. This organisation gradually moved into resistance without entirely renouncing its Pétainist values. The Prisoners of War had a privileged target of Vichyist propaganda, central to its vision of redemption through suffering. Indeed, the difference between Mitterrand and de Gaulle could be encapsulated in the fact that Mitterrand's imprisonment was a defining experience of his life, while de Gaulle lived his experience as a prisoner in the First World War as a period of frustration away

---

[94] F. Mitterrand, *Le Coup d'Etat permanent* (Paris, 1964).
[95] F. Mitterrand, *Ma Part de vérité* (Paris, 1969), 23–4; also Mitterrand in Wieviorka, *Nous ntrerons*, 343–5.

from the scene of action. De Gaulle therefore had reservations about the whole idea of a Resistance movement run by POWs: 'a Resistance movement of POWs? Why not one of hair dressers?'[96]

For much of his career Mitterrand was silent about his Vichyite past, but in his last years he made it clear that he was not happy with the Manichean simplicities of the Gaullist view. From 1987, as President, he had a wreath placed on the tomb of Pétain on each armistice day; he made clear that he disapproved of the continued pursuit of alleged former collaborators; and he co-operated in a book on his early career which showed the extent of his Vichyite involvement.[97] In all this Mitterrand's aim was pedagogic: to teach the French that the past should be embraced in all its complexity. Mitterrand, who had in 1982 amnestied the putschist army officers of the Algerian War, now attempted a reconciliation over the memory of the war. He offered himself as the Henri IV for whom the right had called in 1944. But the attempt failed: his revelations caused an uproar and he was forced to abandon his practice of placing a wreath on Pétain's tomb. The language of reconciliation remained too bound up with the agendas of anti-Gaullism.[98]

In the end, anti-Gaullism achieved very little: de Gaulle triumphed over his enemies, and contemporary France is more modelled in his image than theirs. There is no doubt that anti-Gaullism was built around a stock of myths and wishful thinking. The idea that the Liberation could have been a painless process of national reconciliation was hardly a disinterested reading of the situation in France in 1944. The right wanted de Gaulle to be a French Mihailovic and believed he had become a Tito instead – but Mihailovic had failed, and de Gaulle was no Tito. The anti-Gaullist critique is not entirely without validity: there were patriots at Vichy; in the long run the armistice probably did serve the interests of the Allies (even if this was certainly not the intention of its signatories); the Resistance, whatever its moral importance, made no significant difference to the conduct of the war; it is arguable that France's position in the world would have been no different after 1945 if de Gaulle had never existed; de Gaulle's nationalism was in some respects anachronistic; and the Gaullist myth about the war delayed France's coming to terms with the past.

In this context, I would like to conclude with a few words about the recent trial of Maurice Papon for crimes against humanity. The historical implications of the trial were complex because although

---

[96] E. Conan and H. Rousso, *Un Passé qui ne passe pas* (Paris, 1994), 187.

[97] P. Péan, *Une Jeunesse française. François Mitterrand 1934–1947* (Paris, 1994).

[98] Conan and Rousso, *Un Passé quine passe pas* Mitterrand's last thoughts on the subject were: F. Mitterrand, *Mémoires interrompues* (Paris, 1996), 70–82, 123–4.

Papon was judged as a servant of Vichy his defence was partly built around the fact that he became a loyal Gaullist, and many historic Gaullists testified in his favour. The Gaullist President Jacques Chirac has made clear that he believes France should accept responsibility for her role in the Holocaust, but in the early days of the trial the current leader of the Gaullist party Philippe Séguin sounded a note of alarm: was the trial of Papon, he warned, not in danger of becoming the trial of France and accrediting the notion that Vichy France really was France, and by implication de Gaulle technically a dissident rather than the representative of the true France? Séguin argued that the trial risked becoming the pretext for an anti-Gaullist campaign which would destabilise the contemporary Gaullist Party. If that occurred, he argued, there would be nothing between the Socialists and the National Front of Le Pen.[99]

Clearly, Séguin's remarks were part of current political debate more than a dispassionate analysis of the standing of Gaullist history, but they were not entirely baseless. Jean-Marie Le Pen, one of the historic leaders of anti-Gaullism from his participation in Isorni's election campaign in 1951 through his defence of *Algérie française* in 1960–1 to his organisation of Tixier's campaign in 1965, was quick to leap in and observe that it was easier to resist the Germans in London than it had been in France (the implication being that de Gaulle was an emigré). As for Papon's defence counsel, Jean-Marc Varaut, he was himself an anti-Gaullist veteran, the last in that brilliant line of defence counsels which stretches from Isorni in 1945 to Tixier in 1960. Varaut had defended *L'Esprit publique* in 1961 when it was banned by the government; he had defended Jacques Laurent in 1965 when he was prosecuted for insulting the head of state. Varaut's defence of Papon, then, was not innocent: it was the act of a man with a lifelong anti-Gaullist pedigree. The moral perhaps is that if France confronts the Occupation in a balanced way the objective should not be, as some conservatives once hoped, to detach de Gaulle from Gaullism, or, as Soustelle hoped, to detach Gaullism from de Gaulle, but to detach what is valid in anti-Gaullism from the anti-Gaullists.

[99] *Le Figaro*, 21 October 1998.

THE POLITICS OF ENGLISH BIBLE TRANSLATION
IN GEORGIAN BRITAIN[1]

The Alexander Prize
By Neil W. Hitchin

READ 24 APRIL 1998

THE eighteenth century is a lost era in the history of English bible translation. The long tenure of the King James, or Authorised Version (AV), has caused historians to overlook the existence of the scores of translations which were attempted between 1611 and 1881–5, when the Revised Version was published. Darlow and Moule's *Historical Catalogue of English Bibles* lists the publication of at least forty-four new English translations of bibles, testaments, individual books, or groups of books between 1700 and 1800.[2] There were many more translations of biblical texts than these, however, as the recent and more comprehensive catalogue by W. Chamberlin has conclusively demonstrated.[3] Many have been lost to historical sight, or were never published, which could have easily been the fate of the celebrated translation by Anthony Purver, were it not for the patronage of the wealthy physician and fellow Quaker, Dr John Fothergill.[4]

To be fair, it has been easy to overlook them, awash in the great sea of the AV's global distribution by the bible societies in the nineteenth

---

[1] Earlier versions of this essay were given at the British Society for Eighteenth-Century Studies conference at St John's College, Oxford, 4 January 1997, and to the Cambridge Inter-faculty seminar 'Restoration to Reform, 1660–1832' at Pembroke College, 10 June 1997.

[2] *Historical Catalogue of English Bibles* ..., ed. H. Darlow and F. Moule (Cambridge, 1966).

[3] W. Chamberlin, *Catalogue of English Bible Translations: a Classified Bibliography* (New York, 1991), *passim*. Christopher Hill's opinion that the Bible was ignored in the eighteenth century must be modified in the light of such a large amount of material. *The English Bible and the Seventeenth-Century Revolution* (London, 1993), 7.

[4] P. Sjolander, *Some Aspects of Style in Twentieth Century English Bible Translation. One Man Versions of Mark and the Psalms* (U.M.E.A., Stockholm, 1979) points out the existence of many manuscript and privately printed translations beyond those included in her study of translation this century. There is good reason to believe the same was true of the eighteenth century.

century.[5] The combination of the royal copyright monopoly on printing bibles[6] and the cheap production and mass distribution systems of the British and Foreign Bible Society created a culture in the English-speaking world in which the AV *was* the bible.

The classicist Richard Lattimore wrote some years ago that 'no translator can escape being coloured by his own time ... One cannot translate in a vacuum.'[7] To an historian, the translation and publication of the English bible in the eighteenth century provides a splendid opportunity to probe the cultural politics of religion. Bible translation committees, bibliographers and historians of the Bible have been aware of the existence of these 'intermediate' translations, but as their interests differ from those of historians[8] there is no historically interpretive

---

[5] For the British and Foreign Bible Society's publishing and distribution operations, see L. Howsam, *Cheap Bibles: Nineteenth-Century Publishing and the British and Foreign Bible Society* (Cambridge, 1991). William Newcome, Archbishop of Armagh, saw that 'a translation by authority ought to supersede all others from its intrinsic excellence; and would of course supersede them by the frequency, correctness, and cheapness of its editions, as King James's Bible did that of Geneva, notwithstanding the preference given to it by the Calvinists'. Newcome, *An Historical View of the English Biblical Translations: the Expediency of Revising our Present Translation: and the Means of Executing such a Revision* (Dublin, 1792), 202–3.

[6] For which, see G. E. Bentley, 'Bible Illustrations and Sales' and *idem*, 'The Holy Pirates: Legal Enforcement in England of the Patent in the Authorised Version of the Bible, c. 1800', *Studies in Bibliography* (University of Virginia), 50 (1997), 372–89, which discusses the debate over whether the Crown had copyright over *all* bibles, all *English* bibles, or merely over the current AV, which had been produced specifically by royal command; 'Images of the Word: Separately Published English Bible Illustrations, 1539–1830', *Studies in Bibliography*, 47 (1994), 103–28 (esp. 107–8). The question of royal copyright was raised in the light of the modern patent of Elizabeth I to the publisher Barker in 1577, which stated 'All and singular Bibles and New Testaments whatsoever, in the English tongue or in any other tongue whatsoever, and any translation with or without notes.' It was a decision of 1769 which clarified the Crown's copyright. 'Mr Salkeld, after positively and expressly denying any prerogative in the Crown over the press, or any power to grant an exclusive privilege, says "I take the rule in all these cases to be, that when the Crown has a property or right of copy, the king may grant it. The Crown may grant the sole printing of Bibles in the English translation, because it was made at the king's charge." ' Quoted by Lord Mansfield, CJ, in Millar v. Taylor (1763–9), 4. Burrows Reports, 2303, from Salkeld's MS report, 2403–4, cited in H. Carter, *A History of Oxford University Press, vol. 1, to 1780* (Oxford, 1975), 351, 348.

[7] R. Lattimore, 'Practical Notes on Translating Greek Poetry', *On Translation*, ed. R. A. Brower (Cambridge, Mass., 1959), 148.

[8] H. Pope and S. Bullough, *English Versions of the Bible* (London, 1952) is the fullest treatment of the subject by far. B. F. Westcott's *A General View of the History of the English Bible* (5th edn, 1905) is dismissive of the eighteenth-century translation activity. W. F. Moulton, *The History of the English Bible* (London, Paris, New York, 1878), ignores it completely. Mention must be made of New Testament scholar F. F. Bruce's compact survey *The English Bible* (Lutterworth, 1961), published to coincide with the launching of the New Testament of the *New English Bible*. These books are among the few to note seriously any activity between 1611 and 1881 but, like all others, lack an interpretive scheme.

scheme within which to situate Georgian bible translators. It is a primary aim of this essay to provide one.

The centrepiece of the story is an unsuccessful campaign to get the Crown to convene a committee to produce a new authorised version. Dissatisfaction with King James's version had been manifest from its publication in 1611. By the eighteenth century desire for a new authorised translation of the Bible in English embraced biblical critics and bishops, dons and dissenters. The latitudinarian position, increasingly the mainstream in the Church, participated in a European protestant ecumenism which expected 'an apocalyptic union of all protestants'.[9] Since, as William Chillingworth famously wrote, 'the Bible, I say, the Bible only, is the religion of Protestants',[10] it should be no surprise to discern political influences at work beneath the scholarly and aesthetic justifications for a new translation under royal authority.

It had long been recognised that the existence of a 'canonical' bible translation was an expression of power relations. It was this awareness which had been behind the king's convening of the Hampton Court conference of 1604, which led to the creation of the AV, and marginalised the Geneva bible, though not without resistance from the puritans.[11] After 1662, partly in an exercise of anti-Calvinist spleen, the AV was again established by Convocation as the text for public worship. By the eighteenth century dissenters, and fellow-travellers within the Church of England, called the AV the 'common version',[12] which hints that both their acquiescence to the 'canonical' translation and their support for the project of a new authorised translation had a political significance.

[9] H. Schwartz, *The French Prophets. The History of a Millenarian Group in Eighteenth-century England* (Berkeley, Ca., 1980), p. 53.

[10] N. Sykes, 'The Religion of Protestants', *The Cambridge History of the Bible. The West from the Reformation to the Present Day*, ed. S. L. Greenslade, III (Cambridge, 1963), 175, citing Chillingworth, *The Religion of Protestants: a Safe Way to Salvation* (1638).

[11] For which, see Hill, *Bible*, 64–5. The revisions and distribution of the Catholic Douai–Rheims translation were similarly politicised, though the main purpose in providing a Roman Catholic translation in English was to give a safe alternative bible to Catholics. It need hardly be said that in the political climate of eighteenth-century Britain, there were no plans to invite Catholic scholars to join any translation committee. For the history of Catholic bibles in eighteenth-century Britain, see H. Cotton, *Rhemes and Doway. An attempt to shew what has been done by Roman Catholics for the diffusion of the Holy Scriptures in English* (Oxford, 1855). More accessible is Pope and Bullough, *English Versions*, 337–90. There is no discussion of Catholic bible translation in *Challoner and his Church. A Catholic Bishop in Georgian England*, ed. E. Duffy (Cambridge, 1981), though there is a chapter in E. H. Burton's earlier biographical treatment, *The Life and Times of Bishop Challoner (1691–1781)* (London, 1909), I, 270–89.

[12] For example, James MacKnight, 'Essay IV', *A New and Literal Translation ... of all the Apostolical Epistles* (London, 1795 [1821 edn]), I, 85. Anthony Purver, *A New and Literal Translation of all the Books of the Old and New Testament...* (London, 1764), 202. Nathaniel Scarlett, *A Translation of the New Testament from the Original Greek; humbly attempted...* (London, 1798), i.

The dissenters' support for a new official version seems to reflect an assurance that they had a stake in the nation's religious life. If so, theirs was a sophisticated use of a key national text to redefine the assumptions of national religious culture either to obtain the limited goal of toleration for themselves, or even to reconstruct a nationally comprehensive, protestant Church of England.

The historical memory of King James's translation committee of 1611 exercised the imaginations of these new reformers. The scholarly dissenter Philip Doddridge wished that 'our Governors in church and state would favour us with a version of the scriptures with all possible improvement'. But he thought it would be useful if 'private Divines' would 'supply the defect, and ... give us improved versions' until it was 'undertaken under the patronage of supreme authority',[13] which is what eventually happened. Much later, in the 1780s, Cambridge divine Richard Ormerod still believed 'a revisal upon a plan somewhat similar [to the King James Version], conducted under proper authority, and under due restriction, by men of acknowledged erudition, and with abilities every way competent to such an undertaking, could hardly fail of being generally approved'.[14] Still, some opponents objected that the correcting translators would differ among themselves, as those offering their own translations already did. William Newcome, the Irish bishop and translator, reflected on the committee of 1611:

> Undoubtedly King James's translators often disagreed as individuals; and adopted in a body what seemed most agreeable to the sound rules of interpretation. Let a like number of able judges decide, on the same principle, between the biblical critics of the present age.[15]

Others, not necessarily opponents of an authorised translation to be used in public, felt that it was desirable to have numerous translations for the sake of comparision, a view which had advocates among the early church Fathers too.

In addition to the search for increased ecclesiastical latitude, the desire for a new authorised translation was an affirmation of national resistance to popery, the common cause of all British protestants.[16]

---

[13] Philip Doddridge, 'Preface', *Family Expositor: or, a paraphrase and version of the New Testament: with critical notes*, 12-vol. edn (London, 1765). Cited in Newcome, *Historical View*, 133.

[14] Richard Ormerod, *A short specimen for an improvement in some parts of the present translation of the Old Testament* (Cambridge and London, 1792).

[15] Newcome, *Historical View*, 226.

[16] For a discussion of the role of the Authorised version in constructing a protestant British identity before 1800, albeit a contested identity, see S. Mandelbrote, 'The bible and national identity in the British Isles, c. 1650–c. 1750', *Protestantism and National Identity. Britain and Ireland, c. 1650–c. 1850*, ed. T. Claydon and I. McBride (Cambridge, 1998), 157–81.

James MacKnight, the eminent moderator of the General Assembly of the Church of Scotland, a biblical critic who worked for thirty years on his translation of the epistles, thought that 'the inaccurate and misleading translation of the modern version derive, in many cases, from the Vulgate translators'. He did not dislike the Vulgate for its stylistic influence, for 'with all its faults the Vulgate ... hath preserved much of the beautiful simplicity of the original, and in many passages its translations are more just than those in some of the modern versions'.[17] MacKnight viewed the AV, rightly, as a mere amendment to its predecessor the Bishop's bible. Following previous historians,[18] he showed how the first English versions all depended on the Vulgate, and that the translators of the 1611 version were required to follow 'the ordinary Bible read in the churches', the Bishop's bible, deviating 'as little as the original would permit'. This rule meant, explicitly, keeping words like *church* instead of *congregation* for ecclesia, a particularly important point of ecclesiastical and political translation.[19] He showed his protestant conviction when he wrote: 'It is ultimately from the Scriptures, and not from creeds or systems, by whomsoever composed, nor even from the decrees of councils, whether general or particular, that the genuine doctrines of the gospel are to be learned.'[20] On the other hand, the 1611 AV had acquired sufficient cultural authority through use by this time that it had itself become an expression of reformed protestant Britain, an expression of national identity. The Bible, whether the conservative, episcopal AV or a new version, was treated as a part of the protestant constitution of Britain.

The point is reinforced by the differences in word choice between the Catholic Douay version and the AV. Where the AV has Jesus tell Peter 'when thou art converted, *strengthen* thy brethren', the Douay–Rheims has 'and thou, being once converted, *confirm* thy brethren', reiterating the sacrament of confirmation, which the Anglicans already accepted, but dissenters did not (Matt. xxii. 32). The use of the word *chalice* instead of the AV *cup* asserts the liturgical and latinate image of the Last Supper (Matt. xxii. 17, 20). The final charge of the risen Christ is translated to read 'that *penance* and remission of sins should be preached', rather than *repentance* and remission of sins (Matt. xxiv. 47).

---

[17] MacKnight, 'Preface', *Apostolic Epistles*, 1 and 9.

[18] He referred to Anthony Johnson, *An Historical Account of the several English translations of the Bible: and the opposition they met with from the Church of Rome* (London, 1730), and the low church whig John Lewis's *Complete History of the several translations of the Bible in English* (2nd edn, 1739). Lewis's 'strong protestant bias' 'excited the open hostility of his hearers' in 1712 when he preached a visitation sermon in Canterbury. *DNB*. His was the first published edition of Wycliffe's bible, in 1731.

[19] MacKnight, 'Preface', *Apostolic Epistles*, 11–24.

[20] MacKnight, 'Preface', *Apostolic Epistles*, 49.

Finally, the awkward phrase, 'the ancient to the lady Elect' (i.e. her name is Elect, which has a strangely puritan feel to it), seeks to undermine the doctrine of predestination and the presbyterian system of church government, readings possible with the AV's 'the elder unto the elect lady' (2 John i. 1).[21]

Great care was taken over particular word meanings because, beyond its bearing of sacred knowledge, the AV was a text which carried a legal significance. The purpose of the AV was to provide a common text, a lingua franca from which to reinforce decisions about doctrine and organisation, and to orient worship and devotion around a common axis. The medieval and early protestant view of the Bible as a divine law underlay the search for a godly political state, ruled by this divine law. The translation of the sacred books had to be literal and precise, because legal codes could not be ambiguous. Just as legal conflicts led to the discovery of clearer laws, controversies over biblical texts led to more accurate translations. The Gospel was the 'nova lex', or new law.[22] The apologetic theme of the 'evidences of Christianity' was more than a metaphor, more than a method; it suggested an idea of a legal system sanctified and corrected by a higher law. This approach to translating, which advocated refinement of the traditional text, reflected the legal traditions of the common law.[23]

There was a noticeable overlap between reformers and the desire for a new *translation*, and between constitutional moderates and the desire for a *revision* of the presently authorised translation. Dissenters often described literal translations as '*slavish* and literal', suggestive of this deeper significance of translation as an act. Liberty and freedom in translation were prized by translators in the republican or the neo-Roman tradition.[24] To be dependent, or perpetually liable to the authority of a tyrannous system, was slavery. A slave may not always be coerced, but he is always liable to coercion. The AV, and all other authorised versions before it, with their verbal dependency on the Roman Vulgate bible, were slavish translations, as were literal trans-

---

[21] *Douay Rheims New Testament* (1899 edition).

[22] F. C. Grant, *Translating the Bible* (Edinburgh, 1961), 6–7.

[23] M. Lobban, *The Common Law and English Jurisprudence, 1760–1850* (Oxford, 1991), 7–16. Jeremy Bentham's proverbial hostility to religion did not prevent him making the rather interesting observation that 'The forming of a Digest of the Law' was 'to lawyers, what the making of a translation of the bible was to churchmen'. That is, Bentham thought bible translation would expose priestcraft. Presumably he was describing pre-Reformation churchmen, though contemporary lawyers. Univ. Lond. MSS: UC. xxvii. 124, cited in D. Lieberman, *The Province of Legislation Determined. Legal Theory in Eighteenth-Century Britain* (Cambridge, 1989), 253.

[24] For discussion of the neo-Roman idea of liberty, especially as it relates to the problem of monarchy and public liberty, see Quentin Skinner's inaugural lecture as Regius Professor, *Liberty before Liberalism* (Cambridge, 1998), 52–5.

lations. In terms of the biblical translation debate, the rationalist, who thought the existing version to be corrupt, often at the source, which was Latin and popish, wanted a wholly new translation, which would reflect the 'rational Christianity' to which all 'consistent protestants' adhered.[25] The moderate sought an improvement of the translation only at the points which had been discovered to be inaccurate or inadequate. To have gone further would have been disruptive of people's confidence in the faith itself, since it would have seemed to call into question the reliability of the fundamental evidence for the truth of the faith. Again, it was not unlike the common law, where the points of law were resolved as they arose and codified from time to time, rather than the law being wiped away at a stroke to be replaced by a new 'rational' system.

I have described some general political tensions impinging on plans to produce a new authorised English bible, and I shall return to the point shortly. But political reasons, as I have noted above, were not the reasons actually cited by those who wanted to see a new AV. The publicly stated reasons were those of taste and scholarship.

Scholarship and the English language had moved on since 1611.[26] It was widely agreed among the learned that the increased knowledge of Greek and, increasingly, Hebrew texts presented irrefutable evidence that however attractive the AV rendering might be as an English translation it was now out of date on text-critical grounds. Considerable advances had been made towards a more accurate Greek and Hebrew text since the AV was first published, so there was, in a sense, a new bible to be translated.

Translation theory and aesthetic values had changed since 1611 and continued to do so during the eighteenth century. There was 'almost unrestrained freedom' among translators of classical secular works in the later seventeenth century, in contrast to their more rigid approach to scripture. The classics were acknowledgedly artifical; the Bible, however, was another expression of the natural law, and had to be

---

[25] Joseph Priestley was a notable exception to dissenting norms in preferring a revision, even to the point of resisting the views of strong-willed friends, like Thomas Belsham, William Frend and Theophilus Lindsay, whom he had commissioned to assist him in making a new translation. Priestley wanted to stay much closer to the wording of the AV than, specifically, Newcome and Blayney. See his Preface to the English edition of his *Harmony of the Evangelists* (III), and, despite some inaccuracies, Marilyn Brooks, 'Priestley's plan for a "Continually Improving" translation of the Bible', *Enlightenment and Dissent*, no. 15 (1996), 89–106. The new translation was within days of completion when it was destroyed in the fire of July 1792. Also Jenny Graham, 'Priestley and his Bible', *Enlightenment and Dissent*, no. 14 (1995), 88–104.

[26] 'To be a useful instrument of social intercourse, language must be able to admit new knowledge and new organisations of knowledge. In a sense, it must fit reality or it is useless.' E. Nida, *Toward a Science of Translating* (Leiden, 1964), 3.

treated with due respect. The notion that there might be rhetoric or artifice in scripture was a disturbing one. In translating foreign works, the general idea of the original was the goal, rather than a literal rendering. Dryden challenged the propriety of calling such efforts translations in 1680, and declared that there were three types of translation: word for word, or metaphrase; paraphrase, in which the author's work is kept carefully in view, but in which the sense is followed rather than the words; and imitation, which could leave both words and sense behind in favour of the spirit of the original. He thought imitation and metaphrase were undesirable extremes, and paraphrase to be preferred.[27] It was probably this critical preference which lay behind the fashion for scriptural paraphrases in the 1690s and after.[28] Beginning on the continent some time after mid-century, there was a return to the preference for more literal renderings which preserved the ordering of words and ideas.[29] Indeed, the increasingly conservative archbishop Secker held this view personally, though permitting others their own conscience in practice. In a letter of September 1761 to the Cambridge Hebraist William Green he wrote

> I dare neither add nor strike out nor alter words, nor even the order of words, on little or no ancient authority, merely to make the Sacred Text appear what seems to me more beautiful or methodical, or less exceptionable, where it is already fairly defensible. I heartily wish you success. For I am fully persuaded of your good intentions.[30]

Wesley's revised translation of 1755 related the technical problems of theology and exegesis to secular conceptual words, recognising the bearing which key words could have on doctrine. George Campbell's *The Four Gospels* (1789), 'an outstanding work on the history and theory of translation', offered a new summary of the principles of good translation: the just representation of the sense of the original; the author's spirit and manner; and that a translation should seem enough of an original performance to be natural and easy.[31] The ideas were picked up by Tytler in his more widely read *Principles of Translation* (1790), through which book they were transmitted into the next century.

---

[27] Dryden, 'Preface', *Ovid's Epistles* (1680), in *Essay on Dramatic Poesy and other Prose Works*, ed. George Watson, I, 262–73. Also Nida, *Science*, 17–18.

[28] See literature review in 'Preface' to John Locke, *Paraphrase and Notes on the Epistles of St. Paul*, ed. A. W. Wainwright (2 vols) (Oxford, 1987), I, 22–5.

[29] Batteux (1760) in France, and Herder and Schlegel in Germany. Nida, *Science*, 18.

[30] John Nichols, *Illustrations of the Literary History of the Eighteenth Century* (8 vols, London, 1817–58), IV, 853.

[31] Nida, *Science*, 18, citing G. Campbell, *The Four Gospels* (2 vols, London, 1789). Nida also appreciated Campbell's introductory volume, which he called 'an outstanding scholarly treatment of translation principles and procedures, especially as they are related to the problems of the Bible translator' (5, note).

By the century's end much less licence was permitted to translators. Many felt that the old translation left much to be desired from the point of view of English-language usage. Diction and style were much changed in the intervening time. Whereas the style of seventeenth-century writing was typically expansive and erudite, piling detail and example upon one another in an hortatory fruitcake, the style of the early eighteenth century was self-consciously modelled with clean Palladian lines, aspiring to epigrammatic precision.

In this harmonious world of 'pleasing to instruct', the scriptures were often described as the 'Sacred Classics'.[32] The presbyterian critic Edward Harwood's study of the New Testament consisted of 'critical observations, explanatory remarks, parallel passages from Greek and Roman authors, accounts of customs and usages mentioned or alluded to in the New Testament, and a list of the most eminent authors, with the best editions of their works, who have illustrated the sacred classics'.[33] This was a self-conscious effort to connect the study, criticism and translation of the Bible with the classical literature into which all truly educated people were initiated in the neoclassical culture of Georgian Britain. Even the autodidact Quaker tradesman Anthony Purver thought it a disgrace that 'this deference is paid to the *Heathen Classics*, that they may appear beautiful and not barbarous; many of which are translated often.[34] Why should the Scripture meet with less Regard? Is it to be exposed to Ridicule and Contempt, in our Libertine Age?'[35]

Despite its sometimes pompous expression, Edward Harwood's translation of the New Testament showed this style well. He had modelled it on the Latin translation of Castalio, and on Hume, Robertson, Lowth, Hurd, Johnson, Samuel Pratt and others in the English language.[36] His plan, pointedly, was 'to translate the sacred writers of the New Testament with the same freedom, Impartiality and Elegance' of the recent Greek classical translations.[37] It was, he thought, decidedly difficult to make modern elegant language 'the vehicle of inspired truths ... conscious that the ... barbarous language of the old vulgar version hath acquired a venerable sacredness from length of time and custom'.[38] He aimed to induce 'persons of a liberal education and polite taste to

[32] Anthony Blackwall, *The Sacred Classics defended and illustrated; or, an essay humbly offer'd towards proving the purity, propriety, and true eloquence of the writers of the New Testament* (London, 1725–31).

[33] Edward Harwood, *A New Introduction to the Study and Knowledge of the New Testament* (2nd edn, London, 1773), xiii.

[34] See his appendix concerning classical Greek and bibles.

[35] Purver, 'Introductory Remarks', *New and Literal Translation*, v.

[36] Harwood, 'Introduction', *A Liberal Translation of the New Testament, being an attempt to translate the sacred writings* (London, Bristol and Warrington, 1768), iv.

[37] Harwood, Advertisement of subscription for *Liberal Translation* (1765), 3.

[38] Harwood, *Liberal Translation*, v.

peruse the sacred volume', especially educated young gentlemen and women, whom he hoped might be lured through 'the innocent strategem of a *modern style* [his italics], to read a book, which is now, alas! too generally neglected and disregarded by the young and gay, as a volume containing little to amuse and delight, and furnishing a study congenial only to the gloom of old age, or the melancholy of a desponding visionary'.[39] Harwood and others had realised the very modern idea that it is the reader's experience which should be at the centre of the translator's attention. The twentieth-century idea of formal equivalency 'focuses attention on the message itself' and is intended to enable a reader to enter and identify with a person in the source-language, while dynamic equivalency 'aims at complete naturalness of expression, and tries to relate the receptor to modes of behaviour relevant within the context of his own culture; it does not insist that he understand the cultural patterns of the source language in order to comprehend the message'.[40]

Though well intentioned, Harwood failed to adhere to his plan of simplicity. His reviewer John Hirons thought his failure was partly due to the fact that the life of Christ is better in the simplicity of Luke or John than in the 'elegant fluency of Livy or the pointed energy of Tacitus' which Harwood had aimed for. His use of polished words and phrases often degrades the style of sentiment, and 'such polite expression may sometimes expose him to ridicule'. The usual passage trotted out is the Parable of the Prodigal Son, which begins, 'A gentleman of a splendid family and opulent fortune had two sons...' (Luke xv. 11ff). Another familiar passage, John iii. 16, 'For God so loved the world, that he gave his only begotten Son, that whosoever believeth in him should not perish, but have everlasting life', is rendered:

> For the supreme God was affected with such immense compassion and love for the human race, that he deputed his son from heaven to instruct them – in order that everyone who embraces and obeys his religion might not finally perish, but secure everlasting happiness.[41]

His rendering of Acts is rather good, possibly because it is better suited, as a narrative, to the style of Livy or Tacitus. Harwood's biographer summed it up, a little bluntly, as 'good scholarship but turgid prose'.[42] The high style of classical elegance inclined to a latinate

[39] Ibid.

[40] The model of formal and dynamic equivalent in translating was proposed by the twentieth-century missionary translator Eugene Nida. Nida, *Science*, 159.

[41] The shift in emphasis away from the traditional christology of redemption through sacrifice in favour of redemption through moral instruction is noticeable in Harwood's translation of this passage.

[42] *DNB*.

diction and was preferred by the more cultured, critical and literary minds. The criticism of the AV for its Latin heritage did not apply here, so long as the translation was a new one, based on the Greek testament, for it was the objection to the popish Vulgate, rather than Latin as such, that was the real point for some translators.

A taste for the primitive which surfaced in the 1760s contrasted with the artifices of classicism. Where the Bible was the religion of protestants, nature was the religion of deists, and the naturalistic search for the origins of society and for the true natural religion were one fruit of several decades of deist polemic. The idea that English words with Saxon roots were preferable to latinate words was dictated by political and religious considerations as much as by linguistic knowledge. In the sixteenth century, protestant translators of the English bible thought that Greek and Hebrew were closer in spirit to English than they were to Latin, a view that was held as late as Addison, who remarked that Hebrew could easily be translated directly into English without losing any of its power, since both ancient Hebrew and Saxon were manly and earthy languages.[43] The debate over Saxon versus Latin words had a parallel in the religious mentality of candour amongst dissenters.[44] Saxon words, like dissenting belief, were forthright, manly, honest and independent; so would a translation be which utilised words of English origin.[45] Latinate words were sophisticated, popish, dissimulating and effete. The same conflict over the political culture of diction emerged in an affectation of less refined language in Commons debates and in pamphlet literature in the 1770s.[46] Anthony Purver wanted the English bible to compete with classical literature aesthetically, but in his translation he sought to purge the use of linguistic corruptions to restore the purity of the English words, to which end he included an appendix of unacceptable words. So the rationale for using Saxon words was shifting.

The new style of protestant primitivism continued to reflect a suspicion of Catholic urbanity, but now addressed deist naturalism too. If there was an original natural religion then it had to be found in the Bible. When Robert Lowth discovered the parallelism of repeating metaphors in Hebrew poetry he regarded it as a literary structure

---

[43] Addison, *Spectator*, No. 405, 14 June 1712.

[44] For the importance of candour to dissenters, see R. K. Webb, 'Rational Piety', *Enlightenment and Religion. Rational Dissent in Eighteenth-Century Britain*, ed. K. Haakonssen (Cambridge, 1996), 219–40.

[45] A debate which persists even today among translators of the English bible.

[46] Edmund Paley noted that while writing *Principles of Moral and Political Philosophy* his father 'fell in with times when uncourtly language became the fashion in politics'. E. Paley, *An Account of the Life of William Paley, D.D.* (London, 1825), 344–5. Also E. Barker, *Traditions of Civility. Eight Essays* (Cambridge, 1948), 232.

which proved that the poetry was very ancient. The ancients, like children, learned by repetition. His lectures on the subject helped to consolidate the growing fashion for primitivity and naturalness. Lowth and his followers went on to produce translations of Hebrew poetry which reinforced this impression of natural and primitive language and thought patterns in the biblical text.

A different angle on the roots of the primordial language was given by William Jones of Nayland, the Hutchinsonian divine, who thought the real content of scripture was in the figurative elements or principles. Though 'there is a certain obscurity in the language of the Bible', it does not arise from the language or the grammar. All language is subject to ambiguity. But our ideas of 'all sensual things stored in our minds and memories' provides the means for us to apprehend the invisible things which revelation points out to us. 'Whatever difficulties remain in the original are removed for all common readers by the translation of the Bible into their mother tongue.'[47]

Another indication that the ideology of nature was quietly displacing the reformation ideology was in the modern idea of 'science' being applied to biblical texts. The substance and style of early eighteenth-century divinity were modelled on scientific precision and sobriety, according to Hans Frei, reflecting Baconian ideas.[48] Jones described a critical technique which treated the Bible as a parallel of nature and the biblical student as a scientist.[49] In early 1789 Edward King's *Morsels of Criticism* advocated an 'application of modern science to biblical texts', which his reviewer found 'very interesting'.[50] Marks of the method may be seen in MacKnight, too, for whom text critics provide the raw data, like experimental scientists, and theologians, like natural philosophers, act as the interpreters. If the data of scripture were contradictory, he wrote, why should it be concealed in translation or in interpretation?[51] It would not be good scientific practice, so why should it be good critical practice?

Finally, the 'natural' was related to the emergent fascination with the 'oriental'. There is no reason to disagree with Edward Said's argument that interest in 'the East' was driven by domestic needs and

---

[47] W. Jones, *A Course of Lectures on the Figurative Language of the Holy Scripture, and the Interpretation of it from Scripture itself* (London, for the author, 1787), 2–10. See also N. W. Hitchin, 'The Evidence of Things Seen: Georgian Churchmen and Biblical Prophecy', *Prophecy. The Power of Inspired Language in History, 1300–2000*, ed. B. Taithe and T. Thornton (Stroud, Glocs., 1997), 133.

[48] H. Frei, *The Eclipse of Biblical Narrative. A Study in Eighteenth- and Nineteenth-Century Hermeneutics* (New Haven and London, 1974), 52.

[49] W. Jones, *Figurative Language*, 1.

[50] *Monthly Review* (1789), 110–17.

[51] MacKnight does not himself use the scientific metaphor, but the practical point is evident in his writing. 'Preface', *Apostolic Epistles*, 45.

power relations,[52] in order to maintain that biblical scholars had a legitimate interest in seeking greater understanding of the book. E. S. Shaffer wrote, some years before Said and with more lucidity:

Orientalism ... is very much more than a fanciful and ignorant borrowing from the translations of the Arabian Nights ... or from the tall stories of the travellers, or a taste for Chinese gardens or bric-a-brac. It is closely bound up with the new textual and historical scholarship exercised on the Bible since the Reformation, and drew on a very considerable body of new and challenging knowledge, geological, chronological, and anthropological, though its interpretation was still moulded by Christian apologetics ... If indeed it created a 'pseudo-Orient', it did so not as escapism, but on the contrary, as a subtle harmonizing of the urgently conflicting readings of the significance of primitive religious experience.

This orientalism was one aspect of a broader Hellenism, associated with bible studies rather than classical antiquity.[53] The improving access to near eastern lands was a boon to translators. Comparing Arabic and Syraic words with ancient Hebrew words was increasingly treated as an indispensable adjunct for biblical philology.[54] For 'rational' dissenters and churchmen, the political usefulness of knowing more about the primitive words and culture was obvious, for it enabled them to argue that the primitive church differed from the contemporary church, and to point to orientalist researches in support.[55] If 'the orient' was often used as cultural polemic in the eighteenth century,[56] reform-minded biblical critics and translators found they could appeal to new knowledge of 'the orient' as a privileged source of textual and cultural authority in making their case for a new translation.

Criticisms of the Hebrew and Greek biblical text from deist critics and the French Catholic Richard Simon forced protestant apologists to justify their reliance on the Bible. Critics might point to discrepancies in various reading of the biblical books but scholars had always been

---

[52] E. Said, *Orientalism* (Harmondsworth, Middx, 1978), 3.

[53] E. S. Shaffer, *'Kubla Khan' and* The Fall of Jerusalem. *The Mythological School in Biblical Criticism and Secular Literature, 1770–1880* (Cambridge, 1972), 14.

[54] For example, Johan-David Michaelis, *Introductory Lectures to the Sacred Books of the New Testament*, translated anonymously (London, 1761). Latterly translated from the 4th German edition by Herbert Marsh, with considerable additional notes (3 vols, Cambridge and London, 1793–1801).

[55] J. White, Laudian Professor of Arabic at Oxford, noted the increased knowledge of ₔastern customs as one reason for a new revision in a sermon of 1778. *A Revisal of the ₔglish Translation of the Old Testament Recommended* (Oxford, 1779).

[56] R. L. Mack, 'Introduction', *Oriental Tales* (Oxford, 1992), xlvii–xlviii.

aware of these discrepancies.[57] Such criticisms were regarded as tactical ploys rather than as attacks to be reckoned with intellectually.[58] Nevertheless, the need to dispel the criticisms prompted a new round of research into the state of the Greek and Hebrew texts, and renewed interest in both text criticism and translation. The publication of John Mill's Greek testament of 1707 was the first significant demonstration of textual improvement.[59] It was widely used in study, but did not set off a rush of translating activity. Richard Bentley made a start on editing the Greek testament, but soon shied away, which left the field open to the continental critics Wetstein and Griesbach, whose editions were as widely used as Mill's towards the latter end of the century. Ironically, given the argument that improvements in textual knowledge had strengthened the demand for a new authorised version, the high profile research into the state of the Hebrew text which dominated the second half of the century played an important role in the diversion of energy away from the campaign.

Obviously, the plans for a new AV never came to fruition, despite apparently strong support from Archbishop Secker. As Bishop of Oxford he had built up a strong network of Hebrew scholars there in the 1750s. Lowth was already in place at New College when he published his influential lectures on Hebrew poetry in 1753. Secker supported Benjamin Kennicott at Exeter, and facilitated the creation of a Hebraists' hive at Hertford College which included Benjamin Blayney, who prepared the Clarendon edition of the AV (1769) and David Durell, 'an ardent advocate of a new translation' of the Bible, who became principal of Hertford College in 1757.[60] William Newcome was also part of the circle working around Secker. His career began at Oxford, where he was elected fellow of Hertford College in 1753, and was subsequently tutor and vice-principal, before his consecration as bishop of Dromore in 1766.[61]

Moreover, Secker was himself actively pursuing research into the improvement of the AV. One of the acts of Dr Andrew Ducarel, who was made keeper of Lambeth Library in 1757 and commissary of the

---

[57] For instance, St Jerome corresponded with St Augustine on the textual discrepancies they encountered.

[58] MacKnight, 'Supplementary Essays', *Apostolical Epistles*, 1, 69–70.

[59] William Whiston's Greek text was based on the eccentric but important codex Beza at Cambridge. It provided the foundation for his English version (1745) which, together with his commitment to the priority of the *Apostolic Constitutions*, formed the core support for his idea of Primitive Christianity.

[60] *Autobiography of Thomas Secker, Archbishop of Canterbury*, ed. J. S. Macauley and R. W. Greaves, University of Kansas Library Series, no. 49, (Lawrence, Kansas, 1988), 169. Durell was also responsible, as vice-chancellor in 1768, for passing sentence against the six evangelical 'martyrs' of St Edmund's Hall.

[61] For all of whom, see *DNB*.

city and diocese of Canterbury from 1758, was to catalogue the English bible translations, apparently at the request of Secker.[62] Numerous notes from Secker's interleaved English bible were included in an appendix to Newcome's *Attempt towards an improved version ... of the twelve minor prophets*.[63] In 1778 Lowth referred to Secker's valuable corrections of the English translation and critical remarks on the Hebrew text which 'will be of infinite service, whenever that necessary work, a New Translation, or a Revision of the present Translation of the Holy Scriptures, for the use of our Church, shall be undertaken'.[64]

With the promotion of Secker to Canterbury in 1757 it looked as if the success of convening a new committee was assured, and perhaps even the political agenda to move the Church further along the protestant road of rational Christianity. In that year Edmund Law, the Master of Peterhouse, and later bishop of Carlisle, purchased a 1606 Geneva bible and began to make extensive annotations.[65] The first volume contains the inscription:

> This Book contains Remarks from various Authors in relation both to ye original Text & Versions, chiefly in ye New Testament, by way of Materials toward a more perfect Edition, as well as a more accurate Translation, wch is extremely wanted.
>
> E Law 1757

Lower on the same page he explained his choice of edition for annotation.

> I made use of this old Translat^n as giving me an opportunity of comparing ye last with it, wch is often chang'd for ye worse & took up with ye present interleaved copy, tho' scribbled in by other hands.[66]

All three volumes contain notes on a variety of cultural, doctrinal and grammatical points His use of the Geneva translation as the basis for

---

[62] *DNB* and Newcome to Toulmin, 7 Sept. 1794, *Monthly Repository [of Theology and General Literature] (1800), vol* I, pp. 519–20. Newcome included the catalogue, *A List of various editions of the Bible, and parts therof, in English from the year 1526 to 1776* (London, 1778) in his *Historical View*.

[63] *Twelve Minor Prophets* (London and Dublin, 1785), 229–46.

[64] Lowth, *Preliminary Dissertation to Isaiah* (London, 1778), lxix.

[65] The tooled inscription 'E. Law 1757' on the front cover of each volume, with the note inside, confirm that he purchased this bible in 1757, the year after he became Master of Peterhouse (1756–87).

[66] *Holy Bible* (Tomson's Geneva version as printed in 1599, without the Apocrypha, 4to), 3 vols (Robert Barker, 1606), I, MS page iii. British Library reference C. 45. g. 13. This bible has hitherto been overlooked by historians and biblical scholars, perhaps because it has been stored in the Early Printed Collections of the British Museum, rather than in the Manuscript Students' Room.

his thinking about the shape of a new AV was a deliberate integration of the reform movement with the puritans of the previous century. Puritanism lay behind his friend Francis Blackburne's radicalism too. While waiting at his uncle's house for an appropriate living to come up after his ordination, he discovered some old books by puritans in the storage room at his great-grandfather's house in Catterick, Yorkshire. He brought them to his room

> and there became acquainted with the manners and principles of many excellent old puritans. I was struck by their unaffected and disinterested piety, and their zeal for the spiritual good of mankind; and from them I learned that a Christian truly such, must ever be in a state of warfare with the world, and particularly the principalities and powers of it.[67]

Law must already have heard that Secker, a proponent of the plan, was to be made archbishop when he bought his annotated Geneva bible in preparation for his probable role in formulating the new translation. It seems unlikely that he was responding to intelligence that the proposed committee was going to be sidelined, though as Law was an old friend of Blackburne there is little doubt that he knew about the Archbishop's manœuvre in short order. In any case Law ended up taking a lead in the cause. His financial, intellectual and moral support for Edward Harwood bore fruit in the celebrated *New Introduction to the New Testament* in 1767 and in his idiosyncratic *Liberal Translation of the New Testament* in 1768.[68] As Master of Peterhouse Edmund Law and his Cambridge colleagues became a third centre, apart from Oxford and Lambeth, for research preparatory to making the new translation. Upon his elevation to the episcopacy in 1768 he made John Disney his chaplain. Law continued to be normally resident at Peterhouse, spending only the long vacations at Rose Castle near Carlisle, so he continued to have regular access to John Jebb, whose New Testament criticism caused a stir when he provided public lectures,[69] and James Lambert, the arian Regius Professor of Greek (1771–80), another useful scholarly asset, a contemporary and close friend of both his son John and of William Paley.[70]

---

[67] Francis Blackburne to Rev Mr Turner, from *Monthly Magazine* (Dec. 1796), 888. Cited in F. Blackburne, 'A Life of Francis Blackburne', *Works*, 7 vols (London, 1804), I, iv–v.

[68] For which, see John Nichols's *Literary Anecdotes of the Eighteenth Century* (9 vols, London, 1812–15), IV, 313, 323, 350–62.

[69] The discovery of Law's annotated bible provides a valuable mirror to Jebb's two heavily annotated Greek testaments. Dr Williams's Library, Jebb MSS, 24, 168–73.

[70] Paley, for his part, undertook the surprising measure of gently introducing the problems of text criticism and translation into his parochial sermons. For example, *Sermons on Several Subjects*, xxii (331) and xxvii (407–8) (2nd edn, London, 1808). Paley's Greek testament, well stocked with annotations, is in the British Library (Add MS 12080).

Why did the projected new AV fail? The evidence suggests, incredibly, that Secker himself killed it. A manuscript fragment of a letter sent from Secker to Robert Lowth, apparently in 1758, was passed from Lowth to Francis Blackburne, the controversial reforming churchman. Blackburne and Secker were old enemies. It would be easy to dismiss Blackburne's testimony as a mere reflection of distrust and conflict between them, except he claims to have the letter itself, and that he will shortly send it to Theophilus Lindsey for his perusal. Such evidence is difficult to refute.

> Pilkington's *Remarks on several passages of Scripture*,[71] where the errors of the Hebrew text are rectified, is worth your notice. His aim is at a new Translation of the Bible, which he and Kennicott and others have made appear is much wanted. The present A.B.C. [Archbishop of Canterbury: i.e. Secker] set a particular person (very capable) upon collecting instances of erroneous Translation in order to the setting forward this desirable end: But he [Secker] was then Bp. of Oxford only. Since his promotion, he has told the poor Fellow, his pains might have been spared – For that – *tempora mutantor.* ie. the Times, now that we can look at them from a greater point of Elevation, appear to be not so *ripe* as we thought them upon lower ground: I have the fragment of the Letter he wrote to this man: and shall insert it in the remarks on Ec[clesiastical] Hist[ory] and if I can meet with it before I write next you shall have a copy on proper Terms of Taciturnity.[72]

Why might Secker have derailed his own project? There was a standing policy between Lambeth and the king's ministers through mid-century that even the discussion of religious reform was undesirable, for it could easily lead to public disorder. Successive archbishops might consider the idea, but drop it quickly. The political significance of a new translation was lost on no one. The new reformers saw a reformed bible as a necessary preliminary to the completion of the protestant reformation.

He replaced Disney as chaplain, and may well have assisted Law in his edition of John Locke's *Works* (1777). N. W. Hitchin, 'Probability and the Word of God: William Paley's Anglican method and the defence of the scriptures', *Anglican Theological Review*, 77 (Summer, 1995), 396.

[71] Pilkington's *Remarks upon several passages of Scripture, rectifying some errors in the printed Hebrew text* (Cambridge and London, 1759) refers to 'the uncouth and obsolete words and expressions that are met with in our English version', though admitting their intelligibility and accuracy. But language had improved in 'politeness and correctness since that version was made', so that some people pretend to have delicate ears, and to be disgusted with every uncouth sound as an excuse for not reading the Bible.

[72] Francis Blackburne to Theophilus Lindsey, 23 Feb. 1759, Dr Williams's Library MSS, 2. 52 (60)/2.

The candle was kept burning for reformation theology by, among others, John Jones, vicar of Alconbury and compiler of the controversial *Free and Candid Disquisition relating to the church of England* (1749). True to protestant convictions the first point raised in the *Disquisitions* is the need for a new translation of the Bible.[73] His private papers also attest to this preoccupation, for we find in them notes on the subject of translation methods and the earlier translators Wyclif and Cranmer.[74] Thereafter the bulk of the argument of the *Disquisitions* concerns simplifying the liturgy. Shortening the service was paramount (presumably in response to the problem of sleeping in church), as was permitting greater flexibility to the parish clergy for local liturgical needs.[75] But it was the Bible that was the religion of protestants, and Jones's emphasis on this point by placing it at the head of the book was signal.

The book represents a correspondence among a number of established and dissenting clergy and laity during the 1730s and 1740s over the question of further reformation and comprehension, in line with the views of the notorious bishop Benjamin Hoadley.[76] With the disgrace of Jacobitism and the fear of popery in the air in January 1746, the correspondents decided to present their views in manuscript to the by-now perfunctory synodical meeting at York, hoping that they might get a hearing there. They would have preferred a revival of convocation, as the most fitting place for the questions to be raised, but, failing this, it was hoped the question of reform and comprehension might be raised in the House of Lords.[77] It was an abortively early response to

[73] *Free and Candid Disquisitions*, 12–21.

[74] Dr Williams's Library MSS, 12. 64/15.

[75] This meant primarily dropping the Trinitarian creeds and prayers. *Free and Candid Disquisitions*, 22–157. Beilby Porteous described a copy of Benjamin Franklin's edited Prayer Book, in which Franklin used the excuse of shortening the service to make heavy amendments in doctrine. Lambeth Palace Library MS 2099/59–62, 130–2. See also A. E. Peaston, *The Prayer Book Reform Movement of the XVIIIth Century* (Oxford, 1940), *passim*.

[76] Reference to the 'Editors of these papers, being intrusted with the care of them, by the Gentlemen, who were principally concerned in drawing them up' (*Free and Candid Disquisitions*, i) seems to suggest that Jones was not alone in editing it. Blackburne disavowed any role in the project, apart from reading it over without making any comment or notation. *The Calendar of the Correspondence of Philip Doddridge, DD (1702–1751)* (Northamptonshire Record Society Publication, xxix), ed. G. F. Nuttall (London, 1979) reveals the identities of several correspondents to include, besides Philip Doddridge, the MP George Lyttelton, Gilbert West and John Barker. The tone of their letters suggests that though friendly towards Jones, they did not hold him in unqualified regard, and were perhaps not wholly aware of the uses Jones was making of their letters. (See letters no. 1225, 1309, 1314, 1323–4, 1481, 1487.)

[77] *Free and Candid Disquisitions*, v–ix. 'The design, it seems, has been under consideration, and carrying on leisurely, from time to time, for some years. When the observations .. were brought together ... [and] digested into some order' it was presented to 'a ver

the 1745 rebellion, and they heard nothing. A letter of 2 February 1747/8 from the presbyterian minister John Barker to Doddridge suggests one reason for the silence was that negotiation was taking place anyway. A leading dissenting minister, Samuel Chandler, met with Sir Thomas Gooch, bishop of Norwich, and Thomas Sherlock, of Salisbury, and discussed the terms and differences at issue for a comprehension to be made possible. While they were doing so Thomas Herring, who had been archbishop of York in 1746, now the archbishop of Canterbury, happened to pass by. 'A very good thing. I wish it with all my heart' he said, when told they were discussing comprehension. He hoped it might be a good time to attempt it, for there were presently many pious, learned and moderate dissenters, and he thought the bench of bishops were of his own mind in wishing to revise the creed into scripture language. Conditions were not always right, however. He had not been so convinced shortly after his translation to Canterbury in 1747, when he expressed his apprehensions of a renewal of the demand for reform in a letter to the Duke of Newcastle. He was clearly referring to the papers sent by Jones to be presented to the synod when he wrote he had 'very particular and ... alarming evidence that some business on the scheme of a reformation of our establishment in its doctrines, discipline and liturgy, was then on foot and ready for publication (having been long digesting)', and although he knew the project to be 'very serious and explained with decency', yet he feared it would be presented with determination and even peremptoriness 'as the united sense of some of the best of the clergy and laity in the kingdom'.[78] Nor were conditions right several years later when he wrote 'These were no times for stirs in the church. ... Our present establishment and liturgy are good enough for me.'[79] This line was followed by Secker when he became archbishop three years after.

Many thought Secker had moved towards a far more conservative outlook as he aged and rose in the Church, a fact he even admitted himself.[80] Originally a presbyterian, he had been a friend to the cause of a comprehensive latitude in the Church for years. Possibly, as his christology moved from a position akin to arianism, under the influence of Samuel Clarke when he had been a curate at St James' Piccadilly, to a clear Trinitarianism, his concern to preserve latitude had dwin-

---

eminent and worthy Prelate, with an humble request to his Lordship, that he would ... communicate the contents of it to the Synod at one of their meetings' (iii).

[78] N. Sykes, *Church and State in England in the XVIIIth Century* (Cambridge, 1934), 385, quoting Herring to Newcastle, 12 Sept. 1748. BL Add MSS 32716/213.

[79] Sykes, *Church and State*, 385, quoting Herring to Newcastle, 10 Oct. 1754. BL Add MSS 35599/217.

[80] *Secker Autobiography*, 170.

dled.[81] The Hutchinsonian don Thomas Patten had been critical of the translation project, but was pleased by Secker's appointment to Canterbury in 1757.[82] It seems Secker was getting cold feet, perhaps shifting uncertainly around the time of his move to Canterbury, wanting to please everyone, aware of his new archepiscopal role as mediator. Nevertheless, his steady encouragement of biblical scholarship, and opinion that a new translation was desirable, are further supported by the existence of a charge intended to have been given to convocation in 1761, still advocating the new translation.[83] As late as 1766, he was providing Durell (as vice-chancellor) and the Clarendon Press with 'the best Information and Advice that I could towards a correct Edition of the English Bible and Prayer Book'.[84]

Did Lowth have an inkling, or indeed already know, that the project might be about to be put off? In a 1758 Visitation sermon in Durham he said

> Here I cannot but mention that nothing would more effectually conduce to this end than the exhibiting of the holy scriptures themselves to the people in a more advantageous and just light, by an accurate revisal of our vulgar translation by public authority. This hath often been represented; and I hope, will not always be represented in vain.[85]

In the light of what we know from Blackburne, the last phrase does sound a little bitter and disappointed. It may be that Secker was told there was no chance of a new authorised version by the king or his ministers. Failing this, and needing to defuse the situation, he may have prevailed upon the monarch for support in redirecting the energies of his bishops and biblical scholars as a compromise. It is undoubtedly significant that two large biblical research projects were undertaken at Oxford.

Benjamin Kennicott[86] had published a dissertation in 1753 'attributing obscurities and conflicting passages to scribal errors and the ambiguities

---

[81] Ibid., xix.

[82] Ibid., xx.

[83] *Eight charges delivered to the clergy of the dioceses of Oxford and Canterbury: to which [is] added ... a Latin speech intended to have been made at the opening of the convocation in 1761. Published from the original manuscripts* by Beilby Porteous, D.D. and George Stinton (London, 1769).

[84] *Secker Autobiography*, 170; Clarendon Press, Orders of Delegates (1758–95), 52 and 56: 12 & 24 June 1766; and Carter, *History of Oxford University Press*, 358.

[85] R. Lowth, *A Sermon preached at the visitation of the Hon. and Rt Rev. Lord Bishop of Durham ... 27 July, 1758* (London, 1758).

[86] W. McCane, 'Benjamin Kennicott: an eighteenth century researcher', *Journal of Theological Studies* (n.s., Oct. 1977), 28: 2, 445–64.

inherent in the script'.[87] Between 1753 and 1759 he had made a survey of all existing manuscripts of the Hebrew bible attributable to the age before printing and a catalogue of those in Oxford libraries.[88] In the key year 1758 Secker encouraged him to issue an appeal for subscriptions to the expensive project, which resulted in £9,119.7.6.[89] Between 1760 and 1780 Kennicott expanded the textual knowledge of the Hebrew bible vastly, supported by money from the king, the Oxford University Press, and with the ready co-operation of the libraries at Cambridge and the British Museum, finally presenting the king with a copy himself.[90] His textual research, published in parallel texts and informed by wide knowledge of Syraic, early Latin, Septuagint and even Samaritan Pentateuch, was a project of international scope.[91] He was assisted significantly by his wife, who was said to have made herself an exceptional Hebraist in order to help him.[92] He concluded in 1780 by saying that 'none of the variants was a threat to essential doctrine or increase[d] historical knowledge'.[93]

In 1788, a few years after the completion of Kennicott's project, Robert Holmes, like Lowth, of Winchester and New College, Oxford, and by then dean of Winchester, began a collation of the Septuagint manuscripts, and like Kennicott with an international network of scholars co-operating, until 1795 when the continental war made it untenable.[94] 'Such a work,' thought William Newcome, with whom he corresponded, 'will furnish important external helps for understanding the Hebrew Scriptures.'[95] He considered the encouragement of such a

[87] *The History of the University of Oxford. The Eighteenth Century*, ed. L. Sutherland and L. Mitchell (Oxford, 1986), v, 540.

[88] *History of the University of Oxford*, v, 540. Antecedently, William Whiston responded to the deist Anthony Collins's argument that the scripture texts were simply too badly corrupted ever to be recovered, by urging ' "a Great Search" for the most ancient Hebrew copies "in all Parts of the World".' J. E. Force, 'Hume and Johnson on Prophecy and Miracles: Historical Context', *Journal of the History of Ideas*, 43 (1982), 469.

[89] Secker contributed 10 guineas a year to this project from 1759 to 1766. *Autobiography*, 170.

[90] He published annual reports for subscribers to the work from 1760 to 1769 (*DNB*).

[91] D. Katz, *Sabbath and Sectarianism in Seventeenth-Century England* (Leiden and New York, 1988), 196.

[92] Madame d'Arblay, *Diaries and Letters, 1778–1840* (6 vols), ed. C. Barnet (London, 1905), III, 237.

[93] *History of the University of Oxford*, v, 541.

[94] The collations included Spanish and Arabic MSS, and especially the text of the Syraic MS of Origen's Hexapla in the Ambrosian library in Milan. 'Assistants are employed by him at Oxford; at the British Museum; at the Grand Duke's Library in Florence; in the ducal librar[ies] at Este [and] Parma; in the royal library at Turin; and in the Vatican, Caranattan, and Vallicellan libraries at Rome, and in that belonging to the College De Propaganda Fide in this last city.' Letter 2: Bishop Newcome to Rev. Dr Joshua Toulmin, Waterford, 24 December 1788. *Monthly Repository* (1806), I, 457–8.

[95] Newcome to Toulmin, 458.

work 'as a national object in a Christian country'.[96] Newcome also thought there was a 'need for a more complete, even if expensive, concordance and lexicon of Hebrew', which editing the Septuagint would clearly make a more feasible prospect.[97] The problem was with the subscription (less than £400 in 1788), since the project was not sufficiently advertised. In 1790, the expenses fell short by more than £200, but Newcome thought that the encouragement of a recent royal subscription and the patronage of the bishop of Salisbury would help. Of course, the Dean and Chapter of Winchester had subscribed already.[98] By 1795 subscriptions were running at £4,445, but even this was far short of expenses. His edition was completed posthumously, twenty-two years after his death, in 1827.[99]

The work of editing the Hebrew text was invaluable; but it was the fag-end of the earlier effort to create a new AV and a new ecclesiastical polity. By 1781 the Hebraist William Green considered that 'we have at length obtained all the assistance probably, that can be expected. ... All that seems wanting is labourers to be employed in the vineyard. Competent labourers, I am told, are very few in number', and there was little financial incentive for any to take up Oriental languages. 'Patrons of scripture learning are not to be found, so that it will be no wonder if the work goes on heavily.'[100] Benjamin Blayney, Oxford Regius Professor of Hebrew from 1787, noted that Kennicott's collations were in use, but had been 'left ... altogether in the hands of a few well intentioned individuals'.[101] In 1794 Newcome opined that 'the only invincible objection to a revised translation by authority is the present low state of Hebrew literature; which ought to be more attended to by divines of every denomination'.[102] The movement was effectively dead.

Out in Ireland Newcome was known to the government as a scholar and a reliable prelate when he was promoted to the archepiscopal see of Armagh in 1795.[103] It was a post he did not wish to take, but 'my duty to my large family induced me to accept'. He preferred Waterford,

---

[96] Newcome, *Twelve Minor Prophets*, xii.

[97] Ibid.

[98] W. Bussby, *Winchester Cathedral, 1079–1979* (London, 1979), 198, citing the Treasury Books.

[99] The particulars of the project are related by Newcome in two letters (Newcome to Toulmin, Waterford, 24 Dec. 1788 and 26 April 1790) published in the *Monthly Repository* (1806), I, 457–8 and *DNB* for Holmes.

[100] William Green, *Poetical Parts of Old Testament: being the blessing of Noah and other poetical pieces* (Cambridge, 1781), vi.

[101] Benjamin Blayney, 'Preliminary Discourse', *Jeremiah, and Lamentations. A new translation, with notes critical, philological and explanatory* (Oxford, 1784), ix.

[102] Newcome to Toulmin, Waterford, 5 March 1794. *Monthly Repository* (1806), I, 519.

[103] R. Mant, *History of the Church of Ireland from the Reformation to the Revolution ...* (2 vols, London, 1840), II, 234.

which was quieter, and where he could get on with his scriptural research.[104] He continued to press for the longed-for committee to the end, and published a limited circulation edition of the whole bible in 1798, which was thereafter published posthumously in 1800. This same version became the basis of the 'Unitarian' bible edited by Thomas Belsham and published in 1813. It was a strangely fitting conclusion to the work of the previous generation.

By the 1790s the work had truly moved outside of the establishment. One group around the publisher Nathaniel Scarlett is of particular interest. They continued the traditions of ecumenicity, and exemplify much of the religious and cultural climate in the London of the 1790s.

Nathaniel Scarlett's *New Testament* of 1798 was an unusual exercise in translation by ecumenical committee. Scarlett became a noted shipwright after his education at the Merchant Taylors' school, and then an accountant, before he opened a bookshop on the Strand. He also traversed the religious cityscape, passing from Wesleyan to Universalist and then Baptist. He brought together a small circle of learned acquaintances to work on his proposed publication of an 'improved' translation, 'intended chiefly for the unlearned'.[105]

His circle provides some insights into the complexities of religion in late eighteenth-century London. Three of the members attended a universalist Baptist congregation on Artillery Lane in Parliament Square. William Vidler, the minister, had started up as a bookseller and editor of successive magazines, which were later bought out in 1805 by Robert Aspland to produce the influential dissenting organ, the *Monthly Repository*. Scarlett came to the congregation through Vidler, with whom he had a brief publishing partnership on the heels of the production of the *New Testament*. They fell out over Scarlett's continued publication of a series of plays called 'The British Theater', in another example of the tensions within the dissenting communities over the relationship of sacred and profane literature.

Within the Artillery Lane chapel, there was a small society devoted to the discussion of points of religious controversy, of which Vidler and another of the translators, John Cue, were members. Cue, a 'very tolerable Hebrew scholar, of warm passions, a Sandemanian and Trinitarian' was one of the heads of the society. This group had been meeting every Tuesday evening since 1778 in a large room in Shoreditch, and was frequented by Established and dissenting clergy alike. Through Cue's friendship with Elhanan Winchester, the preacher who preceded Vidler, the group was induced to move to Artillery Lane, on the condition that they could meet in the vestry. Although they were a

---

[104] Newcome to Toulmin, Dublin, 6 March 1795, *Monthly Repository* (1806), I, 520.
[105] N. Scarlett, 'Preface', *New Testament*.

small fellowship of intellectuals meeting outside of regular worship, for purposes which both antedated their joining the chapel and which would have been inappropriate within a worship setting, inevitably the existence of such a group within the congregation aroused controversy, and they soon became known as 'the Church'. It was almost certainly through this group that Scarlett met the Wesleyan Anglican curate, James Creighton, whose manuscript translation of the New Testament formed the basis of their discussion and publication.

Scarlett's main concern was accessibility, and as a publisher he put considerable emphasis on the physical presentation of the book and the text. The book was a pocket volume with an easy-to-read layout. It had a smaller but spacious print, divided into sections separated by ornamental designs. Each section began with a title heading intended to assist the reader to comprehend the substance of the passage. Within each passage the speakers were identified as if in a dramatic text, partly on the assumption that the book would be more easily read aloud at home or among friends. The chapters and verses were relegated to the margins so that the sections were emphasised for the reader. The limited number of notes were intended to provide only the most necessary guidance.

These very compressed notes reflect much hard work within the group. For example, the inclusion, in parentheses, of 1 John v. 7 was noted as a matter of long-running controversy. But a carefully worded footnote informed Trinitarians that even if the passage were excised, the doctrine could be demonstrated from other places in the scriptures; while at the same time, arians could take comfort that their views received support by the exclusion of the passage. Before meeting each week at Scarlett's, Vidler and Cue would provide translations for Scarlett to collate with his own. Then, at an early hour, they would breakfast together and proceed to compare Creighton's translation with these collations, and with the standard Greek text, until teatime. They would dispute over the translations seeking consensus. But when they continued to differ, they would return home with the material to privately reconsider it, and send in their opinion to Scarlett. The most votes would carry the point.[106]

The personal dynamics of the group must have been terribly complex. Vidler was described in an otherwise admiring obituary as 'habitually irascible' when younger, and 'easily thrown into paroxysms of passion which were very dreadful'.[107] The fact that Scarlett's conversion to universalism was due to Vidler must have made it difficult for Scarlett

---

[106] *DNB* and *Monthly Repository* (1817), xii, 1-, 65-, 193-; (1818), xiii, 5-; Scarlett's 'Preface', *New Testament.*
[107] *Monthly Repository* (1817), xii, 66.

to chair their meetings, especially when passages bearing on the doctrine of the Trinity were under discussion, since it was Cue and Creighton who upheld that end. Additional tensions may have been added by the emotional religious temper provided by Cue's Sandemanianism and Creighton's methodism. The fact that these men could work their way through the translation of the whole new testament meeting weekly would have been impressive even apart from these personal considerations. Evidently, Vidler continued to speak well of Scarlett even after their business enterprise ceased,[108] which suggests that they may all have been better men for having worked together. But the lion's share of praise must go to Scarlett, who maintained discipline and kept the work moving for many years.[109]

Scarlett's *New Testament* made a particular point of utilising an improved English style to break out of the odd English syntax which resulted from retaining Greek and Hebrew forms. The new style 'reversed' the word orders to update them, so that Matt iii. 5, 'Then went out to him Jerusalem and all Judea', now read more naturally as 'Then Judea and all Jerusalem went out to meet him.' The preferred use of more euphonious words at the close of sentences was another improvement in Scarlett's bible. 'Worship God alone', rather than 'Worship God only' was chosen for its iambic foot. Obsolete words were laid aside; redundant words omitted. The Scarlett circle attempted to use the English idiom of the 1790s, without being either too literal or periphrastic.

Ideas of taste, of elegance and primitivity, helped to shape the work of translation, and were themselves expressions of the protestant constitution in Britain. But even 'consistent protestants' were not quite agreed about the aesthetic principles upon which a new translation should be based. Was the best hedge the latinate classicism of the educated or the primitive Saxon words of the common people? It depended who was perceived as the greater enemy: polite mockers, or papists?

If I am correct in identifying a political agenda behind the pressure for a new authorised translation, then one or two speculative points are worth considering. The drive to complete the reformation was a holdover of the commonwealth period, and it was this which provided the energy which had been going into the preparations for the new translation. In a letter of 1766 Dr Johnson wrote to William Drummond about a work of translating the Bible into Gaelic for the use of Scots

---

[108] Ibid., 193.

[109] A time-conscious man, Scarlett 'estimated that it took 1 hour, 8 minutes to read the Gospel of Matthew; 1 hour, 9 minutes the Gospel of Mark; 2 minutes 2 John; the whole New Testament 14 hours' (noted in E. Carpenter, 'The Bible in the Eighteenth Century', *The Church's Use of the Bible, Past and Present*, ed. D. E. Nineham (London, 1963), 113.

highlanders which was receiving opposition from the reformed church.

> I did not expect to hear that it could be, in an assembly convened for the propagation of Christian knowledge, a question whether any nation uninstructed in religion should receive instruction; or whether that instruction should be imparted to them by a translation of the holy books into their own language ... The Papists have, indeed, denied to the laity the use of the bible; but this prohibition, in few places now very rigorously enforced, is defended by arguments, which have for their foundation the care of souls. To obscure, upon motives merely political, the light of revelation, is a practice reserved for the reformed...[110]

The point at issue in the debate over the English version was whether the old translation illuminated or obscured the Gospel, and whether a new one was likely to be hijacked by heretics. All sides had doctrinal agendas. In a nation with a constitutional church reformed by law, any effort to change the official documents of faith was inherently political. The failure to undertake what was, in effect, a codification of one part of constitutional law, was one step closer to the final division of the orthodox protestants into established and nonconforming denominations.

The hope that with a new bible it might be possible to formulate doctrinal positions and liturgies which would have enabled the Church to encompass the whole protestant nation again was eroded in the 1760s, as the pressure for a new translation by authority was adroitly redirected into less controversial scholarly channels by Thomas Secker. Calls for liturgical reform, a subject which could well use a closer analysis, ran parallel to the reform of the Bible, and it was not long after Secker's manœuvre that more overtly political organisation began to take place. The legal and political issue of clerical subscription is not one which has been much looked at, but from what we know, it seems pointed that Blackburne's *Confessional* was published only a few years after the failure of the movement for bible reform had become obvious. The subsequent failure of the Feathers Tavern petition in February 1772 led inexorably onward to the breaking apart of liberal churchmen and dissent. It is probably too much to claim that the deflection of the campaign to get a new bible led directly to a more openly political collision of reformers and conservatives in the Church. It must be agreed, however, that with the frustration of this aspect of the search for latitude and comprehension, it was inevitable that other areas of conflict would shortly emerge, which they did in 1772.

[110] S. Johnson to W. Drummond, 13 Aug. 1766, Letter 184, *Letters of Samuel Johnson, LLD*, ed. G. Birkbeck Hill (2 vols) (Oxford, 1892).

NARRATIVES OF TRIUMPH AND RITUALS OF SUBMISSION: CHARLEMAGNE'S MASTERING OF BAVARIA

By Stuart Airlie

READ 22 MAY 1998 AT THE UNIVERSITY OF EAST ANGLIA

AMONG the more striking literary creations of Herman Melville is a short story entitled 'Bartleby'. The eponymous hero is a law-clerk who gradually withdraws from his employer's power, and ultimately from the world, by meeting all requests – to copy texts, to quit the premises, to co-operate with the authorities of the prison to which his intransigence finally leads him – with the phrase, 'I would prefer not to.' Melville's existential fable is disquieting on all sorts of levels and it has, perhaps, a special resonance for historians. The story's narrator is Bartleby's employer, a tranquil elderly man baffled by the latter's stubbornness. One of the problems the narrator faces is the shortage of sources: 'this man ... was one of these beings of whom nothing is ascertainable, except from the original sources and ... those are very small'. After Bartleby's death, the narrator learns that he had worked in the Dead Letter Office in Washington, and the story ends with a vision of piles of lost 'dead' documents and artefacts whose texts and meanings remain unread and beyond recall. As a text haunted by notions of unknowability and by the crushing weight of dead letters, 'Bartleby' seems to speak directly to some of the pre-occupations of historians in a post-modernist era.[1]

More concretely, though no less disquietingly, it also reminds us of (buried) acts of resistance or dissent. Neither the seemingly self-evident reasonableness of his employer's demands nor the power of the prison authorities can shift Bartleby from his negating position. I would like Bartleby's words – 'I would prefer not to' – and his figure, known to us only through a problematic narration not his own, to stand as motto and emblem for what follows, which is an examination of some aspects of the empire-building of Charlemagne (768–814). All too often seen in the modern period as an avatar of some form of western European identity or authority, Charlemagne, we do well to remind ourselves, was a fearsome figure seen by many of his contemporaries as a man

---

[1] 'Bartleby' is a product of the 1850s and is available in a variety of editions; see Herman Melville, *Billy Budd, Sailor & Other Stories*, ed. H. Beaver (Harmondsworth, 1970).

of force and violence whom it was legitimate to resist. In other words, for much of his lifetime he was not Charlemagne, the legend-encrusted Charles the Great, in the eyes of others or indeed of himself.[2]

In this essay I am concerned with one of Charlemagne's most dangerous opponents, Duke Tassilo of Bavaria (748–88), whose career reveals not only the sort of problems Charlemagne faced in his effort to establish Carolingian hegemony in western Europe but also the ruthlessly skilful way in which he solved them. Although the following analysis is intended to cast light on some of the processes through which the Carolingian empire was created, its focus is deliberately narrow. It would be possible to sketch a history of Bavaria in the eighth and ninth centuries as part of a broad tableau of the integration of south-eastern Europe into the Frankish world. Such a tableau would depict the intensification of Bavarian Christian culture through the activities of luminaries such as Boniface and the grand bishops of Salzburg: Rupert, Virgil and Arn. It would also chart the military and political expansion eastwards of this great empire until its famiiiar administrative structures can be found along the Danube as revealed in the Raffelsteter toll-list of the early tenth century.[3] It would be a valuable exercise to examine Bavarian history from this perspective, not least because that is how Bavarians came to see the story of their absorption into Charlemagne's empire. Like the Saxons, Bavarians of the ninth century saw that process as welcome, even providential. The aura of Charlemagne worked its magic early and lasted long.[4]

[2] The sneeringly hostile remarks on Charlemagne and the Franks ascribed to an abbot of San Vincenzo al Volturno in the 780s may be an isolated survival but cannot have been an isolated phenomenon: 'Codex Carolinus', no. 67, ed. W. Gundlach, *Monumenta Germaniae Historica* [hereafter *MGH*], *Epistolae*, III, *Epistolae Merowingici et Karolini Aevi*, I, 595; see M. McCormick, 'The Liturgy of War in the Early Middle Ages', *Viator*, 15 (1984), 1–23, at 3–4.

[3] For the resources of Christian culture in Bavaria, see, for example, B. Bischoff, *Die südostdeutschen Schreibschulen und Bibliotheken der Karolingerzeit* (2 vols, Wiesbaden, 1974 and 1980), and M. Garrison, 'The *Collectanea* and medieval florilegia', in *Collectanea Pseudo-Bedae*, ed. M. Bayless and M. Lapidge (Dublin, 1998), 42–83. The text of the Raffelstet toll ordinance is in *Inquisitio e Theloneis Raffelstettensis*, ed. A. Boretius and V. Krause, *MGH, Capitularia regum Francorum*, II (Hanover, 1897), 249–52; see also M. Innes, 'Franks and Slavs c. 700–1000: the problem of European expansion before the millennium', *Early Medieval Europe*, 6 (1997), 201–16, at 215.

[4] Bavarians: F. Losek, *Die Conversio Bagoariorum et Carantanorum und der Brief des Erzbischofs Theotmar von Salzburg, MGH, Studien und Texte*, 15 (Hanover, 1997); Saxons: *Poeta Saxo*, ed. P. von Winterfeld, *MGH, Poetae Latini Aevi Carolini*, IV (Berlin, 1899), 1–71, and cf. K. Leyser, *Rule and Conflict in an Early Medieval Society* (1979), 5–6. By the seventeenth century, Bavarian writers saw the struggle between Tassilo and Charlemagne as a moral drama in which the latter's piety triumphed, according to A. Kraus, 'Tassilo und Karl der Grosse in der bayerischen Geschichtsschreibung des 17. Jahrhunderts', in *idem, Bayerische Geschichtswissenschaft in drei Jahrhunderten* (Munich, 1979), 34–53; for the rather more regional views of Tassilo in Bavaria in this century, see L. Kolmer, 'Zur Kommendation und

For Tassilo, however, Charlemagne was a sinister figure and his story may unfold for us here under the aegis of Melville's Bartleby as a tale of resistance and buried narratives. Tassilo's fate as a victim of Charlemagne has given him a walk-on part in histories of medieval political structures, specifically in histories of feudal relations.[5] The principle reason for this is that a master narrative of Tassilo's fate was constructed by an annalist at the court of Charlemagne after the duke's fall. According to this text, known to us as the *Royal Frankish Annals*, the duke of Bavaria was the disloyal vassal of the Frankish king and had been given Bavaria as a benefice by Charlemagne's father Pippin III in 748, swearing an oath of vassalage to Pippin in 757, but had deserted the Frankish host in 763, and had then gone on to defy Charlemagne despite renewing oaths to him in 781 and reiterating his status as vassal in 787. The long-suffering Charlemagne finally summoned Tassilo to trial in 788 and he was duly deposed. The narrative of the *Annals* is thus a rising crescendo of outrages as a chain of oaths and obligations come to enmesh Tassilo, and this has long been repeated by a chorus of commentators.[6] But this narrative has itself been subject to a crescendo of criticism which has focused on the partiality of the annalist as well as the fact that he wrote after the events he describes. The recent devastating critique of the *Annals* by Matthias Becher, coinciding with Susan Reynolds's demolishing of the conceptualising of early medieval feudalism, very much a Futile System in Sellars's and Yeatman's immortal phrase, means that Tassilo's conviction now looks unsafe.[7]

Absetzung Tassilos III', *Zeitschrift für bayerische Landesgeschichte*, 43 (1980), 291–327, at 291, n. 2, and 327, n. 219.

[5] P. Roth, *Geschichte des Beneficialwesens von den älteren Zeiten bis ins zehnte Jahrhundert* (Erlangen, 1850), 388–9; H. Krawinkel, *Untersuchungen zum Fränkischen Benefizialrecht* (Weimar, 1937), 48–65; such references could be multiplied. See also n. 7 below.

[6] *Annales Regni Francorum*, ed. F. Kurze, MGH, *Scriptores rerum germanicarum* (Hanover, 1895); K. Reindel, 'Bayern im Karolingerreich', in *Karl der Grosse*, I, *Persönlichkeit und Geschichte*, ed. H. Beumann (Düsseldorf, 1965), 220–4; K. Reindel, 'Die politische Entwicklung', in *Handbuch der Bayerischen Geschichte*, ed. M. Spindler (Munich, 1967), 127.

[7] Peter Classen, 'Bayern und die politischen Mächte im Zeitalter Karls des Grossen und Tassilos', most conveniently available in P. Classen, *Ausgewählte Aufsätze*, ed. J. Fleckenstein (Sigmaringen, 1983); Kolmer, 'Zur Kommendation und Absetzung Tassilos'; Matthias Becher, *Eid und Herrschaft. Untersuchungen zum Herrscherethos Karls des Grossen* (Sigmaringen, 1993), 21–77; Rosamond McKitterick, 'Constructing the Past in the Early Middle Ages: The Case of the Royal Frankish Annals', *Transactions of the Royal Historical Society*, sixth series, 7 (1997), 109–29. On the 'feudal' debate: Susan Reynolds, *Fiefs and Vassals* (Oxford, 1994), 84–105, together with the exchange on this book between Johannes Fried and Susan Reynolds in *German Historical Institute, London: Bulletin*, 19.1 (1997), 28–41, and 19.2 (1997), 30–40. For alternative perspectives on both debates, see P. Depreux, 'Tassilon III et le roi des Francs: examen d'une vassalité controversée', *Revue Historique*, 293 (1995), 23–73, and D. Barthélemy, 'La théorie féodale à l'épreuve de l'anthropologie', *Annales. Histoire, Sciences Sociales*, 52 (1997), 321–41.

The problematic nature of the *Annals* means that it is most profitable to avoid forensic arguments on the nature of Tassilo's vassalage and instead to concentrate on the events of 787 and immediately afterwards where the testimony of sources such as the *Annals* is agreed, even by Matthias Becher, to be credible, if not reliable. The advantage of this approach is that it focuses attention not just on what the *Annals* and other texts say, but on the reasons for them being written in the first place. Here some formulations by the literary critic Edward Said may be illuminating. Said has stressed the importance of the 'power to narrate, or to block other narratives from emerging' in the construction of imperial identities. Such power is all the more important where there is 'uncertainty about whether the past really is past, over and concluded, or whether it continues...'.[8] In this light the *Annals* can be seen as being written, in part, to quell Tassilo and their narrative is a sign of Carolingian anxiety, not of Carolingian strength. Tassilo was dangerous and had to be crushed by Charlemagne through an elaborately constructed overwhelming authority.

What made Tassilo so dangerous? The dukes of Bavaria can be placed alongside the Aquitanian and Alemannian dukes as princely figures who took advantage of the troubles of the Frankish kings towards the close of the Merovingian period to assert a greater or lesser degree of independence from those kings. It was the task of Charles Martel and his descendants, who gained the crown in 751, to re-assert Frankish hegemony and to ensure that their own family did not split in these conflicts, a task they undertook with grim determination, launching a series of military expeditions throughout the eighth century. The brutality of this warfare should not be underestimated, but more sophisticated weapons were also deployed. The historiography of the new dynasty stigmatised its ducal opponents as 'tyrants' and traitors who allied with non-Christian peoples. For their part, the dukes thought little of the pretensions to authority of their would-be masters.[9] The seizure of the crown by Pippin III in 751 marked only a stage within this conflict, not an end of it.

The dukes of Bavaria have a special place in this story. It is not necessary here to offer a general survey of the history of the duchy of

---

[8] Edward Said, *Culture and Imperialism* (1993), xiii, 1.

[9] Einhard, *Vita Karoli*, c. 2, ed. L. Halphen, *La Vie de Charlemagne* (Paris, 1938), 10; *The Fourth Book of the Chronicle of Fredegar with its continuations*, trans. and ed. J. M. Wallace-Hadrill (London and Edinburgh, 1960), *continuationes*, c. 13, 90–1, with Roger Collins, 'Deception and misrepresentation in early eighth century Frankish historiography', in *Karl Martell in seiner Zeit*, ed. J. Jarnut, U. Nonn and M. Richter (Sigmaringen, 1994), 239; on the general situation, see Timothy Reuter, *Germany in the Early Middle Ages c. 800–1056* (1991), 54–60, and Ian Wood, *The Merovingian Kingdoms 450–751* (1994), 273–92.

Bavaria.[10] What needs to be stressed is the particular status of the dukes and the nature of their relationship to the Carolingians. Probably of Frankish origins, the dukes rose to power in Bavaria sometime in the sixth century, thanks to the support of the Merovingian kings, and quickly established important connections with Alemannia to the west and Lombard Italy to the south. The fact that the origins of the Bavarian ducal family, known as the Agilolfings, may be obscure is not surprising. What is surprising is that we know the name of the family and the way in which its very high status was enshrined in the law of the Bavarians, the *Lex Baiwariorum*. According to this text, the Agilolfings had a hereditary claim to rule Bavaria: 'The duke who presides among the people of the Bavarians always has been and ought to be of the family of the Agilolfings (*de genere Agilolfingarum*), as the kings our predecessors granted to them; so that whoever of that family was faithful to the king, they established him as duke for ruling that people.'[11] We may recall that the Carolingians had no explicit hereditary right to the Frankish crown. In fact, as Einhard stated in his *Life of Charlemagne*, the traditional Frankish royal family was the Merovingian dynasty.[12] The law-code may only have found its final written form in the eighth century (though there seems little reason to doubt its validity) but that makes the contrast with the Carolingians even more telling. Beside the Agilolfings, rich in heritage and buttressed by a legal text, the latter may appear as parvenus.[13] Yet this law-code also highlights the tensions in the duke's position in its reference to the king's concession of the duchy in the first place and in a further reference to obedience to royal commands as a condition of office.[14]

Ducal power was not untrammelled. If the law-code gave the duke

---

[10] Good surveys, with extensive bibliographies and notes that render more extensive references here redundant, are J. Jahn, *Ducatus Baiuwariorum. Das bairische Herzogtum der Agilolfinger* (Stuttgart, 1991) [hereafter Jahn, *Ducatus Baiuwariorum*] and H. Wolfram, *Österreichische Geschichte 378–907. Grenzen und Räume* (Vienna, 1995) [hereafter Wolfram, *Grenzen und Räume*]; Wolfram's monograph can be supplemented by the essays contained in his *Salzburg, Bayern, Österreich: die Conversio Bagoariorum und die Quellen ihrer Zeit, Mitteilungen des Instituts für Österreichische Geschichtsforschung*, Ergänzungsband 31 (Vienna, 1995). An important study by C. Hammer is forthcoming; I am grateful to him for letting me see a copy of 'Those Wicked Men, Odilo and Our Cousin Tassilo': Two Studies in Eighth-Century Rule in advance of publication.

[11] *Lex Baiwariorum*, Titulus III, ed. E. von Schwind, *MGH, Legum Sectio I, Legum nationum Germanicarum*, v. ii (Hanover, 1928), 313.

[12] Einhard, *Vita Karoli*, c. I, 8.

[13] H. Siems, 'Lex Baiuvariorum', in *Handwörterbuch zur Deutschen Rechtsgeschichte*, II, ed. A. Erler and E. Kaufman (Berlin, 1978), cols 1887–8 and 1894–5; Jahn, *Ducatus Baiuwariorum*, 1–3. The anqituity and depth of Agilolfing–Carolingian rivalry are stressed by J. Jarnut, 'Genealogie und politische Bedeutung der agilolfingischen Herzöge', *Mitteilungen des Instituts für Österreichische Geschichtsforschung*, 99 (1991), 1–22.

[14] *Lex Baiwariorum*, Tituli II. 1, II. 8a, II. 9 and III, 291, 302–3 and 313.

status it also placed him in a relationship with the Frankish king. Nor was the duke the only Bavarian potentate to have his authority asserted in the code, as five other families are named in it as being the first after the duke. Such privileges were probably won in the time of Tassilo's father, Duke Odilo (736–48), who seems to have stemmed from a branch of the Agilolfings in Alemannia and whose authority in Bavaria was far from unchallenged.[15] Further, Odilo's troubles with members of the Bavarian nobility saw him turn to the Carolingian ruler, Charles Martel, for support and assistance. It was while he was at Charles's court that he contracted the fateful liaison with the former's daughter that resulted in the birth of Tassilo, who was thus a cousin of Charlemagne.[16] All this means that the Agilolfings cannot be seen as straightforward enemies of the Carolingians; if Odilo clashed with Charles Martel's sons Pippin and Carloman in 743, it was Pippin who helped establish his nephew Tassilo as duke of Bavaria after Odilo's death in 748. These relationships were made more complicated by the struggles for power within the Carolingian family itself. Pippin preferred to have his Agilolfing nephew as duke of Bavaria rather than to be faced with his dangerous half-brother Grifo in that position.[17] The exact nature of Pippin's regency over Tassilo need not detain us here.[18] What is clear is that Tassilo's position, once he reached maturity around 757, was exalted but ambiguous. An Agilolfing duke, he was the hereditary prince of Bavaria with a title to rule much older than that of the Carolingians, to whom he was nevertheless related. He was also, however, a junior partner to the Frankish kings. In the charters of ducal Bavaria Tassilo might be styled *vir inluster dux Baiouariorum* but he could not use the *gratia Dei* formula in his *intitulatio* as his royal Carolingian cousins did.[19] He could, however, do much else.

Tassilo worked hard to make himself into a prestigious ruler. He married Liutpirga, a princess of the Lombard royal family in Italy; this was sometime before 768 and preceded Charlemagne's own marriage

[15] H. Wanderwitz, 'Quellenkritische Studien zu den bayerischen Besitzlisten des 8. Jahrhunderts', *Deutsches Archiv für Erforschung des Mittelalters*, 39 (1983), 27–84, esp. 68–77; Jahn, *Ducatus Baiuwariorum*, 221–54.

[16] Jahn, *Ducatus Baiuwariorum*, 125–32, 172–8, and see below.

[17] I. Haselbach, *Aufstieg und Herrschaft der Karlinger in der Darstellung der sogenannten Annales Mettenses priores* (Lübeck and Hamburg, 1970), 87–102, 107–11; Jahn, *Ducatus Baiuwariorum*, 172–92, 277–82.

[18] Becher, *Eid und Herrschaft*, 25–35, and Depreux, 'Tassilon III et le roi des Francs', 28–37, review the evidence.

[19] H. Wolfram, *Intitulatio I. Lateinische Königs- und Fürstentitel bis zum Ende des 8. Jahrhunderts*, Mitteilungen des Instituts für Österreichische Geschichtsforschung, Ergänzungsband 21 (Vienna, 1967), 155–84, esp. at 181–2; see also Wolfram, *Grenzen und Räume*, 132.

into that family. The son of this marriage, Theodo, was baptised by the pope in Rome in 772 and the same year saw Tassilo gain a great victory over the Carantanians in the south-east.[20] Associated with this victory is a remarkably flattering letter written by the Insular scholar Clemens to Tassilo and the bishops and magnates of his duchy.[21] The letter deserves comment here. First, as an exhortatory text written by a scholar from the British Isles for a continental prince, it is rather precocious in that it predates a similar letter to Charlemagne from the Anglo-Saxon Cathwulf by about three years. The patronage of the Bavarian court was thus a cultural magnet attractive enough to rival that of Charlemagne. It is possible that the writer was attached to the church of Freising, a detail worth bearing in mind.[22]

The contents of the letter cast revealing light on the literary representation of Tassilo's power. Weaving together biblical allusions and references with what one modern scholar has described as 'unrelenting fluency', Clemens asks for God to aid Tassilo as he aided Abraham, Moses, Joshua and Gideon. Joshua and Gideon are striking figures: they are invoked in masses for the army in texts from Carolingian Francia (and it is with such texts and ceremonies that we ought, perhaps, to associate Clemens's letter).[23] They are, however, figures from a particular time in Israel's history: 'In those days there was no king in Israel.'[24] In fact Clemens prays for God to give victory as he gave it to the *dux* Gideon who crushed kings. The chosen people could be led by dukes, and such a wish surely had a special resonance in Agilolfing Bavaria. The emperor Constantine is also invoked.[25]

All this is pitched pretty high but lets us catch something of the

[20] Wolfram, *Grenzen und Räume*, 89.

[21] Letter of Clemens *peregrinus*, ed. E. Dümmler, *MGH, Epistolae*, IV, *Epistolae Karolini Aevi*, II (Berlin, 1895), 496–7.

[22] Cathwulf's letter is edited by E. Dümmler in *MGH, Epistolae*, IV, *Epistolae Karolini Aevi*, II, 501–5; for comment, J. M. Wallace-Hadrill, *Early Germanic Kingship in England and on the Continent* (Oxford, 1971), 100–2, and M. Garrison, 'The English and the Irish at the Court of Charlemagne', in *Karl der Grosse und sein Nachwirken: 1200 Jahre Kultur und Wissenschaft in Europa*, ed. P. L. Butzer, M. Kerner and W. Oberschelp (Turnholt, 1997), 102. On Clemens and Freising, see Bischoff, *Die südostdeutschen Schreibschulen*, I, 61–2, and II, 264.

[23] Garrison, 'English and the Irish', 102, 116; cf. the references to Gideon, Moses and Aaron in the sacramentaries of Gellone and Angoulême: *Liber Sacramentorum Gellonensis*, at, e.g., no. 2091 and no. 2755, ed. A. Dumas and J. Deshusses, *Corpus Christianorum, Series Latina*, vol. 159 (Turnholt, 1981), 296, 432; *Liber Sacramentorum Engolismensis*, at, e.g., no. 2308, ed. P. Saint-Roch, *Corpus Christianorum, Series Latina*, vol. 159C (Turnholt, 1987), 358, and see M. McCormick, *Eternal Victory* (Cambridge, 1986), 347–62. The Sacramentary of Angoulême's reference to 'tyrants' (loc. cit.) is worth juxtaposing with Einhard's use of this term, as cited at n. 9 above.

[24] Clemens *peregrinus*, 496; cf. Judges 18.1 and J. L. Nelson, 'Kingship and empire in the Carolingian world', in *Carolingian Culture: emulation and innovation*, ed. R. McKitterick (Cambridge, 1994), 57.

[25] Clemens *peregrinus*, 497.

brazen fanfares of majesty that attended Tassilo. We may juxtapose with this text a precious object, the well-known Tassilo chalice. Again, the workmanship is Insular and testifies to the talent at the command of Tassilo's court. It may have been given to the monastery of Kremsmünster in 777; it may be associated with the wedding of Tassilo and Liutpirga.[26] What I wish to stress now is the dynastic character of this religious object. The names of Tassilo and his wife appear at the base of the chalice: '*Tassilo dux fortis: Liutpirc virga regalis*'. They represent, as it were, the masculine and feminine principles of ducal dynastic rule and authority. Tassilo is defined by his title and by his quality of strength, or bravery; more surprisingly, perhaps, Liutpirc's royal status is explicitly proclaimed in dynastic terms: '*virga regalis*', royal rod, is an 'allusion to the family-tree of the Lombard royal line'.[27] Contemporaries were aware of this facet of Liutpirga's identity and here we find it emblazoned on a holy object, or at least an object associated with holy ceremonies. The linking of both names and the allusion to a family tree surely also generates an association, not merely of ancestry, but of progeny. These associations ought to be borne in mind. It might also be worth recalling here that the women of the ducal house were anchored in a sacred institution, the convent of St Erintrudis on the Nonnberg in Salzburg, which functioned as an *Eigenkloster* of the ducal family.[28] The great building of the cathedral church of Salzburg itself and the founding or lavish patronage of monasteries such as Mondsee and Kremsmünster is also worthy of note. Kremsmünster was showered with ducal largesse and its dedication ceremony in 777 was a splendid display of ducal majesty, while its location and properties on the eastern frontier tied it in with a more worldly programme of the expansion of ducal power.[29]

Perhaps some of the great men of Bavaria remained unimpressed by all this. As we have seen, Tassilo's father Odilo could not command unchallenged loyalty from his aristocracy and the Bavarian nobility was a force to be reckoned with.[30] We should be careful not to exaggerate Agilolfing insecurity. All early medieval dynasties were insecure and

[26] Wolfram, *Grenzen und Räume*, 120, 135.

[27] J. L. Nelson, 'The Siting of the Council at Frankfort: Some Reflections on Family and Politics', in *Das Frankfurter Konzil von 794*, ed. R. Berndt (Mainz, 1997), 155.

[28] M. Hasdenteufel, 'Das Salzburger Erintrudis-Kloster und die Agilolfinger', *Mitteilungen des Instituts für Österreichische Geschichtsforschung*, 93 (1985), 1–29.

[29] Wolfram, *Grenzen und Räume*, 130–6; C. Bowlus, *Franks, Moravians and Magyars* (Philadelphia, 1995), 37–8; valuable surveys of Agilolfing Salzburg in *Virgil von Salzburg Missionar und Gelehrter*, ed. H. Dopsch and R. Juffinger (Salzburg, 1985).

[30] Jahn, *Ducatus Baiuwariorum*, 125–31, 172–3, 248–59. In general, see W. Störmer, *Früher Adel. Studien zur politischen Führungsschicht im Fränkisch-Deutschen Reich vom 8. bis 11. Jahrhundert*, 2 vols (Stuttgart, 1973), and Wanderwitz, 'Quellenkritische Studien zu den bayerischen Besitzlisten'; see also n. 31.

had to tread warily with their aristocracy. This is true of even so formidabie a ruler as Charlemagne, as we shall see. The particular problem posed by the Agilolfings is one of perception. It is clear that Charlemagne could not have taken over Bavaria in the way that he did without the support or at least the non-resistance of the Bavarian aristocracy. But the attitude of this aristocracy to the unnerving figure of Charlemagne in 787–8 does not necessarily tell us much about its general attitudes before that date. Hindsight can be misleading. Some historians, most notably Friedrich Prinz, have argued that a pro-Carolingian faction existed in western Bavaria and that this undermined ducal authority there, as well as preparing the way for Carolingian infiltration.[31]

Despite often acrimonious debate, the verdict on the existence of such a 'fifth column' must remain as not proven. Let us take the example of the monastery of Schäftlarn. This monastery, situated in western Bavaria, was founded by members of a family that can be shown to have been pro-Carolingian; further, it was dedicated to St Dionysius, i.e. St Denis, the particular patron of the Carolingian dynasty; the abbey had close links with the bishop of Freising, a church whose loyalty to the Agilolfings may have been suspect. The problem is that none of these points are conclusive. Schäftlarn enjoyed the patronage of Tassilo himself and, far from seething with anti-Agilolfing feeling, seems to have preserved favourable memories of him. As for the dedication to St Denis, the import of dedications can be difficult to measure and this dedication may refer to a Dionysius of Augsburg rather than his more famous western homonym.[32] On the basis of material such as this it is difficult to claim that the duke's writ did not run in the south-west of his duchy.

We may now turn to the ecclesiastical nobility of Bavaria. Again, the west has been seen as the problem area, with the key figure in this

---

[31] F. Prinz, 'Herzog und Adel im agilulfingischen Bayern', *Zeitschrift für bayerische Landesgeschichte*, 25 (1962), 283–311, and reprinted in *Zur Geschichte der Bayern*, ed. K. Bosl, *Wege der Forschung*, 60 (Darmstadt, 1965), 225–63, from which citations are taken; contrast Jahn, *Ducatus Baiuvariorum*, e.g. 319–34, 349–56. A variety of views can be consulted in *Früh- und hochmittelalterlicher Adel in Schwaben und Bayern*, ed. I. Eberl, W. Hartung and J. Jahn, *REGIO. Forschungen zur schwäbischen· Regionalgeschichte*, 1 (Sigmaringendorf, 1988), and there is a brief summary in English in Bowlus, *Franks, Moravians and Magyars*, 34.

[32] Prinz, 'Herzog und Adel', 235; for more nuanced views, see G. Diepolder, 'Schäftlarn: Nachlese in den Traditionen der Gründerzeit', in *Früh- und hochmittelalterlicher Adel in Schwaben und Bayern*, 180–2; W. Störmer, 'Die bayerische Herzogskirche', in *Der hl. Willibald − Klosterbischoff oder Bistumsgründer?*, ed. H. Dickerhof, E. Reiter and S. Weinfurter (Regensburg, 1990), 134–6; Becher, *Eid und Herrschaft*, 42–4; Depreux, 'Tassilon III et le roi des Francs', 46. On some problems of identification concerning the founders' family, Wolfram, *Grenzen und Räume*, 137; the monastery of Scharnitz-Schlehdorf also repays examination in this context, see Jahn, *Ducatus Baiuvariorum*, 407–48.

landscape being the bishop of Freising from 764 to 783, Arbeo, recently described as an 'implacable' Carolingian sympathiser and an author of saints' *Lives* as anti-Agilolfing propaganda. It is true that we have an explicit reference in a Freising charter to how 'duke Tassilo and his wife Liutpirga' injured the church of Freising because of the resentment (*invidiam*) which they felt towards Arbeo, 'saying that he was more faithful to the lord king Charlemagne and to the Franks than to them'. This charter, however, dates from 804 and may therefore tell us more about the church of Freising's effort to accommodate itself to the Frankish takeover than about the circumstances of Arbeo's own time.[33] As for the saints' *Lives*, Arbeo does describe clashes between saints and the Agilofling house as in Corbinian's disapproval of duke Grimoald's marriage of his brother's widow, the dangerous Pilitrud. Such early eighth-century clashes are, however, balanced by descriptions of the richness and power of the dukes and the sites of their rule. It is difficult to describe saints' *Lives* as propaganda, and one might add that if any ruler of the 770s was to be criticised for marital misbehaviour it was Charlemagne whose unceremonious returning of his Lombard wife to her father seems to have provoked moral criticism from within his own family.[34]

We should remember that our sources do not necessarily fit neatly into our categories of political faction and that they refuse to do so tells us something of the complexity of contemporary categories. Let us shift our focus from the church of Freising to that of Salzburg. In the commemoration book of St Peter's, Salzburg, we find the names of the Lombard king Desiderius and his wife Ansa. Professor Nelson has pointed out that their being commemorated there must stem from the initiative of their daughter Liutpirga, and we may note here that this corresponds to and confirms the Tassilo chalice's view of her as '*virga regalis*' (and it also conforms to the pattern of women acting as bearers of family memory and identity in early medieval Europe). Professor

[33] *Die Traditionen des Hochstifts Freising*, ed. T. Bitterauf, 2 vols (Munich, 1905, 1909), I, no. 193(b); this is trusted by Nelson, 'Siting of the Council at Frankfort', 155, and see also M.J. Enright, 'Iona, Tara and Soissons (Berlin and New York, 1985), 101, and Bowlus, *Franks, Moravians and Magyars*, 33, 37; a more sceptical view in J. Jahn, 'Bischof Arbeo von Freising und die Politik seiner Zeit', in *Ethnogenese und Uberlieferung: angewandte Methoden der Frühmittelalterforschung*, ed. K. Brunner and B. Merta (Vienna and Munich, 1994), 157–8.
[34] Compare Arbeo's *Vita Corbiniani*, c. 24, in *Arbeonis Episcopi Frisingensis Vitae Sanctorum Haimhrammi et Corbiniani*, ed. B. Krusch, *MGH, Scriptores rerum germanicarum* (Hanover, 1920), 215, with Paschasius Radbertus, *Vita Sancti Adalhardi Corbeiensis Abbatis*, c. 7, ed. J. P. Migne, *Patrologia Latina*, 112 (Paris, 1852), cols 1511–12; on Adalhard's response to the ending of Charlemagne's Lombard marriage, see B. Kasten, *Adalhard von Corbie* (Düsseldorf, 1985), 18–35. On Arbeo's *Vitae*, see K. Bosl, 'Der Adelsheilige', in *Speculum Historiale. Festschrift für Johannes Spörl*, ed. C. Bauer, L. Boehm and M. Müller (Freiburg and Munich, 1965), 167–87.

Nelson associates this memory-keeping with Liutpirga's influence at the heart of politics in the Bavarian court. That Liutpirga had such influence is undeniable and Frankish hostility to her pays grudging tribute to it.[35] But the appearance of the Lombard names in the Salzburg book cannot be explained solely by reference to hostility to the Carolingians. The name of Desiderius might have surprised any supporter of Charlemagne who came across it but the bishop oi Salzburg at this time was Virgil, who can hardly be considered as anti-Carolingian. What matters is that the name of Desiderius appears in its proper place, i.e. in the *ordo* of deceased kings and he thus appears alongside dead rulers of the Carolingian line, just as Liutpirga's mother and brother appear alongside their living Carolingian rivals.[36] Political enmities are dissolved in the architecture of the source which reflects liturgical priorities and arrangements.

The great churchmen of Bavaria were complex figures in a complex world and resist pigeonholing, though they can scarcely have been immune to the political pressures that swirled round them. The bonds of the Christian community transcended political boundaries, though the existence of such boundaries cannot have been forgotten. The career of Arn, who became bishop of Salzburg, is instructive here. A member of the church of Freising, he was also a member of the Frankish monastery of Saint-Amand and became its abbot by 782. This did not mean the end of his Bavarian career, for in 785 he succeeded Virgil as bishop of Salzburg, an appointment that may have owed as much to Charlemagne as it owed to Tassilo.[37] Arn's career shows something of the gravitational pull of the Frankish court; the church of Freising trained not only Arn but several churchmen who headed west and into the Carolingian world.[38] It is hard to believe, however, that Arn would have been completely unacceptable to Tassilo as bishop of Salzburg in 785. Perhaps it was his very closeness to the Carolingian world that made him so valuable to the duke, just as his Bavarian

---

[35] *Das Verbrüderungsbuch von St. Peter in Salzburg. Vollständige Faksimile-Ausgabe im Originalformat der Handschrift A1 aus dem Archiv von St. Peter in Salzburg*, ed. K. Forstner (Graz, 1974), pag. 10 and pag. 20; Nelson, 'Siting of the Council at Frankfort', 155; on hostility to Liutpirga in Frankish sources, Kolmer, 'Kommendation und Absetzung Tassilos', 315.

[36] *Das Verbrüderungsbuch von St. Peter in Salzburg*, pag. 10 and pag. 20; J. Semmler, 'Geistiges Leben in Salzburg (5.–10. Jahrhundert)', in *Virgil von Salzburg*, 367; H. Wolfram, 'Virgil als Abt und Bischof', ibid., 345; Wolfram, *Grenzen und Räume*, 117–18. Family membership could, however, have a bearing on how names were entered into an *ordo*: see K. Schmid, 'Über das Verhältnis von Person und Gemeinschaft im früheren Mittelalter', *Frühmittelalterliche Studien*, 1 (1967), 225–49, esp. at 242–6.

[37] Wolfram, *Grenzen und Räume*, 170–2.

[38] J. Semmler, 'Zu den bayrisch-westfränkischen Beziehungen in karolingischer Zeit', *Zeitschrift für bayerische Landesgeschichte*, 29 (1966), 344–424; Störmer, 'Die bayerische Hezogskirche', 134–6.

connections made him so useful to Charlemagne. This made him the ideal candidate as go-between, a role in which Tassilo cast him in 787 when he sent him to Rome to try and persuade the pope to adopt a less pro-Frankish stance in the looming conflict. As a bishop Arn was, almost *ex officio*, involved in politics but he was more than a political figure. After all, his father had dedicated him as a youth to the church of Freising as a thanks-offering to heaven after he recovered from wounds after an attack. Men such as Arn were aware of the fragility of earthly institutions. The Bavarian church may have contained figures who looked to the Frankish king as the duke's superior, but that is what the Bavarian law-code said and we cannot conclude that the church as a whole was poised to defect from Tassilo.[39]

Arn's career demonstrates the existence of important links between Bavaria and the Frankish world. Bavarian troops travelled west to participate in Charlemagne's campaign in Spain in 778 and Carolingian patronage settled lands of the church of Auxerre on favoured Bavarians.[40] Bavaria was not isolated or remote and its connections were not simply the result of Carolingian patronage; Bavaria was an active partner. Tassilo's father Odilo stemmed from a branch of the Agilolfings that was rooted in Alemannia and links between Alemannia and Bavaria remained close. Perhaps such links served to draw Bavaria into the Carolingian orbit after the harsh subjection of Alemannia in the 740s.[41] But not everything was subject to Carolingian control. Study of the entries found in the commemoration books of the great abbeys of Reichenau and St Gall suggests that memories of links to the Agilolfings survived the Carolinglan conquest.[42] Furthermore, Tassilo was married to a Lombard princess and this not only gave him a wife of royal stock, as we have seen, but connected him to Duke Arichis of Benevento, who also married a daughter of Desiderius. The fact that Charlemagne himself was for a time married to a Lombard princess shows how valuable such women were; the fact that Arichis's widow appears to have acted as leader of opposition to Charlemagne in Benevento shows how formidable they could be.[43]

[39] For Arn as envoy, *Annales Regni Francorum*, a. 787, 74; on Arn's being given to Freising in 758, *Traditionen des Hochstifts Freising*, 1, no. 11, with Wolfram, *Grenzen und Räume*, 170–1; judicious summing-up in Störmer, 'Die bayerische Herzogskirche', esp. at 136.

[40] Reindel, 'Bayern im Karolingerreich', 221–2; Wanderwitz, 'Quellenkritische Studien zu den bayerischen Besitzlisten', 78; Jahn, *Ducatus Baiuwariorum*, 175–6.

[41] W. Hartung, 'Bertolde in Baiern', in *Früh- und hochmittelalterlicher Adel*, though this should be compared with J. Jahn, 'Bayerische Pfalzgrafen im 8. Jahrhundert?', ibid.

[42] G. Diepolder, 'Freisinger Traditionen und Memorialeinträge im Salzburger Liber Vitae und im Reichenauer Verbrüderungsbuch', *Zeitschrift für bayerische Landesgeschichte*, 58 (1995), 147–89, esp. at 180–8.

[43] 'Codex Carolinus', nos 80, 82, 611–14, 615–16; R. Collins, *Charlemagne* (Basingstoke and London, 1998), 72.

The reach of the Agilolfings in fact stretched dangerously close to the centres of Carolingian power. In 725, Charles Martel marched into Bavaria, 'subjugated' it and 'returned home with great treasure and also with a certain lady Beletrudis and her niece Swanahildis'.[44] The bracketing together of women and treasure is noteworthy here; women were currency. If the Agilolfing Swanahild was to leave a baleful memory in Francia she was also recalled in Bavaria in the commemoration book of St Peter's, Salzburg. There she was placed in the entry of the kings and their wives and children, and at some stage the name of her son by Charles Martel was also recorded, the ill-omened Grifo, whose struggles for a share in his Carolingian inheritance had affected Bavaria after the death of Odilo.[45] The connections between the Carolingians and the ducal house of Bavaria were close and were remembered.

Tassilo himself embodied such connections. Sometime in 741 Odilo took Charles Martel's daughter to wife, with the connivance of her stepmother Swanahild and to the horror of her brothers, according to a Carolingian source. A century later, this episode was still remembered as an outrageous *scandalum*.[46] From the death of Charles Martel to Pippin's becoming king in 751, members of the Carolingian family fought not only to gain the supreme prize of the crown but struggled among themselves to ensure that only one line of the family would triumph. The loss of control of one of their women, Charles Martel's daughter, was a serious blow. Women could create new enmities as well as heal old ones. That is surely why no daughter of Pippin III or Charlemagne was permitted to marry.[47] Tassilo was the offspring of this fateful union. If his Agilolfing identity was the key element that Charlemagne had to break, as we shall see, his intimate connection with the Carolingians means that the relationship between Francia and Bavaria can be seen as a tortuous working out of relations within one large family group. In Charlemagne's reign such relationships gained in intensity. For a time he and Tassilo shared a Lombard king as a father-in-law. In marrying Hildegarde in 772, Charlemagne was marrying a woman from the Alemannian branch of the Agilolfings.[48] In a sense, Tassilo was Charlemagne's 'significant other'.

[44] *The Fourth Book of the Chronicle of Fredegar*, 'continuationes', c. 12, 90; R. Schieffer, 'Karl Martell und seine Familie', in *Karl Martell und seiner Zeit*, 303–15.

[45] *Das Verbrüderungsbuch von St. Peter in Salzburg*, pag. 20; Wolfram, *Grenzen und Räume*, 83, 117.

[46] *The Fourth Book of the Chronicle of Fredegar*, 'continuationes', c. 25, 98; Astronomus, *Vita Hludowici Imperatoris*, c. 21, ed. E. Tremp, *MGH, Scriptores rerum germanicarum* (Hanover, 1995), 348; relevant discussion in M. Becher, 'Zum Geburtsjahr Tassilos III', *Zeitschrift für bayerische Landesgeschichte*, 52 (1989), 3–12, and Jahn, *Ducatus Baiuwariorum*, 176–8.

[47] J. L. Nelson, *The Frankish World 750–900* (London and Rio Grande, 1996), xxv, 232.

[48] Wanderwitz, 'Quellenkritische Studien zu den bayerischen Besitzlisten', 55; Jahn, *Ducatus Baiuwariorum*, 184; Becher, *Eid und Herrschaft*, 29. On Hildegarde, S. Airlie, '*Semper*

We can now grasp something of the scale of the problem Tassilo posed for Charlemagne and we can also see that the former's fall was not inevitable. Bavaria was not a fruit ripe for the plucking. The details of the complicated manœuvrings that gave Charlemagne the advantage do not concern us here. It is, however, worth remembering that relations between the two rulers were not consistently hostile. Further, when hostility came to the surface Tassilo was subject to pressure but retained a certain independence of action. Even if the *Royal Frankish Annals* can be trusted in their account of Tassilo's journey to Worms in 781 where he is said to have given hostages and renewed oaths to the Frankish king, Tassilo remained uncowed. His son Theodo remained prominent as a reminder of Tassilo's hopes for continuity and in a clash between Franks and Bavarians at Bolzano in 784, the former were worsted.[49] For us, the 780s may seem to mark the ascent of Charlemagne and the Franks to superpower status, with Saxons, Beneventans and even discontented members of his own nobility being forced to yield to a king at the height of his powers. For contemporaries, however, the picture, while impressive. may not have been quite so clear.[50]

In 787 time seemed to run out for Tassilo. According to the *Royal Frankish Annals* Charlemagne, busy in Italy strong-arming the duke of Benevento into submission, was consulted by the pope as to what reply should be given to envoys of Tassilo. The envoys got a very dusty answer indeed, with the pope, according to the *Annals*, outlining with grisly relish what would befall the territory of Bavaria if Tassilo should persist in his insubordination. One can be sure that the anger of the successor of St Peter was broadcast in Bavaria and Francia. Tassilo remained undaunted, however, and later that year refused to come into Charlemagne's presence. Charlemagne responded by mobilising three armies to fall on Bavaria from the west, north and south. Confronted with this, and with the prospect of defection among his own followers, Tassilo came to the Frankish king and, as the *Annals* put it, 'gave himself by his hands in to the hands of the lord king Charles in vassalage and yielded (*reddens*) the dukedom entrusted to him by the lord king Pippin, he recognised that he had sinned and acted wickedly

---

Fideles? Loyauté envers les Carolingiens comme constituant de l'identité aristocratique', in *La Royauté et les Elites dans l'Europe carolingienne*, ed. R. Le Jan (Lille, 1998), 131.

[49] On events of 781, see *Annales Regni Francorum*, a. 781, 58, and Becher, *Eid und Herrschaft*, 51–8; on Theodo's prominence, see *Traditionen des Hochstifts Freising*, I, no. 106 (a. 782) and Jahn, *Ducatus Baiuwariorum*, 531–2; on the clash at Bolzano, Jahn, ibid.

[50] D. Bullough, *The Age of Charlemagne*, 2nd edn (1980), 59–67.

in all things. Then, renewing his oaths, he gave twelve chosen hostages and as a thirteenth his son Theodo'.[51]

Whether Tassilo here became a vassal of the Frankish king for the first time or had his status as vassal simply reiterated is not now my primary concern. What is undeniable is that Tassilo was a vassal of the Frankish king as a result of 787. The testimony of the *Royal Annals* is backed up by other texts.[52] The course of events, and Tassilo's status, now look so clear that his fall seems inevitable. In fact, the distinguished historian Percy Ernst Schramm has telescoped 787 and 788 in a casual reference to the events of 787 and to Tassilo's tonsuring and loss of office as happening at the same time.[53] Even Homer nods. But 787 was not the end and the meaning of the events of that year for contemporaries remained, it not problematic, far from cut and dried.

The events of 787 deserve attention as they cast light not only on the specific nature of relations between Charles and Tassilo but also more generally on what one might call the political *mentalité* of the age and on the medium of its politics. As we shall see, the medium is indeed the message. As a preliminary, however, we must spend a little time in the rocky terrain of the Futile System. Tassilo's status as vassal was special, i.e. his is a special case and as such a difficult case from which to draw conclusions about the status of vassals in general. Susan Reynolds has done more than anyone recently to make this sort of rocky terrain fruitful and I can only agree with her view of the (supposed) earlier commendation of 757 as 'poor evidence either that great men were normally vassals or that a similar rite was undergone by normal vassals'.[54] Tassilo's guilt was indeed constructed in 'feudal' terms, but these terms were the product of Charlemagne's court of the 780s and 790s, and are thus very unsound bases for generalising back before that date, or from generalising out from Tassilo's case. Tassilo's case is dealt with in language by the annalist that points less to vassalage narrowly defined than to broader concerns of lordship. We should remember that Matthias Becher's forensic analysis of the annalist's text stems from his book's concern with oaths and lordship. The conspiracy of Hardrad and his fellows in 785 meant that oaths were not an academic subject in that decade and Tassilo's vassalage should be seen, not as the tip of the iceberg of pre-787 developments in vassalage, but

[51] *Annales Regni Francorum*, a.787, 72–8; for the English translation of this and many other relevant texts, see P. D. King, *Charlemagne: Translated Sources* (Kendal, 1987).

[52] Kolmer, 'Zur Kommendation und Absetzung Tassilos III', 306–11; Becher, *Eid und Herrschaft*, 59–63, and see nn. 56 and 59 below.

[53] P. E, Schramm *Kaiser, Könige und Päpste*, iv. i (Stuttgart, 1978), 212.

[54] S. Reynolds's response to J. Fried, as above at n. 7, 38.

as part of the constructing of Charlemagne's kingship through oaths.[55] While Tassilo's status as vassal is hard to fit into a general framework of the development of feudal bonds the meaning of the events of 787 also remains elusive. Tassilo was annihilated, so to speak, in 788, not in 787. What did happen then?

Certainly, Tassilo did suffer humiliation. His yielding up his own son as a thirteenth hostage struck contemporary observers as significant, though it was not a unique example.[56] Charlemagne was ensuring that Tassilo's designated successor was in his hands before he launched the final attack. In taking away the son and successor, Charlemagne was striking at the Agilolfing dynasty and he was beginning to chip away at its status in 787. Tassilo was humiliated, but not completely so; that was not to happen until 788 or later. What counted in 787 was the fact and nature of Tassilo's subordination and deference: Bavaria was not be the inheritance of the Agilolfings but an *honor* held by com-mendation.[57] The events of 787 are therefore simultaneously precise in so far as they were laying the grounds for the 'show-trial' of 788 and murky in so far as they form part of the tricky process of dissolving the Agilolfings as a dynasty. And it is the significance of this process that becomes clearer if we tear our gaze away from the ceremony of vassalage that has so mesmerised historians.

Let us start broadening our perspective by looking at some of the other surrenders of the 780s, that decade which saw Frankish and Carolingian power reach new heights. In 781, Tassilo came to Charles at Worms, but only after he had received hostages from the king. In 785, defeated Saxon leaders reluctantly agreed to come to Francia but only after they had negotiated safe conduct and, it seems, insisted on hostages. In 787, in Italy, Charlemagne bounced the duke of Benevento into submission and the latter gave hostages, including his son, but later Frankish sources seem to admit that the duke had slipped out of the king's clutches by a 'cunning plan' (*salubre consilium*).[58] Perhaps most significantly of all for us is the account in some annals (*not the Royal*

[55] Becher, *Eid und Herrschaft*, 78–87 and 144–212.

[56] *Annales Laureshamenses*, a. 787, ed. G. H. Pertz, *MGH, Scriptores*, I (Hanover, 1826), 33; Becher, *Eid und Herrschaft*, 62; M. Innes, 'Kings, Monks and Patrons: Political Identities and the Abbey of Lorsch', in *La Royauté et les Elites dans l'Europe carolingienne*, 315–16.

[57] Depreux, 'Tassilon III et le roi des Francs', 69, 73, though Depreux follows other writers in seeing the ceremonies of 787 as humiliating for Tassilo, see art. cit., 28, nn. 40 and 57.

[58] Tassilo: *Annales Regni Francorum*, a. 781, 58, and Collins, *Charlemagne*, 84; Widukind: *Annales Regni Francorum*, a. 785, 70, and G. Althoff, *Spielregeln der Politik im Mittelalter* (Darmstadt, 1997), 174; Benevento: *Annales Regni Francorum* (revised), a. 786, 75, and one should juxtapose this with the taking of hostages from still recalcitrant Lombards, *Annales Nazariani*, a. 787, ed. G. H. Pertz, *MGH, Scriptores*, I, 43, and Bullough, *Age of Charlemagne*, 59.

Frankish Annals) of how very intense negotiations, including the activity of the abbot of Fulda as a go-between, preceded the surrender of the conspirators of 785 to a smoulderingly angry Charlemagne.[59]

Such stories, of negotiated settlement rather than unconditional surrender, do not make Charlemagne look any less powerful; negotiations were precisely the instrument that made surrender possible and thus enabled Charlemagne to display his triumph in, for example, Saxony, on a western European stage. But these stories do highlight the fact that Charlemagne's power was not absolute, and when he did have overwhelming power the face of the victim had to be saved.[60] The events of 787 fit into this pattern. The *Royal Frankish Annals* tell us that Charlemagne mobilised awe-inspiring resources against Tassilo and that Tassilo saw that his own nobles would not fight for him. But the awe-inspiring force was not unleashed; this is surprising. Peace was concluded; this is surprising too. What happened when Tassilo came to Charlemagne at the Lechfeld, just on the borders of Bavarian terriory? While other (contemporary, or near-contemporary) sources confirm the fact of vassalage, they focus, not on the ceremony of hands, but on the handing-over by Tassilo of his son as hostage and on the handing-over of something else: 'Tassilo, duke of the Bavarians, came to him there and yielded that land to him through a staff (*baculum*) on the head of which there was a likeness of a man: and he was made his vassal. And he gave his son Theodo to him as a hostage.'[61] The result: Tassilo retained his dukedom. A thousand years before Teddy Roosevelt, the Bavarian duke had realised the wisdom of speaking softly and carrying a big stick.

This was a public ceremony that we can call a ritual act in in some of the senses spelt out by Karl Leyser, via anthropology: 'individual life-crisis ceremonials' and 'means of social communication to re-affirm status differences'.[62] We are concerned with something that is highly plastic, so plastic in fact that what we have here is probably something invented for the specific circumstances of 787. One hardly needs to stress the creativity and fertility of ritual for an English-language audience but these features have recently been taken up and forcefully developed in German-language historiography, particularly in the work of Gerd Althoff.

[59] *Annales Nazariani*, a. 786, 41–2; K. Brunner, 'Auf den Spuren verlorener Traditionen', *Peritia*, 2 (1983), 1–22, at 6–12; Innes, 'Kings, Monks and Patrons', 313–16.

[60] McCormick, *Eternal Victory*, 359–60; Althoff, *Spielregeln der Politik*, 99–125.

[61] *Annales Nazariani*, a. 787, 43; Brunner, 'Auf den Spuren'; Jahn, *Ducatus Baiuwariorum*, 537–8 with 182–4 on the Lech as part of a border zone; Becher, *Eid und Herrschaft*, 61–3.

[62] K. Leyser, 'Ritual, Ceremony and Gesture: Ottonian Germany', in *idem*, *Communications and Power in Medieval Europe: the Carolingian and Ottonian Centuries* (London and Rio Grande, 1994), 189, citing A. van Gennep.

One of Althoff's starting-points is a critique of the views of Jürgen Habermas. For Habermas, political modernity begins in the eighteenth century when citizens' associations and coffee-house intellectuals engaged critically with authority rather than being merely passive and 'awe-struck' subjects before its representation. As Professor Blanning has put it: 'the culture of the old regime is "representational", by which is meant the "making present" of authority by dress, ritual, painting, architecture ... or any other form of display. Its audience – the sovereign's subjects – are involved only as passive spectators.'[63] So, for Habermas, there is essentially no 'public sphere' in the pre-modern world. Althoff has argued powerfully against this, stressing that there was such a public sphere (for the elite) in the medieval period and that it would be easier for us to recognise this if we remember that it was dominated not so much by discussions and the verbal power of argument as by non-verbal communication: acts of ritual and ceremony. The Middle Ages were not an era of 'passivity' or rigid representation but one of dramatic display, and *through* this display arguments and statements were made. Early medieval rituals, e.g. of surrender, of granting of mercy, of bestowing charity, were carefully controlled and negotiated acts, consciously designed as ceremonies in which the resolution of conflicts over loyalty, status and honour could be expressed. They do not merely reflect the turning of discord into harmony, they are the means by which that final cadence is reached.[64]

Let us now return to Tassilo, whom we left on the Lechfeld, handing over his staff to Charlemagne. What was that staff? It has not survived, and so we cannot look at it and gaze upon it as a 'savage thing', to borrow the terms of observers of the Sutton Hoo 'sceptre'. In fact, Tassilo's staff has been compared with the Sutton Hoo sceptre and thus placed within a very broad context of symbols of authority in the northern world, though dangers of circularity of argument here and the sheer breadth of that context mean that I wish to keep my own focus fairly narrow.[65] German-language scholars have characterised

---

[63] T. C. W. Blanning, 'Frederick the Great and German culture', in *Royal and Republican Sovereignty in Early Modern Europe. Essays in memory of Ragnhild Hatton*, ed. R. Oresko, G. C. Gibbs and H. M. Scott (Cambridge, 1997), 529–30.

[64] Althoff, *Spielregeln der Politik*, 229–32. Such rituals mattered even in the relatively text-based societies of the Carolingian world though they may have possessed greater intensity in the more oral society of the Ottonian Reich; see Leyser, 'Ritual, Ceremony and Gesture', 192–6, and H. Mayr-Harting, *Ottonian Book Illumination*, 2 vols (1991), I, 62. In general, J. L. Nelson, *Politics and Ritual in Early Medieval Europe* (1986) remains indispensable.

[65] Nuanced views of the Sutton Hoo 'sceptre' can be found in J. Campbell, 'The Impact of the Sutton Hoo Discoveries on the Study of Anglo-Saxon History', in *Voyage to the Other World*, ed. C. B. Kendall and P. S. Wells (Minneapolis, 1992), 84, and S. Keynes, 'Raedwald the Bretwalda', ibid., 116 (from where the quotation is taken); M. Ryan, 'The Sutton Hoo Ship Burial and Ireland: Some Celtic Perspectives', in *Sutton*

Tassilo's staff as an 'ancestral staff acting as a sign of lordly status' (*Ahnenstab als herrscherliche Würdezeichen*). This seems reasonable; according to our source, Tassilo gives Charlemagne the staff and the duchy. The staff is therefore associated with rule and seems to be the instrument by which the duchy is given up. It seems fair, therefore, to see it as an *Ahnenstab*, and even to see the figure on it as a (saintly?) ancestor.[66] We may recall that the *Law of the Bavarians* enshrined Agilolfing rule as based on hereditary claims.

What was this special object doing at the Lechfeld near Augsburg? Presumably it had been brought there. And presumably it had been brought there because it had been requested by Charlemagne. Medieval princes such as Tassilo travelled with treasure, but they did not travel with all that they possessed. When Charles had Tassilo seized at Ingelheim in 788, he sent some of his henchmen into Bavaria specifically to get Tassilo's treasure.[67] If Charles did not specifically ask for the staff in 787 it was part of the package that he had demanded and to which Tassilo had agreed. That is to say, there must have been much backstage preparation and negotiations resulting in a ritual which could clearly express the relationship it created.[68] These negotiations were probably very tough and Tassilo must have been given something in return: a promise to be re-defined, but not erased. The ceremony of 787 was staged with care. Consider the timing: close to the feast-day of St Denis, the particular patron of the Carolingians. Consider the location: a border zone. Charlemagne had three armies poised to strike, and they were assembled at key points. Charles and his host, assembled at the Lechfeld, had gathered on the site of a Frankish victory over Tassilo's father. Time and space combined to provide good auguries for Charlemagne who could confidently demonstrate what he could do

---

Hoo – Fifty Years After, ed. R. Farrell and C. N. De Vegvar (Oxford, Ohio), 85–90. Tassilo's staff is placed in a broad context by G. Waitz, *Deutsche Verfassungsgeschichte*, III (Kiel, 1883), III–12, 249–51; P. E. Schramm, *Herrschaftszeichen und Staatssymbolik*, Schriften der MGH 13, 3 vols (Stuttgart, 1954–6), II, 192–210, 286–7; A. Gauert, 'Das Zepter Tassilos III.', *Deutsches Archiv für Erforschung des Mittelalters*, 18 (1962), 214–23.

[66] *Annales Nazariani*, a. 787, 43; Schramm, *Herrschaftszeichen und Staatssymbolik*, II, 209; Wolfram, *Grenzen und Räume*, 91. Among other contemporary objects that connected holiness with a dynastic sense, one might point to the Tassilo chalice itself, and it is possible that the ring of St Arnulf, holy ancestor of the Carolingians, was preserved at Metz; it certainly featured in a story that Charlemagne recounted: see K. Hauck, 'Die Ausbreitung des Glaubens in Sachsen und die Verteidigung der römische Kirche als konkurriende Herrschaftsaufgaben Karls des Grossen', *Frühmittelalterliche Studien*, 4 (1970), 138–72. Breton leaders yielded their swords to Charlemagne when they surrendered to him in 799: J. L. Nelson, 'Kingship and Royal Government', in *The New Cambridge Medieval History II c. 700–c. 900*, ed. R. McKitterick (Cambridge, 1995), 428.

[67] *Annales Nazariani*, a. 788, 43–4; Brunner, 'Auf den Spuren verlorener Traditionen', 15–16.

[68] H. Keller, 'Die Investitur', *Frühmittelalterliche Studien*, 27 (1993), 51–86, at 56, 67–8.

(a threat) without actually doing it (a sign of grace for wavering Bavarians).[69] Tassilo, laden with symbolic treasure, journeyed to Charlemagne, but did not have to go deep into Francia and Bavarian territory was spared the devastation the pope had threatened, and Tassilo remained as duke.

In giving up his staff and his dukedom, Tassilo was giving up part of his Agilolfing identity and that is why he also had to give up his son, who must have travelled west as another treasure. Tassilo was giving up his ancestors and his descendants and publicly acknowledging his status as vassal. Tassilo's Agilolfing identity was beginning to be dissolved and his status was that of holder of an *honor* from the king of the Franks. For Tassilo and the audience this was a melancholy music, shot through with the elements of 'darkness' and 'emotional power' that, for Geoffrey Koziol, differentiate ritual from mere ceremony.[70]

Such ritual, however, can be attended not only by 'emotional power' but by conflict, ambiguity and contradiction. The point to stress here is that Tassilo survived 787. Charlemagne was not ready, or able, to destroy him and had to be content with re-defining him. Tassilo's new status can in fact be seen as that of honoured subordinate, not grovelling wretch. This is confirmed by a final piece of evidence for 787, the Latin poem addressed to Charlemagne by an anonymous Irish writer, Hibernicus Exul. As it has come down to us, this text is a fragment, but it offers a vivid account of the encounter between Charles and Tassilo. Events are depicted on a Christian moral plane. Tassilo's failure to be faithful is depicted as being the work of that old serpent, the devil, and his failure to obey Charles is a sin.[71] But Tassilo is described as a 'distinguished duke' (*'dux inclitus'*) and, on his surrender to Charles (the events of the Lechfeld are not in the portion of the text that has come down to us) he receives splendid gifts from the king and, while he has to display his subordinate status through kissing the king's knees,

---

[69] Tassilo surrendered on 3 October at the Lechfeld; see J. F. Böhmer, *Die Regesten des Kaiserreichs unter den Karolingern*, revised by E. Mühlbacher and J. Lechner (Innsbruck, 1908), 290g and 290h. The feast of St Denis is 9 October; for the importance of such dates in Carolingian political life, see M. Sierck, *Festtag und Politik* (Cologne, Weimar and Vienna, 1995). On Carolingian victory on the banks of the Lech in 743, *Fourth Book of the Chronicle of Fredegar*, continuationes', c. 26, 99. Charlemagne's seemingly surprising failure to crush Tassilo is noted in Becher, *Eid und Herrschaft*, 61.

[70] G. Koziol, *Begging Pardon and Favor: Ritual and Political Order in Early Medieval France* (Ithaca and London, 1992), 7–8, 316.

[71] The text of Hibernicus Exul is edited by E. Dümmler in *MGH, Poetae Latini Aevi Carolini*, 1 (Berlin, 1881), 396–9; there is a partial English translation in P. Godman, *Poetry of the Carolingian Renaissance* (1985), 174–9. For the serpent and Tassilo's sin, see Hibernicus Exul, lines 62–8, p. 397; on the poem's moral concerns, see P. Godman, *Poets and Emperors* (Oxford, 1987), 62, and C. Ratkowitsch, *Karolus Magnus – Alter Aeneas, Alter Martinus, Alter Iustinus* (Vienna, 1997), 41.

this gesture, and the giving of the gifts, show Tassilo as being re-integrated into a properly ordered world.[72]

This interpretation gains force if we recall the context sketched for Carolingian panegyric by Mary Garrison, namely, it was extremely 'ephemeral and occasional'. Developing this in more positive language, we can see this poem as being designed for a very specific contemporary purpose. In other words, I believe that it dates from 787 itself (or 788) and thus reveals that at the Carolingian court Tassilo could realistically be depicted in positive terms.[73] In fact, one might go further. As current literary criticism insists, texts can be worldly, i.e. active in the world; they are part of the social world and do not merely reflect it.[74] This text can itself therefore be seen as part of the apparatus that redefined Tassilo; it is not merely a source that supplements our picture of 787 but was designed (through performance? through distribution?) to help people at Charlemagne's court grasp Tassilo's new status. And that status was not entirely negative. Tassilo had salvaged something, though we know that all he had gained was time. Tassilo himself may have been relatively optimistic after his encounter with Charlemagne. He had been, in a word, disciplined, but he had also been treated with honour. Some echo of this optimism may be heard in a Bavarian source transmitted to us via the early modern period: 'duke Tassilo came to king Charles, received the whole of Bavaria from him and gave him great gifts ... in return the king gave the duke much more. And duke Tassilo went home again to Regensburg, with great joy.'[75]

Any joy Tassilo may have felt was short-lived. Charlemagne spent the winter and spring at Ingelheim, probably preparing the show trial that was to follow. An assembly was summoned to be held there and Tassilo

[72] Hibernicus Exul, lines 94–103, p. 399; on such gestures, Gauert, 'Das Zepter Herzog Tassilos III', 221, and, for broader context, J. L. Nelson, 'The Lord's anointed and the people's choice: Carolingian royal ritual', in *Rituals of Royalty*, ed. D. Cannadine and S. Price (Cambridge, 1987), 168.

[73] M. Garrison, 'The emergence of Carolingian Latin literature and the court of Charlemagne (780–814)', in *Carolingian Culture*, ed. McKitterick, 128; see also her 'English and the Irish', 100, and, for dating and context, A. Ebenbauer, *Carmen Historicum: Untersuchungen zur historischen Dichtung im karolingischen Europa* (Vienna, 1978), 18–29, esp. at 28–9.

[74] E. Said, *The World, the Text and the Critic* (1984), 4, 31–53; on the 'active' nature of ninth-century Carolingian historical writing, see J. L. Nelson, 'History-writing at the courts of Louis the Pious and Charles the Bald', in *Historiographie im frühen Mittelalter*, ed. A. Scharer and G. Scheibelreiter (Vienna and Munich, 1994), 435–42.

[75] S. Riezler, 'Ein verlorenes bairisches Geschichtswerk des achten Jahrhunderts', *Sitzungsberichte der königlichen bayerischen Akademie der Wissenschaften, Philosophisch-Philologisch-Historische Klasse*, 1 (1881), 247–91; cited in the translation of King, *Charlemagne: Translated Sources*, 342.

attended, along with other vassals of the king. The fact that Tassilo attended suggests strongly that he thought that he had gained a level of security after the Lechfeld. He was wrong. He was denounced by Bavarians as having plotted to turn to the Avars for help, taking his oaths lightly, expressing deep resentment of Charlemagne, etc. According to the *Royal Frankish Annals* his wife was explicitly linked with his wickedness. Then the assembly recalled (*reminiscentes*) how he had abandoned Pippin's army (*harisliz*) and was worthy of death. At that point, Charles intervened on behalf of his kinsman (the first time Tassilo is so called in these *Annals*) for mercy's sake and asked for less than the death penalty. On being asked what he wanted, Tassilo expressed enthusiasm for the monastic life and he was given permission to be tonsured, to enter a monastery and there do penance for his great sins.[76]

The trial of 788 has occasioned much scholarly comment and it is not my place to repeat it here. Instead, I propose to offer a few comments on how the *Annals'* report works as part of its overall narrative of triumph, a triumph of justice. To have abandoned the army, the *exercitus*, was to have deserved death and within the text of the *Annals* up to this point, the army has been bathed in the aura of Carolingian lordship. We are told, for example, of how no *exercitus* was summoned in 745 as Carloman prepared to enter a monastery; it is the *exercitus* that benefits from 'divine grace' when water miraculously appears to end a drought in a campaign in Saxony; part of Charlemagne's royal mastery is apparent in the way he is constantly depicted as commander of the army, and it is an imperial army (contingents in 778 include Lombards and Bavarians); in 787, the army is depicted as the instrument of Charlemagne's justice.[77] For Tassilo to leave the *exercitus* was to put himself outside the political community of warriors under their rightful leader.

In focusing on military treachery, the annalist also highlights Tassilo's unreliability in a key activity of rulership. The *Law of the Bavarians* states that the duke should remain safe from challenge from his son or successor while he is still able to 'march with the army, judge the people, leap upon his horse and carry arms'. Tassilo's non-performance flouted contemporary norms, above all those enshrined in the *Royal Frankish Annals*, whose narrative is a rough charcoal sketch of Christian

---

[76] *Annales Regni Francorum*, a. 788, 80–4; Becher, *Eid und Herrschaft*, 64–71, provides a clear guide to events, but cf. R. Schieffer, 'Ein politischer Prozess des 8. Jahrhunderts im Vexierspiegel der Quellen', in *Das Frankfurter Konzil von 794*, 179–82. On the accusations of colluding with the Avars, see Kolmer, 'Zur Kommendation und Absetzung Tassilos III', 323–5, and W. Pohl, *Die Awaren: Ein Steppenvolk in Mitteleuropa 567–822 n. Chr.* (Munich, 1988), 313–14.

[77] *Annales Regni Francorum*, a. 745, a. 772, a. 775, a. 778, a. 787, a. 788, 4, 34, 40–2, 50, 76–8, 80.

warriorship in advance of Einhard's full-length portrait.[78] He was no longer the *dux fortis* of the Tassilo chalice.

Significantly, Tassilo's treachery is located in the past, in the reign of Pippin. His condemnation is therefore rightful judgement of his sinful essence. He is revealed as what he had always been. Most importantly, he is revealed and condemned by the peoples of the empire: his treachery is 'recalled' not only by Franks but also by Bavarians, Lombards and Saxons who are thus retrospectively involved by the text in the history of the empire before they were part of it.[79] Thus Tassilo becomes part of a legitimating imperial narrative. As penitent sinner, he becomes recipient of the mercy of the Frankish king and of God, who are thus associated through the quality of mercy. Charlemagne petitions the assembly for mercy by addressing the *fideles* of God and himself. Tassilo thus ceases to be a historical actor and leaves the world of politics for that of penance.[80] He exits from history precisely as he exits from the narrative. He is not mentioned again in the text of the *Royal Frankish Annals*, whose Tassilo narrative now attains closure. This is hardly a casual or accidental omission. Why was the annalist so keen to depict Tassilo as finished? We may recall Edward Said's comments on narratives that are uncertain that the past really is past. From this angle, the narrative of the *Annals* can be seen as being paralleled by the lapidary statement of a charter issued in 788 by Charlemagne in Bavaria whose preamble refers to 'the wicked men, Odilo and Tassilo, our kinsmen, who faithlessly took the duchy from the kingdom of the Franks but now the God of justice has restored it...'[81] It is easier, however, to reach closure in a text than in history itself. The year 788 was not in fact the end of Tassilo's story.

But before tracing the final phase of Tassilo's disappearance, his final ritual of submission, I wish to make two more comments on 788. First, according to another annalistic source, Tassilo begged Charles not to have him tonsured in the palace in the presence of the Franks because of the shame and disgrace that would entail. This was the final degradation which he had avoided in 787; this was real transformation into a non-secular figure. Secondly, Tassilo's whole family was involved in his fall. The same source tells us that Tassilo's wife and children, together with his treasure, were brought west. Much of the treasure was probably distributed among Charlemagne's followers but the family was not. The children shared the fate of their father and mother:

---

[78] *Lex Baiwariorum*, Titulus II.9, 302–3. On Einhard's description of wars, J. M. Wallace-Hadrill, *Early Medieval History* (Oxford, 1975), 30–1.

[79] *Annales Regni Francorum*, a. 788, 80; Schieffer, 'Ein politischer Prozess', 175.

[80] *Annales Regni Francorum*, a. 788, 80; cf. n. 87 below.

[81] See Charlemagne's charter no. 162, ed. E. Mühlbacher, *MGH, Diplomata Karolinorum*, 1 (Hanover, 1906).

monastic imprisonment, where they were not only safe but where they were, in the case of at least one daughter, re-educated and taught to pray for their rivals in the Carolingian women's abbey of Chelles.[82] They were too volatile to be married off and in thus cancelling their status Charlemagne revealed how dangerously prestigious it was. He too would have remembered the importance of marriage for the Agilolfings and the children of Tassilo and Liutpirga carried Agilolfing, Carolingian and Lombard 'royal' blood. The only royalty in the new empire was to be Carolingian royalty.

Absorbing Bavaria into the *regnum Francorum* was therefore a rather more delicate business than the *Royal Frankish Annals* would have us believe. Admittedly, there was no upheaval comparable to that in England after 1066. Charlemagne won over the Bavarian aristocracy by letting it retain land, probably free from certain obligations imposed by Tassilo and Odilo.[83] But he had to tread cautiously. We know that some Bavarian nobles did remain loyal to Tassilo and his family and had to be exiled. The Bavarian church was worried about its hold on its possessions being recognised and there was a flurry of documentary activity to secure its hold on its property, culminating in Charlemagne's confirmation, at the end of 793, of grants made by 'kings, queens, dukes and other God-fearing men'. Nor was the Agilolfing connection snapped: Bavaria may no longer have had a duke but the *praefectus* Gerold to whom it was entrusted had Agilolfing blood.[84]

Of course, the point about such activities is that they were successful. Charlemagne himself stayed in Bavaria from 791 to 793 and launched great attacks on the Avars. Bavaria was integrated into his kingdom. The problem was, however, that it was too well integrated. Charlemagne's stay in Regensburg witnessed not only the launching of great military expeditions and the crushing of heresies but a full-blown conspiracy against his rule, led by his son Pippin the Hunchback in 792. In so far as Pippin's followers can be identified they seem to have

---

[82] *Annales Nazariani*, a. 788, 44; Brunner, 'Auf den Spuren verlorener Traditionen', 15–16; Jahn, *Ducatus Baiuwariorum*, 542; J. L. Nelson, *The Frankish World*, 236.

[83] Wanderwitz, 'Quellenkritische Studien zu den bayerischen Besitzlisten', 81–4.

[84] *Annales Regni Francorum*, a. 788, 82, reports the exiling of supporters of Tassilo; testimony of such supporters is preserved in the texts collected in B. Bischoff, *Salzburger Formelbücher und Briefe aus Tassilonischer und Karolingischer Zeit*, Bayerische Akademie der Wissenschaften, Philosophisch-Historische Klasse, Sitzungsberichte Jahrgang 1973, part 4 (Munich, 1973). For church concerns, see the *Notitia Arnonis* and *Breves Notitiae* drawn up by the church of Salzburg in *Salzburger Urkundenbuch*, ed. W. Hauthaler, 1 (Salzburg, 1910), no. I.A and no. I.B; Charlemagne's confirmation is his charter no. 168 (to be dated to 793; see Wolfram, *Grenzen und Räume*, 72–3). On Gerold, see M. Borgolte, *Die Grafen Alemanniens in Merowingischer und Karolingischer Zeit. Eine Prosopographie* (Sigmaringen, 1986), 119–21. In general, Jahn, *Ducatus Baiuwariorum*, 545–8.

come from Francia but one cannot doubt that there was a Bavarian dimension to the plot. The acquisition of new territories by kings could be a trigger for marginalised sons to revolt.[85] Like Grifo, Pippin was fighting the sons of another mother and, like Grifo, he failed. His failure resulted in permanent imprisonment in Prüm. With his failure, the Carolingian royal family assumed its 'definitive' narrow, slimmed-down form. All Carolingian kings and emperors of the ninth century were descended from Charlemagne and just one of his wives: Hildegarde. The last 'irrelevant' segments of the family were shed in Bavaria between 788 and 792–3. The progeny of Charles Martel and Swanahild (i.e. Grifo), of Hiltrud (Charles Martel's daughter) and Odilo (i.e. Tassilo) and of Charlemagne and Himiltrud (i.e. Pippin the Hunchback) all failed to establish themselves in Bavaria. Family structure had been radically simplified.

The fact that Charlemagne's Bavarian settlement was tricky, a grumbling process that had to be carefully negotiated, and which had hit a bump with Pippin's conspiracy, is surely confirmed by Tassilo's surprising reappearance on the political stage in 794. This was at the great meeting in Frankfurt where all sorts of theological matters were aired. But much unfinished political business was also dealt with. A bishop who had supported Pippin negotiated a return to royal grace and Tassilo, explicitly described as Charlemagne's cousin, appeared to beg forgiveness for his offences against Pippin, Charlemagne and the Franks.[86] Tassilo thus appeared within 'a penitential frame of reference' which rendered lack of political obedience in 'terms of guilt and penance' as Mayke de Jong has put it.[87] But within this framework explicitly political claims could be articulated or, as in this case. renounced. For Frankfurt 794 marks the end of that process of dissolution of Agilolfing dynastic identity and claims that began on the Lechfeld in 787. Tassilo spoke as head of the Agilolfing house in order to utter its political death sentence. The record of proceedings tells us: 'all rights and allodial property whatsoever in the duchy of the Bavarians

---

[85] A. Krah, *Absetzungsverfahren als Spiegelbild von Königsmacht* (Aalen, 1987), 36–8; Kolmer, 'Zur Kommendation und Absetzung Tassilos', 316, and Becher, *Eid und Herrschaft*, 73, see the connection between Bavarian unrest and Pippin's revolt; a rather different perspective in Nelson, 'Siting of the Council at Frankfort', 160–3. I intend to discuss Pippin's conspiracy more fully elsewhere.

[86] Synod of Frankfurt, c. 3, ed. A. Boretius, *MGH, Capitularia Regum Francorum*, 1 (Hanover, 1885), 74; contemporary texts dealing with Charlemagne's activities at Frankfurt in 794 are conveniently gathered together in E. Orth, 'Frankfurt', in *Die deutschen Königspfalzen*, ed. T. Zotz, vol. I, *Hessen*, parts 2, 3 and 4 (Göttingen, 1985–96). Comprehensive treatment of the council in *Das Frankfurter Konzil von 794*.

[87] M. de Jong, 'What was public about public penance? *Paenitentia publica* and justice in the Carolingian world', in *La Giustizia nell'alto Medioevo (secoli IX–XI), Settimane di Studio del Centro Italiano di Studi sull'alto Medioevo*, 45 (Spoleto, 1997), 880–1.

which ought lawfully to belong to him or to *his sons or daughters* he abandoned ... and surrendered irrevocably and, together with his sons and daughters, commended to the king's mercy...' In return Tassilo received Charlemagne's forgiveness.[88]

Perhaps that was enough for Tassilo. His essential status remained the same after Frankfurt: he was a penitent monk. He had re-entered history only to underline his and his family's absence from it. This appearance at Frankfurt is not mentioned in the text of the *Royal Frankish Annals* which had hoped for closure in 788. The closure of 794 was intended to be definitive and, again, a text, an 'active' text, played a key role in this procedure. Three written copies of Tassilo's statement were drawn up, one of which was to be kept 'in the palace' (Frankfurt?), another in the chapel, and one was to stay with Tassilo in his monastery.[89] Tassilo's story was finished and he was given the script. There was to be no ambiguity over this ceremony. Its meaning was to be fixed. Tassilo was no longer an independent element; he was inscribed within a single system. The mercy of Charlemagne and God enfolded and obliterated Tassilo, and his family. The significant other had been rendered insignificant.

The danger of the Agilolfing connection with Francia had been neutralised. The wires may still have been there but no dangerous current could now pass through them. There is a sombre paradox here. Tassilo and his family could indeed travel along the networks of the Bavarian–Frankish world to the centres of the Carolingian kingdom but they did so only as impotent prisoners, not as dangerously active figures. Tassilo travelled to Ingelheim and St Goar (a dependency of the great Carolingian abbey of Prüm) in 788 and then to Jumièges and Frankfurt; his daughter travelled to Chelles. The Agilolfings had finally penetrated the power centres of Francia but their journeying there took them into oblivion.

The fate of the Agilolfings, and their treasures, forms part of a larger phenomenon. The Franks did not always have to travel to newly conquered lands to grasp the fact that they had mastered an empire. The fruits of empire, and the victims of conquest, travelled to them: Saxon hostages and deportees; Lombard and Beneventan hostages (contemporary with Tassilo); Avar treasures. The arrival of the pope in Paderborn and the appearance of envoys from the church of Jerusalem at Charlemagne's court in 799 was the culmination of a process.[90] The

---

[88] Synod of Frankfurt, c. 3, 74; translation in King, *Charlemagne; Translated Sources*, 224; my emphasis.

[89] Synod of Frankfurt, c. 3, 74; Wolfram, *Grenzen und Räume*, 92–3; Schieffer, 'Ein politischer Prozess des 8. Jahrhunderts', 167–9.

[90] Saxons: 'Indiculus Obsidum Saxonum Moguntium Deducendorum', ed. A. Boretius, *MGH, Capitularia*, I, 233–4; Lombards and Beneventans: as above at n. 58; Avar treasure:

removal of Tassilo from Bavaria and his absorption into Francia was indeed part of a grander drama than merely the subduing of the dukes and the re-establishing of the integrity of the *regnum Francorum*. We should recall the suggestiveness of the *Royal Frankish Annals'* narrative of Tassilo's being condemned, not just by the Franks, but by many peoples under Charlemagne's lordship: Bavarians, Lombards and Saxons.[91] Notions of empire were abroad. At Frankfurt in 794, Tassilo appeared on a stage that was already looking imperial: the Christian faith was defended against threats from west and east; Charlemagne forgave his Bavarian cousin and issued charters for St Emmeram in Regensburg as well as for churches in Spain; a host was summoned for campaigns in Saxony. All this took place before a gathering that included papal legates, the patriarch of Aquileia, the Archbishop of Milan, the Anglo-Saxon Alcuin and bishops, and presumably secular magnates, from all over the kingdom.[92] All roads led to Frankfurt and would soon lead to Aachen and Rome.

For the Agilolfings it had been a long journey. They had descended from being enshrined as hereditary dukes in the Bavarian law-code to being pilloried in the *Royal Frankish Annals* as disloyal vassals. From there it was but a step to a walk-on part in Einhard's *Life of Charlemagne*, where Tassilo and Liutpirga served merely to point a moral and adorn a tale.[93] Distraught supporters of Tassilo found that only tears, not words, sufficed to express their sorrow at the outcome but it was surely clear to all contemporaries that the Agilolfings had been brought to book.[94]

Einhard, *Vita Karoli*, c. 13, 38–40; pope and envoys from Jerusalem: *Annales Regni Francorum*, a. 799, 106–8.

[91] *Annales Regni Francorum*, a. 788, 80; on the political creativity necessitated by acquisition of empire, see H. Mayr-Harting, 'Charlemagne, the Saxons and the Imperial Coronation of 800', *English Historical Review*, 111 (1996), 1113–33.

[92] Orth, 'Frankfurt', 178–82; cf. D. Bullough, '*Aula Renovata*: the Carolingian Court before the Aachen Palace', *Proceedings of the British Academy*, 71 (1985), 267–301, esp. at 295–301.

[93] Einhard, *Vita Karoli*, c. 11, 34–6; later in the ninth century Tassilo's dangerous Carolingian connections were neutralised in a haze of benevolent nostalgia: see *Vita S. Hugonis*, c. 1, c. 2, ed. J. van der Straeten, 'Vie Inédite de S. Hugues Evêque de Rouen', *Analecta Bollandiana*, 87 (1969), 235–6.

[94] Bischoff, *Salzburger Formelbücher und Briefe*, III.23, p. 57, and cf. p. 25. My own text has been assembled in more positive circumstances; versions of this paper were presented to research seminars in the University of Glasgow and All Souls College, Oxford, and I am grateful to the participants on these occasions for comment and advice as I am to the audience who attended the final version at the University of East Anglia. For advice on particular points I am grateful to Simon Dixon, Mary Garrison and Sarah Hamilton.

THE MIDDLE AGES THROUGH MODERN EYES.
A HISTORICAL PROBLEM

The Prothero Lecture

By Otto Gerhard Oexle

READ 1 JULY 1998

I

THE title of this essay can be interpreted in two ways. One possibility might be to show how our times in their thinking, patterns of behaviour, and institutional structures still continue to be shaped by that distant era of the Middle Ages. In other words, one could show the lingering impact of the Middle Ages until the present day. This sort of approach brings many things to mind: the division of Europe into East and West, through the Roman and the Byzantine church; medieval philosophy and the influential reception of Roman law and its effects which can still be discerned today; knighthood and courtly culture; the development of the 'modern' state; the continuing influence of social groups and their systems of values and institutions such as vassalage, the university, and the city state; and last but not least, the division into competing states and nations that is so distinctive for Europe.

I would like, however, to approach my topic in another way. I am interested in exploring this topic in terms of a history of interpretation, a history of a constellation of problems, a 'history of meaning' (*Sinngeschichte*).[1] I am concerned with the problem of how the Middle Ages are interpreted in the modern era (since the end of the eighteenth century) and especially how they are interpreted in relation to the modern era.[2] I would like to examine this problem from two different angles. On the one hand, I am concerned with the way certain, often

---

[1] See J. Assmann, *Ägypten. Eine Sinngeschichte* (München–Wien, 1996), p. 11.

[2] For a more detailed discussion of this, see O. G. Oexle, 'Die Moderne und ihr Mittelalter. Eine folgenreiche Problemgeschichte', in P. Segl, ed., *Mittelalter und Moderne. Entdeckung und Rekonstruktion der mittelalterlichen Welt* (Signaringen, 1997), pp. 307–64. See also O. G. Oexle, 'Das entzweite Mittelalter', in G. Althoff, ed., *Die Deutschen und ihr Mittelalter. Themen und Funktionen moderner Geschichtsbilder vom Mittelalter* (Darmstadt, 1992), pp. 7–28, and 'Das Mittelalter und das Unbehagen an der Moderne. Mittelalterbeschwörungen in der Weimarer Republik und danach', in *idem, Geschichtswissenschaft im Zeichen des Historismus. Studien zu Problemgeschichten der Moderne* (Göttingen, 1996), pp. 137–62.

unreflected, assumptions and views of the Middle Ages influence the way we see the modern era – this also means our own time. On the other hand, I am talking about the way certain, often unreflected, assumptions about modernity, modernisation, and the path of occidental culture from the Middle Ages to the modern era influence the way we see the Middle Ages.

I would like to demonstrate what I mean by looking at two current examples; here I am referring to two books which appeared simultaneously in the autumn of 1993, one in Germany, the other in France. The German author's book, entitled *Das Ende des Individualismus* (The End of Individualism), bears the subtitle *Die Kultur des Westens zerstört sich selbst* (Western Culture Is Destroying Itself).[3] The author, Meinhard Miegel, works in the fields of law, economics and sociology and is currently the director of the Institut für Wirtschaft und Gesellschaft in Bonn. In 1992 he also became professor and director of the Centre for International Trade Relations at the University of Leipzig. What his book 'is about' is clear from the very first page: it is based on a 'comprehensive study of the causes of the declining birth rate in Germany'. According to Miegel, his study has arrived at the conclusion 'that the populations of highly industrialized countries, including Germany, are in a demographic dilemma which could easily lead to a loss of their cultural identities'.

For if these populations were to maintain 'their long practised behaviour in terms of birth', Miegel continues, they would 'within a short time age dramatically and quickly decline in numbers, or be infiltrated by so many immigrants that the integration of these immigrants may become very difficult'. The cause of all this is, in Miegel's opinion, the 'individualistic cultures which the populations of these countries have internalized over centuries'. Their hallmark: 'the extreme emphasis on the interests of the individual as opposed to the community'. Individualisation has become here an end in and of itself with grave negative consequences. All of this is resulting in the declining birth rates of the individualistic cultures of the 'West' which in the end are, thus, destroying themselves

One could now, depending on one's political position, have a controversial discussion about such ideas or one could simply let them rest, if the author had not chosen to support his theses with sweeping historical generalisations. The Middle Ages play a key role in this, for the Middle Ages are for Miegel the exemplary time of 'community orientation'. 'Individual, community, and nature form an indissoluble unity in medieval thinking', he says. This, according to Miegel, ended

---

[3] M. Miegel and S. Wahl, *Das Ende des Individualismus. Die Kultur des Westens zerstört sich selbst* (München, 1993).

with the Renaissance. He explains this by employing Jacob Burckhardt's book from 1860 on the *Kultur der Renaissance*. In the eyes of our author, the dissolution of the community and mankind's emancipation from the dogmas of faith meant the end of the Middle Ages and the beginning of the modern era. After that, as our author assures us, a 'wave of individualization' began, which continued with Humanism and the Reformation, the Enlightenment, Liberalism and Socialism. All of this, then, flowed into the 'individualistic culture' of today. According to Miegel, there is only one antidote to the imminent self-destruction of Western culture, the one called for by the title of the book: the *End of Individualism*. The author could just as well have said, 'We need a New Middle Ages.'

The New Middle Ages is also the title and theme of the second book I would like to discuss. It bears the title *Le nouveau Moyen Age*.[4] Alain Minc, a French industrialist and intellectual, wrote it. No less a figure than Jacques Delors said about Alain Minc's concept of the New Middle Ages that it is 'a concept which would permeate all political debates'. This prognosis now seems to be somewhat outdated. Although in the presidential election of Mitterand's successor, Alain Minc did rise to become the most influential adviser and main ideologue of then French Premier, Edouard Balladur, it was of no avail.

Minc sees Europe after the collapse of Communism as marching doggedly towards a New Middle Ages. The collapse of Communism, according to him, meant a fatal upheaval of the world order which can only be compared to the end of the Roman Empire. Minc does not wish for a New Middle Ages – he dreads it. His New Middle Ages is completely different from that of the German professor. Minc's New Middle Ages is – as he says – a 'synonym for fragmentation and chaos'. World-wide deregulation, on the increase since 1989, the surge in local conflicts, disintegration of national societies through powerful private groups (*vulgo*: the Mafia), new migration movements, Aids as the new plague, the loss of belief in progress, the end of Liberalism which has lost its most important pillar along with Communism – all of these are signalling the end of the modern era and the beginning of a New Middle Ages.

II

Both of these publications show very clearly just what this history of the problem constellation or 'history of the meaning' (*Sinngeschichte*) of the modern era and the Middle Ages is really about. Here the Middle

[4] A. Minc, *Le nouveau Moyen Age* (Paris, 1993).

Ages means an imagined point of reference against which the modern era is evaluated, against which the modern era is measured. At the same time the concept of a New Middle Ages is intended to say something about the future, its challenges and the necessity of shaping it. This is done in two diametrically opposed ways. On the one hand, the Middle Ages represents the imagined memory of happy times of unity, community, and wholeness. At the same time it also represents the imagined promise of a better future in which the negative, even disastrous, characteristics of modernity are obliterated. In other words, the allegedly fatal path which European history has followed since the Renaissance, Humanism and the Reformation up until the end of our century will be revised. On the other hand, the New Middle Ages is imagined as 'chaos' and 'fragmentation', which are now threatening to return. Everything possible must be set in motion to prevent the 'End of the Modern Era', *la fin des Temps Modernes*. In both cases we are dealing with imagined notions of the Middle Ages which are partially based on 'real' history, but for the most part founded on a certain history of interpretations of the Middle Ages. I have already mentioned Jacob Burckhardt's Renaissance book from 1860.

These imagined notions of the Middle Ages contribute to the discussion of two cardinal problems of modernity. And for each of these problems there are, depending on your point of view, two contrasting answers.

The one problem is progress and how one should evaluate it. This issue brings up two questions. First, whether overcoming the Middle Ages is a sign of progress, or, on the contrary, whether the progress which occidental culture has made since the end of the Middle Ages and in the course of the modern era, when measured against the Middle Ages, has revealed itself as a disaster – a disaster which must be revised by a New Middle Ages. In other words, here we are dealing with the issue of whether the diagnosed New Middle Ages which is replacing or should replace the modern era means a fatal threat to modernity or the long-awaited end to it.

These questions about progress are linked to a second problem which centres on the topic of individuality. The solution of this problem can also be justified in two contradictory ways. The first problem concerns the emancipation of the individual, which Jacob Burckhardt defined in 1860 as the end of the Middle Ages and the beginning of modernity. According to Burckhardt, this was a double emancipation: on the one hand from the powers of the community and on the other hand from the powers of religion. Does this double emancipation represent a step forward, or a disaster? Should one understand the European process of civilisation since the Renaissance as a process of man's increasing liberation from his self-inflicted dependence and the constraints of intellectual and social bondage and ignorance, or are the Renaissance, Humanism, Enlightenment, etc., to be viewed as processes which tore mankind from its natural bonds and order? From this point of view the Middle Ages must seem to be the epitome of a lost world of ties, security and meaning in the spiritual as well as the social sense.

What is being so hotly debated here as a fundamental question of modernity is, in other words, the issue of social and spiritual ties and freedom. With respect to this issue, too, the Middle Ages become a unique example with which – in the dialectic of rejection or identification – the process of modernity can be either illuminated or condemned.

In terms of the history of this problem constellation one could be tempted to understand the position of the German writer as typically German, that of the French writer as typically French. This would, however, be an oversimplification. We encounter the problem of the Middle Ages and the modern era and of the New Middle Ages in different combinations everywhere, though in very different mixtures. Here I am talking about a comprehensive comparison of modern national mentalities which I cannot go into here. I will need to limit myself largely to Germany, in particular to three aspects of the history of this problem constellation.

(1) First – in connection with the examples I gave at the beginning – I will note something about the virulence of this problem in today's culture, especially in the systematic sciences such as philosophy or the social sciences. (2) Secondly, I say something about the history of these patterns of interpretation in Germany. (3) Thirdly, I shall briefly look at the effects of these patterns of interpretation on medieval and modern scholarship. Here I am talking about a historisation of historiography. At the end of my considerations I will address the question of the 'purpose' of such a historisation of historiography and how we can profit from it.

III

First, let us consider the histories of the Middle Ages and the modern era in the systematic sciences of the present.

Authors such as the writers of the two books from 1993 always tend to think of their ideas as new and original. The possibility that they are following previously well-trodden paths of thinking, that they are moving down already long-established paths of modern historical thought, generally transcends their reflections.

(1) It is enough to take a look at one author who is an expert on modern medieval ideologies, an author who uses these ideologies

knowledgeably, cleverly and in a superior manner and in doing so at the same time nourishes these ideas again and again. Here I am referring to Umberto Eco.[5] His marvellous medieval novel from 1982 (*Il nome della rosa*) is outstanding precisely because he fulfils modern expectations by using all the modern notions of the Middle Ages, in all their contradictions. As early as 1972 Eco published an essay entitled 'Heading Towards a New Middle Ages'. In this essay Eco claims that our epoch *is* the New Middle Ages. The only question which remains open is whether with this statement we are dealing 'with a prognosis' or 'an assertion of fact'. Eco's essay was based on an analysis by the Italian sociologist Furio Colombo. He also used a book by the Italian philosopher Roberto Vacca, *Il medioevo prossimo venturo* (1971), which also appeared in English in 1974 as *The Coming Dark Ages*. In this book Vacca fantasised about a collapse of the current technological culture (just like Alain Minc twenty years later). In a short time, he claimed, this breakdown will also lead to a dissolution of social and political structures, to a re-feudalisation of the world, to a division of power on a local and regional level, to the formation of militias and self-organised groups, to the return of epidemics and migrations, and to the decline of the cities. Vacca suggested, as a preventative measure, thinking about the foundation of new monasteries in order to store and preserve the knowledge of the present until a 'new Renaissance' should come and culture can revive.

There are – especially in Italy and the United States – numerous discussions on the end of modernity and the coming of a New Middle Ages with specific motifs of imagined Middle Ages which have been handed down and which one can also find in places where no one is explicitly talking about the 'Old' Middle Ages or the New Middle Ages. Consider, for instance, Daniel Bell, *The Cultural Contradictions of Capitalism* (1976), Christopher Lasch, *The Culture of Narcissism* (1978), and Richard Sennett, *The Fall of Public Man* (1977). One could also include David Riesman's *The Lonely Crowd* from 1950.[6]

(2) Other examples of the influential presence and the clearly indisputable power of the imagined notions of the Middle Ages to shape ideas about modernity are provided by the German sociologist, Niklas Luhmann, and his work. His work shows how the imagined notions of the Middle Ages manipulate or steer reflections on modernity.

Luhmann's *Rechtssoziologie*, for instance, works with a three-stage model for the development of the legal system.[7] He describes the first stage as the legal system of archaic societies which is based on a system

[5] Oexle, 'Die Moderne und ihr Mittelalter', pp. 314–15.
[6] Ibid., pp. 315–16.
[7] N. Luhmann, *Rechtssoziologie* (Opladen, 3rd edn, 1987).

of relationships, of violent self-preservation and of revenge. The second stage is the legal system of the advanced civilisations of the pre-modern era (including the occidental Middle Ages). Finally, the third stage is the introduction of positive law in the modern era. Advanced civilisations of pre-modern character (in other words: the Middle Ages) form hierarchically structured societies with incomplete functional differentiation, as Luhmann explains. The concept of law upon which these societies are founded is, according to Luhmann, that of 'good old law' or traditional law.

One could criticise Luhmann's evolutionary model by pointing to the 'legislative revolution' of the twelfth and thirteenth centuries, that is, the whole range of positive legislation established by medieval governmental authorities between 1100 and 1350. According to Luhmann's theory, no such legislation could have existed in the Middle Ages. This objection, based on empirical facts, however, cannot touch Luhmann's theory because it already 'knows' everything. The structure of the model appears to be unshakable even though, or rather because, Luhmann's entire evolutionary model is held together by the very notion of the Middle Ages it implies (a chronologically ill-defined, extended Middle Ages).[8] One could also say that this model assumes a contradiction between the Middle Ages and modern times.

Luhmann's general theory about modernity and its genesis is also shaped by certain, unarticulated assumptions about the Middle Ages. In his four-volume work, *Gesellschaftsstruktur und Semantik* (1980–95), Luhmann tries to show the 'interplay of structural and semantic changes' which 'led' from the medieval system of estates 'to modern society'. The chapter on 'Individual, Individuality, Individualism' plays a central role in the third volume of this work (1989).[9] Its topic is the genesis of modernity, to the extent that modernity differentiates itself from the Middle Ages by constructing an opposition between the individual and the community. The individual in the Middle Ages, according to Luhmann's thesis, could only live within his commitments to home and family or, as Luhmann says, in 'inclusion'. And only in this 'inclusion', as a member of a community that was pre-determined and pre-arranged, was it at all possible for him to be something like an individual. Luhmann argues, then, that there was an evolutionary process from medieval inclusion to modern exclusion of the individual, or from the community to individuality. This kind of a thesis is doomed, of course, for many reasons of which every medievalist is aware; for

[8] See J. Rückert, *Autonomie des Rechts in rechtshistorischer Perspektive* (Hanover, 1988), pp. 16–35.

[9] N. Luhmann, *Gesellschaftsstruktur und Semantik. Studien zur Wissenssoziologie der modernen Gesellschaft*, vol. 3 (Frankfurt/M., 1989), pp. 149–258.

instance, the formation of groups in medieval society and the binding of individuals to contracts. And at the same time this thesis is anything but new. Its roots lie in the famous book by the German sociologist Ferdinand Tönnies on *Gemeinschaft und Gesellschaft* from 1887. In what follows I will have occasion to refer to this work several times. The example of Luhmann's sociology demonstrates just how extensively sociological interpretations of the modern era and modernity are influenced by unarticulated, unconscious assumptions about the Middle Ages. What seems to be even more problematic is that we are dealing here with assumptions about the Middle Ages which are themselves products of the historical process of modernity.

In a similar manner one could mention numerous reflections in contemporary philosophy, political science and sociology. These always have something to do with the topic of the individual and the community in the modern era and the origin of early modern and modern individualism in contrast to the Middle Ages, be it that one affirms individualism (like, for example, the German sociologist Günther Dux in his latest book *Geschlecht und Gesellschaft* from 1994) or that one declares the protection of the integrity of communal relationships against modern individualism to be the fundamental problem of contemporary ethics (like, for example, the Canadian philosopher Charles Taylor in his much-quoted book *Sources of the Self. The Making of Modern Identity* from 1989).

IV

It is astonishing that this widespread discourse about modernity gets away with using so few basic elements – the contrast between the Middle Ages and modernity and the individual and community. The debate on so-called postmodernism which has been raging in Germany for more than fifteen years and is on the verge of dying out is, of course, also fertile ground for the creation of such theories.[10] I cannot go into this in general or in detail. I would just like to raise one voice among the many voices on postmodernism. In particular, I would like to do this because we can go step by step back in time to the origin of the German debate on the New Middle Ages which started around a hundred years ago. With this I will turn to the second part of my lecture, the history of such patterns of interpretation in Germany.

In 1989, a turning-point in world history, the Hanover philosopher Peter Koslowski published a book with the programmatic title *Die*

---

[10] See W. Welsch, *Unsere postmoderne Moderne* (Weinheim, 3rd edn, 1991).

Prüfungen der Neuzeit (The Trials of the Modern Era).[11] His thesis is that the validity of modernity as a philosophical, artistic and scholarly model and of modernism as a *Weltanschauung* is not taken for granted anymore today. For 'postmodern philosophy questions modernity and whether the thinking of modernity is up-to-date'. What is meant, however, by the thinking of modernity? The answer is that it is the thinking based on 'the autonomy of the subject and the destruction of metaphysics'. In this critique of modernity and modernism, that is, in these 'trials of the modern era' in which 'postmodernism' challenges modernity, 'the outlines of a new attitude toward the absolute, toward nature and toward the person at the centre of the human self, which is not absorbed by the subject, become visible'. According to Koslowski this is 'postmodernity'. He argues that with postmodernity a new, 'fourth era' has begun. Moreover, he maintains that the only thing that is still not clear is whether this 'postmodern epoch will be an epoch on the same level as the modern era or simply a transitional epoch'.

Koslowski believes that the idea of 'postmodernity' emerged as a result of the oil crisis in 1973. This is, of course, a convenient illusion. Its purpose is obviously to conceal just how completely traditional these allegedly new ideas about modernity and postmodernity really are. For the historically minded reader of the book it soon becomes obvious that Koslowksi's train of thought has little to do with the oil crisis in 1973. It has a great deal more to do with another book which appeared as early as 1950 under the title *Das Ende der Neuzeit* (The End of the Modern Era). It was written by the Catholic theologian Romano Guardini.[12] The theme of Guardini's book is the thesis that the modern era is 'coming to an end', that something 'coming' is on the move. He argues that a 'coming epoch, not yet christened by historiography' is beginning to 'develop'. What is indicative of this new epoch? According to Guardini it is the ascendance of a new evaluation of the autonomy of the individual, it is the looming end of the 'culture of personality'. Koslowski's 'postmodernity' from 1989 is nothing more than Guardini's 'coming epoch, not yet christened by historiography' from 1950.

Guardini's book – published after the German disaster of 1945 – compared the 'attitude toward life and the world view of the Middle Ages' with the early modern and particularly with the modern era. According to Guardini, there was a 'medieval desire' to 'design and construct the world as a whole and to assign each individual their somehow fixed place within this world'. This was then propagated by Guardini as an exemplary norm for modernity, against which the early

---

[11] P. Koslowski, *Die Prüfungen der Neuzeit. Über Postmodernität, Philosophie der Geschichte, Metaphysik, Gnosis* (Wien, 1989).
[12] R. Guardini, *Das Ende der Neuzeit. Ein Versuch zur Orientierung* (Würzburg, 1950).

modern and modern era should be measured and then condemned. Filled with the spirit of the norms of community and wholeness, Guardini put modernity on trial, filed suit against the destructivity of the early modern and modern era, and called for and announced the 'end of the modern era'. According to Guardini the destructiveness of the modern era began in the fourteenth century, namely with nominalism. Nominalism, he argues, destroyed the holistic thinking of medieval metaphysics and similarly crushed the medieval social world's concept of community.

Guardini's thesis from 1950 that the nominalism of the fourteenth century destroyed medieval community and wholeness was, however, by no means new. It stemmed from another, older book, entitled *Die Welt des Mittelalters und wir* (The World of the Middle Ages and Us). It was published in 1922 by the then 21-year-old philosopher Paul Ludwig Landsberg, a student of Max Scheler. The book was a great success and it was reprinted several times in just a short period of time. Landsberg acted as a speaker for the younger generation after the German disaster of 1918.[13] He described a 'new love for the Middle Ages'. The 'Middle Ages' in Landsberg's writing was not so much meant to refer to a specific epoch, but rather 'a fundamental and intrinsic possibility for humanity'. The Middle Ages represented, according to Landsberg, for this reason a 'realisable goal or model' against which modernity could measure itself. And just what was Landsberg's own time supposed to learn from the Middle Ages? It should learn to understand the world as a cosmos, to believe that the world is a 'rationally organised whole'. By means of its teleological order of the world, the Middle Ages seemed to Landsberg to be an exemplary model for modernity. According to Landsberg, the loss of spiritual and social ties characterised the spiritual and social chaos of the post-medieval world from Humanism to the present. Landsberg also maintained that chaos began with nominalism, with William of Ockham. For this reason Landsberg, just like Guardini thirty years later, called for the end of the modern era. He demanded 'the death of modern European society'. Landsberg declared that the youth, the new 'Us', would take this path in order to create a new order, or a New Middle Ages, from the anarchy of a revolution. This revolution was, according to Landsberg, 'that which is developing and already exists in the present hour'. In his eyes a new age was dawning. This, as Landsberg said, was a consequence of the 'conservative revolution' which he propagated as a 'revolution of the eternal'.

[13] P. L. Landsberg, *Die Welt des Mittelalters und wir. Ein geschichtsphilosophischer Versuch über den Sinn eines Zeitalters* (Bonn, 1922, and 3rd edn, 1925). On Landsberg and his book, see Oexle, 'Das Mittelalter und das Unbehagen an der Moderne', pp. 139–42.

Landsberg's book on the Middle Ages from 1922 is, oddly enough, in turn based on another book that appeared several decades before. It is the work, published in 1887, by the German sociologist Ferdinand Tönnies, *Gemeinschaft und Gesellschaft* (Community and Society) which I have already mentioned.

Tönnies defined 'community' as a person's 'organic' ties to intimate social life, to family and relatives, to neighbourhoods and friendships, to village and city.[14] He viewed 'society', on the other hand, as the epitome of human 'mechanical' relationships shaped by conflicts of interest and contractual relationships, by mechanical production and economic exchange, by individualism and rationalism, and finally by the loss of all ties, loyalties and values. The entire culture, Tönnies wrote in 1887, changed suddenly into a civilisation of society and state. And thus, according to Tönnies, culture itself was coming to an end. He maintained that there are two eras in history. These are set against each other: an era of society succeeds an era of community, the modern era followed the Middle Ages. The latter, in Tönnies's, view, is the superior age. In 1913 and once again in 1926, Tönnies concluded with the same judgement with which we are already familiar from Koslowski, Guardini, and Landsberg: 'Modern culture is in the middle of an unstoppable process of decay. Its progress is its decline.' Thus, as early as 1887 in his plea for 'community', Tönnies called for the 'annihilation' of modern society.[15]

V

All of this represents a German mentality, a way of 'thinking' 'history' whose stubborn perseverance is baffling.

The foundation for these concepts was laid by the German Romantics, namely by Novalis in his speech *Die Christenheit oder Europa* (Christendom or Europe) from 1799.[16] Novalis was the first to celebrate the historical Middle Ages as a joyous, but remote epoch of wholeness, unity, and community; as a time of unified Christian culture under the beneficent leadership of the Church. According to Novalis, this epoch

[14] F. Tönnies, *Gemeinschaft und Gesellschaft. Abhandlung des Communismus und des Socialismus als empirischer Culturformen* (Leipzig, 1887). *Idem, Gemeinschaft und Gesellschaft. Grundbegriffe der reinen Soziologie* (1912). On this, see Oexle, 'Die Moderne und ihr Mittelalter', pp. 325–6.

[15] F. Tönnies, 'Individuum und Welt in der Neuzeit', *Weltwirtschaftliches Archiv*, 1 (1913), pp. 37–66, p. 66; *idem, Fortschritt und soziale Entwicklung. Geschichtsphilosophische Ansichten* (Karlsruhe, 1926), pp. 34–5.

[16] Novalis, *Werke, Tagebücher und Briefe Friedrich von Hardenbergs*, 2: *Das philosophisch-theoretische Werk*, ed. Hans-Joachim Mähl (München–Wien, 1978), pp. 731–750. See Oexle, 'Die Moderne und ihr Mittelalter', pp. 326–9.

was brought to an end by Humanism and the Reformation, and this in turn was the beginning of the evils of modernity which were taken up by the Enlightenment. In Novalis's text we also find the vision of a New Middle Ages, which is, as yet, only visible in traces, but inevitably approaching. 'With definite certainty', as he writes at the end of his tract, he discerns the 'first signs of a new world', of a new epoch of the 'resurrection of Europe' in conjunction with 'a new Church'. 'Be patient, it will, it must come, the holy era of eternal peace where the new Jerusalem will be the capital of the world.'

While the Enlightenment interpreted European history as a history of progress and divided it into Antiquity, the (bad) Middle Ages and the modern era, Novalis replaced this three-part model with a new one. The new model was composed of an (exemplary) Middle Ages, (bad) early modern and modern era and a coming New Middle Ages. This interpretive model tells the story of a decline (namely from the Middle Ages to the modern era) and at the same time adds the promise of a (better) future. According to Novalis, this New Middle Ages is preceded by the present anarchy which will end in the destruction, the 'annihilation of the present' in order to make room for something new, something better.

The real boom of ideas concerning a New Middle Ages in Germany does not begin in the Romantic era, but rather much later, in the 1870s. It begins under the influence of the rapid disintegration of the belief in progress, which was at the same time kindled by the so-called Great Depression of the Bismarck era (1873–96). The Great Depression released a wave of pessimism and anxieties, fear of the 'Reds' and revolution, waves of class animosity and anti-Semitism and the passionate intensification of religious conflicts, the 'increasing volume of nationalist bellowing', and a 'widespread tendency toward radicalization' (Hans Rosenberg).[17] We can add to this the effects of the increasing modernisation of the 1880s and 1890s, which were experienced as a burden: *Historismus* and relativism, positivism, and mechanisation. Growing anti-modernism railed violently against these trends.[18]

Scholarship has not devoted enough attention to the salient indicators of these controversies. What I am referring to here is the power of images, the imagined notions of different epochs which were expressed in the sciences, but even more so in literature, art and architecture as

---

[17] H. Rosenberg, *Große Depression und Bismarck-Zeit. Wirtschaftsablauf, Gesellschaft und Politik in Mitteleuropa* (Frankfurt/M.–Berlin–Wien, 1976), pp. 56–7. See also W.J. Mommsen, *Das Ringen um den nationalen Staat. Die Gründung und der innere Ausbau des Deutschen Reiches unter Otto von Bismarck, 1850–1890* (Berlin, 1993), p. 283.

[18] Oexle, 'Die Moderne und ihr Mittelalter', pp. 329–34.

well as in theories of art and architecture.[19] There are two epochs which I am talking about particularly: the Renaissance and the Middle Ages. The imagined notions of the Renaissance always affirm progress which supposedly led from the Renaissance to modernity. The imagined notions of the Middle Ages, on the other hand, are critical of progress and anti-modern.

It is interesting and at the same time extremely telling to observe the appearance of 'Renaissancism' and 'medievalism' in art, architecture, and literature as well as in the popular press and scholarship from the 1870s on. This is significant because by looking at this conflict and examining the visible shift of emphasis from Renaissancism to medievalism it is possible to see the dramatic changes in mentality German society experienced. Tönnies's book, *Gemeinschaft und Gesellschaft*, from 1887 is a good example of this. I cannot describe this complex process here. Instead I will limit myself to a discussion of medievalism which has manifested itself more and more clearly since the turn of the century.[20]

Enthusiasm for the Renaissance, for example in German literature, ran out of steam at the end of the nineteenth century. The Middle Ages took the lead and became the central epoch in the modern era. Let me give you some examples.[21] For instance, in 1908 the art historian Wilhelm Worringer called for a new modern art, which should be anti-individualistic and oriented towards the community. It should be a new kind of Gothic, able to establish new values for society. In 1913 the art critic Karl Scheffler wrote a book on Italy which contained a harsh rejection of the Renaissance. For him, this rejection was a 'matter of life or death' for Germany. Scheffler also propagated a 'secret Gothic' as an art form he defined as bound to the community, anti-modern, anti-individualistic, and national. The journalist Paul Fechter wrote in 1914: 'This time is yearning for a new Gothic.' He wrote this in a book on Expressionism, which he identified as this new Gothic. In 1914 Stefan George published his new collection of poetry entitled *Der Stern des Bundes* (The Star of the Covenant). In it he outlined a programme which rigorously rejected modernity while waving the banners of the Middle Ages, which he saw as represented by the covenant of his disciples, with himself the master. The German scholar Richard Benz published his manifesto *Die Renaissance, das Verhängnis der deutschen Kultur* (The Renaissance, the Downfall of German Culture) in 1915. Stefan George started working on his poetry collection *Das Neue Reich* (The

---

[19] Ibid.
[20] Ibid.
[21] M. Bushart, *Der Geist der Gotik und die expressionistische Kunst. Kunstgeschichte und Kunsttheorie 1911–1925* (München, 1990).

New Reich) in 1919, whose title already announces what he means by the 'secret Germany' he propagates in his poems. In the 1919 founding manifesto of the Bauhaus, the architect Walter Gropius evoked the model of the medieval church masons' guild and called the Gothic cathedral, as a synthesis of the arts, a suitable ideal for modernity.[22]

Political medievalism blossomed, especially in the period after the disaster of 1918 and during the Weimar Republic. We have already seen this in the 1922 publication by Paul Ludwig Landsberg (see note 13), which initiated a broad discussion and was for the most part positively received. Elsewhere I have shown how especially sociologists and philosophers, scholars of constitutional law and Protestant theologians evoked the Middle Ages during the Weimar Republic.[23] All of this took place against the background of a 'turning away from individualism', in the sense of a 'revolution', a 'reversal of world spirit', in the form of a 'Counter-Renaissance', as the Austrian sociologist Othmar Spann expressed it in 1931.[24]

It is also worth while to analyse art and literature of the Weimar Republic in terms of how they thematised the debate on the 'Renaissance' and 'the Middle Ages' in their portrayal of the present. Here I would like to mention Fritz Lang's films and their effects on the audience, for instance *Die Nibelungen* (1924) or *Metropolis* (1927). These movies contrast the soulless, mechanised civilisation of the future with a New Middle Ages. I would also like to recall the analysis of the problem in Robert Musil's work, *Der Mann ohne Eigenschaften* (The Man Without Qualities), from 1930 or in Thomas Mann's *Der Zauberberg* (The Magic Mountain) from 1924. In the *Zauberberg* the discussions between Settembrini, the Humanist and philosopher of the Enlightenment, and Naphta, the Jesuit and representative of the New Middle Ages, cover the entire spectrum of themes. Let me add the novels on the Middle Ages written by Gertrud von Le Fort, Werner Bergengruen and Wilhelm von Scholz, all of which appeared in the final crisis of the Weimar Republic, in 1930.[25] Further examples include Hermann Hesse's *Narziß und Goldmund* (also from 1930) and his novel *Das Glasperlenspiel* (begun in 1930, published in 1943). This novel represents a perfect description of the New Middle Ages which is depicted as already having

[22] Ibid.
[23] Oexle, 'Das Mittelalter und das Unbehagen an der Moderne'. See *idem*, 'Das Mittelalter als Waffe. Ernst H. Kantorowicz' "Kaiser Friedrich der Zweite" in den politischen Kontroversen der Weimarer Republik', in *idem, Geschichtswissenschaft im Zeichen des Historismus*, pp. 163–215.
[24] O. Spann, *Der wahre Staat. Vorlesungen über Abbruch und Neuaufbau der Gesellschaft* (Jena, 3rd edn, 1931), pp. 3 and 26.
[25] B. Hey'l, *Geschichtsdenken und literarische Moderne. Zum historischen Roman in der Zeit der Weimarer Republik* (Tübingen, 1994), pp. 280–316.

begun.[26] One could also mention the works of devout anti-modernists and medievalists such as Stefan George (and his disciples) and Rudolf Borchardt.[27] One could also recall that Hermann Broch, in his trilogy and contemporary analysis *Die Schlafwandler* (The Sleepwalkers) from 1931–2, reflected on the 'depraved' era of the Renaissance and the 'decline of values' triggered by it.

In his *Doktor Faustus* (1947), Thomas Mann characterised the debates of the first half of the century about medieval and modern in a critical way as a sort of pandemonium of German intellectuals and professors. He also pinpointed that moment when communal 'authority' in thought and interpretation became a real 'force'.

It is noteworthy that this kind of political medievalism also turned up in places where there was no discussion of the Middle Ages. This is, for example, true of a key work on the debates surrounding the Weimar Republic such as Ernst Jünger's *Der Arbeiter* (The Worker) from 1932.[28]

In 1932 Ernst Jünger proclaimed that the age of the third estate, or the bourgeoisie, simultaneously the age of the masses and the individual, was coming to an end. According to Jünger one stood 'in front of the gates' of a new era 'in which talk will again be of real authority, order and subordination, command and obedience'. This new, coming age of which traces are already discernible, will be characterised by a 'different concept of freedom', a concept of freedom in which 'authority and service will mean the same thing'. For this reason, Jünger claimed that a new 'type' will succeed the individual of the early modern and modern era. This type has already appeared in the form of the uniformed front-line soldier and uniformed worker, as a 'real figure', as a representative of a new epoch. Its hallmark, according to Jünger, will be a wholeness which is more than simply the sum of its parts.

VI

These kinds of statement on the New Middle Ages accumulated in the fatal year of 1933. In other words, one can see here what made National Socialism so fascinating for so many German scholars of the humanities: discontent with modernity and suffering from individualism, rationalism, relativism. All of this was supposed to be cured by the influence of 'community' and 'wholeness' in a new era. Of course, these scholars did not confine themselves only to thinking and interpreting. 'Der

---

[26] Oexle, 'Das Mittelalter und das Unbehagen an der Moderne', pp. 151–2.
[27] Oexle, 'Die Moderne und ihr Mittelalter', pp. 342–3.
[28] Ibid., pp. 347–8.

Führer' was to bring the 'New Middle Ages' – this was the hope and expectation which filled many art historians (for instance, the famous Wilhelm Pinder), many legal scholars, many legal historians and philosophers, German scholars, historians and sociologists. They expressed their hopes with this notion of the New Middle Ages.[29]

The Protestant theologian Friedrich Gogarten welcomed National Socialism because it overcame humanism (defined by Gogarten as the fatal autonomy of human reason) and its final stage, modern *Historismus*, by propagating a new community. Gogarten rejected *Historismus*, which he defined as infinite variations of subjectivity promoted as absolute norms. In his notorious speech as rector of the University of Freiburg held in May 1933, Martin Heidegger explicitly banished the much-celebrated academic freedom from German universities. For, Heidegger claimed, this freedom was only 'negative'. Instead, Heidegger demanded that the true meaning of the notion of freedom be revived; that is, 'loyalty and service'. He defined scholarship as 'service'. For him it was 'labour service', 'military service' and 'academic service', bound to the national community. In his speech on *Art in the New German State* given in August 1933 the art historian Wilhelm Pinder declared the end of the long-standing crisis of modern art.[30] For by then, according to Pinder, art and the people had become aware of their insoluble, indestructible bond. Pinder rejected the art of modernity, beginning with the end of the eighteenth century, as 'unhealthy' and 'not normal'. For, in his eyes, this art was shaped by a 'freedom to choose between different styles' and an 'unrestrained independence of these styles from political ideologies'. The styles of pre-modern art, however, were shaped by the 'community'. Now, Pinder emphatically exclaimed, 'we' are again 'on our way to a new community'. Then, rather than problems with styles, there will once again be one style, for style is 'faith and community and communal faith'. Both of these mean, as Pinder explained, the beginning of a New Middle Ages.

While Pinder, surely without intending to, was paving the way for the destruction of modern art as 'unhealthy' and 'degenerate', these fatal services of contemporary art historians were being topped by those of legal scholars.[31] In proactive obedience, without ever being urged by anyone, brilliant young representatives of German jurisprudence (whose careers, by the way, did not end in 1945) were of crucial assistance to the supposed New Middle Ages of National Socialism in 1933–4. They rejected the idea of individual rights, in other words, the rights of

[29] Oexle, 'Das Mittelalter und das Unbehagen an der Moderne'; *idem*, 'Die Moderne und ihr Mittelalter', pp. 348–58.

[30] Oexle, 'Das Mittelalter und das Unbehagen an der Moderne', pp. 155–8.

[31] Oexle, 'Das Mittelalter und das Unbehagen an der Moderne', pp. 158–9; *idem*, 'Die Moderne und ihr Mittelalter', pp. 354–8.

freedom and the equality of the individual, and replaced them with a concept of law bound to the community. As Franz Wieacker declared at the time, the subjective rights of the individual should be overcome in favour of legal norms of 'authentic communities, communities with a leader'. These communities were soon defined in a *völkisch* and racist way. The decisive factor for the legal position of the individual was no longer, as Karl Larenz maintained back then, his 'existence as a person' (*Personsein*), but rather his 'concrete membership in a community' (*konkretes Gliedsein*). For the 'German concept of law', as Larenz pointed out, replaces the mere coexistence of individuals with 'the community and replaces abstract equality with the membership of the individual in the community'. The idea of man as a morally free person, as an individual, he claimed, must be relinquished in favour of the idea of man as a 'personality' essentially 'defined by species and community'. Surely, the inventors of this new communal law cannot have wanted to help the National Socialists on their way towards the exclusion, persecution, abuse and finally the extermination of humans who were not protected by this new communal law. But they did help them on their way. Here, too, the ideas about a New Middle Ages were activated.

VII

It is also important to mention this because this anti-modern medievalism, as we all know, survived the second German disaster, that of the year 1945, in many cases untouched. This anti-modern medievalism had no trouble entering the service of Western ideology.[32] I do not want to discuss this any further, but rather would like to change our focus once again. Without going into too much detail, I would like as my third observation to talk about the effects of political medievalism on historical research, including contemporary scholarship and the work of medievalists and modern historians.

Whenever one wants to explain epoch-making breakthroughs and changes, the interpretive models of the individual and community and of the emancipation of the individual are always close at hand.[33] The modern historian Thomas Nipperdey, for example, interpreted the development of the modern association (*Verein*) around 1800 as a symptom of modernisation, as emancipation of individuals, and explained it with the dissolution of medieval communities during the Enlightenment. This explanatory model could, by its very nature, be applied to any other point in history. It also works, for example, to

---

[32] Oexle, 'Das Mittelalter und das Unbehagen an der Moderne', p. 159.
[33] *Idem*, 'Die Moderne und ihr Mittelalter', pp. 358–62.

explain not only modernisation around 1800, but also the beginning of the modern era around 1500. Medievalists also like to employ this model, whether it be to depict the Middle Ages on the whole as an epoch of 'wholeness' and 'community' and 'types' or to define internal medieval periods, for example, by contrasting a 'static', 'immobile' or 'archaic' early Middle Ages and a 'dynamic' time of new departures (*Aufbruchsepoche*) which put an end to the early Middle Ages. Of course, there is still much controversy about whether this dynamic *Aufbruch* took place in the eleventh or twelfth centuries, or not until the thirteenth century.

Perhaps it is valuable, just once, to recognise the topical character of such interpretations of the Middle Ages, whose almost serial usage shows nothing more than their lack of value. The unlimited usability of this topos in all the nooks and crannies of European history demonstrates that this explanatory model really does not explain anything. This is also true of a long list of other motifs from the political medievalism starting at the end of the nineteenth century. They are found in the work of Stefan George, Ernst Jünger and Martin Heidegger. These motifs, namely, the concept of 'power as service' or 'freedom as service', were, and partly still are, virulent in the research on the Middle Ages itself. Based on these concepts medievalists like Theodor Mayer, Walter Schlesinger and Karl Bosl formulated questions which strongly influenced research after 1945.[34] Here one could also mention the model of medieval man as a 'type' (until recently in vogue among art historians), or the model of the 'whole house' (Otto Brunner), which is at the moment a recurrent topic of controversial and heated debates.[35] Especially in view of the highly intense discussions about Otto Brunner, I would like to emphasise that a critique of such models that focuses solely on their complicity with National Socialism does not go deep enough. The problem is not confined to how scholars compromised with National Socialism. Rather, it encompasses the much broader spectrum of the interpretations of modernity against the background of an imagined Middle Ages. National Socialism was able, in its own way, to profit from these interpretations in which, however, much broader

[34] See Karl Kroeschell, 'Führer, Gefolgschaft und Treue', in Joachim Rückert and Dietmar Willoweit, eds, *Die Deutsche Rechtsgeschichte in der NS-Zeit, ihre Vorgeschichte und ihre Nachwirkungen* (Tübingen, 1995), pp. 55–76; Dietmar Willoweit, 'Freiheit in der Volksgemeinde. Geschichtliche Aspekte des Freiheitsbegriffs in der deutschen rechtshistorischen und historischen Forschung des 19. und 20. Jahrhunderts', ibid., pp. 301–22.
[35] G. Algazi, 'Otto Brunner – "Konkrete Ordnung" und Sprache der Zeit', in P. Schöttler, ed., *Geschichtsschreibung als Legitimationswissenschaft 1918–1945* (Frankfurt/M., 1997), pp. 166–203.

and more fundamental interpretive models of modernity were and are involved.

Here I am not only talking about concepts like 'the whole house' or research concepts like 'freedom through service', not only about constellations of problems like 'community and society' or 'individual and type', but also about the broad field of the history of progress and decline which steers historical research in broad diachronics. We are already familiar with two variations of 'individual and society' (Jacob Burckhardt, 1860, and Ferdinand Tönnies, 1887).[36] One could also mention here works of history describing a progressive process of civilisation ('From Brutish to Civilized Society', according to Norbert Elias) or increasing rationalisation ('From a Magical to a Rational Understanding of the World') or vice versa, works of history that calculate the costs of modernisation by portraying increasing moral decay ('From the Christian World Order to Relativism') or the over-powering of the individual by societal and state powers, in other words, the history of the process 'From the Original State of Man to His Social Disciplining'. Here I would like to mention two French examples. The French social historian Philippe Ariès based his history of death in Europe on the – at first glance – convincing thesis that death in the Middle Ages was 'humane' ('la mort apprivoisée'). Modern man, on the other hand, suffers a difficult, lonely, inhumane death. It is obvious that this thesis takes a predominantly critical view of civilisation.[37] The opposing thesis – of a dull, 'dark' Middle Ages leading to the light of modernity – is represented by Georges Duby in numerous more recent studies, especially on the history of gender. Like Ariès, Duby insists that the Middle Ages and modernity are complete opposites. In Duby's case, however, this opposition is reversed. Duby's Middle Ages is an epoch of brutal, instinctive sexuality.[38] 'Love' and 'marriage' appear as male institutions to promote the securing of property, etc. I think that both of these authors in these books have unwittingly fallen victim to the interpretive models I have been describing.

VIII

With these reflections I would like to support a historisation of his-toriography. Let me add some concluding remarks.

[36] Above, pp. 124 and 131. See also O. G. Oexle, 'Die mittelalterliche Zunft als Forschungsproblem. Ein Beitrag zur Wissenschaftsgeschichte der Moderne', *Blätter für deutsche Landesgeschichte*, 118 (1982), pp. 1–44.

[37] Philippe Ariès, *L'homme devant la mort* (Paris, 1977).

[38] Georges Duby, *Mâle Moyen Age. De l'amour et autres essais* (Paris, 1988).

I do not in any way intend simply to contribute to the so-called reception of the Middle Ages in modern times, just as I do not intend to deliver some kind of superficial ideological critique. So what do I mean, then, by a historisation of historiography? I am talking about optimising research itself, about improving the questions research addresses. The question is how can research, in particular research on the Middle Ages, profit from such a historisation of historiography? In conclusion, I would like to make five suggestions.

(1) First, research on the Middle Ages could regain some of its freedom, some of its autonomy. It could free itself from pre-set approaches which appear legitimate by the very same traditional nature that makes them dubious. Research on the Middle Ages could thus gain a clear picture of itself. Furthermore, by reflecting on its own historicity, on its own historical mediation and determination, research on the Middle Ages could gain the possibility of new options.[39] The historisation of old, traditional questions opens up possibilities for asking new questions.

(2) Secondly, through reflecting on the context and traditions of the history of problem constellations, scholarship on the Middle Ages could partly regain access to modernity and to the present. Perhaps it is precisely this which is particularly important for scholarship on the Middle Ages.

(3) Thirdly, cultural studies on the whole can profit from this kind of historisation of historiography. For these interpretive models, which are themselves the product of a historical process, often form the basis not only of historical concepts, but also are the basis for the concepts of art history, theology, the history of law and the legal sciences in general, of philosophy, sociology and political science. In the case of sociology, for example, it is astonishing that far-reaching sociological theories are based on inherited historical interpretive models. The fact that several branches of cultural studies use these models again and again has the undesirable side-effect that these inherited interpretive models affirm and confirm themselves in circular arguments.

(4) Fourthly, we can learn from the history of these patterns of interpretation that not only the daily life of historians, but also historical research is closely connected to *Erinnerungsbilder* (visual memories) of the past, as the Egyptologist Jan Assmann recently formulated.[40] These images and everything connected to them enter the collective 'cultural memory' (das 'kulturelle Gedächtnis'),[41] the 'culture of remembrance'

[39] Oexle, 'Die mittelalterliche Zunft', pp. 38–40.

[40] Assmann, *Ägypten*, pp. 475–87.

[41] J. Assmann, *Das kulturelle Gedächtnis. Schrift, Erinnerung und politische Identität in frühen Hochkulturen* (München, 1992).

(*die Erinnerungskultur*) or, better yet, the 'cultures of remembrance' (Jan Assmann) of daily life as well as scholarship. We can almost understand the historical disciplines as the collective 'cultural memory' of modernity.[42] This, of course, also means that the elements, the images and notions which constitute, form, and differentiate this collective 'cultural memory' must constantly be re-examined and analysed. Precisely because, however, such *Erinnerungsbilder* of past epochs and cultures are present in the collective 'cultural memory', in the 'culture of remembrance' of the present, they define its 'self-image', and because they define its self-image they are present. Whenever such visual memories which apply to entire cultures, for example, 'the Middle Ages', are made visible in their diachronic sequence, entire 'histories of meaning' (to use another one of Jan Assmann's concepts) emerge.[43] By 'histories of meaning' I mean historical clusters of interpretations, interpretations of the entire history referring to single epochs. Such a 'history of meaning' was recently outlined by Jan Assmann using the example of Egypt.[44] He showed how Egypt has been interpreted from Ancient Israel to Greece, Rome, the Middle Ages, the Renaissance and on up to modern Egyptology. Precisely these stages of a 'history of the meaning' of Egypt point to other similar histories of meaning which one can roughly define as 'Rome', 'the Middle Ages', 'the Renaissance', etc.

(5) And fifth, I am also talking about a *comparative* 'history of meaning', to the extent that since the beginning of the nineteenth century, every national scholarly culture has developed its own specific patterns of interpretation, for example, for the Middle Ages. Post-revolutionary France, for instance, developed a liberal-revolutionary view of the Middle Ages during the Restoration and the July Monarchy. This view of the Middle Ages meant, to some extent, also a national 'myth', namely an assessment of the Middle Ages as the beginning of modernity and modern society. In the interpretation of the Middle Ages advanced by this specific period in time, the Middle Ages constituted the 'crucial historical reference point'. It stood in stark contrast to the interpretations of the Middle Ages propagated by the Nostalgics and Legitimists who also existed in France in that time.[45] As we already know, the history of dominant interpretations of the Middle Ages in Germany was very

---

[42] See O. G. Oexle, 'Memoria als Kultur', in *idem*, ed., *Memoria als Kultur* (Göttingen, 1995), pp. 9–78, pp. 69–78.

[43] Assmann, *Ägypten* (see n. 1).

[44] Assmann, ibid.

[45] D. Hoeges, 'Der Kampf um die Geschichte: Das Mittelalter in Restauration und Juli-Monarchie – Ein Paradigma selektiver Rezeption', in R. R. Grimm, ed., *Mittelalterrezeption. Zur Rezeptionsgeschichte der romanischen Literaturen des Mittelalters in der Neuzeit* (Heidelberg, 1991), pp. 227–42.

different.[46] We have already become somewhat acquainted with a particularly relevant interpretation (concerning the Middle Ages and the New Middle Ages). A comparative analysis of these kinds of patterns of historical interpretation (for instance in Germany and in France, in daily life and scholarship) would be extraordinarily illuminating.

In his famous lecture 'Pour une histoire comparée des sociétés européennes' (For a Comparative History of European Societies) Marc Bloch, who was murdered by the Germans in 1944, called for a comparative European social history as early as 1928.[47] Medieval scholarship was not yet mature enough for this back then, and especially not in Germany. Perhaps, in the meantime, we have come a little closer to this approach. In his 1928 lecture, however, Marc Bloch called for far more. He also called for a comparative history of terminology and approaches: 'une histoire comparée de nos terminologies et de nos questionnaires'.[48] It is remarkable that Bloch did not call for standardisation, but rather for a reconciliation, 'une réconciliation de nos terminologies et de nos questionnaires'. In other words, he argued that it should be possible to combine and compare national interpretations of history and the terminology and approaches resulting from these interpretations. We are still a long way away from this today. It does not seem, however, to be too early to finally begin. The comparative historisation of historiography could bring us closer to this goal. This goal, I think, is an essential precondition for a true history of Europe and for truly European historical scholarship.

---

[46] See also M. Frank, *Gott im Exil. Vorlesungen über die Neue Mythologie*, II. Teil (Frankfurt/M., 1988).

[47] M. Bloch, 'Pour une histoire comparée des sociétés europénnes', in *idem*, *Histoire et historiens. Textes réunis par Étienne Bloch* (Paris, 1995), pp. 94–123.

[48] Ibid., pp. 122–3. See O. G. Oexle, 'Marc Bloch et l'histoire comparée de l'histoire', in P. Deyon, J.-Cl. Richez, L. Strauss, eds, *Marc Bloch, l'historien et la cité* (Strasbourg, 1997), pp. 57–67.

MAKING MERCANTILISM WORK: LONDON MERCHANTS AND ATLANTIC TRADE IN THE SEVENTEENTH CENTURY

By Nuala Zahedieh

READ 23 OCTOBER 1998 AT THE UNIVERSITY OF ABERDEEN

AUTHORS of the surge of economic tracts and treatises published in late seventeenth-century England generally agreed that foreign trade underpinned the wealth, health, and strength of the nation. The merchant was hero:

> the same to the body politick as the liver, veins and arteries are to the natural; for he both raises and distributes treasure the vital blood of the common weal. He is the steward of the kingdom's stock which by his good or ill-management does proportionably increase or languish. One of the most useful members in a state without whom it can never be opulent in peace nor consequently formidable in war.[1]

Yet these agents of national economic advancement remain shadowy figures, particularly in the fastest growing branch of commerce, the plantation trade. This neglect reflects the difficulty in identifying colonial merchants as a group, for the openness of the trade meant large numbers took part and high risks meant a rapid turnover. An examination of the leading players derived from a detailed analysis of the London port books of 1686 reveals insights into the ingredients of personal success and contributes to a better understanding of the structure of the trade and its links with the broader metropolitan and national economies: a look at the merchants who succeeded in making the mercantile system work.[2]

The colonial trade stood at the centre of what Adam Smith described

---

[1] Anon., *Character and Qualifications of an Honest, Loyal Merchant* (1686), 1.

[2] The London port books surviving for 1686 record imports (excluding bullion) and exports of English manufactures. Records of re-exports were not found. Values are taken from official valuations assembled by D. W. Jones from the Inspector General's Ledgers. PRO E190/139/1; 141/5; 136/4; 143/1; 137/2. The commission business of a number of these West India merchants was discussed in K. G. Davis, 'The Origins of the Commission System in the West India Trade', *Transactions of the Royal Historical Society* (1951), 89–101.

as the 'mercantile system'.[3] By 1660 English people had settled permanent plantations on the American mainland in New England and the Chesapeake and in the Caribbean islands of St Christopher, Barbados, Nevis, Antigua, Montserrat, and Jamaica. A three-way pattern of exchange had been established. The southern plantations and the islands produced valuable cash crops for export including tobacco, sugar, indigo, ginger, cotton, and dyewoods. New Englanders provided fish, timber, ships, and shipping services to the southerners. Old England provided all colonies with manufactured goods, food, labour (white servants and black slaves taken in Africa) and commercial services.[4] Once the potential for profit was proven the state took steps to ensure that the benefits of colonial commerce were reserved for the mother country. It was particularly anxious to exclude the Dutch who had established a strong foothold in the Atlantic trades. The Navigation legislation of 1651, refined and improved after the Restoration, confined the colonial carrying trade to English and colonial ships and attempted to ensure that, with some exceptions, all trade to and from the colonies was funnelled through England. In so far as the Acts could be enforced the English created a self-contained commercial system.[5] Within this framework, in the decades after the Restoration, the English consolidated and extended settlement taking in new territories in the middle colonies and the lower south; expanding the colonial population threefold by 1700; and ensuring that an increasing share of a growing colonial commerce remained in their hands with London as the hub of the system.[6] The precarious figures which survive suggest that the value of London's plantation trade more than doubled between the 1660s and the end of the century comprising about 20 per cent of London's overseas trade but, on account of the long distances involved, a far higher proportion of the shipping and shipping services (probably around 40%).[7] Contemporaries such as Josiah Child were convinced that without the Navigation Acts 'we had not now been owners of one half of the shipping, nor trade, nor employed one half of the seamen which we do at present'.[8] John Cary praised the legislation for making

[3] Adam Smith, *An Inquiry into the Nature and Causes of the Wealth of Nations* (2 vols, 1776), II, Book 4.

[4] John J. McCusker and Russell R. Menard, *The Economy of British America, 1607–1789* (Chapel Hill, N.C., 1985).

[5] L. A. Harper, *The English Navigation Laws: A Seventeenth Century Experiment in Social Engineering* (New York, 1939); G. L. Beer, *The Origins of the British Colonial System, 1578–1660* (New York, 1908).

[6] Nuala Zahedieh, 'Overseas Expansion and Trade in the Seventeenth Century', in *The Oxford History of the British Empire*, ed. Nicholas Canny (Oxford, 1998), 398–422.

[7] Ralph Davis, *The Rise of the English Shipping Industry in the Seventeenth and Eighteenth Centuries* (Newton Abbot, 1962), 15.

[8] Josiah Child, *A New Discourse of Trade* (1692), 91.

England 'the sun in the midst of its plantations' and it was fitting that it should be so as 'this was the first Design of settling plantations abroad that the people of England might better maintain a commerce and trade among themselves, the chief profit whereof was to redound to the centre'.[9]

Within the bounds of the national monopoly the trade between England and its colonies was open to all its own subjects. Leading merchants tried from the first days of settlement to restrict entry on the model of other branches of overseas commerce which were regulated by chartered companies. Collective trading was justified as a means to enhance merchants' strength in negotiations with powerful local rulers, facilitate defence of shipping and trading bases, and secure a 'well and ordered trade'. But company organisation was also a familiar vehicle for obtaining a monopoly and other privileges from the crown. In return for using part of their profits to provide loans and gifts to the state, merchants were able to limit competition and reduce the costs of risky enterprise by squeezing suppliers who were paid less and consumers who paid more.[10] However, joint stock companies proved singularly inappropriate for the work of American colonisation which was not merely a trading project. The native economy was not organised on lines which could provide Europeans with regular supplies of desired commodities (except perhaps furs) but native society was such that Europeans were able to appropriate territory and, after a number of failed attempts, the plantation established in Virginia in 1607 laid the foundations of successful English settlement in America. The success depended on the slow, hard work of clearing land and creating the entire physical fabric of new communities which required, not only a very large investment, but also close, careful supervision to secure a profit. Progress was most rapid when those overseeing had proprietary rights. Absentee management by English merchants proved ill-suited to the task. The trading system which emerged had large numbers of competing producers selling commodities to ships' captains and colonial merchants or consigning them to English merchants on their own account. The diversity within the colonial trade made it less amenable to regulation and restricted entry than other branches of commerce

[9] John Cary, *An Essay on the State of England in Relation to its Trade* (Bristol, 1695), 68.

[10] E. L. J. Coornaert, 'European Economic Institutions and the New World: The Chartered Companies', in *The Cambridge Economic History of Europe*, ed. E. E. Rich and C. H. Wilson (8 vols, Cambridge, 1967), IV, 223–74; *Companies and Trade: Essays on Overseas Trading Companies during the Ancien Regime*, ed. L. Blussé and F. Gaastra (The Hague, 1981); A. M. Carlos and S. Nicholas, 'Theory and History: Seventeenth Century Joint Stock Trading Companies', *Journal of Economic History* (hereafter *J. Ec. Hist.*), 56 (1996), 916–44; S. R. M. Jones and S. Ville, 'Efficient Transactors or Rent-seeking Monopolies? The Rationale for Early Joint Stock Companies', *J. Ec. Hist.*, 56 (1996), 898–915.

and viewing its growth and vigour most contemporaries were anxious to protect this freedom. In the words of one pamphleteer 'Nothing is more ... pernicious and destructive to any kingdom or commonwealth than monopolies ... [trade] is like dung which being close kept in a heap or two stinks, but being spread abroad, it doth fertilize the earth and make it more fructible.'[11]

Thus practicalities and politics combined to ensure that the Atlantic trades, apart from the Hudson's Bay and slave trades, remained open to all Englishmen and many took part. The London port books of 1686 list around 1,800 persons participating in colonial trade; high numbers in a period when a London directory lists a total of 1,953 overseas merchants.[12] But most of the entrants were involved in a small way. About 60 per cent of the exporters consigned goods worth less than £50 and over 40 per cent of the importers received less than £50 worth. Furthermore, around half the names do not appear in the port books surviving from years on either side of 1686 suggesting that their adventure in that year was a once only gamble. As Price and Clemens have shown for the Chesapeake commerce a small number of merchants quickly came to dominate the entire Atlantic trade.[13] In 1686, 19 merchants exported English goods worth over £1,000 to North America and 22 to the West Indies. In the import trade seven merchants imported over £5,000 value from North America and 28 from the West Indies. Despite its celebrated openness a group of 61 merchants (including the agent importing the 4.5 per cent duty for the King, the Royal African Company, and the Hudson's Bay Company) controlled well over one-third of these important branches of the plantation trade (Tables 1 and 2). Information about the background and qualifications of the group of 58 individuals pieced together from miscellaneous sources suggests patterns for success among those who made the mercantile system work.[14] It suggests that colonial trade was less of a

[11] Anon., *A Discourse Consisting of Motives for the Enlargement and Freedom of Trade* (1645).

[12] Samuel Lee, *The Little London Directory of 1677* (1878).

[13] Jacob M. Price and P. G. E. Clemens, 'A Revolution of Scale in Overseas Trade: British Firms in the Chesapeake Trade', *J. Ec. Hist.*, 47, 1–43.

[14] The 58 merchants are: Paul Allestree, William Barnes, Moses Barrow (otherwise known as Anthony Lauzado), William Baxter, Jospeh Bueno, Edward Carleton, Richard Cary, Thomas Clarke, William Coward, William Crouch, John Crow, Robert Curtis, John Daveson, Thomas Ducke, Thomas Elliot, John Eston, Francis Eyles, John Eyles, Christopher Fowler, Paul Freeman, John Gardner, Antony Gomezsera, William Gore, Bartholomew Gracedieu, Samuel Groome, Henry Hale, John Harwood, Gilbert Heathcote, Peter and Pierre Henriques, John Hill, Thomas Hunt, John Jackson, John Jefferies, Jeremy Johnson, Thomas Lane, John Lovero, Jacob Lucy, Joseph Martin, Manuel Mendez, Richard Merriweather, Arthur North, William Paggen, Emanuel Perara, Micajah Perry, Joseph Perkins, John Pitt, George Richards, Stephen Skinner, Benjamin Skutt, Thomas Starke, John Taylor, Dalby Thomas, William Thornburgh, Richard Tilden, Thomas Tryon, William Walker, William Wrayford. The biographical information

Table 1

Merchants exporting English goods to the colonies, 1686

Value of trade £ sterling	0–99	100–999	1,000–4,999	5,000–9,999	TOTAL
West Indies					
Number of	521	166	20	2	709
Value of trade, £	14,355	54,393	31,303	11,341	111,392
% of total	13	49	28	10	100
North America					
Number of merchants	476	176	18	1	671
Value of trade, £	13,379	51,500	29,780	5,881	100,540
% of total	13	51	30	6	100

Source: PRO E190/139/1; 141/5; 136/4. Values are taken from official valuations assembled by D. W. Jones from the Inspector General's Ledgers.

level playing field than enthusiastic contemporary observers and later Adam Smith were to suggest.

The age distribution of these 58 leading merchants shows that the first requirement of success was physical survival. The mean age of these top traders in 1686 was 44. None of these men was aged below 30 and the eldest was 72 but there was heavy clustering with almost 50 per cent in their 30s and a marked falling off in older age groups with around 20 per cent in their 40s and 20 per cent in their 50s.[15] Mean age of death among this group was 66 which suggests that (unless there was a dramatic change in merchant life expectancy in one generation) after taking around 20 years to build up a substantial trade many withdrew by choice. Surviving wills and inventories show that these merchants managed to accumulate sufficient capital to diversify investment into joint stocks, government debt, urban property for rent, shipowning, and industry.[16] A preference for a relatively secure rentier life-style rather than the intensely hard work and high risks of overseas trade is unsurprising. It seems plausible that the accumulation of commercial capital and the demand for investment opportunities offering high liquidity and a relatively secure return helped stimulate the

available in wills, inventories, court records and business papers is uneven. For fuller discussion, see Nuala Zahedieh, *The Capital and Commerce. London and the Plantation Trade in the Late Seventeenth Century* (forthcoming).

[15] The best sources for data on age were court depositions. Age data was obtained for 48 men. PRO HCA 13/77–80; HCA 14/55–7; C24/1129–35; Corporation of London Record Office (hereafter CLRO) Mayors Court Depositions, MCD 40–2.

[16] For example, see inventory of William Walker, CLRO, CSB v, 184.

Table 2

Merchants in London's colonial import trade, 1686

Value of trade £ sterling	0–99	100–999	1,000– 4,999	5,000– 9,999	10,000 +	TOTAL
West Indies						
Number of merchants	742	427	86	15	13	1,283
Value of trade, £	25,845	101,847	187,533	118,104	217,186	674,518
% of total	3.5	20	28	17.5	32	100
North America						
Number of merchants	339	172	38	5	2	556
Value of trade, £	10,972	57,923	77,078	32,992	28,166	207,131
% of total	5	28	37	16	14	100

Source: PRO E190/143/1; 137/2. Values are taken from official valuations assembled by D. W. Jones from the Inspector General's Ledgers.

London-based 'financial revolution' of the 1690s.[17] A number of these men bought a country house in the style of a weekend retreat in a village adjacent to London: Stoke Newington, Hackney, Kingston and Richmond all being popular. Only a handful, such as Gilbert Heathcote who bought land in Lincolnshire and Rutland, bought sizeable country estates and proved able or desirous of making the transition into the landed gentry.[18]

The leading colonial merchants of 1686 were 'new men' not only in the sense of having built up capital through accumulation in trade but also in the sense that only around one-third of the group were born in London. Almost half of the men were born in the country and the remainder came from overseas including the major tobacco merchant Micajah Perry who was born in New England and a number of Jews born in France, Portugal, and Spain. Thus, few were stepping into an established family firm although in the 30 cases where the father's occupation is known, 51 per cent were merchants, 26 per cent were

[17] P. G. M. Dickson, *The Financial Revolution in England: A Study in the Development of Public Credit, 1688–1757* (1967).
[18] Evelyn D. Heathcote, *An Account of Some of the Families Bearing the Name of Heathcote* (Winchester, 1899). Romney Sedgwick, *The History of Parliament: The House of Commons, 1715–1754* (2 vols, Oxford, 1970).

tradesmen, 15 per cent were gentlemen, and 7 per cent were yeomen or husbandmen.

These middling origins are not surprising. Any examination of the day-to-day workings of Atlantic commerce makes clear that although a thorough classical education was viewed as unnecessary a good basic education was essential. Every merchant needed to write large numbers of letters (every cargo consignment in and out involved several letters sent in duplicate and one copy retained for reference) and although family members, apprentices, and clerks shared the burden the merchant wrote many himself as his handwriting was a guarantee of authenticity. The first prerequisite for the intending merchant was the command of a pen and the acquisition of a good hand preferably 'not crampt up to a set secretary like a scrivener's boy; not scrawling long-tails like a wench at boarding school, but a neat charming mixture of Roman and Italian flowing with a kind of negligence'. In addition he needed good arithmetical skills and a thorough knowledge of 'that noble method of debtor and creditor' double-entry book-keeping.[19] These skills could be learnt at school and the number of establishments teaching writing and arithmetic for merchants proliferated in the late seventeenth century.[20]

In addition to receiving a basic education most men in the sample seem to have served an apprenticeship with a merchant (even when the father's citizenship made the son free of a livery company). This was the way to learn about the intricacies of charter parties, bills of lading, invoices, contracts, bills of exchange, insurance policies, weights and measures, and other details of business which included a host of unwritten, customary practices. It was important too to acquire some knowledge of the goods traded and an eye for quality and price. Above all, it gave access to networks of tried and tested correspondents. Merchants in this sample were bound between the ages of 14 and 18 (with a mean age of 15.6) to masters from a wide range of livery companies: Clothmakers, Dyers, Embroiderers, Fishmongers, Grocers, Haberdashers, Ironmongers, Mercers, Merchant Taylors, Upholders, Vintners, and Weavers. The premium was £200 to £300: a substantial sum equal to that Gregory King suggested as the typical annual income of a family from the merchant classes.[21] An additional premium was payable if the apprentice served abroad and it was clearly commonplace

[19] *Honest, Loyal Merchant*, 7.

[20] An advertisement for instruction of merchants' accounts allow the most 'exact, plain, short, full and practical method' is in BL *Tracts on Trade*, 41.

[21] Discussion of the appropriate education for an intending merchant is often found in wills and subsequent litigation. For example, PRO Prob 11/401, Will of Thomas Brailsford, 16 Sept. 1690; PRO C9/177/28, Brailsford and Taylors v. Peeres and Tooke.

but not universal.[22] The training aspect of apprenticeship was more valued than access to civic political and social life. Only 65 per cent of those apprenticed took up freedom of the city although this meant that they were liable for less duties and customs on their goods than unfreemen.[23] Furthermore, many delayed taking the freedom until years after ending their apprenticeship. Fourteen men in the group (around a quarter) did become involved in city politics as common council men or aldermen.[24]

An intending merchant did not need great financial resources beyond the premium paid on being apprenticed. It was usual to start trading on one's own account before completing service and accumulated savings were augmented with loans from family, inheritance, and marriage.[25] The average age of marriage among this group of leading merchants was 27, by which stage they would have been several years out of an apprenticeship. Almost two-thirds of the wives were London bred coming overwhelmingly from the merchant/tradesmen classes. In the limited number of cases where information is available portions were as high as £1,000 or more: a large sum among London's middling sort. A rich widow or an heiress drew covetous glances. A wife with a fortune was a great asset to the aspiring merchant, especially if she also possessed literacy, numeracy, and good household management skills.[26]

All businessmen augmented their capital base through credit. Every link in the long chain of transactions involved in transporting goods to and fro across the Atlantic was joined by credit which was, remarked Nicholas Barbon, 'the value raised by opinion' or reputation.[27] Reputation was built on a code of conduct which combined rules of reason and religion; interest and honour; a blend of pragmatism and idealism which promised deviants punishment from God, a stinging conscience, and damage to pocket and pride. The prototype merchant of reputation appears in contemporary print literature as a paragon of prudence,

[22] PRO Prob 11/360, fos. 321–323 Will of John Gould, 15 Apr. 1678; CLRO MC6/452A Case of John Booth and Basil Booth v. William Coward.

[23] Unfreemen (such as William Freeman) could avoid higher duties by trading in partnership with a freeman (William Baxter) to whom goods were consigned. Institute of Jamaica, Kingston, Jamaica (hereafter IJ), MS. 134, Letterbook of William Freeman, Letter, 6 Sept. 1680.

[24] William Barnes, Thomas Clarke, John and Francis Eyles, John Gardner, William Gore, Bartholomew Gracedieu, Gilbert Heathcote, John Jeffries, Jacob Lucy, Joseph Martin, Benjamin Skutt, Richard Tilden, William Walker.

[25] Massachusetts Historical Society, Boston (hereafter MHS), Jeffries Family Papers, VII, Francis Clarke to David Jeffries, fo. 66.

[26] Josiah Child claimed that attention to the education of women as well as men was a reason for Dutch success in commerce. Josiah Child, *A Discourse Concerning Trade* (1693), 4–6.

[27] Nicholas Barbon, *A Discourse of Trade* (1690), 27.

wisdom, and justice.[28] He was knowledgeable about his business (familiar with countries, ports, shipping routes, commodities, financial and legal instruments and much else). He knew, understood, and abided by merchant custom. He was diligent but careful not to overreach his mental or physical resources. He was cautious in extending and taking credit. He regulated his domestic expenses for 'expensive living ... [is] sure to kill: for it feeds upon the two most essential branches of his trade, his credit and his cash'.[29] He kept careful accounts and often inspected his affairs. He displayed 'justice' or fairness in his dealings; performed his promises; paid and demanded a fair price for his goods; was exact about weights and measures and provided good quality produce. He paid his bills and debts promptly and took especial care not to go bankrupt 'upon design' in order to defraud creditors of their dues for here was 'stealing, notorious hypocrisy and dissimulation; contempt of God's law and justice and injury to men'.[30] The first task for a young man embarking on a career in trade was to establish his own reputation in order to attract custom and credit. In a very real sense a man's reputation was his capital, 'wealth is the result of credit and credit is the effect of fair dealing'.[31] When Claypoole recommended business with John Bawden, London's leading West India merchant in partnership with John Gardner, he pointed to his having as great estate and repute as few beyond him in the city.[32] Both were essential. Business with a poor man was risky but business with a dishonest man was simply foolishness.

A good training and reputation were necessary but they were not sufficient ingredients for success and they were shared by many less successful merchants. The task of deciding who to trust was where the real difficulties lay. As Richard Steele warned,

> Great prudence is necessary in the choice of ... whom to trust, for it is not always the metal that glitters most that is always the richest. Men are often deceitful and make it their business to enrich themselves with the spoils of the unwary and credulous. It is better therefore to be at the pains of a diligent inquiry after their abilities for the trust that we repose in them; than endure the grief of sad experience that we were mistaken in our apprehensions concerning them. Certain it is that there is prudence in trusting some, and

[28] Examples include *Honest, Loyal Merchant*; Richard Steele, *A Tradesman's Calling* (1686); *A Description of Plain Dealing, Truth and Death which all Men Ought to Mind whilst they do Live on Earth* (1686).

[29] Steele, *Tradesman's Calling*, 31.

[30] Ibid, 58.

[31] Anon., *Case of the Fair Trader* (1686).

[32] *James Claypoole's Letterbook, London and Philadelphia, 1681–1684*, ed. Marion Balderston (San Marino, 1967), 173 and 183.

charity in trusting others; so there are many whom it is neither prudence nor charity to trust at all.[33]

Examination of the lengthy, complex round of transactions involved in colonial exchange reveals the heavy need to trust the fidelity, diligence, and honesty of others. The first task was to assemble a wide range of manufactures and provisions for shipment outwards. Goods were drawn from London, the provinces, and abroad and as every parcel could not be checked suppliers were trusted to provide the quantity and quality required at a fair price.[34] The goods needed to be packed with skill and care to ensure minimum damage: hats and books were packed in boxes; Cheshire cheeses were sewn in canvas and tarred to protect them from rats; in 1679 a coach was packed with masses of haircloth and almost 30 yards of flannel.[35] The cargo was then consigned to a ship's captain who needed to be trusted to make the long, dangerous transatlantic sea-crossing as quickly as possible with minimum damage and embezzlement.[36] On arrival in the colonies an agent collected the consignment, dealt with the freight and legal formalities, put the goods into merchantable condition, and sold for the best possible price to good paymasters without cheating on the returns.[37] Back in London there was no central market place for colonial goods. They were sold with a great deal of haggling and great skill was needed in judging the depth of the purchaser's pocket. As Claypoole retorted on being told he was outsold by another, it was easy to sell for a high price to a man who was about to go broke.[38] The entire round of transactions extended well beyond a year – often as many as three – and at every stage agents were in a position to undo the principal. Accidents such as fire, bad weather, or plunder could be insured against for between 3 and 7 per cent in peacetime and analysis of the naval officer's returns in Jamaica suggests that this reflected the real level of risk even in the pirate-infested Caribbean.[39] The much greater frequency with which mishaps and disappointing returns are reported in letters and court records suggests a screen for bad judgement or, worse, perfidy. Captains wanting to explain shortfalls in the cargo claimed goods were thrown overboard; entire cargoes were eaten by rats; fire on board was caused by a slave woman smoking between the decks. Disappointing prices

[33] Steele, *Tradesman's Calling*, 28.

[34] Barbon, *Discourse*, 12.

[35] MHS, Jeffries Family Papers, VII, fo. 124.

[36] Davis, *English Shipping Industry*, 122–32.

[37] Richard Ligon, *A True and Exact History of Barbadoes* (1657), 111; Letters from the Halls in Port Royal, Jamaica, 1688–92, provide a detailed insight into the work of colonial correspondents. PRO C110/152, Brailsford v. Peers and Tooke.

[38] *Claypoole's Letterbook*, ed. Balderston, 149.

[39] PRO CO 142/13, Naval Officer's Returns, Jamaica, 1682–1705.

were explained by gluts, scarcities, or poor quality goods: the beer was sour, the colour ran in the stockings, the shoes were all for left feet, the hats were too small.[40] Excuses abounded but, not surprisingly, merchants often suspected the defendants' veracity. Suppliers, packers, captains, colonial correspondents were all in a position to undo him and as misplaced trust was the major source of loss, fraud limitation was the main preoccupation of players in the game.

Information about character and wrong doing was eagerly sought. In London each man's credit was determined by talk at the merchants' meeting place, the Royal Exchange. Claypoole visited daily and was scathing about the less conscientious. Merchant correspondence is full of requests for information about others and what amounts to informal character references. One merchant advised his correspondent against trusting Charles Tumer who is a 'young man of little experience and has too many sorts of trade to thrive. I like him none the better for bragging.' He was more encouraging about another who although 'a soft unthinking man' had a 'noteable, stirring wife' who 'by her diligence hath put him in a way to live'. Haitswell was strongly recommended as 'very diligent and capable to do business' being honest, sober and not given to any extravagance. But information travelled slowly from the colonies and was only as good as the provider who was often as distant from retribution as the subject of enquiry.[41] Collusion was commonplace.

Various incentives were offered for good behaviour. Remunerations were higher in colonial trade than in other branches of commerce. Captains were paid 20 per cent more than those engaged on European voyages.[42] Factors in the colonial trades were paid 8 to 10 per cent commission compared with 2 or 3 per cent in France, Spain, and Portugal and as little as 1.5 per cent in Holland.[43] Every effort was made to ensure loyalty through offering repeat business and exclusive agency. Undertaking reciprocal services which ensured mutual dependence was perhaps the most promising strategy for promoting good behaviour. Every effort was made to reinforce all strategies by nurturing goodwill through exchange of news and gifts.[44] Unfortunately, for many

[40] Examples abound in High Court of Admiralty depositions. PRO HCA 13/79–81, 131, 132.

[41] *Claypooles Letterbook*, ed. Balderston, 183, 119–20, 127, Thomas Knight to Thomas Brailsford, 24 April 1690, PRO C110/152, Brailsford v. Peers and Tooke.

[42] Masters in the West India trade were paid £6 per month in the 1680s and given the benefit of free freight to the value of £200 or so. PRO HCA 13/79.

[43] H.N. *The Compleat Tradesman* (1686), 155.

[44] Printed and manuscript merchant correspondence are rich sources. Examples include: *Claypoole's Letterbook*, ed. Balderston; *The Correspondence of the Three William Byrds of Westover Virginia, 1684–1776* (Charlottesville, Va., 1977); *William Fitzhugh and his Chesapeake World, 1676–1701. The Fitzhugh Letters and Other Documents*, ed. R. B. Davis (Chapel Hill, NC, 1963) MHS, Jeffries Family Papers; PRO C110/152, Brailsford v. Peers and Tooke.

merchants the returns to cheating were so high and the risks of quick discovery so low that generous commissions and mutuality often counted for little. It took William Freeman (William Baxter's partner) eight years to realise the extent of his losses in Montserrat at the hands of 'a crafty, undermining sophister' who through embezzlement had 'raised to himself a very considerable estate'.[45] Freeman's plight was commonplace and the law, regarded by many as a blunt instrument for recovering losses at home, was an even blunter instrument for preventing or punishing crime across the Atlantic. The difficulty of obtaining evidence and witnesses who could testify from 'beyond the sea' left many merchants without effective legal remedy.[46]

Given the very high risks of colonial trade it is not surprising that while large numbers participated relatively few survived and flourished. Small traders and first-timers had less leverage than large, repeat customers and were most likely to suffer neglect or fraud on the part of agents. The importance of well-chosen agents in the success of the 58 merchants considered here is reflected in high levels of regional specialisation. Only six of the leading merchants had trade with both North America and the West Indies and 44 of the group concentrated over 80 per cent of their trade to one destination on the mainland or in the Caribbean. It seems plausible to suggest that this strong specialisation by port stemmed from the overwhelming necessity of firm, reliable credit networks dependent on little more than the fragile ties of reciprocity and reputation and the difficulty of maintaining more than very few such relationships.

Ready-made trust networks were clearly important tools for the aspiring merchant but for most people they were confined to kin networks. Many merchants echoed Ashurst's pleadings to his cousin Hampden that 'upon the score of relation as well as your own interest you will do what you can in the sales'.[47] Gilbert Heathcote, the most successful of the merchants treated here, had six brothers spread between Jamaica, New York, the Baltic, and London. Bartholomew Gracedieu had a brother in Jamaica and Dalby Thomas had a brother in Barbados. Others had similar family links. However, families frequently failed to meet expectations: cousins, nephews, siblings, and even fathers and sons often proved disappointing. Merchant correspondence is littered with tales of recalcitrant kin folk.[48] The pool of family members was limited (the merchants in the sample had an average of three children) and the number with talent often even more

[45] IJ, MS. 134, 'Letterbook of William Freeman', fo. 387, letter, 14 Sept. 1682.
[46] PRO E112/475/2127.
[47] Bodleian Library, Ashurst Letterbook, MS Dom. c 169 p. 35, Letter 5 Aug. 1684.
[48] *Claypoole's Letterbook*, ed. Balderston, 184, 219, PRO C110/152, Brailsford v. Peers and Tooke.

so. Sentiment was more likely to cloud information and judgement when dealing with family members; family members' fortunes were likely to be positively correlated reducing their efficacy as a safety net in a crisis; family discipline was often undermined by inheritance arrangements, particularly among those from the landed classes where primogeniture (giving one child an unconditional inheritance and the rest little) was the norm but also among the middling sorts where, although there might be a more even division, sons often received little beyond the cost of training and apprenticeship.[49] Exclusion from the family circle was not always viewed with horror.

Although the livery companies had no formal role in regulating colonial trade it might have been expected that their dinners, their courts of arbitration, and their various social arrangements would promote information exchange and offer possibilities for mutual support. Five of these leading merchants belonged to the Haberdashers' Company, whose members had always been overseas merchants and traditionally specialised in importing the types of wares now exported in large quantites to the colonies.[50] However, the remaining merchants were spread so thinly between different companies that it does not seem that these associations played a major role in Atlantic trade.

Religious networks proved more robust. Religion is difficult to determine and is reasonably certain for only 31 of these 58 merchants. The ten or so Quakers and seven Jews (together comprising almost one-third of the sample) are most readily identified underlining the separateness which seems to have given them an advantage in colonial trade.[51] A hint at the reason for the heavy representation of these religious minorities is gleaned from the structure of their trade. Whereas, in general, merchants focused trade on one destination, these merchants spread their trade and trust more widely.

The importance of Quakers in colonial commerce is well established but a secular explanation is as important as the usual emphasis on the content of their beliefs and code of conduct which differed little from that exhorted in all contemporary advice manuals designed to deal with problems presented in an increasingly impersonal commercial

[49] Y. Ben-Porath, 'The F-Connection: Families, Friends and Firms and the Organization of Exchange', *Pop. Dev. Review*, 6 (1980), 1–30.

[50] The Haberdashers were Francis Eyles (it is usually assumed that John Eyles was also a Haberdasher but there is no record of his membership in company records), Joseph Martin, Richard Merriweather, Micajah Perry, Thomas Starke. On the company, see Ian W. Archer, *The History of the Haberdasher's Company* (Chichester, 1991).

[51] Probable and certain Quakers include William Barnes, Thomas Clarke, William Coward, William Crouch, John Crow, Robert Curtis, John Daveson, Samuel Groome, Henry Hale, John Harwood, John Taylor, William Wrayford. Jewish merchants were Moses Barrow (otherwise Anthony Lauzado), Joseph Bueno, Anthony Gomezsera, Peter and Pierre Henriques, Manuel Mendez, Emanuel Perara.

world revolving around reputation and trust.[52] What set the Quakers apart was their ability to enforce the code and transmit information about character and wrong doing. By the late seventeenth century there was a Quaker meeting in almost every colony as well as in every county of England with a yearly meeting in London acting as the hub for both information and regulation. Meetings sent regular communications and when the Yearly Meeting compiled a code of conduct it was copied out and sent to meetings everywhere.[53] Quaker doctrines, wrote William Crouch, were 'short and plain' eschewing the 'contemplation and speculation of difficult things which are more curious than useful to piety and goodness'. Their 'most conspicuous virtue', he continued, was a 'diligent love, care and watchfulness over those of their faction especially as to their religious concerns'.[54] Friends were instructed to watch over one another, and correct any ill-conduct in personal or business matters, ensuring adherence to rules against over-trading or breaking trust in any way and they were notoriously hard on those who failed in business. Culpable bankruptcy was ground for disownment, that is expulsion from the meeting, which was a powerful deterrent to men like Crouch who participated in a total Quaker life-style: living in a Quaker neighbourhood and attending meetings most days.

The discipline of the meeting was reinforced by the communication networks between meetings. Distant Quakers would not only provide detailed business information about their own members but also good general intelligence.[55] Friends needed to carry certificates of clearance and introduction when they travelled between meetings. Finally, they provided solid support to all members whether familiar or strangers, helping Friends to get apprenticeships, set up in business, providing custom and financial assistance in time of crisis.[56] The journal of George Welch, a young Quaker who in 1671 travelled to the West Indies 'to improve himself', records the warmth and hospitality of his reception by his co-religionists although they had no previous acquaintance with him.[57]

Jewish success was equally striking and again may be attributed to effective communication and trust networks based on an enforceable

[52] F. B. Tolles, *Meeting House and Counting House. The Quaker Merchants of Colonial Philadelphia, 1682–1763 (Chapel Hill, NC, 1948)*.

[53] Friends House, London, Yearly Meeting Minutes, I, 19–20, 27 March 1675.

[54] William Crouch, *Posthuma Christiana or a Collection of Some Papers of William Crouch Being a Brief Historical Account under his own Hand* (1712), 131, 182.

[55] Friends House, Epistles Received, Vol. 1 (1683–1706); Minutes, I, 19–20, 27 March 1675.

[56] T. Story, *A Journal of the Life of Thomas Story* (Newcastle, 1747).

[57] American Philosophical Society Library, Philadelphia (hereafter APSL), MS. 917, 29/WH55, George Welch, 'A Journal of My Voyage in 1671'.

code of conduct. Jewish commercial success had long rested on importing and processing colonial products together with the bullion and jewel trades and export of manufactured goods to Iberian America. The community had a number of advantages when operating in high-risk enterprises. Firstly, the universal precariousness of Jewish life favoured subjection to discipline and authority. Boards of elders nominated each year from among a congregation's wealthiest members could exert authoritarian, even despotic, rule. It was not simply a question of upholding the Torah and pursuing the moral ideals of Judaism. Anything likely to disrupt the unity of the congregation or provoke popular hatred was seen as a threat to the community. Boards of elders controlled charity, sick care, and education; exercised moral and intellectual censorship; arbitrated in business disputes; and maintained a formidable grip over any aspect of Jewish life. Congregants, unless they wished to be cast adrift among the gentiles, had little choice but to comply. Secondly, the history of persecution and expulsion had moulded a tradition of adaptability and mobility to mitigate the relentless and repeated hardships of the wandering Jew. Thirdly, the scattered community was linked not only by religion but also by kinship, language, culture and commercial interest across boundaries between different empires and all to some extent in the mid-seventeenth century revolved around the hub of Sephardim in Amsterdam.[58]

The Sephardi transit trade between Europe and Iberian America took new shape in the 1650s. The Jews were expelled from Brazil after the Portuguese defeated the Dutch in 1654 and the community of 4,000 or so fanned out all over the Caribbean. At this time new opportunities opened up in the English system with the establishment of sugar planting in Barbados and the capture of Jamaica which provided a base for illicit trade with the Spanish colonies.[59] The Navigation Acts made it strategic for those wishing to participate in English colonial commerce to have representatives in the English plantations and London. At the same time arguments were gaining ground for readmitting the Jews to England and benefiting from their commercial expertise and connections. A new community was established in London in 1657;

[58] J. I. Israel, *European Jewry in the Age of Mercantilism, 1550–1750* (Oxford, 1985), 154–8. Herbert I. Bloom, *The Economic Activities of the Jews in Amsterdam in the Seventeenth and Eighteenth Centuries* (Williamsburg, 1939). The depositions of an Admiralty Court Case of 1672 provide detailed information about the wandering careers of a group of prominent Jewish merchants. PRO HCA 13/77, Abraham Perera and Anthony Gomezsera v. Jacob Calloway, 25 Sept. 1672.

[59] On the rapid penetration of Jews into Jamaica's contraband commerce, see Nuala Zahedieh, 'The Capture of the Blue Dove, 1664, Policy, Profits, and Protection in Early English Jamaica', in *West Indies Accounts, Essays on the History of the British Caribbean and the Atlantic Economy in Honour of Richard Sheridan*, ed. R. McDonald (Kingston, Jamaica, 1996), 29–47.

in Barbados in the 1650s; and in Jamaica in the 1660s. All numbered around 300 by the 1680s.[60] In 1686, although there were only a few hundred Jews in London all told, there were 7 among the 22 largest exporters from London to the West Indies. Access to reliable information about reputation backed by strong guarantees of good behaviour provided the Jews with a competitive advantage which underpinned their substantial role in Atlantic commerce.

England's westward expansion in the seventeenth century opened up a wide range of opportunities for economic advancement. These were pursued with a vigour and enthusiasm which resulted in the rapid rise of colonial trade after the Restoration and contributed to a substantial restructuring of the national economy which underpinned accelerated growth in the eighteenth century. Although in the interests of national security, the colonial trade was closed to foreigners it was open to all Englishmen. Many men of middling background with sound education and modest means could (and did) enter but close examination of the trade suggests that, although necessary, these were not sufficient grounds for success. Colonial trade was attended with high risks. The commerce was based on a long chain of promises: promises to provide goods, promises to deliver, promises to pay. The importance of trust required merchants to pay careful attention to publicising their own probity while taking adequate steps to ensure the good character of others. The pivotal role of trust and reputation was reflected in the structure of the trade which, despite being celebrated as open to all, quickly became concentrated in relatively few hands with high levels of regional specialisation. Merchants reduced risks not by spreading business between as many agents as possible but by confining themselves to a few well-tried and trusted correspondents with whom a standing relationship was reinforced where possible by mutuality and repeat business. Furthermore, the nature of risk in colonial commerce placed groups such as the Quakers or Jews in a strong position which is reflected in their numbers among the most successful (far higher than would be predicted from their total numbers in the population) and the more dispersed nature of their trade. Their strength drew partly on their 'awe of God and conscience' but perhaps more on the community leaders' ability to enforce good conduct and information flows. A somewhat revised and secularised version of the Weber thesis reinstates the importance of the discipline and integrity achieved by some religious groups in the forefront of explanations of economic change: making mercantilism work.

---

[60] Maurice Woolf, 'Foreign Trade of London Jews in the Seventeenth Century', *Jewish Historical Society of England Transactions (hereafter JHSET)*, XIII (1932–5), 1–97. Richard S Dunn, *Sugar and Slaves. The Rise of the Planter Class in the English West Indies, 1624–1713 (Chapel Hill, NC, 1972)*, 106–8, 183.

ORAL HISTORY, MEMORY AND
WRITTEN TRADITION

ORAL HISTORY, MEMORY AND WRITTEN TRADITION: AN INTRODUCTION

By Patricia M. Thane, University of Sussex

WHEN, in the 1970s, historians of the recent past began seriously to explore the uses of oral history they were, as Alistair Thomson points out in this volume, much criticised for uncritical reliance upon the frailties of human memory. Not all such criticism was misplaced, but, as Thomson describes, the past quarter-century of scepticism and experience has immensely refined the ways in which the method is used and its outcomes interpreted. Yet many historians continue to value documentary over oral sources to a surprising degree, given the extent to which documents throughout history have been derived from oral sources, or were written versions of unspoken memories. If there are serious methodological problems confronting interpretations of the recent past which depend upon memory, such problems arise at least equally for other time periods. The value of the essays which follow, and of the conference at which they were read, is in the focus on the common methodological problems posed to historians and anthropologists of very different time periods and cultures by memory and its oral and written expression: issues of what people do and do not remember, of why and how memory is used to interpret past and present.

An influential interpretation of historical change, which all of the essays challenge, is of a long-run shift from almost purely oral to purely literary cultures, in the course of which individual memory came to be less important to society and less valued. On one level, of course, this is so. In the ninth century the great majority of people, and even in the seventeenth century a very high proportion of people, even in the most highly developed societies, could not read and had little direct contact with literary texts. In the twentieth century the great majority of people in such societies can read and literary, and also visual, artefacts play extensive and inescapable roles in their lives. Yet a fascinating theme connecting the essays which follow is the importance of literary texts from very early times and the continuing importance of oral transmission in the late twentieth century; the extent to which orality and literacy have always interacted, and exploration of the circumstances in which they do so.

Patrick Geary discusses what has been seen as the classic period of transition in Europe from the oral culture of the early Middle Ages to a culture of the written word in the late eleventh and twelfth centuries. He emphasises the importance of written records in early medieval Europe, especially in relation to legal transactions, and focuses particularly upon their use in land disputes. These were not purely literary documents but records of oral statements and indeed they were often written to be read aloud in court. They were not of trivial importance because land was overwhelmingly important to the families of medieval Europe who possessed it or aspired to do so. To safeguard against disputes about title to land, written legal records were produced which were often derived from memories of how and by what means the family had acquired the land. Such title could be challenged only by competing memories. Illiterate juries called upon to decide in such disputes were dependent upon oral testimony and the reading aloud of documents. The outcome of disputes of such importance to early medieval society depended upon the interpretation of fallible, or manipulable, human memory and upon written as well as oral testimony. Written testimony could be doubly unreliable, for documents could be forged. As Geary concludes, in this period at least 'orality and literacy are not competing ways of understanding the retention and communication of the past'. Rather they were inseparably connected and neither oral nor literary sources are indisputably reliable.

Sarah Foot points to the similar interaction of oral and documentary evidence in the different context of the construction of representations of the past in early medieval England. In general at this time documents, like the legal sources described by Geary, existed primarily as aids to memory and as records of oral transactions. Such historical texts as survive, such as Bede's *Historia Ecclesiastica*, make clear their dependence upon oral testimony, placing great weight upon the trustworthiness of the memories of eyewitnesses. In certain circumstances memory and oral history became especially salient in the construction of understandings of the past, especially when surviving documents were destroyed by war or other catastrophes. Our knowledge of the distant past is heavily dependent on past oral histories. Foot describes the cataclysmic effects of the Danish wars of the ninth century. The upheavals especially disrupted ecclesiastical communities and as monasteries disappeared so did archives. With the loss of so many documentary sources, memory, forgetfulness and silence played a central role in shaping the understandings of the past of later generations, since this was all they had. Similar processes were to follow other profound disruptions, such as the sixty-year silence of the chroniclers following the Norman Conquest.[1]

A caesura of this kind presents an opportunity not only for historians

---

[1] Elisabeth van Houts, *Memory and Gender in Europe, 900–1200* (London, 1999).

of later generations seeking to reconstruct some more-or-less accurate understanding of past events, but also for myth-makers seeking to construct a version of the past convenient for their present purposes. In Foot's account King Alfred took advantage of the historical silence to invent a past which filled the void left by the Viking wars, a new version of a political past which promoted and legitimated the ideal of a single people. The 'invention of tradition' is itself no modern invention, as Hobsbawm oddly claims, nor is it clear that it has quite distinctive modern forms.[2] The narrative inspired by Alfred was preserved in written chronicles, but re-told orally, so that future generations mistook for pure oral tradition tales originating in written texts.

Fox illustrates this process at work as he describes the continued intersection of orality and literacy in sixteenth- and seventeenth-century England, both in the law courts and in constructions of history. He and also Wood challenge the narrative which represents literacy as a modernising force thrusting inexorably through medieval and early modern European culture, eroding oral tradition, diminishing the importance of locality, memory and the status of the guardians of memory – old people, or, rather, old men – reinforcing the power of the social and political elite, who wielded their literacy to subordinate the illiterate.

The story told below by the early modernists as by the medievalists is more complex and interesting, and stresses the continuing importance of orality in certain circumstances in early modern England. Both Fox and Wood describe the continuing importance of old men's memories in disputes over customary law. Legal documents were still primarily written *aides-mémoire* constructed from 'memories', which might be far from pure disinterested recollection if elicited, for example, from a venerable member of a community engaged in defending what it believed were its common rights. As Wood points out, illiterate village communities were, when necessary, as ready as their landlords to construct written texts to defend their version of history: 'even illiterate villagers were not intimidated by the written word'. There was not a straightforward conflict between literate elite and illiterate mass. Both could manipulate written and oral sources, and in consequence both types of source were suspect. The process of negotiation between the sides created new versions of tradition to be handed on to subsequent generations.

Fox describes a similar intertwining of oral and literary influences on perceptions of the past in early modern England. In this period, when a modern conception of scholarly history was only beginning to emerge, both written and oral accounts of the past could be confused

---

[2] Eric Hobsbawm and Terence Ranger, *The Invention of Tradition* (Cambridge, 1983), 1.

and mythic. The confusions in oral accounts noted by contemporaries were not only due to the fallibility of memory, but to confusions, errors and inventions in the written texts from which 'oral traditions' often derived. As newly arrived gentry produced bogus versions of their family histories to promote their status, and as towns and institutions fabricated and cherished myths of their antiquity and venerability, such inventions were often absorbed as fact into oral accounts. Oral culture drew on literary culture. As written sources proliferated in the forms of sermons, broadsheets, poetry, drama and much else, they enriched rather than impoverished oral 'tradition'. Fox concludes: 'written culture was probably more culpable than oral in the fabrication and perpetuation of distorted, exaggerated and spurious versions of the past'.

It might be thought that in the highly literate cultures of twentieth-century Europe and North America at last the importance of individual memory and its oral expression would be diminished and the culture of literacy dominate, whilst, as Pat Caplan describes, orality retains more obvious prominence in African and other cultures. Yet Thomson describes below the importance of story-telling for a marginalised community in New York State in the late twentieth century, and he and Kedward clearly demonstrate that memory, expressed orally, is still an important resource for understanding central features of recent European history. As Kedward puts it, modern archives, though they may delight, can also disappoint with their silences on important issues. Oral history became an influential technique in 1970s Britain, with its relatively peaceable recent domestic history, as an adjunct to the growth of social history and the accompanying recognition that aspects of everyday life in which there was growing interest, such as relationships within families, were poorly recorded in documentary sources, but potentially available through the careful use of oral history. In this respect oral history has enriched the resources of the twentieth-century historian. But its value is not confined to the study of the private and the domestic. In less peaceable environments, which have been regrettably no less prevalent in the twentieth century than in earlier periods, oral history can, as in earlier times, be the only means to explore more public and more violent episodes. Thomson and Kedward demonstrate that in the recent as in the distant past, war and other situations of extreme danger, such as occupation by a foreign power or an oppressive political system, as in eastern Europe before 1989, in South Africa under apartheid, in some colonial regimes, can force communication into secrecy, disrupt the documentary record and give greater saliency to oral communication and memory. Kedward describes how waitresses in a Warsaw cafe during the Nazi occupation memorised overheard conversations of drunken officers of the Wehrmacht and provided essential intelligence to the allies.

As Kedward points out, memory is important not only *of* war but *in* war. Memory in war, or other form of crisis, can be important in differing ways. As Kedward describes, memories of past traditions, real or invented, can inspire individuals and communities to resist unwanted forms of rule when other sources of leadership and inspiration are lacking, as in the anti-colonial struggles in southern Africa in the 1970s, or in east European communities before 1989. The trials of Papon and other suspected criminals of the Second World War have been dependent upon the memories *of* war, of victims and observers, in the absence of documentary evidence of many of the atrocities of twentieth-century Europe (and still fewer are the documents directly recording other horrors of the century in Cambodia and elsewhere). The trials have often been equivocal in their outcomes due to the difficulty of judging incontrovertibly among competing memories, between truth and falsehood. Major catastrophes in the twentieth as in the ninth or the eleventh centuries leave behind few or inadequate written records, leaving the historian dependent upon competing interpretations derived from memory, forgetfulness and deliberate falsification.

Awareness of their dependence upon memory and its oral transmission has made modern historians increasingly conscious of the problems of interpreting memories and of understanding why some things are remembered and others forgotten. This was first thoroughly explored in Luisa Passerini's study of the silences and inconsistencies in Italian working-class recollections of Mussolini's regime.[3] The difficulty of interpreting memory is another theme connecting the essays below and is most thoroughly discussed by Thomson and also by Caplan.

Thomson shows in his interviews with Australian veterans of the First World War that in the twentieth century, as in the seventeenth, oral accounts incorporate narratives drawn from documents, such as newspapers, which he can demonstrate were not strictly accurate. Some would dismiss such accounts as evidence of the unreliability of memory. Thomson rather treats them not as misrepresentations but by asking what they represent, as a resource which may not tell us about the subject's actual experience but can tell us much about how he or she has made sense of and learned to live with traumatic experiences. How human beings cope with catastrophe is as important to the historian as the fact of catastrophe. Recent developments in the interpretation of oral histories, influenced by anthropology, literary studies and psychoanalysis, combined with awareness, which is not just a product of postmodernism, that knowledge is always subjective, provisional and

---

[3] Luisa Passerini, *Fascism in Popular Memory: The Cultural Experience of the Turin Working Class* (1987).

partial, assist the interpretation of oral testimony and can bring us closer to understanding such terrible experiences as those of survivors of the Nazi concentration camps. Questions of why memories are presented in certain ways, why some 'memories' are borrowed, others drawn from personal experience, some hidden and some revealed reluctantly and partially have obvious relevance for historians of earlier as of later periods.

Another theme which connects these essays is: whose memory is recorded? The disputes about land transactions in early medieval Europe discussed by Geary revolved around 'the memories of know-ledgeable and trustworthy local men'. Young boys were present at important transactions in the hope that they would remember them in their later years, sometimes with the *aide-mémoire* of a good beating. A question remains about the reliability of such memories, a reliability more likely to be compromised the greater the self-interest involved, as Wood suggests about seventeenth-century conflicts over customary rights. Male recollection was normally publicly more credible than that of women and the reliability of female memory was much debated in medieval Europe, even though, as van Houts and Fox describe, stories which were part of the common culture were often passed down the female line. Van Houts finds that in medieval as in early modern times, the testimonies of 'good women' were accepted in cases involving sexuality (such as rape) or motherhood, about which women were thought – reasonably enough – to have special knowledge. But this gendered separation of spheres of public testimony can provide incom-plete histories. The silence of women in documentary sources and public accounts of past events was one reason for the growth of oral history in recent times. Kedward, when interviewing male members of the French Resistance, came gradually to notice the woman listening in the background, providing the drinks, occasionally intervening and correcting the man's account, and to wonder whether 'the woman in the doorway' perhaps played a similar unobtrusive, unremembered but essential role in the Resistance, 'prolonging police enquiries, misleading their search, feigning ignorance, covering tracks'. As indeed she did, but this was unremembered in conventional narratives of the Resistance because such actions were apparently unheroic and merely an extension of women's everyday role; just as Wehrmacht officers fatally forgot that waitresses carrying out unremarked everyday duties in a Warsaw cafe could have and use reliable memories. By widening the range of memories that are drawn upon, oral historians can extend the range of questions available to us and deepen our understanding of important events.

A related theme of several of the papers is the distinction and possible conflict between individual memory and what Halbwachs called 'collective' or social memory, the interpretation of the past accepted by a whole community.[4] Sarah Foot acutely questions whether 'memory' is an accurate or useful term for the process whereby a collective conception of a common past emerges. As she describes: 'the act of memory is personal and fallible, constructed by complex processes which influence selection and omission', rather than a conscious construct. Collective memories may emerge in this largely unguided way, as several of the essays suggest, but especially in situations of political sensitivity they may be the outcome of manipulation and control, as by King Alfred, or the seventeenth-century villagers safeguarding their customary rights by the conscious selection of memories for a particular purpose. Shaw interestingly discusses the different contexts in which elites stabilised the politics of fifteenth-century Siena by appealing at one time to a collective memory of traditional broadly based participation in government, at another to personal memories of the qualities of a small number of individuals.

In all time periods historians are dependent for the study of historical questions of central importance upon the transmission of memory, and we share difficulties of understanding how memories are constructed and are or are not made available, as well as the enormous problems of interpretation. In all periods memories have been transmitted in both oral and written forms. A particular problem for historians of the distant past, when oral transmission was the more common form, is their dependence upon written accounts of oral transactions, often, as with legal depositions, in stylised forms. An oral culture is peculiarly difficult to reconstruct historically. However, the problem that oral sources must be presented and interpreted in written form, and of how this is to be done, faces historians of all time periods, and also anthropologists, as Caplan recognises in her thoughtful reflections on the close methodological relationship between historians and anthropologists. Even Cabinet minutes are documentary representations and summaries of speech, and may select, distort or misrepresent the live speech. In Thomson's account of his interviews with two Australian veterans the historian is throughout as present as the speaker, interpreting the content, the modes of speech, the silences. Modern historians who have access to oral sources have a different set of problems from medievalists who do not. The sources of the former can answer back, as we can see in Kedward's description of the confrontation between veterans of the Resistance and the historians who questioned their collective interpretation of their own experience. Such conflicts raise ethical as well as methodological problems: should the historian responsibly challenge an interpretation of a difficult personal experience with

[4] Maurice Halbwachs, *Le Mémoire Collective* (Paris, 1950).

which the subject feels comfortable; how far should he or she go in stirring up deeply painful memories, such as experiences of the Holocaust, vital though such memories might be for our understanding of historical events of the greatest importance? There are no simple answers, but growing awareness in recent years of the issues raised in the papers which follow has broadened the interpretive scope and skills of historians of all time periods.

LAND, LANGUAGE AND MEMORY IN EUROPE
700–1100
By Patrick J. Geary

READ 27 MARCH 1998 AT THE UNIVERSITY OF SUSSEX[1]

LITERACY and property have been among the dominant themes of early medieval history for more than a decade. Since the work of Rosamund McKitterick, Janet Nelson and others, contrary to the assumptions of an earlier generation of scholars, scholars have recognised that the written word profoundly influenced the transmission of the past and the control of the present in early medieval Europe.[2] This was true not only in the highest circles of ecclesiastical and royal life, but also at much more humble levels across Europe. If, as Janet Nelson reminds us, even freedmen could still be referred to in the ninth century as '*cartularii*', literally charter-men, 'because of the written *carta* of manumission required by law courts as symbol and proof of liberation', the written word reached indeed deeply into society.[3]

Nowhere is the influence of the written word more evident than in questions of property. The recent volumes of essays on property and power edited by Wendy Davies and Paul Fouracre remind us forcefully of the way that land property dominates not only the exercise of power but more generally the archival record of the past.[4] Indeed, so thoroughly has land been the dominant subject of surviving archival material from before the twelfth century that the earlier volume produced by this remarkable group of scholars on the settlement of disputes in the early Middle Ages might almost have been subtitled

---

[1] Versions of this essay were delivered at the meeting of the Illinois Medieval Studies Association in February 1998 and at the Royal Historical Society conference, 'Oral History, Memory and Tradition', held at the University of Sussex in March 1998. The author benefited enormously from the discussions with participants at both meetings and wishes to thank in particular Elisabeth van Houts, Simon Keynes and Pongracz Sennyey for their advice and suggestions.

[2] Especially Rosamond McKitterick, *The Carolingians and the Written Word* (Cambridge, 1989), and Rosamond McKitterick, ed., *The Uses of Literacy in Early Mediaeval Europe* (Cambridge, 1990).

[3] Janet L. Nelson, 'Literacy in Carolingian Government', in *Uses of Literacy*, ed. McKitterick, 262.

[4] Wendy Davies and Paul Fouracre, eds, *Property and Power in the Early Middle Ages* (Cambridge, 1995).

'the settlement of disputes about land in the early Middle Ages'.[5]

Of course, conveyances and confirmations are one of the earliest and most significant forms of documentation, both in England and on the continent, to have survived from the early Middle Ages. While certainly not the only form of administrative instruments produced before the year thousand, they are the most common form of documentation that was deemed worth keeping through the centuries. We know, largely from formula collections, of the wide spectrum of instruments used in the early Middle Ages to establish or prove right. But those concerning persons, as the Janet Nelson's *cartae*, or those concerned with movables, normally ceased to have any use with the death or disappearance of the persons or things that they concerned. Unless they were written into a book or document that also preserved the most enduring of possessions, real property, normally they were allowed to disappear. Likewise, judicial records prior to the twelfth century only occasionally include actions concerning persons or movables.[6] They are overwhelmingly *placita* concerning disputes over real property, preserved because the judgment or settlement, properly textualised, became itself a record of possession. Indeed, many texts that purport to record settlements of disputes over property may be legal fictions, *Scheinprocesse* undertaken not in an adversarial spirit but simply to produce a written judgment of lawful possession.

Land and written memory of land work together in a variety of obvious and perhaps not so obvious ways. The extent to which written record of ownership was as important to lay landowners as to ecclesiastical varied by region of Europe and by period. Here again, however, the work of McKitterick and her colleagues as well as that of the Davies and Fouracre team have demonstrated, from differing perspectives, that the value of written evidence of ownership reached widely into secular society in England and on the continent, even though individual and family archives tended to vanish with the death or extinction of the family, thus leaving the erroneous impression that book land was largely a matter for the Church.[7]

Family lands, and thus the means of remembering and demonstrating possession, were, of course, the bedrock of a family's wealth, social position, and identity. The ability to demonstrate a family's possessions

---

[5] Wendy Davies and Paul Fouracre, *The Settlement of Disputes in Early Medieval Europe* (Cambridge, 1986).

[6] An exception to this rule are judgments against serfs claiming freedom. However, this exception may be only apparent, since *servi casati* were in a sense part of the real property to which they were bound.

[7] On Anglo-Saxon Charters the work of Simon Keynes is fundamental. See, in particular, 'Royal Government and the Written Word in Late Anglo-Saxon England', in *Uses of Literacy*, ed. McKitterick, 226–57.

was thus a central pragmatic need in this agrarian society. But the relationship between land and family was more than a pragmatic one. Land not only formed the basis of a family's wealth and power: land was the means by which a family knew itself in historical perspective. Certainly in the twelfth century, as European aristocracies completed the process of forming lineages, the symbolic meaning of land was enormous. Whether it was the castle or property that provided a family toponymic, the *Hantgemal* or symbolic free tenure that was the proof of a family's free and noble status, or the accounts of how one's ancestors came into land and office in the often mythical past of the ninth or tenth centuries, land was a symbolic capital that constituted a family's identity. Its memory, often textualised, was fundamental to self-identity. Even earlier, before the toponymic came to be the distinguishing feature of a lineage, families used property and its devolution as one way of conceiving and talking about themselves. Inheritance of land established and clarified ego-centric kinship networks, while broad kindreds recognised their relationship through the description of, for example, the lands of the Huosi that appear in Bavarian charters. Current scholarship on monastic property is demonstrating how families used donations and precarial holdings to channel wealth from one generation to another, in a real sense creating relationship through the symbolic medium of land, recorded and accessible in monastic archives.[8]

Thus it is not enough to argue that land was essential to a family's status and power. Land can also be described as that which created families as well as sustained them. Property was the symbolic language through which people discussed, negotiated, affirmed, and delimited the boundaries of family. In the eighth century, for example, one can observe property transfers, sales, exchanges, and the like operating within two spheres: one, explicit kinship groups involving parents and children, brothers and sisters, uncles, aunts and cousins. The second, and larger, was a circle of implicit kin who bought and sold land among themselves, reuniting and redefining ancestral lands and, thus, the families that this ancestry created.[9] In the ninth century, inheritance

---

[8] On the *Hantgemal*, see John Freed, 'The Counts of Falkenstein: Noble Self-Consciousness in Twelfth-Century Germany', *Transactions of the American Philosophical Society*, 74:6 (Philadelphia, 1984). On the use of donations for family strategies in Bavaria, see Joachim Jahn, 'Tradere ad sanctum. Politische und gesellschaftliche Aspekte der Traditionspraxis in agilolfingischen Bayern', in *Gesellschaftgeschichte. Festschrift für Karl Bosl zum 80. Geburtstag*, 1 (Munich, 1988), 400–16; and, in Alsace, Hans Josef Hummer, 'Monastic Property, Family Continuity and Central Authority in Early Medieval Alsace and Southern Lotharingia' (PhD dissertation, UCLA, 1997), chapter two, 'Family structure and family memory: The Rodoins and the Saargau section of the cartulary of Weissenburg', 79–105.

[9] Patrick J. Geary, *Aristocracy in Provence: the Rhône Basin at the Dawn of the Carolingian Age* (Stuttgart, Philadelphia, 1985), 115–19.

defined kindred and proximity, not simply blood. In her book of advice for her son, Dhuoda describes his *proximi* and *propinqui*, his close kindred, as those who leave him land in inheritance and urges him to pray for them in proportion to the bequests that they leave him. The bonds of giving and the bonds of praying overlay each other.[10]

No wonder, then, that the origins of lands, their extent, and the means by which they were acquired took on more than merely practical significance. Memory of the family as a family began with the memory of the acquisition of the family's land, and this primordial acquisition could become the subject of family legend and myth. The most famous is perhaps that of the Welfs, whose foundation legend told of Henry with the Golden Plough reported by the Annalista Saxo sometime in the 1130s.[11] This legend tells of Eticho-Welf, a great prince who refused to do homage for land to anyone, even to his son-in-law Emperor Louis the Pious. His son Henry, by contrast, was willing to pay feudal homage provided Louis would give him the amount of land in Swabia he could encircle at noontide with a plough. The father was so incensed that he retired for the rest of his life into the Scharnitzwald. Henry, however, tricked the emperor by taking off on a race through the countryside with a golden plough, using a relay of fresh horses to encircle a vast amount of land that became the centre of the Welf patrimony.[12] This legend, combining a variety of folkloric motifs, shows close interaction between land and the memory of family identity. No wonder, likewise, that land, its conveyance, and its boundaries was the stuff not only of elaborated family traditions, but of archival record.

But, of course, textualisation was not the only or even the most important means by which something as fundamental as land and identity were preserved and transmitted. Orality and a variety of oral practices were equally important. McKitterick herself, summarising the state of the question, wrote: 'Orality, with literacy, nevertheless retained its centrality in early medieval societies. This was most manifest in the many discussions of charters. At whatever other levels they need to be appreciated, one essential function of the charter was to serve as a written record of an oral transaction.'[13] Orality and literacy, then, are not competing ways of understanding the retention and communication

---

[10] Patrick J. Geary, 'Echanges et relations entre les vivants et les morts dans la société du Haute Moyen Age', *Droit et Cultures*, 12 (1986), 3–17. Translated as 'Exchanges and Interactions between the Living and the Dead in the Early Middle Ages', in *Living with the Dead in the Middle Ages* (Ithaca, 1994), 77–92.

[11] Karl Schmid, 'Welfisches Selbstverstándnis', in *Gebetsgedenken und adliges. Selbstverstándnis im Mittelalter*. Ausgeváhlte Beitráge. Festgabe zu seinem sechzigsten Geburtstag (Sigmaringen, 1983), 424–53.

[12] Annalista Saxo, *MGH SS*, 6, 164.

[13] Rosamond McKitterick, ed., *The Uses of Literacy*, 320–1.

of the past in the early Middle Ages as has been suggested by some continental scholars.[14] They are, rather, inseparably connected. Brian Stock, writing on orality and literacy, distinguishes between the 'strong thesis' of orality and literacy and the 'weak thesis'. While the strong posits a major transformation associated with the advent of literacy in a previously oral society, the weak thesis 'attempts to account for the interaction of the oral and the written after the initial steps are taken. It assumes that a knowledge of writing is not completely new.'[15]

Much of the recent work of British scholars on the subject of orality and literacy has focused on demonstrating that the 'strong thesis' is not particularly helpful in understanding early medieval culture. As such, it has emphasised the literate side of the equation. This has been entirely proper and necessary because of the misconception prevalent until recently that the world of the early Middle Ages was an oral culture that transformed into a culture of the written word sometime in the late eleventh or twelfth centuries. Thus a corrective was both necessary and salutary. However, we must not forget the second half of McKitterick's equation: orality did indeed retain its centrality. Our problem, however, is how to examine or evaluate this centrality, how to understand the intimate relationship between oral and textual transmission, given that our sources must necessarily derive from the second half of the equation, that which survives as written record.

Of course, oral and literal transmission are not the only or even the primary means by which the experiences and values of the past were communicated to the future. Much that society needs to know is transmitted experientially: neighbours observing a family working a particular portion of land or a lord exercising, through the collection of rents and the demand of services, the concrete rights of possession; the boy observing as his father works a rough piece of wood into a useful tool; the daughter assisting her mother in gathering herbs for a poultice or healing broth; the youth observing the warriors he serves as he learns to be a knight. The primary 'how to' books of the Middle Ages were people, and much that was at the very core of cultural reproduction was probably never vocalised or textualised. Verbalisation was necessary only for specific kinds of knowledge and under certain specific circumstances.

We must attempt to understand these specific circumstances, and the complex interplay between orality and textuality that they elicited. I want to concentrate specifically on the intimate relationship between

[14] Especially Michael Richter, *The Formation of the Medieval West: Studies in the Oral Culture of the Barbarians* (Dublin: Fourcourts Press, 1994), and his *The Oral Tradition in the Early Middle Ages*, Typologie des Sources du moyen âge occidental, fasc. 71 (Turnhout, 1994).
[15] Brian Stock, *Listening for the Text: On the Uses of the Past* (Philadelphia, 1996), 5–6.

orality and textuality in the transmission of certain memories concerning the past. Of course, the specifically oral aspects of such transmission are irretrievably lost to us. Unlike the ethnographer or the contemporary oral historian, we cannot listen to the voices of the past. We have then only three possibilities. First, we can examine texts that purport to record oral tradition. These texts are never what some philologists would call *Verschriftung*, that is, the simple transference from phonetic to graphic medium.[16] In medieval texts, we are always faced with *Verschriftlichung*, that is, the more complex conceptual process by which textualisation creates a qualitative difference between that which is oral and that which is written.

The second possibility is to look for descriptions of how literate authors describe their interaction with those for whom the text is always mediated. This approach too is problematic, since the presentation of the encounter is entirely in the hands of the literate party. The extent to which his or her construction of the party who is providing access to oral modes of communication and transmission will be to a great extent constructed from assumptions, literary topoi, and values that pertain to the literate world. Moreover, as Franz Bäuml has argued concerning literature,

> In referring to the oral tradition, the written text fictionalizes it. Since the one is given a role to play within the other, since oral formulae in the garb of writing refer to 'orality' within the written tradition, the oral tradition becomes an implicit fictional 'character' of literacy.[17]

A third possibility is to look for the evidence of oral performance within texts. Written texts in the Middle Ages were created and performed orally: thus most texts have an essentially oral characteristic – they were vocalised at the time that they were transcribed and were intended to be vocalised in their reading, whether for an individual reading aloud to himself or herself, or as a performance before others.[18] Thus, at the level of representation of vocality, examination of such descriptions provides a vital if partial entry into the operations of the 'weak thesis' in the world of medieval orality. This is especially true in

[16] Peter Koch, Distanz im Dictamen. Zur Schriftlichkeit und Pragmatik mittelalterlicher Brief- und Redemodelle in Italian. Freiburg (maschinenschriftl. Habil. arbeit), 94. Cited by Ursula Schaefer, *Vokalität. Altenglische Dichtung zwischen Mündlichkeit und Schriftlichkeit* (Tübingen, 1987), 17. n. 24; Wulf Oesterreicher, 'Verschriftung und Verschriftlichung im Kontexte medialer und konzeptioneller Schriftlichkeit', in Ursula Schaefer, ed., *Schriftlichkeit im frühen Mittelalter* (Tübingen, 1993), 267–92.

[17] Franz Bäuml, 'Medieval Texts and the Two Theories of Oral–Formulaic Composition: A Proposal for a Third Theory', *New Literary History*, 16 (1984–5), 43. Cited by Schaeffer, *Vokalität*, 115–16, n. 49.

[18] See especially Schaeffer, *Vokalität, passim*.

examining charters and *placita* or court proceedings. Formalised and 'fictionalised' they certainly are, but nevertheless they not only record agreements, transactions, or donations. They are also records of performances. Moreover, they are scripts for future performances.

It is the evidence of performance of the past that this essay will address, particularly in terms of the primary concern about land and its history that had to be accessible to a lay audience whose concern about property was paramount. How did one perform the scripts, what was needed to be certain that those who spoke the past did so in a way that brought that past to life in an immediate way?

Performing scripts, seeing as well as hearing, were fundamental in establishing right in early medieval courts. This aural aspect was as true in Roman law areas of Europe as it was in areas of customary law. I have elsewhere examined cases from Languedoc and Provence in which this vocalisation of texts was essential. To cite but one example, at Narbonne in 955 the local bishop judged on the validity of a deathbed donation only after he had seen and heard it, *vidit et audivit.*[19] This is a standard phrase in dispute settlement charters. Seeing and hearing, as Horst Wenzel has argued in other contexts, was an essential part in determining the past.[20]

But what exactly did one need to hear? The past had to be revived through the performance of a text in a way that made its content immediately accessible to those who had to judge its right. In land cases, this meant essentially two things: possession of land and the description of that land. Charters recorded transfers, agreements, and oaths concerning the location and ownership of land. That which had been sworn was textualised so that, on reading, an audience could hear once more the description and the oath that confirmed it.[21] But what sounds did a lay audience need to hear? While portions of a charter might be performed in Latin and translated or explained by a *litteratus,*

---

[19] Cl. Devic et J. Vaissete, *Histoire générale de Languedoc avec des notes et les pièces justificatives,* 15 vols in 17 (Toulouse, 1872–92), V, 222. See Patrick J. Geary, 'Oblivion between Orality and Textuality in the Tenth Century', in Gerd Althoff, Johannes Fried, and Patrick J. Geary, eds, *Imagination, Ritual, Memory, Historiography: Concepts of the Past* (Cambridge: in press).

[20] Horst Wenzel, *Hören und Sehen, Schrift und Bild: Kultur und Gedächtnis im Mittelalter* (Munich, 1995).

[21] This is true not only of ordinary disputes and judgments but even, or perhaps especially, of royal decrees. As Simon Keynes writes, 'As regards tenth- and eleventh-century legislation, what counted was the king's oral pronouncement of the law, and many of the extant written texts were more in the nature of "minutes of what was orally decreed, rather than statute law in their own right".' 'Royal Government and the Written Word', in *Uses of Literacy,* ed. McKitterick, 228, quoting Patrick Wormald, '*Lex Scripta* and *Verbum Regis*: legislation and Germanic kingship, from Euric to Cnut', *Early Medieval Kingship,* ed. P. H. Sawyer and I. N. Wood (Leeds, 1977), 105–38.

some portions were so important that they might be put directly into the vernacular. This was particularly true in the descriptions of property. Names and places were so intimately tied together that in these cases the vernacular had to bleed through the Latin text, usually in the naming of places, but at times in the directional indications as well.

I first noticed this tendency while working with a document from the high Middle Ages. In the 1180s Count Siboto IV of Falkenstein, a Bavarian noble who held lands in the region of the Kemsee in modern Bavaria as well as in what is today upper Austria, grew so exasperated with one Rudolf of Piesting that he decided to get rid of him. He had written a letter to one of his vassals, Ortwin of Merkenstein, in which he bluntly asked Ortwin to cut down Rudolf, or at least to blind him.[22] If Ortwin would be so good as to do this favour for him, Siboto wrote, 'I will do for you whatever you wish. I grant you the property along the Panzenbach from its source to where it flows into the Piesting.' The letter, one of the earliest letters between laymen from the Middle Ages, is from every perspective a remarkable and unusual document, written, perhaps, not only to communicate the request to Ortwin, something that could probably have been done as well or even better orally, but also to provide proof for Ortwin, after the fact, that he had acted on behalf of his lord, was free from personal responsibility, and should receive the reward that he was promised.[23] The one aspect of the letter that I wish to note today, however, is the language in which Siboto describes the reward awaiting Ortwin. The original of the passage I just quoted reads: *quecumque vultis, faciam vobis. Concedo vobis itaque bonum da der Panzinpach also er oueralbe in den Piesnic vellet unde dase da springet*. In other words, while the letter is written in what passed for Latin in aristocratic circles of Bavaria, the passage in which Siboto describes what he will give Ortwin for carrying out the hit contract is in Middle High German. The vernacular will be emerging increasingly into German documents in the next generation. Indeed, sometime in the early thirteenth century Siboto's son had the whole codex in which the letter appears translated. However, the use of the vernacular in this Latin letter is not the beginning of that tradition but rather the end of a much more ancient and complex tradition central to questions of memory, land, and language.

As Anglo-Saxonists well know, English charters from at least the time of Alfred, even when written in Latin, often contain significant passages in Old English. Most frequently these are, just as in the case

---

[22] *Codex Falkensteinensis: die Rechtsaufzeichnungen der Grafen von Falkenstein*, ed. Elisabeth Noichl, Quellen und Erörterungen zur bayerischen Geschichte, n.s., 29 (Munich, 1978), no. 183, 163–4.

[23] See John B. Freed and Patrick J. Geary, 'Literacy and Violence in Twelfth-Century Bavaria: the "Murder letter" of Count Siboto IV', *Viator*, 25 (1994): 115–29.

of Siboto's hit contract, descriptions of boundaries. Simon Keynes in particular has explored the importance of these boundary descriptions in the Anglo-Saxon world, and I do not intend to develop them further here.[24] In his recent unpublished dissertation on boundaries in pre-Conquest England, the American medievalist Mark Rabuck has discussed these passages and rehearsed the various interpretations that have been offered to explain them.[25] To some, they have been seen as evidence of the decline of Latinity. This is highly unlikely, since the scribes were perfectly capable of preparing the rest of the charters in Latin. Others see this as part of the Anglo-Saxon linguistic renaissance encouraged by Alfred. If this were so, it would be difficult to understand why only these passages were prepared in English. Rabuck argues convincingly that the choice was anything but arbitrary and had everything to do with the importance of reading aloud to people not fluent in Latin.[26]

But there is even more to the use of the vernacular in describing and discussing land. This impression is supported by an examination of the appearance of the vernacular in continental legal and administrative documents. Here, too, in places as widely separated as Germany and Italy, the vernacular first begins to emerge in administrative practice in those aspects of disputes and transactions involving precise descriptions and statements concerning land, its boundaries, and the nature of its tenure. I would like to suggest that this practice is closely related to the demands of memory, and its public recitation, under specific ritualised circumstances in the early Middle Ages. These words, phrases, or extended passages are in a sense Bäuml's fictional characters embedded within the text, characters who can be made to speak again what was said about the past.

Unlike in England, boundary descriptions were not the usual way of designating property in the East Frankish world. The most common practice was to follow a formula that simply gave the place-names of donated properties. For example, in a donation by Charlemagne to which we shall return, 'We give to the monastery of Fulda in the pagus

---

[24] Simon Keynes, 'Royal Government and the Written Word' in *Uses of Literacy*, ed. McKitterick, 225–57. See, in particular, his description of two versions of the boundaries appearing in a treaty between Alfred and Guthrum, 233–4. As he explains, the treaty is 'ostensibly a record of oral agreements made between the two parties and confirmed on a particular day by the swearing of oaths'. On the wider literature concerning Anglo-Saxon boundary clauses, see, in addition, for an earlier survey, Nicholas Brooks, 'Anglo-Saxon charters: the work of the last twenty years', *Anglo-Saxon England*, 3 (1974), 211–31, esp. 223–4; and C. P. Biggam, 'Sociolinguistic aspects of Old English colour lexemes', *Anglo-Saxon England*, 24 (1995), 51–65.

[25] Mark Rabuck, 'The Imagined Boundary: Borders and Frontiers in Anglo-Saxon England' (PhD dissertation, Yale University, 1995), chapter 6, 'Ðis sin þe land gemære ... Vernacular Boundary Clauses', 149–65.

[26] Rabuck, ibid., 150–1.

of Gaaffelt ... our property of Hammelburg situated in the Salgau on the Sale river, integrally, with all its adjacencies and appendices on the Eschenback, Diebach, and Ertal, whatever we are seen to have in these above mentioned places.'[27]

As Hanna Vollrath observes, however, such designations in a charter, even if it can be termed a legal title, could have only a very limited function since the precise property bounds had to be expanded through a topographical knowledge of the location. Only oral testimony could make good such written evidence.[28] Occasionally, however, one learns more about the donated property. Either because of its unusual dimensions or, more frequently, because the specific limits of the property are subject to dispute, a charter will provide that information normally left to oral testimony. The determination of these boundaries, and the establishment of a charter recording the transfer or establishing the result of a judicial or quasi-judicial process, demanded explicitly the ritual action and vocalisation of the boundaries by a group of knowledgeable and trustworthy men. These individuals had to lead a circumnavigation of the bounds, stating explicitly what the boundaries were that they were showing. Their sworn statement had to be heard and recorded first in the memory of witnesses and then, secondarily, in a document that could be used as an *aide-mémoire* of the events. Such documents are particularly telling of the relationship between ritual action, oral performance, and memory. One also sees with particular clarity the importance of accessibility to the words spoken and remembered by those participating in the circumnavigation, an importance that favoured the use of the vernacular in place-names and, at times, just as in England, in the presentation of the entire description of boundaries in the vernacular.

Just such a dispute developed in the first quarter of the ninth century concerning the Hammelburg property donated to Fulda by Charlemagne. We know this because of a document, surviving in a contemporary copy, of the boundaries of this property. This so-called Hammelburg Boundary description, along with a somewhat similar description from Würzburg, is among the most ancient vernacular texts in Old High German.[29] The Hammelburg document states that in the

---

[27] DKar I, 162, no. 116. For a detailed discussion and edition of this diploma, see Edmund E. Stengel, *Urkundenbuch des Klosters Fulda*, 1 (Marburg, 1958), 140–7.

[28] Vollrath, *Rechtexte*, 329.

[29] Ed. Elias von Steinmeyer, *Die Kleineren althochdeutschen Sprachdenkmäler* (Berlin, 1916), XII, 62–3; and by Stengel, *Urkundenbuch des Klosters Fulda*, 1 (Marburg, 1958), no. 83, 151–4. See J. Knight Bostock, *A Handbook on Old High German Literature* (Oxford, 1976), 113–14; Dieter Geuenich, 'Zur althochdeutscher Literatur aus Fulda', *Von der Klosterbibliothek zur Landesbibliothek: Beiträge zum zweihundert-jährigen Bestehen der Hessischen Landesbibliothek Fulda*, ed. Artur Brall (Stuttgart, 1978), 114–15. One should note that the majority of Continental boundary descriptions concern much larger territories than those of Anglo-Saxon charters

third year of King Charles (777) counts Nithard and Heimo, along with two royal vassals, invested Abbot Sturm with the property granted by the king, an investiture witnessed by twenty-one named individuals. The witness list follows with the statement (in Latin) that this place had been described and designated with these boundaries, and then the most noble people of the land (*nobiliores terrae illius*) swore that they had spoken the truth of this portion of the fisc. Then follows a detailed description, essentially in German, that traces the boundaries. The document has been accepted as essentially genuine in its Latin portion since it agrees with the earlier diploma of Charlemagne. The boundary description, however, is in a German that must date philologically from no earlier than the 820s and thus has been dismissed as a forgery, of which a considerable number were generated in Fulda at this time. This may be so. However, the text, when examined as part of an inquest following a dispute rather than as part of the original investiture, is subject to an alternative interpretation. The document does not identify the *nobiliores terrae illius* as the twenty-one witnesses of the investiture. They may be rather those who in the 820s recalled and swore to the earlier boundaries, swearing, naturally, in their spoken language, not in an archaic vernacular. Alternatively, it may indeed be a forgery, but even then its fabrication shows that for Fulda, the precise boundary, described in words that anyone at a court could understand, were deemed sufficiently important to record in the contemporary spoken language. Only through such an utterly transparent document, capable of being revocalised before a lay audience, could a donation of some fifty years previous be defended.

The importance of the vernacular oath demonstrating the boundary of land that could be revocalised for an assembly is shown in the second such boundary description, the Würzburg boundary description from 14 October 779. This exists in two versions, one entirely in German, one in Latin with significant interpolation of German.[30] The German version begins in Rabanesbrunnen and traces a series of landmarks connected by directional indications until it returns again to its start. It is followed by the names of eighteen men who have sworn that these are the proper boundaries.[31] The Latin–German version, which is not

---

and might be considered more political treaties than ordinary land delimittions. However, the charter evidence discussed below suggests that while full descriptions survive in such cases, the vernacular phrases in charters suggest a similar process lay behind them as well.

[30] Ed. von Steinmeyer, *Kleineren althochdeutschen Sprachdenkmäler*, XXIV, 115–17. See Bostick, *Handbook*, 114–15.

[31] Diz sageta Marcuuart, Nanduuin, Helitberaht, Fredthant, Heio, Unuuan, Fridurih, Reginberaht, Ortuuin, Gozuuin, Iuto, Liutberaht, Baso, Berahtolf, Ruotberaht, Sigifrid, Reginuuart, Folcberaht. Ed. von Steinmeyer, *Kleineren althochdeutschen Sprachdenkmäler*, 116.

an exact duplicate of the information in the German version, is divided into three vernacular boundary descriptions and one Latin description, each followed by the names of those who went around them with the royal missi and who swore that they were accurate.[32] The divergence of the two again suggests a dispute or disagreement on the exact bounds, and the documents with their heavy vernacular content were means to preserve oaths about those bounds for later vocalisation before the kind of audience that would want direct access to the sounds of the oaths taken by those who rode the bounds in 779.

A similar process of riding the boundaries with a group of men who swear to their locations appears in other Frankish charters of the eighth and ninth centuries. In some cases the boundaries are presented in Latin, in most the place-names are designated in German and in others all or significant portions of the entire boundary, including directional prepositions, are presented in the vernacular, as, for example: 'That is, at Kazozeheim, Chungsheid and Chriestadt with the above designated boundaries to the place called Sampinsaolla to Cozeheim and then it follows the flow of the stream to the large bush that is called in the vernacular *nidar pi deru labhun za deru mihilun eihi*...'[33]

---

[32] The procedure by which the boundaries were established is explained in the text:

In nomine domini nostri Ihesu Christi. Notum sit omnibus sanctae dei ecclesiae fidelibus, qualiter Eburhardus missus domni nostri Karoli excellentissimi regis cum omnibus obtimatibus et senibus istius prouinciae in occidentali parte fluuii nomine Moin marcham Vuirziburgarensium iuste discernendo et ius iurantibus illis subter scriptis optimatibus et senibus circumduxit.

Incipientes igitur in loco, qui dicitus Ôtuuinesbrunno, danan in daz haganina sol, danan in Herostat in den uuidenen seo, danan in mittan Nottenlôh, danan in Scelenhoue. Isit sunt, qui in his locis suprascriptis circumduxerund et iuramento firmauerunt: Zótan, Ephfo, Lantold, sigiuuin, runzolf, Diotmar, Artumar, Eburraat, Hiltuuin, Eburkar, Germunt, Árberaht, Folcger, Theotger, Theodolt.

The second section continues:

Incipiebant uero in eodem loco alii testes perire et circumducere. Id est fon demo Scelenhouge in Hibiscesbiunta, danan in das Ruotgises houc, danan anan Amarland, danan in Moruhhesstein, danan after dero clingun unzan Christesbrunnon. hucusque preibant et circumducebant et iuramento firmabant, qui subter nominiti sunt: hoc est Batolf, gerfrid, Haduger, Lanto, Marcuuart, Vodalmaar, Adalbrabt, Utto, Hatto, Saraman, Húnger, Vuigbald, Aato., Eggihart, Strangolf, Haamo, Francho, Enistriit, Gerhart, Gatto, Hiltiberaht, Ruotberaht, Hanno, Nantger, Hunband, Rihholf, Ramftger.

Ed. von Steinmeyer, *Kleineren althochdeutschen Sprachdenkmäler*, 115.

[33] *Die Traditionen des Hochstiftes Freising*, ed. Theodor Bitterauf, Quellen und Erörterungen zur bayerischen und Deutschen Geschichte, n.f., 4 (Munich, 1905), no. 166a, 162: 'id est Kaozesheim, Chuningesheid et Chriechesstat cum omni confino supradicto ad loco qui dicitur Sampinsaolla usque ad Cozesheim et exinde tendit in iusu iuxta rivulum usque ad magnum rubum quod vulgo dicitir *nidar pi deru lahhun za deru mihilun eihi*, deinde per locas terminatas, id est in longitudine antlanga Caozeslahhun usque ad Caozesprunnun, similiter et in illa silva quae pertinet ad Uuemodinga'.

Some have suggested that the heavy use of vernacular in these descriptions stems from the inability of scribes to write Latin when needing to diverge from set formulae. I find this highly unlikely – the Latin is never elegant, but the charters are capable of some variety of description and variety in other respects. Rather, I believe that the high importance of vernacular is related to the ritual process by which these documents were produced, including the riding of the boundaries and especially the oral statement of their limits and the oath that the statements had been heard and were true. The testimony of witness, not in a document but pronounced in the hearing of others, was what mattered. As one Regensburg charter from 819 puts it, 'These are the names of those who heard this judgment and who rode this boundary and who were present.'[34]

As Susan Kelly has argued in the case of English vernacular charters, vernacular clauses could provide not only more precision in certain terminology than Latin, but the vernacular recorded a verbal statement of intent or agreement.[35] What the witnesses said was directly related to the names of the land, and the physical description, experienced and verbalised, had to be immediately accessible should the document be revocalised. In the case of such vocalisation in Latin, the charter would be, again in Susan Kelly's words, 'doubly inaccessible to the uneducated. Not only did it have to be read out to them; it also required translation into the vernacular.'[36] In cases as fundamental to the identity and significance of an aristocracy as land, there was greater emphasis on the ability to hear the sounds of the past that directly linked the property to the action.[37]

---

[34] 'Haec sunt nomina eorum, qui audierunt rationem istam et cauallicauerunt illam commarcam et fuerunt in ista pireisa.' Throughout, the charter emphasises what has been heard as in the testimony of two episcopal witnesses: 'Tunc dixit Rodolt et Betto [the episcopal huntsman and episcopal vicar]: "nos audemus hoc dicere et confirmare, etiam si fuerit coram domno imperatore, quod ista omnis commarca, sicut hunc eundem episcopum Baturicum circumducentes consignauimus, debet consistere cum omni iustitia ad sanctum Petrum et sanctum Emmerammum in traditione ducum, qui istam patriam possiderunt."' *Die Traditionen des Hochstifts Regensburg und des Klosters s. Emmeram*, ed. Josef Widemann, Quellen und Erörterungen zur bayerischen Geschichte, n.f., 8 (Munich, 1943), no. 16, 16.

[35] Susan Kelly, 'Anglo-Saxon Lay Society and the Written Word', in *Uses of Literacy*, ed. McKitterick, 56.

[36] Ibid., 56–7.

[37] The same practice of providing boundaries in the vernacular appears in the earliest Hungarian royal charters. The foundation charter of the Benedictine Abbey at Tihany, written in 1055, reads, for example, 'Adhuc autem est locus *Mortis* dictus, cuius incipit terminus *a Sar feu eri iturea*, hinc *Ohut cutarea*, inde ad *holmodi rea*, postea *Gnir uuege holmodia rea* et exinde *Mortis uuasara kuta rea* as postea *Nogu azah feherea*, inde ad *Sastelic et Feheruuaru rea meneh hodu utu rea*, post haec *Petre zenaia hel rea*.' György Györffy, *Diplomata Hungariae Antiquissima* (Budapest, 1992), 150. Since the individual responsible for this diploma of King Stephen is most likely 'Herebert C',who had been active in the German imperial

The two versions of the Würzburg boundary description suggest that the process by which the document was created began with a vernacular description of the boundaries and a list of those who participated in the riding. Then a more careful Latin text was prepared, which nevertheless preserved in the vernacular the specific, detailed vernacular boundaries and the names of the individuals who had sworn to them.[38]

Preserving boundaries is not the only kind of oral testimony about land that was deemed sufficiently important to be transparent to a lay audience that it would be recorded in the vernacular. So too were oaths sworn about such boundaries. The earliest documents in the Italian language are four *placiti* and one memorandum (or memoratorio) from the 960s concerning the property of Montecassino. In each case, a dispute (real or fictive) with the monastery over a portion of land is announced before a judge. The boundaries of the disputed property are described in a Latin closely related to the vernacular. Then individual witnesses are called to swear to the veracity of the boundaries and to the possession by the monastery for more than thirty years. These oaths are unambiguously in the vernacular: *sao ko kelle terre per kelle fini que ki contene trenta anni le possette parte sancti benedicti.*[39] These are hardly attempts to record the verbatim formulations of individuals unable to speak Latin: all are pronounced by clerics or notables who would presumably have been capable of expressing themselves in Latin that was at least as good as the rest of the documents. Moreover, the repetition is so precise that they are obviously formulas betraying even in their orthography hints of formal, notarial usage.[40] They are, rather, part of a ritualised performance intended not for the judges and

---

chancellery, one can assume that this practice, and probably the type of vernacular inquest that produced such vernacular boundary descriptions, were introduced from the west. I am grateful to Professors Pongracz Sennyey and Janos Bak for bringing the Hungarian material to my attention.

[38] The process was probably similar in the preparation of Anglo-Saxon charters. Two such original documents containing only boundary descriptions have survived and a number of others have been preserved in post-Conquest cartularies. These were probably the drafts prepared by the sheriff immediately after the riding of the bounds and eventually would have been incorporated into the charter. Normally, these preliminary drafts would not have been needed after the completion of the charter and thus need not have been preserved. Communication from Simon Keynes.

[39] Placitum of Capua, March 960. D. M. Inguanez, ed., *I placiti cassinesi del secolo X con periodi in volgare* (La Badia di Montecassino, 1934), 18. The other formulae are very similar: Placitum of Sessa, March 963: 'sao cco kelle terre per kelle fini que tebe monstrai pergoaldi foro que ki contene, et trenta anni le possette.' 22; First placitum of Teano, July 963: 'Kella terra per kelle fini qi bobe mostrai sancte marie e et trenta anni la posset parte sancte marie.' 26; Second placitum of Teano, October 963: 'sao cco kelle terre per kelle fini que tebe mostrai, trenta anni le possette parte sancte marie.' 29.

[40] See the discussion in Bruno Migliorini, *Storia della Langua Italiana* (Florence, 1978), 93–6.

principals but for others attending the solemn court assembly: lay neighbours and landowners around Montecassino. It is not enough to prove possession by Latin documents or oaths. Those for whom land matters must be able to hear about it in a language immediately meaningful to them, and by recording these oaths as vernacular formulae, a record is created that allows the revocalisation of the solemn oaths should they be needed in the future. Again, these oaths, in a highly stylised vernacular, become fictionalised characters in the construction of the record of a legal procedure. If we take the suggestion that these processes were themselves rituals in which there was no real dispute but simply the desire to create formal recognition of monastic right, then we have the double fictionalisation of a play within a play.

This fictionalisation returns us to the question of forgery, both in the Fulda boundary description and in Anglo-Saxon charters. Nicholas Brooks pointed out long ago that these vernacular boundaries were among the most frequently forged aspects of Anglo-Saxon charters. More elaborate vernacular bounds were added to earlier charters, bounds that might include more than the original donation.[41] We have seen the same process at Fulda and, possibly, at Würzburg, where the two versions cannot be made to coincide. Rather than dismissing these 'forgeries' as simply fraud, one can see them as evidence of the deeply contested field of memory: differing views about how the past was to be reactualised. Memory, always creative and transformative, can be seen to be at work in these disputes, recreating in dynamic and original ways the past.

These brief examples suggest that while we have no direct contact with pure orality from the Middle Ages, we have abundant evidence of vocality, of performance of texts. This is a different orality from that which most people are interested in, since it is the orality of a literate minority, even if they, through reading, reach a much wider audience. Nor is it a fossilised orality, formulae transmitted verbatim through the ages. Rather, it is a constantly renewed and disputed past, vocalised for the present with an eye to the future.

Thus, at the level of representation of vocality, examination of documents handling land provides a vital if partial entry into the operations of the 'weak thesis' in the world of medieval orality. This is especially true in examining charters and *placita* or court proceedings. Formalised and 'fictionalised' they certainly are, but nevertheless they not only record agreements, transactions, or donations. They are also records of performances. Moreover, they are scripts for future performances. In our cases, statements of the boundaries, oaths acknowledging these boundaries or declaring uninterrupted possession of

---

[41] Brooks, 'Anglo-Saxon charters', 223.

disputed lands are vital parts of the scripts for these performances. The performance had to be accessible to a lay audience whose concern about property was paramount, not only the first time that it was given, but in case of necessity, for future audiences. To become relevant in disputes, they had once more to be heard by learned judges and by the *nobiliores terrae*. Most scripts were prepared in Latin and would no doubt be retranslated into the vernacular. But some vital elements of the vernacular, whether place-names, boundaries, or oaths, might be so crucial that a notary or scribe might incorporate them into his document. In this way the past could not only be memorialised in a text but it could be re-enacted, as the sounds made before a judge in a distant past could once more reach the ears and the eyes of those who looked to land as the key to their very identities.

REMEMBERING, FORGETTING AND INVENTING: ATTITUDES TO THE PAST IN ENGLAND AT THE END OF THE FIRST VIKING AGE

By Sarah Foot

READ 26 MARCH 1998 AT THE UNIVERSITY OF SUSSEX

'REMEMBER', King Alfred wrote to his bishops, sending them a copy of the translation he had made of Pope Gregory the Great's *Cura pastoralis*, 'remember what punishments befell us in this world when we ourselves did not cherish learning nor transmit it to other men'.[1] To remedy the twofold disaster consequent on this intellectual and pedagogic failure – not just the ransacking of the churches throughout England and loss of their treasures and books, but, worse, the loss to the English of the wisdom the books had preserved – King Alfred arranged to have the young men among his subjects taught to read in the vernacular. Set-texts for this programme were to be supplied by the translating of 'certain books which are the most necessary for all men to know'.[2] Among these was Boethius' *Consolation of Philosophy*, generally thought to have been translated by the king himself and to include some of Alfred's own musings. Towards the end of this text in the context of a discussion of the nature of God, eternity and the place of humanity in the divine plan, Alfred had Wisdom declare: 'we can know very little concerning what was before our time, except through memory and inquiry, and even less concerning what comes after us. Only one thing is certainly present to us, namely that which now exists. But to God all is present, what was before, what is now, and what shall be after us.'[3] The central point at issue here is the disjunction between what an omniscient deity and frail humanity can know of the past, but it usefully introduces this discussion by linking the process of obtaining information about the past with that of personal memory. Much of the force of Alfred's hortatory letter to his bishops is derived from the king's

---

[1] Alfred, prose preface to the *Cura pastoralis*, transl. S. Keynes and M. Lapidge, *Alfred the Great: Asser's 'Life of King Alfred' and Other Contemporary Sources* (Harmondsworth, 1983), 125.

[2] Ibid., p. 126. See D. A. Bullough, 'The Educational Tradition in England from Alfred to Ælfric: Teaching *utriusque linguae*', *La Scuola nell'Occidente Latino dell'alto medioevo*, Settimane di Studio del Centro Italiano di Studi Sull'alto medioevo, 19 (1972), 453–94, at 455–63.

[3] *King Alfred's Old English Version of Boethius De Consolatione Philosophiae*, XLII (ed. W.J. Sedgefield, Oxford, 1899, 148; transl. Keynes and Lapidge, *Alfred the Great*, 136).

appeal to their shared experience of the vicissitudes of the second half of the ninth century and their apparently common notion of a prior golden age.

The significance of the process of remembering, the conscious shaping and fixing of individual and shared experience and observation into recollectable form, has long been recognised as an important element in the preservation of information about the past by both oral and partially (or transitionally) literate societies.[4] By the eleventh century the written word was being increasingly used for a variety of purposes in Anglo-Saxon England, and familiarity with letters and the meanings they might convey had spread far beyond the primarily clerical elite of the professionally literate.[5] It is generally agreed, however, that the upsurge in the use of writing beyond the cloister post-dates the First Viking Age and the Alfredian educational programme;[6] in the period before the late ninth century the use of writing in lay society remained restricted, documents serving a primarily mnemonic purpose to assist in the recollection of transactions effected (and thereby made valid) by word of mouth.[7] The means by which the past could be accessed in early Anglo-Saxon England were highly dependent upon individual memory, the recollection of personal involvement in events later perceived to have been significant, individual acquaintance with notable figures, and the oral transmission of those reminiscences to others within the familial, tribal, or institutional group. Such historical texts as survive from England before the Viking Age indeed make their debt to reliable oral testimony explicit, placing considerable weight on the word of the trustworthy eyewitness.[8] In the process of the preservation

---

[4] For discussion of these issues in a Carolingian context, see M. Innes, 'Memory, Orality and Literacy in an Early Medieval Society', *Past and Present*, 158 (1998), 3–36.

[5] Michael Clanchy, *From Memory to Written Record* (2nd edn, Oxford, 1993), 26–32; Patrick Wormald, 'The uses of literacy in Anglo-Saxon England and its neighbours', *Transactions of the Royal Historical Society*, 5th series, 27 (1977), 94–114; Simon Keynes, 'Royal Government and the Written Word in late Anglo-Saxon England', in *The Uses of Literacy in Early Medieval Europe*, ed. Rosamond McKitterick (Cambridge, 1990), 226–57.

[6] The fullest discussion is by Susan Kelly, 'Anglo-Saxon lay society and the written word', in *The Uses of Literacy*, ed. McKitterick, 36–62.

[7] An early tenth-century charter of King Edward the Elder explains succinctly the purpose for which written record of an oral conveyance was made: because the Church had long ago resolved 'that the gifts of most pious kings should be delivered with the records of charters on account of the changeable vicissitudes of the times and concluded with the testimony of a title-deed, lest the source of truth should be brought to nothing by the assault of misty oblivion'. S 362 [S: P. H. Sawyer, *Anglo-Saxon Charters: An Annotated List and Bibliography* (London, 1968)]; transl. *English Historical Documents, I, c.500–1042*, ed. D. Whitelock (2nd edn, 1979) [hereafter *EHD*], no. 100.

[8] Most notable in the pages of Bede's *Historia ecclesiastica*, where the testimony of named oral witnesses is accorded privileged status in comparison with vulgar report; for discussion of Bede's network of informants, see D. P. Kirby, 'Bede's Native Sources for the *Historia ecclesiastica*', *Bulletin of the John Rylands Library*, 48 (1966), 341–71.

of memory the religious community played a significant role, not purely because it was ecclesiastics who composed and physically created the charters and wills preserved in their archives, or recorded in writing the lives of their spiritually celebrated predecessors, but more significantly through their role in the liturgical commemoration of the dead. It was via such celebratory recollection that monastic communities defined and maintained their own corporate identity as well as offering a form of immortality to lay benefactors or those who entered into confraternity with their congregations.[9]

The purpose of this essay is to investigate the effect of dislocation on attitudes to the past and the mechanisms for its preservation in early Anglo-Saxon society by exploring the immediate impact of the political and religious upheavals of the ninth century. The argument is contingent on two propositions: first that the Danish wars, or at least their aftermath, had cataclysmic effects on the political and religious life of the country and that these disrupted the machinery available for remembrance; and secondly that memory as an individual mental process should be distinguished from the constructed accounts of shared pasts, however much these may claim to draw on multiple memories. I am uncomfortable not so much with the concept of 'social' or 'collective memory' as with the use of that particular label for the process to which it refers, which seems to me semantically flawed.[10] The act of memory I take to be a personal one, particular (exclusive) to the mind recalling past events, although what the mind may remember is mutable (under the influence of time, age and experience, and through the intrusion of subsequent events, or conflicting recollections) and hence frequently fallible, often erroneous. That memory is itself constructed by many of the same mechanisms of selection and omission that will shape collective accounts and formal histories is taken to be self-evident. Yet the notion of a common past,

---

[9] The formulaic phraseology of early Anglo-Saxon charters always attributed pious motives to secular donors to churches and monasteries, but some texts spelt out in some detail the spiritual benefits anticipated from the gift; for example, the Kentish ealdorman Oswulf and his wife Beornthryth gave land early in the ninth century to Christ Church, Canterbury, on condition that they might be in the fellowship of the community there and that their anniversay be celebrated each year with religious offices [*on godcundum godum*] and with the distribution of alms: S 1188; transl. F. E. Harmer, *Select English Historical Documents of the Ninth and Tenth Centuries* (Cambridge, 1914), no. 1, 39.

[10] The concept of 'collective' memory was defined by Maurice Halbwachs (*Les cadres sociaux de la mémoire* (Paris, 1925); *La Mémoire collective* (Paris, 1950, English translation, New York, 1980). His ideas about the ways in which memory is structured by group identities have been developed in a slightly different direction by James Fentress and Chris Wickham, *Social Memory* (Oxford, 1992). See also Patrick Geary, *Phantoms of Remembrance: Memory and Oblivion at the End of the First Millennium* (Princeton, NJ, 1994), especially 3–22.

a pool of shared remembrance to which the members of a specific social, political or, for example, religious community have access by virtue of their individual and collective ownership of the elements of which it is constructed, I wish to differentiate from 'memory'. For such commemoration – whether oral or written – is memorial (in the sense of celebrating recollection, co-mingling remembrance) but not reminiscent, in that the mental process involved in its recovery is that of retrieving a learned pattern, not the process of drawing out an experienced one. This distinction cannot be absolute – relived experiences are often when retold gilded with learned glosses supplied by other witnesses or auditors of earlier, unrefined versions – yet the cognitive acts are discrete. Indeed, it may be argued (and will be here) that what is nominally recollected by commemorative activity is, in fact, more likely to be recent fictive construction than long-acknowledged and collectively remembered 'truth'. Commemoration (collaborative remembrance) transmogrifies separate memories by embodying them in a common narrative; this is true even where the commemorative narrative is required to function mnemonically.[11] Here I shall be exploring how the loss of personal memories affected English mechanisms for recalling the past following the various disasters of the middle years of the ninth century. But to categorise this period as disastrous is to presuppose my first condition: that the Danish wars had cataclysmic consequences.

Political correctness has so overtaken viking studies in the last thirty years or so that it is no longer thought appropriate to attribute the political upheavals of ninth-century England or the misfortunes suffered by English churches and monasteries in the period to the ravages of marauding bands of heathen Danes.[12] The vikings' incontrovertibly bad press should rather be attributed to prejudicial reporting by reactionary ecclesiastics responsible for the recording of behaviour to which they were particularly (but temporarily) victim than to the extraordinary or excessive violence of Scandinavian raiders.[13] This particular debate is irrelevant to my concern here which is to explore the consequences of the dislocations of the ninth century, not to argue about why they

[11] I must acknowledge the assistance of Michael Bentley in clarifying my thoughts about memory, and his suggestion that commemoration is a more useful term than social memory.

[12] The revisionist position was first articulated by Peter Sawyer, *The Age of the Vikings* (1962), and has acquired numerous adherents since then.

[13] On the panic-stricken mood of many of the Frankish sources in particular, see J. M. Wallace-Hadrill, *Early Medieval History* (Oxford, 1975), 218–20. That the Danes were notably more violent than their contemporaries has been questioned, for example by G. Halsall, 'Playing by whose Rules? A Further Look at Viking Atrocity in the Ninth Century', *Medieval History*, 2.2 (1992), 2–12. For a contrary view, see David N. Dumville, *The Churches of North Britain in the First Viking Age*, Fifth Whithorn Lecture (Whithorn, 1997).

occurred. It can certainly be shown that Christian kings and nobles attacked churches for their movable wealth and that native dynasties were eradicated or demoted by the military actions of their rivals – the eighth-century Mercian king Offa perpetrated both evils. But the middle years of the ninth century stand out as a period of particular political and ecclesiastical turbulence.[14]

Remembering monks and saints

The detrimental effects of Danish raiding, and perhaps even more importantly of Scandinavian settlement, were felt most keenly in the ecclesiastical sphere where these apparently affected the provision of pastoral care for the lay population.[15] That three bishoprics disappeared entirely from the historical record during this period (both of the East Anglian sees and that at Hexham) suggests that little episcopal control of the clergy could be maintained in these areas and raises severe doubts as to the practicability of the exercise of routine priestly duty.[16] Similar questions must surround the continuance of ecclesiastical activity in the dioceses of Leicester and Lindisfarne, both of whose sees were transferred to new locations during the ninth century,[17] as well as in Lindsey (whose see was vacant between c. 875 and 953) and Lichfield, where the bishop may well have been able to exercise authority solely

[14] Space does not permit the cataloguing of these largely familiar details; for summaries, see Keynes and Lapidge, *Alfred the Great*, introduction, 11–26; D. P. Kirby, *The Earliest English Kings* (1991), 210–20. That the effects of the vikings in England were 'very serious indeed' was argued by Patrick Wormald, 'Viking Studies: Whence and Whither', in *The Vikings*, ed. R. T. Farrell (1982), 128–53, at 139.

[15] Anxieties about the provision of pastoral care were expressed in Northumbria long before the start of the Viking Age (Bede, *Epistola ad Ecgbertum*, ed. C. Plummer, *Venerabilis Baedae Opera Historica*, 2 vols, Oxford, 1896, I, 405–23); the contention here is not that such problems were new, nor that they were solely prompted by Danish warfare, but that they were felt more acutely in this period.

[16] No bishop of Hexham is recorded beyond Bishop Tidferth who died in 821: Simon Keynes, 'Episcopal succession in Anglo-Saxon England', in E. B. Fryde *et al.*, *Handbook of British Chronology* (3rd edn, 1986), 209–24, at 217. The last known bishop of Dunwich was Æthelwold, who acceded 845 x 870, the date of his death is unknown: ibid., 216; D. Whitelock, 'The pre-Viking Church in East Anglia', *Anglo-Saxon England*, I (1972), 1–22, at 17–19. The see of Elmham was revived in the later tenth century, following a century of interruption after the death of Bishop Hunberht in 845 or 856x? or ? November 869: Keynes in Fryde *et al.*, *Handbook*, p. 216; Whitelock, 'The pre-Viking Church, 21–2.

[17] For Leicester, see Mary Anne O'Donovan, 'An Interim Revision of Episcopal Dates for the Province of Canterbury, 850–950: Part 1', *Anglo-Saxon England*, I (1972), 23–44, at 27, 43–4. The see of Lindisfarne transferred to Chester-le-Street in c. 883; Keynes in Fryde *et al.*, *Handbook*, 219; A. P. Smyth, *Scandinavian York and Dublin* (2 vols, Dublin, 1975–9), I, 41–4, 96–103.

over those parts of his diocese which fell under West Saxon control.[18] Odd instances can be cited of priestly congregations that persisted despite the vicissitudes of the times, and even of their assumption of an active role in the conversion of the pagan Danish settlers.[19] Generally, however, the monastic life would seem, at least from the silence of the sources, to have suffered particularly within those dioceses where episcopal discontinuity is evident. In the northern and eastern parts of England, especially, religious congregations known from the pages of Bede's *Ecclesiastical History* and from references in early saints' lives as well as from the evidence of surviving sculpture cease to find mention in the historical record beyond the middle and later years of the ninth century.[20] With a few exceptions, most evidence for continuity in monastic observance derives from southern and western England. Most strikingly, although it is usually presumed that charters were written in Northumbria to provide written record of gifts of land made to religious communities, not one authentic diploma has survived from pre-Viking Age Northumbria.[21] While most of the accounts of the savage destruction of monastic houses and the murder of their inmates by pagan barbarians date from after the Norman Conquest and are of no historical value, the disappearance of religious houses from view leads to the assumption (albeit one derived from silence) that this reflects both the demise of those institutions and − more pertinently to this discussion − the loss of the means for the preservation of their corporate memory. Not only had the repositories of written record, the monastic archives, been lost but, worse, the dispersal of the communities responsible for their safe-keeping and the secularisation of their lands had put an end to organised forms of corporate remembrance, as the interruption to liturgical life severed the commemoration of the cults of the dead around whom a congregation's identity was shaped and sustained.[22]

Individual memories could, however, outlive the collective for-

---

[18] Mary Anne O'Donovan, 'An Interim Revision: part 2', *Anglo-Saxon England*, 2 (1972), 91–113, at 91–6. It is, of course, possible that men were still performing the role of bishop across this period when their names were not recorded, the dislocation being simply one of record-keeping, but this seems distinctly implausible in cases where the episcopal seat was relocated.

[19] For example, the *congregatio clericorum* at Horningsea mentioned in the *Liber Eliensis*, II, 32 (ed. E. O. Blake, 1962), 105; see Whitelock, ibid., xi–xii.

[20] A list of sorts may be found in David Knowles and R. Neville Hadcock, *Medieval Religious Houses: England and Wales* (2nd edn, London, 1971), appendix 1, 463–87. See, however, David N. Dumville, *Wessex and England from Alfred to Edgar* (Woodbridge, 1992), 33–49.

[21] Demonstration of the generally parlous state of Latin learning in ninth-century England is given by Michael Lapidge, *Anglo-Saxon Literature, 600–899* (1996), 409–39.

[22] See C. Cubitt, 'Universal and Local Saints in Anglo-Saxon England', in *Local Saints and Local Churches*, ed. Richard Sharpe and Alan Thacker (Oxford, forthcoming).

getfulness of a broken community and personal devotion might safeguard relics until times improved. Although there survive no contemporaneous accounts of the sufferings (or indeed of the miraculous redemption) of Northumbrian monastic communities, the cults of many Northumbrian male saints were re-remembered beyond the lacuna of ninth-century sources. The most potent example of a male community able, despite being displaced from its original home, to preserve its institutional memory through the preservation of the all-important relics of its patron saint is that of the community of St Cuthbert. The island monastery at Lindisfarne fell victim to the first datable viking raid on England in 793, yet remained in its exposed location until the 870s. The community, with the body of its most famous saint, books and presumably its land-charters,[23] set out on a seven-year wandering from 875 to 882 or 883, resting briefly at Crayke and at Norham-on-Tweed and conceivably getting as far as Whithorn, before settling finally at Chester-le-Street.[24] The continuing significance of this cult (perhaps because it could act as a focus of local Northumbrian identity in the face of West Saxon expansion) is indicated by the visit made to Cuthbert's shrine by King Æthelstan on his way to Scotland in the summer of 934;[25] the king's name was prominently recorded in the community's *Liber vitae* and he bestowed various gifts of liturgical vestments and manuscripts on the saint, one of which contains a portrait of the king making his gifts to Cuthbert himself.[26]

---

[23] E. Craster, 'The Patrimony of St Cuthbert', *English Historical Review*, 69 (1954), 177–99.

[24] *Historia regum Anglorum*, part I, *s.a.* 875 (*Symeonis Monachi Opera Omnia*, ed. T. Arnold, 2 vols, Rolls Series, London, 1882–5, II, 82) reports a nine-year wandering; part 2, *s.a.* 875 (ibid., II, 110) allocates seven years. A fuller account of the seven-year wandering is found in *Historia de Sancto Cuthberto*, ch. 20 (ibid., I, 207–8); the fully developed story in *Historia Dunelmensis ecclesiae*, II, 6–13 (ibid., I, 54–71). See Dumville, *The Churches*, 24, and n. 68, and E. Cambridge, 'Why did the Community of St Cuthbert Settle at Chester-le-Street?', in *St Cuthbert His Cult and His Community*, ed. G. Bonner *et al.* (Woodbridge, 1989), 367–86, at 379–86. That the community rested at Crayke was reported in the *Historia de Sancto Cuthberto*, ch. 20; the one-time presence of Cuthbert's relics at Norham finds mention in the earliest surviving list of saints' resting-places: *Die Heiligen Englands*, II.4 (ed. Felix Liebermann, Hanover, 1889, 10).

[25] Anglo-Saxon Chronicle 934, BCDE 933; *Historia de Sancto Cuthberto*, ch. 26 (ed. Arnoold, I, 211); Craster, 'The Patrimony', 191–2; G. Bonner, 'St Cuthbert at Chester-le-Street', in *St Cuthbert*, ed. Bonner *et al.*, 387–95, at 389–92.

[26] Corpus Christi College, Cambridge, MS. 183, fo. IV; S. Keynes, 'King Æthelstan's Books', in *Learning and Literature in Anglo-Saxon England*, ed. Michael Lapidge and Helmut Gneuss (Cambridge, 1985), 143–201, at 170–85. For other examples of relics moved (sometimes only temporarily) by their guardians away from Danish attack, compare Ermentarius, *Miracula S. Philiberti*, ch. 1 (ed. O. Holder-Egger, *MGH*, SS XV.1, Hanover, 1887, 298–9); Adrevald of Fleury, *Miracula S Benedicti*, ch. 34 (ed. Holder-Egger, ibid., 495–6); Annals of Ulster 831, 849, 878, ed. and transl. Sean Mac Airt and Gearoid mac Niocaill, Dublin Institute for Advanced Studies (Dublin, 1983).

The memory of other Northumbrian and Mercian male saints was somewhat differently constructed, or perhaps 'reinvented' after the First Viking Age. Some cults were revived via the foundation of new religious houses at the site of the former shrine, for example the refoundation of a monastery at Winchcombe in the 970s under the auspices of the reformed house at Worcester was accompanied by the revival there of the cult of St Kenelm.[27] Other relics were removed from their original resting-places and translated to areas of West Saxon hegemony. Such moves are generally interpreted by historians as representing the expression of West Saxon political dominance: as part of the process of building new *burhs* Æthelflæd (daughter of King Alfred and wife of ealdorman Æthelred of Mercia) translated the relics of luminous saints venerated in the Mercian past. Thus St Oswald's remains were taken from Bardney to Gloucester and Ealhmund's from Derby to Shrewsbury.[28] According to William of Malmesbury, King Edmund, while campaigning in the north, arranged for the removal of various Northumbrian saints including Ceolfrith of Wearmouth–Jarrow and Aidan of Lindisfarne to a new resting-place at Glastonbury, a minster with close connections with the West Saxon royal family.[29] The relics of St Wilfrid, formerly preserved at Ripon, were translated to Canterbury, probably in the aftermath of King Eadred's burning of the minster at Ripon in 948;[30] it was not solely the ravages of the Danes that denuded holy places of religious to sustain the cults of their saints.

Although the institutional memories of many religious houses appear (from the silence of the sources) to have been lost in the destruction or dissolution of minsters in the areas of the densest Danish warfare and settlement, the relocation of the cults of some of their more prominent saints to religious houses in southern and western England demonstrates that their cults had not in the interim been forgotten. The political connotations of these actions cannot be denied. The hijacking by the West Saxons of the religious history of areas they were bringing under their control enabled the conquerors to share in the spiritual benefits of their new territories and made them co-heirs of their subjects' pasts. The Northumbrian golden age was remembered enviously by King Alfred (who reminisced at the beginning of his prefatory letter to the

---

[27] A. T. Thacker, 'Kings, Saints and Monasteries in pre-Viking Mercia', *Midland History*, 10 (1985), 1–25, at 8–12.

[28] A. T. Thacker, 'Chester and Gloucester: Early Ecclesiastical Organisation in two Mercian Burhs', *Northern History*, 18 (1982), 199–211, at 203–4, 209–10; D. Rollason, 'Relic-Cults as an Instrument of Royal Policy c. 900–1050', *Anglo-Saxon England*, 15 (1986), 91–103, at 95; Thacker, 'Kings', 18.

[29] William of Malmesbury, *De gestis pontificum Anglorum*, §91 (ed. N. E. S. A. Hamilton, Rolls Series, London, 1870, 198).

[30] Anglo-Saxon Chronicle 948. Rollason, 'Relic-cults', 94.

Cura pastoralis about the happy times there were formerly throughout England when there were men of learning in religious and secular orders[31]) and Bede's *Ecclesiastical History* was one of the works translated as part of the king's programme of making significant texts available in the vernacular. It can also be argued that the monks themselves (not just the saints of whose memory they had charge) were remembered; in his vernacular account of King Edgar's monastic reform Bishop Æthelwold made direct appeal to the historic past and the monastic ideals then represented in order to justify his promotion of a complete reorganisation of the religious life, describing a lost golden age to which, in his own era, only the minster at Glastonbury was heir.[32] He thus relocated the religious memories of the pre-Viking Age, re-employing them to new ends.

Forgetting women

In the rhetoric surrounding the tenth-century monastic revolution (much of it written by Æthelwold) and in the contemporary and near-contemporaneous accounts of the process of reform, women religious attracted much less attention than their male counterparts. They were a part of the movement to the extent that the precepts of St Benedict's rule were to be introduced to women's as much as to men's houses, yet little direct attention was paid to the means by which the rule was imposed on individual congregations of women.[33] Once one looks beyond the general admonitions in the prescriptive literature in search of contemporaneous references to individual religious women or their congregations, it is striking both how poor the evidence is and how far it focuses on a small cluster of houses lying in southern and western Wessex, all with close connections to the West Saxon royal house.[34] The invisibility of women's religious houses in the literature relating to

[31] Alfred, prefatory letter, transl. Keynes and Lapidge, *Alfred the Great*, 124.

[32] Æthelwold, 'Account of King Edgar's establishment of ministers', ed. and transl. D. Whitelock *et al.*, *Councils & Synods with other Documents Relating to the English Church: I 871–1204*, 2 vols, part I, 871–1066 (Oxford, 1981), no. 33, 148–9.

[33] The only nunnery explicitly to be mentioned in any contemporaneous account of the process by which the precepts of the Rule of St Benedict were introduced was the Nunnaminster at Winchester: *Wulfstan of Winchester, The Life of St Æthelwold*, chs 16–18 (ed. and transl. M. Lapidge and M. Winterbottom, Oxford, 1991, 30–3).

[34] The women's houses that dominate the contemporary sources and later historiography are Amesbury, Barking, Horton, Romsey, Shaftesbury (and its cell at Bradford-on-Avon), Wherwell, Wilton, and the Nunnaminster at Winchester. Their prominence in the literature arises primarily because these are the only houses for which extant charters have survived. I provide here a summary of the argument defended in full in my book *Veiled Women: the Disappearance of Nuns from Anglo-Saxon England* (2 vols, Ashgate Publishing, forthcoming): the role of women in the tenth-century Benedictine revolution is analysed in vol. I, ch. 4.

the Benedictine movement is merely a part of a larger picture: nunneries are not only less well-evidenced in the tenth and eleventh centuries than male houses of the same period, but the sources for the study of women in religion after the First Viking Age are both qualitatively and quantitatively inferior to those surviving for women's houses and double communities from the period before *c.* 900.

Having been working for some time now with these evidential problems, I began my consideration of the functioning of memory beyond the ninth century from the premiss that the answers to my questions would be gendered, in that the dislocation in memory and the consequences of the loss of shared pasts would be more severe for women (and perhaps for women religious in particular) because of the demonstrable diminution and change in the nature of the evidence for the communal female religious life in England across the Viking Age. In recognising that large numbers of female houses appear, from the silence of the sources, to have been destroyed or abandoned, I presumed that they would therefore largely have been forgotten. In the coastal areas of Kent and Northumbria where Danish attack was most frequent not one of the communities of women known to have existed in the late seventh century was still active at the Norman Conquest; most had disappeared from the historical record by the early tenth century. It is just possible that descendants of the community of St Mildrith on Thanet were still active in the city of Canterbury in 1086.[35] Elsewhere in England the only site where female congregations of religious were located in the seventh and eighth centuries still housing nuns at the Conquest was at Barking, and there it is unclear if that community had a continuous existence or whether the tenth-century nunnery was refounded on the site of the earlier minster.[36] A few additional tenth- and eleventh-century female houses could trace their origins back into the early period,[37] but none of these proved able to support a con-

---

[35] At the time of the Domesday survey the lands of Minster-in-Thanet had come into the possession of St Augustine's, Canterbury, and there was only a church with one priest left on the island, but a congregation of St Mildrith's is attested in the eleventh century and four nuns who held land in alms of the abbot of St Augustine's in 1086 might, conceivably, have been the remnant of the former Thanet community: Domesday Book, 1, fo. 12ra–b.

[36] There is no evidence for the continuation of the female house at Barking between the early eighth century and the 950s, when a monastic community there received a grant from King Eadred (S 552a) and was beneficiary of the will of Ealdorman Ælfgar: ibid., no 1483. It is not, however, necessary to believe the late eleventh-century account of Goscelin of St-Bertin's that the abbess and nuns were burnt to death by the Danes in 870: *Lecciones de sancta Hildelitha*, ch. 2 (ed. M. L. Colker, 'Texts of Jocelyn of Canterbury which Relate to the History of Barking Abbey', *Studia Monastica*, 7 (1965), 383–460, at 455).

[37] These houses are Berkeley, Boxwell, Castor, Cheddar, Leominster, Wareham, Warwick, Wenlock, Wimborne, and Winchcombe.

gregation of religious women to the end of the Anglo-Saxon period.

There are, however, two problems with my over-simplistic explanation that women were somehow peculiarly disadvantaged in the preservation of memory, not having recourse to the same mechanisms as their male counterparts. First, it cannot be argued that all female saints of the pre-Viking Age were forgotten, together with the congregations who had promoted their cults; the relics of women saints also were translated from the areas of Danish settlement to western and southern England. Æthelflæd moved the remains of St Werburg from Hanbury to Chester, Hild of Whitby was supposedly removed to Glastonbury along with other celebrated figures from the Northumbrian golden age, and there is even one community of women that seems to have retained something of its corporate identity around the relics of its most famous former member. The nuns of St Mildrith were certainly forced away from their island home in the ninth century, taking refuge first at Lyminge and later perhaps with that congregation inside the walls of Canterbury,[38] but a mid-tenth-century charter defined a Kentish estate in terms of its relationship to the community's boundary for St Mildrith ('þæs hiredes mearc to sancte Mildryþe')[39] and an abbess Leofrun captured in the Danish siege of Canterbury in 1011 was identified by John of Worcester as head of a monastery dedicated to St Mildrith.[40] Female cults may not have been prominent in the tenth and eleventh centuries but some holy women from the pre-Viking Age were remembered and commemorated.

Second, the inadequacy of the evidence for women's religious houses after c. 900 (whether demonstrated via the silences of texts from the late Anglo-Saxon period or from their invisibility in the work of later medieval historians and antiquaries) should not be attributed to a deliberate suppression or obfuscation of the role of women in religion. Nuns had access to the same mechanisms for the preservation and promotion of their collective pasts as had monks. The silence of the sources more plausibly reflects the realities of the position of women religious during and after the Viking wars: groups of nuns did indeed suffer disproportionately in time of war, perhaps because their congregations afforded undeniable attractions to marauding sea-borne warbands, but perhaps less dramatically because their blood families had the sense to confine their daughters to better-defended sites

---

[38] Goscelin, *Libellus contra inanes sanctae uirginis Mildrethae usurpatores*, ch. 4 (ed. M. L. Colker, 'A Hagiographic Polemic', *Mediaeval Studies*, 39 (1977), 60–108, at 74–5). Lyminge was granted a refuge from the Danes at Canterbury in 804: S 160.

[39] S 535, AD 948.

[40] Anglo-Saxon Chronicle, 1011 CD; EF have wrongly 'Leofwine'. *The Chronicle of John of Worcester, II The Annals from 450 to 1066, s.a. 1011* (ed. R. R. Darlington *et al.*, Oxford, 1995, 468–9).

before their chastity could be compromised. Equally pertinent to the discontinuance of female religion may have been the need for their monastic lands for the defence of the kingdom against this external threat. In the face of frequent military incursions, the maintenance of strategically vulnerable women's religious houses and their protection from destruction must have looked like a luxury no prudent king or nobleman could afford to sustain. And once a community had been dissolved, who was to preserve its corporate memory? A lay acquisitor of its lands might acquire its earlier charters as proof of ownership (and the charters of some early Anglo-Saxon women's houses have indeed survived, preserved in the archives of male monasteries and cathedral churches), but such an individual or institution had greater need to bolster his own claim to the title than to record the circumstances of the women's renunciation of their estates.

Further, other reasons can in fact be adduced to account for the discontinuities in the historical record for women's religious houses across the First Viking Age which are not illusory. The start of the decline in the number of female communities can in fact be perceived as early as the middle years of the eighth century and seems to reflect changes in patterns of aristocratic landholding, coupled with an apparent reluctance on the part of the nobility to continue alienating land permanently from the kin group to congregations of women whose liturgical function was limited by their inability to say masses for the dead. Since the dislocations of war followed closely upon this apparent change, it was only in the tenth century that its effects first become visible; then, although there were few congregations of nuns living enclosed lives on permanently endowed estates, there were many more small, informally organised groups of religious women, living on the margins of the secular world on estates which either belonged to one of their number by inheritance or had been assigned to her use for her lifetime while still ultimately belonging to her male kin. These *Deo deuotae* contrived to maximise their own entitlement to the usufruct of land in order to satisfy their religious devotion without compromising the desire of their male kin to retain the land within the family. The distinction between the professed nun (*mynecena*) and the secular *nunne* is made explicit in the prescriptive literature of the later tenth and eleventh centuries but the significance of this dichotomy has hitherto escaped historians:[41] the religious woman appears invisible in the sources for the later Anglo-Saxon Church precisely because she more commonly

---

[41] V Æthelred, chs 4–4.1 (ed. Felix Liebermann, *Die Gesetze der Angelsachsen*, 3 vols, Halle, 1903–16, I, 238): ', huruþinga Godes þeowas—biscopas , abbudas, munecas , mynecena, preostas , nunnan—to rihte gebugan , regollice libban , for eall Cristen folc þingian georne'. Compare VI Æthelred, ch. 2.2 and I Cnut, ch. 6a (ibid., 246 and 288).

expressed her devotion outside the royal structure of the cloistered monastery, remaining within her own family nexus as a vowed, veiled woman. Communities established around such women were necessarily ephemeral; one might more reasonably remark on the number that have left written record than lament the paucity of sources in which they find mention. The pattern of the evidence for religious women in pre-Conquest England thus reflects practical realities; it cannot be used either to argue for a gendered perception of the validity of the female past, or for the possibility that groups of women failed to exploit routes of commemoration that were available to their male counterparts.

Inventing a political past

Following his decisive victory over the Danes at Edington in 878 and the agreement with their defeated leader over a division of land that would exile the Danes from his realm, Alfred, king of the West Saxons, seems to have sought to extend his authority over all the Anglo-Saxon peoples outside the Danelaw and to unite them in common cause. His political dominance of the south and west of England was formally acknowledged in 886 in a ceremony at which the Anglo-Saxon chronicler reported that all the *Angelcynn* not subject to the Danes submitted to Alfred's authority.[42] This political label, as I have previously argued, is significant in that it provided a name for the imagined community to which all Alfred's newly united subjects might now belong;[43] at the same time the king adopted a new regnal style calling himself 'king of the Angles and Saxons', or 'king of the Anglo-Saxons', a name suggesting a new vision rather than an appeal to history.[44] Yet, in order to legitimise and promote the ideal of a single people, Alfred invented a notion of a past common to all his subjects in which all the members of his new realm might share, by means of historical texts translated (and in the case of the Anglo-Saxon Chronicle constructed) as part of his programme of educational reform. By appropriating his subject people's separate – Christian – pasts, Alfred drew their separate threads together in order to weave a single story that showed how former

---

[42] Anglo-Saxon Chronicle 886; Asser, *Life of King Alfred*, ch. 83, ed. W. H. Stevenson, *Asser's Life of King Alfred* (Oxford, 1904; new impression, 1959), 69; transl. Keynes and Lapidge, *Alfred the Great*, 98.

[43] S. Foot, 'The making of *Angelcynn*: English identity before the Norman Conquest', *TRHS*, 6th series 6 (1996), 25–49, at 27–37.

[44] S. Keynes, 'King Alfred and the Mercians', in *Kings, Currency and Alliances: the History and Coinage of Southern England, AD 840–900*, ed. M. A. S. Blackburn and D. N. Dumville (Woodbridge, 1998), 1–45, at 24–6; S. Keynes, 'The West Saxon Charters of King Æthelwulf and his Sons', *English Historical Review*, 109 (1994), 1109–49, at 1147–9.

disunity was a necessary precursor to present unity.[45] He thus envisaged
a past sufficient to fill the void left by the erasure of memory across
the Viking wars, and in offering a teleological explanation of what had
gone before spoke also to the future. It would be possible to claim this
as an instance of memory restored, but what the texts of the Alfredian
court promote is rather a given, gilded past, one constructed in the
image of the present, that above all serves present needs in its appeal
to a former golden age. Although the king's endeavour could be
interpreted as constructing a collective memory, there was in fact little
reminiscent about the past that Alfred invented.[46]   Narrating the past
imbues it with meaning; narration establishes relationships between
disparate fragments of imperfectly recollected time, providing a sense of
direction and repairing the traumatic break of dislocation by providing
substitute for the memory that has been lost. The historical writings of
the Alfredian court fit the English past into the divine plan; they
demonstrate the part played by the English within God's larger, linear
scheme for humanity's progression to salvation, by restoring the English
to the path of grace. Memory and inquiry appear to be working
together. But this is illusion. In fact narrating a supposed common past
in this fashion dislocates the story from memory. What all the freeborn
young men among the English were to know is what they had learnt
through reading such texts. Their common past was not known to them
by experience; it could not be remembered. The political advantage of
this from the point of view of Alfred (and even more so of his yet more
ambitious successors) is that it could not be challenged; the Alfredian
historical vision supplied a post hoc justification for a new political
reality achieved by military prowess and the force of the king's own
personality. I return to Alfred's preface to his translation of Pope
Gregory's *Cura pastoralis*:[47]

When I reflected on all this I recollected how – before everything
was ransacked and burned – the churches throughout England
stood filled with treasures and books. Similarly, there was a great
multitude of those serving God. And they derived very little

[45] Foot, 'The making of *Angelcynn*', 28–9 and 35–7; the relevant texts are Bede's *Historia ecclesiastica*, Orosius, Seven books of histories against the pagans, and the Anglo-Saxon Chronicle. See also A. P. Smyth, 'The Emergence of English Identity, 700–1000', in *Medieval Europeans: Studies in Ethnic Identity and National Perspectives in Medieval Europe*, ed. Smyth (1998), 24–52, at 39–44; and for historical writing, A. Scharer, 'The Writing of History at King Alfred's Court', *Early Medieval Europe*, 5 (1996), 177–206.
[46] Compare the fabrication of a collective past by the Carolingians, discussed by Innes, 'Memory', 11, and particularly by R. McKitterick, 'Constructing the Past in the Early Middle Ages: the Case of the Royal Frankish Annals', *TRHS*, 6th series, 7 (1997), 101–29, at 113–17 and 125–9.
[47] Alfred, prose preface, transl. Keynes and Lapidge, *Alfred the Great*, 125.

benefit from those books because they could understand nothing of them, since they were not written in their own language. It is as if they had said: 'Our ancestors, who formerly maintained these places, loved wisdom and through it they obtained wealth and passed it on to us. Here one can still see the track, but we cannot follow it'. Therefore we have now lost the wealth as well as the wisdom, because we did not wish to set our minds to the track.

Alfred's preservation of the past in writing restored the track for his people to follow. His construction of a new identity was aimed at an (expanded) literate elite and he was explicitly trying to disseminate his ideas as widely as possible, but I hesitate to call this an appeal to 'memory'. What the Alfredian texts did was to create a notion of a shared past that could be co-memorated, but was no more capable of being 'remembered' than were the forgotten pasts of male and female monastics whose liturgical commemoration had been broken. Memory cannot survive across caesura (or may not be allowed to do so by a new regime), but an imaginative man with a vision can invent an idea of the past and then ensure that it is taught for co-memoration (and as is clear from the appeal that was made to this past later in the tenth and eleventh centuries, it rapidly in fact became the accepted orthodoxy).

The difference between this kind of learnt memorial and the genuinely recollected past was made clear by the tenth-century chronicler Æthelweard. A layman, related to the West Saxon royal house, Æthelweard produced a Latin epitome of the Anglo-Saxon Chronicle for his relative Matilda, abbess of Essen. In explaining how he had set about recounting the migration of 'our nation' Æthelweard reported that he had turned to the help of God and drawn on 'the annalists from the beginning of the world', but where he would dwell upon his and Matilda's joint family in modern times and the re-affirmation of their relationship he would recount 'so far as memory provides proof and as our parents taught us'.[48] Æthelweard located memory (both recollection and implicitly forgetfulness) firmly in the sphere of the individual and of the family group. Although memories recalled in this fashion are patently themselves constructed and shaped by interaction with other members of the family and the wider social group (and are not notably more accurate or 'truthful'), there is a meaningful distinction to be sustained between

---

[48] *The Chronicle of Æthelweard*, prologue (ed. and transl. A. Campbell, 1962, 1–2): 'in quantum memoria nostra argumentatur et sicut docuere parentes'.

this reminiscent process and the invention of a past to which all Alfred's subjects were supposedly heir.

Well, you see the first thing is I don't believe in public memory. A memory's a biochemical change in an individual brain, and that's all there is.[49]

[49] Pat Barker, *Another World* (1998), 84–5.

GENDER AND AUTHORITY OF ORAL WITNESSES IN EUROPE (800–1300)

By Elisabeth van Houts

READ 26 MARCH 1998 AT THE UNIVERSITY OF SUSSEX

BETWEEN 1068 and 1070 an extraordinary dispute was settled at Bonneville-sur-Touques in Normandy. Duke William, who had recently become king of England, and his wife Matilda, heard the story of a contested property at Bayeux which centred on the identity of a rented child. The story goes as follows. A man called Stephen had married a widow called Oringa by whom he had a small son (*puerulus*) who lived only a short while. When the boy died, Oringa substituted for him, without her husband's knowledge, the son of a woman called Ulburga at Martragny (Calvados, c. Creully), to whom she paid an annual sum of 100 *solidi*. Stephen made the boy his heir and left him his property. When first Oringa and then Stephen died, the boy's natural mother emerged and demanded rent from the couple's surprised relatives. The family refused to pay and Ulberga turned to Duke William and his wife Matilda. Having heard the case Duke William, in consultation with Archbishop John of Rouen, Roger of Beaumont and others, decided that an ordeal of the hot iron would be the most appropriate way to establish the truth. William and Matilda sent their chaplain Rainald to Bayeux to organise the ordeal, which took place in the monastery of Saint-Vigor in the presence of Rainald himself, two named archdeacons, Robert *Insule* and his wife Albereda, Euremarus of Bayeux and many other good men (*meliores homines*) of Bayeux. Ulburga emerged unscathed from the ordeal by fire and therefore her son was returned to her. The property involved, however, returned to the duke who gave it to his wife Matilda, who in turn gave it to Rainald. He retired to Jumièges as a monk and before he died wrote down the story of the property, which ultimately passed to the monastery of Jumièges.[1]

The case of the rented child is interesting because it illustrates several points pertinent to my essay.[2] The case highlights the close collaboration

---

[1] *Regesta Regum Anglo-Normannorum. The Acta of William I (1066–87)*, ed. D. Bates (Oxford, 1998), no. 162, 530–3.

[2] For the aspect of the exchange of young children, see J. Boswell, *The Kindness of Strangers. The Abandonment of Children in Western Europe from Late Antiquity to the Renaissance* (New York, 1988), 447–8.

between Duke William of Normandy and his wife Matilda: she not only sat with the duke when the case was first heard but also acted as a witness in the property dispute.[3] It also tells us about the witnesses to the ordeal. The most important of those named, some of them priests and some laymen, are described as 'good men' of Bayeux, the normal collection of jurors and witnesses who testified to this kind of case in customary medieval law.[4] Unusually and importantly, however, the story also gives the name of a female lay witness Albereda, the wife of Robert *Insule*, who testified to the outcome of Ulberga's ordeal. Three women, then, played an important role in the outcome of this property dispute: Ulberga whose insistence to have her child back initiated the whole case; Duchess Matilda who, with her husband, heard the case, acted as witness to the property dispute and, briefly, held the property before she passed it on to Rainald; and Albereda, the only female witness to the ordeal of the hot iron, whose presence was specifically recorded. The question why Albereda's name was singled out is one of a series of questions related to the status of witnesses in medieval law. In particular, the value of testimonies by women and the authority (or lack of it) of their stories about the past will be the subject of this essay. The present investigation thereby complements my recent work based primarily on historiographical and hagiographical sources, rather than on legal records.[5]

In Roman law free men could act as witnesses, but free women could not, because they were not admitted to any public office:

> a woman is subject to the power of a man and has no authority, nor is she able to instruct nor to be a witness nor to make a promise nor to make a legal judgement.[6]

The sixth-century law-codes of Emperor Justinian also stipulate that women are banned from public office and that they cannot act as judge, advocate or witness in court:

> Women are debarred from all civil and public functions and therefore cannot be judges or hold a magistracy or bring a lawsuit or intervene on behalf of anyone else or act as procurators. Likewise, someone

---

[3] For Matilda's role, see *Regesta*, ed. Bates, 93–4.

[4] K. Nehlsen-van Stryk, *Die boni homines des frühen Mittelalters unter besonderer Berücksichtigung der fränkischen Quellen* (Berlin, 1981), 242–54 and 344–8.

[5] E. van Houts, *Memory and Gender in Medieval Europe, 900–1200* (London, 1999).

[6] Gratian, *Decretum*, Part II, Causa 33, question 5, no. xvii (*Corpus Iuris Canonici*, ed. A. Friedberg (Leipzig, 1879), 1255; *Woman Defamed and Woman Defended. An Anthology of Medieval Texts*, ed. A. Blamires (Oxford, 1992), 83–7, at 86. The original quote for this passage is said by Gratian to be St Ambrose but is in fact the Ambrosiaster.

who is not grown up must abstain from all civil functions.[7]

All references to people mentioned in the codes which are not gender specific, therefore, must be assumed to refer only to men. Canon law – the law of the Church – evolved directly from Roman law and repeated its prohibition for women to act in public capacities. Gratian in his *Decretum*, written in *c.* 1140, repeated Roman law and thereafter through the Middle Ages Canon lawyers advised that women should not act as witnesses, not even in marriage litigation, and that if they did so their evidence should be treated with the greatest possible scepticism.[8] As James Brundage has noted, much of what such academic writers had to say about the law of evidence, in particular with regard to marriage, concubinage, prostitution and sex offences, was biased in favour of men. The Canonists were well aware of this. One of them, the influential Cardinal Hostiensis (d. 1271), put his thoughts into writing and stated why the law is often against women. Women cannot be judges or arbitrators, they cannot teach, preach, hear confessions, or exercise other types of spiritual power, nor may they receive holy orders, plead in court or act as notaries or guardians (except for their own children). In addition, continued Hostiensis, women cannot bring criminal accusations, adopt children, hold public office, act as agents, be witnesses to wills or work as silversmiths. Nevertheless, women could act as sureties for debts and were indeed preferred to men in that capacity, although many assumed that if they did act as sureties they still did not know the law. They could also secure the discharge of unqualified guardians of their minor sons. And as Hostiensis tantalisingly concludes: 'there are many other examples but these will suffice in order to keep the discussion brief'. Of roles which women may play we would like to know precisely what other roles he had in mind.[9] As we will see later, the practice was often very different from the theory which excluded women.

Thus far the Roman and Canon law. What, on the other hand, was the attitude of the medieval Germanic lawyers? The position of witnesses in early customary law is difficult to assess. Firstly, no court cases along the lines of Roman law existed. Instead disputes were settled by arbitration, consensus and compromise. In complicated or tricky cases when other forms of arbitration failed, people resorted to 'irrational methods' of proof: the ordeals of the hot iron or fire, the *duellum*, that

---

[7] Justinian, *Digesta*, 50, 17, 2, see *The Digest of Justinian*. Latin text edited by T. Mommsen with the aid of P. Krueger; English translation edited by A. Watson, 4 vols (Philadelphia, 1985), IV, 957.
[8] J. A. Brundage, *Law, Sex and Christian Society in Medieval Europe* (Chicago–London, 1987), 483, n. 325.
[9] Brundage, *Law*, 485.

is trial by battle, or compurgation.[10] The purgatory oath was the sworn affirmation by the accused or the plaintiff of his own innocence or the justness of his case, and each was normally assisted by members of his family or neighbourhood who swore to his good character and joined their oaths to his.[11] The difficulty for our subject is that compurgators and oath helpers are witnesses of a sort, even though they were not witnesses like the witnesses of Roman or Canon law. In practice, as we shall see, the distinction between them is very difficult to draw.[12] They did not need to be eyewitnesses or to be particularly knowledgeable about the matter in hand, as long as they were prepared to swear in good faith and back up the person whom they supported. Amongst oath helpers women can be found, though their presence is rarely singled out. The nearest to the type of Roman and Canon law witnesses were the *boni homines*, the good men of the law, chosen from the free men who would confirm customs and practices or denounce new customs as not being valid. They always operated in groups and never individually.[13]

No evidence has been found that a woman could act as a *bonus homo*, but the *Très ancien coutumier de Normandie*, the oldest surviving customary law-code of France written not later than 1199, refers to a comparable group of 'good women and lawful matrons' (*bonae mulieres et legales matronae*).[14] The female group is cited in the section 'on girls' (*de puellis*) that deals with rape, the wounds caused by sexual violation and the trial of rapists, who could be convicted on the oath and testimony of the 'good women' alone. The context of sexual violence and the role of women to assess the damage and bring to trial the accused men explains the gender-specific role of (medical) assessors fulfilled by women whose expertise was clearly recognised. It was valued so much that if

---

[10] F. L. Ganshof, 'La preuve dans le droit franc', *La Preuve*, Recueils de la Société Jean Bodin (4 vols, Paris, 1965), II, 71–98; For the ordeals, see P. Hyams, 'Trial by ordeal. The key to proof in the early common law', *On the Laws and Customs of England. Essays in Honor of Samuel E. Thorne*, ed. M. S. Arnold *et al.* (Chapel Hill, 1981), 90–126; R. Bartlett, *Trial by Fire and Water. The Medieval Judicial Ordeal* (Oxford, 1986), 13–33.

[11] M. Boulet-Sautel, 'Aperçu sur les systèmes des preuves dans la France coutumière du moyen âge', *La Preuve*, 275–326, at 304–15. R. C. van Caenegem, *Legal History. A European Perspective* (London–Rio Grande, 1991), 71–114 at 73–82.

[12] P. Wormald, 'Oaths', *The Blackwell Encyclopaedia of Anglo-Saxon England*, ed. M. Lapidge *et al.* (Oxford, 1999), 338–9.

[13] Nehlsen-van Stryk, *Die boni homines*, 250–1. The author does not explicitly discuss the gender of the *boni homines*; for a nobilis matrona, see 251, n. 44.

[14] *Coutumiers de Normandie. Textes Critiques, I: Le Très Ancien Coutumier de Normandie*, ed. E. J. Tardif (Rouen, 1881), 40–1. S. Shahar, *The Fourth Estate. A History of Women in the Middle Ages*, transl. C. Galai (London–New York, 1983), 14–15. The office of the legal matron thus is older than suggested by J. Murray, 'On the origins and the role of "wise women" in causes for annulment on the grounds of male impotence', *Journal of Medieval History*, 16 (1990), 235–49, esp. 241, 243, where the beginning of the thirteenth century is given.

the women did not find evidence of rape, a girl complaining that such a violation had taken place would not be believed and would be whipped instead. The continuing role of the good women and legal matrons is well attested for Normandy and from the thirteenth century onwards in the rest of France and England as well.[15] Its origin, however, is more difficult to establish. The Norman charter of 1068x70, in which Albereda *Insule* is named as a lay witness, is perhaps the earliest evidence from Normandy. The case did not involve rape and Albereda is not explicitly described as a 'good woman'. It is reasonable to suppose, however, that because the case involved motherhood, female witness was thought necessary in addition to the 'good men'; Albereda was surely present in a legal capacity.

The lack of explicit statements on the legal role of women in law-codes, combined with the fluid boundaries between *boni homines* and witnesses, precludes drawing firm conclusions about the validity of women's presence at court. Many cases can be cited where women attended dispute settlements in an ill-defined capacity. If they were neither the accused, nor the plaintiff, witness and oath helper, why would the recorders of such cases bother to list their names and cite their presence? A well-known Carolingian case will illustrate that sometimes the presence of one or more women was considered to be vital. In 861 a large group of twenty-three men and seventeen women, of whom ten brought their children, came before Charles the Bald. They were *coloni* of the villa of Mitry, which belonged to the monastery of Saint-Denis, and had travelled some 60 km to attend the royal court at Compiègne.[16] Their complaint was that they wished to be treated by Saint-Denis's agent Deodadus as free *coloni* and not as slaves (*servi*). Charles ordered that the testimony of the twenty-three men be confirmed by a similarly large group of other *coloni* from the same villa. The second group, however, stated that since the time of Louis the Pious the men and their ancestors had always been serfs and had done more work than the *coloni* had. The king accepted this testimony and the case was settled in Saint-Denis's favour. The intriguing question is what the women and children did at this tribunal. Serfdom passed on in the female line and the children of a non-free woman were not themselves free whether their father was or not. The women and children in the Mitry case had made the long journey to attend the

---

[15] K. Gravdal, *Ravishing Maidens. Writing Rape in Medieval French Literature and Law* (Philadelphia, 1991), 122–40.

[16] *Actes de Charles II le Chauve*, ed. G. Tessier (Paris, 1952), II, no. 228, pp. 7–9. J. Nelson, *Charles the Bald* (London, 1992), 62–3, where the distance between Mitry and Compiègne is highlighted as a factor. The numbers of men and women involved is confusing because one person, *Lurduinus*, a man's name, is said to have brought his children. Nelson counts him as a woman implying a scribal mistake for *Lurduina*.

tribunal because, it can be suggested, their knowledge about their status might have been needed by the men, legally the plaintiffs, in pleading their case. Not only knowledge about their origin and past, but knowledge for the future was an essential ingredient of any lawsuit. The mothers, single women and children were present to hear the outcome so that they would know what new knowledge to pass on to their children, grandchildren or great-grandchildren.[17] Technically, therefore, they were not *boni homines* or witnesses or oath helpers, and therefore did not play any legal role in the proceedings,[18] but in practice their presence meant that they could have been, and probably were, consulted about their past. It also meant that the women would have picked up vital details for the future. For the scribe of Saint-Denis (presumably Grimbald the notary who is mentioned) the names of the women, and where applicable their status as mother, were as essential information as the names of the men. In order to avoid future problems, Grimbald – like Rainald of Jumièges in the Norman case discussed above – recorded the names of all those present. Clearly, the line between the (legally) active and the (legally) passive participants of this dispute is a fine one.

The presence of children at Compiègne, too, raises the question whether they were there only because of their mothers and the lack of alternative childcare at Mitry. The boys and girls are referred to as *infantes*, and thus were still young. Children could not act as witnesses in Roman and Canon law and they are not mentioned in any Germanic law-code as such. Other documentary evidence shows, however, that young people not infrequently attended events of which their memories might later come in useful. As in the case of the 'good women and legal matrons', the evidence comes from Normandy. Several mid-eleventh-century Norman charters mention small boys attending ceremonies of grants of land to the monastery of Saint-Pierre at Préaux and the cathedral of Rouen. They were there as witnesses so that later on in life they might testify that property had been handed over to the monks. To make sure that they did not forget, the Rouen adults 'whipped many little boys and [then] refreshed [them] in record and

---

[17] For the assumption that knowledge about unfreedom could be stated by the great-grandchildren of an unfree woman, see *Philippe de Beaumanoir: Coutumes de Beauvaisis*, ed. A. Salmon (Paris, 1899–1900), and *The Coutumes de Philippe de Beaumanoir*, transl. F. R. P. Akehurst (Philadelphia, 1992), ch. 45, paras 1433–4, p. 511 (all page references are to Akehurst's translation).

[18] Ganshof does not draw attention to the female presence (Ganshof, 'La preuve', 81–3), while Nelson assumes that their legal incapacity was the reason that they themselves did not testify (J. Nelson, 'Dispute Settlement in Carolingian West Francia', *The Settlement of Disputes in Early Medieval Europe*, ed. W. Davies and P. Fouracre (Cambridge, 1986), 45–64, at 51–2).

memory of this deed', while at Préaux three boys were beaten.[19] When one of them asked Humphrey de Vieilles, the founder of Saint-Pierre, why he had hit him, Humphrey answered: 'because you are younger than I and perhaps you will live a long time and you will be a witness of this business when[ever] there is a need...'.[20] Thus the children were made to remember these occasions by whipping and slapping them, a primitive but no doubt effective method to ensure that they would not forget the grants. In Normandy, as elsewhere, common sense encouraged fathers to bring their sons with them to watch momentous events long before they were called to testify as witnesses,[21] and they evidently took it for granted that should the boys be called upon in later life to act as witnesses their testimony would be accepted as valid, despite their having been only boys at the time. There is no similar evidence from other parts of France or from England, but it was permissible there for sons to provide hearsay evidence in court about events at which they had not been present themselves; they could testify on the basis of what they had been told by their fathers who had witnessed grants or settlements of disputes.[22] Interestingly, the practice of passing on knowledge from one generation to another in twelfth-century French and English chronicles was considered valid as long as the chain of informants was restricted to three generations: father, son and grandson.[23]

Written records of inquests (*inquisitiones*) have survived from the Carolingian period onwards though with a gap for the tenth and eleventh century. Despite this gap historians agree that as an administrative tool the Carolingian inquest survived without too many differences, especially in Normandy.[24] Very rarely do the inquests contain references to women as members of the jury or as witnesses. None of the Anglo-Saxon law-codes explicitly forbids women to sit on a jury or to act as witness, but their general absence from juries is usually taken

[19] *Recueil des actes des ducs de Normandie de 911 à 1066*, ed. M. Fauroux (Caen, 1961), no. 10, pp. 81–2, at 82: ... et flagelaverunt [sic] ibi plures puerulos atque bene refocillaverunt in recordatione et memoratione hujus facti; the translation comes from E. Z. Tabuteau, *Transfers of Property in Eleventh-Century Norman Law* (Chapel Hill–London, 1988), 148.

[20] *Recueil des actes*, ed. Fauroux, no. 89, pp. 230–1, at 231: '...quia tu junior me es et forte multo vives tempore erisque testis hujus rationis cum res poposcerit'. Translation Tabuteau, *Transfers*, 148.

[21] For an example from Marmoutiers, see Tabuteau, *Transfers*, 149, and from Poitou, see J. Martindale, 'His special friend?' The settlement of disputes and political power in the kingdom of the French, tenth to mid-twelfth century', *TRHS*, 6th series, 5 (1995), 21–57, at 57.

[22] Y. Bongert, *Recherches sur les cours laiques du Xe au XIIIe siècle* (Paris, 1949), 256–7, n. 3; *The Treatise on the Laws and Customs of the Realm of England commonly called Glanvill*, ed. G. D. G. Hall (London, 1965), Book II, ch. 17, pp. 34–5.

[23] Van Houts, *Memory and Gender*, 27–8.

[24] M. Boulet-Sautel, 'La preuve', 308–15, and esp. 310, n. 2; Bongert, *Recherches*, 263.

as evidence that they were not supposed to testify.[25] They could, however, be present and the men who acted as jurors or witnesses may well have drawn upon their memories.[26] Even when they were not present they could be consulted and their word would be accepted.[27] The most famous eleventh-century inquest is the one of 1085 that resulted in the *Domesday Book* survey. This great record contains only one explicit reference to a female witness, Edith the nun, as the woman to whom land had been leased and for which she was prepared to do service in King Edward's time. In King William's time she had returned the land. *Domesday Book* concludes its reference to her by stating that 'she is still living and this is her testimony' (*ipsa adhuc vivens inde est testis*), words that carry the clear implication that anyone who wished to check the information could go and see her.[28] Another famous example of an inquest, the so-called *Roll of the Ladies and the Boys and Girls*, also comes from England and dates from one century later.[29] It is devoted exclusively to women and children, and is based almost entirely on information which ultimately derived from the women themselves. The list of widows and their dependant children was drawn up at the orders of King Henry II (1154–89) to establish the numbers of widows and wards in his kingdom for tax and marriage purposes. Knowledge of the ages of the women and children involved enabled the king to calculate how many of the widows were still available in the marriage market as rewards for young landless knights, and for how many under-age children he could levy wardship fines. The list was divided by shire and in each shire the evidence was collected by two investigative judges.

---

[25] A. L. Klinck, 'Anglo-Saxon women and the law', *Journal of Medieval History*, 8 (1982), 107–21, at 116–17. R. Fleming, 'Oral Testimony and the Domesday Inquest', *Anglo-Norman Studies*, 17 (1994), 101–22, and C. P. Lewis, 'The Domesday Jurors', *The Haskins Society Journal*, 5 (1993), 17–44.

[26] This was clearly the case when the widow Siflaed spoke against Bishop Aethelwold (963–84) at eight combined hundred courts of Northamptonshire and East Anglia, *Liber Eliensis*, ed. E. O. Blake (London, 1962), Book III, ch. 11, pp. 84–6, and Fleming, 'Oral testimony', p. 103. For other cases where women spoke on oath or were said that they could do so, see *Anglo-Saxon Charters: An Annotated List and Bibliography*, ed. P. Sawyer (London, 1968), no. 1187, p. 349, and no. 1454, p. 408; cf. commentary by C. Hough, 'Women', *The Blackwell Encyclopaedia of Anglo-Saxon England*, ed. M. Lapidge *et al.* (Oxford, 1999), p. 486.

[27] The widow of Herefordshire spoke to the thegns sent to her to hear her view, which was accepted (ibid., no. 1462; *English Historical Documents, c. 500–1042*, ed. D. Whitelock (Oxford, 1955), no. 135, p. 556; E. van Houts, *Memory and Gender*, 79–80.

[28] R. Fleming, *Domesday Book and the Law. Society and Legal Custom in Early Medieval England* (Cambridge, 1998), p. 260, no. 1658; ibid., p. 45, n. 66. Fleming suggests that Edith's testimony may have been submitted in writing.

[29] *Rotuli de Dominabus et Pueris et Puellis de XII Comitatibus*, ed. J. H. Round, The Pipe Roll Society (London, 1913). For an analysis of the information pertaining to the history of the family, see J. S. Moore, 'The Anglo-Norman family: size and structure', *Anglo-Norman Studies*, 14 (1991), 153–96.

It has been assumed that locally the information was presented to the hundred courts by male juries and that none of the women were interrogated by the judges themselves. Ultimately, however, the information on ages of the women and the children must have come from them even though it was passed on to the judges by the local male authorities. Women under forty were listed with their precise age, but if they were older their age was given in round numbers of decades. After the age of forty few women were expected to be able to bear children and therefore they were not attractive any longer as potential marriage partners. As witnesses for the ages of themselves and of their children the list is valuable, but there is an added interest. Many women gave the names of their fathers, grandfathers and occasionally great-grandfathers as well as their husbands' names and sometimes backgrounds. These mini-histories of women are a potentially rich but as yet untapped source for local memorial family traditions, which illustrate women's knowledge of their background. Moreover, the nature of the list, concentrating on widows and fatherless children, is a conclusive proof how the absence of men turned women into bearers of testimony.

A completely different form of inquest is the ecclesiastical inquest which developed towards the end of the twelfth century as a means of establishing someone's sanctity.[30] Despite the Canon law prohibitions that women could not act as witnesses, the legal depositions prepared for the Curia in Rome contain a considerable number of witness accounts from women, in particular in cases of female saints.[31] A good example is the case of St Elisabeth of Hungary who lived from 1207 to 1231. Born as the daughter of King Andrew II of Hungary, she married Landgrave Louis IV of Thuringia in 1221. After his death six years later she was evicted from her home by her brother-in-law and began a life of much greater austerity than the one she had led thus far. She founded a hospital in Marburg where she helped the sick and the poor, and where she died of self-inflicted suffering in 1231. Within four years she was canonised by Pope Gregory IX on the basis of hundreds of witness accounts claiming her holiness and miracles. One of the central documents to the case was the so-called 'Book based on the testimonies of four servants of St. Elisabeth'. It consisted of a life composed entirely from the testimonies of four women who knew her well. The first two were Guda, her exact contemporary, who had been educated with her

---

[30] For a more general study of witnesses in ecclesiastical courts, see C. Donahue, 'Proof by witness in the church courts of medieval England: an imperfect reception of the learned law', *On the Laws and Customs*, ed. Arnold, 127–58.

[31] A. Vauchez, *Sainthood in the Later Middle Ages*, transl. J. Birrell (Cambridge, 1997), 33–58; D. Elliott, *Spiritual Marriage. Sexual Abstinence in Medieval Wedlock* (Princeton, 1993), 266–87.

from the age of five and who later entered her service as her companion, and Isentrudis, who as a widow became one of Elisabeth's maids after her marriage to Louis of Thuringia. Between them Guda and Isentrudis covered her life from childhood to marriage. The others were the nuns (*ancillae*) Elisabeth and Irmengard, who shared Elisabeth's life at the hospital in Marburg. The stories told by these women illustrate the daily world of an aristocratic woman, her life at court, and her later life of charity and care for the sick in Marburg. The private world of women is central to their testimonies which were, as it turned out, absolutely essential. A first attempt to establish the case for Elisabeth's canonisation, based on a life written by her chaplain Conrad of Marburg, had failed due to a lack of witnesses testifying specifically to her sanctity. The evidence which the women were in a position to provide – e.g. that Elisabeth had demonstrated profound piety when still a child by tricking her playmates into following her into the chapel and by persuading them to kneel and pray there – made all the difference. In the document which contains their accounts there is no sign of doubt expressed concerning the fact that as women they were not trustworthy.[32]

Thus far it seems that despite a lack of written evidence in law-codes that women and children were permitted to give evidence in court they did in practice provide vital testimony in cases concerning property, the settlement of disputes involving personal freedom, care of a child, the establishment of the ages of children, and the sanctity of close associates. What prevailed in the Carolingian period and the following centuries was the use of common sense allowing women and children, normally barred from official legal positions to be present, to look on, to remember in case their knowledge had to be tapped on a later occasion. This trend certainly continued into the twelfth and thirteenth centuries, a period in which the first customary law-codes, like the *Très ancien coutumier* in Normandy, emerged. What do these sources have to say about women as witnesses? Amongst the later secular lawyers from France none is more explicit than Philippe de Beaumanoir in his *Coutumes de Beauvaisis*, written in the early 1280s.[33] Philippe ranks women with bastards, serfs and lepers as groups of the population who cannot act as witnesses, except in a few cases, namely inquests on personal

---

[32] *Der sog. Libellus de dictis quatuor ancillarum s. Elisabeth confectus*, ed. A. Huyskens (Kempten–Munich, 1911), and P. G. Schmidt, 'Die zeitgenössische Uberlieferung zum Leben und zur Heilgsprechung der heiligen Elisabeth', *Sankt Elisabeth Fürstin, Dienerin, Heilige. Aufsätze, Dokumentation, Katalog; Ausstellung zum 750. Todestag der hl. Elisabeth, Marburg, Landgrafenschloss und Elisabethkirche 19. November 1981–6. Januar 1982* (Sigmaringen, 1981), 1–6.
[33] *Coutumes de Beauvaisis*.

property, chattels, defamation or real property.[34] He echoes the Canon lawyers by stating that a woman cannot act as an advocate for another person for a fee, and that she cannot act as advocate or attorney or do any work that has to do with law enforcement or guard duty.[35] She can speak for herself, for her children or for someone in her lineage, provided she is not paid to do so; if she is married, however, she can do so only with her husband's consent.[36] A married woman cannot be called as a witness for her son or for her husband or a relative if they are accused of a crime, for no one will believe her. But if she testifies against her male kin (a son, husband or relative) her testimony is believable and hence admissible.[37] Philippe also confirms the Canonists in accepting women as witnesses for debt collection.[38] His clearest definition of women as witnesses can be found in Chapter 39 where he put all his scattered remarks to women into one succinct passage which is worth quoting in full:

We have said above in this chapter that women are admitted to give testimony to prove the age of children, and they are also heard according to our custom in cases which are conducted by an inquest, for it sometimes happens that they know what is being inquired into and the men do not know, and if they were not believed in such a case, certain truths could be concealed. Cases of crime, are an exception, for in cases where the penalty is loss of limb, women are not to be heard in testimony unless it is a case of a well-known fact, something done before so many honest men that it is clearly known, for example, in the presence of six or more persons of good reputation; and women are also heard in testimony when virginity is put to proof, as it happens in certain cases in the ecclesiastical courts, but because there is no need for it in secular courts we will say no more about it.[39]

Interesting here is the notion that women are useful witnesses only by default. If there is no man about, a woman's testimony is acceptable. Secondly, the notion of women as witnesses who confirm what is already known is significant if only because one would expect them not

[34] *Coutumes de Beauvaisis*, ch. 40, para. 1259, p. 456; cf. also ch. 5, para 185, p. 72; ch. 39, paras 1175–6 and par. 1177, p. 426, adds lepers.

[35] *Coutumes de Beauvaisis*, ch. 5, para. 190, p. 73 (cannot act as advocate for fee); ch. 29, para. 821, pp. 300–1 (no work to do with law enforcement or being an advocate).

[36] *Coutumes de Beauvaisis*, ch. 5, para. 190, p. 73 (speaking without a fee for herself, her children or a relative).

[37] *Coutumes de Beauvaisis*, ch. 39, para. 1182, p. 427. Cf. W. Ullman, 'Defence of the accused in the medieval inquisition', *Law and Jurisdiction in the Middle Ages*, ed. G. Garnett, no. xv, 481–9, at 486.

[38] *Coutumes de Beauvaisis*, ch. 29, para. 815, p. 297.

[39] *Coutumes de Beauvaisis*, ch. 39, para. 1197, p. 433.

to be necessary if the fact had already been established. Thirdly, the testimony with regard to the age of children and cases of virginity were clearly felt to belong too much to the female domain to be ignored. Age was tied in with birth and its proper establishement was important for legal reasons, e.g. in the case of male twins it was important to decide who was the eldest and thus the heir,[40] and in cases of marriage which could only be consummated at the legal age of adulthood. For girls virginity could only be checked by internal examination, a task normally reserved for women like the 'good women and legal matrons' from Normandy and the midwives found in other parts of Europe.

Further on in the *Coutumes de Beauvaisis*, in Chapter 41, Philippe sets out the position of women who are independent, that is, those who are of high rank, unmarried and in possession of a fief. They cannot give judgement in court, but they can give it as a mediator, for a mediator is appointed by two parties who seek advice, even though this advice is not legally binding. He then goes on to say that a woman holding a fief and owing homage and being unmarried can be compelled to go to judgements or send a man on her behalf. 'But it is a courteous and kind thing to excuse women, since there are plenty of men to be jurors.' Nevertheless, if the lord wishes her to come she has to comply.[41]

Thus, on the whole, women are excused and not really wanted as witnesses or mediators except in certain circumstances. Clearly, women were discouraged from being involved and they were given to understand that their role was a subordinate one. The reasons for wishing them to play a minimal part are sometimes given. The context is usually a passage in which the author explains why women cannot be trusted. In the chapter on illegitimacy, for example, Philippe begins by saying that judges should never believe a mother against her children if she says they are bastards, because she almost always has ulterior motives. However, a judge should question her carefully and gently and if he thinks she speaks the truth, 'for example if she admits her wickedness' or 'when she told on confessing' she should be believed.[42] How exactly the judge was to know this remains unstated by Philippe.

The question of women's capacity for stating the truth in the first place was an area of great debate in the Middle Ages. The misogynistic literature collectively doubted that women were capable of telling the truth. The Canonists were unanimous that women lacked strength, physical and moral, and therefore were unfit for more central roles in human affairs. Women's inferiority resulted from their biological constitution. They were said to be variable and changeable because of

---

[40] *Coutumes de Beauvaisis*, ch. 39, para. 1175, p. 426.
[41] *Coutumes de Beauvaisis*, ch. 41, paras 1287–8, pp. 464–5.
[42] *Coutumes de Beauvaisis*, ch. 18, para. 580, p. 205.

the delicacy of their physical constitution and, for the same reason, soft-hearted and yielding. How could women be believed if men saw them in such negative light?[43] The secular texts offer differing degrees of understanding towards women in this respect. Philippe de Beaumanoir, as we have seen, advised judges on the ways of interrogating women, and in one case was prepared to give a grandmother the benefit of the doubt for lack of evidence.[44] There is other evidence which can be usefully compared with Philippe de Beaumanoir's legal writing. Like several other lawyers in thirteenth-century France, he wrote romances in his spare time.[45] In this he may have followed his father, also called Philippe and also, like him, a law officer.[46] As practising baillis the two Philippes had an intimate knowledge of the practice of law. Both, too, were married, had children and thus, we may assume, had intimate knowledge of women as life companions and as mothers of their children. Whether any practical experience of daily conversations with their wives helped or hindered them in assessing a woman's capacity to speak the truth is a matter for speculation. As we have seen, Philippe de Beaumanoir Jr, is not universally sceptical about women's truthfulness. Some of his sidelines in the *Coutumes de Beauvaisis* are quite revealing; for example, I have already referred to his careful guidance to judges as to how to interogate women to assess whether a woman speaks the truth, or the case quoted by him where he is prepared to give a grandmother the benefit of doubt due to lack of evidence. These hints of leniency in dealing with women, however, hardly prepare us for his astonishingly favourable portrayal of women in his poetry and fiction. This may be partly due to the romantic nature of the verses, consisting as they do of love poetry composed when he was a young man. His first and longest poem, entitled *Le salut d'amour*, is autobiographical (the main protagonist is Philippe) and depicts his emotial struggle after having fallen in love.[47] The setting is, unsurprisingly, a court case. As a young lover he defends himself in court against the prosecutors Envy, Hatred and Lust and justifies his love for his lady supported by a messenger called Wisdom. But the most intriguing role in the poem is played by the judge called Love, who is … a wise woman. The gender of the judge, who ultimately lets Philippe

[43] Brundage, *Law*, 426.

[44] *Coutumes de Beauvaisis*, ch. 30, para. 929, pp. 328–9 (advice to judges), and ch. 63, paras. 1813–14, pp. 663–4 (grandmother, daughter and granddaughter case).

[45] H. L. Bordier, *Philippe de Remi, sire de Beaumanoir: jurisconsulte et poète national du Beauvaisis 1246–1296* (Paris, 1869).

[46] There is controversy whether father or son wrote the fictional works, see most recently, M. Shepard, *Tradition and Re-creation in Thirteenth-Century Romance: 'La Manekine' and 'Jehan et Blonde' by Philippe de Remi* (Amsterdam, 1990), 9–20.

[47] Bordier, *Philippe de Remi*, 268–70.

off the hook, is significant because it is a direct inversion of the juridical reality of Philippe's life in which no woman could act as a judge. The fictional judge is wiser than any real judge can be because her inspiration for justice comes directly from God. Interestingly, an echo of the female wisdom can be found in the introduction of the *Coutumes de Beauvaisis*, which sums up the ten characteristics of a judge. The first and most important one is wisdom:

> In our opinion a man who wants to be an honest judge and a just one should have ten virtues, one of which is and should be the lady and mistress of all others, for without it the other virtues cannot be controlled. And this virtue is called wisdom, which is the same thing as being wise. Therefore we can say the person who wants to hold the office of a judge and do justice should be wise for otherwise he would not be able to perform the duties of a judge.[48]

Is it not surprising that the most important qualification of a judge, Wisdom as 'the lady and mistress of all others' is described in terms of the opposite sex? The long classical tradition of the personification of morals might go far to explain Philippe's positive image of women, it cannot be the whole explanation. The rest of the explanation is provided by his romances. In *Jehan et Blonde* and *La Manekine*, the female heroines are faithful, they keep their promises in the face of severe adversity, they are caring, loving and above all sensible women.[49] Not only do they have these qualities as young independent women, both Blonde and Manekine are heiresses of royal or aristocratic backgrounds, who continue to behave in a trustworthy manner after marriage and well into motherhood. One may easily imagine these women testifying in court on behalf of their children, or relatives, or in any circumstance the legal texts tell us they can appear. The two faces of Philippe de Beaumanoir, as a secular lawyer and as a poet and novelist, show us a man who was perceptive, sensible and sensitive. As a lawyer he was prepared to give women the benefit of the doubt and as romantic author he painted a remarkable positive picture of women.

By comparison the attitude of another northern French lawyer, Mathieu of Boulogne, who lived in the second half of the thirteenth century, is straightforwardly misogynistic.[50] After an excellent education in the law faculty at Orléans, a flourishing career as a Canon lawyer,

---

[48] *Coutumes de Beauvaisis*, ch. 1, para. 12, p. 14.

[49] *Jehan et Blonde de Philippe de Remi. Roman du XIIIe siècle*, ed. S. Lécuyer (Paris, 1984). The edition of *La Manekine* can be found in Bordier.

[50] *Les Lamentations de Matheolus et le Livre de leesce de Jehan le Fevre de Ressous*, ed. A. G. Hamel (2 vols, Paris, 1893, 1905). The Latin text, known from a unique manuscript now at Utrecht, is given in the apparatus criticus of the French text which is published in vol. I.

and a distinguished performance at the council of Lyon in 1274, he fell in love with Petronella, a widow, whom he married. Apparently the ecclesiastical authorities then sacked him from his job, arguing that as a clerk he was banned from marriage. Petronella turned out to be a devil in disguise and twenty years later, in 1298, he wrote a satirical poem about his wife, his children, his failed marriage and the loss of his job as Canon lawyer.[51] He could see no good in women, reproached Petronella of being made of rock (a pun on her name Petra) and interlaced his tirade with *exempla* illustrating woman's duplicitous nature. His practical experience as husband and father, it seems, enforced his doubts about women and their capacity to speak the truth. Whereas Philippe de Beaumanoir was prepared to give women the benefit of the doubt in law as well as in fiction, Mathieu of Boulogne is anti-women on all fronts. Perhaps, his schooling in Canon law as opposed to secular law lies at the bottom of his hatred and disappointment. The vicious circle of misogyny as found in schoolbooks is beyond doubt: clerics were educated on the basis of misogynistic literature which permeated their minds, their legal schooling reinforced their low opinion of women because all literature underlined their inferiority and their lack of truthfulness.[52] When they entered marriage they attributed to their female partners, consciously or unconsciously, all the bad characteristics they had learned. From the perspective of Petronella, we can only conclude that faced with so much scepticism she had very little opportunity to prove that women could be trusted.

Thus far, the mixed views of men on the subject of women and the truth have been discussed. Are there any sources written by women themselves? Several fictional works written by women originated from England and France, e.g. Clemence of Barking's *Life of St. Catherine*, the poems of the Occitan troubaritz Comtessa de Dia; and, in addition, the anonymous romance *Daurel et Beton*, which contains an important passage on women and their handling of the truth. In the last quarter of the twelfth century Clemence, a nun of Barking, translated the Latin *Life of St. Catherine* into Anglo-Norman and used the occasion to insert her own comments into the narrative.[53] Clemence presents St Catherine as a royal heiress, the daughter of a king, who after her father's death succeeded him in his kingdom. Her education had been entirely focused on her accession to the throne, so she was learned, skilled in debate,

---

[51] For the biographical details, see *Les Lamentations*, ed. Hamel, II, cx–cxxxix.

[52] *Woman Defamed*, ed. A. Blamires, gives an excellent range of Latin and vernacular texts through which this process can be easily traced.

[53] *The Life of St. Catherine by Clemence of Barking*, ed. W. Macbain, *Anglo-Norman Texts*, 18 (Oxford, 1964), translated in *Virgin Lives and Holy Deaths. Two exemplary biographies for Anglo-Norman Women*, transl. J. Wogan-Browne and G. S. Burgess (London, 1996), 3–43.

had been taught how to be wise and how to conduct a disputation.[54] In other words, she had been taught how to act as judge and advocate and how to plead for herself, skills which as we have seen were supposedly reserved exclusively for men. Admittedly, the legal texts allow women in possession of fiefs to act in public roles but even Philippe de Beaumanoir encouraged his readers to excuse women and appoint men instead.[55] According to the legend, St Catherine was forced to appear before the Roman emperor Maxentius, a pagan, who denounced her Christianity. St Catherine answered him skilfully, defeated not only him in debate but also his imperial philosphers called in to defend paganism. In the end, despite her masculine defence, she was condemned to death. After a lengthy torture she was killed and died a martyr's death. Approximately one-quarter of the Anglo-Norman life is devoted to St Catherine's role in Maxentius's court where she is pleading for her own case, namely the freedom to choose Christianity.[56] Her arguments are culled from the works of St Anselm of Canterbury, the encyclopedia of Honorius Augustodunensis, and other twelfth-century theological works. What is interesting from our perspective is that the nun Clemence of Barking used this piece of fiction to portray a formidably independent woman, a heiress in her own right, in the male role of defending herself in a courtroom setting. The contrast between Clemence's defence of a woman pleading for herself in court and the stereotyped women in French romances who are usually described in misogynistic terms as not being capable of telling the truth is very striking.[57] Like Clemence of Barking, the Comtessa de Dia was a female author who wrote poetry. She was one of the female troubaritz who stood up for herself. In one poem she depicted herself in the role of advocate, a role she admitted is most unusual for a woman:

> I know well that it pleases me, even though everyone says it is very improper for a lady to plead her own case with a knight, and make him so long a sermon all the time. But whoever says this is not discerning for I want to plead my cause before I let myself die, since in beseeching I find such sweet succour when I beseech the man who causes me such anguish.[58]

According to the rules of Canon and secular law, women were allowed

[54] *The Life of St. Catherine*, ed. Macbain, ll. 140–4, p. 5; *Virgin Lives*, p. 5.

[55] *Coutumes de Beauvaisis*, ch. 41, paras 1287–8, pp. 464–5.

[56] *The Life of St. Catherine*, ed. Macbain, ll. 199–498, 612–1158, and pp. 7–16 and 20–37; *Virgin Lives*, pp. 6–10, 12–20.

[57] Simon Gaunt, *Gender and Genre in Medieval French Literature* (Cambridge, 1995,) 229–32. The inspiration for the exceptional portrayal of St Catherine might have been Clemence's older contemporary Empress Matilda, the heiress of King Henry I, who so recently had tried to gain the throne of England in her own name.

[58] Gaunt, *Gender and Genre*, 175, quoted from the manuscripts.

to defend themselves in exceptional circumstances, but women were not encouraged to do so. Pleading for themselves was such a taboo that women had to resort to fiction to explore the potential of such actions, pleading on behalf of others, in court or otherwise in public, was an action from which women were formally barred. Little wonder, then, that women explored in fiction the possibilities of court action which in reality they were dissuaded from starting. Occasionally female fiction can fill in the gaps in our knowledge of how such an action by a woman might have been viewed by women in reality. From the south of France originates the Occitan romance called *Daurel et Beton*, which is contemporary to the *Life of St. Catherine*. In it Ermenjart, wife of Bovis, frequently warns her husband against the treacherous intentions of his best friend Gui, emphasising the truth (*vertatz* and *verdat*) of her allegations. Her veracity, however, is discounted by the king on the grounds that she is a woman and thus can say what she likes, because – and here comes the crux of the male argument – a woman can never be invited to defend herself in combat and thus is never asked to prove the truth of what she has said in a *duellum*, the trial by combat from which women are excluded. In the story Ermenjart's alternative offer to prove the truth of what she said was ignored:

> King, Lord Emperor, what I say is the truth, for he did kill him and this will be proved; let a fire be prepared out there on the plain, I will pass through it before all your barons; if just one of my hairs is burnt may I be consumed by the flames, and may you have no mercy upon me. So help me God and in truth, let this traitor be quartered![59]

Not only was Ermenjart's request for a trial by fire to prove her version of events ignored, the king also brushed aside her verdict, which as a woman she was not supposed to give, that the traitor should be quartered, a punishment often given to those accused of treason.

Despite the formal prohibition of women to act as judges or advocates there is a body of evidence to support the suggestion that in practice all through the Middle Ages women did fulfil those functions. On behalf of their absent or deceased husbands, aristocratic women could act as judges or mediators and could preside over trials and disputes: Queen Matilda I as wife of William the Conqueror in Normandy and England,[60] Empress Matilda (d. 1167) as wife of Henry V of Germany

---

[59] *Daurel e Beton*, ed. C. Lee (Parma, 1991), ll. 607–14; transl. Gaunt, *Gender and Genre*, 66–7.

[60] *Regesta*, ed. Bates, no. 200, pp. 634–5, and as regent, D. Bates, 'The origins of the justiciarship', *Proceedings of the Battle Conference*, 4 (1981), 1–12, at 6–7.

in northern Italy,[61] Countess Adela of Blois-Chartres (d. 1137) in Blois,[62] Countess Eleanor of Saint-Quentin (c. 1201) in the Vermandois and the queen-mother Queen Adela of France in 1190.[63] In none of these examples is there any evidence of male hostility to the fact that women acted in a function normally reserved for men.[64] From France, however, comes the late twelfth-century example involving an unidentified queen A.,[65] who presided over a dispute between the Cistercian monastery of Écharlis (Dep. Yonne, arr. Joigny) and the Order of Hospitallers in the diocese of Sens.[66] On the advice of the bishops, the queen judged in favour of the Cistercians whereupon the Hospitallers refused to execute her order on the grounds that a woman could not act as a mediator and therefore the judgement was invalid. The case was put before Pope Innocent III (1198–1216) who in a letter of 1202 argued that in respect of Roman civil law this was true, but that this case was exceptional because the queen had acted under powers of customary law.[67] Thus some scepticism against female judges was current even though in this particular case one might suspect that the Hospitallers were not so

[61] M. Chibnall, *The Empress Matilda* (Oxford, 1991), 33–4.

[62] Martindale, 'His special friend?', 55.

[63] Bongert, *Recherches*, p. 266, n. 2 (Countess Eleanor), and 268 (Queen Adela).

[64] Surprisingly, Countess Matilda of Tuscany's admirer Bonizo of Sutri writing c. 1090, argued that no woman should govern as secular ruler. Taking examples from the Old Testament and early Frankish and Lombard history he argued that as soon as women got involved in secular rule they caused chaos (*Bonizo, Liber de vita Christiana*, ed. E. Perels, *Texte zur Geschichte des römischen und kanonischen Rechts im Mittelalter*, 1 (Berlin, 1930), p. 249). Half a century later Gratian rejected counter-arguments from people who used the biblical examples of women acting as judges on the grounds that the Ancient Law had permitted women to do so but that presently (*hodie*) this was no longer allowed for the sins committed by women and that by way of punishment women were subjected to the authority of men and had to keep their heads covered (Gratian, *Decretum* C. 15, q. 3, principium, ed. Friedberg, *Corpus Iuris Canonici*, 1, 750).

[65] *Patrologia Latina*, ed. J.P. Migne, 214, 1094–5; *Regesta pontificum romanorum*, ed. A. Potthast (Berlin, 1874), 1, p. 152, no. 1749. The queen is only mentioned with her initial A and has been identified by Potthast as Queen Aelinor=Eleanor of Aquitaine as wife of Louis VII. This is unlikely because she ceased to be queen of France in 1153. More likely candidates are either Queen Adela, the queen-mother, who together with her brother Archbishop William of Reims stood in during her son's absence in the Holy Land in the period June 1190– December 1191 (J.W. Baldwin, *The Government of Philip Augustus. Foundations of French Royal Power in the Middle Ages* (Berkeley, 1986), 102–4) or Agnes de Méran (d. 1201), who was never officially recognised as queen.

[66] A similar case involving King Louis VII and Countess Ermengard of Narbonne in 1164 is discussed in L. Patterson. *The World of Troubadours* (Cambridge, 1993), 222–3.

[67] For a discussion, see R. Metz, 'Le statut de la femme en droit canonique médiéval', *La Femme*, Recueils de la Société de Jean Bodin, 12 (4 vols, Brussels, 1962), II, 59–113a at 104. Cf. *Coutumes de Beauvaisis*, ch. 41, paras. 1287–8, pp. 464–5, where the distinction is made between judgements given by independent women in criminal trials, which are not allowed, and judgements by them as arbitrators which are allowed.

much against the queen as judge *per se*, but simply used her as a legal excuse to avoid the negative ruling against them.

Finally, there is some evidence that women faced with a dispute may have exploited the system that was supposedly against them by appealing to prevalent ideas about supposed female weaknesses, including the widespread scepticism that they could be truthful. Patricia Skinner has used compelling evidence from Lombard Italy, to show that some women turned the disadvantage of legal incapacity into an advantage by making unusual demands.[68] The use of delaying tactics was one of them. Under Lombard law a woman could not herself bring a case or appear in court as a witness or defendant. She had to be represented by an advocate, who usually was a male member of her family. By claiming not to be able to have found a suitable advocate, or by delaying to send someone in her place a woman could protract the proceedings. There is indeed evidence from other parts of Europe that this might have happened elsewhere. A good Norman example dates from 1207 and shows a dispute where Basilia de Glisolles, presumably a widow, had the truth on her side but confessed to have done wrong in order to have the case settled.

Basilia de Glisolles's case centred on the claim against her by the monks of La Noë, near Evreux, that certain lands granted by her to the monastery had been mortgaged. The document which tells us about the allegation is a record drawn up by the monks of Basilia's denial of the claim and her confession of 'the manifest, scandalous and wicked falsehood'.[69] She then bound herself and her heirs to confirm the lands in the possesion of the monastery in a new document (i.e. the present surviving one) and appended her seal to it. It ends with the following statement: 'I confess and recognise the truth of this case and the truth of my dower in God's truth.' We may wonder why Basilia is pictured as making a confession when, as Leopold Delisle has shown conclusively, all other surviving documents clearly exonerate her and confirm the truth of her case, namely, that she had given the lands unburdened by a mortgage. Perhaps Basilia realised that the easiest way out of the dispute was to play the system, pretend to have made a mistake and simply confess to a sin she did not commit. This was what the baillis believed, judging by Philippe de Beaumanoir's advice that if a woman confessed she surely spoke the truth.[70] Thus Basilia exonerated herself in a humiliating ritual surrounded by men, who had been trained to

[68] P. Skinner, 'Disputes and disparity: women in court in medieval southern Italy', *Reading Medieval Studies*, 22 (1996), 85–105, at 94.

[69] *Cartulaire normand de Philippe Auguste, Louis VIII, Saint Louis et Philippe-le-Hardi*, ed. L. Delisle, Mélanges de la Société des Antiquaires de Normandie (Caen, 1852), no. 145, p. 25. I am grateful to Mathieu Arnoux for kindly drawing my attention to this charter.

[70] See above, p. 212.

believe only women who 'confessed': the monks of La Noë, the bishop and seven of his ecclesiastical clerks: two archdeacons, one precentor, one dean and one priest who was the chanter's brother. No reference is made to any of Basilia's children nor to anyone who supported her. Left to her own devices she cannot be blamed for the way she gave in to the monks and other men present. The fact that she was a person of authority on account of the seal she carried and appended to the document seems not to have made the slightest difference.[71]

What does the evidence from law books, legal practice and fiction reveal about the gender and authority of oral witnesses? Firstly, law books excluded women, and children, as witnesses even though gradually categories of exceptions were being devised to accommodate the many instances in which women were testifying. Even where women were not supposed to witness or testify, their presence at disputes and in courts was noted in documents, which may indicate women's potential usefulness as informants of relevant knowledge. Where women do appear in a less invisible role they act on behalf of their own, usually as widows. The absence of men turned them into useful, acceptable and even sometimes authoritative sources of information. Thus, public recognition of their legal status was usually couched in terms of exceptions to rules, and their testimonies were accepted by default. Amongst the lawyers the secular ones, e.g. Philippe de Beaumanoir, were ready to gradually accept greater legal responsibility for women, while the Canon lawyers on the whole remained sceptical and even hostile. The picture that has emerged from the present legal investigation is surprisingly similar to the one that emerges from historiographical and hagiographical sources. Little public acknowledgement is given to women who report their memories, their testimonies or other stories about the past. Women's knowledge of the past and present, however, was vital for the functioning of society and most people knew this. Their memorial role in law as well as history was an oral one.[72]

---

[71] B. Bedos-Rezak, *Form and Order in Medieval France. Studies in Social and Quantitative Sigillography* (Aldershot, 1993), ix, 61–82, at 65–67 for the relative large number of noble and non-noble Norman women to have possessed seals.

[72] I should like to acknowledge my gratititude to C. A. J. Coady for the inspiration provided by his book *Testimony. A Philosophical Study* (Oxford, 1992).

MEMORY AND TRADITION IN SIENESE POLITICAL LIFE IN THE FIFTEENTH CENTURY

By Christine Shaw

READ 26 MARCH, 1998 AT THE UNIVERSITY OF SUSSEX

WHEN someone who is not a specialist thinks of Italian Renaissance politics, he or she probably thinks first of Machiavelli – Machiavelli the cynical, Machiavelli the revolutionary. But if you read the writings of Machiavelli's contemporaries – not so much perhaps the political theorists (except for Francesco Guicciardini, to my mind a far more interesting political thinker than Machiavelli), as the active politicians of the day, Machiavelli does not seem anything like so revolutionary. Next to their clear-eyed realism and knowledge of men and affairs, Machiavelli's extremism can seem naïve.

Men who took an active part in public affairs were prompted to think about politics by (among other factors) two major, arguably defining, characteristics of the political system of Renaissance Italy. The first was how intricately and intimately connected the numerous states crammed into the Italian peninsula were. Even before the development of permanent resident embassies in the major diplomatic centres – especially Rome and Milan – in the second half of the fifteenth century, governments and private citizens took an intense interest in the internal affairs of other states. Many Italians of the political classes spent at least some part of their careers away from home, as merchants, bankers, soldiers, teachers, clergy or as itinerant judges (in many cities the leading judicial officials had to come from outside, and were appointed for fixed, comparatively short terms), or even as officials, diplomats or councillors of princes (republics rarely used foreigners in such political positions). Many Italians thus had first-hand knowledge of how other states were governed, and the wide variety of institutions and structures of government, of political mores and assumptions and conventions, stimulated reflection. Most notably, Florentine observation of and reflection on the political system of Venice influenced political thinking and political reforms in Florence around the turn of the century.[1] There were stores of knowledge and experience, of memory that were shared by many politically active

---

[1] Felix Gilbert, 'The Venetian Constitution in Florentine Political Thought', in *Florentine Studies: Politics and Society in Renaissance Florence*, ed. Nicolai Rubinstein (1968), 463–500.

Italians, and on which they would draw when taking part in discussions on internal politics or in diplomatic negotiations.

The second factor that prompted Italians to think about political principles and practice was the lack of clearly defined sovereignty characteristic of all but a few Italian states. The political institutions of most Italian cities had developed in the absence of any effective ruler. Even towns and cities which acknowledged the overlordship of the emperor or the pope often still regarded themselves as being *de facto*, if not *de jure*, sovereigns. Siena was nominally subject to the Holy Roman Emperor, and in 1432 the Imperial eagle was painted on the façade of the Palazzo della Signoria,[2] but the great majority of Sienese regarded any intervention by the emperor in the affairs of their city as an unwelcome intrusion. (I do not say all Sienese because some had been ready to invoke the intervention of the emperor in the later fourteenth century, and there were fears when an emperor came to Siena in the fifteenth century that others might do so too – as we shall see later.) The improvisation, the invention of institutions that characterised the civic governments of Italy over several centuries, brought innovations in thinking about politics and the nature of political authority, but also led to the 'invention' of authority (rather in the sense of the Invention of the Cross). Tradition became an important – arguably the major – source of legitimacy, even when those 'traditions' had developed almost within living memory. For all the history of innovation and the readiness to go on innovating that characterised Italian political life in the Renaissance, how things had been done, or how it was thought they had been done, was for many of those active in civic politics how things ought to be done.

The Sienese for centuries had a reputation for conservatism, for adherence to their own traditions, a characteristic that perhaps finds expression today in their passionate attachment to the rituals of the Palio and to their *contrade*. The rituals of the Palio cycle go on throughout the year without so much as a glance at tourists. And, of course, Sienese youths will still taunt Florentine rivals with cries of 'Montaperti' – recalling the battle the Sienese Ghibellines won against the Florentine Guelfs in 1260. The traditions of the dedication of the city to the Virgin to implore her help by placing the city keys before her venerated image in the cathedral, first noted before that battle, was last revived in 1944, before the allied forces arrived in the city. The Sienese need not have worried too much. As a plaque on one of the city gates recalls, the French commander of the approaching troops told his men that they could fire anywhere they liked but they must not hit anything older than the eighteenth century – quite difficult to avoid in most of Siena

---

[2] Now called the Palazzo Pubblico, and still the seat of the civic government.

within the walls. Frequently, indeed, buildings put up or radically altered, even in the nineteenth century, imitated Sienese Gothic, the style characteristic of the city's heyday in the thirteenth and early fourteenth centuries. Memorably, even in the later seventeenth century, not generally characterised by respect for fourteenth-century archi- tectural styles, additions to the Palazzo della Signoria were made to copy exactly the design of the rest of the façade.

One interesting example of the deliberate copying of revered models in Siena in the fifteenth century is a commission in the 1440s by the main executive council, the Concistoro, of three tapestry panels which were to copy the famous frescoes painted in the Palazzo by Ambrogio Lorenzetti over a century before.[3] Now known as the Allegory of Good and Bad Government, and The Effects of Good and Bad Government in the City and the Country, in the fifteenth century they were known simply as Peace and War. These frescoes and their images were well known to the Sienese of the day. Saint Bernardino of Siena referred to them in sermons preached in the *piazza* (now known as the Campo) before the Palazzo, when he was urging on the citizens the virtues of peace and unity.[4] Peace and unity were threatened in the later 1440s, at the time the tapestries were commissioned, by war in Tuscany, and by conspiracy among some citizens dissatisfied with what had become regarded as the traditional, broadly based Sienese government, and who wanted greater prominence and power to be given to an elite distinguished by wealth or education or (of course) both.[5]

The discovery of the conspiracy in 1456 brought a realisation that the conspirators had been prepared to compromise the independence of Siena in order to achieve their aim of a more elitist form of government. They had contacts with King Alfonso of Aragon and Naples, and may have offered him some kind of lordship or suzerainty over Siena.[6] The revelations of their treachery reinforced the attachment of the Sienese to what they had come to regard as their traditional form of government. In fact, this tradition dated back only to the

---

[3] Edna Carter Southard, *The Frescoes in Siena's Palazzo Pubblico, 1289–1539: Studies in Imagery and Relations to Other Communal Palaces in Tuscany* (New York, 1979), 268–70; Deborah Lubera Kawsky, 'The Survival and Reappraisal of Artistic Tradition: Civic Art and Civic Identity in Quattrocento Siena' (PhD thesis, Princeton University, 1995), 126–38; G. Cecchini, 'L'Arazzeria Senese', *Archivio Storico Italiano*, 120 (1962), 158, 172.

[4] For example, S. Bernardino da Siena, *Le Prediche Volgari Dette nella Piazza del Campo l'Anno MCCCCXXVII*, ed. P. Bargellini (Siena, 1936), p. 991.

[5] For the political ideas of this group, see P. Pertici, *Tra Politica e Cultura nel Primo Quattrocento Senese. Le Epistole di Andreoccio Petrucci (1426–1443)* (Siena, 1990); and see P. Pertici, 'Una "Coniuratio" del reggimento di Siena nel 1450', *Bullettino Senese di Storia Patria*, 99 (1992), 9–47.

[6] Luciano Banchi, 'Il Piccinino nello Stato di Siena e la Lega Italica', *Archivio Storico Italiano* 4th series, 4 (1879), 44–58, 225–45.

beginning of the fifteenth century – to 1404, to be precise. Ironically, in the aftermath of the conspiracy there were a number of institutional experiments with executive and legislative Balìe. These new bodies did not long survive the death of Alfonso and the cessation of fears that the exiled conspirators would return backed by the king. But the return of those conspirators who had survived twenty-five years in exile, and of their families, in 1480 marked the beginning of decades of institutional innovation, with the (increasingly distorted) tradition of Sienese government never forgotten but of decreasing practical effect, until a new equilibrium was imposed by the Medici regime after the Sienese lost their independence in the 1550s.

The subjection of the city to Duke Cosimo de' Medici was the bitter resolution of a struggle the Sienese had waged for centuries, first to challenge the Florentines for domination in Tuscany, and then, once Florence had clearly emerged as the stronger power, to keep their powerful neighbours at bay. When the Sienese were able to benefit from alliance with Naples during the Pazzi War against Florence in 1478–80 to take possession of a few small towns on the Florentine border, they bitterly resented being forced to give them back.[7] Consequently, when the citizens of Montepulciano took advantage of the distraction of the Florentines by the rebellion of Pisa in 1494 to rebel in their turn, and place themselves under the protection of Siena (the Sienese thought of it as subjection), the Sienese were delighted and determined this time to hold on to their prize. Memories of the long history of their rivalry were present in the minds of both the Sienese and the Florentines, and made settlement of the dispute far more difficult. To the Sienese *popolo*, Montepulciano was theirs by right anyway, having briefly been under Sienese dominion about a century before. The Sienese political elite could not afford to take quite so simple a view of the situation, but felt that they had the Florentines, for once, at a disadvantage, and savoured the moment. The Florentines found it distasteful, not to say humiliating, to have to parley with the Sienese over what they regarded as a rebellious subject. Sometimes reminders of the past were used as gambits in negotiations. The Sienese should beware of becoming involved in hostilities against Florence, a Florentine envoy warned his Sienese interlocutors in 1497. They could bring war on their territory, and would be forced to put themselves into the power of others, as had happened with Giangaleazzo Visconti a century before, and had threatened to happen after the Pazzi War

[7] Lorenzo de' Medici, *Lettere V (1480–1481)*, ed. Michael Mallett, 327–37; Christine Shaw, 'Politics and Institutional Innovation in Siena 1480–1498', *Bullettino Senese di Storia Patria*, 103 (1996), 28–30, 36–9, 93–5.

with Alfonso, Duke of Calabria.[8] Certainly, he admonished them, the last thing any good Sienese citizens, remembering those times, should think of would be making war on the Florentines. They admitted that what I said was true, the envoy reported, but they said the Florentines should recall what Cosimo de' Medici (who had been dead for thirty years) had said – leave the Sienese alone, he's mad and he has bread (that is, he has corn to export).[9]

The internal politics of Siena were complicated and difficult to follow and I shall not attempt to describe them in detail here.[10] One aspect I do want to discuss was the most distinctive feature of Sienese government in the fifteenth century – the *monti*. There were five *monti* – the Gentiluomini, Nove, Dodici, Riformatori and Popolari – whose members were, broadly speaking, the descendants of those who had first held office in the major executive council in Siena under the five regimes that had succeeded one another in the thirteenth and fourteenth centuries. Only members of a *monte* could hold political offices, which were divided among members of those *monti* who were in the regime in strict rotation. Only Genoa had a system remotely like this, with political offices being explicitly distributed among what could be described as official factions. The *monti* had no internal organisation, no official leadership, no recognised meeting-places, no banners or symbols, or rallying cries other than the name of the *monti*. All that held the members together was their descent from those who had first held office during a particular period of Sienese history.

For much of the fifteenth century not all the *monti* were admitted to the regime. From 1404 to 1480, the Dodici were completely excluded from government. The Gentiluomini were also excluded for much of the time, although they held some offices (particularly castellanies) during the first couple of decades. They were also briefly and grudgingly admitted to the Concistoro and to the major legislative body, the Consiglio del Popolo, during the pontificate of Pius II, Enea Piccolomini, who was a member of one of the families of the Gentiluomini. It had taken considerable persuasion, not to say threats, from Pius to accomplish this, and as soon as he died in 1464, the Gentiluomini (except for the Piccolomini) were excluded again. Pius had tried hard to have the

---

[8] After Siena sided with Giangaleazzo Visconti in his war against the Florentines, the city became subject to him from 1399 to 1403. There were fears in the aftermath of the Pazzi War that Alfonso would use the troops he had with him in Tuscany to enforce Neapolitan suzerainty over the city, but he was summoned back to the kingdom to deal with the Turks who had captured the city of Otranto in August 1480.

[9] Florence, Archivio di Stato, Archivio della Repubblica, Dieci di Balìa, Carteggi, Responsive, 45, cc. 119–20: Antonio Guidotti, 11 Jan. 1496(7), Colle.

[10] For a detailed account of Sienese internal politics in the later fifteenth century, see Shaw, 'Politics and Institutional Innovation in Siena', *Bullettino Senese di Storia Patria*, 103 (1996), 9–102, and 104 (1997), 194–307.

Dodici admitted to the regime, too, but on this the Sienese would not budge. To let the Dodici into the regime would be the ruin of the city, the Sienese ambassador told the pope.[11] In 1480, when another pope, Sixtus IV, asked for some individual Dodici to be made members of the Consiglio del Popolo, he was told by the Sienese ambassadors 'that this was a really hard and difficult matter for our regime, because of our factions and ancient enmities'.[12]

The Dodici had come to power in the fourteenth century with the help of the Emperor Charles IV when he had been passing through the city on his way to coronation in Rome in 1355, and they turned to him for help when they were ousted from power in 1368. Charles, trying to support them on his way through Siena in January 1369, found himself humiliated by being besieged by the Sienese *popolo* in the house where he had taken refuge.[13] The Dodici continued to be associated, in the minds of the Sienese at least, with the Emperor. When the Emperor Sigismund came to the city in 1432, and the Emperor Frederick in 1451, leading Dodici were exiled from Siena as a precautionary measure. They were also exiled when the city was emptied by an epidemic in 1436 and in 1447, when King Alfonso was campaigning in Tuscany.[14] But it was not the Dodici who conspired with Alfonso in the 1440s, and who constituted a danger to the regime – it was the disaffected members of the *reggimento*, mostly of the Monte dei Nove, who wanted a greater share of government office for themselves. In fact, once the Dodici were brought into the government in 1482, they caused no trouble and seem to have been quickly accepted.

The Gentiluomini had been admitted to the regime again in 1480, this time at the behest of Alfonso, Duke of Calabria. Briefly expelled in June 1482, they were soon readmitted. There is evidence of some resentment of them among the *popolo*, and some reports that they might be ejected again, but they remained members of the regime. Some Gentiluomini were nostalgic for their ancient pre-eminence and dreamt of returning to what they regarded as their rightful place at the head of government. We gentlemen are biding our time, wrote one of them, Giovanni Malavolta, to Lodovico Sforza, Duke of Milan in June 1495. But we hope one day to recover 'our old way of governing' (*nostro*

[11] Irene Polverini Fosi, '"La Comune, Dolcissima Patria": Siena e Pio II', in *I Ceti Dirigenti nella Toscana del Quattrocento* (Florence, 1987), 515.

[12] Siena, Archivio di Stato (hereafter ASSiena), Balìa 502, 39: Francesco Petrucci and Sinolfo da Castel'Ottieri, 3 Oct. 1480, Rome.

[13] P. Rossi, 'Carlo IV di Lussemburgo e la Repubblica di Siena (1355–1369)', *Bullettino Senese di Storia Patria*, N.S., 1 (1930), 4–39, 178–242.

[14] ASSiena, Concistoro 1638, fo. 197r, Concistoro 421, fos 38r, 43r–v, Concistoro 490, fos 41r, 44v–45r, 46r–v; Concistoro 512, fo. 23v; Paolo Nardi, *Mariano Sozzini, Giureconsulto Senese del Quattrocento* (Milan, 1974), 28, 40, 65.

governo antico).[15] That day never came, and the Gentiluomini became fully integrated into the Sienese *reggimento*.

The opportunity for the Dodici and the Gentiluomini to have a share in the government had come about because of the divisions which had grown up among the three *monti* which had constituted the regime in Siena from 1404 to 1480 – that is, the Nove, the Riformatori and the Monte del Popolo. The Riformatori were blamed by some Noveschi for the exiles of 1456 and for resisting the return of the remaining exiles in 1480. The Riformatori were excluded from the regime for two years from 1480 to 1482, and many were exiled in their turn. They never recovered what they regarded as their rightful third share of all political offices, and resentment rankled. In 1483, it was the turn of the Nove to be expelled from office, by an increasingly extremist Popolare regime; many hundreds went into exile. The Noveschi exiles returned in 1487, but the bad blood between members of the Monte dei Nove and some of the Monte del Popolo and of the *popolo minuto* (the 'little men' with no access to political office) persisted for several decades. Such divisions, and the animus they created among those three *monti*, eclipsed the long-standing animus against the Dodici and Gentiluomini.[16]

The period of nearly eighty years during which political offices had been divided between members of the Monti dei Nove, dei Riformatori and del Popolo had made such a tripartite regime the 'traditional' government of Siena. The Sienese came to believe that the regime had been deliberately modelled on 'the Holy and indivisible Trinity, under whose Name this government, with the orders of the Nove, Popolo and Riformatori, was established and created',[17] thus giving it an additional sanction. How to accommodate the members of more than three *monti* in the regime was a problem that was never satisfactorily solved during the remaining years of Sienese independence. Experiments were made with having only one government *monte*, in which all members of the *monti* in the regime would participate, but there were always suspicions that some *monte* was getting more than their share of office, or some other *monte* less, and another attempt would be made to divide up the members of the *monti* of the *reggimento* into three government *monti*.

Another aspect of Sienese government that came to be regarded as a Sienese tradition was the important role assigned to the Consiglio del

[15] Milan, Archivio di Stato, Archivio Sforzesco, Potenze Estere, b. 1263: Giovanni Malavolta, 4 June 1495, Siena.

[16] See Shaw, 'Politics and Institutional Innovation in Siena'; Judith Hook, 'Habsburg Imperialism and Italian Particularism: The Case of Charles V and Siena', *European Studies Review*, 9 (1979), 283–312.

[17] Siena, Biblioteca Comunale degli Intronati, MS. A.VII. 26., fo. 184r.

Popolo. All those who held a seat in the Concistoro became members of the Consiglio del Popolo for life. With the members of the Concistoro holding office for only two months at a time, and with the electoral purses into which their names were placed being compiled for several years at a time, this meant that several hundred men, in a city of perhaps 15,000 inhabitants, had a right to a seat for life in the main legislative assembly. Unlike similar bodies in other Italian cities, the Consiglio del Popolo in Siena kept the right to debate and to modify proposals put before it, as well as to accept and reject them. It was a true political forum, and membership in it was considered a privilege and an honour.[18]

The recurrent political crises that engulfed Siena from 1480, however, led to the establishment of a new executive council, the Balìa, that gradually took from the Concistoro much of its political significance and left much less scope for the Consiglio del Popolo. There had been Balìe earlier in the century, commissions of senior politicians appointed to support the Concistoro in deliberations on particularly difficult or important matters. One of the innovations of the mid-1450s was that the Balìe that were appointed to deal with the problems arising from the war in Tuscany began in 1455–6 to meet on their own, as did some of the Balìe appointed to deal with the wars in Tuscany from 1477 to 1480. The Balìe that were in office almost continuously from 1480 were significantly different, taking over many of the functions of the Concistoro.[19]

Apart from during periods of political turmoil, there was significant continuity of membership from one Balìa to the next. The number of members varied under different dispensations, but was usually from twenty-five to forty. The continuity of membership, particularly during the 1490s, when Balìe were appointed for five years at a time, rather than from two to six months at a time, meant that a group of a couple of dozen men were exercising full executive power in Siena continuously. This was, of course, precisely the situation that the system of appointment to the Concistoro was designed to avoid, and there were occasional rumbles of discontent. In 1493, for example, there were demands that there should be a return to 'the old style of government [*governo antiquo*], as being more civil and peaceful, that is, that all matters should be

---

[18] See Mario Ascheri, 'Siena nel Rinascimento: Dal Governo di "Popolo" al Governo Nobiliare', in *I Ceti Dirigenti nella Toscana del Quattrocento*, 415–20; Mario Ascheri, *Siena nel Rinascimento* (Siena, 1985), 31–9, 57–108; Christine Shaw, 'Political Elites in Siena and Lucca in the Fifteenth Century', *Bulletin of the Society for Renaissance Studies*, 14 (Oct. 1996), 8–12.

[19] Mario Ascheri, *Siena nel Rinascimento*, 39–42; G. Prunai and S. De' Colli, 'La Balìa dagli Inizi del XIII Secolo fino alla Invasione Francese (1789)', *Bullettino Senese di Storia Patria*, 65 (1958), 33–96 (this account requires revision on some points).

referred freely to the councils', but the leaders of the other *monti* saw this as an attempt by the Popolari to increase their own power and united to resist these calls for a return to the traditional ways.[20]

In theory, the powers of Balìe were delegated to them and circumscribed by the Consiglio del Popolo and the Consiglio had to appoint them, indeed elect the members. It was, on occasion, difficult to have a new Balìa approved by the Consiglio, but those who favoured the Balìa generally got their way. The Balìa became the instrument of a group who consciously sought power for themselves, consciously wanted to change the government of Siena to one in which a small group of men exercised effective control. The Balìe were justified by arguments that they were needed to deal with crises, with difficult times, that a steady hand was needed to guide the city. All the citizens who had been consulted, it was claimed in October 1487, had agreed that 'it is not only useful but necessary that a Balìa should be created so that there will be a rudder [*timone*] and good guide to conduct, establish and confirm your regime [*reggimento*] so that no one will dare to plot against it'.[21] Ten years later, it was 'the situation in which your city finds itself and the discords there are in Italy and outside Italy [which] are of such a nature that they will not be settled very soon', which, it was argued, made the reappointment of the Balìa expedient.[22]

What was needed was government by men whose authority came from their personal qualities and experience, not by men whose authority derived from their being selected by lot to hold office for a short period in the traditional way. The authority of experience, of the memory of what had been done and seen by an individual, was to take precedence over the authority of tradition. It had been recognised earlier in the century, too, that the traditional ways of appointing to political office might not always produce the right man for the right job, that there were some tasks that called for more deliberate selection of men with the required qualities. The very practice of appointing Balìe to assist the members of the Concistoro was a recognition of the fact that some men had qualities of judgement and experience that made their counsel particularly valuable. In August 1456 it was thought needful to revise the rule governing scrutinies, and the composition of the electoral purses for the Concistoro to ensure that all those drawn at one time would not be 'novices and young men', which could bring damage and shame to the republic; and to ensure that those drawn for the position of Capitano del Popolo, the head of the Concistoro, should

[20] Florence, Archivio di Stato, Medici avanti il Principato, b. 19, 437: Alessandro Braccesi to Piero de' Medici, 11 Oct. 1493, Siena.

[21] ASSiena, Consiglio Generale 240, fo. 158v.

[22] ASSiena, Consiglio Generale 241, fo. 33r.

be 'the principal and most capable [*atti*] citizens of your city and republic'.[23]

There was no tradition in Siena, as in Florence, of individuals writing *ricordanze*, family memoirs, or of writing political commentaries. The political beliefs of individual Sienese have to be gleaned from letters, and from the rare surviving accounts of speeches to the councils. But much can be learned about the political ideas of the Sienese from the expositions of principles in the prologues to legislation. These show that the Sienese shared in the Italian culture of self-conscious reflection on the nature of political life.

Sometimes they drew conclusions from observing other states. 'Seeing that all the good signorie and republics of Italy have in their government a measure of politic conduct [*qualche politico vivare*] and are governed with some discretion, and rather more secrecy' than the Sienese had had, particularly of late, there were to be controls on the contacts of citizens with visiting dignitaries or ambassadors, it was decided in August 1456. Sometimes it was reflection on Sienese experience which prompted legislation. Considering how often commissions and Balìe overstepped their terms of reference, quite contrary to the will of the councils, 'so that there has never been a Balìa which did not attend more to particular than to public business', as all citizens know, and that in consequence the councils would not agree to appoint such Balìe, a reluctance which 'might threaten the ruin of the city', new rules were made governing the work of Balìe in 1465.[24] It is clear that experience was valued, and regarded as a guide. 'Reason says, and experience shows',[25] the preamble to one piece of legislation began; 'reason shows and experience proves',[26] began another; and in a third, experience was described as the teacher of all things.[27]

The authority of personal memory, of personal experience was perhaps even more valued in Florence, where there was the same conflict as in Siena between those who prized what was seen as the traditional government by councils whose members were elected by lot to serve for short terms, and those who argued the claims of men of experience, education and wealth to a leading role in the regime, to a permanent place in government.[28] Restriction of the numbers involved, and narrowing of the social recruitment of those participating actively in government, was a feature not just of Sienese and Florentine political

[23] ASSiena, Concistoro 2118, fos 109r–110r.

[24] ASSiena, Concistoro 2118, fo. 100bisr.

[25] ASSiena, Concistoro 2117, fo. 296r.

[26] ASSiena, Consiglio Generale 240, fo. 79v.

[27] ASSiena, Concistoro 777, fos 56v–58r.

[28] For a recent, stimulating discussion of the question, see Carlo Varotti, *Gloria e Ambizione Politica nel Rinascimento. Da Petrarca a Machiavelli* (Milan, 1998).

life in the fifteenth and early sixteenth centuries, but of virtually all Italian towns and cities, independent or not. This long-term change in the nature of Italian civic government had profound (and imperfectly understood) roots in changes in the Italian economy and society, and I would not wish to make excessive claims for the significance of the contrast I am drawing. But, while the proponents of broadly based government – *governo largo* – appealed to the collective memory of tradition, the proponents of more elitist government – *governo stretto* – appealed to the personal memory of experience, and the triumph of *governo stretto* marked the subordination of the authority of tradition to the authority of experience.

REMEMBERING THE PAST IN EARLY MODERN ENGLAND: ORAL AND WRITTEN TRADITION

By Adam Fox

READ 26 MARCH 1998 AT THE UNIVERSITY OF SUSSEX

FOR students of the interaction between oral and written forms of communication the early modern period provides an important case study. England in the sixteenth and seventeenth centuries was far from being an oral society; and yet it was not a completely literate one either. On the one hand, old vernacular traditions had long been infused and supplemented, or corrupted and destroyed, by the written word; on the other hand, only a certain part of the population could read and write or ever relied on the products of literacy. Indeed, as Keith Thomas has suggested, 'it is the interaction between contrasting forms of culture, literate and illiterate, oral and written, which gives this period its particular fascination'.[1]

Long before the early modern period, records, documents and literary productions of all kinds were structuring the mental world of English people at all social levels. Written texts were commonplace in recording economic transactions, in providing witness and proof at law and in conveying the fruits of artistic and imaginative achievement. If the spoken word remained the principal mode of communication and cultural transmission, it was inextricably and increasingly intertwined with the written. And yet oral exchange and tradition, however derivative from textual sources, remained a vital and innovative force throughout these centuries and beyond. For that majority of men and women who could not read, and for all people in certain contexts, information was learned by listening and stored in memory.

In this paper I want to focus on the relationship between oral and written tradition in the formation of memories and perceptions of the past in early modern England. In this sphere, too, the mutual infusion of the oral and the written was thorough and of long standing. Whatever the provenance of historical tales or traditions, however, there is no doubt that the majority of people received their knowledge of the past

[1] Keith Thomas, 'The Meaning of Literacy in Early Modern England', in *The Written Word: Literacy in Transition*, ed. Gerd Baumann (Oxford, 1986), 97.

233

most readily from the mouths of others. This was a world evoked so vividly by John Aubrey's reminiscences of his Wiltshire childhood in the 1630s when, 'before woomen were readers, the history was handed downe from mother to daughter' and it was common 'for the maydes to sitt-up late by the fire [to] tell old romantique stories of the old time'. In particular, his own nurse, a local woman, Katherine Bushell of Ford, 'was excellent at these old stories', and 'had the history from the conquest downe to Carl. I in ballad'. Indeed, it was Aubrey's mistaken belief, which he seems to have shared with John Milton, that historical facts would have been lost altogether under the Saxons had it not been for oral transmission: William of Malmesbury had 'pickt up his history from the time of Ven: Bede to his time out of old songs: for there was no writer in England from Bede to him'.[2]

Many of these old fireside stories remained unwritten because they were essentially local and too circumscribed in interest to make the recording of them either necessary or desirable. They had meaning for the community and it was this parochial relevance which both kept them alive and ensured their confinement. Thomas Bewick's Tyneside village of Mickley in the 1750s was probably typical, where 'the winter evenings were often spent in listening to the traditionary tales and songs, relating to men who had been eminent for their prowess and bravery in the border wars, and of others who had been esteemed for better and milder qualities, such as their having been good landlords, kind neighbours, and otherwise in every respect being bold independent and honest men'.[3]

It was thus events which were significant to the neighbourhood that were remembered, while even historical incidents or individuals of national renown tended to be conceived of within a familiar setting. Many traditions served an aetiological function, purporting to explain the origin of local place-names or account for the evolution of the topographical landmarks which provided people with their mental reference points. Indeed, the landscape all around was a vast repository of memory.[4] Memories of the past, then, comprised part of that local

---

[2] John Aubrey, 'Remaines of Gentilisme and Judaisme', in *Three Prose Works*, ed. John Buchanan-Brown (Fontwell, 1972), 289–90, 445; John Milton, *The History of Britain*, ed. G. P. Krapp, in *The Works of John Milton* (18 vols, New York, 1931–8), x, 232, 237–8.

[3] Thomas Bewick, *A Memoir of Thomas Bewick Written by Himself*, ed. Iain Bain (Oxford, 1979), 8.

[4] On the importance of landscape as a mnemonic of historical traditions, see, for example, Jan Vansina, *Oral Tradition as History* (London and Nairobi, 1985), 45–6; James Fentress and Chris Wickham, *Social Memory* (Oxford, 1992), 87, 93, 113, 121, 166; Walter Johnson, *Folk Memory: or the Continuity of British Archaeology* (Oxford, 1908); Jacqueline Simpson, 'The Local Legend: A Product of Popular Culture', *Rural History*, 2 (1991), 25–35; David Rollison, *The Local Origins of Modern Society: Gloucestershire 1500–1800* (1992), 70–1.

knowledge from which people derived a sense of identity and pride based upon place. They provided an imagined heritage which helped to underscore the emotional solidarity of the community and they were expressed in the 'common voice', 'common fame' or 'common report' of the inhabitants which antiquaries and travellers frequently encountered as they toured the country.[5]

The fanciful fables which some small towns or villages liked to cherish about their former greatness, for example, were often sustained by local memory and by the physical evidence all around rather than by any written documents. In the 1530s the 'commune voyce' at Billericay in Essex informed the passing John Leland that the town had once been much greater, and they could show had a fine ceremonial horn and mace to prove it. The Elizabethan inhabitants of Overburrow in Lancashire were equally keen to tell visitors that their 'small country village' had been 'formerly a great city', as they knew 'by a tradition handed down from their ancestors' and a variety of Roman remains confirmed. By the same token, large foundations uncovered in the village of Coggs, Oxfordshire, made the 'vulgar people that live here think that in old time here was a castle', but there was seemingly no documentary evidence to support this idea.[6]

Just as the survival of such physical evidence could be crucial in the preservation of local tradition, so it was likely to die out if the landmarks or monuments which kept it in mind once faded. 'Notwithstanding the eagerness of the vulgar in harkening to stories relating to parochial churches to which themselves particularly belong', observed the Oxford antiquary Thomas Hearne, 'when such churches fall or are destroyed, they soon forget what they had been, or even what benefactions had been made to them.'[7] A good example of this is provided by the case of the statue of Our Lady of Gillingham and the Rood of Chatham which stood in the churchyard of this Kentish village. They were described in the 1570s by the local antiquary, William Lambarde, who also recorded the legendary miracle associated with them 'as I have often heard (and that constantly reported)', and he thought it 'not amisse to commit faithfully to writing, what I have received credibly by hearing'. But when John Weever came to the same monuments

---

[5] D. R. Woolf, 'The "Common Voice": History, Folklore and Oral Tradition in Early Modern England', *Past and Present*, 120 (1988), 26–52.

[6] *The Itinerary of John Leland in or About the Years 1535–1543*, ed. Lucy Toulmin Smith (5 vols, 1906–10), IV, 67; William Camden, *Britannia*, ed. Edmund Gibson (1695), 794; British Library (hereafter BL) Sloane MS., 241, fo. 35v; *Parochial Collections (First Part) made by Anthony a Wood, M.A. and Richard Rawlinson, D.C.L., F.R.S.*, ed. F. N. Davis (Oxfordshire Record Society, Oxford, 1920), 100; Anthony Wood, *The Life and Times of Anthony Wood, Antiquary, of Oxford, 1632–1695, Described by Himself*, ed. Andrew Clark (5 vols, Oxford Historical Society, xix, xxi, xxvi, xxx, xl, Oxford, 1891–1900), I, 253.

[7] *The History and Antiquities of Glastonbury*, ed. Thomas Hearne (Oxford, 1722), xiv.

over half a century later he found the images 'now many yeares sithence defaced' and thus the legend, although 'received by tradition ... from the elders', and 'long since both comonly reported and faithfully credited by the vulgar sort', was now not to be 'learne[d] at man's mouth'. Yet, Weever conceded, 'many of the aged number remember it well'.[8]

As this comment suggests, the memories of aged inhabitants could be crucial in the retention of local tradition. The evidence here confirms the picture given of other societies with strong oral traditions that older people are of vital importance in the preservation and transmission of customary practice and intellectual capital. They provide a direct human link with the past and are often revered as the repositories of ancient wisdom and the custodians of communal memory.[9] 'We old men are old chronicles', says the 'countryman' in a dialogue of 1608, 'and when our tongues go they are not only clocks to tell only the time present, but large books unclasped; and our speeches, like leaves turned over and over, discover wonders long since passed.'[10] The importance of long memories in early modem England was no more evident than in the many disputes which arose during these centuries over customary law. For the customs of manors, towns and parishes were very often unwritten, retained only in the memories of the eldest inhabitants, and it was thus of crucial importance to the preservation of economic rights and the maintenance of livelihoods to be able to remember exactly what had gone on in the community 'within the memory of those yet living' and beyond.[11]

Customs were just one of the pieces of local information for which there was no alternative but to rely upon the recollection of ancients. Where transmission was relatively shallow, spanning no more than one or two generations, it might remain a reasonably accurate guide to past practice. Thus, when the vicar of Radwinter in Essex, William Harrison, wanted to learn of the changes in domestic comfort which had taken place during the sixteenth century, it was the 'old men yet dwelling in the village' to whom he turned. In 1630 Thomas Westcote reported the innovations in agricultural practice in Devon, 'begun within the memory

[8] William Lambarde, *A Perambulation of Kent: Conteining the Description, Hystorie, and Customes of that Shyre* (1576), 287; John Weever, *Ancient Funerall Monuments* (1631), 343–4.

[9] Jack Goody, *The Interface Between the Written and the Oral* (Cambridge, 1987), 150, 164; M. T. Clanchy, *From Memory to Written Record: England 1066–1307* (2nd edn, Oxford, 1993), 25–6; Keith Thomas, 'Age and Authority in Early Modern England', *Proceedings of the British Academy*, lxii (1976), 233–4.

[10] *The Great Frost* (1608), in *Social England Illustrated: A Collection of XVIIth-Century Tracts*, ed. Andrew Lang (1903), 166.

[11] For recent discussions, see *The Experience of Authority in Early Modern England*, ed. Paul Griffiths, Adam Fox and Steve Hindle (Basingstoke, 1996), 96–9, 266–73.

of old men'.[12] As a young boy growing up in Wiltshire before the Civil Wars, John Aubrey 'did ever love to converse with old men, as living histories'. Among many gleanings from such sources, he picked up local customs and anecdotes from his grandfather Isaac Lite who had heard them, in turn, from his own father; he listened to reminiscences of notable events past from old Mr Jacob, of Wootton Bassett who was eighty years of age in 1648; and he lapped up the stories of other ancients, like his 'old cosen' Ambrose Brown of Winterbourne Basset 'who lived to 103', 'old Jaquez' of Kington St Michael and old Bartholomew of Malmesbury.[13]

The length of this memory could thus be reliable at least for the period of a long life. In the mid-seventeenth century the Lancashire clergyman Henry Newcome learned of the last great famine to afflict the county from old aunt Key of Bury who told him that it 'was then sixty years past'. A curious visitor to Skenegrave on the Cleveland coast sometime before had heard 'ould men, that would be loath to have their credytes crackt by a tale of a stale date, reporte confidentlye' an incident said to have taken place 'sixty years since, or perhaps eighty or more'. Aubrey talked to Goodwife Dew of Broad Chalke in south Wiltshire who died in 1649, also at the age of 103, and remembered Edward VI visiting the county almost a century before. And when more than one generation was involved, inherited memory could reach back with some reliability for far longer. John Smyth of Nibley, estate steward to the earls of Berkeley in Gloucestershire, lived between 1567 and 1640 and during this period he 'often heard many old men and weomen' of the neighbourhood, born in the reign of Henry VII, 'relate the report of their parents, kinsfolks and neighbours' who as children themselves had witnessed the great local battle of 1469 between William, marquis of Berkeley, and Thomas Talbot, Viscount Lisle, over land rights. Smyth heard in vivid detail how Lisle had been slain by the arrow of one 'Black Will' and carried from the field, together with 'many other perticularyties ... not possible almost by such plaine country people to be fained'. Old Mr Charles Hiet was able to tell the same story in 1603, as 'delivered from the relation of his father and grandfather as if the same had been but yesterday'. The inherited

[12] William Harrison, *The Description of England*, ed. Georges Edelen (Ithaca, NY, 1968), 200; Thomas Westcote, *A View of Devonshire in 1630*, ed. George Oliver and Pitman Jones (Exeter, 1845), 56.

[13] John Aubrey, *Brief Lives*, ed. Andrew Clark (2 vols, Oxford, 1898), I, 43; John Aubrey, *The Natural History of Wiltshire*, ed. John Britton (1847), 76; Bodleian Library (hereafter Bod Lib) MS. Aubrey 3, fos 3, 25v, 57v, 59, 76v, 80v, 92, 97, 98, 185v; Aubrey, *Three Prose Works*, ed. Buchanan-Brown, 162, 353; Michael Hunter, *John Aubrey and the Realm of Learning* (1975), 168–9.

memory here, then, spanned at least a century and a half.[14]

In many of the reminiscences of eldest inhabitants is a nostalgia for the old days which can be characteristic of any age. It had been, after all, a much 'merrier world' in the past: hospitality was greater and life was simpler, there were fewer lawyers and all things were cheap.[15] To this extent there could be something inherently subversive about popular perceptions of the past. What ordinary men and women remembered was not usually the stuff of learned or officially approved versions of the past but instead interpretations of events which attempted to make sense of and justify the world as they saw it. As such their memories could be irreverent and even seditious in the details which they chose to retain, or forget, and the way in which they chose to construe them. Thus at the time of the Civil War the inhabitants of Evesham in Worcestershire were eager to relate the exploits of Simon de Montfort, earl of Leicester, who had fallen there while leading the baronial revolt against Henry III, for such tales sat well with their view of the present monarchy. 'It is reported the dead body of the earl of Leicester being fouly and barbarously deformed with wounds was there discovered, whom neverthelesse the vulgar sort reverence as a martir, because as they said he suffered all this for the Commonwealth, but not for the King, who forbad this the people's cannonizacion....'[16]

Just as the versions of manorial custom remembered by the tenants could differ completely from those understood by their landlords, so too other popular traditions might bear little relationship to the significant historical events as recorded by antiquarian scholarship in this period. Take, for example, the disafforestation, drainage and enclosure of Hatfield Chase on the Yorkshire–Lincolnshire border in the reign of Charles I. This was apparently consented to by the 'better sort' of the inhabitants of the area at the time and, after initial protests by some of the dispossessed, occasioned no further contention. Sir William Dugdale was to write up this history of 'improvement' in 1662 and no other verdict on the issue would be recorded were it not for the enquiries of Abraham de la Pryme who became vicar of Hatfield in November 1696. De la Pryme was a great collector of local traditions and here, as elsewhere, he was always 'examining and talking with ...

---

[14] *The Autobiography of Henry Newcome, M.A.*, ed. Richard Parkinson (2 vols, Chetham Society, xxvi–xxvii, Manchester, 1852), I, 82; *The Topographer and Genealogist*, ed. John Gough Nichols (3 vols, 1846–58), II, 416; Aubrey, *The Natural History of Wiltshire*, ed. Britton, 69; John Smyth, *The Berkeley Manuscripts*, ed. Sir John Maclean (3 vols, Gloucester, 1883–5), II, 114–15.

[15] Keith Thomas, *The Perception of the Past in Early Modern England* (Creighton Trust Lecture, 1984), 11–22.

[16] Thomas Habington, *A Survey of Worcestershire*, ed. John Amphlett (2 vols, Worcestershire Historical Society, Oxford, 1895–9), II, 82.

my eldest parishioners ... about what was memorable relating thereto'. He found that the 'old men' of Hatfield would often talk nostalgically of the days before the destruction of the chase when 'the poor people got a good liveing out of the same and venison was no greater a rarity then in a poor man's kitchen than mutton is now'. They also related in loving detail the intricacies of their poaching technique, seeming to delight in its skill and craft as well as in its defiance of authority. Moreover, they had a popular hero in Sir Robert Swift, the last Bowbearer to the king in the chase, whose responsibility it was to protect the game but whose loveable incompetence seems to have endeared him to all and occasioned 'many traditional stories'.[17]

Exactly the same kind of discrepancy in interpretations of the past may be detected in the rather different versions of an eventually famous tale collected at Tilney Smeath in Norfolk. In the churchyard there stood a monument commemorating the deeds of one Hikifricke. In 1631 John Weever recorded the tale, 'as it hath gone by tradition from father to son', of how 'upon a time (no man knowes how long since)', Hikifricke had saved the rights of the seven villages in the parish over the large common which they surrounded from the encroachments of the local landlord.[18] When, however, the heralds Elias Ashmole and William Dugdale were touring the fenlands in the early summer of 1657, they both seem to have derived different versions of events from the locals at Tilney. Ashmole understood their hero to have 'killed a gyant and recovered marshland from him', while Dugdale believed that Hikificke himself had been the lord of Tilney and had fought not for but against the inhabitants over the bounds of the common.[19] Such variance provides signal evidence of the way in which interpretations of a tale might depend upon the disposition of both tellers and recipients. In the minds of some Hikifricke was a champion of the common cause of the people, while in the view of others he was invoked as a defender of the rights of property and lordly authority.

---

[17] Sir William Dugdale, *The History of Imbanking and Drayning* (1662), 145–9; Keith Lindley, *Fenland Riots and the English Revolution* (1982), 13–14, 23–4, 64, 71–2; *The Diary of Abraham de la Pryme, the Yorkshire Antiquary*, ed. Charles Jackson (Surtees Society, liv, Durham, 1869–70), 71; BL Lansdowne MS., 897, fos 50–1, 55r.

[18] Weever, *Ancient Funerall Monuments*, 866; and cf. Sir Henry Spelman, 'Incenia: Sive Norfolciae Descriptio Topographica', in *Reliquiae Spelmannianae* (Oxford, 1698), 138; Francis Blomefield and Charles Parkin, *An Essay towards a Topographical History of the County of Norfolk* (5 vols, Fersfield and Lynn, 1735–75), IV, 691–2. Equally, local tenants might seek to deface or destroy such monuments when there were traditions associated with them which were prejudicial to their land rights and usages: Sampson Erdeswicke, *A Survey of Staffordshire* (1723), 192.

[19] *Elias Ashmole (1617–1692). His Autobiographical and Historical Notes, his Correspondence, and other Contemporary Sources Relating to his Life and Work*, ed. C. H. Josten (Oxford, 1966), 708–9; Dugdale, *History of Imbanking and Drayning*, 244.

Many communities seem to have cherished hero figures such as Hikifricke who had at some time defended the rights of the common people or flouted authority. Outlaws, in particular, were the epitome of those who spurned the conventions of society and appeared to live a life of freedom outside the bounds and burdens which usually kept people in their place. Theirs were deeds of daring and adventure, romantic and exceptional. To hear of them was to be transported momentarily to a time and a place in which the powerful might be defied and even conquered. Such had been the appeal of Hereward the Wake in the centuries after the Norman Conquest and then of Robin Hood who by the thirteenth century seems to have taken his place in the popular imagination.[20]

Ubiquitous as Robin was in popular legend, he had plenty of local equivalents who may have been unknown other than in the parochial context and were probably remembered only in oral tradition. Thus, the people living around the Forest of Exmoor in Devon would tell of one Symon, 'another Robin Hood', who 'standing in outlary, kept this forest'. Among the trees was 'a large deep pool which they name Symon's Bath ... and in the moors of Somerset there is a burrow or fort called, by the inhabitants, Symon's Burrow, which he made his winter strength to retire unto'. Such tales suggest all the swashbuckling elements of the conventional Robin Hood narratives and many seem to have adopted the motif of man of high birth forced to live on the margins of society. At Myddle in Shropshire, for example, they had a local hero in 'wild Humphry' Kinaston, a knight-errant turned fugitive of whom 'the people tell almost as many romantick storyes, as of the great outlawe Robin Whood'. Among these was the tale of how 'wild Humphry' had escaped from the ambush of the sheriff and 'a considerable company of men' by leaping over the river Severn. He sought shelter in a cave near Nescliffe 'which, to this day, is called Kinaston's Cave'. Such also was the history of Poole's Hole, an underground cave by Buxton in Derbyshire, the refuge of 'one Pool, of Pool's Hall in Staffordshire, a man of great valour who, being outlawed, resided here for his own security', and yet to be seen were his stone table, bed and shelf. Likewise, at Bristol in the years before the Civil War one could still hear tell 'as fresh as but of yesterday' of the exploits of 'black Will' Herbert, the first earl of Pembroke, 'a mad fighting young fellow' who in the reign of Henry VIII had killed one of the sheriffs and escaped through the city gates to France.[21]

[20] On this aspect of Robin Hood's appeal, see Christopher Hill, 'Robin Hood', in his *Liberty Against the Law: Some Seventeenth-Century Controversies* (1996), 71–82.

[21] Westcote, *A View of Devonshire in 1630*, ed. Oliver and Jones, 95; Richard Gough, *The History of Myddle*, ed. David Hey (Harmondsworth, 1981), 56–7; Ralph Thoresby, *The Diary of Ralph Thoresby, F.R.S.*, ed. Joseph Hunter (2 vols, 1830), I, 91–2; Edward Browne,

Thus, the memories of ancient inhabitants could provide a strong and relatively reliable link with the recent past. Knowledge of events stretching back for a century or more might be passed down the generations with some degree of consistency. The further away from the incidents or individuals in question that oral transmission took an historical tradition, however, the more prone to distortion it might become. Moreover, there was a large gap in the terms of factual accuracy between what was inherited directly at first or second hand from elders and ancestors and what was believed to have taken place in the very distant past. When the short limits of memory were exhausted, myth began.[22]

For most people their understanding of long ago was vague and episodic: theirs was a past with little sense of chronology, in which names and places, dates and events could be hopelessly compressed and confused. Certain great historical figures loomed so large as to explain almost any landmark or occurrence of note. There was a tendency to 'telescope', to shorten or omit entire portions of the past, which is familiar in many societies with strong oral traditions.[23] A vivid example of conflation would be uncovered by John Byng in his travels around England in the late eighteenth century. He found that wherever he went the people attributed the destruction of any ruined building to Oliver Cromwell. Moreover, they tended to muddle the Lord Protector with his namesake, Henry VIII's first minister. Thus at Wingfield manor in Derbyshire his guide 'spake of the seige it sustain'd in the civil wars; shew'd every rent in the walls as if made by cannon balls; and was puzzled, as all countrymen are, about the two Cromwells; the destroyer of monasteries, and the destroyer of castles'.[24] Such observations indicate the importance of great events such as the Reformation or the Civil

---

'Journal of a Tour in Derbyshire', in *Sir Thomas Browne's Works*, ed. Simon Wilkin (4 vols, 1833–4), I, 35; Aubrey, *Brief Lives*, ed. Clark, I, 314–15; Anthony Powell, *John Aubrey and his Friends* (1948), 31–2. The celebrated escape of the border reiver Kinmont Willie from Carlisle Castle in April 1596 continued to be remembered in Cumberland: Edmund Sansford, *A Cursory Relation of all the Antiquities and Familyes in Cumberland*, ed. R. S. Ferguson (Cumberland and Westmorland Ant. and Arch. Soc., 4, Kendal, 1890), 49. Sir Walter Scott was later to transcribe from oral tradition and immortalise in print the ballad of this triumphant episode: *Minstrelsy of the Scottish Borber*, ed. Thomas Henderson (1931), 179–90.

[22] On the large gap between what is personally remembered and some imagined mythical past, see Johnson, *Folk Memory: or the Continuity of British Archaeology*, 13; M. T. Clanchy, 'Remembering the Past and the Good Old Law', *History*, 55 (1970), 167; Thomas, *The Perception of the Past in Early Modern England*, 8–9; Rosalind Thomas, *Oral Tradition and Written Record in Classical Athens* (Cambridge, 1989), 283.

[23] On this 'telescoping' of the past, see Jan Vansina, *Oral Tradition: a Study in Historical Methodology*, transl. H. M. Wright (1965), 101–2; David Henige, *Oral Historiography* (1982), 100–1.

[24] John Byng, *The Torrington Diaries*, ed. C. Bruyn Andrews (4 vols, 1970), II, 199.

War as dating tools in popular perceptions of the past, even if they failed to engender any firm sense of chronology.[25]

This vague sense of date was no less evident among 'the country people' of Lincolnshire who were reported to labour under the 'notion that the Foss road is the oldest in England, and that it was made by William the Conqueror'. Ethelbert's Tower in Canterbury was not in fact built by Ethelbert himself, 'as vulgar tradition will fabulously tell you it was', but merely in his honour in about 1047. Castles seemed particularly prone to this kind of fanciful dating. Some were post-dated, like Reigate in Surrey, actually built by the Saxons, 'tho a vulgar error has generally given credit of it to one of the Warrens, earls of Surrey'. Most, however, were dignified with a more or less bogus antiquity, as was Bamburgh Castle on the Northumbrian coast, built, so the local people affirmed, 'before our Saviour's time'.[26]

Julius Caesar seems to have impressed himself on the popular imagination as the natural builder of fortifications, whatever age they may have been. 'Vulgar chronology will have Norwich Castle as old as Julius Caesar', it was said, while the castles at Chepstow, Exeter, Canterbury and Dover, where visitors could inspect his 'old brass trumpet', were among those similarly attributed.[27] Patrons in an alehouse at Woodstock, Oxfordshire, boasted to one Elizabethan tourist that the Roman conqueror had been responsible for a 'palace' there; nor were such notions mere village fancy, for even in the capital city 'common opinion' erroneously ascribed the Tower of London to his offices.[28] Small wonder, then, that 'the vulgar' were thought to be 'generally uncapable of judging of antiquities'.[29]

---

[25] On great events as dating tools, see Fentress and Wickham, *Social Memory*, 99, 110–12.

[26] William Stukeley, *Itinerarium Curiosum* (1722), 99; William Somner, *The Antiquities of Canterbury* (1640), 40; John Aubrey, *The Natural History and Antiquities of the County of Surrey* (5 vols, 1718), IV, 189; 'Journeyings through Northumberland and Durham Anno Dom. 1677', in *Reprints of Rare Tracts and Imprints of Antient Manuscripts*, ed. M. A. Richardson (7 vols, Newcastle, 1843–9), VII, 11.

[27] Sir Thomas Browne, *Hydriotaphia Urne-Burial* (1658), in *The Works of Sir Thomas Browne*, ed. Geoffrey Keynes (4 vols, 1928), I, 142; Marmaduke Rawdon, *The Life of Marmaduke Rawdon of York*, ed. Robert Davies (Camden Society, 1st series, lxxxv, 1863), 187; James Brome, *Travels Over England, Scotland and Wales* (1700), 21; John Hooker, *The Description of the Citie of Excester*, ed. W. J. Harte, J. W. Schopp and H Tapley-Soper (Devon and Cornwall Record Society, Exeter, 1919), 31; Camden, *Britannia*, ed. Gibson, 205; 'A Relation of a Short Survey of the Western Counties', ed. L. G. Wickham Legg, in *Camden Miscellany Vol. XVI* (Camden Society, 3rd series, lii, 1936), 19, 24; BL Sloane MS., 1911–13, fo. 195r.

[28] *Thomas Platter's Travels in England, 1599*, ed. Clare Williams (1937), 223; John Stow, *A Survey of London*, ed. C. L. Kingsford (2 vols, Oxford, 1908), I, 44, 136.

[29] *The History and Antiquities of Glastonbury*, ed. Hearne, vii.

This confused sense of chronology was not merely the product of popular ignorance or the distortion caused by oral transmission, however, but was in essence the fruit of learned fiction and often derived from written sources. At a time when studious historical scholarship was only just beginning to develop standards of documentary reference and corroboration and to question many of the long-established legends, inherited from the medieval chronicles, which continued to dominate the learned view of the past, ignorance was by no means confined to 'the vulgar'. Moreover, new and spurious versions of the past were being written in the early modern period which did as much to generate error. It was the arriviste gentry of Tudor England, with the aid of the heralds, who were as responsible as anyone for the creation of bogus versions of history in the fantastic genealogies which they fabricated in an attempt to dignify family lines with spurious longevity.[30]

This can be seen, for example, in the elaborate 'charter myths' fabricated and cherished by many towns and institutions in support of their antiquity and venerability. In the late fifteenth century the Warwickshire antiquary John Rous had claimed the foundation of Cambridge, both town and university, for Cantaber, a Spaniard who came to Britain in the time of King Gurguntius, about 375 BC. This was the view endorsed by John Caius in the 1570s, among others, so that the Duke of Wurttemberg, visiting the town in 1592, was rightly told that this was the orthodoxy 'as affirmed by the principal historians'.[31] At Oxford, meanwhile, it was possible for the curious enquirer to choose from a number of contending hypotheses about origins, all of them derived from learned written authorities. Some attributed its provenance to one Mempric 'who was king of the Britannes in the year of the world 2954 and before Christ 1009'; others gave the plaudits to his son Ebranc; while still others preferred the claims of Olenus Calenus

---

[30] On these bogus genealogies, see Michael Maclagan, 'Genealogy and Heraldry in the Sixteenth and Seventeenth Centuries', in *English Historical Scholarship in the Sixteenth and Seventeenth Centuries*, ed. Levi Fox (1956), 41–2; Lawrence Stone, *The Crisis of the Aristocracy, 1558–1641* (Oxford, 1965), 23–5; A R. Wagner, *English Genealogy* (2nd edn, Oxford, 1972), 358–66; Felicity Heal and Clive Holmes, *The Gentry in England and Wales, 1500–1700* (Basingstoke, 1994), 34–7.

[31] John Rous, *Historia Regum Angliae*, ed. Thomas Hearne (2nd edn, Oxford, 1745), 25–6; John Caius, *De Antiquitate Cantebrigiensis Academiae* (1574), in *The Works of John Caius, M.D.*, ed, E. S. Roberts (Cambridge, 1912), 11–14; *England as seen by Foreigners in the Days of Elizabeth and James the First*, ed. William Brenchley Rye (1865), 33; T. D. Kendrick, *British Antiquity* (1950), 25–6. Cf. 'Diary of the Journey of Philip Julius, Duke of Stettin-Pomerania, through England in the Year 1602', ed. Gottfried von Bulow', *Transactions of the Royal Historical Society*, n.s., vi (1892), 33; 'Thomas Baskerville's Journeys in England, Temp. Car. II', in Historical Manuscripts Commission, *Thirteenth Report, Appendix, Part II* (1893), 284.

'a Roman, about 70 years before Christ'. But it was equally possible to find support for the view that it had been the creation of 'certain philosophers out of Graece', a theory which the existence of 'Aristotle's well' near Walton did much to confirm; 'that Cassisbulan, king of the Britaines about 58 years before Christ, built it; as he did Exeter, Colchester and Norwich'; that it was 'originally founded by a British king called Avizagus about 70 years after our Saviour's nativity'; that it had been 'built or at least restored' by King Voritgen in 474; or, finally, that it was the work of King Alfred '(as some, and these not mean historians, assert) in the year 872'.[32]

Such myths were hardly mere 'vulgar errors', therefore, but learned fictions‛endorsed in the universites and supported by the most respected antiquarian opinion. Many of them derived from Geoffrey of Monmouth's *Historia Regum Britanniae* or else from the elaborations and imaginings of subsequent monastic writers. Scholarly opinion in the sixteenth and early seventeenth centuries did little to dispel, and often much to encourage, such legend. It is hardly surprising, therefore, that the majority should have accepted and rehearsed what were no more than long-established commonplaces of historical understanding. Thus, when the 'old attendant' at the Angel Inn in Leicester assured three soldiers resting there in 1634 that the town had been 'built by the British King Leir, neare 1000 yeeres before Christ', he was doing no more than repeating the testimony of Geoffrey. And his *Historia* was also the source of the tale which these same three travellers found in York, 'as tradition and story tells', that the town was founded by King Ebraucus 'in the reign of K[ing] David' of Judaea.[33]

This sense of learned fiction feeding into popular lore is evident in much of what can be recovered of generally held versions of the past. In practice few historical narratives which circulated orally were completely 'pure', in the sense of owing nothing to the written word. A number of recent studies drawing upon evidence gathered from societies around the world and over time have demonstrated the interaction and reciprocal infusion of written and unwritten sources in the communication of information about the past, whether in story or

---

[32] Rous, *Historia Regum Angliae*, ed. Hearne, 21–2; Anthony Wood, *'Survey of the Antiquities of the City of Oxford', composed in 1661–6, by Anthony Wood*, ed. Andrew Clark (3 vols, Oxford Historical Society, xv, xvii, xxxvii, Oxford, 1889–99), I, 41–3, 354–5. Cf. *England as seen by Foreigners*, ed. Rye, 21; Charles Deering, *Nottingham Vetus et Nova* (Nottingham, 1751), 12.

[33] *A Relation of a Short Survey of 26 Counties*, ed. L. G. Wickham Legg (1904), 14, 64, deriving directly from Geoffrey of Monmouth, *Historia Regum Britanniae*, ii. 11, ii. 7. Touring the south of England in 1478–80, William Worcestre discovered chronicles in a number of abbeys and libraries which detailed the fabulous origins of British towns: William Worcestre, *Itineraries*, ed. John H. Harvey (Oxford, 1969), 94, 96, 278.

song.[34] So, too, in Tudor and Stuart England, much of the historical tradition which circulated among ordinary people had some basis in literary and learned culture even if the embellishment and corruption effected by generations of transmission had taken it far from its origins. By the early modern period, centuries of chronicle and hagiographic writing, of chivalric romance, sermon exempla, poetry and drama, had been providing a variety of written sources of knowledge about the past and they provide the key to understanding the genesis of a large part of popular tradition.[35] Time and again, the kind of local anecdote which was increasingly coming to be dismissed as erroneous by antiquarian scholarship in the seventeenth century can be found to derive from some written source, perhaps long forgotten. As Sir Thomas Browne put it in the 1640s with characteristic acuity: 'there is scarce any tradition or popular error but stands also delivered by some good author'.[36]

In addition to initiating much of what subsequently passed into oral circulation, the written word was also responsible for augmenting and enhancing it; for reviving an oral narrative which might otherwise have died out were it not for its preservation, elaboration and dissemination in text. Again, written culture was probably more culpable than oral in the fabrication and perpetuation of distorted, exaggerated and spurious versions of the past. Thomas Westcote commented perceptively in the 1630s that 'some things seem more fabulous, interposed by some augmenting transcribers' than many others 'left unto us as tradition ... from mouth to mouth'. By the same token, it was said of the tales told of the miraculous deeds of St William of Lindholm in south Yorkshire, that they remained purely local and rather muted as a consequence of never having been writtten down: 'the pitty is that this worthy saint has not had any one to set forth his strang works or else perhaps they might have been as great, wonderfull and fabulous as K[ing] Arthur's are'.[37]

Even contemporaries who believed that they were witnessing pure

---

[34] See the evidence reviewed in Ruth Finnegan, *Oral Poetry: its Nature, Signifiacance and Social Context* (Cambridge, 1977), ch. 5; Ruth Finnegan, *Literacy and Orality: Studies in the Technology of Communication* (Oxford, 1988), ch. 6. The point is made with regard to early modern England in Thomas, *The Perception of the Past*, 7–8.

[35] See, for example, G. R. Owst, *Literature and Pulpit in Medieval England* (2nd edn, Oxford, 1961), esp. 126–34, 158–61; P. R. Coss, 'Aspects of Cultural Diffusion in Medieval England: the Early Romances, Local Society and Robin Hood', *Past and Present*, 108 (1985), 35–79; C. L. Kingsford, *English Historical Literature in the Fifteenth Century* (Oxford, 1913); E. K. Chambers, *English Literature at the Close of the Middle Ages* (Oxford, 1945).

[36] Sir Thomas Browne, *Pseudodoxia Epidemica* (1646), in *The Works*, ed. Keynes, II, 52.

[37] Westcote, *A View of Devonshire*, ed. Oliver and Jones, 30; BL Lansdowne MS., 897, fo. 73r. On the way in which writing can infuse and augment oral traditions, see Henige, *Oral Historiography*, 81–7.

oral tradition passing down the generations unadulterated by the infiltration of writing were usually mistaken in this. Elias Ashmole seems to have thought that the legend of St Joseph of Arimathea and the Holy Thorn of Glastonbury Abbey provided an example of one such tradition, for until the work of a few recent writers he could 'not remember to have read any author who hath taken notice of this thorne in print'. Otherwise, 'all the remembrance we have of it, hath past along among us by tradition only, which I have often heard spoken of...'. In reality, however, the monks at Glastonbury had been fabricating miraculous stories of St Joseph since the twelfth century and they had enjoyed wide manuscript circulation long before the Tudor herbalists popularised the legend of the Thorn.[38]

Many such legends of saints and their miracles which still enjoyed widespread currency in the early modern period probably had their origins in this kind of monastic fabrication. Accounts of their lives had been written by chroniclers since the early Middle Ages and by the twelfth and thirteenth centuries had assumed a standard format. In this guise they became a staple of manuscript culture and sermon exempla and represented some of the most widely known of all traditionary tales in late medieval England. Given that they were, in Gerald Owst's words, 'definitely presented as true history, not to be confused in the popular mind with lighter forms of pulpit illustration', it is hardly suprising that they were widely and faithfully believed by the majority. Many of them were included in compilations such as the famous *Golden Legend*, the thirteenth-century continental collection which was to be translated and printed by Caxton in 1483 and reissued seven times by 1527. There were scores of individual lives, too, especially of English martyrs like St Thomas of Canterbury, St Oswald and St Edmund.[39]

Thus the origin of a tradition in Canterbury that the devil had once tried to prevent St Augustine preaching at the chapel of St Pancrace, was, according to William Somner, the work of some monastic chronicler which he had seen. But it had passed subsequently into popular tradition and 'of latter time ... became vulgarly received'. Similarly, the tales which travellers often encountered from the mouths of local people at Crowland Abbey in Lincolnshire, of the torments once inflicted by frightful devils upon St Guthlac and the monks, could be

---

[38] *Elias Ashmole (1617–1692)*, ed. Josten, 1286–7; and cf. *The History and Antiquities of Glastonbury*, ed. Hearne, 302. Antonia Gransden, 'The Growth of the Glastonbury Traditions and Legends in the Twelfth Century', *Journal of Ecclesiastical History*, 27 (1976), 358; C. E. Raven, *English Naturalists from Neckam to Ray* (Cambridge, 1947), 21.

[39] Owst, *Literature and Pulpit in Medieval England*, 126–6; Keith Thomas, *Religion and the Decline of Magic* (1971), 26; *The Golden Legand*, transl. William Grainger Ryan (2 vols, Princeton, 1993); G. H. Gerould, *Saints' Legends* (Boston, 1916).

traced back, so it was said, to 'the chronicler Felix.[40] The scores of other local saints' legends to which communities loyally adhered were all just as likely to be the products of written hagiographic tradition. This was to end at the Reformation, of course, but the continuation of such stories throughout the eighteenth century and beyond in some cases is testimony to their survival in oral tradition.[41]

The large role played by the devil in so many popular traditions was also a product of centuries of preaching and didactic writing which had played upon the notion of a malevolent fiend active in the temporal world who tempted mankind and whose evil projects to wreak havoc explained the shape of so much of the landscape. Rocky outcrops, stone circles, caves, ditches and gorges were all likely to be attributed to the work of 'old nick'. 'It is a strange taste which our ancestors had', William Cobbett could later muse, 'to ascribe no inconsiderable part of these wonders of nature to the devil.'[42] Equally, large man-made structures such as dykes, causeways or Roman roads were just as likely to be explained in these terms: 'for the vulgar', observed William Stukeley, 'generally think these extraordinary works made by the help of the devil'.[43]

Another prominent theme in popular tradition was tales about dragons. These, too, had a long lineage in the bestiaries and emblematic writings of the Middle Ages, but many owed their popularity in the early modern period to another series of spurious charter myths. From an early date it had been common for noble or gentle families, and

[40] Somner, *The Antiquities of Canterbury*, 61–2; Camden, *Britannia*, ed. Gibson, 460–1; Daniel Defoe, *A Tour Thro' the Whole Island of Great Britain*, ed. G. D. H. Cole (2 vols, 1968), II, 495.
[41] For the continued vibrance of saints' legends in the eighteenth century, see, for example, Defoe, *A Tour Thro' the Whole Island of Great Britain*, ed. Cole, I, 49, II, 480, 682, 694; Richard Pococke, *The Travels through England of Dr Richard Pococke*, ed. James Joel Cartwright (2 vols, Camden Society, n.s., xlii–xliv, 1888–9), I, 136; Francis Grose, *The Antiquarian Repertory* (4 vols, 1775–84), II, 76–7; William Hutchinson, *A View of Northumberland* (2 vols, Newcastle, 1778), II, 23.
[42] William Cobbett, *Rural Rides* (2 vols, Everyman edn, n.d.), I, 205. For a selection of examples, see Fynes Morrison, *An Itinerary Containing His Ten Yeeres Travell* (4 vols, Glasgow, 1907–8), IV, 152, 154; BL Additional MS., 38599, fo. 98v; *The Topographer and Genealogist*, ed. Nichols, II, 409, 425; Camden, *Britannia*, ed. Gibson, 495, 716; John Aubrey, *Monumenta Britannica*, ed. John Fowles and Rodney Legg (Sherborne, 1982), 95, 107, 109–12, 823; Robert Plot, *The Natural History of Oxford-shire* (Oxford, 1677), 343; Robert Plot, *The Natural History of Staffordshire* (Oxford, 1686), 398; Defoe, *A Tour Thro' the Whole Island of Great Britain*, ed. Cole, I, 461–2, II, 627–8; Pococke, *Travels through England*, ed. Cartwright, II, 52.
[43] Stukeley, *Itinerarium Curiosum*, 171. For examples, see Camden, *Britannia*, ed. Gibson, 85; Aubrey, *Monumenta Britannica*, ed. Fowles and Legg, 273, 381, 881, 891, 923, 925; Aubrey, *The Natural History and Antiquities of the County of Surrey*, IV, 187; Defoe, *A Tour Thro' the Whole Island of Great Britain*, ed. Cole, II, 592; Hutchinson, *A View of Northumberland*, I, 80.

institutions or corporations, to try to explain their origins, justify their ownership of a piece of land, or account for the heraldic dragon on their coat of arms, by claiming for an ancient forbear some feat of heroism or conquest. Such inventions might then pass into the popular lore and become generally believed in the locality. The Lordship of Moston in Cheshire, for example, had been in the possession of the Venables family for many generations when it was recorded in 1560 that their ancestor, Thomas, had earned the inheritance by slaying 'a terrible dragon' which had once terrorised the neighbourhood, piercing it with an arrow while in the very act of devouring a child. The dragon on the Berkeley family crest derived, so an early seventeenth-century document explains, from the dragon-slaying exploits of Sir John Berkeley at Bisterne in Hampshire, where a Dragon Field can be seen to this day. At Sockburn, in County Durham, a monument in the church commemorated the valiant deeds of Sir John Conyers, who 'before the Conquest', tradition told, had fought and slain the dragon, 'a monstrous venom'd and poison'd wiverne, ask or worme, which overthrew and devour'd many people in fight, for the scent of the poyson was so strong that noe person was able to abide it'. In the reign of Charles I people were still showing the spot known as Graystone where the dragon had fallen, and the deeds of Sir John were commemorated in local ceremonial into the nineteenth century.[44]

Finally, together with the legends of saints and the fabulous exploits of devils and dragons, tales of giants also occupied a central place in English folk tradition. Once again, the literary origins of these are well attested. It was Geoffrey of Monmouth's *Historia* which popularised notions, probably much older, that the island of Albion had been populated by giants before the conquest of the Trojan Brutus. The belief that giants had once inhabited the earth had Old Testament authority, of course, and these ideas were taken up again by the historians of the sixteenth and early seventeenth centuries. In 1610 the astrologer Simon Forman wrote a genealogy of all the giants from the days of Noah, while at the same time the antiquary William Burton could invoke a variety of scriptural and other authorities to prove their former existence.[45] Gigantic figures adorned the frescoes and murals in palaces, cathedrals and great houses.[46] And, naturally enough, images

[44] BL Harleian MS., 2119, fo. 40. Jennifer Westwood, *Albion: A Guide to Legendary Britain* (1985), 45, and cf. 250–1, 341–2; BL Harleian MS., 2118, fo. 39r; W.C. Hazlitt, *Tenures of Land and Customs of Manors* (1874), 285n.

[45] Genesis, vi, 4; Bod Lib MS. Ashmole, 244, fos 192–9; William Burton, *The Description of Leicestershire* (1622), 277.

[46] See, for example, *Itinerary of John Leland*, ed. Smith, I, 95; *Thomas Platter's Travels in England*, ed. Williams, 165–6; Aubrey, *Monumenta Britannica*, ed. Fowles and Legg, 477; *The Diary of Henry Machyn*, ed. John Gough Nichols (Camden Society, 1st series, xlii, 1848), 186.

of giants and the legendary stories of Albion found their way into the great poetry and literature of the day.[47]

Once again, then, it is hardly surprising to find this weight of written tradition feeding into popular historical consciousness. Camden believed that the many tales told by Cornish folk of the giants who occupied St Michael's Mount, still much talked of in the late nineteenth century, owed their creation to verses penned in the reign of Henry II.[48] As with the devil, giants provided an explanation for much that was gargantuan or unusual in the landscape. Stonehenge had been known as 'the Giant's Dance' since Saxon times.[49] The lone boulder next to the stone circle at Stanton Drew in Somerset was believed to be the quoit of the giant Hakewell, while Wookey Hole was designated, in typical fashion, 'the gyant's table'.[50] Large man-made structures were similarly explained. Oxfordshire had a number of Grim's ditches, for example, and 'the country people will tell you that this Grymes was a gyant', while the Roman road on Wheeldale Moor in the North Riding was known as Wade's causeway after the giant and his wife who were said to have built it in an instant.[51]

In general, Roman buildings were 'so very stately', observed Camden, that 'the common people will have these ... to be the work of gyants'. That giants lived in castles was something which readers of *Pilgrim's Progress* would have accepted without a second thought. Typically enough, of the great ruins above Aldridge in Staffordshire the locals

---

[47] Among the most famous examples are Edmund Spenser, *The Faerie Queene* (1596), in *Spenser: Poetical Works*, ed. J. C. Smith and E. De Selincourt (Oxford, 1912); Michael Drayton, *Poly-Olbion* (1613), in *The Works of Michael Drayton*, ed. J. William Hebel (5 vols, Oxford, 1961), IV, 26. For discussion, see C. B. Millican, *Spenser and the Round Table* (Cambridge, Mass., 1932); Ernest Jones, *Geoffrey of Monmouth 1640–1800* (Berkeley and Los Angeles, 1944), 406–17.

[48] Camden, *Britannia*, ed. Gibson, 4. For legends of Cornish giants, as they were recorded in the mid-nineteenth century, see Robert Hunt, *Popular Romances of the West of England* (1865), 44–75.

[49] L. V. Grinsell, 'The Legendary History and Folklore of Stonehenge', *Folklore*, 87 (1976), 5–20.

[50] Aubrey, *Monumenta Britannica*, ed. Fowles and Legg, 46. 68; Rawdon, *The Life of Marmaduke Rawdon of York*, ed. Davies, 178. For other examples of giants' boulders, see Plot, *The Natural History of Staffordshire*, 397–8; Martin Martin, *A Description of the Western Islands of Scotland circa 1695* (Glasgow, 1884), 152–3, 220, 364; Joseph Taylor, *A Journey to Edenborough in Scotland*, ed. William Cowan (Edinburgh, 1903), 19–20; Ralph Thoresby, *Ducatus Leodiensis: or, the Topography of the Ancient and Populous Town and Parish of Leedes* (1715), 194; Sir Robert Atkyns, *The Ancient and Present State of Gloucestershire* (2nd edn, 1768), 188; James Hardy (ed.), *The Denham Tracts* (2 vols, Folklore Society, 1892–5), II, 217. There was another 'giant's table' outside Penrith: Celia Fiennes, *The Journeys of Celia Fiennes*, ed. Christopher Morris (1947), 201. There were also numerous giants' caves, chairs and gravestones.

[51] *The Remains of Thomas Hearne*, ed. John Buchanan-Brown (1966), 199, 205; Westwood, *Albion: A Guide to Legendary Britain*, 344–5.

had 'a tradition that there lived a gyant ... and another att a castle in Wall[sall] and that when either went from home he used to throwe the key to the other'. Once upon a time, the story went, a throw fell short and the key plummeted into a pit of water below where it was found by a poor man who used it as 'a share and coulter for a plow'.[52] The benign and friendly, almost comical, character evidenced by the giants in this tale, as in so many similar anecedotes, attests to the way in which they had been adopted and absorbed to fit local needs. Frequently they milked cows, fought on behalf of the community or bequeathed some enormous gift. At Brent Pelham in Hertfordshire there was a monument in the church to their particular giant, Shonk. An 'old farmer ... who valued himself for being born in the air that Shonk breathed', explained to Nathanial Salmon in the 1720s how 'Shonk was a giant that dwelt in this parish, who fought with a giant of Barkway, named Cadmus, and worsted him; upon which Barkway hath paid a quit rent to Pelham ever since.'[53]

To the manuscript culture of the Middle Ages, then, can be traced the foundation of much of what passed into oral tradition, where it was to take on a life of its own. Moreover, by the early modern period these written sources were being enhanced by printed ones which would, in turn, enormously stimulate the creation and augmentation of the legendary repertoire. In particular, the tremendous growth of antiquarian writings in the form of chronicles, county histories and itineraries from the sixteenth century was responsible not only for recording much popular belief but also for helping to create and sustain it. Once again, this cautions against the notion that writing necessarily destroys memory and undermines oral tradition. Rather, it is more instructive

[52] Camden, *Britannia*, ed. Gibson, lxv; John Bunyan, *The Pilgrim's Progress*, ed. J. B. Wharey and Roger Sharrock (Oxford, 1960), 113–19, 281–3; Aubrey, *Monumenta Britannica*, ed. Fowles and Legg, 387–9. Among other examples of giants' castles, see *Itinerary of John Leland*, ed. Smith, I, 59, V, 57; Habington, *A Survey of Worcestershire*, ed Amphlett, I, 187; Pococke, *Travels through England*, ed. Cartwright, I, 6, 31. The castle of Abergavenny in Monmouthshire was built after the Norman Conquest, 'as auncient monuments and writtings make mencion', on the same spot 'where before time, a gyant called Ayres had builded a stronge forte or holde': Public Record Office, SP12/219/17.

[53] Nathanial Salmon, *The History of Hertfordshire* (1728), 289–90, and cf. 184. For other examples of giants or men of extraordinary stature, said to have performed heroic deeds for the community, see Camden, *Britannia*, ed. Gibson, 126; Thomas Machell, *Antiquary on Horseback*, ed. Jane M. Ewbank (Cumberland and Westmorland Ant. and Arch. Soc., extra series, 19, Kendal, 1963), 126–7; Sir Daniel Fleming, *Description of the County of Cumberland*, ed. R. S. Ferguson (Cumberland and Westmorland Ant. and Arch. Soc., 3, Kendal, 1889); 18; Sandford, *A Cursory Relation of all the Antiquities and Familyes in Cumberland*, ed. Ferguson, 37; Westwood, *Albion: A Guide to Legendary Britain*, 258.

to view it in many cases as an agent of invigoration and recreation.

A number of examples of printed history infusing oral culture are discernible. Thus local tradition in London knew the great building in Basing Lane as 'Gerrards Hall' after its supposed one-time inhabitant Gerard the Giant. When the curious John Stow went to investigate in the 1590s he was assured by the master of the house that the story was true and was advised to 'reade the great chronicles, for there he heard it'. This was a reference to the mention of Gerard in Harrison's *Historicall Description of the Iland of Britaine* which in 1577 had been included in the first part of Holinshed's *Chronicles*.[54] In the late seventeenth century, the clergyman White Kennett discovered the view among the inhabitants around Ot Moor in Oxfordshire that the Roman road, Akeman Street, had run north–south across the county between Wallingford and Banbury, when it actually ran east–west through Thame and on to Bath. The origin of this error he attributed to William Camden, who had indeed published it in the sixth edition of his *Britannia* in 1607, and now the misapprehension had 'resolv'd into the oral tradition of the common people'.[55]

A good example of this process of 'feedback' is also evident in the tradition of the 'Danish yoke'.[56] One of the most potent themes in the popular memories of the past in early modern England was a strong sense of the ravages and atrocities committed by the Danish armies during their occupation from the ninth century. Hundreds of communities up and down the country harboured traditions about battles once fought between local people and the brutal armies who oppressed them. Place-names and buildings, barrows and natural features of all sorts were explained in these terms.[57] But it is doubtful that there was much continuous folk memory of such events passing in oral tradition

[54] Stow, *A Survey of London*, ed. Kingsford, I, 348–9, II, 353; Raphael Holinshed, *Holinshed's Chronicles of England, Scotland and Ireland* (6 vols, 1807–8), I, 21.

[55] White Kennett, *Parochial Antiquities attempted in the History of Ambrosden, Burcester, and other adjacent parts in the Counties of Oxford and Bucks* (Oxford, 1695), 16; William Camden, *Britannia* (6th edn, 1607), 267.

[56] On the concept of 'the Danish yoke', see Thomas, *The Perception of the Past*, 26; D. R. Woolf, 'Of Danes and Giants: Popular Beliefs about the Past in Early Modern England', *Dalhousie Review*, 71 (1991), 193–7.

[57] For a selection of such traditions, see Bod Lib MS. Aubrey 3, fos 23–4, 25v, 35r, 104v, 151r; Aubrey, *Monumenta Britannica*, ed. Fowles and Legg, 807, 817; Aubrey, *The History and Antiquities of the County of Surrey*, IV, 217, 261; BL Additional MS., 6223, fos 11r–13v; Camden, *Britannia*, ed. Gibson, 352, 747; *The Topographer and Genealogist*, ed. Nichols, II, 411; Tristram Risdon, *The Chorographical Description or Survey of the County of Devon* (1811), 143; Sir William Dugdale, *The Antiquities of Warwickshire* (1656), 299; Plot, *The Natural History of Stafford-shire*, 432; Salmon, *History of Hertfordshire*, 220; John Morton, *The Natural History of Northamptonshire* (1712), 530–48; Stukeley, *Itinerarium Curiosum*, 10, 22, 107; Defoe, *A Tour Thro' the Whole Island of Great Britain*, ed. Cole, I, 15; Pococke, *Travels through England*, ed. Cartwright, I, 46.

from the time of their occurrence down to the seventeenth century when they are most plentifully recorded. Instead, the demonisation of the Danes seems to be a product quite specifically of the late fifteenth century. The historian John Rous may have been responsible for initiating it in his influential *Historia Regum Angliae*, which recounts the Danish conquest of Mercia. In the fields of his native Warwickshire he pointed to the red flowering dwarf elder (*Sambucus ebulus*), or walwort as it was popularly known, which marked the spots where blood had been shed. By the time that William Turner published his list of plant names in 1538, walwort was called for the first time danewort. By 1590 Camden was using the name 'danes-bloud' when he discovered it growing on the Bartlow Hills in Essex and found that the 'country people' knew it 'by no other name'. It has been suggested that the etymological derivation of walwort from the Old English *wealh* could imply the shedding of foreign, or specifically Welsh, blood. Could it be that Rous, whose *Historia* was fulsomely dedicated to Henry VII, replaced the association of battle grounds long regarded as the scenes of victory over the old Welsh enemy with that of a new foe in order to flatter, or not to offend, his new Tudor master? If so, he may have instigated a rich theme in English folklore which was to last for a least two centuries.[58] Credence to this theory is given by the fact that the famous Hocktide plays performed on the second Monday and Tuesday after Easter seem also to have become widely popular from the late fifteenth century. This drama, together with the processions led through towns, and symbolic fights enacted between men and women which commemorated the defeat of the Danes must have done much to create and keep alive these traditions.[59]

Another equally ubiquitous series of traditions which the Tudor dynasty and the new technology of print did much to reinvent and nourish were those of King Arthur. The fabulous legends of Geoffrey

---

[58] Rous, *Historia Regum Angliae*, ed. Hearne, 101–6; Wood, '*Survey of the Antiquities of the City of Oxford*', ed. Clark, I, 326; William Turner, *Libellus De Re Herbaria Nouus. In Quo Herbarum Aliquot Nomina Greca, Latina, & Anglica Habes* (1538), sig. A4r; William Camden, *Britannia* (3rd edn, 1590), 352; Westwood, *Albion: A Guide to Legendary Britain*, 103–4.

[59] Hockday is mentioned by Rous as commemorating the 'liberation of England from Danish servitude': *Historia Regum Angliae*, ed. Hearne, 106. On these Hocktide ceremonies and plays, see John Brand, *Observations on the Popular Antiquities of Great Britain*, ed. Sir Henry Ellis (3 vols, 1849), I, 186–91; E. K. Chambers, *The Mediaeval Stage* (2 vols, Oxford, 1903), I, 154–6, 187, II, 264–6; Ronald Hutton, *The Stations of the Sun: A History of the Ritual Year in Britain* (Oxford, 1996), 207–13. They were staged in Coventry as early as 1416 but do not seem to have become widely popular until later in the century: Charles Phythian-Adams, 'Ceremony and the Citizen: the Communal Year at Coventry, 1450–1550', in *Crisis and Order in English Towns, 1500–1700*, ed. Peter Clark and Paul Slack (1972), 69. For a useful discussion of the mnemonic value of ceremony and ritual, see Paul Connerton, *How Societies Remember* (Cambridge, 1989), 41–71.

of Monmouth had been much popularised by the renaissance in chronicle and romance writing during the fifteenth century. Thomas Malory's *Morte d'Arthur*, completed in 1469, was first printed by Caxton in 1485 and would be reprinted in a furthur six editions by the mid-seventeenth century. It was under the Tudors, for whom Geoffrey's Welsh Arthur had particular appeal, that his myth reached the status of cult with the help of an outpouring of poetry, prose and drama.[60] The dissemination of such literature was clearly widespread. The Elizabethan mason from Coventry, Captain Cox, was said to have a copy of 'king Arthurz book' in his remarkable little library of vernacular literature, while the 'book of king Arthures knights' was one that the 'poore husband-man' proposed to buy for his son in a tract of 1586. Whatever evidential basis there may have been for an historical Arthur figure, 'the many incredible stories that have been reported of this prince', lamented one contemporary, had long 'made his history little better than a romance'.[61]

The development of the broadside ballad must have been greatly influential in bringing the legend of Arthur to the widest possible audiences. *A pleasaunte history of an adventurus knighte of kynges Arthurs Couurte* was printed by Richard Jones in 1566. The great ballad-writer Thomas Deloney was responsible for *The noble Actes nowe newly found of Arthure of the round table* which was entered in the Stationers' register in June 1603. In 1598, Fynes Moryson was already describing the many monuments attributed to Arthur's name as 'famous among all ballad-makers'. 'Tis great pity', John Aubrey was later to lament, 'that so famous and great a worthie should have ever been abused, either by monkish verses, or vile painting in an alehouse.'[62]

Despite this view, however, Aubrey, who still believed that 'antiquaries, when they cannot meet with better authority, will not disdayn to give an old ballad in evidence', borrowed Elias Ashmole's copy of Robert Laneharn's *A Letter* (1575), which contained a song said to be taken from 'king Arthurz book', and transcribed it into his *Monumenta*

---

[60] Sir Thomas Malory, *Le Morte D'Arthur* (2 vols, Everyman edn, 1906), I, viii; Kendrick, *British Antiquity*, ch. 3; Millican, *Spencer and the Round Table*; Irving Ribner, *The English History Play in the Age of Shakespeare* (2nd edn, 1965), ch. 8; Sydney Anglo, 'The British History in Early Tudor Propaganda', *Bulletin of the John Rylands Library*, xliv (1961–2), 17–48; E. K. Chambers, *Arthur of Britain* (1927); R. F. Brinkley, *Arthurian Legend in the Seventeenth Century* (Baltimore, 1932).

[61] Robert Laneham, *A Letter* (1575), 34; John Ferne, *The Blazon of Gentrie* (1586), part ii, 23; *Antiquities of Glastonbury*, ed. Hearne, 145; and cf. Mathias Prideaux, *An Easy and Compendious Introduction for Reading All Sorts of Histories* (4th edn, Oxford, 1664), 292–3.

[62] Hyder E. Rollins, 'An Analytical Index to the Ballad-Entries (1557–1709) in the Registers of the Company of Stationers of London', *Studies in Philology*, xxi (1924), 169, 183; Morrison, *An Itinerary Containing his Ten Yeeres Travell*, II, 118; Aubrey, *Monumenta Britannica*, ed. Fowles and Legg, 543.

Britannica. Meredith Lloyd had told him that at Cynllwyd near Bala in Merionethshire 'the common people to this day' would show the 'heap of stones of the length of four pershes' at the foot of a great hill which they said was 'Bedd Rita Gawr' or 'the grave of Rita the Giant', slayn upon that spot by King Arthur. The tale comes straight from Geoffrey of Monmouth's account of the giant Ritho of Mount Aravius, or Snowden, who has a cloak made of the beards of the kings he has killed and taunts Arthur to shave off his. Here, it seems, is a good example of the intersection of medieval chronicle, popular print and oral tradition. It is likely that the legend of Ritho and Arthur had been handed down by word of mouth in North Wales well before Geoffrey wrote it down in the early twelfth century. There is evidence here of unbroken oral transmission over at least seven centuries, therefore, although it is likely that the widespread influence of the printed ballad had done much to elaborate, invigorate and keep this story fresh in the minds of people by John Aubrey's day.[63] It is interesting to consider that two of the major episodes in the *Historia* which Professor Tatlock considers obviously to be drawing upon twelfth-century oral tradition, this story of Arthur and that of King Lear's foundation of Leicester, should also be among the few legends in Geoffrey that were found still to be alive in the popular memory of the early modern period.[64]

As the example of Arthurian legend suggests, the influence of cheap print in the form of the broadside ballads, chapbooks and plays which poured from the presses in this period, was clearly of great importance in inventing and sustaining popular versions of the past. The Elizabethan puritan Nicholas Bownd believed that the arrival of the printed ballad after the Reformation had, far from undermining oral tradition, actually revived it when it was in danger of dying out: for 'the singing of ballads (that was rife in Poperie) began to cease, and in time was cleane banished away in many places', but with the broadside there was a 'sudden renewing of them, and hastie receiving of them everywhere'. The content of such material, thought his contemporary George Puttenham, was 'for the most part stories of old time, as the tale of Sir Topas, the reportes of Bevis of Southampton, Guy of Warwick, Adam

---

[63] Bod Lib MS. Aubrey 2, fo. 145; Aubrey, *Monumenta Britannica*, ed. Fowles and Legg, 540–3, 809; Laneham, *A Letter*, 53–4; Geoffrey of Monmouth, *Historia Regum Britanniae*, x, 3. For a selection of the many topographical features with which an Arthurian legend was associated, see *Itinerary of John Leland*, ed. Smith, iii, 106, 119, v, 48; Sampson Erdeswicke, 'Certaine Verie Rare Observations of Cumberland, Northumberland, etc.', in *Reprints of Rare Tracts*, ed. Richardson, vii, 9; Camden, *Britannia*, ed. Gibson, 11, 545, 620, 628–9; Sir Daniel Fleming, *Description of the County of Westmorland*, ed. G. F. Duckett (Cumberland and Westmorland Ant. and Arch. Soc., 1, Kendal, 1882), 30; Aubrey, *Monumenta Britannica*, ed. Fowles and Legg, 955.

[64] J. S. P. Tatlock, *The Legendary History of Britain: Geoffrey of Monmouth's Historia Regum Britanniae and its Early Vernacular Versions* (Berkeley and Los Angeles, 1950), 381–2, 388–9.

Bell, and Clymme of the Clough, and such other old romances or historicall rimes'.[65]

The most famous of these, the rhymes of Robin Hood, were again not born so much of popular oral tradition as of the literary romances written for performance among the social elite.[66] But it was probably the widespread dissemination of his story in the famous *Gest*, which was reprinted several times during the sixteenth century, together with broadsides such as *A ballett of Robyn Hod* (1562), and the play-books informing mummings and May games, which was responsible for fixing the legend in its present form.[67] It also ensured the place of Robin in local folklore. For Robin Hood's Bay is not known to have been so named before 1544 and his many 'strides', hills and mills, or the examples of his butts which are to be found in a least six counties of England, were probably attributed no earlier.[68] His famous well with accompanying chair at St Anne's, about a mile to the north of Nottingham, is of similar date, while there is no reference to that by the side of the Great North Road between Doncaster and Pontefract before the first quarter of the seventeenth century.[69] Robin Hood's grave at Kirklees in the West Riding was first noted by Richard Grafton in 1565. A generation later, the early fifteenth-century tomb of Elizabeth Fitz Walter in the church at Little Dunmow, Essex, was reinvented as the resting-place of Matilda the Fair, or Maid Marion, thanks to two plays by Anthony Munday, *The Downfall of Robert, Earl of Huntingdon* (1601) and its sequel *The Death* (1601), which ensured the currency of the fable well into the nineteenth century. It may also have been around

---

[65] Nicholas Bownd, *The Doctrine of the Sabbath* (1595), 241–2; George Puttenham, *The Arte of English Poesie*, ed. G. D. Willcock and A. Walker (Cambridge, 1936), 83–4. For a seemingly typical selection of these historical ballads, see the collection begun by John Selden and expanded by Samuel Pepys: *The Pepys Ballads*, ed. W. G. Day (5 vols, Cambridge, 1987), I, 63–104, II, 97–138.

[66] Coss, 'Aspects of Cultural Diffusion in Medieval England', 38–40.

[67] *Rymes of Robyn Hood: an Introduction to the English Outlaw*, ed. R. B. Dobson and J. Taylor (2nd edn, Gloucester, 1989); Rollins, 'An Analytical Index to the Ballad-Entries', 199–200; Stephen Knight, *Robin Hood: A Complete Study of the English Outlaw* (Oxford, 1994), chs 3–4; David Wiles, *The Early Plays of Robin Hood* (Cambridge, 1981); Hutton, *Stations of the Sun*, 270–4.

[68] Westwood, *Albion: A Guide to Legendary Britain*, 206–8. For a variety of contemporary references to these topographical landmarks, see *Elias Ashmole (1617–1692)*, ed. Josten, 625, 961; Aubrey, *Monumenta Britannica*, ed. Fowles and Legg, 273; Brome, *Travels Over England, Scotland and Wales*, 160, 217; Pococke, *Travels through England*, ed. Cartwright, II, 271; Byng, *The Torrington Diaries*, ed Bruyn Andrews, II, 192.

[69] Roger Dodsworth, *Yorkshire Church Notes 1619–1631*, ed. J. W. Clay (Yorkshire Archaeological Society Record Series, xxxiv, 1904), 12; *A Relation of a Short Survey of 26 Counties*, ed. Wickham Legg, 13; Brome, *Travels Over England, Scotland and Wales*, 85; Deering, *Nottingham Vetus et Nova*, 73; Robert Thoroton, *The Antiquities of Nottinghamshire*, ed. John Throsby (3 vols, Nottingham, 1790–6), II, 164–71; J. C. Holt, *Robin Hood* (2nd edn, 1989), 176–9.

this time that the huge grave in Hathersage churchyard, Derbyshire, 'with one stone set up at his head, and another at his feete, but a large distance between them', was first ascribed to Little John, whereafter local people would show part of his bow hanging up in the church.[70]

Memories of the past in early modern England reflect the nature of this society as one in which oral and written tradition overlapped and interacted in reciprocal and mutually reinforcing ways. Verbal communication remained the medium through which knowledge was most often transmitted. A powerful quasi-autonomous oral tradition thrived at a time in which literacy levels were limited and popular culture could be highly parochial. And yet the influence of the written word, and increasingly of print, lay behind so much of this repertoire, informing it, structuring it and sustaining it. In this period, as for many centuries before, writing had supplemented and complemented the vernacular repertoire rather than necessarily undermining it. What began with the pen of a learned author could very quickly pass into the oral tradition of the people and even more quickly be assumed to be ancient. In 1812 Sir Walter Scott visited Rokeby. His guide, J. B. S. Morritt, observed that he 'was but half satisfied with the most beautiful scenery when he could not connect it with some local legend, and when I was forced sometimes to confess ... "Story! God bless you! I have none to tell, sir" – he would laugh, and say, "then let us make one – nothing so easy to make as a tradition".'[71]

---

[70] Holt, *Robin Hood*, 41; Westwood, *Albion: A Guide to Legendary Britain*, 118–19; Dodsworth, *Yorkshire Church Notes*, ed. Clay, 52; *Elias Ashmole*, ed. Josten, 625. Little John's bow was later removed to Cannon Hall near Barnsley where it may still be seen: *Folklore; Myths and Legends of Britain* (1973), 294.
[71] Quoted in Westwood, *Albion: A Guide to Legendary Britain*, 371.

CUSTOM AND THE SOCIAL ORGANISATION OF WRITING IN EARLY MODERN ENGLAND

By Andy Wood

School of History, University of East Anglia

READ 27 MARCH 1998 AT THE UNIVERSITY OF SUSSEX

SOCIAL historians of sixteenth- and seventeenth-century England have tended to see literacy as a modernising force which eroded oral tradition and overrode local identities. Whereas the increasing literacy of the period has long appeared an important constituent element of Tudor and Stuart England's early modernity, custom has been represented as its mirror image. Attached to cumbersome local identities, borne from the continuing authority of speech, bred within a plebeian culture which was simultaneously pugnacious and conservative, customary law has been taken to define a traditional, backward-looking mind-set which stood at odds to the sharp forces of change cutting into the fabric of early modern English society.[1] Hence, social historians have sometimes perceived the growing elite hostility to custom as a part of a larger attack upon oral culture. In certain accounts, this elite antipathy is presented as a by-product of the standardising impulses of early capitalism.[2] Social historians have presented the increasing role of written documents in the defence of custom as the tainting of an authentic oral tradition, and as further evidence of the growing dom-

[1] The most nuanced accounts of the modernising force of literacy are to be found in K. Thomas, 'The meaning of literacy in early modern England', in G. Baumann (ed.), *The Written Word: Literacy in Transition* (Oxford, 1986), 97–131; and in K. E. Wrightson, *English Society, 1580–1680* (London, 1982), ch. 7. For enduring influences, see, especially, W.J. Ong, 'Writing is a technology that restructures thought', in Baumann (ed.), *Written Word*, 23–50; J. Goody and I. Watt, 'The consequences of literacy', in J. Goody (ed.), *Literacy in Traditional Societies* (Cambridge, 1968), 27–68. For a study which sites the domination of literacy alongside the growth of industrial modernity, see D. Vincent, 'The decline of the oral tradition in popular culture', in R. D. Storch (ed.), *Popular Culture and Custom in Nineteenth Century England* (London, 1982), 20–47. For an important critique of this view, see P. Joyce, *Visions of the People: Industrial England and the Question of Class, 1848–1914* (Cambridge, 1991), chs 8, 11–12.

[2] D. Rollison, *The Local Origins of Modern Society: Gloucestershire, 1500–1800* (London, 1992), 12–15, 67–83; M. Johnson, *An Archaeology of Capitalism* (Oxford, 1996), ch. 5.

257

ination of writing over speech.[3] Crudely stated, orality, and hence custom, is seen as 'of the people'; while writing was 'of the elite'. In this respect as in others, social historians have therefore accepted all too readily John Aubrey's nostalgic recollections of the late seventeenth century that

> Before printing, Old Wives tales were ingeniose and since Printing came in fashion, till a little before the Civil warres, the ordinary Sort of people were not taught to reade & now-a-dayes Books are common and most of the poor people understand letters: and the many good Bookes and the variety of Turnes of Affaires, have putt the old Fables out of dores: and the divine art of Printing and Gunpowder have frighted away Robin-good-fellowe and the Fayries.[4]

This essay will challenge the established historiographical opposition between custom and writing. In its place, it will emphasise the complex interplay of speech and writing in the creation and renewal of customary knowledge. It will subsequently discuss the social organisation which underlay the production and preservation of written documents. I am interested primarily in the cultural worlds of those of non-gentle status; that is, with what historians used to call 'popular culture'.[5] As we shall see, this does not presuppose that either elite or plebeian worlds were hermetically sealed. Neither should we conceive of writing as a weapon of a literate elite; following Jack Goody, we will rather see that 'the written code does not initiate either oppression or justice; [instead] it gives them a different format'.[6] While elites were certainly able to use their greater access to written documentation and to the central legal system to undermine claims to local custom, some defenders of custom responded with creativity to this challenge. We will see from this that the distinction between orality and literacy has been overdrawn. While speech remained a vital constituent of customary law and local memory

[3] See, especially, A. Fox, 'Custom, memory and the authority of writing', in P. Griffiths, A. Fox and S. Hindle (eds), *The Experience of Authority in Early Modern England* (Basingstoke, 1996), 89–116. I managed to persuade myself of this connection too: see A. Wood, 'Social conflict and change in the mining communities of north-west Derbyshire, c. 1600–1700', *International Review of Social History*, 38, 1 (1993), 41–2, in which I drew far too easy a division between a literate (elite) interest and a popular (oral) culture. The subject is, of course, contradictory. Edward Thompson could see the importance of written documentation in sustaining custom: *Customs in Common* (London, 1991), 153, 159. Yet, elsewhere, he continued to present 'customary consciousness' as synonymous with 'oral tradition': *Customs in Common*, 179.

[4] BL, Landsdowne MS. 231, fo. 140. For the uncritical use of Aubrey in other contexts, see, especially, D. E. Underdown, *Revel, Riot and Rebellion: Popular Politics and Culture in England, 1603–1660* (Oxford, 1987), esp. ch. 4.

[5] For the historiographical deconstruction of popular culture, see, most recently, T. Harris (ed.), *Popular Culture in England, 1500–1850* (Basingstoke, 1995).

[6] J. Goody, *The Logic of Writing and the Organization of Society* (Cambridge, 1986), 133.

throughout the early modern period, the written word had long been an important means of retaining and transmitting local knowledge prior to the sixteenth century.[7] The modernising, unitary transition imagined in earlier histories ought therefore to be replaced by an emphasis upon the contradictory dynamism which developed between writing, speech and custom. Those contradictions were felt most keenly in the early modern period, as oral and literate cultures twisted ever more closely into one another. Finally, this essay will contest the claim that 'literacy dislocated memory' (that is, literacy removed the junction between collective memory and local identity) and that literacy 'marginalised local and regional cultures'.[8]

Cultural histories of writing, speech and custom in early modern England make little sense without an appreciation of contemporary contests over the rights and resources guaranteed by customary law. The legal and political authority of custom shifted over the course of the sixteenth and seventeenth centuries, but in order for a custom to be accepted as legitimate by central courts, it had to be shown to conform to three important criteria.[9] Firstly, the custom had to be reasonable, and of benefit to the person(s) exercising the claim. Secondly, the custom had to lie 'beyond memory of man', or 'time whereof the memory of man is not the contrary'. Formally, this meant that a custom had to originate at some point prior to 1189; but in the practise of courts, evidence that the custom was known within the memory of the oldest inhabitants, and that such memory was not contradicted by earlier written sources, was sufficient. Finally, custom had to have been exercised continuously prior to its being called into question. Custom necessarily operated within a defined administrative unit: typically, the manor or parish; less typically, the lordship, borough or city. The defenders of custom therefore presented the concept in highly normative terms as the quintessential form of local knowledge.

In so far as custom regulated production and exploitation and defined the spatial, moral and legal boundaries of rights and responsibilities, custom had always been political.[10] Since its conception, customary law

---

[7] The classic study is M. T. Clanchy, *From Memory to Written Record: England, 1066–1307* (1979; 2nd edn, 1993). But, see also, Z. Razi and R. Smith (eds), *Medieval Society and the Manor Court* (Oxford, 1996).

[8] Rollison, *Local Origins*, 71, 73.

[9] The best contemporary introduction to the subject is C. Calthorpe, *The Relation between the Lord of a Mannor and the Coppyholder his Tenant* (London, 1635). For a useful discussion, see A. Kiralfy, 'Custom in medieval English law', *Journal of Legal History*, 9, 1 (1988), 26–39.

[10] For the politics of custom, see A. Wood, 'The place of custom in plebeian political culture: England, 1550–1800', *Social History*, 22, 1, (1997), 46–60; K. E. Wrightson, 'The politics of the parish in early modern England', in Griffiths, Fox and Hindle (eds), *Experience of Authority*, 22–5.

had been a source of contention. Lord and tenant argued over fines, rents, the extent of demesne and seigneurial enclosures. Inhabitants of one village argued with those of another over boundaries and mutual responsibilities. Landed and landless argued over encroachment on commons, rights of gleaning, and the stinting of common right. But in the sixteenth and seventeenth centuries such conflicts both intensified and broadened. Increasing population put more pressure on resources; inflation encouraged lords to raise rents and change tenures; social and cultural polarisation between villagers diminished the moral standing of the rights of the parochial poor in the eyes of their wealthier neighbours. In relation to such structural and cultural changes, central courts based in Westminster and Chancery Lane heard an increasing number of cases concerning matters of custom, thereby extending their own authority over the subject. With every judgment issued by central courts concerning local custom, English state formation advanced another scarcely perceptible step.

It is a cliché of structural anthropology that 'pre-industrial' systems of thought are only revealed to the historical record at the moment of their dissolution. For all that this insight both obscures earlier changes in customary law and assumes the inevitable defeat of custom, it none the less remains important to our discussion. Rarely can the provisions of customary law be reconstructed with such accuracy, or the ambivalences of the language of custom be heard so clearly, as in the records of proceedings before central courts. Of special importance are the records of depositions, in which the verbal evidence of inhabitants was transcribed by clerks of equity courts adjudicating in customary disputes. In such evidence, deponents spoke of the character of customary law, how they learnt about it, how it had changed in their lifetime, and often discussed the roles of writing and speech in the maintenance of such knowledge.

In early modern legal transactions, the spoken word had a power it lacks today: in 1596, for instance, the Court of the Duchy of Lancaster heard evidence that the custom of Godmanchester allowed property to be conveyed by word of mouth.[11] Just as accepted communal opinion could be used to damn somebody's sexual or moral reputation at the consistory court, so it could also be presented as a common assumption of rights. Hence, a village or town could be imagined as speaking in a 'common voice' or as holding a 'common opinion' which held that a custom had existed 'time out of mind'.[12] Custom therefore both legitimated and defined collective memory. Whereas in our own society writing is conceived of as a means of avoiding dependence upon

---

[11] PRO, DL4/29/54, deposition of Baldwyn Easdall.
[12] See, for instance, PRO, DL4/14/36, deposition of Robert Marsham.

memory, in the early modern period writing was more likely to be thought of as providing a support to memory.[13] The social function, and politico-legal meanings given to both memory and writing were therefore quite different from today. Early modern plebeians who were unable to read or write could none the less gain access to writing. Institutional settings such as court meetings provided mnemonic contexts within which complicated texts concerning local custom were read aloud.[14] Illiterate men and women remembered having 'heard read' and thereby 'knowing' the customs of the manor or parish. For many, memory remained the equivalent of knowledge. Hence, a dying man might be described as 'in the pangs of death wthowte any memorye sence or understandinge'.[15] In his deposition of 1580, Arthur Watts, a yeoman of Hockwold (Norfolk), stated consistently that 'he doth not remember' or 'he remembreth not' in order to make the point that he did not *know* something. Conceived of as immediate and communal, memory was understood by many deponents as a normative, moral force which imposed duties of maintenance and transmission. The aged were expected to pass on their memories to the young, and thereby to maintain the common voice: Edmund Burden, aged 68 in 1584, remembered how 'about fiftie yeres sithence he was tolde by one daynes an olde man beinge a maker of fursse there that the Towne of wells (Norfolk) had a certaine libtie for the feade of theire milche neate there from Michelmas til Martylmas And so had longe before his tyme'.[16] To Burden, his recollections of the old man's words seemed to carry him back into the (often deliberately) ill-defined 'ancient time' within which custom had been born. The duty of transmission was important enough to intrude into the dying moments of the early modern plebeian: John Coatman of Thetford (Norfolk) recalled how 'old Mr Torrell upp[on] his death bedd' had confirmed to him the extent of common rights upon the town's fens, linking his testimony of his own use of the fens with the common voice, and thereby with time immemorial.[17]

Such memories present themselves as cosy, consensual and widely accepted. Those claims are, of course, highly ideological and often quite fictional. In actions concerning the defence of common rights against a lord, for instance, plebeians had an obvious interest in projecting a united front. Differences and contradictions in knowledge

---

[13] J. Fentress and C. Whickham, *Social Memory* (Oxford, 1992), 9–10.
[14] See, for instance, PRO, E134/11ChasI/Mich45; PRO, DL4/105/1661/22; P. Griffiths, 'Secrecy and authority in late sixteenth and early seventeenth century London', *Historical Journal*, 40, 4 (1997), 940–1.
[15] PRO, STAC5/S70/24.
[16] PRO, DL4/26/37, deposition of Edmund Burden.
[17] PRO, E134/3JasI/Mich30, deposition of John Coatman.

about the history and past use of such land, or the character of legal title to it, lie concealed beneath the surface of these texts. None the less, careful study and cross-reference reveal layers of uncertainty and contradiction in the stories told by lower-class deponents to the commissioners of Westminster courts. In reality, communal memory was not homogeneous. Rival factions of villagers might contend against one another, producing wildly different accounts of local custom and local history. Certain aspects of the past – such as the lord's or the church's right to a particular duty – might be conveniently forgotten.[18] More simply, there may just be confusion or contradiction in local memory, as with the 'ylde men' of Haddenham (Cambridgeshire) amongst whom 'there grewe some dyversitie of speche' as to whether a certain ditch was a fen drain or not.[19] It is easy for historians to be gulled by such sources, and to reify 'local memory' into a composite, unchanging whole which was gradually marginalised by equity and common law, and undermined by the written word. The reality was rather more complex.

For all that the relationship between speech, writing and custom may have been more elaborate than it seems upon initial enquiry, conflicts over customary law typically expressed a blunt opposition of material interest. We will concern ourselves primarily with one such opposition: that between lord and tenant. Amongst the advantages held by the seigneurial interest in such confrontations was lords' possession of an organised body of written evidence which could be produced to undermine the 'common report' of their tenants. Where early modern central courts were presented with such a choice, they seem to have increasingly favoured written evidence over oral.[20] This trend became more noticeable over time as estate owners, seeing the growing import-ance of written evidence in legal process, grew more concerned to protect and collect manorial documents, customaries, surveys and the like into their muniment rooms.[21] Where a lord wished to raise entry fines, or enclose common land, such documents could therefore be set in opposition to the 'common report' of plebeian community. For this

[18] For a colourful example of the deliberate loss of collective memory, see PRO, DL4/55/47.

[19] PRO, E134/25Eliz/Trin1, deposition of Robert Page.

[20] Fox, 'Custom, memory'; A. Wood, 'Custom, identity and resistance: English free miners and their law, c. 1550–1800', in Griffiths, Fox and Hindle (eds), *Experience of Authority*, 268–73.

[21] For example, when Edward Phipers of Haddenham found 'a writinge in the Bottome of his Chest', concerning the tithes of Haddenham, he exchanged it with the Earl of Suffolk for the remittance of his debts and two stone of wool to make a gown for his wife: PRO, E134/9JasI/Trin2, deposition of Elizabeth Cordell. Keith Thomas has pointed to the growing importance of historical records to landowners: K. Thomas, *The Perception of the Past in Early Modern England* (London, 1983), 2.

reason, gentlemen who gave evidence to central courts adjudicating in disputes over local custom were much more likely to cite their readership or possession of written documents than were those further down the social scale.[22] The role of the estate steward on larger estates was of particular importance in this regard. Such men were often equipped with a degree of legal training, and sometimes doubled as attorneys. As such, they were responsible for the maintenance and renewal of the estate archives. Making trips to the Tower, the Rolls Chapel or the muniments room of a near-by great house, stewards might return bearing transcriptions or the originals of key documents which were felt to shed light upon a particular custom. In commissioning surveys, maps, rentals and customaries, the estate steward again contributed to the stock of written evidence concerning local custom and history.[23] Similarly, the growth of litigation over matters of custom helped to produce a more document-conscious and legalistic culture amongst lesser gentlemen (again, often possessed of a degree of legal training) concerned to raise revenue upon their smaller estates or to find employment as attorneys in legal cases.[24] It is a strange irony that it has been the survival of those catalogued and ordered manuscripts in the muniments rooms of great houses, or in the document chests of the gentry, that has allowed twentieth-century social historians to reconstruct the plebeian communities against which those documents were so often opposed in the legal contests engendered by early capitalism.

It is therefore more than possible to sustain the argument that writing was a source of power in early modern England. The tenants of Gillingham Forest in Dorset, the commoners of the Cambridgeshire and Lincolnshire fens and the miners of Wirksworth in the Peak Country of Derbyshire certainly made the claim that the written word was an agent of elite domination. In the years of the Personal Rule of Charles I, all of these groups complained of being conned by cunning royal patentees who had threatened and cajoled them into setting their hands to agreements which they were too 'unlearned' to make sense of, and which subsequently proved to prejudice their rights.[25] In so

---

[22] For representative examples, see PRO, DL4/38/17, 60/7.

[23] For a remarkable case study, see A. Bagot, 'Mr Gilpin and manorial customs', *Transactions of the Cumberland and Westmorland Antiquarian and Archaeological Society*, n.s., 62 (1962), 224–45. For depositions given by such antiquarian stewards examples, see PRO, DL4/56/12, 117/8. See also J. H. Bettey, 'Manorial stewards and the conduct of manorial affairs', *Dorset Natural History and Archaeology Society*, 115 (1993), 15–19.

[24] See especially C. W. Brooks, *Pettyfoggers and Vipers of the Commonwealth: the 'Lower Branch' of the Legal Profession in Early Modern England* (Cambridge, 1986).

[25] For the Peak, see PRO, DL44/1121; PRO, DL4/91/16. For Gillingham Forest, see PRO, E134/3ChasI/East17. For the fens, see K. Lindley, *Fenland Riots and the English Revolution* (London, 1982), 31.

doing, these foresters, commoners and miners may have protested too much. No doubt they were, as they insisted, laboured and intimidated by the arbitrary proceedings of 'great men'. But the bloody-minded defence of custom formed the cornerstone of a bifurcated plebeian political culture in all three regions. Moreover, customary law in all three areas was heavily dependent by the late 1620s upon written documentation.[26] The point backs up one of the key findings of the 'new' social history of the period: that not only were the early modern lower classes notoriously litigious, but in many cases their local cultures were based upon a highly legalistic mind-set in which understandings of custom occupied a central place.[27]

We should not, therefore, be surprised to find that as equity and common law process became dependent upon the written word, so too did local customary law. In increasing proportion from the mid-sixteenth century, accounts of parish and manorial bounds were written down, vague local rights given new clarity in customaries, documents such as account books, manorial rolls, surveys, depositions and inquisitions collected into parish chests. One result was to standardise parochial, manorial and regional difference. Another was to provide a more concrete vision of community from which certain groups were closed out, and within which others were silenced. In spite of the well-known participation of women in the assertion of key common rights, and in the maintenance of oral tradition, women featured very rarely in accounts of custom. In my sample of about 12,000 depositions held in the archives of central courts, around 90 to 95 per cent of deponents were male. Similarly, written customaries almost invariably defined custom as a male property, held by the 'Men' or (still more exclusive) the 'Substanciall Men' of the place concerned. While this may not have had much practical effect upon the day-to-day operation of custom, given the lower levels of female literacy in the period, one long-term repercussion was to restrict women's participation in the growing document-conscious culture of custom.[28]

The effect of the transliteration of custom was therefore to reorder

---

[26] On the fens, see, for instance, W. Cunningham, 'Common rights at Cottenham and Stretham in Cambridgeshire', *Camden Miscellany*, n.s., 12 (1910), 173–289; on Gillingham, see John Rylands Library, Nicholas MS., 65 [Customary book of Gillingham Forest]; on the Peak, see A. Wood, *The Politics of Social Conflict: the Peak Country, 1520–1770* (Cambridge, 1999), ch. 6.

[27] On popular ideas about the law, see J. A. Sharpe, 'The people and the law', in B. Reay (ed.), *Popular Culture in Seventeenth Century England* (London, 1985), 244–70, and, more recently, *idem*, 'The law, law enforcement, state formation and national integration in late medieval and early modern England', in X. Rousseaux and R. Levy (eds), *Le Pénal dans tous ses états: justice, états et sociétés en Europe (XIIe–XXe siècles)* (Brussels, 1997), 65–80.

[28] I hope to write about the changing relationship between gender and custom elsewhere.

the priorities and logic of local systems of law, and to a lesser extent to redefine the memories upon which they depended. Where lord and tenant sat down to negotiate the content of a customary, they created an ideologically charged piece of writing. For the creation of a customary represented more than the simple description of agricultural, industrial or communal practice, or of the rights and dues owed by one social group to another. Rather, the customary froze a fluid set of relations, imposing a rigidity and homogeneity upon custom which had important implications for the future. Both lord and tenant were aware of the ramifications of deciding upon a fixed statement of custom, and to that end (dependent upon local circumstance) might be more, or less, interested than the other in agreeing a specific statement. Customaries were therefore the product of a complex web of local political interests, in which the rendering of custom into writing represented not the necessary domination of literacy over orality, or of elite over plebeian interest, but rather a formal, ideal statement of the balance of power at one given moment. Just as in their encounters with legal authority the plebeians of eighteenth-century England were not to be 'mystified by the first man who puts on a wig' so their predecessors of the sixteenth and seventeenth centuries were unlikely to roll over at the production of pen and ink.[29]

The point is best illustrated by example. In 1589, John Manners of Haddon, a powerful Derbyshire gentleman, purchased the Peak Country manor of Holmesfield. Knowing the Holmesfield copyhold tenants to be a troublesome bunch – they had been had up before the Court of Star Chamber for a collective assault upon their bailiff only eight years earlier – he wrote to the copyholders, telling them that he wished to avoid 'Sute and contensyon' and therefore wanted to have 'the customary of the Lordship set downe in certainty ... whereby I may know what to demand, & they the better performe what is their Duty to doe'. To that end, Manners intended to convene a jury of copyholders whose duty it would be to describe their customs, 'therefore I will be well content therewith, that I may be ascertained what the Law is, which I will willingly yield unto'.[30] The subsequent customary detailed the nature of copyhold tenure, the extent of common rights,

---

[29] Quoting E. P. Thompson, *Whigs and Hunters: the Origins of the Black Act* (London, 1975), 262.

[30] Sheffield Archives, MD3401/1; B. Bunker, *All Their Yesterdays: the Story of an Ancient Derbyshire Village on the South-Eastern Foothills of the Pennines* (Sheffield, 1973), 78–80. On the Manners' role in disputes over custom in the Peak, see Wood, *Politics of Social Conflict*, chs 7–11. The creation of the customary was important enough to lodge in the mind of Arthur Mower, who led the tenants' negotiations. Many years later, the production of the customary was one of the events which he singled out as noteworthy enough to enter into his brief autobiography. See BL, Add MS. 6671, fo. 163; Bunker, *All Their Yesterdays*, 85–6.

the organisation of the common field system, the antique military service owed to the lord, the circumstances under which the tenants' labour services had been commuted to a cash payment some twenty years earlier, and the lord's monopoly over milling. The tenants stood to benefit from the bulk of the customs listed by the jury, which amounted to a fulsome statement of popular rights. Knowing the Manners to be harsh and interventionist lords, however, the jury added a series of riders to the customary, by which they hoped to provide fuller legal protection. They asked to see the lord's court rolls, 'for their further & better memory & instruction'. Furthermore, the customary of 1589 should 'remeane of record perpetually', as a statement of all the rights which they could recall at the moment of the passage of the manor into the Haddon estate. But they were keen to ensure that the customary itself should not provide the lord with a means of denying any wider claims which the tenants might make in the future, adding also that 'if any custome or matter materiall now in this short time not come to theire memory concerninge the Lord or them be omitted and forgotten, & shall hereafter come in their memory or aryse in question', then such additional customs should be entered alongside those of 1589.

The Holmesfield customary pointed to a very careful, hard-headed appreciation on the part of the tenants of the significance of writing. There was no sense that the relatively poor and largely illiterate villagers of 1589 were intimidated by the written word. They seem not to have regarded writing as a definitive statement of solid, permanent rights, but rather as a contingent product of their recent encounter with Manners. To that end, the tenants assumed that the customary could be overridden by the advance of memory, stating that any customs they had omitted to mention in 1589 should be added in thereafter. To the tenants, it was memory which carried authority within custom, rather then the means by which it was communicated. Yet, in spite of the pragmatic attitude displayed by the tenants to writing, we ought also to note that the new customary was felt to be of sufficient importance that it should 'remeane of record perpetually'. The invention of past tradition was therefore intended to reach into the future.

Larger material conflicts between lord and tenant were sometimes reducible to contest over the 'writings' of a manor. Arrangements for access to such documents codified the uneasy relationship between interest groups: thus the keys of the 'greate chyste standinge in Wighton churche' (Norfolk) which contained the evidences of the manor were divided between the tenants and the bailiff.[31] Writing could sustain as much as deny popular rights. The inhabitants of Huntingdon claimed

[31] PRO, DL4/17/27.

freedom from all market tolls in the kingdom, by virtue of charters of 1205, 1348, 1381, 1402, and 1559 which were held by the town bailiffs. All seven deponents in an action of 1563 (two were yeomen, one a gentleman, one a minister, one fisherman, one pewterer and one unidentified) said that they had seen these charters, and had heard them read.[32] Fifteen years later, Thomas Amborough, a shepherd of Godmanchester (Huntingdonshire), claimed a similar right and explained that when he used to trade at other town markets he always carried with him a copy of the Charter of Godmanchester which showed his exemption from market tolls.[33] The increasing use of written documentation by plebeians in the defence of their rights at law did not replace the spoken word in the articulation and definition of custom. Rather, it supplemented orality. By the late sixteenth century in East Anglia and by the Restoration in the Peak Country, it was common for equity court commissioners to hear from plebeian deponents that a custom existed time out of mind, that it was known by common report, and that the deponent had read or had heard read ancient documents which further proved the right. Depositions in earlier actions concerning the same or similar rights might also be produced, having been carefully safeguarded upon victory at law.[34] The source for such depositions was more likely to have been 'common report', memory and speech alone; but at the moment of their words being transcribed by the clerks of central courts, illiterate deponents also joined in the growing role played by writing within custom.

Yet the place held by writing within custom remained anomalous. In 1595, the 76-year-old John Martin of Clare (Suffolk) remembered that in his youth a board displaying details of lands belonging to the almshouses had hung in the chancel of the parish church. He recalled that he had heard the contents of the board read aloud many times: as he told commissioners of the Court of the Duchy of Lancaster, 'He doth not knowe how long it is since the same was sett upp there but by reporte he sayth it was longe there before he was borne.' The board was removed, together with much else, in the reign of Edward VI.[35] The Clare board, like the 'auncient booke of the towne of Clare' which John Martin remembered as 'covered wth a whyte parchment' functioned as a mnemonic device. For Martin the significance of the board lay not so much in its precise text, but in its place and function in his memory, calling to attention rights and duties to the community, and placed in a sacred spot within the church. Like the stained glass

[32] PRO, DL4/5/12.
[33] PRO, DL4/20/24, deposition of Thomas Amborough.
[34] For an example, see PRO, DL4/30/28, deposition of Thomas Gunthorpe.
[35] PRO, DL4/37/51, deposition of John Martin.

in the parish church of Haxey (Lincolnshire), which depicted John de Mowbray holding the deed which he granted in the fourteenth century to his tenants, and which provided the basis for the legal defence of their commons in the seventeenth century, the board in Clare church spoke to local inhabitants about their rights and duties, its meaning known to literate and illiterate alike.[36] For all that barriers between orality and literacy may have been rising in early modern England, they were rather less fixed and stable than they were to become by the eighteenth and nineteenth centuries. By the eighteenth century, the character of this transition in the place and relative strength of writing within popular culture was becoming clearer. Literate yeoman had their own chests, in which they kept documents proving individual and collective titles and rights; they bought newsbooks from London, linking them to the wider world of national and international print culture; sometimes they wrote indexed and ordered descriptions of their local laws, transcribed earlier customaries or the evidences on which they were based, or kept precedent books and extracts from manorial court rolls as points of reference to be produced in the case of dispute. From all this, the illiterate were being *gradually* excluded. But this process was long, slow and uneven. For many generations, writing and speech acted together to define remembrance and custom, and to strengthen local identities.

Writing was an important means of conserving memory and custom. But even in the eighteenth century, it was still not the only one. By 1700, its position in custom was becoming hegemonic; but that domination never became monolithic. Orally communicated memory, and the assumptions of everyday usage, habit and opinion bound up in 'the common report of the neighbours' remained key constituents of customary law, and hence of local identity. Indeed, local identity could be strengthened by the increasing authority of writing. Written documents helped to uphold custom, and hence in some part local identity, before central law courts. Written accounts of parochial and manorial bounds gave a clearer, and in some respects a sharper, sense of local difference. Written customaries and depositions, where preserved and widely communicated, helped to articulate and refine local loyalties, and could even become totemic emblems of a spatial identity: witness the 'Book of Dennis' whose widely known provisions gave a solidity to the collective identity of the Free Miners of the Forest of Dean.[37]

---

[36] C. Holmes, 'Drainers and fenmen: The problem of popular political consciousness in the seventeenth century', in A. Fletcher and J. Stevenson (eds), *Order and Disorder in Early Modern England* (Cambridge, 1985), 191–2.

[37] For the 'Book of Dennis', see, especially, C. E. Hart, *The Free Miners of the Forest of Dean and the Hundred of St. Briavels* (Gloucester, 1953). For a revealing case study of the

In noting the peculiarities of folk culture and local tradition, Gerald Sider has pointed out that we tend to perceive of the origins of tradition as lying 'in the hazy dawn of time' – a perception, of course, which the lower orders of early modern England both consciously played on and persuaded themselves of – and that we all too often see tradition in constant retreat before 'the expansion and consolidation of supralocal institutions'. So much has been true of the historiography of orality, literacy and custom in early modern England. But as Sider goes on: 'Clearly, incorporative structures of power *do* undermine and destroy differentiation; but they must also, simultaneously, create it.'[38]

---

long preservation of legal records by tenants, see J. L. Drury, 'Sir Arthur Hesilrige and the Weardale chest', *Transactions of the Architectural and Archaeological Society of Durham and Northumberland*, n.s., 5 (1980), 125–37.

[38] G. M. Sider, *Culture and Class in Anthropology and History: a Newfoundland Illustration* (Cambridge, 1986), 93.

RESITING FRENCH RESISTANCE

By H. R. Kedward

READ 27 MARCH 1998 AT THE UNIVERSITY OF SUSSEX

EXCEPTIONS, minorities, non-conformities, individual refusals and small group actions, these are words with which historians of the French Resistance learn to live. The words allow social detail to flourish, but they stand in the way of general social conclusions and question the kind of class representation which seems so convincing in René Clément's film of the resistance of railway workers, *La Bataille du rail* (1946), but which cannot be sustained for the working class as a whole.[1] Is there a social history of the Resistance? Are all generalities suspect? The French nation as a category is far too large, so is the working class, and equally so the bourgeoisie and the peasantry: it has often been argued that social and political categorisation of the Resistance is nothing but a captivating mirage, tantalising every new interpreter who sets out to give much needed structure to empirical research.

Happily social history is more than a passion for generalisation, and in the last ten years historians of the Resistance have learnt not only how to live with discrete details but also how to approach a social history of the Resistance through an insistent emphasis on *spécificité*.[2] The rigour which this gives to current research, as the archives alternately disappoint and surprise, cannot be overestimated. Discovering what is specific to those places, groups, events and institutions, which created or sustained resistance, has replaced the search for generalised categories; and, of course, specificity operates also in the other direction. To take an emblematic example: the focus of Vichy's compulsory labour service was sharpened by Pierre Laval on 13 February 1943 in the form of the STO (Service du Travail Obligatoire), which targeted twenty-to-twenty-two-year-old male youths and eventually led to tens of thousands of *réfractaires* who sought refuge in the countryside. The specificities of the legislation and its complex mechanisms provoked several forms of resistance both among those who refused to go and those who gave them refuge: conversely, these

---

[1] For a detailed analysis of the film, see Martin O'Shaughnessy, '*La Bataille du rail*: Unconventional Form, Conventional Image?', in H. R. Kedward and Nancy Wood (eds), *The Liberation of France: Image and Event* (Berg, 1995), pp. 15–27.

[2] A social history of the Resistance was finally deemed to be possible in 1997. See Antoine Prost (ed.), *La Résistance, une histoire sociale* (Editions de l'Atelier, 1997).

forms of resistance had their own specificity which helps to explain why certain rural areas were actively involved, some only passively, and others not at all.[3] It is still surprising to realise that it is only recently that this question of what resistance had to offer to certain places and people has come to supplement the previously dominant question of what places and people had to offer to resistance. The shift of perspective entrains whole new areas of knowledge and theory. The history of the Resistance is now far more than an empirical catalogue of more or less dislocated actions: its denotations may be too scattered and fragmented for some historians, but its connotations within the layered history of France, which now includes the history of memory, offer to the historian a deep and rich vein of intellectual possibilities, more than compensating for the absence of general social categories.

A comparative study of resistances, across time and place, and moving beyond national frontiers, has begun to suggest itself as analagous to the older study of revolutions. The decades of East European resistance to the pathology of Stalinism, modified but perpetuated under Brezhnev, or the long years of resistance against apartheid in Southern Africa, allow models of clandestine activity to emerge, which fit closely with paradigms of resistance within Nazi-occupied Europe. As Vladimir Kusin and Gordon Skilling have shown for Czechoslovakia,[4] many of these models are cultural in origin and expression, and such is the diversity of cultural practice within these different societies that there must be a turn to anthropology for new discipline and enlightenment. This step has been taken; so that alongside the search for specificity within the details of French experience of the Occupation there exists a search for wider and more generic categories of motivation, cultural practice and behaviour. Taken together, these two prongs of resistance research, specific and generic, break new ground: they turn over the soil, much of which has lain undisturbed since the war, through design or neglect.

Memory, collective and individual, public and private, has been a key player in the debates which have accompanied the growth and application of these two methods of approach: it has enabled explorations to be undertaken far beyond the previous confines of resistance historiography. It is, for example, localised memory which has enabled historians to reconstruct the ways in which communities with specific cultural traditions were instrumental in fashioning ways of resistance.

[3] See François Marcot (ed.), *Lutte armée et maquis* (Annales littéraires de l'Université de Franche-Comté, 1996), and H. R. Kedward, *In Search of the Maquis* (Oxford University Press, 1993).

[4] Vladimir Kusin, *Intellectual Origins of the Prague Spring* (Cambridge University Press, 1971); Gordon Skilling, *Czechoslovakia's Interrupted Revolution* (Princeton University Press, 1976).

In a recent conference paper, the historian of Greek resistance, Riki van Boeschoten, has suggestively utilised Bourdieu's concept of the 'habitus' to contrast different cultural systems which operated within the northern Pindus during the German Occupation. She finds that the truly collective expression of the resistance was not the habitus of the mountain brigands and outlaws, the klephts, with its apparently direct issue in the formation and actions of the maquis, but the day-to-day village habitus of autonomy and struggle against the personal power of elites. It was this that created the new habitus of resistance. If there was continuity with the klephts in the region of Grevená, she says, it was only in the idealised public image of the klephts as national heroes of 1821. The more significant social values and structures of resistance derived from schoolteachers, peasant smallholders, the lower echelons of the Communist and Agrarian Party and salaried employees. Memory from these social milieux stress co-operation and shared civic attitudes within the resistance (EAM), and emphasise the aspiration towards an egalitarian society based on local self-rule.[5]

Conflict within this specific memory lies between its own collective model of society and models imposed from outside and above. The communities of Protestant resisters in French villages of the plateau Vivarais-Lignon and the Cévennes have emerged from oral evidence in the same way. Pastor André Bettex of the village of Le Riou confirmed that the hiding of Jewish refugees on the plateau was a direct expression of a religious culture in which parents taught their children through the Psalms to love the Jews, and transmitted the biblical imperatives to give food and shelter to those in need.[6] 'Every Protestant of the plateau', argues François Boulet, 'is something of a historian, a guarantor of the heritage of memory.'[7]

At the Toulouse conference on 'Les Français et la Résistance' in 1993, the first of six international conferences with the aim of locating French resistance within a comparative framework, I indicated how relevant I found the anthropological concepts of James C. Scott and David Lan and the writings in *Subaltern Studies* in assessing the significance of cultural traditions in both the practice and memory of resistance.[8] Scott uses the phrase 'weapons of the weak' to designate

---

[5] Riki van Boeschoten, 'Pour une géopolitique de la résistance grecque: le cas du Pinde nord', in *La Résistance et les Européens du sud* (Pré-actes du Colloque d'Aix-en-Provence, UMR Telemme, 1997), no pagination.

[6] Oral contribution to a discussion at the 1990 Conference at Le Chambon-sur-Lignon, published in Pierre Bolle (ed.), *Le Plateau Vivarais-Lignon. Accueil et Résistance 1939–1944* (Société d'Histoire de la Montagne, 1992), p. 434.

[7] Ibid., p. 427.

[8] James C. Scott, *Weapons of the Weak. Everyday Forms of Peasant Resistance* (Yale University Press, 1985); David Lan, *Guns and Rain. Guerrillas and Spirit Mediums in Zimbabwe* (James

the day-to-day methods employed by the Malaysian peasants of the Kedah in their struggle against impositions by landlords and external authority. Such methods comprise 'foot-dragging, dissimulation, false compliance, pilfering, feigned ignorance, slander, arson, sabotage'. 'The peasantry', he adds, 'has no monopoly on these weapons, as anyone can easily attest who has observed officials and landlords resisting and disrupting state policies that are to their disadvantage.'[9] He could easily have pointed to civil resistance against all unwelcome forms of occupation in the Second World War, in situations where more military forms of resistance or classic forms of industrial action were not available. Exactly the same methods were employed.

Claudio Pavone gives evidence for such comparisons in his attempt to delineate civil resistance in Italy, to distinguish it from passive resistance and from the 'grey zone' of survivalism which he borrows from Primo Levi's writings on the concentration camps. Civil resistance he defines as actions which do not in principle exclude violence, and may in fact have recourse to violence as the ultimate necessity, but which mainly include 'acts of support for those in need and the persecuted (soldiers, escaped allied prisoners, wounded partisans, Jews), refusal of obedience, small acts of sabotage within factories and public administration, refusal to surrender agricultural produce to official collection depots, and finally the provision of burial rites for the dead, withheld or forbidden by the German and Fascist authorities'.[10] He admits that his list does not solve definitional problems occasioned by the similarity of some survivalist actions and some actions of *double-jeu*, but it is a list which all national and local histories of resistance produce, regardless of the nature of the enemy.

The adoption of the concept of the 'habitus' and the work mentioned on resistance in Greece, the Protestant Vivarais, peasant Malaya and Italy, all depend on memories, oral and written, which the anthropologist and the historian have collected or found available, but equally they focus new research on the function of memory *at the very time* of the resistances which are being studied. There is endless polemic inside and outside France about the nature of resistance memory in the years since 1944, and we shall return to this, but it is barely recognised that historians are now asking probing questions about the content of memory and the process of oral transmission during the Occupation itself. I was drawn into a new understanding of the subtlety of oral

Currey, 1985); Ranajit Guha, *Elementary Aspects of Peasant Insurgency in Colonial India* (Oxford University Press, 1983).

[9] James C. Scott, *Weapons of the Weak*, pp. 29–30.

[10] Claudio Pavone, 'Les objectifs de la Résistance: le cas d'Italie', in *La Résistance et les Français: villes, centres et logiques de décision* (Actes du Colloque international, Cachan, IHTP, 1995), p. 456.

transmission by David Lan's anthropological study, *Guns and Rain. Guerrillas and Spirit Mediums in Zimbabwe*. With astonishing insight Lan demonstrates how the spirit mediums in the Dande district of the Zambezi valley gave legitimacy to the guerrilla resistance against the British in the 1970s by providing them with access to the spirits of the chiefs of the past, the *mhondoro*, at a time when the chiefs of the present were widely felt to be too compromised with the colonial authority. It was not, argues Lan, the decision of the mediums or the guerrilla leaders to turn from the present to the past, but rather it was the ordinary people themselves whose memories prompted them to shift their allegiance backwards in time. This shift gave new and unexpected power to the mediums, and established an alternative discourse of power, located in the past but expressed in the present, which challenged the authority of the colonial state.[11] An amazingly similar process of story-telling, memory and empowerment operated in parts of France during the Occupation, when generations of local history, rural know-ledge and tactics were transmitted by peasants and villagers to the *réfractaires* and to the maquisards during the autumn and winter of 1943 and the spring of 1944. This is memory as cognition.

The memories harnessed by the resistance in this way are there to be studied as representations and images of the past which prevailed at the time of the Occupation, and the historian has to be careful not to confuse them with post-war representations which come later. In avoiding this confusion we are on familiar conceptual ground, trodden by Paul Thompson in *The Voice of the Past*, by Pierre Nora in *Les lieux de mémoire* and by Pierre Laborie in *L'opinion française sous Vichy* and in several theoretical articles by Laborie on resistance and represen-tations.[12] There is also some methodological confusion with the genre of history which focuses on the understanding of the 'imaginaire social', society's representation of any phenomenon at any given time or place. Luc Capdevila, a Breton historian, has recently completed a thesis on the 'imaginaire social' of the Liberation in Brittany between the summer of 1944 and the winter of 1945/6: it will, I am sure, become a classic of this genre, and he makes it clear in his opening pages why his methodology excludes an oral investigation which he might easily have undertaken. He explains that he did not seek or use the oral testimonies of those who experienced the period of the Liberation, his main concern being the unsatisfactory ethics of any oral interview that

---

[11] David Lan, *Guns and Rain*, pp. 136–53.
[12] Pierre Laborie, 'Opinion et représentations: la libération et l'image de la résistance', *Revue d'Histoire de la Seconde Guerre Mondiale et des Conflits Contemporains*, no. 131 (1983); 'Sur les représentations collectives de la résistance dans la France de l'après Libération et sur l'usage de la mémoire', in Robert Frank and José Gotovitch (eds), *La Résistance et les Européens du Nord (Pré-actes du Colloque de Bruxelles, GREHSGM/IHTP, 1994)*.

he might have conducted. The interviewer, he writes of himself, 'would have been looking for representations, while the witness would have been confiding his or her memory'. He calls this 'an involuntary but inherent ambiguity, created by the very aim and problematic' of his research.[13] In these words he is articulating the accepted and scrupulous distinction between representations of the Liberation produced at the time and those produced subsequently by memory.

But there is, none the less, a viable function for oral history in researching the representations and memories which were significant at the time, and this is no different from its conventional function in exploring events and actions. In short, it is one of the pre-eminent functions of oral history to provide the historian with hypotheses of what the past contained, whether in terms of action, thought or memory. The hypotheses are constructed from the whole scenario of the *témoignage*, from its location, content, language and gestures, and from the very process of transmission which is consciously staged in the historian's presence, or, more often, autonomously and independently. Extrapolating ideas and hypotheses from the process itself has enabled us to envisage resistance roles and behaviour more clearly, particularly in cultural and gender terms. Arriving to interview old maquisards in rural areas of the south of France in the 1970s, I found that the process was remarkably similar from one household to the next. I was given a seat opposite the maquisard with the tape-recorder on the table between us. The wife, sister or daughter brought drinks to the table and positioned herself at the doorway, intervening with corrections to the story when the man's memory failed or distortions crept into his account. It gradually seemed probable, and then certain, that this had been the rural woman's household position at the time of the Occupation, and indeed, once I started looking for corroboration of this hypothesis in police reports, I found endless archival evidence of the woman at the doorway, prolonging police enquiries, misleading their search, feigning ignorance, covering tracks. As a vantage-point of power, this otherwise marginalised position came into its own in the resistance.

---

[13] 'En ce qui concerne le champ des représentations, ils n'apportaient pas un complément aux sources écrites, la mémoire s'étant constituée pour l'essentiel au moment de l'événement. Quand il s'agissait de vérifier des points précis, les souvenirs des témoins se révélaient peu fiables; certes, leurs silences, leurs tâtonnements, leurs erreurs avaient du sens. Mais le problème le plus délicat concernait l'éthique de l'entretien: l'enquêteur guettait des représentations et les témoins confiaient une mémoire. Cette ambiguïté, involontaire, mais inhérente aux entrevues (en raison de la problématique de cette étude), décalait le chercheur par rapport à son interlocuteur, ce qui n'était pas satisfaisant.' Luc Capdevila, 'L'Imaginaire social de la Libération en Bretagne (été 1944–hiver 1945/1946). Contribution à une histoire des représentations mentales.' (Thèse nouveau régime. Université de Rennes 2, 1997), p. 16. I wish to thank the author for his kindness in sending me a copy of this excellent thesis.

Its specific significance under the Occupation had been missed by historians, perhaps because it was culturally so accepted and so conventional a part of gender relations.[14] It operated in places other than the home. The widow of Count Michael Sobanski told Janine Ponty of the café in Warsaw where from twenty to thirty bourgeois women acted as waitresses. All understood German, and their role was to listen from their vantage-points to the conversation at the tables, memorising information exchanged after heavy drinking by officers of the Wehrmacht. They were essential links in intelligence networks, playing out their accepted gender roles.[15]

A summary of these recent departures in the specific and the generic location of French Resistance would seem to indicate that a certain resiting has been in progress. It is not so much a move away from military and political history as a widening of the social and cultural matrix within which resistance is seen to have originated and developed, and a burgeoning of an interdisciplinary area which might well set up its own canon of texts and enter academic practice as 'resistance studies'. Given the importance of memory in both history and in anthropology it can at least be claimed that memory *within* resistance and memory *of* resistance must have a position of some significance in this new constellation of research. And yet curiously enough the relationship between memory and resistance in France appears to be more problematic at the present time than at any other point since the war. This needs its own historical and contextual explanation.

It is not memory itself which is at issue in France but rather individual memory or *témoignage*. Studies of national myths, collective memories and representations have flourished: Pierre Nora's volumes, *Les lieux de mémoire*, published between 1984 and 1993, were a cultural watershed, and Henry Rousso's *Syndrome de Vichy* made it imperative to understand Vichy in terms of its post-war representations.[16] In-depth analyses of

[14] Laurent Douzou took up this concept of 'the woman at the doorway' and developed it with reference to the interviews with Alexis and Louis Grave in the film by Marcel Ophuls, *Le Chagrin et la pitié*, where the wife of Alexis positions herself precisely 'au seuil de la porte'. See his article 'La Résistance, une affaire d'hommes?', in *Les Cahiers de l'IHTP: Identités féminines et violences politiques*, no.31 (1995), pp. 11–24. Hanna Diamond's wide range of evidence from women in one locality is available in 'Women's experience during and after World War Two in the Toulouse area, 1939–1948: choices and constraints' (DPhil thesis, University of Sussex, 1992); Margaret Collins Weitz has successfully structured the details of women's memories in *Sisters in the Resistance. How Women Fought to Free France 1940–1944* (John Wiley, 1995). See also Claire Gorrara's perceptive literary study, *Women's Representations of the Occupation in Post-'68 France* (Macmillan, 1998).
[15] Janine Ponty, 'Etre résistant dans une ville de Pologne', in *La Résistance et les Français: villes, centres et logiques de décision*, p. 112.
[16] The whole corpus of Nora's work is in Pierre Nora (ed), *Les lieux de mémoire* (Paris, Gallimard, 7 vols, 1984–93). See also Nancy Wood, 'Memory's Remains: *Les lieux de mémoire*', in *History and Memory*, vol. 6, no. 1 (1994), pp. 123–49. Henry Rousso's *Le syndrome*

the Vichy regime preoccupied contemporary historians in France throughout most of the 1980s. In 1993 the Institut d'Histoire du Temps Présent (IHTP) turned its research to a similar multiple study of the Resistance, by which time the new theories of memory and representation had already ensured a collective view of resistance memory and an enumeration of myths, most prominently the Gaullist myth of 'la nation résistante' and the Communist myth of 'le parti des fusillés'. These were seen to have disputed public consciousness throughout most of the post-war years, and a strong drive within the programme of *spécificité* was towards demythologising resistance memory. Ex-resisters, attending the international conferences as participants, but also as non-historians, offered their memories to clarify or dispute points of fact. The rejoinder from authoritative historians was repeatedly the same: memory does not constitute history; it constitutes representations of history. In reply the most persistent of the *témoins* continued to insist that their memories and presence be treated with more academic respect. This led to some caustic exchanges across the floor, and most recently to the staged discussion of Raymond and Lucie Aubrac's memories by five leading IHTP historians and Daniel Cordier, the biographer of Jean Moulin, on 17 May 1997. The newspaper *Libération* published a twenty-four page transcription of the whole exchange between the Aubracs and the historians, with an introduction which claimed its singular importance as an event in oral history, giving 'an exciting insight into the process of memory and the profession of the historian'. In effect it led to the realisation that the historians control the appellation and evaluation of both representation and fact. In the context of public accusation and litigation which has surrounded the history of the war years in France, this is disturbing.

The prolonged presence of the judicial dossiers, trials and detection relating to Leguay, Bousquet, Barbie, Touvier, and, lastly, René Papon, has pushed academic historians into courtroom drama and heightened the burden of proof which lies at the heart of archival, historical work. Memory is not proof enough: hence the constant reminder that memory must be located as representation, shading into memory as mythification, or media-conscious commemoration, the very stuff of Nora's *lieux de mémoire*. This has excitingly prioritised public memory, but it has made it difficult for many French historians to know what to do with individual memories. The law both cherishes and interrogates the individual witness. Historians can do no less; but they are seen to

---

de Vichy, 1944–198... (Seuil, 1987, updated 1990) is now a classic, and of all Rousso's shorter writings on the subject I particularly like the small piece he did in 1991 looking back on his own contribution, and rethinking certain aspects of memory in the widest sense of the word: 'Pour une histoire de la mémoire collective: l'après-Vichy', *Les Cahiers de l'IHTP. Histoire politique et sciences sociales*, no. 18 (1991), pp. 163–76.

do more. To discover the guilt or innocence of players under the Occupation, the law and the media need access to the archives: the expert is the historian. The media and the law expect historical research to have the answers, and as a result the historians have become the prime witnesses. They decide not just how and why memory is influential as representation; they now feel they have to replace individual memory with their own statements of fact. The law and the media expect it of them. They have come to expect it of themselves. In the last twenty years in France it is the professional historian who has claimed to be the shaman, the spirit medium, the raiser and guardian of the dead, the voice of the past.

This is precisely the role which historians should leave to the actors, the *témoins*, the story-tellers at the evening *veillées* round the fire or over a glass of wine at the café. We know that oral transmission of the past to the present happens everywhere, with or without the presence of the historian. Actors (*témoins*) transmit the representations of the past which continually form attitudes and opinions and influence actions. It is they who are the spirit mediums. They link the past and the present; they facilitate the understanding of experience, the workings of representation, the power of images and previous histories, the oscillation between continuity and change. Why usurp their role? There now exists a prestigious academic approach to memory studies, to commemoration and to monuments of the past, and within this the role of oral history is more or less clear. Resiting French Resistance has made this specific place more, and not less, valuable to the historian's research. The courtroom mode endangers the separation of roles on which both testimony and history depend.

Finally, to return to the minority status of resistance, there is a politics in the theory of oral history, and in the generic search for patterns of resistance, which coincides with the function of much resistance testimony. The vast literature in France of local publications dedicated to resistance memories, accounts, commemorations, biographies and diaries, constitutes an immense archive of individual memory. Taken together they constitute a singular process of remembering, adapting and overcoming, which is place and time specific. The process is a clear sign of what Nora calls the democratisation of the commemorative spirit, which signifies, he believes, 'the democratization of history itself, for history is no longer the privileged domain of the historian'.[17] Whereas Nora is ambivalent about the value of this development, there is little doubt in my mind that a widespread determination to record specific resistance experience in local pamphlets

[17] Pierre Nora, 'Le présent', in J. Le Goff *et al.* (eds), *La nouvelle histoire* (Editions CEPL, 1978), p. 470.

and publications is a perpetuation of the nature of resistance itself, and accurately reflects the sense that resistance elevated the ordinary individual's choice and commitment to a level of moral and historical meaning that few, if any, other national events have achieved. Its distinctiveness, compared with the experience of the First World War, lay in its voluntarism and its minority status. However unfocused at the Liberation it had seen people taking charge of their own lives at all levels of society and this essential force of democratisation has chimed precisely at local level, if not always at national level, with the enabling practice of oral history.

A keen awareness that resistance had never been a unifying property of the whole nation informs much of the local literature and many of the individual testimonies. There can be endless dispute about what is public and what is private in this democratic process of history-making, with obligatory references to the collective memory theory of Halbwachs. But it is precisely the complex fusion of private and public that is the domain of resistance experience and memory, a conscious fusion which has never surrendered its minority consciousness.[18] Tassoula Vervenioti, investigating the memory of Greek women organised into resistance by EAM and the Greek Communist Party, stresses the move from traditional gender roles in the period 1941–3 to a more public role after the surrender of Italy and the onset of widespread armed struggle. 'It was the first time', she writes, 'that the social context gave women the chance to enter the public sphere. But the historical conjuncture was not sufficient to subvert old traditions ... Organised women were thought to be "disgraced" and "corrupted" because EAM's organisations were mixed.'[19] It is a form of post-war protest against continued confinement to the private sphere that those she has interviewed give priority to their first encounter with social equality.

In France, equally, women's memories of resistance repeatedly underline a certain felt equality within organised resistance, even though the gender inequalities can be easily perceived. 'Although the historical record appears to be different,' Paula Schwartz notes in her classic article of 1989, 'women activists remember the Resistance as an experience of equality with men: they shared tasks, responsibilities and risks.' She sharply exposes the inequalities but she also analyses with great subtlety the element of gender displacement in the organised

[18] Note the astute comments on the post-war discourse of ex-resisters in Olivier Wieviorka, *Une certaine idée de la Résistance: Défense de la France 1940–1949* (Seuil, 1995), pp. 397–410.

[19] Tassoula Vervenioti, 'Les résistantes grecques, membres des organisations du Front national de la Libération (EAM) et les contraintes imposées à leur action (1941–-44)', in *La Résistance et les Européens du sud*, no pagination.

Resistance which helps to explain 'why women report that there was little or no distinction between men and women in the underground'.[20] They did, indeed, report and recollect in this way, and the notion of equality was given its most expressive form in the 1975 conference and publication *Les femmes dans la Résistance*, initiated by the Union des Femmes Françaises and held at the Sorbonne, a high point in women's reclamation of their resistance history. The evidence of Camille Tauber, the first woman on the Conseil Général of the Haute-Garonne, reconstructed the political assertiveness of women resisters in Toulouse at the Liberation, and stated that women's memory of these actions became an educative force in the civic instruction of women across the region in post-war France.[21] As in Greece, the equality remembered was equality demanded. It is not just in academic conferences that ex-resisters have become assertive. Remembering resistance in France has frequently been a conflictual process, and many of the recurrent conflicts are with dominant social and political practices which have failed to fulfil the democratic expectations of change.

This political agenda in much of resistance testimony points to the need for a cautious note to accompany the resiting of French Resistance within a larger field of resistance studies. In generic terms, resistance as conflict is not the monopoly of any one political creed or cause, and it is instructive to see how Dominique Venner's memoirs of his political involvement in the minority defence of Algérie française, recuperates the moral prestige of resistance action for the extreme Right, to the point where he claims that the rebellious OAS, in its resistance to decolonisation, derived its legitimacy from the political Right under Vichy which he credits with creating and leading the national resistance to the Germans.[22] Apart from the outrageous bravura of its revisionism, which has become the characteristic style of those seeking to rehabilitate Pétain and Vichy, the perspective of Venner is challenging to those historians who are not willing to problematise the wider notion of resistance. It is crucial from the outset of any research to insist that generic descriptions of resistance behaviour, whether in terms of clandestine revolt, local community practices or transgressive weapons of the weak, are complementary to historical and political analysis, and not a substitute. The structural insights of anthropology both illuminate

[20] Paula Schwartz, '*Partisanes* and Gender Politics in Vichy France', *French Historical Studies*, vol. 16, no. 1 (1989), pp. 138–9.

[21] Camille Tauber, 'Evolution de la participation des femmes à la vie civique, telle qu'elle apparaît à la Libération', in *Les Femmes dans la Résistance* (Editions du Rocher, 1977), pp. 286–9.

[22] Dominique Venner, *Histoire critique de la Résistance* (Pygmalion, 1995). See the review article by Hugo Frey on this and Venner's *Le Cœur rebelle: guerres d'Algérie* (Belles Lettres, 1994) in *Modern and Contemporary France*, vol. n.s. 4, no. 4 (1996), pp. 509–12.

the workings of resistance behaviour, and allow the resistance memories of ordinary people to be situated within cultural parameters. They provide means of comparative study which allow resistance studies to range imaginatively across time and continents, but each precise historical setting, with its specific politics, its function and its legacy, still has to be located. Mapping the specific sites still falls to the historian. It follows therefore that that the resiting of resistance reflects something in which we are all involved, the constant resiting of history.

ANTHROPOLOGY, HISTORY AND PERSONAL NARRATIVES: REFLECTIONS ON WRITING 'AFRICAN VOICES, AFRICAN LIVES'

By Pat Caplan

READ 27 MARCH 1998 AT THE UNIVERSITY OF SUSSEX

Historians and anthropologists have a common subject matter, 'otherness': one field constructs and studies 'otherness' in space, the other in time.[1]

Introduction: anthropology and history

ALMOST half a century ago, the famous British anthropologist Evans-Pritchard suggested that anthropology is actually a form of historiography,[2] thus initiating a debate about the relationship between the two disciplines which has continued sporadically ever since. His statement was a reaction to the claims of Radcliffe-Brown, a founding 'father' of British social anthropology, that social anthropology was a kind of science,[3] whereas Evans-Pritchard sought to claim it for the humanities.

In 1966, the Association of Social Anthropologists held a conference on anthropology and history, and a volume, edited by Ioan Lewis, was published in 1968.[4] This placed history firmly on the anthropological agenda, but it was very much a view of history as being about the past, about historical records, and temporal causation.

Twenty years later, Marshall Sahlins showed how social anthropology had created 'islands of history' by its insistence on studying wholes.[5] He argued that this stance had led to the estrangement of anthropology and history by suggesting that studies of change and stability were two different endeavours. Sahlins maintained that such a concept of history

[1] Bernard Cohn, 1980. 'History and Anthropology: the State of Play', in *Comparative History and Society*, vol. 22.

[2] E. Evans-Pritchard, 1950. 'Social Anthropology: past and present', *Man*, 198; 1961, 'Anthropology and History', Simon Lecture delivered at Manchester University: Manchester University Press. Reprinted in 1962 in *Essays in Social Anthropology*, London.

[3] R. Radcliffe-Brown, 1952. *Structure and Function in Primitive Society*, London, Cohen and West.

[4] I. Lewis (ed.), 1965. *History and Social Anthropology*, ASA Monograph 7. London: Tavistock Publications.

[5] M. Sahlins, 1985. *Islands of History*. Chicago University Press.

has been exploded by the anthropological experience of culture, thus the allegation that history is preoccupied with 'fact' and social science with theory is untenable.

In a recent volume, the Danish social anthropologist Kirsten Hastrup considers some of the debates of the last forty years about the nature of 'historical anthropology'[6] and points out that dealing with this question immediately raises the nature of time itself. As Hastrup notes, many anthropologists have pointed out that the western view of time is a very particular one. Lévi-Strauss drew attention to the existence of a linear view of time in the west,[7] and Johannes Fabian how 'the other' is created by being excluded from 'our' history and placed in a different time frame.[8] Nowhere is this more evident than in the 'traditional–modern' dichotomy which is so ubiquitous, including in discussions of development. Eric Wolf, in his book *Europe and the People without History*, has argued strongly that all societies are 'in history', and that they should be allowed their own histories.[9]

Hastrup maintains that the apparent unity of history as linear and causative is a discursive rather than a social fact, since analysis reveals the non-synchronicity and discontinuity of social experience: 'In the social life of people, tradition and change are two sides of the same coin, not separate entities with distinct historicities.'[10]

Hastrup argues that anthropologists appear to deal in space, and historians in time, but historical anthropology must include reference to both – an examination of the 'state' which obtains in a particular time-space. This objective condition is matched by a subjective reality, a world of experience. Hastrup's argument is that anthropology's specific contribution is to rewrite world history as a non-domesticated multiple history. This is because anthropology provides abundant evidence that the world is neither stable nor structurally coherent, although discourse may mask this, thus 'in order to understanding the complexity of "modern" histories, we must take such disjunctures into account'.[11]

Furthermore, images of 'self' work their way into historical realities – people live in different plot-spaces in one world. Here, as Blok points out in his article in Hastrup's collection, the intersection of history and memory is central to any purportedly historical anthropology, since

[6] K. Hastrup, 1992. 'Introduction' to her edited collection, *Other Histories*, Routledge, London and New York.

[7] C. Lévi-Strauss, 1966. *The Savage Mind*, London, Weidenfeld and Nicolson.

[8] J. Fabian, 1983. *Time and the Other: How Anthropology Makes its Object*, New York, Colombia University Press.

[9] E. Wolf, 1982. *Europe and the People without History*. University of California Press, Berkeley and Los Angeles.

[10] Hastrup, 'Introduction', p. 3.

[11] Ibid., p. 7.

'For events to become part of "history" they have to be or to have been experienced as significant.'[12] Formerly, only records provided acceptable historical evidence, but from an anthropological perspective, recollections are equally valid, given that in both, culture is significant. The rise of oral history is also an acknowledgement of the validity of popular recollection, and a recognition of human beings as both subjects and objects of history. With such an approach, people are seen as the authors of their own concepts, since they are responsible for their own actions.

Anthropologists and historians

In recent years, historians have increasingly made use of oral history, and there has been a growth of interest in the everyday, and in the lives of ordinary people, which is sometimes referred to as 'subaltern history' after the work of Guha and his colleagues.[13] Social anthropologists, too, have published various forms of personal narrative including life histories, biographies, and autobiographies.

I would thus argue that historians might read with profit the work of anthropologists, just as anthropologists will benefit from reading the work of historians.[14] The work of Carlo Ginzburg, Jonathan Spence, and several of the books of Le Roy Ladurie[15] also reveal how the sensitive handling of documents can enable a historian to produce a kind of history which is also a kind of anthropology.

More recently, the work of many feminist historians has clearly shown the interconnections between the private domestic worlds in which women act, and the public world; indeed, the very notion of

---

[12] Ibid., p. 9. A. Blok, 'Reflections on "making history" ', in K. Hastrup (ed.), 1922 (see fn. 6).

[13] R. Guha (ed.), 1982. *Subaltern Studies vol. I: Writings on South Asian History and Society*, Delhi: Oxford University Press (this volume has been followed by numerous others in the same series).

[14] In my own thinking on the topic, I have been influenced by a number of historians, including Alan Macfarlane, a historian turned anthropologist, who, in the 1970s, published the diary of a seventeenth-century clergyman, which he subtitled 'An Essay in Historical Anthropology' (A. Macfarlane, 1970. *The Family Life of Ralph Josselin: a Seventeenth Century Clergyman: An Essay in Historical Anthropology*, Cambridge University Press); later he wrote a study of witchcraft in Tudor and Stuart England which drew heavily upon anthropological studies of witchcraft in sub-Saharan Africa to make sense of happenings in Essex several centuries ago (A. Macfarlane, 1976. *Witchcraft in Tudor and Stuart England: a Regional and Comparative Study*, London).

[15] C. Ginzburg, 1980. *The Cheese and the Worms: the Cosmos of a Sixteenth Century Miller* (London and Henley, 1978). Jonathan Spence *The Death of Woman Wang: Rural Life in China in the 17th Century* (London, 1978); E. Le Roy Ladurie, 1980 [1978]. *Montaillou: Cathars and Catholics in a French Village, 1294–1324*, Penguin; E. Le Roy Ladurie, 1987 [1983]. *Jasmin's Witch: an Investigation into Witchcraft and Magic in South-West France during the Seventeenth Century*. Penguin Books.

'public and private' has been repeatedly shown to be a false dichotomy.[16] At the same time, such work has also revealed the micro-practices of power and the significance of subjectivity, inter-subjectivity and the emotions. A particularly useful example in this regard is the work of Shula Marks on the contrasting yet intertwined lives of three South African women.[17]

The intersection of anthropology and literature: the anthropologist as author

In recent years, anthropology has been influenced by a 'literary turn'[18] which was manifested first in an interest in texts and their meaning,[19] and later, influenced by the work of Derrida, in an interest in texts and their deconstruction. The ensuing postmodern displacement of authorial authority has led to a recognition that knowledge is always subjective and partial and this is as true of the writing of ethnography as it is of other forms of knowledge production.

Other questions arising in such debates include the issue of translation and the way in which the ethnographer interprets another culture; another is the significance of the voice of the subject and how this may best be retained. Finally, there is the problem of the relationship between ethnographer and informants and the issue of power which is exemplified by the former's use of the data provided by the latter. Do we, for example, ennoble our informants, leaving out less pleasant traits? Furthermore, utilising texts such as conversations, life histories and the informant's own diaries and letters to produce a monograph does, of necessity, include the anthropologist, not only as translator and editor, but also as interpreter, bringing in her own knowledge gathered from field data as well as comparative material from other anthropological work.

The debate on authorial authority has raised a number of questions. First of all, what is the role of the ethnographer in the field: initiand, employer, recorder, confidante, therapist, provider of reflecting surfaces, collaborator, extracting confessions?[20] Secondly, what stance does the

---

[16] See, for example, L. Davidoff and C. Hall, 1987. *Family Fortunes: Men and Women of the English Middle Class 1780–1850*, London, Hutchinson.

[17] S. Marks (ed.), 1987. *Not Either an Experimental Doll: the Separate Worlds of Three South African Women* (London); S. Marks, 1989, 'The context of a personal narrative: reflections on "Not Either an Experimenal Doll"', in Personal Narratives Group (eds), *Interpreting Women's Lives: Feminist Theory and Personal Narratives*, Bloomington: Indiana University Press.

[18] J. Clifford and G. E. Marcus (eds), 1986. *Writing Culture: the Politics and Poetics of Ethnography* (Berkeley, University of California Press); for a critical view, see B. Scholte, 'The Literary Turn in Contemporary Anthropology', *Critique of Anthropology*, 7, 1: 33–47.

[19] C. Geertz, 1975. *The Interpretation of Cultures: Selected Essays* (London).

[20] For some varying views of the anthropologist's role in the field, see V. Crapanzano, 1980. *Tuhami: Portrait of a Moroccan* (University of Chicago Press); B. Myerhoff, 1979. *Number Our Days* (New York).

ethnographer adopt when writing up: translator, interpreter, editor, or someone who also plays a part? How do we select what is important? how decide what to leave out?

A third question is that of the style which one adopts. One possibility is to write a seamless narrative, removing ourselves from a picture which has been 'tidied up'.[21] Another is to present a text which is as close to the original as possible and let the reader do the work.[22] How much explanation do we add and where do we put it?[23] Can we bring together texts obtained in different ways at different times, if their content is common?

Do we write in the first, second or third person? Do we produce a monologue, a dialogue or polyphony? And do we leave in the voice of the ethnographer?[24] How do we deal with time: do we impose a linear chronology or do we leave time fluid if that is what our informants do? Do we include photographs, especially if these risk breaching confidentiality? Finally, how do we deal with the issues of subjectivity and emotions – both theirs and ours – by leaving them in, or cutting them out?[25]

One mode of dealing with the above questions is through the genre of personal narratives, which is also a genre utilised by both anthropologists and historians. Personal narratives can take many forms: diaries, journals, letters, life histories, biographies, autobiographies. They can be spoken or written or both. They may be of individuals or families. In the next section, I consider the problems raised by the writing of one particular personal narrative.

African Voices, African Lives: the genre of personal narratives

'African Voices, African Lives' is a personal narrative focusing on the life of one man, Mohammed, together with his wife Mwahadia and one of their daughters, Subira, who are Swahili peasants living in a village on Mafia Island, Tanzania, where I have been carrying out fieldwork since 1965. The book seeks to explore Mohammed's world

---

[21] See M. Shostak, 1983 [1981]. *Nisa: the Life and Words of a !Kung Woman* (Harmondsworth).

[22] See, for example, K. Dwyer, 1982. *Moroccan Dialogue: Anthropology in Question* (Baltimore and London).

[23] Some have used footnotes (M. Smith, *Baba of Karo*, New Haven, CT; M. Strobel, 1989. *Three Swahili Women: Life Histories from Mombasa, Kenya* (Bloomington, IN)); others have placed their explanations at the beginning of each chapter (e.g. Shostak (see fn. 21)).

[24] Many writers of personal narratives have eliminated their own voices altogether, e.g. E. Burgos-Debray, 1984. *I, Rigoberta Menchu: an Indian Woman in Guatemala* (London) or M. Shostak – see fn. 21).

[25] Compare the relatively unemotional life histories of Strobel (see fn. 24) with the emotionally charged one of Shostak (see fn. 21).

largely through his own words – some written, some spoken – and those of his relatives, friends, enemies and neighbours gathered over almost three decades from the 1960s to the 1990s. The texts include notes on conversations, letters between the subjects and myself, my own field diary, Mohammed's diary, and transcripts of tapes. Dealing with such eclectic material raised considerable problems, one of which was whether it should be arranged chronologically or by themes, two modes which I now explore briefly in turn.

There are many kinds of time involved in seeking to understand Mohammed and his world. For me, time is historical and linear, as I observed changes through my repeated visits, and through my readings on developments in Tanzania. Yet there is relatively little in Mohammed's diaries or conversation about the historical changes which were taking place in Tanzania over this thirty-year period, only an awareness of the increasing poverty of the area in general, and of his own family in particular.

Time also concerns the life-cycle and the domestic cycle, both Mohammed's and my own, with all the changes that it brings, yet which also implies elements of circularity as children grow to adults, and the older generation dies. Time is also spirit time, which is thought of by Mohammed as timeless. Yet we know from the work of historians of the coast that spirit cults wax and waned, and are themselves subject to change.[26]

A personal narrative can also be viewed as a series of themes which relate both to individuals and to society as a whole. It is a kind of soap opera: 'an everyday story of country folk' with their births, deaths, marriages and divorces. In the case of Mohammed, as with most human beings, there is both pleasure and pain: the happiness of his early relationship with his wife, followed by their protracted and unhappy separation, the joys of having children, and the pain of losing them: a son aged nineteen from drowning at sea, a daughter in her thirties from illness, their eldest son, also in his thirties, from illness, leaving only four daughters and one son from the original eight children who survived to adulthood.

At the same time, the texts constitute an ethnography of the village, the island and the Swahili coast, a portrait of a society and its culture. They include such topics as making a living on the land and sea, the life-cycle with its attendant relationships, conflict and emotions, ways of dealing with misfortune, illness and death and the search for knowledge and explanation of these mysteries through both Islam and spirit cults.

In the end, I decided to use both chronological and thematic devices

---

[26] T. Ranger, 1975. *Dance and Society in Eastern Africa 1890–1970* (London).

by dividing the book into four parts. In the first, Mohammed tells his life story in 1994, looking back over his life. He told it more or less chronologically, and it required very little editing. In effect, this section is an autobiography, or perhaps an oral life history.

In the second part of the book, I make use of Mohammed's diary, which he kept at varying times when I was present in the village, and his letters, which were sent to me when I was away. Mohammed wrote the diary at my behest, but the choice of material is his own and I have thus entitled this second section of the book 'The informant as ethnographer' because I wanted to stress his agency and his ability to look at and analyse his own society.

The third part of the book relies heavily on my own field notes, including notes of many conversations over the years not only with Mohammed, but also with his wife, Mwahadia, and one of their daughters, Subira. It is entitled 'Other texts, other voices: three encounters 1965–85', and introduces the counter-voices of Mwahadia and Saidia, with their accounts of their lives and their relationship with Mohammed.

The fourth part of the book is based partly on my final encounter in 1994 with Mohammed, his (by now) ex-wife and daughter, and again partly on his diary, a document which enables the reader to see the world through his eyes. A constant concern was spirit possession and many of his explanations for events in his own life and that of others were given in terms of the activities of spirits. One of the aims of the book, then, was to enable readers, most of whom it was expected would be from another culture, to make sense of a mode of explanation so apparently different to their own and to gain insight into the phenomenon of a cult of spirit possession seen as a way of explaining and coping with the vagaries of life.

Around 1991, Mohammed began to be possessed by his ancestral spirit, with whom he had had a relationship for many years. During that time, we had worked on the spirit possession cults together: he had accompanied me to rituals, and translated and explained songs and seances which I had recorded, but he had himself remained carefully distant. In seeking to understand why he had become possessed and started to be initiated into the cult of his ancestral spirit, I had to grapple with ethnography in a different kind of way, if I was not to do violence to the material, his material. Saidia, too, after several unsuccessful marriages and the loss of many of the children she had borne, began in 1994 to be possessed by two spirits: one of her father's and the other of her mother's ancestry and her father began to teach her to serve his spirit.

Spirit possession raises the issue of difference and otherness in a very stark way. It speaks not only about the relation between religion, ritual and society, but also about the relationship between the individual and society and people's problems and emotions. It cannot be explained, or explained away, in any simple fashion. In this case, it was a good example of where the anthropologist not only learned a good deal from her informants, but had to shift her epistemological stance.

Conclusion

In conclusion, then, I return to the issue posed at the beginning of this paper – the relation between history and social anthropology. Much, of course, depends on what kind of history, and what kind of anthropology. In writing this paper I would propose that in the genre of personal narratives, whether these be of contemporary or historical persons, anthropologists and historians find much in common because, as was noted at the beginning of the paper, this is a way of dealing with the problem of 'otherness'.

Writing the personal narrative of someone from another culture involves consideration of the relationships between space and time, culture and history, individual and society. What, then, is the 'truth' in a life history and does this matter since there are always many truths? Why do them? I would suggest that there are several reasons. One is an attempt to transcend through empathy the self–other dichotomy which risks the objectification of our subjects, and deal with cultural or historical difference. A second is that it is a way of giving voice to informants and enabling subjects to be agents in the construction of ethnography, authors of cultural representations. Thirdly, personal narratives and life histories reveal the complex construction of self, including that of a gendered self, as well as the relationship between the individual and society. Fourthly, personal narratives can be highly successful in explaining how the semantic structures of religion, culture and ideology interact with economic, political and social structures. Finally, personal narratives illuminate both history and anthropology from the bottom up, showing historical transformations as experienced by ordinary people.

In the case of 'African Voices', Mohammed's observations of events and people around him, his relationship with his wife Mwahadia and their children, strike a universal chord; they are about those aspects of life which concern us all: birth, illness, death, attachment and separation. In this respect, then, Mohammed's story, like other personal narratives, is about the human condition, the common subject matter of both anthropology and history.

MAKING THE MOST OF MEMORIES: THE EMPIRICAL AND SUBJECTIVE VALUE OF ORAL HISTORY

By Alistair Thomson

READ 27 MARCH 1988 AT THE UNIVERSITY OF SUSSEX

ORAL history, defined by Ronald Grele as 'the interviewing of eye-witness participants in the events of the past for the purposes of historical reconstruction', is an invaluable and compelling research method for twentieth-century history.[1] It provides access to undocumented experience, including the life of civic leaders who have not yet written their autobiographies and, more significantly, the 'hidden histories' of people on the margins: workers, women, indigenous peoples, ethnic minorities and members of other oppressed or marginalised groups. Oral history interviews also provide opportunities to explore particular aspects of historical experience that are rarely recorded, such as personal relationships, domestic life, and the nature of clandestine organisations. They offer rich evidence about the subjective or personal *meanings* of past events: what it felt like to get married, to be under fire, to face death in a concentration camp. Oral historians are unique in being able to question their informants, to ask the questions that might not have been imagined in the past and to evoke recollections and understandings that were previously silenced or ignored. We enjoy the pleasures – as well as the considerable challenges – of engaging in active, human relationships in the course of our research.

But those relationships, and the use of memories as historical evidence, have been subjected to severe criticism. At the core of criticisms of oral history in the early 1970s was the assertion that memory was distorted by physical deterioration and nostalgia in old age, by the personal bias of both interviewer and interviewee, and by the influence of collective and retrospective versions of the past. For example, the Australian historian Patrick O'Farrell wrote in 1979 that oral history was moving into 'the world of image, selective memory,

---

[1] R. K. Grele, 'Directions for Oral History in the United States', in *Oral History: An Interdisciplinary Anthology*, ed. D. K. Dunaway and W. K. Baum (2nd edn, 1996), 63. For an overview of recent developments in oral history, see A. Thomson, 'Fifty Years On: An International Perspective on Oral History', *Journal of American History*, 82, 2 (1998).

291

later overlays and utter subjectivity ... And where will it lead us? Not into history, but into myth.'[2]

Goaded by the taunts of documentary historians, early oral historians developed guidelines to assess the reliability of oral memory (while shrewdly reminding the traditionalists that documentary sources were no less selective and biased). From social psychology and anthropology they showed how to determine the bias and fabulation of memory, the significance of retrospection and the effects of the interviewer upon remembering. From sociology they adopted methods of representative sampling, and from documentary history they brought rules for checking the reliability and internal consistency of their sources. These guidelines provided useful signposts for reading memories and for combining them with other historical sources to find out what happened in the past.[3]

During the 1970s oral historians in different parts of the world began to question this emphasis on the 'distortions' of memory and to see 'the peculiarities of oral history' as a strength rather than a weakness. One of the most significant shifts in the last twenty-five years of oral history has been this recognition that the so-called 'unreliability' of memory might be a resource, rather than a problem, for historical interpretation and reconstruction. For example, Luisa Passerini analysed the silences and inconsistencies in Italian working-class memories of Mussolini's inter-war Fascist regime to show how Fascist ideology had become deeply entangled in everyday life and personal identity, and to explore the difficulties of remembering involvement in a discredited regime.[4] Another Italian, Alessandro Portelli, noticed that interviewees in the factory town of Terni 'misremembered' the date of the death of the worker Luigi Trastulli. Trastulli had died during a small demonstration against the North Atlantic Treaty Organisation (NATO) in 1949, but local people remembered his death as a martyrdom during the course of a catastrophic strike and lockout in 1953, involving the whole town, that led to defeat for the union and the end of work security. Portelli argued that the mistaken memory was a vital clue to understanding the *meanings* of these events for individuals and for the working-class community, as they happened and as they lived on in memory. He concluded that 'what is really important is that memory is not a passive

[2] P. O'Farrell, 'Oral History: Facts and Fiction', *Oral History Association of Australia Journal*, no. 5 (1982–3), 3–9.
[3] See P. Thompson, *The Voice of the Past: Oral History* (1st edn, 1978). The second, 1988, edition was expanded to outline the new approaches to memory developed in the intervening decade.
[4] L. Passerini, 'Work Ideology and Consensus Under Italian Fascism', in *The Oral History Reader*, ed. R. Perks and A. Thomson (1998, article first published in 1979), 53–62. See also L. Passerini, *Fascism in Popular Memory: the Cultural Experience of the Turin Working Class* (1987).

depository of facts, but an active process of creation of meanings'.[5]

Though initially unaware of these European writings, in the 1970s a number of North American oral historians also began to imagine more sophisticated possibilities for the interpretation and use of memory. Writing in 1972 about Studs Terkel's influential book, *Hard Times: An Oral History of the Great Depression*, Michael Frisch argued against the attitude that oral memory was 'history as it really was', and asserted that memory – 'personal and historical, individual and generational' – should be moved to centre stage 'as the object, not merely the method, of oral history':

> What happens to experience on the way to becoming memory? What happens to experiences on the way to becoming history? As an era of intense collective experience recedes into the past what is the relationship of memory to historical generalization?

If memory were treated as an object of historical analysis, oral history could be 'a powerful tool for discovering, exploring, and evaluating the nature of the process of historical memory – how people make sense of their past, how they connect individual experience and its social context, how the past becomes part of the present, and how people use it to interpret their lives and the world around them'.[6]

A more detailed cultural and intellectual history is needed to explain how and why the ideas and approaches exemplified in the writings of Passerini, Portelli, Frisch and others moved from the margins to the mainstream of oral history within the space of a decade. In the memories of several key figures, one particular event stands out, the international oral history conference held at the University of Essex in 1979, which brought together North American and European oral historians in a significant cultural exchange. Ron Grele recalls this event as an 'epiphany':

> As I look back on it I think the excitement for many of us was that we had all been working around the same set of problems in oral history almost alone in our own countries and now we had found one another. These problems had much to do with the tensions of social history, but it was really the issue of how to deal with interview material beyond some form of empirical and positivististic attitude – what we would now call subjectivity – around which our interests orbited. I remember listening to Luisa [Passerini] present her work

---

[5] A. Portelli, 'What Makes Oral History Different', in *The Oral History Reader*, ed. Perks and Thomson, 69 (first published in 1979). See also A. Portelli, *The Death of Luigi Trastulli and Other Stories: Form and Meaning in Oral History* (1991).

[6] M. Frisch, *A Shared Authority: Essays on the Craft and Meaning of Oral and Public History* (1990), 188. See also R. Grele, *Envelopes of Sound: The Art of Oral History* (2nd edn, 1985).

on Italian workers and fascism and saying to myself, 'Of course, of course. That's it.' ... A major part of the excitement at Essex was political. We were for the most part products of the movements of the Sixties and many of the issues we brought to our work were issues of that generation: subjectivity, spontaneity, populism versus elitism, collective memory, working class culture, problems of culture in general, and what is now called 'reflexivity'. It's odd in retrospect how the 1980s and '90s devised the terms for what we were then doing and the problems about which we were thinking. Because we were coming from the same place politically, which did not take us too long to discover, our work resonated with the work of each other. The connections were inherent; grounded by the experiences.[7]

The rich cross-fertilisation of new theoretical approaches apparent at Essex was repeated at subsequent international conferences, and many key papers articulating these new approaches were published over the next few years, in the *History Workshop* and *Oral History* journals in Britain, and in *Oral History Review* and the new *International Journal of Oral History* published in the United States. By the early 1990s the critical literature about the theory and practice of oral history was heavily informed by these earlier writings, and oral history articles and books frequently demonstrated an impressive theoretical sophistication in their interpretation and use of oral testimony.

Oral historians were not alone in this development of more theoretically sophisticated approaches to remembered life stories. The 1980s and 1990s saw an explosion of research using both oral and written life stories in a wide range of intellectual fields which often crossed traditional disciplinary boundaries, such as life story sociology, auto/biographical approaches in literary studies, anthropology, cultural studies, narrative psychology, linguistics and communication studies, and related work which explored the relationships between identity, memory and personal narrative.[8] While theoretical and methodological developments in each of these fields have enriched the practice of oral history, oral historians have themselves made substantial contributions to the theory, method and politics of life story research through their interdisciplinary reflections on interview relationships and on ways of interpreting and using oral testimony.

Over the last few years there have been rumblings that perhaps this theoreticism has gone too far, and that the important initial motivations

[7] R. Grele, 'Memories of a Movement', *Words and Silences: Bulletin of the International Oral History Association*, 1, 3 (1998); P. Thompson, 'I Piccoli e Il Grande', *Oral History*, 23 (Autumn 1995), 27-8.

[8] For references to relevant literature in these fields, see *The Oral History Reader*, ed. Perks and Thomson, 5.

for oral history – to provide empirical evidence about undocumented experience, and to empower social groups that had been hidden from history – were being submerged under the weight of poststructuralist and postmodernist theories. At the New York international oral history conference in 1994 Michael Frisch noted that theoretical debates about subjectivity and narrative had sometimes displaced connections with 'real culture and lives', and warned of the danger of appropriating experience for theory rather than using theory to make sense of experience and enable change.[9]

An important emerging trend is the renewed effort to link theoretical sophistication about narrative and memory with the political commitment to the history of oppressed and marginal groups which motivated the first generation of feminist and socialist oral historians. For example, in an article about women factory workers Canadian historian Joan Sangster explores feminist debates about the social construction of memory and theoretical dilemmas posed by poststructuralist and postmodernist approaches to language and representation. She concludes that 'without a firm grounding of oral narratives in their material and social context, and a probing analysis of the relationship between the two, insights on narrative form and on representation may remain unconnected to any useful critique of oppression and inequality'.[10]

A stunning recent article by Elizabeth Lapovsky Kennedy demonstrates how her oral history of working-class lesbians in New York State has been enriched by a variety of interpretative strategies that heed the empirical, subjective and narrative qualities of oral testimony. The exquisite storytelling styles of her informants reveal the significance of storytelling in a community that needed to create alternative identities and 'guidelines for living'. By embracing 'the uniquely subjective nature of life stories', Kennedy could explore how her narrators coped with and resisted heterosexism and homophobia, and how individuals 'decide to construct and express their identity'. Where narrators' memories were internally contradictory or in conflict with each other, they 'conveyed precisely the freedom and joy and the pain and limitation that characterized bar life in the mid-twentieth century'. Differences between gay male and lesbian memories of the Stonewall riots (a key event in gay liberation), and the ways in which only some stories were inscribed in the myth or meta-narrative of Stonewall, expressed 'the

[9] M. Frisch, 'Oral History, Questions of Identity and the Representation of Culture', Paper presented at the International Conference on Oral History, New York, 1994. See also D. K. Dunaway, 'The Interdisciplinarity of Oral History', in *Oral History: An Interdisciplinary Anthology*, ed. Dunaway and Baum, 9.

[10] J. Sangster, 'Telling Our Stories: Feminist Debates and the Use of Oral History', in *The Oral History Reader*, ed. Perks and Thomson, 97 (first published in 1994).

ambiguous position of women in gay culture' and captured 'the cultural processes of making lesbians and women invisible in history'. Kennedy demonstrates that 'there is a tremendous amount to be learned by fully exploring the subjective and oral nature of oral histories', but her conclusion – that the empirical and subjective values of oral evidence are 'fully complementary to one another' and should not be 'falsely polarized' – is an essential recommendation for all oral historians.[11]

My own interviews with Australian working-class veterans of the Great War of 1914–18, conducted in the 1980s, illustrate ways in which the so-called 'unreliability' of memory can be a resource rather that a problem for historical interpretation, and the need to utilise both the empirical and subjective evidence of oral testimony.[12] The two extracts I reproduce below focus on memories of enlistment, on how and why two young Australians joined the army and went overseas to fight on the European Western Front. In the memories of many of the old men I interviewed the story of enlistment is highly significant and fraught with anxiety and contradiction. It reveals a struggle to make sense of a decision that may have been difficult at the time, that sometimes had disastrous consequences, for which public regard has varied dramatically – from patriotic enthusiasm and admiration through to doubt and even opposition to participation in 'a European war' – and that could be remembered with either pride or regret. In short, enlistment is an emotional minefield in the memory of many veterans.

Percy Bird volunteered for the Australian Imperial Force (AIF) midway through 1915, about a year after the outbreak of war. At 26 years of age he had been working as a clerk with the Victorian railways, and he was engaged to be married. To make sense of Percy's account of his enlistment and wartime experience you really need to hear the tape and to know about Percy Bird as a storyteller. The ways in which people remember their lives, and the forms of the narrative, are often as revealing about the meaning of the account as what is actually said. Percy Bird was a performer, a singer and a fabulous storyteller, with an anecdotal style akin to that of a stand-up comedian. He had developed his singing and storytelling abilities at wartime concert parties and amongst his mates in the trenches, and even in old age he loved to spin a yarn for the other residents of his retirement home. Percy's performance drew upon a fixed repertoire of short, discrete anecdotes, loosely arranged in approximate chronological order but also prompted by cue words in a previous story or a question, or by the established

---

[11] E. Lapovsky Kennedy, 'Telling Tales; Oral History and the Construction of Pre-Stonewall Lesbian History', in *The Oral History Reader*, ed. Perks and Thomson, 344–56 (first published in 1995).

[12] For a more detailed account of my own oral history of Australian soldiers of the First World War, see A. Thomson, *Anzac Memories: Living with the Legend* (1994).

sequence of the story. Each story had a punch line or 'tag' which had helped to fix it in Percy's memory, and which gave it a purposeful theme and made it a 'good' story.

The main themes through which Percy articulated his war memory were the humour of trench life, lucky escapes from enemy shells, his successful participation in army concerts, and the impressive abilities of the Australian soldiers (who shared the 'Anzac' nickname with the New Zealanders). In Percy's remembering the war was never horrifying or disillusioning, and he avoided talking about his experiences in the line and under fire. When I met Percy for our first interview he presented me with a twelve-page set of these stories, titled 'The 5th Battalion, 1916 and 1917, France', and then proceeded to retell these same stories with great glee and with little regard for my questions. I realised that over the years Percy Bird had composed an account of his war years that was popular with a variety of audiences, and that provided him with a relatively safe and comfortable way of remembering the war.

This is how Percy Bird responded to my questions about his enlistment.

Can you remember where you were when the war broke out, and your response to the war?

Oh well, oh yes, I was here. I was in Melbourne on the 4th August 1914, and in the train from Williamstown going to Melbourne. A number of us got in the same carriage and we saw a boat going down the river, the Yarra. 'Hello. Look at that.' It was the *Holtz*, I think they named it. A German boat trying to get out, and they were, the artillery fired to stop them. He had to fire two or three shots to stop them. So they grabbed them.

What was your initial response to the war?

Oh well, nothing particular. But I was going to join up somewhere about February, 1915, but my father was put into hospital seriously ill, and my mother said, 'Don't do anything until we see how Dad gets on.' So I enlisted on the, somewhere early in July 1915, because they had tried to operate on my father, but his heart wouldn't take it, so they said, 'Well, we'll let him have another twelve months.' You see, so he died on the 4th of March, no the 4th of April, 1916.

Why did you want to enlist?

Oh (awkward laugh). Be like all the others (awkward laugh). I wanted to enlist like all the others, you know. Well, like lots of the others, I should say, because I thought I was ... well, I was ...

should enlist. Being a member of ... being an Australian. So then, when I did go on the boat going over...

The story about the German ship the *Holtz* that Percy told me when I first asked him about the outbreak of war was a typical Percy Bird story. It offered a useful hook to remember the start of the war, and linked Percy to a historical public event which would be of interest to his listeners. In fact, the geography of Melbourne's river system and railways makes it very unlikely that Percy could have seen the *Holtz* from his railway carriage. He may have heard the explosions or read about the event in the newspaper, and in time the story became his own with Percy very much in the picture.

Though Percy was happy to talk about the start of the war, he would have preferred to skip the details of his own enlistment and move straight into stories about the trip overseas with reinforcements for the 5th Battalion. The first eighteen months of the war was a difficult time for Percy. On the one hand, there was enormous pressure on eligible young men to join up, and as a one-time member of the Boy's Naval Brigade Percy had a strong sense of patriotism and military duty. On the other hand, the family trauma of his father's illness and the commitment to a new fiancée were countervailing pressures that made enlistment difficult. In effect, enlistment represented a choice between two different masculinities, between the family man and the independent soldier adventurer. After an awkward period of delay, the pressures to join up and be a soldiering man won out.

Yet enlistment never became one of Percy's favoured war stories, because it had been a difficult choice at the time, and because he was later troubled by people who challenged the worth of Australian participation in a European war. Though Percy did return from the war to marry his fiancée, he may also have been wary of talking about leaving her in the first place. When pressed by my questioning, Percy breaks into an awkward laugh and stumbles through an explanation which justifies the decision in terms of duty, patriotism and mateship. Being 'like all the others' and 'being an Australian' were certainly part of the reason why Percy Bird went to war, though in 1915 membership of the Empire meant more to many young recruits than an Australian identity that was strengthened in the course of the war, and that may have been added to the story with hindsight. The silences and awkwardness of Percy's account hint at other influential factors and at the difficulty of recall. As historians we can use Percy's account – with all its gaps and inconsistencies – as rich evidence about the complex experience of joining up, and to illuminate the meanings of enlistment for Percy and other Australians, during and after the war and up to the present day.

Fred Farrall remembered the war and his life in a very different way. Fred's life story is deliberate, detailed and sequential, a well-rehearsed unfolding of the transformations of his life, often superbly told through tensions and twists towards climactic punch-lines. Most importantly, Fred's stories compose a particular meaning in which his war and his life is a process of conversion. Stripped to essentials, Fred's narrative is as follows. The naïve and patriotic farm boy goes to war as a willing recruit but unwitting sacrificial lamb. He becomes a frightened, inadequate and disillusioned soldier on the Western Front, and a confused and traumatised veteran upon his return to Australia. After several years in a personal wilderness he discovers in the labour movement supportive comrades and a new, socialist way of under-standing his life and the world, and regains his self-esteem as a man. He articulates his disillusionment about the war in political terms and thus redefines the war as one stage on the way to his enlightenment. Many of Fred's stories are framed in terms of this movement towards conversion. The narrative is often interrupted and explained by an ironic reflection which situates a particular incident within the larger pattern which he has made of his life. Fred's enlistment story shows how his remembering worked in this way and conveys his skill and style as a storyteller.

The war broke out in 1914. Well of course in August 1914 I was then actually fifteen years of age, and as I'd wanted to be a jockey I wasn't very robust, in fact I was very small. So my father then began to make some changes, politically speaking, because the Labor Party were not very enthusiastic about the war. Although there was a Labor government, Andrew Fisher, who pledged Australia's support to the last man and the last shilling, as politicians can easily do. But there was a fair bit of opposition from other sections of the Labor Party and my father became a staunch supporter for the war. When the landing was made in Gallipoli, of course, we all had to have it read to us from the papers after tea at night. It was sort of . . . almost something like a religious service and we listened to it and we believed it.

The war went on and 1915, in September 1915, I'd reached the age of eighteen. What did I say? Did I say earlier that I was fifteen when the war . . . I was sixteen when the war broke out. In another month's time I was seventeen then, so I'd reached the age of eighteen and having given away the idea of being a jockey I began to build up my physique somewhat. Previous to that I'd, you know, endeavoured to keep my weight down, but after that denial on the part of my father to do what I wanted to do I just sort of grew up more. The physical standard for joining the army in 1914 and early

1915 was very, very high and I had no hope anyway at being able to measure up to that sort of thing, that standard. But after Gallipoli, or while Gallipoli was on, and they'd suffered a lot of casualties, they lowered the standard considerably here.

When we were in the harvest field in November 1915, we were haymaking and dad had one or two or three men working for him in the harvest as we used to have. They would be swagmen that would be picked up in Ganmain and brought out to do some work, you see. So I was working with one of them, Bill Fraser, and I said to Bill one day, 'I'm thinking about going to the war, Bill.' Well he was an Irishman and he gave me some pretty good advice and a bit of a lecture while we were picking up sheaves of hay and putting them in stooks where they belonged. He told me that I should stay on the farm. He said, 'You should remember', he said, 'that next to your life the most valuable thing you've got is your health. You stay here on the farm and look after it because it's worthwhile keeping.' And finished his advice by saying 'Let the rich men fight their own wars.' Well, I didn't take Bill's advice. I had listened to the Prime Minister and his 'last man and last shilling to defend the Empire', the Premier of New South Wales, the Archbishop. I did what they said to do. I enlisted.

This excerpt is a typical example of Fred's storytelling technique. The listener's interest is sustained by the tensions between different characters and courses of action. The narrative works as a story precisely because it is framed by Fred's retrospective vision of his life. The ironies are resonant because we know, as Fred now knows, the consequences of his enlistment, and that Fred should have listened to Bill Fraser's advice. That doesn't mean that the details about how Fred felt and acted at the time are invented, merely that the way in which he has composed his story of enlistment causes him to highlight certain experiences and make sense of them in particular ways.

For example, Fred mentions that his father stopped him from becoming a jockey. Fred hated farm life and desperately wanted to leave the farm, and when a 'Kangaroo' recruiting march came to a near-by town he jumped at the chance to join up. But he does not refer to his distaste for farm life and the desire to escape as a personal motivation for enlistment. Fred prefers to emphasise his patriotic enthusiasm, and to suggest that like other AIF recruits he was duped by patriotic rhetoric. That explanation fits more neatly into his political story of a conversion from patriotism to disillusionment. By contrast, the motivations of escape and adventure are less appealing to Fred the political activist who prefers to emphasise serious and principled motivations, even if they were mistaken. Fred's story draws upon a radical understanding of the war which was developed by socialists and pacifists between the wars, but which was eventually silenced by an 'Anzac legend' which celebrated the achievements of the Australian soldiers through war memorials, commemoration ceremonies and official histories. As an old man Fred still resisted the Anzac legend, and yet, ironically, by continuing to make sense of the war in radical terms he suppressed significant aspects of his own experience.

Fred Farrall's enlistment story, like that of Percy Bird, can be used in several ways. By listening to these stories and reading between the lines of memory, we can see that enlistment was motivated by a complicated mix of factors. The Anzac legend simplifies the historical picture by depicting enlistment primarily in terms of patriotism and adventure. For example, in 1990 publicity for a 75th Anniversary Anzac Commemorative Coin eulogised Australian Great War recruits in the following terms: 'They fought for what they believed in. They fought for freedom. They fought for their country. They fought for us. They fought for our children.' Soldiers' memories suggest a much more complex and nuanced historical understanding of these men's response to the outbreak of war. More than that, veterans' memories provide clues about the continuing significance of the war for participants and other Australians. Percy and Fred's efforts to explain their enlistment and to make sense of the war offer rich evidence about the changing and contested meanings of the Great War, and about the significance of that past in Australian society.

As historians we want empirical evidence about what happened in the past; but we also want to explore how past events have impacted upon individuals and societies, and to understand the subjective meanings of these events for participants, at the time and over the years. Through working with memories – both 'reliable' and 'unreliable' – oral history allows us to explore the relationships between past and present, between experience and meaning, and between individual and collective memory. When we move memory – 'personal and historical, individual and generational' – to centre stage 'as the object, not merely the method, of oral history', we widen the scope of history and our ambition as historians.[13]

---

[13] Frisch, *A Shared Authority*, 188.

MEDIEVAL COMMUNITIES

THE 'CRUSADER' COMMUNITY AT ANTIOCH: THE IMPACT OF INTERACTION WITH BYZANTIUM AND ISLAM

By T. S. Asbridge

READ 26 SEPTEMBER 1998 AT THE INSTITUTE OF HISTORICAL RESEARCH,

LONDON

AT the end of the eleventh century, in the wake of the First Crusade, a Latin principality was established at Antioch, in northern Syria.[1] Founded by the crusade leader Bohemond (1098–*c.* 1105), this Latin community experienced a period of territorial expansion under the energetic rule of his nephew, Tancred (*c.* 1105–12), followed by seven years of less aggressive leadership by Roger of Salerno (1113–19). The principality suffered a serious setback with the defeat of its army at the evocatively named battle of the Field of Blood in 1119, during which Prince Roger was slain. Power then passed to a regent, King Baldwin II of Jerusalem (1118–31), until Bohemond II (1126–30), the son of Antioch's first prince, arrived in northern Syria.[2]

These rulers, drawn from an almost exclusively southern Italian Norman background, laid the foundations of a Latin settlement which

---

[1] The city of Antioch is now known as Antakya. It lies in Turkey, on the Orontes river, to the south of the Gulf of Alexandretta, only a short distance from the border with Syria. The best map of this area in the period of Latin occupation appears in *A History of the Crusades*, vol. 1, ed. K. M. Setton and M. W. Baldwin (Madison, Wisconsin, 1955), p. 305.

[2] To date the seminal study of Latin settlement in northern Syria in the twelfth and thirteenth centuries is: C. Cahen, *La Syrie du nord à l'époque des croisades et la principauté franque d'Antioche* (Paris, 1940). The principality has also received some attention from historians of the Normans, most notably; D. C. Douglas, *The Norman Achievement 1050–1100* (London, 1969); R. Allen-Brown, *The Normans* (Woodbridge, 1984). The brief treatments in these works tend to regard the creation of the community at Antioch as an expression of *Normanitas*. My forthcoming monograph, *The Creation of the Principality of Antioch 1098–1130*, to be published by Boydell & Brewer, will explore the first three decades of the principality's history in greater detail. It should be noted that, to date, historians have treated Roger of Salerno as the regent of Antioch. I will argue, in my monograph, that he should actually be styled as prince of Antioch in his own right.

survived in a hostile political environment until 1268.[3] My research into the early history of this settlement has sought to define the nature of the community which they helped to create. They were, of course, not presented with the metaphorical blank sheet of paper. Nor were they able to fashion the principality according to an idealised vision. Instead, military and political expediency compelled them to establish a functional settlement as rapidly as possible.

My aim has been, therefore, to assess the extent to which the principality's development was influenced by the surrounding Levantine world, western European practice or, perhaps, the founding concepts of crusading. I have also sought to contextualise my findings by comparing the principality with the other Latin settlements created in the Levant, such as the kingdom of Jerusalem, and other medieval frontier societies in areas such as Sicily and Iberia. This article considers what I think makes Antiochene history distinctive; the influence exerted by Islam and eastern Christendom, both within the principality and on its borders. It explores the impact of external military pressure, the survival of Levantine administrative forms and the evidence of Latin Antioch's early interaction with Islam.

The principality was born into an unusual, if not unique, politico-religious environment. The city of Antioch and the northern reaches of the principality appear to have been largely inhabited by Armenian Christians and Greeks, while to the south the indigenous population was predominantly Muslim. Similarly, Antioch was bordered to the south and east by Muslims powers and to the north-west by the remnants of the Byzantine empire's holdings in Asia Minor, which stretched along the Mediterranean coast from Attaleia, to Seleucia and on towards Cilicia.[4]

Studying the impact of the Levantine world upon the principality's development is problematic. There is a shortage of primary material dealing explicitly with cultural interaction. The main Latin narrative sources for early Antiochene history were written by Walter, the chancellor of Antioch between c. 1114 and c. 1122, Fulcher of Chartres, who was based in the kingdom of Jerusalem, and Albert of Aachen, who probably never left western Europe.[5] These accounts reveal little

---

[3] The detailed prosopographical study, which will appear in my forthcoming monograph on the principality's early history, indicates that almost all of Antioch's early settlers were of Norman, if not always southern Italian, background. Although some of his data does not agree with mine, Dr Alan Murray has recently reached a similar conclusion through his own independent study. A. V. Murray, 'How Norman was the principality of Antioch? Prolegomena to a study of the origins of the nobility of a crusader state', *Family Trees and the Roots of Politics*, ed. K. S. B. Keats-Rohan (Woodbridge, 1997), pp. 349–59.

[4] C. Cahen, *La Syrie du Nord*, pp. 109–204.

[5] Walter the Chancellor, *Bella Antiochena*, ed. H. Hagenmeyer (Innsbruck, 1896). The first Latin translation into English of Walter's text will shortly be published by Ashgate

or nothing of the actual relationship between conqueror and conquered and, likewise, generally remain silent regarding Antiochene relations with neighbouring powers which did not involve warfare or conflict. In some ways this fuels our expectations of an environment which was supposedly powered by concepts of crusade and *jihad*.

Are we, then, to assume that the principality developed no cross-cultural interaction with Islam and eastern Christendom; that there was no diffusion of customs, knowledge, trade; that, in effect, an impermeable frontier, an iron-curtain, existed between the Latins and the world around them? This would, of course, stand in sharp contrast with our knowledge of frontiers elsewhere in medieval Europe. Historians have generally acknowledged that the frontiers of Latin Christendom expanded between the tenth and thirteenth centuries at least in part because of entrepreneurial conquest and immigration, described by Robert Bartlett as 'aristocratic diaspora'. This mode of 'adventurous' expansion, which was certainly not limited to individuals or groups of a Norman background, inevitably produced cross-cultural contact and stimulated a degree of interaction and assimilation across Europe.[6] Did the formation of the Latin community at Antioch follow this pattern in any broad sense, even with the heightened possibility of tension with Islam and the legacy of the First Crusade?

The evidence preserved in Arabic and Armenian accounts does provide glimpses of a more interactive environment in northern Syria.[7] Reviewing the scattered evidence of contact, I suggest that the Latins did not create a community in isolation. That, in fact, the principality

---

Press. Walter the Chancellor's *The Antiochene Wars*, transl. with historical notes by T.S. Asbridge and S.B. Edgington; Fulcher of Chartres, *Historia Hierosolymitana*, ed. H. Hagenmeyer (Heidelberg, 1913); Albert of Aachen, 'Historia Hierosolymitana', *Recueil des historiens des croisades. Historiens occidentaux*, vol. 4 (Paris, 1879), pp. 265–713. Susan Edgington's new edition of Albert's account will soon be published by Oxford University Press. References to his work will therefore be cited by book and chapter. A number of other Latin sources provide important information about the principality's foundation. Ralph of Caen, 'Gesta Tancredi in Expeditione Hierosolymitana', *Recueil des historiens des croisades. Historiens occidentaux*, vol. III (Paris, 1866), pp. 587–716; William of Tyre, *Willelmi Tyrensis archiepiscopi chronicon*, ed. R.B.C. Huygens, 2 vols (Turnhout, 1986); Orderic Vitalis, *The Ecclesiastical History*, vol. 6, ed. and transl. M. Chibnall (Oxford, 1978).

[6] R. Bartlett, 'Colonial aristocracies in the High Middle Ages', *Medieval Frontier Societies*, ed. R. Bartlett and A. MacKay (Oxford, 1989), pp. 23–47; R. Bartlett, *The Making of Europe. Conquest, Colonization and Cultural Change, 950–1350* (London, 1993); S. Reynolds, *Kingdoms and Communities in Western Europe, 900–1300* (Oxford, 1984).

[7] Ibn al-Qalanisi, *The Damascus Chronicle of the Crusades*, transl. H.A.R. Gibb (London, 1932); Usamah ibn-Munqidh, *An Arab–Syrian Gentleman and Warrior in the Period of the Crusades*, transl. P.K. Hitti (New York, 1929); Kemal ed-Din, 'La chronique d'Alep', *Recueil des historiens des croisades. Historiens orientaux*, vol. 3 (Paris, 1884), pp. 577–732; Ibn al-Athir, 'Kamel Altevarykh', *Recueil des historiens des croisades. Historiens orientaux*, vol. 1 (Paris, 1872), pp. 189–744; Matthew of Edessa, *The Chronicle of Matthew of Edessa*, transl. A.E. Dostourian (Lanham, New York, London, 1993).

was profoundly shaped by non-Latin influence. Its internal security and patterns of landholding were probably influenced by the presence of a numerically superior subject population, and Antioch's administrative framework was affected by eastern practice. The principality also developed important links with the Muslim world around it which culminated in instances of political and military co-operation.

This openness to contact can be compared with other areas of the medieval world, but seems all the more exceptional in the Levantine context given the fact that the Latins may have continued to be influenced by crusade ideology. Antioch was conquered during the First Crusade, an expedition preached on the basis of pious reconquest and religious conflict with Islam, but did the Latins who settled in the Levant still believe themselves to be engaged in an ongoing Holy War with Islam, a war which would bring them the same spiritual benefits as a crusade? The evidence presented by Walter the Chancellor suggests that they did.

Walter certainly used just war terminology in his account, and seems to have made a conscious effort to present Latin military activity within the context of St Augustine of Hippo's conception of justified violence.[8] He often used variations on the term 'soldiers of God' to describe the Latin armies, noted that they had been 'signed by the Cross' before battle and asserted that they fought with the 'weapons of faith'.[9] At times he even presented 'The Antiochene Wars' as the spiritual equivalent of the First Crusade, suggesting that their participants gained a similar remission of sins in return for military service.[10]

---

[8] In this period the three criteria of legitimate authority, just cause and right intention were required for a conflict to be viewed as just. These were derived from the writings of St Augustine of Hippo by medieval canonists. For further discussion of justified and sanctified violence see: J. Brundage, *Medieval Canon Law and the Crusader* (Madison, Wisconsin, 1969); 'Holy war and the medieval lawyers', *The Holy War*, ed. T. P. Murphy (Columbus, Ohio, 1976), pp. 99–140; H. E. J. Cowdrey, 'The Genesis of the Crusades: The Spring of Western Ideas of Holy War', *The Holy War*, ed. T. P. Murphy (Columbus, Ohio, 1976), pp. 9–32; 'Pope Gregory VII's "crusading plans" of 1074', in *Outremer. Studies in the History of the Crusading Kingdom of Jerusalem Presented to Joshua Prawer*, ed. B. Z. Kedar, H. E. Mayer and J. S. C. Riley-Smith (Jerusalem, 1982); 'Pope Gregory VII and the bearing of arms', *Montjoie: Studies in Crusade History in Honour of Hans Eberhard Mayer*, ed. B. Z. Kedar, J. S. C. Riley-Smith and R. Hiestand (Aldershot, 1997), pp. 21–35; J. S. C. Riley-Smith, *What were the Crusades?*, 2nd edn (London, 1992); I. S. Robinson, 'Gregory VII and the Soldiers of Christ', *History*, vol. 58 (1973), pp. 169–92; F. E. Russell, *The Just War in the Middle Ages* (Cambridge, 1975), pp. 16–39.

[9] Walter the Chancellor, 1.5, p. 73; II.1, p. 79; II.2, p. 82; II.3, p. 84; II.5, p. 87.

[10] For example, he recorded that after the Antiochene army had made confession in 1115 'it was enjoined on each of them by the lord patriarch, instead of a true penance ... that those who would die in the war which was at hand would acquire salvation by his own absolution and also by propitiation of the Lord, while those who returned should all meet at a council arranged for the next feast of All Saints'. Thus, Walter commented, they would be saved 'through a truce and the Church's indulgence' and repeated that

His account is, however, the only extant Latin source for this period to make such extensive use of this terminology. He also naturally wrote from a Christian standpoint, attempting to demonstrate that success and failure in battle was dependent upon God's will. It is, therefore, accordingly natural that he presented a strong spiritual element within 'the Antiochene Wars' and we might question whether this accurately reflected contemporary conviction. With these caveats in mind, it is still worth noting that some evidence does indicate that the Latins continued to espouse the ideology of Holy War during the first decades of settlement in northern Syria. If this were the case then it is all the more remarkable that the Latin community at Antioch was willing to interact at a number of levels with the Levantine world around it.

In terms of internal contact, we know that the principality was a polyglot community, with its Latin population in the minority. Antiochene sources do occasionally make reference to this multicultural society. Walter the Chancellor noted that after an earthquake shook the city of Antioch in 1114 the voices of different nations, 'Latins, Greeks, Syrians, Armenians, strangers and pilgrims', could be heard in the confusion.[11] Arabic sources suggest that the south-eastern portion of the principality, known as the Jabal as-Summaq, had a largely Muslim population.[12] This can be compared to a Latin ruling class which contained perhaps 700 Frankish knights in this period.[13]

This numerical imbalance between conqueror and conquered had several consequences for the principality's establishment. Early in its history, Latin domination of northern Syria seems to have been quite precarious and the principality's frontiers extremely fluid. When the Latins suffered their first serious military defeat in the Levant, at the battle of Harran in 1104, the principality's subjected population revolted en masse and its frontiers shrank radically as a result. This situation may have stabilised to a degree over time, as the next major defeat at the Field of Blood stimulated less of a wholesale territorial disaster.[14]

The aftermath of this second battle, in which the prince of Antioch was killed, prompted Walter the Chancellor to comment upon contact with the indigenous population in the East. He described the vulnerability of Antioch after the defeat at the Field of Blood, but noted that the Latins 'feared much more intensely being deceived by the betrayal of enemies within the city than being in any way vulnerable

---

Bernard 'pronounced absolution from their sins to the people entrusted to him'. Walter the Chancellor, I.4–5, pp. 71–2.
[11] Walter the Chancellor, I.I, p. 63.
[12] Kemal ed-Din, p. 592.
[13] Walter the Chancellor, II.5, p. 88.
[14] T. S. Asbridge, 'The significance and causes of the battle of the Field of Blood', *Journal of Medieval History*, vol. 23.4 (1997), pp. 303–5.

to pressure upon them from external forces'. To cope with the threat of Greek, Syrian and Armenian revolt the Latin Patriarch Bernard organised the defence of the city and ordered 'that the peoples of different nations, wherever they were in the city and wherever they came from, except the Franks, should all remain unarmed and should never venture out of their houses at night without a light'. Walter went on to state in a remarkable aside that he understood why the city's indigenous population might wish to overthrow Latin rule. He wrote, 'Nor was it remarkable if the Antiochenes wanted to return evil for evil ... because that is how the scales of justice change; for indeed the people of Antioch had been deprived of their goods by the force and deviousness of our people and were ... often overcome by despair.'[15] Thus, in the otherwise partisan opinion of the chancellor, the Latins had exploited the local population in the first twenty years of their rule.[16]

The threat of territorial collapse posed by this large and sometimes hostile subjected population, particularly when combined with the threat of Muslim or Byzantine invasion on the principality's vulnerable frontiers, may have influenced the pattern of Antiochene landholding. The desire to assert Latin authority within the localities could explain why the princes of Antioch allowed powerful and semi-autonomous lordships to develop rapidly within the principality. A group of key landholders can be identified and might be usefully compared to marcher lords in the borderlands between medieval England and Wales.

For example, within two decades the first Latin lords of Cilicia, to the north-west of Antioch, attained considerable power. This region played a major strategic role as a buffer zone between Antioch and the Byzantine empire in this period. A succession of Greek military campaigns to Cilicia, combined with the willingness of its Armenian Christian population to switch allegiance, meant that control of the

---

[15] Walter the Chancellor, II.8, pp. 95–6.

[16] Professor B. Z. Kedar has suggested that Walter characterised Latin rule over the principality's indigenous population as 'intolerable' elsewhere in his account. B. Z. Kedar, 'The subjected Muslims of the Frankish Levant', *Muslims under Latin Rule, 1100–1300*, ed. J. M. Powell (Princeton, NJ, 1990), p. 168. The Latin in this passage reads: 'Graecis namque regnantibus ipsorum imperio servisse convincuntur. eisdem ex Asia propulsis Parthorum regnantium cessere domino; tandem, Deo volente, intolerabiliori succubere Gallorum potestati.' In our forthcoming translation of 'The Antiochene Wars' Susan Edgington and I translate this as: 'For while the Greeks ruled they were persuaded to be enslaved to their empire. When those same people had been driven forth from Asia they had yielded to the dominion of the ruling Persians; eventually, God willing, they succumbed to the irresistible power of the Gauls.' Thus, 'intolerabiliori' is read as 'irresistible', that is undefeatable. We suggest, therefore, that although Walter did comment on Antiochene exploitation of the subjected population he did not do so in the passage previously identified by historians.

region changed hands almost continuously in the first decade of Latin settlement.[17] The fertility of the Cilician plain may also have contributed to the region's importance. The history of the Latins who held land there in this period is relatively well documented, and this in itself may be an indication of their standing. The Latin rulers of Cilicia were the only landholders whom we know issued charters in their own name in this period. Before 1114 Guy Le Chevreuil (Guy the Goat), the first lord of the region, issued a charter making grants to the abbey of Our Lady of Josaphat in the kingdom of Jerusalem, including provisions for an annual supply of eels to be provided for the monks' refectory from the fisheries of Mamistra. Guy's grants were subsequently confirmed in 1114 in a charter issued by Roger of Salerno, prince of Antioch from 1113 to 1119.[18]

A man named Sanso the seneschal appeared as the first lay witness to Guy's charter, suggesting that Guy had developed some form of local administrative framework within Cilicia. Guy's importance is also demonstrated by the fact that he was given the honour of commanding the vanguard of the army, alongside Baldwin count of Edessa, in the major battle at Tall Danith in 1115, during which he may have been slain.[19] One Latin source even suggested that, like the rulers of Antioch, he used the title of prince, and was styled 'prince of Tarsus and Mamistra'.[20] Guy was succeeded by Cecilia, 'the Lady of Tarsus', who issued her own charter making grants to the house at Josaphat in 1126. No princely confirmation of this charter survives, but Cecilia herself recorded that she was issuing it 'with the consent of Bohemond (II) prince of Antioch'.[21]

[17] The history of Cilicia's relationship with Antioch and Byzantium between 1097 and 1110 is rather convoluted. The Cilician towns of Tarsus, Adana and Mamistra were first occupied or contacted by the Latins during the First Crusade. Albert of Aachen, III.6–16; Ralph of Caen, pp. 633–9; *Gesta Francorum et aliorum Hierosolimitanorum*, ed. and transl. R. Hill (London, 1962), IV.10, pp. 24–5; Fulcher of Chartres, I.14, pp. 206–8. Latin bishops of Tarsus and Mamistra were consecrated in December 1099. Ralph of Caen, p. 704. By 1100, however, the region was back in Greek hands, only to be re-occupied by Tancred in April 1101. Ralph of Caen, p. 706. Cilicia continued to be an Antiochene possession until at least 1103, but its Armenian populace had rebelled and accepted Byzantine rule by *c.* 1104. Anna Comnena, *The Alexiad*, ed. and transl. S. J. Leib (Paris, 1945), XI.10, p. 41; Ralph of Caen, p. 712. Tancred again achieved at least partial control of the region in *c.* 1107, but then lost it again to Byzantium in 1108. Anna Comnena, XII.2, pp. 57–8; Albert of Aachen, XI.6. Long-term Latin rule was only established by Tancred between 1109 and 1111. Ibn al-Qalanisi, p. 99.

[18] 'Chartes de l'abbaye de Notre-Dame de Josaphat', *Revue de l'Orient Latin*, vol. VII (1890), pp. 115–16, n. 4; *Chartes de Terre Sainte provenant de l'abbaye de N. D. de Josaphat*, ed. H. F. Delaborde (Paris, 1880), pp. 26–7, n. 4.

[19] Walter the Chancellor, I.6. p. 74.

[20] Albert of Aachen, XI.40. It should be noted that as far as we know Albert wrote from western Europe and, therefore, may not provide a reliable record of the titles used in the Levant.

The colourfully named Robert fitz-Fulk the Leper had an extensive lordship. He held the town of Zardana on the eastern frontier, probably from its conquest in 1111.[22] His estate grew in c. 1118, when he became what an Arabic source described as the 'lord of Saone, Balatanos and the adjoining region'.[23] These sites were not in border zones but did have considerable strategic significance. Balatanos, known in Arabic as Qal'at Mehelbe, protected the eastern approach to the port of Jabala, while the impressively fortified Saone defended the region around Latakia and the southern route to Antioch itself.[24] Robert's lordship is of particular interest because it was the first in the principality to show evidence of being disposed of on hereditary principle, with his sons William and Garenton succeeding to Zardana and Saone respectively.[25]

The possession of two key sites on the principality's eastern frontier, namely al-Atharib from c. 1119 and Hisn ad-Dair from 1121, seems to have conferred a special importance upon the man named Alan, especially given the concentration and frequency of military activity between Antioch and Aleppo from 1120 to 1126.[26] In 1123, during the captivity of Baldwin II, Alan led the army of Antioch on a major raiding campaign into the region around Aleppo. His role as commander of the Antiochene army may reflect his high status within the principality at this point.[27] In the Jabal as-Summaq, bordering Shaizar and the dependencies of Aleppo, Bonable of Sarmin and Kafartab appears to have been the most important lay landholder. He probably held Sarmin and Kafartab for twelve years or more, and his importance in the area was second only to that of Peter of Narbonne, the bishop of Albara from 1099, who later became archbishop of Apamea. Bonable donated land to the religious houses of Our Lady of Josaphat in 1114 and the Hospital of Jerusalem in 1118.[28] The only prominent lordship that was established outside the context of a landed frontier with non-Latins was that amassed by Rainald Masoir in the coastal region of Jabala, Baniyas and Marqab. These sites lay to the south of Antioch, but were close to

[21] 'Chartes de l'abbaye de Notre-Dame de Josaphat', p. 123, n. 13.

[22] Ibn al-Athir, p. 278; Kemal ed-Din, p. 621; *Chartes de Terre Sainte provenant de l'abbaye de N. D. de Josaphat*, pp. 26–7, n. 4.

[23] Usamah ibn-Munqidh, p. 149.

[24] P. Deschamps, 'La défense du comté de Tripoli et de la principauté d'Antioche', *Les Châteaux des Croisés en Terre Sainte*, vol. III (Paris, 1973), pp. 220 ff.

[25] Kemal ed-Din, p. 629; *Le Cartulaire du chapitre du Saint-Sépulchre de Jérusalem*, ed. G. Bresc-Bautier (Paris, 1984), pp. 176–83, nn. 76–7.

[26] Walter the Chancellor, II.2, p. 82; Kemal ed-Din, p. 628.

[27] Kemal ed-Din, p. 639.

[28] Albert of Aachen, XI.40; *Chartes de Terre Sainte provenant de l'abbaye de N. D. de Josaphat*, pp. 26–7, n. 4; *Cartulaire général de l'ordre des Hospitaliers de S. Jean de Jérusalem (1100–1200)*, ed. J. Delaville Le Roulx (Paris, 1894), vol. I, p. 38, n. 45; C. Cahen, *La Syrie du Nord*, p. 243, n. 7.

the frontier with the Latin county of Tripoli. The exact date of his acquisition of Marqab is not entirely clear, but it is certain that by 1119 he had an important military role, leading three companies in the battle of the Field of Blood.[29] By 1127 he had been appointed constable of Antioch, and went on to act as regent in the principality in 1132.[30] He also founded one of the most enduring dynasties in the East, with a lordship based around possession of Marqab, and his descendants continued to play an important role in the history of the principality.[31]

These examples serve to demonstrate the rapid rise of the Antiochene nobility. A number of factors – including an individual's personality – may well have combined to produce this situation, but the combination of internal instability and external threat probably did most to encourage the development of localised power in the principality. There has been a long standing historical debate about the relationship between the king of Jerusalem and his nobility and the rise in the second half of the twelfth century of what some have termed a feudal monarchy.[32] Antioch, with its greater territorial instability, developed a potent landed aristocracy even more rapidly.

A more direct connection can be drawn between the principality's institutional development and the Levantine world into which it was born. Our knowledge of institutions in this early period is, admittedly, extremely limited, so any conclusions can only be viewed as tentative. The princes of Antioch did make use of a range of western European officials – constable, chancellor and chamberlain – drawing particularly from a Norman template.[33] They combined these, however, with pre-existing administrative forms. Unlike the Latin kingdom of Jerusalem,

[29] Walter the Chancellor, II.4, p. 87.

[30] William of Tyre, XIV.5, p. 637; 'Liber Jurium republicae Genuensis, I', *Monumenta Historiae Patriae*, vol. VII (Augustae Taurinorum, 1853), pp. 30–1, n. 20.

[31] C. Cahen, *La Syrie du Nord*, p. 543.

[32] J. L. La Monte, *The Feudal Monarchy in the Latin Kingdom of Jerusalem 1100 to 1291* (Cambridge, Mass., 1932); J. Richard, *The Latin Kingdom of Jerusalem*, transl. J. Shirley (Amsterdam, 1979); J. Prawer, *The Latin Kingdom of Jerusalem* (London, 1972); J. S. C. Riley-Smith, *The Feudal Nobility and the Kingdom of Jerusalem, 1174–1277* (London 1973); S. Tibble, *Monarchy and Lordships in the Latin Kingdom of Jerusalem* (Cambridge, 1989).

[33] For early references to the constable of Antioch see: Albert of Aachen, VII.30; *Liber Privilegiorum ecclesiae ianuensis*, ed. D. Puncuh (Genoa, 1962), p. 42, n. 25; Ibn al-Athir, p. 205; *Italia Sacra*, vol. IV, ed. F. Ughelli, pp. 847–8; 'Liber Jurium republicae Genuensis, I', pp. 30–1, n. 20. For early references to chancellor of Antioch see: Walter the Chancellor, II.Prologue, p. 78; II.3, p. 84; 'Liber Jurium republicae Genuensis, I', pp. 30–1, n. 20. For the earliest reference to the chamberlain of Antioch see: Walter the Chancellor, II.3, p. 84. We should, of course, be wary of assuming that the use of a western European title indicates that its powers and responsibilities would be the same in the Levant. For further discussion of Antiochene institutions see: C. Cahen, *La Syrie du Nord*, pp. 435–71; H. E. Mayer, *Varia Antiochena: Studien zum Kreuzfahrerfürstentum Antiochia im 12. und frühen 13. Jahrhundert* (Hanover, 1993).

Antioch had, only a decade before its conquest, been held directly by the Byzantine empire.[34] As a result the principality developed a distinctive institutional framework, particularly influenced by Greek practice in the sphere of local government. Historiographically the kingdom of Jerusalem has dominated the study of Latin administration in the Levant and some historians have tended to assume that its development can act as a universal blueprint for the Latin East.[35] In some areas, however, Antioch followed an independent line.

The most important Latin city official, the duke of Antioch, was probably based on the Greek *dux*. Although the title of duke existed in the West, the duke in the principality of Antioch owed far more to Byzantine precedents. By contrast, in Jerusalem, which had not been under Byzantine rule, the chief local administrator was a viscount, modelled on a western template.[36] Before the Greeks lost Antioch to the Muslim Sulaiman ibn-Qutulmish in 1084 the city and surrounding region was a *theme* of the Byzantine empire and had been governed by a duke.[37] In this period a Greek *dux* represented a local official wielding both military power and a degree of civil authority.[38] Some sense of the powers associated with the principality's Latin *dux* can be gleaned from the events of 1115. In that year Roger of Salerno turned to Ralph the duke of Antioch to resolve the problems caused by the recent earthquake damage to the city. They discussed how to organise the repair of Antioch's walls and towers and then considered what ought to be done by 'the lord and his warriors in regard to the necessities of war'. A policy was formulated at this meeting, which the duke subsequently passed on to the 'the greater and the lesser' (*maiores et minores*) at the council which he himself called. Walter recorded that after having heard the 'prince's decree' all those present agreed to a course of action, almost certainly that suggested by Roger, whereby the responsibility, probably both financial and physical, for repairing damage to walls and towers would be assigned to those holding land and honours and in accordance with their relative resources.

The fact that the prince first consulted the duke on this matter and that Ralph then called and presided over the resultant council

---

[34] M. Angold, *The Byzantine Empire, 1025–1204. A Political History*, 2nd edn (London, 1997), p. 134.

[35] La Monte and Prawer both treated Antiochene institutions as offshoots from the kingdom of Jerusalem. J. L. La Monte, *The Feudal Monarchy in the Latin Kingdom of Jerusalem 1100 to 1291*; J. Prawer, *Crusader Institutions* (Oxford, 1980).

[36] J. L. La Monte, *The Feudal Monarchy in the Latin Kingdom of Jerusalem 1100 to 1291*, p. 106.

[37] J. Laurent, 'Le Duc d'Antioche Khachatour, 1068–1072', *Byzantinisches Zeitschrift*, vol. 30 (1930), pp. 405–11.

[38] H. Glykatzi-Ahrweiler, *Recherches sur l'administration de l'empire Byzantine aux IX–XI siècles* (Athens, 1960), pp. 52–67.

demonstrates his importance. The degree of autonomy which he enjoyed is, however, open to question. Although Ralph summoned the council, we are told that it was done 'by the enjoined command of the lord prince'. Apparently the prince did not simply tell Ralph what to do during their initial meeting but formed a policy with him, but this solution was then presented to the subsequent council as the 'decree of the prince'.[39] In this case Ralph consulted closely with the prince before implementing any policy and acted primarily as his representative and with his authority. From this single example it is, of course, impossible to form any concrete opinions about the duke of Antioch's ability to exert independent control over the civil government of the city, either in the formulation of civil policy or in the ability to summon a council of the city's officials.

This passage also raises the question of the duke's sphere of administrative influence. First, it is not clear whether he was responsible only for the city itself, or also for the territory in the immediate vicinity. Secondly, was Claude Cahen correct to interpret the evidence presented by Walter the Chancellor as indicative that in 1115 the duke exerted authority only over civil matters?[40] The evidence does not fully support this conclusion, as Roger of Salerno apparently discussed 'the necessities of war' with the duke, perhaps indicating that they addressed the problem of military supplies. This discussion may have centred on the prince's forthcoming campaign or on the actual defence of Antioch, but it raises the possibility that Ralph may have acted as some form of quarter-master.[41]

I suggest, therefore, that the duke of Antioch advised on and implemented the prince's decisions regarding civil matters within the city, while also assisting with the logistical preparations for the prince's forthcoming military campaign. Thus, although the Latins adopted the *dux* as the premier local official within Antioch, they also appear to have adapted his role to emphasise civil administration as well as military command. Ralph was certainly a significant figure because he appeared in a princely charter issued between 1113 and 1118 as the second witness after Roger of Salerno and his death in 1117–18 was even reported by the Muslim chronicler Ibn al-Qalanisi.[42] By 1134 the office of *dux* was being used elsewhere in the principality. In that year William of 'Cursibus Altis' the *dux* of Jabala and Theobald of 'Corizo' the *dux* of Latakia appeared in a charter issued by Bohemond II's widow, Alice of Jerusalem.[43] It is not possible to date the creation of

---

[39] Walter the Chancellor, I.2, pp. 65–6.
[40] C. Cahen, *La Syrie du Nord*, pp. 457–8.
[41] Walter the Chancellor, I.2, p. 65.
[42] Ibn al-Qalanisi, p. 157.
[43] H. E. Mayer, *Varia Antiochena*, pp. 110–12, n. 1.

these offices but they may initially have been instituted by Alice to administer her lordship during the struggle for control of Antioch.[44] Two other officers, *praetor* and judge, which are mentioned in relation to the civil administration of the city of Antioch, can also probably be connected with Greek precedents.[45]

The process of adapting the existing apparatus of governance when creating a medieval European community or principality was certainly not unique. For example, institutional development in the kingdom of Norman Sicily was influenced by both Byzantine and Muslim practice, producing offices such as the *diwan*, and a similar use of a *praetor*.[46] In the principality of Antioch this process rapidly produced an administrative framework which differed in some respects from that established in the kingdom of Jerusalem.

I turn now to the principality's interaction with other oriental powers and, in particular, to its links with Islam. On rare occasions the sources do provide us with glimpses of personal relationships which hint at wider contact. For example, the Muslim writer Usamah ibn-Munqidh recalled in his 'Memoirs' that Robert fitz-Fulk the Leper established a close friendship with Tughtegin, the atabeg of Damascus, a story which is, to some extent, confirmed by Walter the Chancellor. This relationship may have been stimulated by Robert's possession of a frontier lordship. Usamah, who had a particular interest in strange twists of fate, probably mentioned this association because it made a good story. He noted that in spite of their friendship, it was Tughtegin who insisted on personally beheading Robert when he was taken captive in 1119. Walter added that Tughtegin then had Robert's skull made into a gold and jewel

---

[44] For the most up to date discussion of Alice's rebellion and its consequences see: J. Phillips, *Defenders of the Holy Land. Relations between the Latin East and the West 1119–1187* (Oxford, 1996), pp. 44–72.

[45] The office described as 'judge (iudex)' may well have been derived from the Greek *krites*. In the Byzantine empire the offices of *krites* and *praetor* were largely interchangeable. They acted as the chief justice of a theme, responsible for passing judgement and implementing any necessary punishment. H. Glykatzi-Alirweiler, *Recherches sur l'administration de l'empire Byzantine aux IX–XI siècles*, pp. 67 ff. Although there is no specific record of a *krites* or *praetor* at Antioch before 1085 the existing reference to a *phorologos* demonstrates that this administrative function was being carried out. H. Glykatzi-Alirweiler, *Recherches sur l'administration de l'empire Byzantine aux IX–XI siècles*, p. 85. In Norman Sicily the office of *praetor* was used to denote a chief judge in control of the municipal judiciary. C. Cahen, *La Syrie du Nord*, p. 456. Although it is likely that the *praetor* and *krites* of Latin Antioch both developed from Byzantine offices it is not possible to state that in this early period their holders acted as judicial administrators. The evidence does not survive to allow any conclusion beyond the fact that these two offices were involved in the administration of the city of Antioch, and given the change of role undergone by the duke of Antioch from its Byzantine antecedent it would seem foolish to base any argument purely on the evidence of an office's previous responsibilities.

[46] D. Matthew, *The Norman Kingdom of Sicily* (Cambridge, 1992), pp. 219–28; C. Cahen, *La Syrie du Nord*, p. 456.

encrusted cup.[47] Alan, lord of al-Atharib on the border with Aleppo, befriended a Muslim living in his town, Hamdan b. Abd al-Rahim, who gave him medical assistance.[48] Perhaps most prominently of all, Roger of Salerno was supposed to have been on close terms with Il-ghazi of Mardin, with one Armenian source even claiming that up to 1118 they were 'very intimate friends',[49] though Il-ghazi led the Aleppan army which crushed the forces of Antioch and slew Roger on the Field of Blood in 1119.

These are, however, only glimpses of a wider picture. What further can be said about early Latin/Muslim interaction in northern Syria?[50] In order to find visible expressions of contact we must examine Antioch's relations with her two closest and most important Muslim neighbours, focusing in turn upon Aleppo, to the east of Antioch, which was held by the Seljuq Turk Ridwan ibn Tutush from 1095 to 1113, and then Shaizar, on the principality's southern frontier, which was under the control of the Arab dynasty of the Banu-Munqidh at the start of the twelfth century.[51]

The Levantine world, into which the principality of Antioch was born in 1098, was not dominated by any single or united Islamic power. Instead, the Muslim world of northern Syria was extremely fragmented. Both Aleppo and Shaizar were classic examples of this disunity. There was little love lost between the Sunni Turks in Aleppo and the Shi'i Arabs in Shaizar, so these two Muslim cities were natural enemies rather than allies.

The creation of the principality altered the balance of power in northern Syria, but did not unite Aleppo and Shaizar in a common cause. Initially, neither power made any concerted attempt to expel the Latins from Antioch. Instead, to a degree, they accepted the principality as another element in the political make-up of a region

[47] Usamah ibn-Munqidh, pp. 149–50. For an excellent discussion of Usamah see: R. Irwin, 'Usamah ibn Munqidh: An Arab–Syrian gentleman at the time of the crusades reconsidered', *The Crusades and Their Sources: Essays Presented to Bernard Hamilton*, ed. J. France and W. G. Zajac (Aldershot, 1998), pp. 71–87. Walter the Chancellor, II.14, pp. 107–9. Walter also actually suggested that Robert had previously paid a tribute to Tughtegin.

[48] Hamdan may also have held an administrative post within the principality and been given two villages by Alan. C. Cahen, *La Syrie du Nord*, pp. 343–4; B. Z. Kedar, 'Subjected Muslims under Latin rule', pp. 156–7.

[49] Matthew of Edessa, III.78, p. 223.

[50] H. Dajani-Shakeel has discussed the series of peace treaties established between Jerusalem and Damascus down to 1153, and alluded to the development of a tribute relationship between these two powers, but did not examine events in northern Syria. H. Dajani-Shakeel, 'Diplomatic relations between Muslim and Frankish ruler 1097–1153 A.D.', *Crusaders and Muslims in Twelfth Century Syria*, ed. M. Shatzmiller (Leiden, 1993), pp. 201–9.

[51] C. Cahen, *La Syrie du Nord*, p. 180.

already fraught by power struggles and both were even willing to pursue policies of co-operation and interaction with the Franks. This turbulent political environment not only facilitated the actual creation of the principality, it also enabled the early princes of Antioch to increase their power through diplomatic manœuvring.

It is helpful to recognise a similarity between this situation and that which existed in the Iberian peninsula during the eleventh century. This era, after the death of al-Mansur in 1002 and the collapse of the caliphate of Cordoba in 1031, characterised as the *taifa* period, saw the break up of Muslim al-Andalus into a large number of smaller political entities. For much of the eleventh century these *taifa* states were embroiled in inter-Muslim power struggles, providing an opportunity for expansion to the surviving Christian states in the north of the peninsula. In this early period of the Reconquest the Christians sought to exploit Muslim weakness and factionalism to increase their own wealth and territory.[52]

One of their primary avenues in this pursuit was the extraction of regular tribute payments (*parias*) from individual *taifas* who either sought to avoid attack or wanted protection from fellow Muslims and other Christian states. Fernando I (1036–65) and Alfonso VI (1065–1109) of Leon-Castile were particularly skilful exponents of this practice. During their successive reigns they established the payment of *parias* from the Muslim cities of Granada, Zaragoza, Badajoz, Seville and Toledo. These payments could represent significant transfers of wealth – it is estimated that in 1074 Alfonso VI gathered *c.* 70,000 gold dinars from *parias* – and thus could fund Christian armies in the field. They also created a relationship of dependence in which a *taifa*'s need for protection afforded its Christian defender increasing influence and authority within that city. This process saw its fullest expression in the peaceful occupation of Toledo by Alfonso VI in 1085 after a long period of *parias* exploitation, a crucial step forward in the Reconquest as a whole.[53] In his study on 'The Contest of Christian and Muslim Spain', B. Reilly wrote that this *parias* system 'had no counterpart elsewhere in western Europe'.[54] This may be true for the West, at least in terms of Christian/Muslim contact, but does not hold for the Latin

---

[52] For further analysis of this period of Iberian history see: R. Fletcher, 'Reconquest and crusade in Spain c. 1050–1150', *Transactions of the Royal Historical Society*, vol. 37 (1987), pp. 31–47; *Moorish Spain*, pp. 79–103; H. Kennedy, *Muslim Spain and Portugal: A Political History of al-Andalus* (London, 1997); D. W. Lomax, *The Reconquest of Spain* (London, 1978), pp. 49–67; J. F. O'Callaghan, *A History of Medieval Spain* (Ithaca, 1975); B. F. Reilly, *The Contest of Christian and Muslim Spain* (Oxford, 1992); D. Wasserstein, *The Rise and Fall of the Party-Kings. Politics and Society in Islamic Spain 1002–1086* (Princeton, 1985).

[53] D. W. Lomax, *The Reconquest of Spain* (London, 1978), pp. 52–5, 63–7.

[54] B. Reilly, *The Contest of Christian and Muslim Spain*, p. 58.

East because it is evident that both the nature of the Muslim weakness in the Levant and the Frankish method of exploitation have marked similarities with the world of the *Reconquista*.

By exploiting Muslim weakness and applying direct military pressure Antioch was rapidly able to establish its own system of regular tribute payments from Aleppo and Shaizar.[55] This process not only enriched the principality while weakening its neighbours' financial resources, but also created a relationship of interdependence, from which both sides could potentially benefit, and which culminated in instances of Latin/Muslim military co-operation. Thus, we can observe a Latin community which existed not in isolation, but in regular, if generally exploitative, contact with Islam.

Aleppo can serve as a case study for the development and impact of tribute links. The city was Antioch's closest Muslim neighbour, with only 90 km separating the two, and potentially its most dangerous enemy. The Muslim disunity of the early twelfth century often left Aleppo politically isolated from other powers in northern Syria, such as Shaizar and Damascus. After 1113 the city was further weakened by the series of succession crises which followed the death of Ridwan ibn Tutush.[56] The early princes of Antioch exploited and exacerbated this frailty by pursuing an aggressive policy of territorial expansion eastwards, towards Aleppo. From 1105 Aleppo began to sue for peace, perhaps confirming a five-year truce in return for a single tribute payment.[57] By 1111 a regular tribute payment to the principality of 20,000 dinars had been established.[58] When Roger of Salerno became prince of Antioch in 1113 one of his first actions was to renew this tribute relationship formally.[59]

The Latin/Muslim contact established by this process produced an atmosphere of interdependence. The first, and perhaps most striking, expression of this was the military co-operation between Antioch and Aleppo in 1108–9. The basic context of this collaboration was an inter-Latin dispute over possession of the county of Edessa. During the Latin defeat at Harran, mentioned above, Baldwin of Le Bourcq, count of Edessa and Joscelin of Courtenay, a major landholder in the county, had both been taken prisoner and they remained in captivity until

---

[55] In some sense the Latins were also following Byzantine precedent in this regard because the Greeks had in the early eleventh century extracted tribute payments from the Muslim powers of northern Syria. *A History of the Crusades*, vol. 1, p. 91.

[56] Kemal ed-Din, p. 602.

[57] Kemal ed-Din, pp. 596–7.

[58] Ibn al-Qalanisi, p. 106; Kemal ed-Din, p. 598; Ibn al-Athir, p. 298. Ibn al-Athir recorded a tribute of 32,000 pieces of gold.

[59] Ibn al-Qalanisi, p. 132.

1107–8.[60] During this period Tancred, ruler of Antioch, took control of Edessa and on Baldwin's release he proved reluctant to renounce his authority over the city. In 1108 Tancred met Baldwin in an inconclusive battle. In this conflict Aleppan troops fought alongside the principality's forces, while Baldwin had, through other means, also secured the assistance of Chavli, the Muslim ruler of Mosul, far to the East. The squabble over possession of Edessa was eventually resolved by negotiation.[61]

This was, however, not the end of hostilities or interdependence, as the forces of both Antioch and Edessa subsequently participated on different sides in a conflict between Ridwan of Aleppo and Chavli of Mosul. In 1109 relations between them had deteriorated to such an extent that the latter led a force to attack Aleppo. In the light of this threat, Ridwan appealed to Tancred for assistance, and Chavli, too, sought Baldwin's military support. Thus, in the resultant battle, the combined forces of Mosul and Edessa met an army, commanded by Tancred, which consisted of 1,500 Antiochene knights, 600 Aleppan horsemen and an unspecified number of infantry.[62]

Antioch and Aleppo joined forces again in 1115. At that point Il-ghazi of Mardin, and Tughtegin of Damascus, had seized temporary control of Aleppo, hoping to ensure that the city did not fall into the hands of the army sent by the sultan of Baghdad under the command of Bursuq of Hamadan.[63] They also decided to seek an alliance with Roger of Salerno.[64] In the early summer he advanced from Antioch to al-Atharib, where he was contacted by Il-ghazi and Tughtegin.[65] Initially, the Latins were alarmed by the gathering of these two Muslim rulers at Aleppo, and Roger actually left Antioch anticipating a military confrontation. Instead, he received an offer of a military alliance against Bursuq. The exact nature of this agreement, in terms of military commitment or numbers of troops, is not clear. At first Roger, Il-ghazi and Tughtegin appear to have all returned to keep watch from their respective cities, but later a contingent from Damascus and perhaps also Aleppo joined the Antiochene army for a short period.[66]

[60] Ralph of Caen, p. 710; Albert of Aachen, IX.39–41; Fulcher of Chartres, II.28, pp. 473–4; Matthew of Edessa, III.18, p. 193.
[61] Ibn al-Athir, pp. 262–3; Matthew of Edessa, III.39, p. 201; Albert of Aachen, X.38; Fulcher of Chartres, II.28, pp. 479–81.
[62] Ibn al-Athir, pp. 266–7.
[63] Ibn al-Athir, p. 296; Kemal ed-Din, p. 608.
[64] Tughtegin also established a treaty with King Baldwin I of Jerusalem. H. Dajani-Shakeel, 'Diplomatic relations between Muslim and Frankish ruler 1097–1153 A.D.', p. 205.
[65] Walter the Chancellor, I.2, p. 66.
[66] Walter the Chancellor, I.2, pp. 66–7; I.4, p. 70; Fulcher of Chartres, II.53, pp. 582–3; Matthew of Edessa, III.70, p. 219; Usamah ibn-Munqidh, p. 149.

Contemporary Latin writers based in the Levant often presented military alliances with Islam in a poor light. Fulcher of Chartres did his best to minimalise Baldwin of Le Bourcq's role in the 1108 pact with Chavli, transferring responsibility for the use of Muslim troops to Joscelin of Courtenay.[67] Fulcher probably decided to shield Baldwin from criticism because he was writing or revising his account during Baldwin's reign as king of Jerusalem. When describing the alliance between Antioch, Aleppo and Damascus in 1115 Walter the Chancellor noted that Tughtegin wished 'to be united with the Christians in a pretended peace, so that he might lead them to disaster',[68] and went on to comment that the pact later dissolved because God 'wished to break up the alliance of the devil with our people'.[69] These examples suggest that there was some tension between the reality of Near Eastern political and military affairs and the ideals espoused by contemporary writers.

Latin involvement in Aleppan affairs continued to increase in the years leading up to 1119. In this period the city had been reduced by internal factionalism to a position of perilous insecurity, and seemed ready to succumb to the constant threat of conquest by other Muslim powers. Antioch exploited this political turmoil by offering the prospect of alliance in return for ever more burdensome financial and territorial concessions, such as possession of al-Qubba, to the south of Aleppo, and the right to extract duty from those pilgrims who passed through the town on their way to Mecca.[70] In 1117 Roger intervened to protect Aleppo, which at this point was almost powerless to defend itself, and so prevented the ruler of Damascus from occupying the city.[71]

This level of dependence could easily have resulted in an actual Frankish occupation of Aleppo, which would have secured Latin domination of northern Syria. In 1119, however, the Muslim ruler of Mardin, Il-ghazi, took control of Aleppo and rejected the policy of alliance with Antioch, deciding instead to embark upon an aggressive military campaign against the principality. This culminated in the disastrous Antiochene defeat at the Field of Blood.[72] For over a decade, however, Antioch had benefited both financially and strategically from the establishment of tributes and alliances with Aleppo, coming desperately close to controlling the city in much the same way as military dependence and *parias* payments had led to the fall of Toledo in the

---

[67] Fulcher of Chartres, II.28, pp. 479–81.
[68] Walter the Chancellor, 1.2, pp. 66–7.
[69] Walter the Chancellor, 1.4, p. 70.
[70] Ibn al-Qalanisi, p. 156; Kemal ed-Din, p. 612.
[71] Kemal ed-Din, p. 613.
[72] T. S. Asbridge, 'The significance and causes of the battle of the Field of Blood', pp. 301–16.

eleventh century. In Iberia this Christian advance was followed by the advent of the Almoravids, a fundamentalist Muslim sect from North Africa, who reinvigorated *al-Andalus*.[73] In northern Syria Il-ghazi renewed resistance to the Latins before Aleppo fell and the initial cycle of exploitation and interdependence was broken.

In 1111 Antioch also established a system of regular tribute payments of 10,000 dinars from the Banu-Munqidh of Shaizar, to the south.[74] Indeed, Walter the Chancellor described the city as a 'tributary' which 'served our men'.[75] This represents the only contemporary Latin acknowledgement that northern Syrian Muslims paid tribute to the Franks. A period of particularly close co-operation with Shaizar can be observed in the 1120s. At this point it was the Latins' turn to be on the back foot. With the death of Roger in 1119 the principality was thrown into a succession crisis. It was left to King Baldwin II of Jerusalem to act as regent until 1126, but Latin prospects briefly deteriorated even further when he, too, was taken captive in June 1123 and ended up as a prisoner of the new ruler of Aleppo, Timurtash. The importance of Antioch's tribute relationship with Shaizar came to the fore in the attempts to secure Baldwin's release from captivity.

The local Muslim writer, Usamah ibn-Munqidh, recorded that Shaizar played an important role in these events, noting that the king was brought to the city so that the Munqidh 'might act as an intermediary in determining the price of his ransom'.[76] Another Arabic source recorded that the emir of Shaizar acted as the mediator between Baldwin and his captor, Timurtash, during this arbitration. The emir even went so far as to send hostages of his own to Aleppo so that the king could be moved to Shaizar. Baldwin remained there for some time, while arrangements were made for Latin hostages to be handed over to the Munqidh as guarantee of his promises to Timurtash, and an initial payment of 20,000 pieces of gold was made. Thus, when Baldwin was actually released on 30 August 1124, and immediately broke his agreement with Aleppo, an unusual situation existed, whereby Timurtash held Munqidh hostages in Aleppo, while Latin hostages were held at Shaizar. Neither of these groups were released before Baldwin led a campaign to attack Aleppo itself later that year.[77]

Usamah also recorded that around this time Baldwin released the Banu-Munqidh of Shaizar from the tribute owed to Antioch.[78] Why

[73] D. Lomax, *The Reconquest of Spain*, pp. 68–73.
[74] Ibn al-Qalanisi, p. 99; Ibn al-Athir, p. 279. Ibn al-Athir recorded that Shaizar's tribute was 4,000 pieces of gold.
[75] Walter the Chancellor, I.2, p. 67.
[76] Usamah ibn-Munqidh, p. 150.
[77] Kemal ed-Din, pp. 644–5.
[78] Usamah ibn-Munqidh, p. 150.

did the king and the emir of Shaizar co-operate in this way? Usamah, who recorded both events, does not enable us to provide a sure answer. Within his text he placed the involvement of the Banu-Munqidh in the negotiations of 1124 immediately before his report that Baldwin cancelled Shaizar's tribute. On this basis it might be assumed that the king exempted the Munqidhs from this payment out of gratitude for their help. The cancellation of this debt may even have been a precondition of the Banu-Munqidh involvement in 1124, a concession which they extracted from the king. Usamah certainly recorded that the Banu-Munqidh 'had him (Baldwin) under great obligation to them' because of the part they played in organising his release. This would explain both Baldwin's and the Banu-Munqidh's actions, although it must be noted that Shaizar may have also hoped to gain something from the assistance it provided to Timurtash of Aleppo. However, in a manner typical to the rather random nature of his work, Usamah confused the matter by suggesting that Baldwin actually cancelled Shaizar's tribute obligations when he first became regent of Antioch in 1119. If this were the case, what could Baldwin's motive have been? As king of Jerusalem and regent of Antioch, Baldwin's resources were severely stretched, in terms of time, money and manpower. He could not neglect northern Syria, but equally he could not fight on all fronts within the principality. The events of the 1120s seem to indicate that he decided to concentrate on the threat from Aleppo. This may have been the reason why he released Shaizar from its debt. Although he may have needed money, there was no guarantee that Shaizar would pay quickly. Improving relations with the Banu-Munqidh, however, would have helped to secure the principality's southern border, allowing Baldwin to deal with the eastern frontier. If this were the case, the king's cultivation of good relations with Shaizar demonstrated both a shrewd understanding of strategic necessity and an ability to manipulate events through diplomatic means. Usamah's confused account of events makes it impossible to affirm categorically what really occurred. There can, however, be no doubt that Baldwin did have a close relationship with Shaizar in the 1120s. Usamah noted that in this period the Banu-Munqidh 'became very influential in the affairs of Antioch'.[79]

Diplomatic relations with the Banu-Munqidh do not seem to have been too badly damaged by the king's duplicity over the terms of his release from captivity in 1124 because Usamah went on to record that when Bohemond II arrived at Antioch in 1126 to take up his inheritance, Baldwin 'was receiving an envoy' from Shaizar.[80] Bohemond died in

---

[79] Usamah ibn-Munqidh, p. 150.
[80] Usamah ibn-Munqidh, p. 150.

1130, perpetuating a further succession crisis, and very little is known of his rule.

Through an examination of tribute systems – one of the only visible modes of interaction, not wholly based on warfare – it is evident that close Latin/Muslim relations did develop in northern Syria during the first decades of Frankish settlement. This culminated in periods of military co-operation and political interdependence, entangling the principality and its Muslim neighbours in each other's affairs. This is not to suggest that Antioch sought long-term peace and co-operation with Islam. Threat and exploitation were still the driving forces behind the implementation and enforcement of tributes. Neither should we imagine that cross-cultural tribute payments were unusual in the overall picture of medieval Europe. In England, for example, Danegeld was used to combat the Danish threat. What is striking is that similar forms of contact could exist in such diverse settings and that even a Catholic community, recently established by a crusading army, interacted with the surrounding Muslim world.

As a postscript it is evident that over the next century Antioch continued to interact with the Islamic and Eastern Christian Levantine world. In the 1180s the Muslim Mansur b. Nabil was the *qadi* of Jabala, acting as chief administrator of the principality's Islamic population.[81] By this point, however, the balance of power had turned in favour of Islam, with the Muslim world united from the Nile to the Euphrates by Saladin. Latin Antioch managed to survive this period of Islamic resurgence at least in part because of its willingness to reach diplomatic accommodations with Saladin both before and after the fateful battle of Hattin.[82] Towards the end of the twelfth century Antioch also perpetuated increasingly close links with the Armenian Christian rulers of Cilicia, culminating in marriage alliances and the accession of the half-Latin, half-Armenian Prince Raymond-Roupen in 1216.[83]

During the first, formative decades of its existence the principality of Antioch established administrative frameworks and patterns of landholding which were influenced by Byzantine precedent and the presence of a predominantly non-Latin population. It also formed diplomatic links with the neighbouring Muslim powers of Aleppo and Shaizar. The principality certainly needs to be examined as a distinct entity rather than an aside to the history of the kingdom of Jerusalem. Antioch developed a potent landed aristocracy more rapidly than Jerusalem, incorporated Byzantine institutions into its local government which

---

[81] B. Z. Kedar, 'The subjected Muslims of the Frankish Levant', pp. 141–2.

[82] Ibn al-Athir, p. 662; M. C. Lyons and D. E. P. Jackson, *Saladin. The Politics of Holy War* (Cambridge, 1982), p. 202; p. 252; p. 362.

[83] C. Cahen, *La Syrie du Nord*, pp. 621–3.

cannot be found elsewhere in the Latin East and interacted and co-operated with Islam more actively than any of its Latin neighbours in this early period. If we can describe the principality as a 'crusader' community, one in which the ideals of Holy War continued to be espoused, then it stands, in comparison to Iberia, Sicily or the wider world of western Christendom, as a significant and distinctive example of the tensions between religious ideology and political reality. Even in the context of the Near East and in the shadow of the crusading movement this frontier community began to partially assimilate and co-operate with the Levantine world within a few years of its creation.

AT THE MARGIN OF COMMUNITY: GERMANS IN PRE-HUSSITE BOHEMIA*

By Leonard E. Scales

READ 26 SEPTEMBER 1998 AT THE INSTITUTE OF HISTORICAL RESEARCH, LONDON

ARGUABLY, the single most important dimension in the existence of any community, medieval or modern, is its members' shared conviction that it exists, and that its existence represents a significant bond between them. The central and later Middle Ages have been viewed as a period of particular importance for the growth of such self-consciousness – and for its growth, particularly among those large political communities which Susan Reynolds suggests we call 'regnal', and which many medievalists appear happy to refer to as 'national'.[1] As Reynolds showed, communities of this sort evolved legitimising mythologies which overlay existing structures of government with notions of ancient and primal ethnic solidarity, and thus placed such communities, imaginatively, outside the normal processes of contingency and change. Challenging questions therefore arise if we call to mind the many new political formations which were established during this period, which saw the extension into neighbouring regions, by both violent and peaceful means, of the political and social forms characteristic of continental western Europe. The new settlements had not only to be organised and defended physically, but also explained and justified. A vocabulary of argument thus evolved to account for their existence and to illuminate their relationships with existing political and social structures. In formulating this vocabulary, however, writers were confronted by the strong impulse in medieval thought to lay upon all significant communities a veneer of timelessness, or at least of antiquity. How this obstacle was overcome for particular new communities doubtless has many specific answers.[2] But an obstacle it must surely

*I am grateful to participants in the Royal Historical Society conference on 'Creating New Communities in the Middle Ages', to the Society's anonymous readers, and to Professor Robin Frame for helpful comments on earlier versions of this paper.

[1] S. Reynolds, *Kingdoms and Communities in Western Europe 900–1300* (2nd edn, Oxford, 1997), ch. 8, esp. p. 254.

[2] Some are indicated in R. Bartlett, *The Making of Europe. Conquest, Colonization and Cultural Change 950–1350* (London, 1993), ch. 4.

have been, and the study of how − or whether − it was surmounted in any given instance is thus inherently worth while.

To this may be added a second potential difficulty. For while medievalists have been happy to find a world of communities − indeed, of 'nations' − in pre-modern times, this view has in certain other quarters been categorically rejected. Benedict Anderson, in a famous book, argued that medieval people had neither the need to imagine large, secular political collectivities nor the social and conceptual means of doing so. Only with the decline of religion and the rise of 'print capitalism' did conceiving of discrete − 'national' − communities become both a possibility and a necessity.[3] Anderson's view is shared by a number of other prominent social theorists who have written on the subject of nation; but elsewhere it has found far from universal endorsement.[4] Medievalists, in particular, must feel that they have available more than adequate responses to so schematic an account of the pre-modern world: we need only peruse the sources, surely, to have weighty proofs that large political communities, communities with characteristics strikingly akin to the modern nation, were eminently imaginable in the Middle Ages; that they lay, indeed, at the unshakeable foundation of medieval views about social organisation.[5] However, as already indicated, one element in medieval thought about communities is the close relationship which it assumed between ethnic solidarities and claims on the one hand and established structures of law, government and power on the other. In modern societies this relationship appears a good deal less fixed. Despite the cogent criticisms which it has attracted, one potential advantage of the 'modernist' approach lies in the effort which its proponents make to explain this important difference, emphasising as they do the rich resources for communication, mobilisation and organisation which modern societies make available, and the diverse and socially penetrating 'imaginative' opportunities which result.[6]

[3] B. Anderson, *Imagined Communities. Reflections on the Origin and Spread of Nationalism* (London, 1983), esp. ch. 2.

[4] Important works broadly supportive of Anderson's distinction between pre-modern and modern societies include: J. Breuilly, *Nationalism and the State* (Manchester, 1982); E. Gellner, *Nations and Nationalism* (Oxford, 1983); E.J. Hobsbawm, *Nations and Nationalism since 1780: Programme, Myth, Reality* (Cambridge, 1990). There is further historiographical guidance in A.D. Smith, 'National identities: modern and medieval?', in *Concepts of Nationality in the Middle Ages*, ed. S. Forde, L. Johnson and A.V. Murray (Leeds, 1995), pp. 21–46. For Anderson's critics, see below, n. 103.

[5] Reynolds, *Kingdoms and Communities*, ch. 8; *idem*, 'Medieval *origines gentium* and the community of the realm', *History*, 68 (1983), pp. 375–90.

[6] Anderson, *Imagined Communities*, p. 40; Breuilly, *Nationalism and the State*, esp. Introduction; Gellner, *Nations and Nationalism*, esp. ch. 2; Hobsbawm, *Nations and Nationalism*, pp. 8–10.

These observations ought to have relevance for the medievalist also, and particularly for the student of new communities, since it is evident that not all the settler groups which found new homes during this period established clearly defined institutional forms. In investigating the self-consciousness of new political communities we must therefore consider not only the imaginative possibilities and constraints of medieval political culture but also the specific social and political characteristics of particular immigrant groups, and their material relationships with their new homelands. Where, we will want to know, did the frontiers of collective self-consciousness lie in the new, colonial communities of the central and later Middle Ages? How constrained, both by conceptual and material factors, were the imaginative resources of such communities? And how did the capacity of contemporaries to conceive of and describe them relate to the existence of established structures of power and authority?

The present paper endeavours to have these questions in mind in investigating the self-consciousness of one particular settler community: the German-speakers who between the twelfth and the fourteenth centuries established themselves in the lands of the Bohemian crown. For a study of the bounds of medieval collective imagination, the Bohemian Germans offer a peculiarly suggestive subject. Two observations come to mind at once: first, that in the organised large-scale immigration of the central Middle Ages lie the roots of a lasting German presence in Bohemia and Moravia; and, second, that the German population of the Bohemian lands has in the present century shown evidence of a powerful collective political consciousness.[7] While the situation of the Sudeten Germans in the recent past was naturally in important ways different from that of their medieval forebears (a fact which has not, however, inhibited both Czech and German commentators from treating the two groups as one),[8] the parallels are sufficient at least to stimulate fruitful reflection – especially in the light of the distinction drawn by Anderson and others between the imaginative capacities of pre-modern and modern political communities. Neither in medieval *nor* in modern times, it should be noted, have the Bohemian Germans existed within distinct political institutions of their own. That fact naturally adds special interest to any investigation of the role played by notions of solidarity, distinctiveness and allegiance among German-speakers in Bohemia during the thirteenth and fourteenth centuries,

---

[7] On the Sudeten German question: E. Wiskemann, *Czechs and Germans* (Oxford, 1938); J. W. Bruegel, *Czechoslovakia before Munich. The German Minority Problem and British Appeasement Policy* (Cambridge, 1973); F. Prinz, 'Vom ersten Weltkrieg bis zur gewaltsamen Beendigung der Zweivölkergemeinschaft am Ende des zweiten Weltkriegs (1914–1948)', in *Deutsche Geschichte im Osten Europas: Böhmen und Mähren*, ed. F. Prinz (Berlin, 1993).

[8] See below, p. 352.

since it promises comparisons, but perhaps also contrasts, with the conspicuous growth of such solidarities in the present century.

In none of the regions into which they penetrated did medieval settlers encounter only empty wilderness; everywhere there were human populations and social institutions already in existence, and in every case the newcomers had to position themselves imaginatively in relation to indigenous peoples and their forms of life. Their responses might be classified in terms of two very broad paths, each followed by some immigrant groups. One entailed the settlers attaching themselves to a pre-existing political community, and thereby to a degree re-making that community. The result was an appearance of substantial continuity and assimilation, but in all likelihood underlain by expansion or modification of previous political identities to accommodate the newcomers.[9] Alternatively, the immigrants might establish themselves as a separate community, either over or alongside the existing inhabitants. In this case, the experience of settlement could stimulate the growth, especially among the leaders of the settler group, of a sense of collective difference, distinguishing them not only from the indigenous population but also − and increasingly so with the passage of time − from the society they had left behind. In this way they might attain the status of a 'middle nation': aliens in the eyes of the natives and of observers in the homeland, and a distinct community in their own estimation.[10]

There are features of the German settlement of Bohemia which might have led the colonists to follow either of these routes. We must note first of all the sheer number of those who came. Nothing beyond the most approximate of estimates is possible, but a realistic figure may be around one in six for the German element in fourteenth-century Bohemia.[11] This is certainly low in comparison with neighbouring regions subject to German immigration, such as Upper Saxony, Lusatia, and Lower Silesia.[12] But it remains a substantial figure, especially in

---

[9] As an example, see A. Grant, 'Aspects of national consciousness in medieval Scotland', in *Nations, Nationalism and Patriotism in the European Past*, ed. C. Bjørn, A. Grant and K. Stringer (Copenhagen, 1994), pp. 68–95. An important instance from the sphere of German settlement is Silesia: T. Jurek, 'Die Entwicklung eines schlesischen Regionalbewußtseins im Mittelalter', *Zeitschrift für Ostmitteleuropa-Forschung*, 47 (1998).

[10] A celebrated example is provided by the English in medieval Ireland. See J. Lydon, 'The middle nation', in *The English in Medieval Ireland* (Dublin, 1984), pp. 1–26; R. Frame, ' "Les Engleys nées en Irlande": the English political identity in medieval Ireland', *Transactions of the Royal Historical Society*, 6th series, 3 (1993). In east-central Europe the regions subject to German crusading saw community-making of this sort. For settler self-consciousness, see P Görlich, *Zur Frage des Nationalbewußtseins in ostdeutschen Quellen des 12. bis 14. Jahrhunderts* (Marbur (Lahn), 1964). For a comparative discussion of settler identities, see Bartlett, *Making of Europe*, ch. 9.

[11] P. Moraw, 'Das Mittelalter', in *Böhmen und Mähren*, ed. Prinz, p. 91.

[12] For the settlement of these regions, see C. Higounet, *Die deutsche Ostsiedlung im Mittelalter* (Munich, 1990), pp. 108–39, 172–89.

the light of the large extent of the Bohemian crown lands, which may at this time have had a total population of around 1.5 million.[13] Most of the newcomers were agriculturalists, and many were engaged in cutting new settlements out of the forest, with the result that areas of concentrated German habitation, and numerous new villages with wholly German populations, were soon a feature of the rural landscape of Bohemia and Moravia.[14] None the less, most of the immigrants would have had Czechs as fairly close neighbours, while others were deliberately settled in the midst of established Czech populations.[15]

More striking is the dominance which German-speakers gained at the focal points of social power in Bohemia. In the higher reaches of the church they had long been conspicuous. Their presence was especially ubiquitous in the religious orders, which represent one of the most important among several channels connecting the Bohemian lands directly to the German world.[16] It was not just that Bohemian monastic houses were themselves filled mostly with German-speaking monks; they were commonly offshoots of older communities on the German side of the frontier, and were thus bound in enduring institutional relationships to the neighbouring German lands. In the towns, the growth of which was such a conspicuous feature of the thirteenth and fourteenth centuries, German-speakers long constituted not only the greater part of the population numerically but, still more clearly, the predominant element in terms of wealth, power and status.[17] The most substantial townsmen were able to acquire rural land and over time to attain a position comparable to the indigenous lower nobility.[18] The thoroughly German tone of urban life in thirteenth- and fourteenth-

---

[13] Moraw, 'Das Mittelalter', p. 91. Moraw points out that the figure assumes population densities per km² comparable with Germany, and may be too high.

[14] K. Richter, 'Die böhmischen Länder im Früh- und Hochmittelalter', in *Handbuch der Geschichte der böhmischen Länder*, 1, ed. K. Bosl (Stuttgart, 1967), pp. 336–47; Moraw, 'Das Mittelalter', pp. 76–92. Older literature is reviewed in F. Graus, 'Die Problematik der deutschen Ostsiedlung aus tschechischer Sicht', in *Die deutsche Ostsiedlung des Mittelalters als Problem der europäischen Geschichte*, ed. W. Schlesinger (Vorträge und Forschungen, 18, Sigmaringen, 1975), pp. 31–75.

[15] Moraw, 'Das Mittelalter', p. 90.

[16] Richter, 'Die böhmischen Länder', pp. 293–300; Moraw, 'Das Mittelalter', pp. 102–9.

[17] Richter, 'Die böhmischen Länder', pp. 323–31; Moraw, 'Das Mittelalter', pp. 59–75; F. Kavka, 'Die Städte Böhmens und Mährens zur Zeit des Přemysliden-Staates', in *Die Städte Mitteleuropas im 12. und 13. Jahrhundert*, ed. W. Rausch (Linz, 1963), pp. 137–53; J. Kejř, 'Die Anfänge der Stadtverfassung und des Stadtrechts in den böhmischen Ländern', in *Die deutsche Ostsiedlung*, ed. Schlesinger, pp. 439–70. For (controversial) estimates of the German element in urban populations during this period, see E. Schwarz, 'Die nationale Zusammensetzung verschiedener Städte in Böhmen und Mähren-Schlesien in vorhussitischer Zeit', in *Sudetendeutscher Atlas*, ed. E. Meynen (Munich, 1955), pp. 15–16.

[18] Moraw, 'Das Mittelalter', p. 72.

century Bohemia is attested not only by the several varieties of town law but also by the early application of the German vernacular in written records.[19] Here, then are elements which might have contributed to a notion of German distinctiveness within the Bohemian kingdom. We can add to them a further potential stimulus, in the hostility which members of native society occasionally directed at socially prominent groups among the settlers. By the fifteenth century the university of Prague had become a particular focus for such tensions; but it is possible to trace an earlier history of periodic conflict, concentrated in those areas where Germans were socially dominant – in the church and in the towns, as well as at the royal court.[20] Precisely this kind of experience may be expected to have stimulated among leading German-speakers a sense of significant things shared, and of common interests to be defended. Yet the elements of conflict surrounding the German presence should certainly not be exaggerated. It is important to remember also that the settlers had entered the kingdom at the invitation and under the protection of native princes, with the Bohemian royal dynasty prominent among them.[21] Despite the violent language which in modern times has been woven around their presence, the settlement of German-speakers in Bohemia was – in stark contrast to many colonising ventures of the period – a peaceful and lawful movement, the major impetus for which came from within the kingdom itself. The overwhelming

---

[19] Ibid., p. 99.

[20] For conflicts at the university, see F. Smahel, 'The idea of the "nation" in Hussite Bohemia', *Historica*, 16 (1969), pp. 163–71; R. Schmidt, 'Die Prager Universitäts-Nationen bis zum Kuttenberger Dekret von 1409 und die Anfänge "nationaler" Gedanken im Königreich Böhmen', in *Deutsche in den böhmischen Ländern*, ed. R. Rothe (Cologne, 1992), pp. 47–65. For tensions in the church, see Bishop John of Prague's establishment, in 1333, of an Augustinian convent in Roudnice, to which only Czechs were admitted: *Regesta Diplomatica nec non Epistolaria Bohemiae et Moraviae*, 3 (1311–33), ed. J. Emler (Prague, 1890), no. 2008, pp. 781–2; for towns, see Charles IV's 1356 settlement of relations between Czechs and Germans in Beroun: ibid., 6 (1355–63), ed. B. Mendl (Prague, 1929), no. 417, pp. 229–30; for the court, see below, p. 000. And see also F. Graus, *Die Nationenbildung der Westslawen im Mittelalter* (Sigmaringen, 1980), pp. 89–116; idem, Die Bildung eines Nationalbewußtseins im mittelalterlichen Böhmen. Die vorhussitische Zeit', *Historica*, 13 (1966), esp. pp. 26–49; R. C. Schwinges, ' "Primäre" und "sekundäre" Nation. Nationalbewußtsein und sozialer Wandel im mittelalterlichen Böhmen', in *Europa slavica – Europa orientalis. Fetschrift für Herbert Ludat zum 70. Geburtstag* (Berlin, 1980), pp. 490–532. For general orientation on Czech and German identities and tensions, see, in addition to the items cited elsewhere, E. Maschke, *Das Erwachen des Nationalbewußtseins im Deutsch-Slavischen Grenzraum* (Leipzig, 1933). The scholarship touching on identities among the Germans is overwhelmingly in German; but see also in Czech: Z. Uhlíř, 'Národnostní proměny 13. století a český nacionalismus', *Folia historica Bohemica*, 12 (1988), 143–70.

[21] Richter, 'Die böhmischen Länder', pp. 323–31, 336–47. For the important reign of Otakar II, see J. K. Hoensch, *Přemysl Otakar II. von Böhmen* (Graz, Vienna, Cologne, 1989), pp. 89–108.

majority of settlers enjoyed a secure, indeed a privileged, legal standing: there is no doubt that, viewed constitutionally, they were full members of a single Bohemian community under a single prince.[22] They were subjects of the monarch like other Bohemians, and if the rhetoric of official documents can be taken seriously, their arrival was held to glorify the king by increasing the number of those giving him their allegiance.[23] It appears, in short, quite reasonable to suppose that the settlers might have followed a path not of forging a separate idea of solidarity but of lending their support to a larger notion of 'Bohemian' community focused on the monarchy, upon which to a significant degree their welfare depended.

At the royal court in Prague, moreover, newcomers from the west ought to have felt fully at home. The ties, both constitutional and dynastic, which the Bohemian monarchy maintained with western, and particularly with German- speaking, Europe, were old-established.[24] The rulers of Bohemia were princes of the western Empire, hereditary imperial cupbearers since the early twelfth century, confirmed as members of the college of imperial (or, as contemporaries habitually called them, 'German') electors from the later thirteenth.[25] The Přemyslids, who ruled to 1306, although a native Czech dynasty with deep roots in Bohemian history and myth, also had strong bonds with the German world: marriages to no fewer than nineteen German princesses can be counted in the course of the dynasty's history.[26] The accession, in 1310, of King John, of the family of the counts of Luxemburg, strengthened further the connection with western Europe, and particularly with the Empire, since John's father was the king and soon-to-be emperor Henry VII.[27] The association between the imperial and Bohemian monarchies, anticipated in John, was realised under his son

---

[22] For the legal status of the settlers, see Graus, 'Problematik', pp. 55–62.

[23] *Reg. Dip. Bohemiae*, 2 (1253–1310), ed. J. Emler (Prague, 1882), no. 499, p. 191 (Otakar II to new town of Polička, 1265).

[24] A note of the kings of thirteenth- and fourteenth-century Bohemia may be helpful here, They are as follows: Přemysl Otakar I (1198/1205–30); Wenceslas I (1230–53); Přemysl Otakar II (1253–78); Wenceslas II (1278–1305); Wenceslas III (1305–6); Rudolf I of Habsburg (1306–7); Henry of Carinthia (1307–10); John of Luxemburg (1310–46); Charles I (IV) (1346–78); Wenceslas IV (1378–1419).

[25] Richter, 'Die böhmischen Länder', pp. 300–5; K. Zeumer, 'Die böhmische und die bayerische Kur im 13. Jahdhundert', *Historische Zeitschrift*, 94 (1905). For the king of Bohemia's primacy among the temporal electors: *Die Goldene Bulle Kaiser Karls IV. vom Jahre 1356: Text*, ed. W. D. Fritz (MGH Fontes iuris Germanici antiqui in usus scholarum, Weimar, 1972), p. 58.

[26] T. Mayer, 'Aufgaben der Siedlungsgeschichtein den Sudetenländern', in T. Mayer, *Mittelalterliche Studien* (Sigmaringen, 1959), p. 430. See also the genealogies in *Handbuch der Geschichte der böhmischen Länder*, ed. K. Bosl, pp. 570–2.

[27] For Henry VII, see H. Thomas, *Deutsche Geschichte des Spätmittelalters 1250–1500* (Stuttgart, Berlin, Cologne, Mainz, 1983), ch. 5.

Charles, who, as the emperor Charles IV, was the first ruler to wear both crowns.[28] Under Charles's patronage Prague flourished as a centre not only of Bohemian, but of imperial rulership, magnificence and *Staatssymbolik*.[29] The personal union of the crowns continued under Charles's son Wenceslas, and both father and son made marriages – just as had their Přemyslid forebears – with German and imperial princesses.[30] The later Přemyslids and the early Luxemburgs were alike in pursuing ambitious policies of territorial acquisition calculated to link the Bohemian lands up with major territorial complexes in German-speaking Europe. Otakar II exercised a short-lived but historically significant rule over the Austrian duchies, while Charles incorporated Bohemia and Moravia into a great dynastic patrimony embracing Brandenburg, Lusatia, Silesia and the Bavarian Upper Palatinate.[31]

It is therefore no surprise that the German language and German aristocratic culture were prominent at court under both the later Přemyslid and early Luxemburg kings. For a time in the second half of the thirteenth century Prague was the most important place in Europe for the composition of aristocratic literature in German.[32] Otakar II's death was lamented by German versifiers outside Bohemia as well as within; and Wenceslas II was a significant German lyric poet in his own right.[33] German literature – especially on religious and devotional themes – was scarcely less important at the magnificent court of Charles of Luxemburg.[34] And given our concern here with the capacity of communities, both settler and indigenous, to (re-) make themselves in response to immigration movements, it is illuminating to observe how the German aristocratic style on display at Prague found a sympathetic reception among elements in native society also. For during the thirteenth century the Bohemian high nobility began to

[28] See F. Seibt, *Karl IV.: ein Kaiser in Europa 1346 bis 1378* (Munich, 1978).

[29] Ibid., esp. pp. 175–9.

[30] *Handbuch*, ed. Bosl, p. 571, for genealogy. In addition to the Wittelsbach Anna of the Palatinate Charles took Pomeranian and Silesian (and French) brides; Wenceslas's two consorts were Wittelsbachs.

[31] On Otakar: Hoensch, *Přemysl Otakar II.*, esp. pp. 38–48; on Charles: Seibt, *Karl IV.*, ch. 7.

[32] H. J. Behr, *Literatur als Machtlegitimation Studien zur Funktion der deutschsprachigen Dichtung am böhmischen Königshof des 13. Jahrhunderts* (Munich, 1987).

[33] On Otakar, see the anonymous German verses incorporated into the Dominican chronicle from Colmar in Alsace: *Chronicon Colmariense*, ed. P. Jaffé (MGH Scriptores, 17, Hanover, 1861), pp. 251–2; on Wenceslas, see Behr, *Literatur als Machtlegitimation*, pp. 239–48.

[34] See, generally, J. Maček, 'Die Hofkultur Karls IV.', in *Kaiser Karl IV. Staatsmann und Mäzen*, ed. F. Seibt (Munich, 1978), pp. 237–41. For two prominent figures: K. Stackmann, 'Heinrich von Mügeln', in *Die deutsche Literatur des Mittelalters: Verfasserlexikon*, ed. K. Ruh et al., 3 (Berlin, New York, 1981), cols 815–27; W. Höver, 'Johann von Neumarkt', in ibid., 4 (1983), cols 686–95.

build their castles in the German style, to derive from them self-consciously Germanised names for their dynasties, and to imitate the festivities, tournaments, modes of dress and literary patronage of the royal court.[35]

The object of common belonging which is most clearly advanced in Bohemian German writings is a notion of Bohemia as a single illustrious political community under great and noble rulers. The first emphasis here is characteristically on the royal dynasty itself, which through its excellent qualities ennobles the Bohemian lands and unites in common benefit the monarch's fortunate subjects. This mode of thought is well represented by the poet Ulrich von Etzenbach in his verse romance *Wilhelm von Wenden*, which dates from the reign of Wenceslas II, and has as a major object the glorification of Wenceslas and his queen.[36] At one point, in the course of praising the royal couple, Ulrich offers an 'etymology' of the name Bohemia (*Bêheim*), which he claims is an amalgam of the Latin *beatus* and the German *heim*, and thus means 'blessed house' or 'blessed land' − 'blessed', of course, in standing under the rule of such illustrious princes.[37] While this must be read as calculated flattery, it does at least suggest that some Germans were disposed to view the Bohemian realm, under its established rulers, as a community with which they could identify and a worthy object of their affections. In his earlier verse epic, *Alexander*, Ulrich explained why he once turned down a chance to serve the archbishop of Salzburg: he had not wished to leave the land of 'the (Bohemian) lion', in which he had been born.[38]

These same points of emphasis are developed at much greater length and more explicitly in the Latin chronicle from the Cistercian monastery of Königsaal (Aula regia) near Prague.[39] This recounts Bohemian and imperial history in the turbulent and, for German-speakers, important period between the reign of Otakar II and the later years of John of Luxemburg. The abbey of Königsaal had been founded on the site of a royal hunting lodge by Wenceslas II, who intended it to serve as a dynastic mausoleum and cult centre.[40] Its German abbots enjoyed a closeness to the king and to royal government exceptional even in

---

[35] Richter, 'Die böhmischen Länder', pp. 297–8; Moraw, 'Das Mittelalter', pp. 110–11.

[36] Ulrich von Etzenbach, *Wilhelm von Wenden*, ed. H.-F. Rosenfeld (Deutsche Texte des Mittelalters, Berlin, 1957).

[37] Ibid., vv. 4696–4707, p. 94.

[38] Ulrich von Eschenbach [*sic*], *Alexander*, ed. W. Toischer (Bibliothek des litterarischen Vereins in Stuttgart, Tübingen, 1888), vv. 27625–8, p. 734.

[39] *Die Königsaaler Geschichts-Quellen mit den Zusätzen und der Fortsetzung des Domherrn Franz von Prag*, ed. J. Loserth (Fontes rerum Austriacarum: Oesterreichische Geschichtsquellen, I Abtheilung, 8, Vienna, 1875).

[40] P. Hilsch, 'Königsaal', in *Lexikon des Mittelalters*, 5 (1991), col. 1325; Richter, 'Die böhmischen Länder', p. 295; Moraw, 'Das Mittelalter', pp. 106–8.

Cistercian circles: in 1310 Abbot Conrad of Königsaal took an instrumental part in bringing John of Luxemburg to Bohemia as king.[41] It is
therefore no surprise that the Königsaal chronicle concentrates on the
glorification of the Bohemian monarchy and of individual rulers –
John's father, Henry VII, his Přemyslid consort, Elizabeth; but above
all the abbey's founder, Wenceslas II.[42] The chronicle, which is in fact
a composite of several pieces, was begun by Otto, Königsaal's second
abbot. However, easily the greater part is the work of Peter of Zittau,
who served as chaplain to Abbot Conrad before going on, in 1316, to
become abbot himself.[43] If we are to find anywhere a resolution of
German and Bohemian identities we will find it in the articulate and,
in general, clear-sighted writings of Peter of Zittau. And such a
resolution, with its focus naturally in the monarchy, is seemingly what
we do find.

Zittau lay just inside the Bohemian frontier in the extreme north of
the kingdom, making Peter by birth a Bohemian, and the abbot
explicitly names himself as such.[44] Nor does he only recognise a
Bohemian political allegiance, but signals a higher level of association:
the Bohemians are his own people, his *gens*.[45] Here, it appears, we find
'kingdom and community' standing in exactly the relationship familiar
from other areas of western Europe: the community of the realm has,
imaginatively as well as constitutionally, absorbed and made a Bohemian
of the German-speaking monk, and was presumably capable of assimi-
lating other Germans in the same fashion.[46] Peter not only saw himself
as Bohemian but identified sympathetically with a single Bohemian
community. He thus tells how, in the deliberations preceding Henry
VII's decision to marry his son to the Přemyslid heiress, Henry's
counsellors had urged the king against the union, branding the Bohemians as regicides.[47] Henry is portrayed responding, to Peter's evident
satisfaction, with an allusion to the comparably violent character of
recent German politics, claiming that it was in fact Germans, not
Bohemians, who were historically responsible for the violent deaths of

[41] Richter, 'Die böhmischen Länder, p. 359.
[42] For the chronicle's treatment of Henry VII, see M. E. Franke, *Kaiser Henrich VII. im
Spiegel der Historiographie. Eine faktenkritische und quellenkundliche Untersuchung ausgewählter
Geschichtsschreiber der ersten Hälfte des 14. Jahrhunderts* (Cologne, Weimar, Vienna, 1992), pp.
202–23. The presentation of Wenceslas II recalls the picture of Louis IX of France
presented in contemporary French royalist historiography: ibid., p. 217.
[43] On Peter, see J. Loserth, 'Peter von Zittau', in *Allgemeine Deutsche Biographie*, 25
(Leipzig, 1887), pp. 476–8; and the biographical note by B. Pabst in *Lexikon des Mittelalters*,
6 (1993), col. 1940.
[44] *Königsaaler Geschichts-Quellen*, p. 177.
[45] Ibid., p. 50.
[46] Reynolds, *Kingdoms and Communities*, pp. 330–1.
[47] *Königsaaler Geschichts-Quellen*, p. 266.

Bohemian rulers, but clinching his argument with the observation that no entire people (*gens*) should be tarred with the crimes of its individual members.[48] Regnal solidarity, moreover, overrode for Peter the appeal of ethnic affinity: German princes from beyond the frontier who aspired to interfere in Bohemian affairs were unwelcome aliens, and the Bohemians were right to oppose them. He thus speaks with understanding of Bohemian resistance to the harsh regency government which the margrave of Brandenburg had sought to impose on the kingdom following Otakar II's death, observing that no one willingly takes commands from strangers.[49] Peter's basic assumptions seem to resemble those expressed in the great confirmation of privileges which John of Luxemburg issued to his new subjects in 1310.[50] There, the language of inclusion and exclusion has reference entirely to the Bohemian kingdom, and nowhere explicitly to notions of ethnicity: the principle of division is between natives – those born within the realm – on the one hand, and foreigners – those born outside – on the other.[51]

Yet to read the Königsaal chronicle more closely is to become aware that the absorption of the 'German' within the 'Bohemian' is less straightforward or complete than at first appears. It is while praising Queen Guta's concern for doing justice to all her subjects that the chronicle reveals most starkly the divisions which lay embedded within the regnal community. The Czechs (*Bohemi*), we learn, have maintained ancient quarrels (*rixae veteres*) against the German population (*Theutonici*).[52] The two groups, it is made clear, are ethnically distinct and naturally antagonistic: they are 'discordant peoples' (*gentes discordes*).[53] A number of things must strike us at once. First, political allegiance has not fully dissolved ethnic affinity after all; habitation of the same land and subjection to the same monarch were in Peter's day still not powerful enough fully to merge natives and settlers into a single *gens*. 'Kingdom and community' form no perfect mirror-image. Second, the material measure of ethnicity is language: *gens* and *linguagium* are here used interchangeably. The idea that command of the Czech ('Bohemian') language was a fundamental element in being Bohemian is not uncommon in writings relating to the Bohemian lands;[54] to cite just one,

[48] Ibid., p. 267.

[49] Ibid., pp. 53–4. Cf. p. 123 with an account of Austrian resentment at the government of Albert of Habsburg's Swabians.

[50] *Reg. Dip. Bohemiae, 2, no. 2245, pp. 973–5.*

[51] Natives: *regnicolae, terrigenae, Boemi vel Moravi*; foreigners: *alienigenae, extranei*.

[52] *Königsaaler Geschichts-Quellen*, p. 69.

[53] Ibid., p. 72.

[54] Graus, *Nationenbildung*, pp. 174, 177, 179, for several examples. A particularly explicit instance is to be found in Bishop John of Prague's 1333 charter for his Augustinian foundation at Roudnice: any candidate admitted had to be 'Bohemus de vtroque parente idiomatis bohemice' (*Reg. Dip. Bohemiae*, 3, no. 2008, p. 782).

celebrated example, the emperor Charles IV – who as the son of a Přemyslid mother had a fundamental claim to be considered a *Bohemus* – recalled in his Autobiography how, returning to Bohemia as a young man, he re-learned the Czech of his childhood until he spoke it 'like another Bohemian'.[55] Third, the language of ethnicity does not merely contradict that of political allegiance, but threatens actually to undermine it. How can the German settlers enjoy as direct a relationship with the Bohemian political community as does the indigenous population when in certain basic contexts they cannot be named as 'Bohemians' at all? The language of ethnicity inevitably relocates the Germans at the margin of community, leaving their position ambiguous, unresolved. And, conversely, however keen Peter of Zittau's own awareness of the distinction between Bohemian and non-Bohemian Germans may have been, he had no language that would distinguish them; when he comes to discuss fractures rather than bonds within Bohemian society all Germans, indigenous and alien alike, merge as *Theutonici*.

Peter's difficulties were compounded by the fact that he was not merely an observer of these divisions, but was himself caught up in them. It is not simply that he naturally took sides with the German element in the population, though he unmistakably did so: it was the 'Bohemians', Peter says, who maintained quarrels against 'the Germans'; the latter people, by contrast, were 'lovers of peace and quiet'.[56] But the hindrances to his articulation of any notion of Bohemian German community were of a different and more fundamental kind. They can be illustrated by his treatment of the subject of warfare. More than once the Königsaal chronicle condemns the wanton plunder to which Bohemian armies inclined, observing at one point that such behaviour is an evil habit characteristic of 'our people' (*gens nostra*).[57] Nor, it seems, did Peter rate very highly the fighting abilities of his fellow-Bohemians, since he records the lucky escape which he claims *nos Bohemi* enjoyed when the German army of Albert of Habsburg, which had in 1304 invaded the kingdom, withdrew without giving battle.[58] In marked contrast to this rather dismal appraisal of native performance are the praises which Peter devotes to the might, the spirit, and the achievements of German armies – not only those engaged in Bohemia, but also Henry VII's forces in Italy.[59] Much of this can be explained in terms of Peter's particular anxieties and motives. Doubtless

---

[55] *Vita Karoli Quarti: Karl IV. Selbstbiographie* (no editor, Hanau, 1979), pp. 68–70: 'ut alter Boemus'.

[56] *Königsaaler Geschichts-Quellen*, p. 69.

[57] Ibid., p. 50.

[58] Ibid., p. 177.

[59] Ibid., pp. 304–5 (John of Luxemburg's entry into Bohemia), 338–43 (Henry VII in ·aly), 347–9 (Henry's army in Rome).

the armies which came together under the Bohemian nobility really were at times ill-disciplined and destructive; and the peculiar vulnerability of great monastic foundations made men such as Peter acutely sensitive to the harm which marauding soldiery could do. His pointed celebration of German arms is likewise explicable, in terms of his concern to legitimise the Luxemburg dynasty through a record of the achievements of the new king and his illustrious father.[60] However, no explanation would be complete which overlooked the literary debt which Peter here attests; for both of these themes – the cruel, chaotic but ultimately unwarlike Bohemians and the militarily incomparable Germans – had roots in a repertoire of ethnic stereotype and self-justification which was by this time well established in German writings.[61] The German account of Bohemian shortcomings conforms closely to the list of stock inadequacies which in this period was often ascribed to peoples geographically at the edge of western European society, in the British Isles, for example, and in other regions of east-central Europe.[62] The Germans' celebration of their own supposedly innate bellicosity also had a context of its own, in arguments justifying German possession of the imperial title – an honour which, it was felt, only a race of military strongmen could bear convincingly.[63]

As a Bohemian German Peter could deploy both *Bohemus* and *Theutonicus* in his writing. Yet the two terms were in themselves inadequate either for marking out a distinct community of Bohemian Germans or for ascribing to the German settlers a stable place within a Bohemian community. They were inadequate precisely because by the time the German settlers set foot on Bohemian soil both names had long been far more than mere labels: they were nodal points in matrices of ideas, arguments and claims. The nature of these varied depending on the cultural and literary traditions to which a particular writer was heir. The authors of the Königsaal chronicle worked in a German tradition, and this posed a double problem, offering a notion of Germanness, which found its richest meanings in contexts of imperial rulership, and a view of 'the Bohemians' which assumed a people both distinct from and culturally firmly subordinate to the Germans. Neither

---

[60] For Henry VII: Franke, *Kaiser Heinrich VII.*, pp. 202–23.

[61] On this subject, see, generally, H. Walther, 'Scherz und Ernst in der Völker- und Stämme-Charakteristik mittellateinischer Verse', *Archiv für Kulturgeschichte*, 41 (1959); L. Schmugge, 'Über "nationale" Vorurteile im Mittelalter', *Deutsches Archiv für Erforschung des Mittelalters*, 38 (1982); H. Zatscek, *Das Volksbewußtsein. Sein Werden im Spiegel der Geschichtsschreibung* (Brünn, Prague, Leipzig, Vienna, 1936).

[62] Bartlett, *Making of Europe*, ch. 9; idem, *Gerald of Wales 1146–1223* (Oxford, 1982), ch. 6. For accusations of cruelty and cowardice directed at the Poles, see Görlich, *Zur Frage des Nationalbewußtseins*, pp. 148, 200.

[63] For the Germans and war: E. Dümmler, 'Über den furor Teutonicus', *Sitzungsberichte der königlich Preussischen Akademie der Wissenschaften zu Berlin* (phil.-hist. Klasse), 9 (1897).

of these outlooks was of any help to a German-speaker who wished also to be a loyal and patriotic Bohemian. For it was clearly no part of Peter of Zittau's purpose to place the *Theutonici* as a whole above the *Bohemi*: he associates himself with Bohemian weakness in arms and accepts the shameful excesses of Bohemian soldiers as those of his own *gens*.[64] But notions of community, once formed, could not cross frontiers and settle strange soils as readily as could the human beings who made them.

When the German immigrants came to Bohemia institutionalised political communities already existed culminating respectively in the Bohemian and German (i.e. imperial) monarchs. Each of these was assimilated to medieval assumptions about the relationship between government and ethnicity: each was held to be the political mani-festation of a quite separate and primal ethnic association. We can test the point by asking how the Bohemian Germans looked from the other side of the frontier. What we find is that, on a conceptual level, they appear to have been almost wholly invisible to other German-speakers of the time. Bohemia was a place apart from 'Germany', and the Bohemians a people apart. Political geography meant the spaces inhabited by distinct ethnic groupings: the publicist Alexander of Roes, writing in 1288, noted how the regions of German settlement were in the east separated by forests from the 'Slavs, Bohemians and Hun-garians'.[65] A mode of thinking which expected power to shadow ethnicity tended to blot out elements of ethnic complexity in political affairs. German accounts of the battle of Dürnkrut, at which Otakar II lost his life, commonly depict it as a clash of Bohemian and German (imperial) armies; yet Otakar's ranks had included the margraves of Meißen and Brandenburg, the landgrave of Thuringia, and contingents from his Austrian lands, as well as Polish and Silesian princes.[66] The fact that large numbers of German-speakers dwelt in the lands of the Bohemian crown is scarcely even hinted at by German writers; even Austrian chroniclers, who might be expected to know that Bohemia was ethnically mixed, are silent on the matter. A rare exception is the striking, if wildly inaccurate, claim made by the Strasbourg chronicler Jakob Twinger that Charles IV so much extended the use of German in Bohemia that it became the most widely spoken language both in

[64] *Königsaaler Geschichts-Quellen*, p. 50.

[65] Alexander of Roes, *Noticia seculi*, ed. H. Grundmann, H. Heimpel (MGH Staats-schriften des späteren Mittelalters, 1.i, Stuttgart, 1958), ch. 9, p. 156.

[66] For the representation of this battle in German sources, see F. Graus, 'Přemysl Otakar II. Sein Ruhm und sein Nachleben', *Mitteilungen des Instituts für österreichische Geschichtsforschung*, 79 (1971), pp. 57–110; F. Seibt, 'Die böhmische Nachbarschaft in der österreichische Historiographie des 13. und 14. Jahrhundnerts', in F. Seibt, *Mittelalter und Gegenwart, Ausgewählte Aufsätze* (Sigmaringen, 1987), pp. 171–96.

Prague and throughout the land, where formerly only Czech (*behemesch*) had been spoken.[67] Yet the overwhelming consensus is that 'Germany' and 'Bohemia' were distinct political communities, resting on fundamental ethnic differences. *Bohemus*, in German writings, means 'Czech'. The 'Bohemians' spoke a different language from the Germans, and had their own distinct character.[68] Their relation to the Germans, indeed, was one not merely of distinction but of polarity and natural enmity: the 'Styrian Rhyming Chronicle', composed in a region close to Bohemia early in the fourteenth century, not only recites, in a sharper form than did Peter of Zittau, the German commonplace that Bohemians had little stomach for fighting, but registers also the 'deceit, envy and hatred' which the chronicler claims characterises Bohemian attitudes to their German neighbours.[69]

Even the Königsaal chroniclers, for all their loyalty to the memory of the Czech Přemyslids, could not wholly outrun the conviction that a people's most natural, and therefore best, governors are those who share the same ethnicity. It finds fleeting expression in their explanation of how those 'ancient quarrels' which we have already encountered were resolved. This was achieved not by Wenceslas II but by his consort, the pious *Theutonica virgo* Guta of Habsburg, who – while naturally dealing with scrupulous fairness between the two peoples – is presented as a special intercessor for the German-speaking population, who thereby gain at last protection from native injustices.[70]

Medieval assumptions about the proper relation of 'kingdoms and communities' did, therefore, raise substantial barriers to the conceptual assimilation of the settlers to a single 'Bohemian' identity. But what of the other possible route for community-making which we have encountered: the notion of German distinctiveness *within* Bohemia – of the Germans as something akin to a 'middle nation'? The omens scarcely look encouraging when we notice that the otherwise articulate

[67] *Chronik des Jacob Twinger von Königshofen 1400 (1415)*, ed. C. Hegel (Die Chroniken der deutschen Städte vom 14. bis ins 16. Jahrhundert, 8, Leipzig, 1870), pp. 484–5. On the representation of Charles IV in contemporary German sources, see B. Frey,*Pater Bohemiae – Vitricus Imperii: Böhmens Vater, Stiefvater des Reichs. Kaiser Karl IV. in der Geschichtsschreibung* (Bern, 1978), esp. pp. 15–34.
[68] As an example, see *Jansen Enikels Weltchronik*, ed. P. Strauch (MGH Deutsche Chroniken, 3.i, Hanover, 1891), vv. 27580–94, p. 537.
[69] *Ottokars österreichische Reimchronik*, ed. J. Seemüller (MGH Deutsche Chroniken, 5.i, Hanover, 1890), vv. 17643–5, p. 234, 17916–19, p. 237 (Bohemian lack of valour); vv. 22440–3, p. 296 ('deceit, envy and hatred'). Abbot Ludolf of Sagan, who had studied at Prague in the 1370s, wrote of the ancient hatreds 'inter ehc duo ydeomata Teutonicorum et Bohemorum', which he compared to the Jews and the Samaritans: quoted in K. Bittner, *Deutsche und Tschechen. Zur Geistesgeschichte des böhmischen Raumes* (Brünn, Prague, Leipzig, Vienna, 1936), p. 101. See also the comments of Seibt, 'Die böhmische Nachbarschaft', pp.190–1.
[70] *Königsaaler Geschichts-Quellen*, p. 69.

Königsaal chronicle cannot even muster a word, or combination of words, to express the idea of being both Bohemian and German.[71] Yet in attitude at least Peter of Zittau does draw a clear distinction between German-speaking insiders and outsiders. The same conceptual distinction is maintained in the only other major piece of Bohemian German historiography to survive from the Middle Ages: a translation into German of the Old Czech chronicle known as 'Dalimil'.[72] This strange work is interesting in taking a long, indeed a thoroughly mythologised, view of Bohemian history. It commands attention here since, if the Bohemian Germans really did conceive of themselves as a single significant body, we can expect to find among them indications of engagement with their own shared past. At the heart of all medieval communities were notions of collective rights, liberties and status, and these were most powerfully articulated and affirmed by reference to their supposedly ancient origins.[73] We might, indeed, expect the German settlers to have felt more need than most for the legitimising authority of a common past, in view of the tensions which their presence generated at certain sensitive points in Bohemian society.

The original, Czech, 'Dalimil' chronicle came into being around 1315, and its characteristic attitudes and prejudices indicate the Czech lower nobility as its probable audience.[74] It provides an account – which the German translator by and large faithfully reproduced – of Bohemian history, from the land's earliest settlement, by the mythical Cech and his six brothers, down to the chronicler's own time. For the remote past it relies on the early twelfth-century Latin chronicle of Cosmas of Prague, which the chronicler, however, embroidered with a great deal of mythical pseudo-history of his own.[75] Composed at a time of tension between the native nobility and the circle of German courtiers around John of Luxemburg, the Czech 'Dalimil' has an anti-German disposition at its heart. It offers not only a detailed account but also an

---

[71] For attempts in Polish sources to describe accurately the German settlers: B. Zientara, 'Die deutsche Einwanderer in Polen vom 12. bis zum 14. Jahrhundert', in *Die deutsche Ostsiedlung*, ed. Schlesinger, pp. 333–48, at 342.

[72] *Di tutsch kronik von Behem lant*, ed. J. Jiriček (Fontes rerum Bohemicarum, 3, Prague, 1882).

[73] A. D. Smith, *The Ethnic Origins of Nations* (Oxford, 1986), p. 2, emphasises the indispensability of shared myths and memories to the existence of political communities. For a well-known example of legitimisation through myth: A. A. M. Duncan, *The Nation of the Scots and the Declaration of Arbroath* (Historical Association, London, 1970).

[74] See Graus, 'Bildung eines Nationalbewußtseins', pp. 26–30; idem, *Lebendige Vergangenheit*, ch. 3.ii; idem, *Nationenbildung*, pp. 91–5; Schwinges, ' "Primäre" und "sekundäre" Nation'. For the older literature, see N. Kerskens, *Geschichtsschreibung im Europa der 'Nationes'. Nationalgeschichtliche Gesamtdarstellungen im Mittelalter* (Cologne, Weimar, Vienna, 1995), pp. 583–7.

[75] Graus, *Lebendige Vergangenheit*, pp. 91–8.

interpretation of Bohemian history, and the baleful influence of the Germans runs like a dark vein through the whole work. For much of the way, the story oscillates between bad dukes and kings, who surround themselves with Germans and live to regret it, and good ones, who make it their special business to persecute Germans, and periodically expel them from the kingdom altogether. Yet this is merely the manifestation of the author's more fundamental underlying message, namely that the Bohemian lands should be inhabited and governed by Bohemians, by which he means speakers of the Bohemian language (*jazyk*): Czechs. Linguistic division was built into his basic historical scheme, and the chronicle opens with the Babylonian confusion of tongues.[76] About the linguistic basis of political community the chronicler is quite insistent. In a famous passage, Duke Udalrich explains to his nobles why he would rather marry a Czech peasant's daughter than a German princess. A foreign bride would teach his children German, and thereby corrupt their customs, sow a division of tongues, and bring about the ruin of the land.[77] The chain of anticipated cause and effect leading back to a violation of Bohemian linguistic purity highlights how strange it is that a Bohemian German should have found such a resolutely exclusivist work any use at all.

The German verse translation can be dated to the years 1342–6, and although its author is unknown, internal evidence indicates that he was a cleric and that he wrote in Prague.[78] In addition to rendering the Czech text into distinctly laboured German, the translator appended his own 546-verse synopsis of Bohemian history, and also made numerous, mostly small but none the less significant, changes to his exemplar. From these, as well as from his own verses, we can establish with some confidence the translator's point of view. Characteristically, he concentrated his attention on the Bohemian monarchy, and identified in the prince the historic key to the welfare of the realm's German-speaking population. In fact his Czech exemplar encouraged him to do this, since he, too, from a very different perspective, had been interested in the rulers' treatment of the Germans. The translator's contribution was to add his own distinctive gloss to the unfolding narrative. Recounting how a Bohemian duke had once persecuted the German population, cutting off their noses and driving them from his land, the translator adds that he acted shamefully.[79] By contrast, Otakar II, criticised by

[76] *Di tutsch kronik*, p. 5.

[77] Ibid., pp. 82–4.

[78] P. Hilsch, 'Di tutsch kronik von Behem lant. Der Verfasser der Dalimilübertragung und die deutschböhmische Identität', in *Ex ipsis rerum documentis: Beiträge zur Mediävistik. Festschrift für Harald Zimmermann zum 65. Geburtstag*, ed. K. Herbers et al. (Sigmaringen, 1991), esp. pp. 111–15.

[79] *Di tutsch kronik*, p. 143, l. 154.

the Czech chronicler for the great favour which he showed to the Germans, is warmly praised by the translator for that very reason. In the German version the account of Otakar's death is followed by verses absent from the original, in which the Germans of the kingdom are portrayed weeping and lamenting their loss.[80] What the translator conveys, more insistently than other Bohemian German writings, is the extent to which prominent and articulate German-speakers looked to the monarch for protection, and viewed their welfare as bound up with the disposition of the ruler. This is a subject to which we shall return.

Like Peter of Zittau, the translator distinguished between Bohemian Germans, with whom he felt an evident affinity, and outsiders, whose incursions he follows the Czech chronicler in denouncing as illegitimate. Indeed, his demarcation of a distinct, Bohemian, community of German-speakers is sharper than in the Königsaal chronicle. The Czech 'Dalimil' depicts Bohemian history of consisting substantially of repeated assaults from beyond the frontier, often perpetrated by Germans, which the Czech community of the realm affirms its solidarity and makes display of its peculiar excellence by repulsing. The translator was anxious to break down this dangerous polarity by keeping Germans within the realm conceptually apart from these wrongful incursions. When the Czech chronicler names the interlopers as 'German' his translator commonly, though not invariably, calls them simply 'foreigners'.[81] Yet the translator's German, just like Peter of Zittau's Latin, lacked a suitable terminology to support the distinction he wished to make: for him, too, Czechs were *Bemin*; Germans were Germans.[82] Despite his own evident identification with Bohemia, the translator could find no language either to establish for German-speakers a status comparable to that enjoyed by the Czech majority or clearly to distinguish them from outsiders, except by periodically suppressing the word 'German' altogether. Here, in contrast to Königsaal, there is not even the first impression of a harmonious regnal community, since the Czech 'Dalimil' had been concerned not with resolving but with reaffirming division – between a wholly Czech realm, within which alone there was solidarity, and the encompassing German menace. The translator could only qualify, not abolish, this gulf.

Perhaps the most insistent question facing any reader of the German 'Dalimil' is why the translator thought such an apparently fruitless task worth undertaking at all. He provides no explicit answer, and it is impossible to know with anything approaching certainty. However, whatever else may be said of it, the original Czech chronicle did have

---

[80] Ibid., p. 196, ll. 139–44.
[81] As examples, ibid., p. 83, ll. 24, 26, 28.
[82] For examples of both forms: ibid., pp. 192–6.

one unusual and important distinction: it offered a full, panoramic sweep of Bohemian history and, in its fashion, gave weight to the role of the Germans in that history. It indicated that Germans had been in the kingdom for a long time, and that problems similar to those of the early fourteenth century had arisen before. It demonstrated, moreover, that certain Bohemian rulers had historically been promoters and protectors of German-speakers. The Czech 'Dalimil' was anything but a justification of the German presence in Bohemia; but it was at least a kind of explanation of it. Could it be, then, that the translator was attempting to establish some historical foundations for the German settlement? The idea is at least worth considering, since historical writings supporting and mythologising the colonisation of Bohemia were something that the settlers conspicuously lacked. If that was the translator's intention, however, we must judge his work a failure. For while it certainly unfolds a long history of German involvement in the kingdom, the translator's debt to his Czech exemplar ensures that the German presence there never appears a settled one. Instead it is surrounded, as it is in other Czech writings, by an undercurrent of flux, contingency and potential impermanence.[83] There is a sense, detectable also in other regions which experienced German immigration, that the relation between land. power and ethnicity was not yet finally resolved, and that a prospect remained of its future resolution by violent means.[84] A notion of what it is tempting to call 'ethnic cleansing' raises its head more frequently than we might expect. In Bohemia, the proximity of German regions rendered expulsions a feasible prospect and, indeed, on a small scale, a periodic feature of Bohemian history. Peter of Zittau recounts how resentments among the native nobility in 1315 forced John of Luxemburg to send his German courtiers out of the kingdom [85] 'Dalimil' and its translator invoke the actuality of the practice, telling how in an earlier incident Duke Spytihněv had given the Germans three days to get out before dumping them in the Bavarian forest, on the German side of the mountains.[86]

The Czech 'Dalimil' placed the Germans at the uncertain edge of

---

[83] See, for example, W. Wostry, 'Ein deutschfeindliches Pamphlet aus Böhmen aus dem 14. Jahrhundert', *Mitteilungen des Vereins für Geschichte der Deutschen in Böhmen*, 53 (1915), p. 232, where their expulsion is advocated. For this text, see Graus, *Nationenbildung*, pp. 221–3, where it is dated to the period 1380–93.

[84] Examples are cited in B. Zientara, 'Foreigners in Poland in the 10th–15th centuries: their role in the opinion of the Polish medieval community', *Acta Poloniae Historica*, 29 (1974), pp. 5–28; *idem*, 'Die deutsche Einwanderer'; J. Strzelczyk, 'Die Wahrnehmung des Fremden im mittelalterlichen Polen', in *Die Begegnung des Westens mit dem Osten*, ed. O. Engels, P. Schreiner (Sigmaringen, 1993), pp. 203–20.

[85] *Königsaaler Geschichts-Quellen*, pp. 371–2.

[86] *Di tutsch kronik*, p. 94, ll. 1–10.

Bohemian society, and that is where they remain in the German translation. In both accounts they appear historically as interlopers. In the upper strata of society, on which historical writings mostly concentrated, there was indeed considerable coming and going, and the sentiments uttered by the poet Reinmar von Zweter, who earned his bread for several years at the court of Wenceslas I, were doubtless shared by other German courtiers also. 'Bohemia I have chosen', he says, but 'more for the lord's sake than the land's' – although both lord and land, he concedes, are good.[87] It was the fate of the German settlers as a group to be burdened, in the polemics of Czech writers, with the rootlessness and opportunism of courtly hangers-on, and as such to be consigned, imaginatively, to the disputed and changeable frontiers of collective identity.

Yet there ought to have been Bohemian Germans articulate enough to have resisted this marginalisation, and to have made their own maps of political community – maps ascribing their fellow German-speakers a more central location within Bohemian society. That they were able to muster nothing more compelling than the feeble 'Dalimil' translation becomes easier to comprehend if we reflect on the characteristics of those myths of settlement which many political communities of the period made for themselves and the Bohemian Germans did not.[88] The familiar characteristics of these stories give pause for thought. Normally they depict migrant bands taking an empty wilderness for their new home, or winning their land by exterminating, subjugating or driving away its aboriginal population. The settlers generally came to the land under the leadership of mighty warriors and princes.[89] Narratives of this kind were developed to glorify and legitimise various colonising movements of the period.[90] But it is clear that such elements could in no sense describe the arrival of the German settlers in Bohemia. They had not come in arms. but as clerics, artists, artisans, miners, merchants and, above all, peasant cultivators. A handful of German nobles also took land under the Bohemian crown, but they, too, came as settlers,

---

[87] Printed in *Politische Lyrik des deutschen Mittelalters*, Texte I, ed. U. Müller (Göppingen, 1972), p. 8.

[88] On settlement myths generally: Graus, *Lebendige Vergangenheit*, ch. 3.

[89] A myth of this sort with especially wide application traced an origin in migrant bands of Trojans: A. Grau, *Der Gedanke der Herkunft in der deutschen Geschichtsschreibung des Mittelalters. Trojasage und Verwandtes* (Leipzig, 1938); C. Beaune, *The Birth of an Ideology: Myths and Symbols of Nation in Late-Medieval France* (English transl. by S. R. Huston, Berkeley, 1991) ch. 8.

[90] Bartlett, *Making of Europe*, ch. 4; A. V. Murray, 'Ethnic identity in the crusader states: the Frankish race and the settlement of Outremer', in *Concepts of Nationality*, ed. Forde, Johnson and Murray, pp. 59–73, which argues for viewing crusading narratives as origin myths.

not warriors, at the invitation of others.[91] Concepts of Germanness derived from beyond the frontier could scarcely have served as a basis for constructing solidarities in the new homeland. They offered no substantial arguments supportive of the settlers' presence in Bohemia, because the reasons for their being there had nothing directly to do with ethnicity. It was not as 'Germans' but as readily available muscle-power and as possessors of valued skills that the rulers of Bohemia called them to their land; and it was not as 'Germans' but as the individual subjects of innumerable specific recruitment ventures that they had come.[92] They had, of course, in their own eyes, a full right to be there; but that right was not touched directly by notions of Germanness. It rested rather upon the many charters of liberties, from the hands of native princes, to which, individually or as local communities, they could make appeal. When these charters made reference, as they often did, to the 'German law' by which the settlers held, the only weight attaching to the word 'German' was to signal material differences from traditional terms of tenure.[93] Of any significant bond among those enjoying *ius Theutonicum* there is not even a hint.

Our sources, few as they are, tell us a good deal about the limits of collective identity among the German population of pre-Hussite Bohemia. They are eloquent in part precisely through being so few. Even when we have allowed for the losses which must have taken place – the Hussite wars took a terrible toll on Bohemian monastic libraries – the tally of writings bearing on Bohemian German self-consciousness is meagre.[94] German-speakers were, after all, a significant element in the population of thirteenth- and fourteenth-century Bohemia, both numerically and socially. But their written statements are not only slight but weak, uncertain and contradictory on the subject of their own common allegiances. Even the learned and politically experienced Peter of Zittau found no satisfactory resolution – or at least none that satisfies the modern reader – between his identification with a Bohemian and a German *gens*. Yet our sources tell us only so much. They tell us that conceptions of a Bohemian German community

[91] Moraw, 'Das Mittelalter', p. 112, emphasising that their settlement was limited to the Egerland and the lands of the church of Olomouc (Olmütz).

[92] Richter, 'Die böhmischen Länder', pp. 336–47; Moraw, 'Das Mittelalter', pp. 76–92; Graus, 'Die Problematik', p. 46.

[93] As examples of this usage, see *Reg. Dip. Bohemiae*, 3, no. 117, p. 46 ('jure hereditario seu teutonico'); no. 1167, pp. 500–1 ('iure theutonico, quod purkrecht dicitur'); no. 1422, p. 614 ('hereditarie seu libere vel iure theutonico'); no. 2824, p. 1236 ('jure theutonicali'). Many more such instances could be cited. Further variants will be found in *Urkunden und erzählende Quellen zur deutschen Ostsiedlung im Mittelalter*, ed. H. Helbig and L. Weinrich, 2 (Ausgewählte Quellen zur deutschen Geschichte des Mittelalters, Darmstadt, 1970).

[94] The German 'Dalimil' translation, for example, survives in only a single manuscript: Hilsch, 'Di tutsch kronik', p. 103, n. 2.

lacked strength and compulsion; but they do not tell us why that was so. They do, admittedly, appear to provide some substantial clues: they suggest that the repertoire of names, concepts and arguments available to Bohemian Germans was too constrained, too much formed by existing political communities, to allow that new, latecomer community to draw life from them. Viewed in this way, the concept of the 'Bohemian German' (not a combination used in writings of the time) becomes an oxymoron. We should, however, beware of supposing that the barrier to a Bohemian German community was solely – or even principally – a conceptual one. New medieval communities were capable of remarkable resourcefulness in veiling recent and unremarkable origins in the smoke and mirrors of legitimising myth.[95] While notions of community failed to crystallise around the Bohemian Germans, they did embrace the German population of neighbouring Silesia, where, by the fifteenth century, elements of settler and indigenous identities were merging around a pronounced sense of Silesian distinctiveness.[96]

It is possible, however, to envisage other sorts of barrier to community-making, about which our sources can reveal little directly, but which may have been no less substantial for that. These are the barriers upon which Anderson and other social theorists concentrated – the sort which flowed from the constraints not of medieval thought but of medieval social life. To consider these constraints it is necessary to turn to more implicit kinds of evidence – to the geographical and social patterns of the German settlement itself. By the thirteenth century Bohemia and Moravia were bounded in most directions by regions which either had old-established German populations or were subject to heavy German immigration: Austria to the south, Bavaria to the south-west and west, Upper Saxony and Lusatia to the north-west and north, Silesia to the north-east. On all fronts except the southern one, the Bohemian lands were separated from adjacent German-speaking regions by areas of largely uninhabited and uncultivated forest and mountain. It was into these ill-defined frontier zones that the settlers first advanced. The result was ribbons of German settlement at the geographical margins of the kingdom, with concentrations of German-speakers spilling forward into the interior, especially in Moravia and around some of the larger towns.[97] The towns were themselves islands of concentrated German speech, in some areas, such as central and eastern Bohemia, lying within an almost wholly Czech-speaking countryside. The map of German settlement had few unities beyond the

---

[95] Noted by Reynolds, 'Medieval *origines gentium*', p. 390; *idem, Kingdoms and Communities*, p. 213.

[96] Jurek, 'Entwicklung eines schlesisches Regionalbewußtseins', esp. pp. 47–8.

[97] E. Schwarz, 'Die deutsche Siedelgebiete in Böhmen und Mähren-Schlesien in vorhussitischer Zeit', in *Sudetendeutscher Atlas*, ed. Meynen, pp. 13–14.

directly experienced local world, and no natural centre. Place-name and dialect evidence makes clear that most of the settlers came only relatively short distances, from adjacent regions of German speech.[98] What they brought to the new land was not some unifying Germanness but, on the contrary, the diversities of their many different homelands. One of the most telling observations which Peter of Zittau offers on the subject of Bohemian German identity is a tangential one: he notes with bemusement how remarkable it is that the Saxon and the Bavarian each rightly calls himself 'German', when neither understands the speech of the other.[99] It is an insight which Peter could easily have tested without leaving Bohemia, since both Bavarian and Saxon dialects were to be heard there. In other things, too, the lines ran outward, not inward. Where the towns of northern Bohemia looked down the Elbe to Magdeburg for their law, southern towns faced south and west, towards Vienna and Nuremberg.[100]

It was not merely a geographical centre that was lacking. The social chains through which medieval identities were elsewhere made and mediated were likewise incomplete. There was, most strikingly, no German nobility to generalise local solidarities in regnal politics and to root generalised affinities in local soil. Instead, socially privileged but politically imperilled elites at court and in the great towns sought the shadow of the monarch or the reassurance of their family networks; and below them, in the Bohemian countryside, local communities nurtured local solidarities, lived, so far as is known, on generally peaceful terms with their Czech neighbours, and were troubled by no urge to imagine more far-reaching or abstract solidarities. The German se~ttlements in Bohemia presented a landscape too meagre -altogether too marginal – for such troublesome plantations to thrive.

When the Sudeten Germans were expelled from Czechoslovakia at the end of the Second World War, the Czechoslovak Communist leader Klement Gottwald justified the action as correcting 'the mistakes of our Czech kings, the Přemyslids, who invited the German colonists here'.[101] In thus placing the medieval settlement in direct relation to the circumstances, sentiments and concerns of his own time, Gottwald merely followed a tradition by that date long established among both

---

[98] E. Schwarz, 'eschichte der deutschen Besiedlung', in *Die Deutschen in Böhmen und Mähren: ein historischer Rückblick*, ed. H. Preidel (Munich, 1952), p. 122 (place-names); *idem*, 'Die deutschen Mundarten in Böhmen und Mähren-Schlesien', in *Sudetendeutscher Atlas*, ed. Meynen, pp. 9–10 (dialects).

[99] *Königsaaler Geschichts-Quellen*, p. 52.

[100] Richter, 'Die böhmischen Länder', pp. 323–31; Moraw, 'Das Mittelalter', pp. 59–75.

[101] Quoted in D. Sayer, 'The language of nationality and the nationality of language: Prague 1780–1920', *Past and Present*, 153 (November 1996), pp. 164–210, at 210.

Czechs and Germans, one which had already spawned and shaped two rival, voluminous and often deeply learned, historiographies.[102] Compressing distant past into present and future is the natural recourse of the nationalist, and a habit of thought characteristic of much of the scholarship dealing with the German presence in medieval Bohemia. In stark contrast is the approach followed by those political scientists, Anderson among them, whose ambitious generalising treatments of the sociology of nation have done so much to shape current debate. Declining to view national loyalties as either inevitable or necessarily benevolent, they endeavoured to open as wide as possible the gap between modern manifestations of national allegiance and the cultures and mentalities of the pre-modern world. In so doing, however, they exposed themselves to criticism from a number of observers, among them specialists in the medieval period.[103] These scholars, whose motives and interests, it need hardly be said, lie far removed from traditional nationalist programmes, have urged the benefits of once again placing pre-modern political solidarities in a closer and more comfortable juxtaposition to modern national loyalties. The concept of nation, it is now argued, is not the recent, and thus perhaps transitory, phenomenon portrayed by the 'modernists', but has deep, ancient and – all the evidence suggests – extremely durable social roots. Nor can it be dismissed as a mere instrument in the hands of sinister regimes, or a vehicle for distorted and unwholesome passions, but it must rather be recognised as a category of sentiment and belonging habitual among human beings, and especially among those whose roots are in the European cultural and religious traditions.[104]

It is beyond question that these critiques have much force, and that they open the way to subtler understandings of the place of 'imagined communities' in different kinds of past society. Yet if the analyses offered by the 'modernist' school are to be set aside as insufficiently nuanced and as empirically unsatisfying, it is naturally important that any general account put in their place should be able to withstand these same objections. The historical role of national solidarities is, however, a subject which notoriously defies general and comparative treatments just as fully as it seems to demand and to presuppose them. Much of

---

[102] Analysed in Graus, 'Die Problematik'.

[103] In addition to Reynolds, *Kingdoms and Communities*, see now, especially, A. Hastings, *The Construction of Nationhood. Ethnicity, Religion and Nationalism* (Cambridge, 1997). The new orientation is also signalled in K. Stringer, 'Social and political communities in European history: some reflections on recent studies', in *Nations, Nationalism and Patriotism*, ed. Björn, Grant and Stringer, pp. 9–34. A more qualified revisionist analysis is developed in Smith, *Ethnic Origins of Nations*; *idem*, 'National identities'. For an explicit critique of Anderson from a medievalist perspective, see L. Johnson, 'Imagining communities: medieval and modern', in *Concepts of Nationality*, ed. Forde, Johnson and Murray, pp. 1–19.

[104] Emphasised by Hastings, *Construction of Nationhood*, ch. 1.

the recent revisionist work has concentrated on the place of 'national' allegiances in medieval patterns of thought and belief.[105] But the actual functioning of such ideas in pre-modern societies, the character and scope of the institutions and media through which they were disseminated, and the breadth and composition of the social groups touched by them, have received comparatively less attention. Yet, particularly here, specific scrutiny is essential, and any full account of the subject, to carry conviction, will need to go beyond general statements about what 'medieval men and women', or 'the cultural community', thought, felt or did.[106] It is important to note at this point that, while medieval and modern notions of political community may have much in common, the opportunities for their dissemination, and thus their social and political consequences, were in important ways different in the medieval world. As Reynolds makes clear, it was only the existence of kingdoms which enabled 'regnal' communities to be imagined at all, and these latter took their contours from established political organisation.[107] More specialised studies likewise indicate the prime importance of structures of power and government in the formation of medieval identities.[108] The rightness of this view is forcefully demonstrated by the patterns of political solidarity in medieval Bohemia, and by the inability of the German settlers clearly to imagine any general political community of their own.

The example of Bohemia, however, is a reminder that the relation between established institutions and the imagining of political solidarities has not at all times been so unilinear. Studies of the development of both Czech and German national movements in the Bohemian lands during the nineteenth and early twentieth centuries have shown them to be grounded above all in the specific circumstances of a modern, industrialising and urbanising society.[109] Although drawing nourishment from imagined continuities with ancient pasts, both communities were essentially new, nineteenth-century creations. Both of them came to maturity within the multi-national Habsburg empire; neither was nurtured by any discrete framework of institutions or power-structures. What did underlie them, however, was a remarkable range of formal

[105] An important recent study with its emphasis in this area is T. Turville-Petre, *England the Nation. Language, Literature, and National Identity, 1290–1340* (Oxford, 1996).

[106] It is worth noting here that the very concept of 'community', understood as a unit of belief and action, has attracted criticism. See: M. Rubin, 'Small groups: identity and solidarity in the late Middle Ages', in *Enterprise and Individuals in Fifteenth-Century England* (Stroud, 1991), pp. 132–50; C. Carpenter, 'Gentry and community in medieval England', *Journal of British Studies*, 33 (1994), pp. 340–80.

[107] Reynolds, *Kingdoms and Communities*, p. 331.

[108] Frame, ' "Les Engleys nées en Irlande" ', p. 89.

[109] In addition to Sayer, 'The language of nationality', see G. B. Cohen, *The Politics of Ethnic Survival: Germans in Prague, 1861–1914* (Princeton, 1981).

and informal cultural networks and stimuli, from gymnastic societies, scientific and cultural associations, through to newspapers, women's magazines, and encyclopaedias in affordable popular editions.[110] Then there were those state-sponsored elements which reflect the power specifically of the modern state, whether in the language of tuition in schools and universities, the contents of textbooks and of public libraries, or the style of policemen's uniforms, the colour and format of road signs, and the historical mythologies condensed into street names.[111] These are just a few of the many daily-experienced points of association and separation through which both Czechs and Germans gradually learned to 'belong to' their respective languages, rather than merely speaking them.[112] It was against this, fundamentally modern, backdrop that the Sudeten Germans moved towards that sense of collective belonging – of community – which is so unmistakable in the history of the twentieth century, and so little to be found in the writings of the Middle Ages. The boundaries which scholars working in the 'modernist' tradition erected between pre-modern and modern political cultures are without doubt too absolute, and too little informed by the medieval evidence. Yet when that evidence is examined, not quite all of it tells against their case, and their insistence upon the distinctive political opportunities to be found in modern societies can teach the medievalist more than some of their critics have allowed. The time may have come if not to revise then at least to refine and to qualify the current emphasis on long-term continuities as the foremost characteristic of political identities. That enterprise ought to include at least a glance at those specific 'imagined communities' – the Bohemian Germans among them – to which the Middle Ages did not and could not give life.

[110] Among the items listed in Sayer, 'The language of nationality', pp. 188–9, 198–201 and *passim*.

[111] As a single example of the role which the everyday artefacts of modern public administration can play in signalling identities, a 1930s observation relating to the town of Teplitz (Teplice) in the Sudetenland: 'The modern town makes a very Reich-German impression; the sign-post at the centre of the town points to Prague and Aussig in small Czech and German Latin print, but to Dresden in large Gothic letters and in German only' (Wiskemann, *Czechs and Germans*, pp. 99–100).

[112] Sayer, 'The language of nationality', p. 181.

THE ROYAL HISTORICAL SOCIETY
REPORT OF COUNCIL, SESSION 1998–1999

THE Council of the Royal Historical Society has the honour to present the following report to the Anniversary Meeting.

1. Activities of the Society during the year

   a) The Anniversary Meeting on 20 November 1998 approved changes in the Society's constitution aimed at making Council a rather more streamlined body without significantly compromising its representative character and thus at making savings in the running costs of the Society. In future Vice Presidents will serve for three years rather than four and three rather than four Councillors will be elected each year. When these changes take effect, they will produce a body of twenty four members in place of thirty under the existing constitution.

   b) The Society is now on e-mail—royalhistsoc@ucl.ac.uk—and will soon have its own website through the co-operation of the Institute of Historical Research, address www.rhs.ac.uk.

   c) The Society has been especially concerned this year with a wide range of issues relating to archives, such as acquisition and collection development policies, access and freedom of information, the application of research funds to archives and the implications of the new technologies for storing documents. This has led to fruitful co-operation with the Public Record Office in particular. The Society participated in the Public Record Office's consultation process on 'The Public Records of Tomorrow' and on its new manual on 'Access to the Public Records'. The Public Record Office will be seeking the advice of the Society on selection policies for particular classes of records. A successful one-day colloquium on 'Historians and Archivists', described more fully in another section of this report, was held on 30 January 1999. This was especially well attended by archivists. The outcome of the colloquium will be that regular meetings of historians to discuss the future of archives will be convened by the Society in future. The report of the colloquium was submitted as the Society's response to the inquiry of the Royal Commission on Historical Manuscripts on 'Archives at the Millennium'. The Society has made responses to the Home Office and to Select Committees of the Lords and Commons on the government's draft Freedom of Information Bill. The report of the Commons Committee took special note of the Society's submission, and both reports endorsed several of its criticisms. It has given its views to the United Kingdom Research Libraries Support Programme and participated in a review being conducted by the National Council on Archives. A response was made to the Court Service's request for views on its proposals for modernising the probate records.

d) The Society has been actively involved in a number of other issues of importance to historians. It continued to work closely with the History at the Universities Defence Group on the scheme for devising benchmark standards for first degrees in history. The Society has also acted as host to a series of meetings at which interested parties considered proposals for a new subject centre in history. It responded to an inquiry undertaken by the History Data Services User Needs Workshop. A questionnaire about the Research Assessment Exercise was answered and a list of names was submitted for the panel in 2001. Names were also suggested for the Arts and Humanities Research Board history panels. The Society submitted views to the British Library's Strategic Review, in particular opposing the proposals, subsequently withdrawn, for charging readers. Comments were sent to the Heritage Lottery Fund on its consultation document on future policies.

e) A wide variety of the Society's publications have appeared this year: the annual volume of <u>Transactions</u> (including eight papers from the 'Identities and Empires' conference), two volumes of the <u>Camden Series</u> went to press and two <u>Camden</u> reprints were published. The reprint volumes will be the last of that series, at least for the immediate future. The <u>Studies in History</u> series goes from strength to strength. It is clearly fulfilling an urgent need, to which other publishers seems to be increasingly less inclined to respond, in providing an outlet for first books of high quality. Six volumes were launched in November 1998 and paperback editions are being issued for some of the books in the series. Council are very happy to announce that under an arrangement with the publishers, Boydell & Brewer, from 2000 <u>Studies in History</u> volumes will be available to Fellows at the heavily discounted price of £15 per volume.

f) Thanks to the generosity of our existing patrons, the Andrew W. Mellon Foundation, the Esmee Fairbairn Charitable Trust and the Isaac Newton Trust and to the most welcome contribution of a new patron, the Arts and Humanities Research Board, the revision of the Society's Bibliography of <u>The History of Britain, Ireland and the British Overseas</u> is now fully funded until 2001, the year of its scheduled completion. The Society owes a great debt to Dr. Julian Hoppit for getting this revision under way as General Editor for the past two years. He has been succeeded by Dr. Ian Archer.

Dr. Austin Gee continues as editor of the <u>Annual Bibliography</u>. His efforts and the invaluable contributions of those scholars who give the Society their time as section editors meant that the largest number of items yet listed, 6762, went into the 1997 volume that was published in October 1998.

2. Meetings of the Society

Five papers were given in London during this year. In addition the Society had the privilege of going to the University of Aberdeen to hear a paper and to participate in a discussion of historical issues of all kinds as part of the celebrations marking one hundred years of the Aberdeen history department. The same pattern of a paper and a discussion was followed on the Society's visit to the University of Reading. The Society has arranged papers to be read at Huddersfield and Warwick during the 1999–2000 session.

A public lecture was given on 11 November 1998 at Gresham College by Professor Geoffrey Hosking on 'Patronage and the Russian State'. This was the first of what is to be an annual series of lectures in association with Gresham College. Their purpose is to present academic history of high quality to a lay audience with the special aim of putting issues of current importance into their historical context. The lectures are published by Gresham College. Professor Hosking's lecture was well attended and provoked lively discussion.

A well-attended Annual Reception was held for members and guests in the Upper Hall at University College London on 1 July 1998.

A one-day conference, 'Creating New Communities in the Middle Ages', was held at the Institute of Historical Research, London, on 26 September 1998. Five papers were given by younger scholars. Approximately 40 people attended.

A conference at Hull on 'Voyages and Journeys' from 29–31 March 1999, for which a most promising programme had been devised by members of the Hull history department, had most unfortunately to be cancelled because of lack of support.

The Society held a one-day colloquium on 30 January 1999 at the Institute of Historical Research on Historians and Archivists. This was attended by some 60 people. It was divided into four sessions in each of which archivists and historians were paired in giving short presentations on themes of common interest. The colloquium clearly aroused great interest and it is intended that it should lead a continuing series of meetings between historians and archivists. The Society is very grateful to the speakers who gave up a Saturday to make the occasion a success.

During the 1999–2000 session, a two-day Conference, 'The British-Irish Union of 1801', is to be held at The Queen's University of Belfast and the Public Record of Northern Ireland, on Thursday 9–Saturday 11 September 1999.

The Society is co-operating with the British Society for the History of Science and the National Museums and Galleries on Merseyside to host a three-day Conference, 'On Time: History, Science, Commemoration', to be held in Liverpool on 16–18 September 1999.

3. Prizes

The Society's annual prizes were awarded as follows:

a) The Alexander Prize, for an essay by a younger scholar, attracted six entries. The Prize for 1999 was awarded to Dr. Magnus Ryan for his essay 'Bartolus of Sassoferrato and Free Cities' which was read to the Society on 23 April 1999.

b) The revised criteria to allow the David Berry Prize to be an essay on any approved topic of Scottish history attracted one entry. The Prize for 1998 was awarded to Mr. C.A. Blake for his essay 'Stuart Policy and Scottish Mercenaries in the Thirty Years War'.

The writer shows a sound grasp of the considerations governing the foreign policies of James I and Charles I and places the levies in this context. The strength of the essay lies in sections which relate policy enforcement, revealing that the men recruited were usually beggars and riff-raff, but it also indicates that little was done to check the work of zealous press-gangs searching for able-bodied but unwilling men. A useful appendix lists levies, numbers involved and destinations, the most interesting finding is that these levies represented a considerable drain to national manpower, which must have exhausted Scotland at least a disastrously as did the civil war, depriving Charles II of the ability to raise large armies in Scotland in the following decades.

c) The Whitfield Prize for a first book on British history attracted 14 entries. The generally high quality of the entries was commended by the assessors.

The Whitfield Prize 1998 was awarded to Amanda Vickery for her book, *The Gentleman's Daughter: Women's Lives in Georgian England*, published by Yale University Press.

In *The Gentleman's Daughter* Amanda Vickery unfolds with grace and sympathy the lives of a network of gentlewomen, principally in Lancashire, across the length of the eighteenth century. Drawing on amazingly rich collections of diaries and letters, she probes deeply into the intimate detail of these women's daily lives—in bed and boudoir, in the home and on the estate, in the shops, assembly rooms and pleasure gardens—and reconstructs not only a way of life but a whole structure of feeling. The result is a vivid picture of one stratum of eighteenth-century society; but it is also an historical argument about the permeable boundaries between the public and the private, about the roles and sensibilities that men and women shared, and about the roles and sensibilities that kept them apart.

d) Thanks to a continuing generous donation from The Gladstone Memorial Trust, the second Gladstone History Book Prize for a first book on a subject outside British history was awarded. There were 13 entries.

The Gladstone History Book Prize 1998 was awarded to Dr. Patrick Major for his book, *The Death of the KPD: Communism and Anti-Communism in West Germany, 1945–1956* (Oxford University Press).

This book constitutes an important contribution to our understanding of the recent history of eastern Europe. It is a fine study both of political culture and of party organisation. It convincingly relates the development of German communism both to its German inheritance and to the pressures of the cold war. Impeccably scholarly, it is also readily accessible to non-specialist readers.

e) Frampton and Beazley Prizes for A-level performances were awarded following nominations from the examining bodies:

Frampton Prizes

The Associated Examining Board: Martin D. Spence, Sudbury Upper School, Suffolk

Edexcel Foundation incorporating the London Examination Board: K.J. Read, Chesham High School, Bucks.

Northern Examinations and Assessment Board: Ronan J. Astin, St. Ambrose College, Altrincham, Cheshire—the second successive year that this prize was awarded to a pupil at this College

Oxford and Cambridge School Examinations Board: J. Clement Power, Charterhouse, Surrey

University of Cambridge Local Examinations Syndicate: Paul Cavill, King's College School, London

University of Oxford Delegacy of Local Examinations: Jane Hilton, Wycombe High School, Buckinghamshire—the second successive year that this prize was awarded to a pupil at this School

Welsh Joint Education Committee: Louisa May Evans, Caerloen Comprehensive School, Newport

Beazley Prizes

Northern Ireland Council for the Curriculum Examinations and Assessment: Catherine J. Haugh, Omagh Academy

Scottish Examination Board: Alice Stevenson, Craigmount High School, Edinburgh.

The Royal Historical Society Centenary Fellowship for the academic year 1998–1999 was awarded to Marcella Simoni registered at University College London and working on a Ph.D. entitled 'Welfare in British Palestine: Education and Health, 1929–1939'. The Fellowship for the academic year 1997–1998 had been awarded to Svetlana Nikitina, who was registered at the School of Slavonic and East European Studies, University of London, for a Ph.D. on a thesis concerning crafts and guilds in Hungary from the fourteenth to the seventeenth centuries.

4. Publications

Transactions, Sixth Series, Volume 8 was published during the session, and *Transactions*, Sixth Series, Volume 9 went to press, to be published in November 1999.

Fleet Street, Press Barons and Politics: The Journals of Collin Brooks, 1932–1940, ed. N.J. Crowson (Camden, Fifth Series, Volume 11) and *Newsletters from the Archpresbyterate of George Birkhead, 1609–1614* ed. M. Questier (Camden, Fifth Series, Volume 12) were due to be published during the session, but were both delayed for various reasons beyond the Society's control. They will appear in August and September 1999 respectively. Further volumes to be published in the Camden, Fifth Series, are *Parliament and Politics in the Age of Churchill and Attlee: The Headlam Diaries, 1935–1951*, ed. Stuart Ball (No. 13); *The diary of Thomas Juxon, 1642-1647'*, ed. K. Lindley (No. 14); *Marital Litigation in the Court of Requests*, ed. J.M. Stretton (No. 15) and a new style themed *Miscellany*, including: 'The Papers of J.C. Langdon', ed. Martin Lynn, and 'The Vanneck Correspondence:

the first eighteen years of Simon Taylor's letters to Chalmer Archdeckne, 1765–1783', ed. W.A. Speck and B. Wood.

Cambridge University Press issued reprints of two Camden volumes during the year. They were *Encomium Emmae Reginae*, ed. S. Keynes and *The Political Correspondence of Mr. Gladstone and Lord Granville, 1868–1876*, ed. A. Ramm, with a new introduction by H.C.G. Matthew. No further reprints were published during the session, and none are planned for the foreseeable future.

The Society's *Annual Bibliography of British and Irish History, Publications of 1997*, was published by Oxford University Press during the session, and the *Annual Bibliography of British and Irish History, Publications of 1998* went to press, to be published in 1999.

The Second Series of the *Studies in History* series continued to produce exciting volumes. As scheduled, the following volumes were published during the session, *Religious Patronage in post- Conquest England, 1066–1135* by Emma Cownie, *Politicians versus Generals: Managing the South African War, 1899–1902* by Keith Terrance Surridge, *Red Flag and Union Jack: Englishness, Patriotism and the British Left, 1881–1924* by Paul Ward and *Conversations in Cold Rooms: Women, Work and Poverty in Northumberland, 1835–1905* by Jane Long.

Science, Religion and Politics in Restoration England: Richard Cumberland's De Legibus Naturae by Jonathan Parkin and *Artful Dodgers: Youth and Crime in Early Nineteenth-Century London* by Heather Shore are scheduled to be published early in the next session. These two volumes, together with *Cornwall Politics in the Age of Reform, 1790–1885* by Edwin Jaggard; *Protection and Politics: Conservative Economic Discourse, 1815–1852* by Anna Gambles; *Patterns of Philanthropy: Charity and Society in Nineteenth-Century Bristol* by Martin Gorsky; and *Charity and the London Hospitals, 1850–1898* by Keir Waddington which are all due to be published in the next session, will feature in a launch to be held after the Anniversary Meeting and Presidential Address on 26 November 1999. As in previous years, the membership of the Society will be invited to attend.

5. Papers Read

At the ordinary meetings of the Society the following papers were read:

'The Middle Ages through modern eyes: an historical problem'
Professor Dr. Otto Gerhard Oexle (1 July 1998: Prothero Lecture)

'Making mercantilism work'
Dr. Nuala Zahedieh (23 October 1998 at the University of Aberdeen)

'Enlightenment and Revolution: Naples 1799'
Dr. John Robertson (22 January 1999)

'Kwame Nkrumah against the chiefs: nationalist struggle for control of the Ghanaian countryside, 1950–1960'
Professor Richard Rathbone (5 March 1999)

'Disputes, Courts and Legal Arguments in Anglo-Norman England'
Dr. John Hudson (21 May 1999 at the University of Reading)

At the Anniversary meeting on 20 November 1998, the President, Professor P.J. Marshall, delivered an address on 'Britain and the World in the Eighteenth Century: II. Britons and Americans'.

At the one-day Conference entitled 'Creating New Communities in the Middle Ages' held at the Institute of Historical Research, London, on 26 September 1998, the following papers were read:

'Imagining Community: Germans in Bohemia, c.1250–c.1400'
Dr. Len Scales

'The Changing role of guilds in the communities of Hungarian towns'
Ms. Svetlana Nikitina [Royal Historical Society Centenary Fellow, IHR, 1997–1998]

'The formation of a "crusader" settlement at Antioch'
Dr. Tom Asbridge

'The Muslim colony at Lucera in thirteenth-century Southern Italy'
Ms Julie Taylor

'The English in Ireland: A colonial community?'
Dr. Brendan Smith

6. <u>Finance</u>

The Society continues to enjoy a healthy financial state overall, as the endowment has increased from £2,546,652 in June 1998 to £2,616,816 in June 1999, an increase of £70,164. Our net investment income decreased from £124,456 to £109,673, primarily as a result of two factors: first, we were affected to an extent by the Asian financial crisis and its attendant aftershocks, as well as by our exposure to global drug stocks; and secondly – and more positively – it seemed safe to modify our fixed income strategy of the previous two years and re-invest some of our investment income in growth stocks. Council continues to support a rigorous control of expenditure across the Society's activities. The Society this year had a surplus of £11,787.

7. <u>Membership</u>

Council was advised and recorded with regret the deaths of

The Rev. Leslie R. Aitken—Associate
Mr. Philip G.W. Annis—Fellow
Professor John M. Barkley—Fellow
Lord Beloff—Retired Fellow
Professor Ian R. Christie—Fellow
Dr. Charles Duggan—Retired Fellow
The Rev. Dr. Cyril C. Eastwood—Retired Fellow
Dr. David Englander—Fellow

Mr. Geoffrey L. Fairs—Fellow
Dr. Robert Farrugia Randon—Fellow
Dr. John Fines—Fellow
Mr. Wyn K. Ford—Retired Fellow
Dr. B.A. [Jim] Holderness—Fellow
Professor Robin A. Humphreys, OBE—Honorary Vice-President [former President]
Dr. Hansjoachim W. Koch—Fellow
Professor Angus I.K. MacKay—Fellow
Professor Callum A. MacDonald—Fellow
Dr. Sheila Marriner—Retired Fellow
Professor Herbert G. Nicholas—Fellow
Mr. J. Gregory Palmer—Fellow
Professor Sidney Pollard—Retired Fellow
Dr. Courtenay A.R. Radford—Fellow
Professor John S. Roskell—Retired Fellow
Mr. Alfred Rubens—Fellow
Miss Alwyn A. Ruddock—Associate
Dr. Robert W. Scribner—Fellow
Mr. E.A. Smith—Retired Fellow
Professor Roger M. Walker—Fellow
Professor Michael J. Wilks—Retired Fellow
Dr. Daniel T. Williams—Fellow.

68 Fellows, 7 Members and 2 Corresponding Fellows were elected. The membership of the Society on 30 June 1999 numbered 2417, comprising 1691 Fellows, 399 Retired Fellows, 25 Life Members, 12 Honorary Vice-Presidents, 93 Corresponding Fellows, 112 Associates and 85 Members.

The Society exchanged publications with 15 Societies, British and Foreign.

8. Officers and Council

At the Anniversary Meeting on 20 November 1998, Professor P. Mandler was elected to succeed Dr. R.E. Quinault as Honorary Secretary; the remaining Officers of the Society were re-elected.

The Vice-Presidents retiring under By-law XVII were Professor P. Collinson and Professor R.D. McKitterick. Professor D.N. Cannadine and Professor P.A. Stafford were elected to replace them.

The members of Council retiring under By-law XX were Professor R.C. Bridges, Professor P.J. Corfield, Professor J.L. Nelson and Professor P.A. Stafford. In accordance with By-law XXI, Dr. W.R. Childs, Professor M.L. Dockrill, Professor V.I.J. Flint and Professor J.L. Miller were elected in their place.

MacIntyre and Company were appointed auditors for the year 1998–1999 under By-law XXXIX.

9. Representatives of the Society

The representation of the Society upon various bodies was as follows:

Mr. M. Roper, Professor P.H. Sawyer and Mr. C.P. Wormald on the Joint Committee of the Society and the British Academy established to prepare an edition of Anglo-Saxon charters;

Professor N.P. Brooks on a committee to promote the publication of photographic records of the more significant collections of British Coins;

Professor G.H. Martin on the Council of the British Records Association;

Professor M.R.D. Foot on the Committee to advise the publishers of *The Annual Register*;

Dr. G.W. Bernard on the History at the Universities Defence Group;

Professor C.J. Holdsworth on the Court of the University of Exeter;

Professor D. d'Avray on the Anthony Panizzi Foundation;

Professor M.C. Cross on the Council of the British Association for Local History; and on the British Sub-Commission of the Commission International d'Histoire Ecclesiastique Comparée;

Miss V. Cromwell on the Advisory Board of the Computers in Teaching Initiative Centre for History; and on the Advisory Committee of the TLTP History Courseware Consortium;

Dr. A.M.S. Prochaska on the National Council on Archives; and on the Advisory Council of the reviewing committee on the Export of Works of Art;

Professor R.A. Griffiths on the Court of Governors of the University of Wales, Swansea;

Professor A.L. Brown on the University of Stirling Conference;

Professor W. Davies on the Court of the University of Birmingham;

Professor R.D. McKitterick on a committee to regulate British co-operation in the preparation of a new repertory of medieval sources to replace Potthast's *Bibliotheca Historica Medii Aevi*;

Professor J. Breuilly on the steering committee of the proposed British Centre for Historical Research in Germany.

Council received reports from its representatives.

24 September 1999

APPENDIX A

ROYAL HISTORICAL SOCIETY
RESEARCH SUPPORT COMMITTEE AWARDS
SESSION 1997–1998

TRAINING BURSARIES:

Nicholas Paul BARON, Centre for Russian and East European Studies, University of Birmingham
Two conferences held at Petrozavodsk and Ryazan, Russia in May and June 1999.

Kimberly CHRISMAN, University of Aberdeen
French Emigre Conference to be held at the Institut Francais, London on 2–4 July 1999.

Meaghan CLARKE, University of Sussex
Conferences to be held at the University of California, Santa Cruz, on 5–8 August 1999, and at Washington, D.C., on 10–12 September 1999.

Lucia DACOME, University of Cambridge
The Tenth International Congress on the Enlightenment to be held in Dublin on 25–31 July 1999.

Sally DIXON-SMITH, University College London
Visit to Humboldt-Universitat zu Berlin in January 1999.

Lisa Lynn FORD, University of St. Andrews
Fifteenth-century Conference, 'Concepts and Pattern of Service', held at the University of Reading on 17–19 September 1998.

Ann Margaret GILETTI, The Warburg Institute, University of London
The International Congress on Medieval Studies held at Kalamazoo, Michigan, USA on 6–8 May 1999.

Natalie J.M.R. HIGGINS, Downing College, Cambridge
NACBS Conference held at Colorado Springs, USA, on 16–18 October 1998.

Matthew MORAN, University of East Anglia
International Medieval Congress to be held at the University of Leeds on 12–15 July 1999.

Liese Marie PERRIN, University of Birmingham
Conference, 'Freedwomen, work and gender in the postbellum south', held at the University of Coastal Carolina, USA on 18–20 March 1999.

Caterina PIZZIGONI, King's College London
Conference for Postgraduates in Latin American Studies held at Newcastle on 5–6 December 1998.

Barbara POLCI, University of East Anglia
International Medieval Congress to be held at the University of Leeds on 12–15 July 1999.

Wigan M.W.T. SALAZAR, SOAS, University of London
Economic History Society Conference held at the University of Sussex on 26–28 March 1999.

Robin McGregor WARD, Birkbeck College, University of London
Conference of the Association for the History of the Northern Seas, to be

held at the Memorial University of Newfoundland, Canada, on 8–15 August
1999.   [14]

RESEARCH SUPPORT:

RESEARCH WITHIN THE UNITED KINGDOM:

Samantha Jane BADGER, University of Wolverhampton
Visit to archives in England.
Nicholas Martin COTT, University of Newcastle upon Tyne
Visit to various archives in the United Kingdom.
Ulrike Carmen EHRET, King's College London
Visit to various Catholic diocesan archives in the United Kingdom.
Lisa Lynn FORD, University of St. Andrews
Visit to the Public Record Office, London.
John Arthur GLEDHILL, University of York
Visit to the premises of Arthur Tooth and Sons, London
Christine Elizabeth JONES, University of Essex
Visit to various archives in the United Kingdom.
Stephen JOYCE, University of Nottingham
Visit to various record offices, etc., in England.
Jennifer Elizabeth KEATING, University of Sussex
Visit to various archives in the London area.
Jonathan David OATES, University of Reading
Visit to various archives in the north of England.
Carl Peter WATTS, University of Birmingham
Visit to Public Record Office and research centres in England.   [10]

RESEARCH OUTSIDE THE UNITED KINGDOM:

Christine BOYANOSKI, Birkbeck College, University of London
Visit to archives in South Africa.
Edward CASTLETON, University of Cambridge
Visit to archives in Paris and Lyon, France.
Bernd Markus DAECHSEL, Royal Holloway, University of London
Visit to various archives in India.
Alexis H.A. DE GREIFF, Imperial College, London
Visit to archives in Austria and Italy.
Paolo DURISOTTO, Royal Holloway, University of London
Visit to various archives in India.
Janet GREENLEES, University of York
Visit to various archives in the USA.
David Stratford GOULD, University of Reading
Visit to various archives in Italy.
Elspeth Leslie JOHNSON, University of Dundee
Visit to archives in Australia.
Lorna Louise KALS, University of Leeds
Visit to archives in Germany.
Monica LAGAZIO, University of Nottingham
Visit to the Centre of United Nations Studies, Yale University, USA.
Emma Louise LAMBERT, University of Birmingham

Visit to libraries in Kansas and South Carolina.
Ilario LOTUFO, University of Cambridge
Visit to Bibliotheque Nationale de Paris.
Timothy John LOVERING, University of Stirling
Visit to the National Archives of Malawi.
Matthew MAYER, Sidney Sussex College, Cambridge
Visit to various archives in Europe.
Matthew MORAN, University of East Anglia
Visit to various libraries in Italy.
Gillian MURPHY, University College London
Visit to the Vatican Archives, Rome.
Jose Lingna NAFAFE, University of Birmingham
Visit to archives in Portugal.
Caterina PIZZIGONI, King's College London
Visit to archives in Mexico.
Camilla Elizabeth RUSSELL, Royal Holloway, University of London
Visit to archives in Italy.
Louis SKYNER, University of Cambridge
Visit to Russian State Historical Archives, St. Petersburg.
Urara TAGUCHI, Royal Holloway, University of London
Visit to archives at Florence, Italy.
Jon Edward WILSON, St. Antony's College, Oxford
Visit to various archives in Bangladesh.
David Colin WORTHINGTON, University of Aberdeen
Visit to archives in Austria, Slovenia and the Czech Republic.   [23]

WORKSHOP FUND: [name of organiser in brackets]:

Society for the study of French History 13th Annual Conference held at the
University of Edinburgh on 29–31 March 1999. [Robert ANDERSON]
'The Reformation Era and Christian Worship', 6th Annual Conference of
The Society for Reformation Studies, to be held at Westminster College,
Cambridge on 7–9 April 1999. [Paul AYRIS]
Conference, 'Women and Brainpower' to be held at Royal Holloway,
University of London, on 4–6 July 1999. [P.J. CORFIELD]
Conference, 'Nowhere—A Place of Our Own: exploring the uses of Utopia',
held at the University of Warwick on 8 May 1999. [Philip M. COUPLAND]
Conference, 'Telling Stories: Personal Testimonies in History', to be held at
the University of Essex on 3 July 1999. [Julie GAMMON]
Conference, 'Aspects of Medieval Administration', to be held at Hatfield
College, Durham University, on 21–22 August 1999. [Beth HARTLAND]
Conference, 'Recent Research in Fifteenth-Century History', to be held at
the University of Southampton on 3–5 September 1999. [M.A. HICKS]
Postgraduate Seminar in International History to be held at the Public
Record Office, Kew, on 24 June 1999. [D.M. KANDIAH]
Conference, 'The Dress of the Poor, 1750–1900—old and new perspectives'
held at Oxford Brookes University on 27–28 November 1999. [Steven KING]
European Reformation Research Group Annual Conference to be held at

the University of the West of England on 2–5 September 1999. [William G. NAPHY]

Conference, 'Alfred the Great, London and Europe, a day colloquium to mark the 1100th anniversary of Alfred's death on 26 October 899', to be held at the Institute of Historical Research, University of London, on 26 October 1999. [J.L. NELSON]

Conference, 'Cruel Necessity: The Regicides and the Execution of Charles I, 1649', held at the Institute of Historical Research, London, on 22–23 January 1999. [J.T. PEACEY]

Conference, 'The Sixteenth-Century French Religious Book' to be held at the University of St. Andrews on 31 August–3 September 1999. [Andrew PETTEGREE]

Conference, 'Thirteenth Century England' VIII, to be held at St. Aidan's College, Durham on 6–8 September 1999. [M.C. PRESTWICH]

Conference, 'Britain and the Baltic: East Coast Connections', held at Van Mildert College, University of Durham on 23–26 March 1999. [P.J.K. SALMON]

Conference, 'The Meaning of Medicine: Cultures of healing in Europe, 16th to 20th centuries', to be held at the University of Amsterdam on 10–12 September 1999. [Pat THANE]

Conference, 'New Perspectives on the British in India, c.1750–1850', held at St. Catharine's College, Cambridge on 24 October 1998. [T.R. TRAVERS]

Conference, 'From Persecution to pluralism: Religious Minorities and the Enforcement of Belief in Western Europe, c.1500–c.2000', to be held at Newbold College on 8–10 September 1999. [David TRIM]

Conference, 'The Commerce of Health: Medicine, Wealth and Leisure, 1650–1900', to be held at the University of Warwick on 5 December 1999. [Chloe UNDERWOOD]   [19]

BURSARIES FOR HOLDERS OF ORS AWARDS:

Megan CLARKE, University of Sussex
Helen Louise DENHAM, Wadham College, Oxford
Jillian Renee MACIAK, University of York   [3]

CENTENARY FELLOWSHIP:

Svetlana NIKITINA, SSEES–1997/1998
Marcella SIMONI, UCL–1998/1999   [2]

THE ROYAL HISTORICAL SOCIETY
FINANCIAL ACCOUNTS
FOR THE YEAR ENDED 30 JUNE 1999

MacIntyre & Co
Chartered Accountants
Registered Auditors
London

LEGAL AND ADMINISTRATIVE INFORMATION

THE ROYAL HISTORICAL SOCIETY
REPORT OF THE COUNCIL OF TRUSTEES
FOR THE YEAR ENDED 30 JUNE 1999

The members of Council present their report and audited accounts for the year ended 30 June 1999.

PRINCIPAL ACTIVITIES AND REVIEW OF THE YEAR

The Society exists for the promotion and support of historical research and its dissemination to historians and the wider community.

The Society expects to continue with these aims in the future.

RESULTS

During the year the Fund's income from members' contributions, donations and bequests totalled £76,267 a decrease of £49,699 from that received in 1998. Expenditure and grants relating directly to charitable activities totalled £191,377, a decrease of £19,744 on that expended in 1998.

The Society's surplus before surplus from investment activities was £11,787 (1998: £52,774).

FIXED ASSETS

Information relating to changes in fixed assets is given in notes 2 and 3 to the accounts.

INVESTMENTS

The Society's investment policy of seeking a higher level of investment income over the longer term has continued.

DONATIONS

The Society made donations to other charities in the year of £Nil (1998: £150).

STATEMENT OF TRUSTEES' RESPONSIBILITIES

The Charities Act of 1993 requires the Council to prepare accounts for each financial year which give a true and fair view of the state of affairs of the Society and of the surplus or deficit of income over expenditure of the Fund for that year. In preparing these accounts, the Trustees are required to:

- select suitable accounting policies and apply them consistently;
- make judgements and estimates that are reasonable and prudent;
- state whether applicable accounting standards have been followed, subject to any material departures disclosed and explained in the accounts;
- prepare the accounts on the going concern basis unless it is inappropriate to presume that the Fund will continue in business.

The Council is responsible for ensuring proper accounting records are kept which disclose with reasonable accuracy at any time, the financial position of the Society and enable them to ensure that the financial statements comply with the By-laws of the Society and the disclosure regulation. They are also responsible for safeguarding the assets of the Society and hence for taking reasonable steps for the prevention and detection of error, fraud and other irregularities.

MEMBERS OF THE COUNCIL

Professor P J Marshall, MA, DPhil, FBA	– President
Professor P Mandler, MA, PhD	– Honorary Secretary
Professor D S Eastwood, MA, DPhil	– Literary Director
Professor A D M Pettegree, MA, DPhil, FSA	– Literary Director
Professor K Burk, MA, DPhil	– Honorary Treasurer
D A L Morgan, MA, FSA	– Honorary Librarian
Professor M D Biddiss, MA, PhD	– Vice-President
Professor D Cannadine, MA, DPhil	– Vice-President
Professor M J Daunton, PhD, FBA	– Vice-President
Professor A J Fletcher, MA	– Vice President
Professor P J Hennessy, PhD	– Vice-President
A M S Prochaska, MA, DPhil	– Vice-President
Professor P A Stafford, DPhil	– Vice President
Professor C J Wrigley, PhD	– Vice President
I W Archer, MA, DPhil	– Member of Council

MEMBERS OF THE COUNCIL

At the Anniversary Meeting on 20 November 1998, Professor P. A. Mandler was elected to succeed Dr R E Quinault as Honorary Secretary, the remaining officers of the Society were re-elected.

The Vice-Presidents retiring under By-law XVII were Professor P Collinson and Professor R. D McKitterick. Professor D. N. Cannadine and Professor P. A. Stafford were elected to replace them.

The members of Council retiring under By-law XX were Professor R. C. Bridges, Professor P. J. Corfield, Professor J. L. Nelson and Professor P. A. Stafford. Following a ballot of Fellows, W. R. Childs, Professor M. L. Dockrill, Professor V. I. J. Flint and Professor J. L. Miller were elected in their place.

STANDING COMMITTEES 1997

The Society was operated through the following Committees during 1999:—

Finance Committee:
Dr. G. W. Bernard
Mr. P. J. C. Firth — non Council Member
Professor J. A. Guy
Professor P. J. Hennessy
Professor A. J. Fletcher
Professor P. Mathias — non Council Member
The six Officers

General Purposes Committee:
Professor D. Bates
Dr. J. C. G. Binfield
Professor D. N. Cannadine
Professor R. I. Moore
The six Officers

Membership Committee:
Professor J. Black
Professor M. L. Dockrill
Professor P. A. Stafford
Dr. J. Martindale
Professor C. J. Wrigley
The six Officers

Publications Committee:
Dr. W. R. Childs
Dr. A. Curry
Professor M. J. Daunton
Professor A. Goodman
Professor J. L. Miller
Professor R. Trainor
The six Officers

Research Support Committee:
Dr. I. W. Archer
Professor M. D. Biddiss
Dr. C. R. J. Currie
Professor V. I. J. Flint
Dr. A. M. S. Prochaska
The six Officers

AUDITORS

MacIntyre and Company were appointed auditors for the year 1998–1999 under By-law XXXIX. A resolution to re-appoint Messrs MacIntyre & Co will be submitted to the Anniversary Meeting.

By Order of the Board

Honorary Secretary

24 September 1999

REPORT OF THE AUDITORS

TO THE MEMBERS OF ROYAL HISTORICAL SOCIETY

We have audited the accounts on pages 373-379 which have been prepared under the historical cost convention, as modified by the revaluation of fixed asset investments, and the accounting policies set out on page 375.

RESPECTIVE RESPONSIBILITIES OF THE COUNCIL OF TRUSTEES

As described on page 369 the Trustees are responsible for the preparation of accounts. It is our responsibility to form an independent opinion, based on our audit, on those accounts and to report our opinion to you.

BASIS OF OPINION

We conducted our audit in accordance with Auditing Standards issued by the Auditing Practices Board. An audit includes examination, on a test basis, of evidence relevant to the amounts and disclosures in the accounts. It also includes an assessment of the significant estimates and judgements made by the Board of Trustees in the preparation of the accounts, and of whether the accounting policies are appropriate to the Society's circumstances, consistently applied and adequately disclosed.

We planned and performed our audit so as to obtain all the information and explanations which we considered necessary in order to provide us with sufficient evidence to give reasonable assurance that the accounts are free from material misstatement, whether caused by fraud or other irregularity or error. In forming our opinion we also evaluated the overall adequacy of the presentation of information in the accounts.

OPINION

In our opinion the accounts give a true and fair view of the state of the Society's affairs as at 30 June 1999 and of its surplus of income over expenditure for the year then ended.

MacIntyre & Co
Chartered Accountants
Registered Auditors

28 Ely Place
London
EC1N 6RL

24 September 1999

THE ROYAL HISTORICAL SOCIETY

BALANCE SHEET AS AT 30TH JUNE 1999

	Notes	1999 £	1999 £	1998 £	1998 £
ED ASSETS					
angible assets	2		3,848		7,711
nvestments	3		2,520,276		2,498,077
			2,524,124		2,505,788
RRENT ASSETS					
tocks	1(c)	30,917		29,968	
ebtors	4	46,104		64,501	
ash at bank and in hand	5	57,263		100,448	
		134,284		194,917	
s: CREDITORS					
mount due within one year	6	(41,592)		(154,053)	
CURRENT ASSETS (LIABILITIES)			92,692		(40,864)
ASSETS			2,616,816		2,546,652
PRESENTED BY:					
Unrestricted – General Fund			2,402,475		2,324,814
Restricted – E. M. Robinson Bequest			105,974		97,517
Restricted – A.S. Whitfield Prize Fund			45,394		42,825
Restricted – BHB Andrew Mellon Fund			62,973		81,496
			2,616,816		2,546,652

proved by the Council on 24 September 1999

sident:

norary Treasurer:

e attached notes form an integral part of these financial statements.

THE ROYAL HISTORICAL SOCIETY

Consolidated Statement of Financial Activities for the Year Ended 30 June 1999

	Notes	Unrestricted Funds — General Fund £	Restricted Funds — E M Robinson Bequest £	Restricted Funds — A S Whitfield Prize Fund £	BHB/ Andrew Mellon Fund £	1999 Total £	1998 Total £
INCOMING RESOURCES							
Members' subscriptions							
—net		67,209	—	—	—	67,209	49,998
—tax recovered on Deeds of Covenant and Gift Aid		3,766	—	—	—	3,766	3,127
		70,975				70,975	53,125
Donations and legacies	7	5,292	—	—	—	5,292	72,841
Total Voluntary Income		76,267	—	—	—	76,267	125,966
Royalties and reproduction fees		59,138	—	—	—	59,138	47,153
Total Income before investment income		135,405	—	—	—	135,405	173,119
Investment income		101,761	2,773	1,347	3,792	109,673	124,456
Gross Incoming Resources in the Year		£237,166	£2,773	£1,347	£3,792	£245,078	£297,575
RESOURCES USED							
Grants and prizes payable	8	(27,285)	(2,200)	(1,000)	—	(30,485)	(29,017)
Direct charitable expenditure	9	(147,647)	—	—	(22,315)	(169,962)	(182,104)
Administration expenses	10	(32,844)	—	—	—	(32,844)	(33,680)
Total Resources used		(207,776)	(2,200)	(1,000)	(22,315)	(233,291)	(244,801)
Net Incoming/Outgoing Resources (Operating surplus)		29,390	573	347	(18,523)	11,787	52,774
Gains and Losses on Investment Assets							
—Realised on Investments		272,686	—	—	—	272,686	38,173
—Unrealised		(224,415)	7,884	2,222	—	(214,309)	291,650
Net Movement in Resources in Year		77,661	8,457	2,569	(18,523)	70,164	382,597
Balance Brought Forward at 30 June 1998		£2,324,814	£97,517	£42,825	£81,496	£2,546,652	£2,164,055
Balance Carried Forward at 30 June 1999		£2,402,475	£105,974	£45,394	£62,973	£2,616,816	£2,546,652
Unrealised Surpluses included in above balances		£680,931	£40,529	£20,196	—	£741,656	£949,368

THE ROYAL HISTORICAL SOCIETY

Notes to the Accounts for the Year Ended 30 June 1999

1. Accounting Policies

(a) *Basis of accounting*
The financial statements have been prepared in accordance with the Charities (Accounts and Reports) Regulations October 1995, the Statements of Recommended Practice 'Accounting by charities' and applicable accounting standards issued by UK accountancy bodies. The particular accounting policies adopted are described below. The financial statements are prepared under the historical cost convention, as modified to include fixed asset investments at market value.

(b) *Depreciation*
Depreciation is calculated by reference to the cost of fixed assets using a straight line basis at rates considered appropriate having regard to the expected lives of the fixed assets.
The annual rates of depreciation in use are:
   Furniture and equipment   10%
   Computer equipment   25%

(c) *Stocks*
Stock is valued at the lower of cost and net realisable value.

(d) *Library and archives*
The cost of additions to the library and archives is written off in the year of purchase.

(e) *Subscription Income*
Subscription Income is recognised in the year it became receivable with a provision against any subscription not received.

(f) *Investments*
Investments are stated at market value. Any surplus arising on revaluation is charged to the income and expenditure account.
Dividend income is accounted for on a received basis.

(g) *Publication costs*
Publication costs are transferred in stock and released to the income and expenditure account as stocks are depleted.

(h) *E.M. Robinson bequest*
Income from the E.M. Robinson bequest is used to provide grants to the Dulwich Picture Gallery.

(i) *A.S. Whitfield Prize Fund*
The A.S. Whitfield Prize Fund is used to provide an annual prize for the best first monograph for British history published in the calendar year.

(j) *Donations and other voluntary income*
Donations are recognised on a received basis.

(k) *Grants payable*
Grants payable are recognised in the year in which they are paid.

(l) *Allocation of administration costs*
Administration costs are allocated between direct charitable expenditure and administration costs on the basis of the work done by the Executive Secretary.

2. Tangible Fixed Assets

	Computer Equipment	Furniture and Equipment	Total
	£	£	£
Cost			
At 1st July 1998	24,904	1,173	26,077
Additions	3,275	—	3,275
At 30th June 1999	28,179	1,173	29,352
Depreciation			
At 1st July 1998	17,286	1,080	18,366
Charge for the year	7,045	93	7,138
At 30th June 1998	24,331	1,173	25,504
Net book value			
At 30th June 1999	£3,848	£—	£3,848
At 30th June 1998	£7,618	£93	7,711

All tangible fixed assets are used in the furtherance of the Society's objectives.

3. INVESTMENTS

	General Fund £	Robinson Bequest £	Whitfield Prize Fund £	Total 1997 £
Cost/market value at 1st July 1998	1,252,744	59,335	17,571	1,329,650
Additions	793,085	—	—	793,085
Disposals	(545,519)	—	—	(545,519)
At 30th June 1999	1,500,310	59,335	17,571	1,577,216
Surplus in revaluation	680,931	40,529	20,196	741,656
Quoted securities at market value	2,181,241	99,864	37,767	2,318,872
Cash awaiting investment	173,788	16,982	10,634	201,404
	£2,355,029	£116,846	£48,401	£2,520,276
Market value at 1st July 1998	2,151,493	91,980	35,545	2,279,018
Additions	793,085	—	—	793,085
Disposals	(545,519)	—	—	(545,519)
Unrealised (loss)/gain on investments . . .	(217,818)	7,884	2,222	(207,712)
Market value at 30th June 1999	£2,181,241	£99,864	£37,767	£2,318,872

4. DEBTORS

	1999 £	1998 £
Trade debtors	33,763	58,660
Other debtors	6,450	238
Prepayments	5,891	5,603
	£46,104	£64,501

5. CASH AT BANK AND IN HAND

	1999 £	1998 £
Deposit accounts	63,607	109,420
Current accounts	(6,344)	(8,972)
	£57,263	£100,448

6. CREDITORS: Amounts due within one year

	1999 £	1998 £
Trade creditors	28,616	137,345
Sundry creditors	6,300	6,206
Subscriptions received in advance	1,226	2,584
Accruals	5,450	7,918
	£41,592	£154,053

7. DONATIONS AND LEGACIES

	1999 £	1998 £
A. Browning Royalties	128	189
G.R. Elton Bequest	2,733	7,134
Donations and sundry income	1,539	61,232
Conference fees and funding	892	4,286
	£5,292	£72,841

8. Grant and Prizes Payable

	Unrestricted Funds £	Restricted Funds £	Total 1999 £	Total 1998 £
Alexander Prize	570	—	570	421
Grants	1,300	—	1,300	150
Research support grants	15,940	—	15,940	15,964
Young Historian Scheme	2,000	—	2,000	1,907
Centenary fellowship	6,175	—	6,175	6,475
A Level prizes	900	—	900	800
A.S. Whitfield Prize	—	1,000	1,000	1,000
E.M. Robinson Bequest				
— Grant to Dulwich Picture Library	—	2,200	2,200	2,200
Gladstone prize	400	—	400	—
	£27,285	£3,200	£30,485	£29,017

9. Direct Charitable Expenditure

	Unrestricted Funds £	Restricted Funds £	Total 1999 £	Total 1998 £
Publishing costs (Note 15)	71,416	—	71,416	74,855
Purchase of books and publications	3,978	—	3,978	3,605
Binding	5,827	—	5,827	5,743
Prothero lecture	902	—	902	352
Studies in History				
— Executive editor's honorarium	4,500	—	4,500	3,667
— Executive editor's expenses	960	—	960	985
— Sundry expenses	1,606	—	1,606	1,827
Other publications (Note 16)	11,071	—	11,071	15,352
British Bibliographies	—	22,315	22,315	35,577
Salaries, pensions and social security	23,499	—	23,499	11,996
Computer consumables, printing and stationery	9,559	—	9,559	9,011
Meetings and travel	12,262	—	12,262	11,647
Conference costs	2,067	—	2,067	7,487
	£147,647	£22,315	£169,962	£182,104

10. Administration Expenses

	Unrestricted Funds £	Restricted Funds £	Total 1999 £	Total 1998 £
Salaries, pensions and social security	10,072	—	10,072	17,993
Postage and telephone	1,432	—	1,432	1,898
Bank charges	1,432	—	1,432	1,303
Audit and accountancy	4,723	—	4,723	5,135
Professional fees	—	—	—	596
Insurance	1,065	—	1,065	883
Depreciation	7,288	—	7,288	3,227
Circulation costs	6,832	—	6,832	2,645
	£32,844	£—	£32,844	£33,680

The average number of staff employed during the year was 1 (1998: 1)

11. Insurance Policies

	1999 £	1998 £
The Society was charged with the following amounts relating to committee and employees' liability:		
Employees liability	78	86
Public liability	78	86
	156	£172

12. Councillors' Expenses

During the year travel expenses were reimbursed to 30 Councillors attending Council meetings at a cost of £6,714 (1998: £5,983).

13. AUDITOR'S REMUNERATION

	1999 £	1998 £
Audit fee	4,723	5,135

14. GRANTS PAID

During the year the Society awarded grants to a value of £15,940 (1998: £15,964) to 75 (1998: 90) individuals.

15. PUBLICATIONS

	Transactions Sixth Series 8 £	Camden Fifth Series 11, 12 £	Guides and Handbooks Reprint Costs £	Camden Classic Reprints £	Total £
Cambridge University Press					
Opening stock	1,037	5,659	7,218	16,054	29,968
Printing	14,758	22,478	—	3,137	40,373
Off prints	2,031	—	—	—	2,031
Carriage	563	1,400	200	—	2,163
Closing stock	(2,067)	(6,507)	(3,472)	(18,871)	(30,917)
	16,322	23,303	3,946	320	43,618
Society's costs	1,477	4,175	20	—	5,672
Paper					3,745
Sales commission					18,381
					£71,416

16. PUBLICATIONS

	1999 £	1998 £
Other publications cost		
Annual Bibliography	12,723	17,662
Less: royalties received	(1,652)	(2,310)
	£11,071	£15,352

17. LEASE COMMITMENTS

The Society has the following annual commitments under non-cancellable operating leases which expire:

	1999 £	1998 £
Within 1–2 years	2,517	176
Within 2–5 years	—	2,517
	£2,517	£2,693

18. CAPITAL COMMITMENTS

	1999 £	1998 £
At the year end, the Society was committed to expenditure to the sum of	£—	£6,842

19. LIFE MEMBERS

The Society has on-going commitments to provide membership services to 25 Life Members on a cost of approximately £28 each year.

20. UNCAPITALISED ASSETS

The Society owns a library the cost of which is written off to the income and expenditure account at the time of purchase.

This library is insured for £150,000 and is used for reference purposes by the membership of the Society.

21. ANALYSIS OF NET ASSETS BETWEEN FUNDS

	General Fund £	E.M. Robinson Bequest Fund £	A.S. Whitfield Prize Fund £	BHB/ Andrew Mellon Fund £	Total £
Fixed Assets	—	—	—	3,848	3,848
Investments	2,355,029	116,846	48,401	—	2,520,276
	2,355,029	116,846	48,401	3,848	2,524,124
Current Assets					
Stocks	30,917	—	—	—	30,917
Debtors	46,104	—	—	—	46,104
Cash at bank and in hand . .	3,013	—	—	54,250	57,263
	80,034	—	—	54,250	134,284
Less: Creditors	(33,588)	(10,872)	(3,007)	4,875	(42,592)
Net Current Assets	46,446	(10,872)	(3,007)	59,125	91,692
Net Assets	£2,401,475	£105,974	£45,394	£62,973	£2,615,816

THE ROYAL HISTORICAL SOCIETY
THE DAVID BERRY ESSAY TRUST

Balance Sheet as at 30th June 1999

	1999 £	1999 £	1998 £	1998 £
Fixed Assets				
1,117.63 units in the Charities Official Investment Fund				
(Market Value £11,444: 1998 £9,524)		1,530		1,530
Current Assets				
Bank Deposit Account	8,989		8,367	
Creditors:				
Amounts falling due within one year	(600)		(250)	
Net Current Assets		8,389		8,117
Net Assets		9,919		9,647
Represented by:				
Capital fund		1,000		1,000
Income and expenditure reserve		8,919		8,647
		£9,919		£9,647

Income and Expenditure Account

	1999 £	1999 £	1998 £	1998 £
Income				
Dividends		391		389
Bank Interest Receivable		231		272
		622		661
Expenditure				
Prize awarded		(250)		(250)
Travel expenses		(100)		—
Excess of income over expenditure for the year . .		272		411
Balance brought forward		8,647		8,236
Balance carried forward		8,919		8,647

The fund has no recognised gains or losses apart from the results for the above financial periods.

1. Accounting Policies
   Basis of accounting.
   The accounts have been prepared under the historical cost convention. The late David Berry, by his Will dated 23rd April 1926, left £1,000 to provide in every three years a gold medal and prize money for the best essay on the Earl of Bothwell or, at the discretion of the Trustees, on Scottish History of the James Stuarts I to VI, in memory of his father the late Rev. David Berry.
   The Trust is regulated by a scheme sanctioned by the Chancery Division of the High Court of Justice dated 23rd January 1930, and made in action 1927 A 1233 David Anderson Berry deceased, Hunter and Another v. Robertson and Another and since modified by an order of the Charity Commissioners made on 11 January 1978 removing the necessity to provide a medal.
   The Royal Historical Society is now the Trustee. The investment consists of 1117.63 Charities Official Investment Fund Income with units. The Trustee will advertise inviting essays every year of the three year period.)
   A resolution was approved by the Charity Commission on the 16 August 1998 changing the purpose of the Charity to provide an annual prize of £250 for the best essay on a subject, to be selected by the candidate, dealing with Scottish History, provided such subject has been previously submitted to and approved by the Council of The Royal Historical Society.

We have audited the accounts on page 380 which have been prepared under the historical cost convention and the accounting policies set out on page 380.

Respective responsibilities of the Council and Auditors
The Trustees are required to prepare accounts for each financial year which give a true and fair view of the state of affairs of the Trust and of the surplus or deficit for that period.
In preparing the accounts, the Trustees are required to:
—select suitable accounting policies and then apply them consistently;
—make judgements and estimates that are reasonable and prudent;
—prepare the accounts on the going concern basis unless it is inappropriate to presume that the Trust will continue in business.
The Trustees are responsible for keeping proper accounting records which disclose with reasonable accuracy at any time the financial position of the Trust. They are also responsible for safeguarding the assets of the Trust and hence for taking reasonable steps for the prevention and detection of fraud and other irregularities.
As described above the Trustees are responsible for the preparation of accounts. It is our responsibility to form an independent opinion, based on our audit, on those accounts and to report our opinion to you.

Basis of opinion
We conducted our audit in accordance with Auditing Standards issued by the Auditing Practices Board. An audit includes examination, on a test basis, of evidence relevant to the amounts and disclosures in the accounts. It also includes an assessment of the significant estimates and judgements made by the Trustees in the preparation of the accounts, and of whether the accounting policies are appropriate to the Trust's circumstances, consistently applied and adequately disclosed.
We planned and performed our audit so as to obtain all the information and explanations which we considered necessary in order to provide us with sufficient evidence to give reasonable assurance that the accounts are free from material misstatement, whether caused by fraud or other irregularity or error. In forming our opinion we also evaluated the overall adequacy of the presentation of information in the accounts.

Opinion
In our opinion the accounts give a true and fair view of the state of the Trust's affairs as at 30th June 1999 and of its surplus for the year then ended.

MacINTYRE & Co
Chartered Accountants
Registered Auditors
London

24 September 1999